Managing Operations

Across the Supply Chain

Third Edition

Morgan Swink
Texas Christian
University

Steven A. Melnyk
Michigan State
University

Janet L. Hartley
Bowling Green
State University

M. Bixby Cooper
Michigan State
University

Mc
Graw
Hill
Education

MANAGING OPERATIONS ACROSS THE SUPPLY CHAIN, THIRD EDITION

Published by McGraw-Hill Education, 2 Penn Plaza, New York, NY 10121. Copyright © 2017 by McGraw-Hill Education. All rights reserved. Printed in the United States of America. Previous editions © 2014, 2011. No part of this publication may be reproduced or distributed in any form or by any means, or stored in a database or retrieval system, without the prior written consent of McGraw-Hill Education, including, but not limited to, in any network or other electronic storage or transmission, or broadcast for distance learning.

2 3 4 5 6 7 8 9 LWI 21 20 19 18 17

ISBN 978-1-259-54430-9
MHID 1-259-54430-3

Chief Product Officer, SVP Products & Markets: *G. Scott Virkler*
Vice President, General Manager, Products & Markets: *Marty Lange*
Managing Director: *James Heine*
Brand Manager: *Dolly Womack*
Senior Director, Product Development: *Rose Koos*
Product Developer: *Camille Corum*
Marketing Manager: *Britney Hermsen*
Senior Director, Digital Content Development: *Douglas Ruby*
Director, Content Design & Delivery: *Linda Avenarius*
Program Manager: *Mark Christianson*
Content Project Managers: *Harvey Yep (Core), Kristin Bradley (Assessment)*
Buyer: *Sandy Ludovissy*
Design: *Egzon Shaqiri*
Content Licensing Specialists: *Ann Marie Jannette (Image), Beth Thole (Text)*
Cover Image: *Liu zishan / Shutterstock*
Compositor: *SPi Global*
Printer: *LSC Communications*

All credits appearing on page or at the end of the book are considered to be an extension of the copyright page.

Library of Congress Cataloging-in-Publication Data

Names: Swink, Morgan, 1959- author.
Title: Managing operations across the supply chain / Morgan Swink, Texas Christian University, Steven A. Melnyk Michigan State University, Janet L. Hartley, Bowling Green State University, M. Bixby Cooper, Michigan State University.
Description: Third Edition. | Dubuque, IA : McGraw-Hill Education, 2016. | Revised edition of
Identifiers: LCCN 2016021249 | ISBN 9781259544309 (alk. paper)
Subjects: LCSH: Business logistics. | Production management. | Industrial management.
Classification: LCC HD38.5 .S95 2016 | DDC 658.5--dc23
LC record available at https://lccn.loc.gov/2016021249

The Internet addresses listed in the text were accurate at the time of publication. The inclusion of a website does not indicate an endorsement by the authors or McGraw-Hill, and McGraw-Hill does not guarantee the accuracy of the information presented at these sites.

The McGraw-Hill Education Series Operations and Decision Sciences

Operations Management

Beckman and Rosenfield
Operations Strategy: Competing in the
21st Century
First Edition

Benton
Purchasing and Supply Chain Management
Third Edition

Bowersox, Closs, and Cooper
Supply Chain Logistics Management
Fifth Edition

Brown and Hyer
Managing Projects: A Team-Based Approach
Second Edition

Burt, Petcavage, and Pinkerton
Supply Management
Ninth Edition

Cachon and Terwiesch
Operations Management
First Edition

Cachon and Terwiesch
Matching Supply with Demand: An
Introduction to Operations Management
Fourth Edition

Finch
Interactive Models for Operations and
Supply Chain Management
First Edition

Fitzsimmons and Fitzsimmons
Service Management: Operations, Strategy,
Information Technology
Eighth Edition

Gehrlein
Operations Management Cases
First Edition

Harrison and Samson
Technology Management
First Edition

Hayen
SAP R/3 Enterprise Software: An Introduction
First Edition

Hill
Manufacturing Strategy: Text & Cases
Third Edition

Hopp
Supply Chain Science
First Edition

Hopp and Spearman
Factory Physics
Third Edition

Jacobs, Berry, Whybark, and Vollmann
Manufacturing Planning & Control
for Supply Chain Management
Sixth Edition

Jacobs and Chase
Operations and Supply Chain Management
Fourteenth Edition

Jacobs and Chase
Operations and Supply Chain Management:
The Core
Fourth Edition

Jacobs and Whybark
Why ERP?
First Edition

Johnson, Leenders, and Flynn
Purchasing and Supply Management
Fifteenth Edition

Larson and Gray
Project Management: The Managerial Process
Sixth Edition

Schroeder, Goldstein, and Rungtusanatham
Operations Management: Contemporary
Concepts and Cases
Sixth Edition

Simchi-Levi, Kaminsky, and Simchi-Levi
Designing and Managing the Supply Chain:

Concepts, Strategies, Case Studies
Third Edition

Sterman
Business Dynamics: Systems Thinking and
Modeling for a Complex World
First Edition

Stevenson
Operations Management
Twelfth Edition

Swink, Melnyk, Cooper, and Hartley
Managing Operations Across the Supply Chain
Third Edition

Thomke
Managing Product and Service
Development: Text and Cases
First Edition

Ulrich and Eppinger
Product Design and Development
Sixth Edition

Zipkin
Foundations of Inventory Management
First Edition

Quantitative Methods and Management Science

Hillier and Hillier
Introduction to Management Science: A
Modeling and Case Studies Approach with
Spreadsheets
Fifth Edition

Stevenson and Ozgur
Introduction to Management Science with
Spreadsheets
First Edition

Dedication

To Jenni, Derek, Rachel, and Sarah, who make my life so full!
Morgan Swink

To my wife and children-Christine, Charles and Beth-for their support and patience.
To four great friends who have been "teachers" to me in my continual quest for more
knowledge-Alan Dunn, Abe Eshkenazi (CEO of APICS), and Colin Seftel (my South African friend).
To these people, this book is dedicated.
Steven A. Melnyk

To my children who make my life complete.
Bix Cooper

To Glenn and Caleb, for their love and support.
Janet Hartley

About the Authors

Morgan Swink

is Professor, Eunice and James L. West Chair of Supply Chain Management, and Executive Director of the Center for Supply Chain Innovation at the Neeley School of Business, Texas Christian University. He holds a BS in Mechanical Engineering from Southern Methodist University, an MBA from the University of Dallas, and a PhD in Operations Management from Indiana University. Before becoming a professor, Dr. Swink worked for 10 years in a variety of manufacturing and product development positions at Texas Instruments Incorporated. He has co-authored three books and published over 75 articles in a variety of academic and managerial journals. Dr. Swink is formerly the Co-Editor in Chief for the *Journal of Operations Management* and past president of the *Decision Sciences Institute*.

Steven A. Melnyk

is Professor of Operations Management at Michigan State University. Dr. Melnyk obtained his undergraduate degree from the University of Windsor and his doctorate from the Ivey School of Business, the University of Western Ontario. He has co-authored 17 books focusing on operations and the supply chain and has published 90 refereed articles in numerous international and national journals. He is Associate Editor for the *Journal of Business Logistics.* He also is a member of the editorial advisory board for the *Production and Inventory Management Journal,* the *Journal of Supply Chain Management,* and the *International Journal of Production Research.* Dr. Melnyk is co-editor (North America) for the *Journal of Humanitarian Logistics and Supply Chain Management.* Dr. Melynk has consulted with over 60 companies. He has also served as a member of the APICS Board of Directors (2014–2016) and the APICS leadership team (2015).

Janet L. Hartley

is Professor and Director of the Supply Chain Management Institute of the Department of Management at Bowling Green State University. She received her BS in Chemical Engineering from the University of Missouri-Rolla, and the MBA and PhD degrees in Business Administration from the University of Cincinnati. Prior to graduate school, she developed new products and designed new manufacturing processes for the Clorox Company. She has published over 28 articles on supply management and supply chain management. She serves as an associate editor for the *Journal of Operations Management, Journal of Business Logistics,* and *Journal of Supply Chain Management.*

M. Bixby Cooper

is Associate Professor in the Department of Supply Chain Management at Michigan State University. He received his BS in Business Administration from the University of North Carolina, MBA from the University of Virginia, and PhD from the University of Alabama. Prior to joining Michigan State, he served on the faculty of Winthrop University and Louisiana State University. He is an active researcher and co-author of several books on distribution and logistics. Dr. Cooper has consulted with numerous organizations including Kellogg, Johnson and Johnson, Mead Johnson, Westinghouse, Novartis, Dayton Hudson (Target), Kerr-McGee, VF Industries, and Siemens.

Preface

We continue to live in dynamic and exciting times. The recent 20 years have seen many changes that have affected nearly every aspect of business-including operations management. In this third edition of our book, we continue to reflect key shifts in operations management, including transitions:

- **From a focus on the internal system to a focus on the supply chain** In today's highly competitive business environment, organizations must leverage the capabilities of their suppliers and customers. Operations managers must look beyond the "four walls" of the firm and take an integrated supply chain perspective of operations.

- **From a local focus to a global focus** As Thomas L. Friedman pointed out,[1] the world is indeed flat. Business solutions generated in Argentina are used to meet needs in the United States, and parts built by suppliers located in China are used to assemble cars in Canada. Commercial needs have overcome, to a large part, national borders, presenting new opportunities and challenges for operations managers.

- **From an emphasis on tools and techniques to an emphasis on systems, people, and processes** To be successful, operations managers must think more broadly than just the application of analytical tools and techniques. They must take a systems view to address important managerial issues such as designing processes, working with people, managing information flows, and building interorganizational relationships.

- **From myopic pursuit of profit to a holistic pursuit of sustainability.** Pressures on businesses have risen to the point that they can no longer ignore or give only lipservice to social and environmental issues. Operations managers have to balance the profit motive with the need to protect and even strengthen both people and the planet.

Managing Operations Across the Supply Chain provides a global, supply chain perspective of operations management for students in introductory courses in operations management and in supply chain management courses that do not require an operations management prerequisite. While the book is primarily written for undergraduates,

it also can be used effectively in MBA courses. There are several features that help to differentiate this book in its view of operations management:

- **Broader Treatment of Operations Management** While many operations management textbooks have revised or added a chapter to address supply chain issues, we developed our book from the ground up to effectively integrate operations management and the supply chain. The primary focus of the book is operations management, but we provide a "supply chain" perspective. Operations management cuts across a firm's boundaries, bringing together its internal activities with the operations of customers, suppliers, and other partners around the world. We clarify the functional roles of operations, supply management, and logistics while examining the integrative processes that make up the supply chain. One unique aspect of the book is that we examine both the upstream (supply-side) and downstream (demand-side) aspects of the supply chain, including a discussion of marketing and customer relationships.

- **Balanced Treatment** The book balances the quantitative and qualitative coverage needed to equip operations and supply chain managers for the challenges and opportunities they face. It describes and applies analytical tools that operations managers use to support decision making. However, we also address the important managerial issues such as systems, people, and processes that are critical in a supply chain context.

- **Use of Integrative Frameworks** The various elements of operations management are introduced and developed using an operations strategy framework that brings together three critical elements: (1) the key customer, (2) the value proposition, and (3) capabilities. Furthermore, the students are introduced to operations management in a structured way that begins with the "big" picture of operations strategy, proceeds to the foundations of operations management, integrating relationships, planning for integrated supply chain operations, and then ending with a discussion of how to manage the system looking to the future.

---

[1]Thomas L. Friedman, *The World Is Flat: A Brief History of the Twenty-First Century* (New York: Farrar, Straus, and Giroux, 2006).

- **Use of Integrating Themes** Three key themes are highlighted throughout the book: global issues, relationships, and sustainability. Because most organizations have supply chains that reach beyond a single country, we examine global issues associated with operations and supply chain management. Organizations must collaborate with customers and suppliers to accomplish many operations activities. Thus, the book show-cases how to build, maintain, and benefit from cross-functional and interorganizational relationships. To reduce costs and be competitive, organizations today must adapt sustainable business practices. We expect sustainability to increasingly become a key metric for operations and supply chain management performance. Accordingly, we have dedicated an entire chapter to sustainability, while also incorporating it throughout the book.

- **Real, Integrated Examples** The book brings operations and supply chain management to life through opening vignettes, Get Real highlights, and rich examples throughout the book.

Managing Operations Across the Supply Chain offers a new, global, supply chain perspective of operations management-a treatment that embraces the foundations of operations management but includes new frameworks, concepts, and tools to address the demands of today and changing needs of the future. The book is organized into five major sections:

- **Part 1 Supply Chain: A Perspective for Operations Management** provides an overview of operations management as a field, and describes the strategic role operations has in business from the perspective of supply chain management.

- **Part 2 Foundations of Operations Management** discusses foundational process concepts and principles that govern all operational activities. This section examines concepts such as product/process innovation, quality, lean, and inventory fundamentals.

- **Part 3 Integrating Relationships Across the Supply Chain** deals with the primary functional relationships between internal operations management activities and other operational functions both inside and outside the firm. This section describes customer relationship management, supply management, and logistics management.

- **Part 4 Planning for Integrated Operations Across the Supply Chain** discusses planning approaches and technologies used at different levels of operations decision making. Key topics such as demand planning, forecasting, sales and operations planning, inventory management, and materials requirements planning are examined.

- **Part 5 Managing Change in Supply Chain Operations** discusses how operations managers use projects, change programs, and technologies to shape a sustainable future for operations and supply chain management.

Acknowledgments

We would like to express our appreciation to the people who have provided assistance in the development of this textbook. We express our sincere thanks to the following individuals for their thoughtful reviews and suggestions:

Samuel Chinnis, Guilford Technical Community College
Madeleine Pullman, Portland State University
John R. Grandzol, Bloomsburg University
Dennis McCahon, Northeastern University
Edward D. Walker, Valdosta State University
Brian Jacobs, Michigan State University
Narendra K. Rustagi, Howard University
Andrew Borchers, Lipscomb University
Sandra Obilade, Brescia University
Rick Bonsall, McKendree University
Helen Eckmann, Brandman University
Nicoleta Maghear, Hampton University
Kelwyn D'Souza, Hampton University
Bruce A. Meyer, Bowling Green State University
Jeanetta Chrystie, Southwest Minnesota State University
Jeff Brand, Marquette University

We also want to express our sincere thanks to the following individuals for their exceptional contributions: William Berry, Professor Emeritus, Queens College, and David Weltman, Texas Christian University, for accuracy checking; Frank Novakowski, Davenport University, and Jody Wolfe, Clarke University, for developing learning resource videos; and Rene Ordonez, for updating the instructor powerpoints and developing guided examples.

We want to thank the outstanding McGraw-Hill/Irwin production and marketing team who made this book possible-including Britney Hermsen, marketing manager; James Heine, managing director; Harvey Yep and Kristin Bradley, content project managers; Sandy Ludovissy, buyer; Doug Ruby, digital content development director; Egzon Shaqiri, designer; and Ann Marie Jannette and Beth Thole, content licensing specialists.

A special thanks to our outstanding editorial team. We greatly appreciate the support, encouragement, and patience shown by Camille Corum, our product developer. Thanks for keeping us on track! Our brand manager, Dolly Womack, provided excellent guidance and leadership throughout the process. We truly appreciate it!

Morgan Swink
Steven A. Melynk
Janet L. Hartley
M. Bixby Cooper

Walkthrough

The following section highlights the key features of the text and accompanying resources, which have been developed to help you learn, understand, and apply operations concepts.

CHAPTER ELEMENTS

Within each chapter, of the text, you will find the following elements. All of these have been developed to facilitate study and learning.

Chapter Opener

Each chapter begins with an opening vignette to help set the tone for the material that follows. Learning objectives provide a quick introduction to the material students will learn and should understand before moving to the next chapter.

Opening Vignette

Each chapter opens with an introduction to the important operations topics covered in the chapter. Students need to see the relevance of operations management in order to actively engage in learning the material.

Key Terms

Key terms are presented in bold and defined in the margin as they are introduced. A list of chapter key terms is also available at the end of the chapter.

supply chain The global network of organizations and activities involved in designing, transforming, consuming, and disposing of goods and services.	A **supply chain** is the global network of organizations and activities involved in (1) designing a set of goods and services and their related processes, (2) transforming inputs into goods and services, (3) consuming these goods and services, and (4) disposing of these goods and services. Think about all the different organizations located in different companies that are

Student Activity

Students are asked to do a personal activity that illustrates the concept being presented or covered, thereby helping them learn to apply the concepts and understand them more deeply.

activity

student

Find a description of digital moviemaking technology on the Internet. Which of the stages and organizations depicted in Figure 1-3 are likely to be most affected by a shift to a completely digital process? How will the structure of the overall supply chain be changed?

Numbered Examples

Numbered examples are integrated into chapters where analytic techniques are introduced. Students learn how to solve specific problems step-by-step and gain insight into general principles by seeing how they are applied.

EXAMPLE 2-1

Suppose that the director of marketing has approached you, as a member of the top management team, with a suggestion that appears very attractive. The proposal begins by noting that because demand is down, the firm (and its supply chain) has much unused capacity. Happily, the marketing group has identified a new potential customer segment. Unlike existing customers (who are price sensitive and who buy large quantities of fairly standard products), these new customers will likely order smaller quantities more frequently. The new customers are also likely to want to make last-minute changes to order sizes, due dates, and product mix. Your current operating system is not really set up to accommodate such changes. However, the marketing director feels that the prices these customers are willing to pay will provide gross margins (30 percent, as compared to the 10–15 percent currently being given by existing customers) that should be high enough to offset any operational problems. The chief financial officer has stated that, in order to enter any new market, it must be expected to generate at least a 25 percent return on assets (ROA).

Given the information provided below, would you recommend accepting the marketing director's proposal?

Category	Estimated First Year Impact	Comments
Sales	$420,000	
Cost of Goods Sold	$294,000	30% gross margin

Figures and Photos

The text includes photographs and graphic illustrations to support student study and provide interest and motivation.

Honda airplane powered by Honda jet engine.
© Kyodo/Landov

FIGURE 2-1 Strategic Planning Hierarchy

Get Real Boxes

Throughout the chapters, readings highlight important real-world applications. They provide examples of operations issues and offer a picture of the concepts in practice. These also provide a basis for classroom discussion and generate interest in the subject matter.

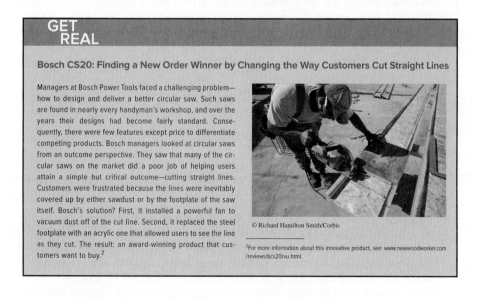

GET REAL

Bosch CS20: Finding a New Order Winner by Changing the Way Customers Cut Straight Lines

Managers at Bosch Power Tools faced a challenging problem—how to design and deliver a better circular saw. Such saws are found in nearly every handyman's workshop, and over the years their designs had become fairly standard. Consequently, there were few features except price to differentiate competing products. Bosch managers looked at circular saws from an outcome perspective. They saw that many of the circular saws on the market did a poor job of helping users attain a simple but critical outcome—cutting straight lines. Customers were frustrated because the lines were inevitably covered up by either sawdust or by the footplate of the saw itself. Bosch's solution? First, it installed a powerful fan to vacuum dust off of the cut line. Second, it replaced the steel footplate with an acrylic one that allowed users to see the line as they cut. The result: an award-winning product that customers want to buy.[2]

© Richard Hamilton Smith/Corbis

[2]For more information about this innovative product, see: www.newwoodworker.com/reviews/bcs20rvu.html.

Logos

Logos are included throughout the text to point out relevant applications of relationships, sustainability, and global issues.

Since most organizations have supply chains that reach beyond a single country, we examine global issues associated with operations and supply chain management.

global

Organizations must collaborate with customers and suppliers to accomplish many operations activities. Thus, the book showcases how to build, maintain, and benefit from cross-functional and interorganizational relationships.

relationships

To reduce costs and be competitive, organizations today must adopt sustainable business practices. In fact, we expect sustainability to become a key metric for operations and supply chain management performance.

sustainability

END-OF-CHAPTER RESOURCES

For student study and review, the following items are provided at the end of each chapter:

Chapter Summary Chapters contain summaries that provide an overview of the material covered.

CHAPTER SUMMARY

This chapter has introduced the operations strategic planning process within the context of supply chain management. In discussing this process, the following points were made within this chapter:

1. Strategic planning defines the specific types of value that the firm will deliver to its customers. It takes place at three levels. Corporate strategy identifies the business units to be included in the firm. Business unit strategy defines how the business will compete. Operations strategy identifies the priorities, capabilities, and resource deployments needed to support the business strategy and associated value proposition. These three levels of strategic planning should be integrated, with planning taking place from the top down, while execution takes place from the bottom up.

2. Operations strategic planning is driven by the business model—an integrative, systematic view of how the SBU generates value. This planning process begins with the

Key Terms Key terms are highlighted in the text, and then repeated at the end of the chapter with page references.

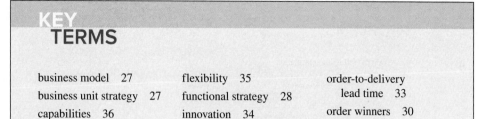

KEY TERMS

business model 27	flexibility 35	order-to-delivery lead time 33
business unit strategy 27	functional strategy 28	order winners 30
capabilities 36	innovation 34	

Discussion Questions Each chapter has a list of discussion questions. These are intended to serve as a student self-review or as class discussion starters.

DISCUSSION QUESTIONS

1. Why should the firm never outsource its core capabilities? What happens if the firm is approached by a supplier who is willing to supply goods and services based on these core capabilities at a significantly lower price? What should the firm do?
2. Apply the corporate/SBU/functional planning hierarchy introduced in this chapter to your university/college or business. What would be the equivalent to corporate planning? SBU planning? Functional planning?
3. How would you define capabilities within a school or business?
4. When can a consumer be a critical consumer? In other words, when does it make sense to focus on consumers such as retail stores, distributors, or buyers, rather than on the end consumer?
5. A critical concept introduced in this chapter was that of the value proposition. Explore

Solved Problems Solved problems are provided to illustrate problem solving and the main concepts in the chapter. These have been carefully prepared to enhance student understanding as well as to provide additional examples of problem solving.

SOLVED PROBLEM

Suppose you have been asked to determine the return on net worth for Great Northwest Canoe and Kayak, a small manufacturer of kayaks and canoes, located near Seattle, Washington. For this task, you have been given the following information:

Categories	Values
Sales	$32,000,000
Cost of goods sold	$20,000,000
Variable expenses	$ 4,000,000
Fixed expenses	$ 6,000,000
Inventory	$ 8,000,000
Accounts receivable	$ 4,000,000
Other current assets	$ 3,000,000
Fixed assets	$ 6,000,000

Problems Each chapter includes a set of problems for assignment. The problems are intended to be challenging but doable for students.

PROBLEMS

1. Given the following information:

Categories	Values
Sales	$32,000,000
Cost of goods sold	$20,000,000
Variable expenses	$ 4,000,000
Fixed expenses	$ 6,000,000
Inventory	$ 8,000,000
Accounts receivable	$ 4,000,000
Other current assets	$ 3,000,000
Fixed assets	$ 6,000,000

  a. What is the net profit margin for this firm?
  b. What is the asset turnover?
  c. What is the return on assets?

Cases The text includes short cases for most chapters. The cases were selected to provide a broader, more integrated thinking opportunity for students without taking a full "case" approach.

CASE

Trail Frames Chassis

Trail Frames Chassis (TFC) of Elkhart, Indiana, is a major manufacturer of chassis for the motor home and van markets. Since it was founded in 1976 by two unemployed truck-manufacturing engineers, TFC has grown into one of the major suppliers in this market. Success in the motor home and van markets is difficult because of the constant rate of change taking place. Increasingly, motor homes and vans are bought by people in their late 40s to 60s. What these people want is a motor home that rides like a car. They are willing to pay for innovations such as ABS (antilock breaking systems),

This approach has served TFC well for a number of years. However, recently sales for TFC have begun to level off. After visiting numerous customers in the field, John Stickley identified what he thought was the reason for this leveling off—the market for high-end, customized motor home chassis had been effectively saturated. There were only just so many customized motor homes that people wanted. Several of the major customers for TFC had strongly hinted that there was another market that TFC could enter that was consistent with its design strengths and its reputation.

INSTRUCTOR RESOURCES

Online Learning Center (OLC) www.mhhe.com/swink3e

The Online Learning Center provides complete materials for study and review. At this book's website, instructors have access to teaching supports such as electronic files of the ancillary materials: Solutions Manual, PowerPoint Lecture Slides, Digital Image Library, and Test Bank.

Solutions Manual. Prepared by the authors, this manual contains solutions to all the end-of-chapter problems and cases.

Test Bank. Prepared by the authors, the Test Bank includes true/false, multiple-choice, and discussion questions/problems at varying levels of difficulty.

EZ Test Online. All test bank questions are available in EZ Test Online, a flexible electronic testing program. The answers to all questions are given, along with a rating of the level of difficulty, chapter learning objective met, Bloom's taxonomy question type, and the AACSB knowledge category.

PowerPoint Lecture Slides. The PowerPoint slides draw on the highlights of each chapter and provide an opportunity for the instructor to emphasize the key concepts in class discussions.

Digital Image Library. All the figures in the book are included for insertion in Power-Point slides or for class discussion.

Operations Management Video Series

The operations management video series, free to text adopters, includes professionally developed videos showing students real applications of key manufacturing and service topics in real companies. Each segment includes on-site or plant footage, interviews with company managers, and focused presentations of OM applications in use to help the companies gain competitive advantage. Companies such as Zappos, FedEx, Subaru, Disney, BP, Chase Bank, DHL, Louisville Slugger, McDonald's, Noodles, and Honda are featured.

CourseSmart (ISBM: 0077535049)

CourseSmart is a convenient way to find and buy eTextbooks. At CourseSmart you can save up to 60 percent off the cost of a print textbook, reduce your impact on the environment, and gain access to powerful Web tools for learning. CourseSmart has the largest selection of eTextbooks available anywhere, offering thousands of the most commonly adopted textbooks from a wide variety of higher education publishers. CourseSmart eTextbooks are available in one standard online reader with full text search, notes and highlighting, and e-mail tools for sharing notes between classmates. Visit www.CourseSmart.com for more information.

TECHNOLOGY

McGraw-Hill *Connect*® *Operations Management*

McGraw-Hill Connect® Operations Management is an online assignment and assessment solution that connects students with the tools and resources they'll need to achieve success through faster learning, higher retention, and more efficient studying. It provides instructors with tools to quickly pick content and assignments according to the topics they want to emphasize.

Online Assignments. *Connect Operations Management* helps students learn more efficiently by providing practice material and feedback when they are needed. *Connect* grades homework automatically and provides feedback on any questions that students may have missed.

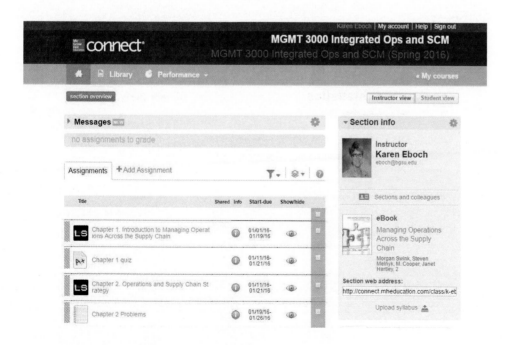

Integration of Excel Data Sets. A convenient feature is the inclusion of an Excel data file link in many problems using data files in their calculation. The link allows students to easily launch into Excel, work the problem, and return to *Connect* to key in the answer.

Guided Examples. These narrated video walkthroughs provide students with step-by-step guidelines for solving problems similar to those contained in the text. The student is given personalized instruction on how to solve a problem by applying the concepts presented in the chapter. The narrated voiceover shows the steps to take to work through an exercise. Students can go through each example multiple times if needed.

LEARNSMART

LearnSmart. LearnSmart adaptive self-study technology with *Connect Operations Management* helps students make the best use of their study time. LearnSmart provides a seamless combination of practice, assessment, and remediation for every concept in the textbook. LearnSmart's intelligent software adapts to students by supplying questions on a new concept when students are ready to learn it. With LearnSmart students will spend less time on topics they understand and instead focus on the topics they need to master.

Simple Assignment Management and Smart Grading. When it comes to studying, time is precious. *Connect Operations Management* helps students learn more efficiently by providing feedback and practice material when they need it, where they need it. When it comes to teaching, your time also is precious. The grading function enables you to:

- Have assignments scored automatically, giving students immediate feedback on their work and side-by-side comparisons with correct answers.
- Access and review each response; manually change grades or leave comments for students to review.

Student Reporting. *Connect Operations Management* keeps instructors informed about how each student, section, and class is performing, allowing for more productive use of lecture and office hours. The progress-tracking function enables you to:

- View scored work immediately (Add Assignment Results Screen) and track individual or group performance with assignment and grade reports.
- Access an instant view of student or class performance relative to learning objectives.
- Collect data and generate reports required by many accreditation organizations, such as AACSB.

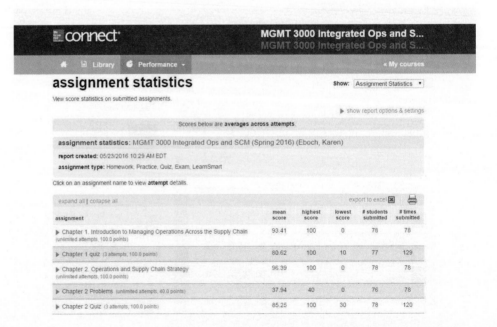

Instructor Library. The *Connect Operations Management* Instructor Library is your repository for additional resources to improve student engagement in and out of class. You can select and use any asset that enhances your lecture. The *Connect Business Statistics* Instructor Library includes:

- eBook
- PowerPoint presentations
- Test Bank
- Instructor's Solutions Manual
- Digital Image Library

Connect® *Plus Operations Management* includes a seamless integration of an eBook and *Connect Operations Management* with rich functionality integrated into the product.

Integrated Media-Rich eBook. An integrated media-rich eBook allows students to access media in context with each chapter. Students can highlight, take notes, and access shared instructor highlights/notes to learn the course material.

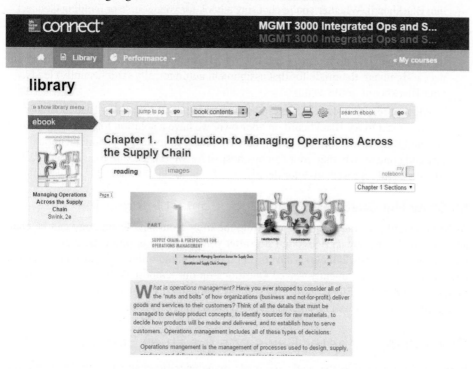

Dynamic Links. Dynamic links between the problems or questions you assign to your students and the location in the eBook where that problem or question is covered.

Powerful Search Function. A powerful search function to pinpoint and connect key concepts in a snap. This state-of-the-art, thoroughly tested system supports you in preparing students for the world that awaits. For more information about *Connect*, go to www.mcgrawhillconnect.com or contact your local McGraw-Hill sales representative.

Tegrity Campus: Lectures 24/7

Tegrity Campus is a service that makes class time available 24/7 by automatically capturing every lecture in a searchable format for students to review when they study and complete assignments. With a simple one-click start-and-stop process, you capture all computer screens and corresponding audio. Students can replay any part of any class with easy-to-use browser-based viewing on a PC or Mac.

Educators know that the more students can see, hear, and experience class resources, the better they learn. In fact, studies prove it. With *Tegrity Campus*, students quickly recall key moments by using *Tegrity Cam-pus*'s unique search feature. This search helps students efficiently find what they need, when they need it, across an entire semester of class recordings. Help turn all your students' study time into learning moments immediately supported by your lecture. To learn more about *Tegrity,* watch a two-minute Flash demo at http://tegritycampus.mhhe.com.

Online Course Management

The **Best** of **Both Worlds**

No matter what online course management system you use (WebCT, BlackBoard, or eCollege), we have a course content ePack available for your course. Our new ePacks are specifically designed to make it easy for students to navigate and access content online. For help, our online Digital Learning Consultants are ready to assist you with your online course needs. They provide training and will answer any questions you have throughout the life of your adoption. McGraw-Hill Higher Education and Blackboard have teamed up. What does this mean for you?

1. **Single sign-on.** Now you and your students can access McGraw-Hill's Connect and Create right from within your Blackboard course-all with one single sign-on.

2. **Deep integration of content and tools.** You get a single sign-on with Connect and Create, and you also get integration of McGraw-Hill content and content engines right into Blackboard. Whether you're choosing a book for your course or building Connect assignments, all the tools you need are right where you want them-inside of Blackboard.

3. **One gradebook.** Keeping several gradebooks and manually synchronizing grades into Blackboard is no longer necessary. When a student completes an integrated Connect assignment, the grade for that assignment automatically (and instantly) feeds your Blackboard grade center.

4. **A solution for everyone.** Whether your institution is already using Blackboard or you just want to try Blackboard on your own, we have a solution for you. McGraw-Hill and Blackboard can now offer you easy access to industry-leading technology and content, whether your campus hosts it, or we do. Be sure to ask your local McGraw-Hill representative for details.

McGraw-Hill Customer Experience Contact Information

At McGraw-Hill, we understand that getting the most from new technology can be challenging. That's why our services don't stop after you purchase our products. You can e-mail our Product Specialists 24 hours a day to get product training online. Or you can search our knowledge bank of Frequently Asked Questions on our support Web site. For Customer Support, call **800-331-5094,** or visit www.mhhe.com/support. One of our Customer Experience Team members will be able to assist you in a timely fashion.

Chapter-by-Chapter Revisions for Third Edition

In this major revision to the book, we made many specific changes to the chapters; the larger changes are highlighted for each chapter below. We updated or replaced most of the opening vignettes and Get Real stories throughout the book. We added about 20 percent more practice problems, as well as more solved problems and examples.

Chapter 1: Introduction to Managing Operations Across the Supply Chain

*   Made stronger linkages of operations to other functions, economies, and business success.

Chapter 2: Operations and Supply Chain Strategy

*   New opening vignette on Redbubble.
*   Added a case on Lil Me, a manufacturer of customized dolls that look like their owner.
*   Additional discussion questions and problems.

Chapter 3 and 3S: Managing Processes and Capacity

*   Included a better focus on the notion of process thinking.
*   Additional discussion questions and problems.

Chapter 4: Product/Process Innovation

- New **Get Real** on Lego.
- New discussion of crowdsourcing and 3D printing.
- Additional problems.

Chapter 5: Manufacturing and Service Process Structures

- New opening vignette on Invisalign and their use of 3D printing, robots, and customer contact.
- Added a discussion of 3D printing.
- Major revision to Capabilities Enabling Technologies section including more on mobile apps, robots, drones, and Internet of Things.
- New **Get Real** on Robots.
- Additional discussion questions and problems.

Chapter 6: Managing Quality

- Updated the Hyundai story to include awards and changes within the last 3 years.
- Updated Get Real on food safety.
- Dropped discussion of Malcolm Baldrige award.
- Additional problems.

Chapter 6 Supplement: Quality Improvement Tools

- Additional discussion questions and problems.

Chapter 7: Managing Inventories

- Additional discussion questions and problems.

Chapter 8: Lean Systems

- Additional discussion questions and problems.

Chapter 9: Customer Service Management

- New opening vignette focusing on Macy's and its attempts to deal with the "Amazon Effect".
- Detailed discussion of how Amazon has changed customer service through its impact on such issues as returns and customer knowledge.
- Additional problems.

Chapter 10: Sourcing and Supply Management

- New opening vignette on sourcing and supply management at Chipotle.
- New **Get Real** on Flextronics and supply chain risk management.
- Updated the supplier quality **Get Real** box to discuss Takata air bags.
- New **Get Real** on K'Nex and reshoring.
- Added a student activity about insourcing/outsourcing.
- Additional discussion questions and problems.

Chapter 11: Logistics Management

- New opening vignette about Amazon's innovations in delivery.
- New **Get Real** on how mobile apps are transforming the trucking industry.
- New **Get Real** on how GameStop depends upon reverse logistics.
- Additional problems.

Chapter 12: Demand Planning: Forecasting and Demand Management

- New **Get Real** on how Lennox uses artificial intelligence to improve demand planning.
- Additional discussion questions and problems.

Chapter 13: Sales and Operations Planning

- Additional discussion questions and problems.

Chapter 14: Materials and Resource Requirements Planning

- Added a new vignette on Blue Apron, a home meal delivery service.
- Additional problems.

Chapter 15 and 15S: Project Management

- Updated opening Pixar vignette.
- Updated to include some of Pixar's recent hit movies.
- Additional problems.

Chapter 16: Sustainable Operations Management-Preparing for the Future

- Updated Unilever vignette with achievements of zero landfill waste.
- New **Get Real** on Patagonia's sustainability efforts.
- Discussion of Starbucks Reserve, a new experiential coffee store in Seattle aimed at making the experience of brewing and enjoying a unique cup of coffee critical and attractive
- Discussion of how the Internet of Things (IoT) is affecting not only the supply chain but also the business model.

Brief Contents

Contents

PART 1

SUPPLY CHAIN: A PERSPECTIVE FOR OPERATIONS MANAGEMENT

		relationships	sustainability	global
1	Introduction to Managing Operations Across the Supply Chain	X	X	X
2	Operations and Supply Chain Strategy	X	X	X

*W*hat is operations management? Have you ever stopped to consider all of the specifics of how organizations (business and not-for-profit) deliver goods and services to their customers? Think of all the details that must be managed to develop product concepts, identify sources for raw materials, decide how products will be made and delivered, and establish how to serve customers. Operations management includes all of these types of decisions:

Operations management is the management of processes used to design, supply, produce, and deliver valuable goods and services to customers.

In Part 1, *Supply Chain: A Perspective for Operations Management,* we define the scope of operations

management, as well as its strategic role in businesses. **Chapter 1** explains what operations management is and why it is important for all managers (accounting, marketing, finance, and other managers) to understand the basics of this management discipline. **Chapter 1** also introduces an important perspective, the *supply chain*, as a way to think about how to coordinate operational activities across different organizations. **Chapter 2** describes how strategic choices in operations management relate to an organization's overall objectives and to choices made in marketing, finance, and other functional areas. In addition, **Chapter 2** explains how to increase competitiveness through effective operations and how to measure the effectiveness of operations activities.

1

Introduction to Managing Operations Across the Supply Chain

LEARNING OBJECTIVES

After studying this chapter, you should be able to:

LO1-1 Explain what operations management is and why it is important.

LO1-2 Describe the major decisions that operations managers typically make.

LO1-3 Explain the role of processes and "process thinking" in operations management.

LO1-4 Explain what the supply chain is and what it means to view operations management using a "supply chain perspective."

LO1-5 Identify the partners and functional groups that work together in operations management.

LO1-6 Define the planning activities associated with managing operations across the supply chain.

Apple often receives praise for its user-friendly and aesthetically pleasing product designs. But a less well-known contributor to Apple's success is its prowess in managing operations across its supply chain. This is the world of manufacturing, procurement, and logistics in which the chief executive officer, Tim Cook, excelled, earning him the trust of Steve Jobs. Apple has built a closed ecosystem where it exerts control over nearly every piece of the supply chain, from design to retail store.

This operational edge is what enables Apple to handle massive product launches without having to maintain large, profit-sapping inventories. It has allowed a company often criticized for high prices to sell its iPad at a price that very few rivals can beat, while still earning a 25 percent margin on the device. Some of the basic elements of Apple's operational strategy include:

- Capitalize on volume. Because of its buying power, Apple gets big discounts on parts, manufacturing capacity, and air freight.

- Work closely with suppliers. Apple engineers sometimes spend months living out of hotel rooms in order to be close to suppliers and manufacturers, helping to tweak the industrial processes and tools that translate prototypes into mass-produced devices.

- Focus on a few product lines, with little customization. Apple's unified strategy allows it to eliminate complexity and cost, while maximizing volume-based economies in its supply chain.

- Ensure supply availability and low prices. Apple makes big upfront payments to suppliers to lock in their capacity and to limit options for competitors.

- Keep a close eye on demand. By selling through its own retail stores, Apple can track demand by specific store and by the hour; then it adjusts sales forecasts and production plans daily to respond quickly to demand changes.

Apple designs cool products. But its enormous profit margins—two to four times the profit margins of most other hardware companies—come in large part from its priority and focus on operations management.

This book, *Managing Operations Across the Supply Chain,* will help you to study "operations management" using a "supply chain" perspective. This perspective means that we will examine operational activities that take place *within firms* as well those *that cross firms' boundaries,* involving suppliers and customers of all types. This larger network of organizations makes up a firm's *supply chain.*

The Apple story illustrates the value of this broad perspective of operations management. The combination of excellence in both internal product design operations and external supply chain operations management makes Apple a dominant player in its industry. Operations management by definition spans a large number of activities that take place both inside and outside the business firm.

A BROAD DEFINITION OF SUPPLY CHAIN OPERATIONS MANAGEMENT

operations management The management of processes used to design, supply, produce, and deliver valuable goods and services to customers.

Operations management is the management of processes used to design, supply, produce, and deliver valuable goods and services to customers.

Operations management includes the planning and execution of tasks that may be long-term (yearly) or short-term (daily) in nature. An operations manager interacts with managers in other business functions, both inside and outside the operations manager's own company. Operations management thus spans the boundaries of any single firm, bringing together the activities of internal operations (i.e., internal to a given company) with the operations of customers, suppliers, and other partners around the world. Operations located around the globe are becoming more tightly interconnected all the time. The supply chain concept can be used to describe connections among business partners.

supply chain The global network of organizations and activities involved in designing, transforming, consuming, and disposing of goods and services.

A **supply chain** is the global network of organizations and activities involved in (1) designing a set of goods and services and their related processes, (2) transforming inputs into goods and services, (3) consuming these goods and services, and (4) disposing of these goods and services.

Think about all the different organizations located in different companies that are involved in converting raw materials into a delivered finished product. Dozens of organizations are involved in producing and delivering even a simple product like bottled water. Together, supply chain organizations perform all the value-creating activities required to innovate, plan, source, make, deliver, and return or dispose of a given set of products and services.[1] Other terms sometimes substituted for *supply chain* include *demand chain, extended enterprise, supply network,* or *supply web.* All of these terms reflect the idea that a supply chain involves connections and relationships among organizations that play various roles for a given set of products.

LO1-1 Explain what operations management is and why it is important.

Operations management activities located throughout a supply chain create and enhance the value of goods and services by increasing their economic value (e.g., lowering delivered cost), functional value (e.g., improving product quality or convenience), and psychosocial value (e.g., improving product aesthetics and desirability). The following statements help define and describe operations management:

- Operations management is mainly concerned with how resources will be developed and used to accomplish business goals.
- Operations management is about designing, executing, and improving business processes.
- Operations management deals with processes that transform inputs, including materials, information, energy, money, and even people, into goods and services.
- Within a supply chain context, operations management brings together four major sets of players: the firm, customers, suppliers, and stakeholders.

---

[1]Supply Chain Council, *Integrated Supply Chain Performance Measurement: A Multi-Industry Consortium Recommendation,* Supply Chain Council Report #5566, p. 1.

- To be effective, operations management must be consistent with the strategic goals of the firm.
- Operations management is dynamic because of changes in customers' demands, resources, competition, and technologies.

relationships

To work in this increasingly interconnected world, you will need to understand the foundational concepts, functional groups, and integrated activities involved in managing operations located across a supply chain. The Get Real box below describes why operations management is important to all of us.

Even if you do not pursue a career in operations management, it will be important for you to understand and appreciate the fundamental challenges associated with managing operations well. First, the decisions you make as a worker in marketing, finance, accounting, human resources, or other areas will have an impact on, and be impacted by, operations. For example, suppose that you work in a hotel where managers want to buy new kiosks that will allow guests to check themselves into the hotel. The effects of this decision extend beyond operational issues such as labor costs and efficiency. The decision will also have implications for the use of capital (a finance

Automated check-in kiosks at a hotel.
© Randy Duchaine/Alamy Stock Photo

GET REAL

Why You Need to Study Operations Management

Because it matters to people:

Operations management plays an important role in determining the quality of life for people around the world. New operational practices and technologies continue to radically improve the effectiveness of governments, not-for-profit institutions, and businesses. Operations management also directly impacts sustainability issues, including the environment, the fair treatment of people, and safety. In doing so, operations management affects social systems and cultural norms, as well as the basic economic prosperity of people everywhere. Consider how your own life is affected. The speed with which organizations provide services to you determines the amount of leisure time you have. In an emergency, the speed and efficiency of a relief organization might even save your life. The cost and quality of products you consume affects your disposable income, your health, even your outlook on life. You can probably think of a good service experience that put a smile on your face, or a bad one that ruined your day! As an operations manager, you may someday have the opportunity and responsibility to positively affect your organization's success. In doing so, you may also be improving the quality of life of the firm's employees, its customers, and even society as a whole.

Because it matters to organizations:

Every product or service offering is a promise of some kind of benefit for someone. Organizations are successful only when they can consistently deliver upon the promises that they make. Operations management determines how well such promises are fulfilled. Research shows that operationally excellent organizations consistently outperform their rivals in financial and other terms. For example, a study[2] showed that companies possessing excellent supply chain operations outperformed their nearest competitors in the following ways:

- 50 percent higher net profit margins
- 20 percent lower sales, general & administration (SG&A) expenses
- 12 percent lower average inventories
- 30 percent less working capital expenses
- Twice the return on assets (ROA)
- Twice the return on equity (ROE)
- 44 percent higher economic value added
- Twice the returns on stock prices
- 2.4 times the risk-weighted stock returns
- 46 percent greater market-value-to-assets ratio

These differences in performance are truly stunning and highlight the important contributions that operations management makes to the financial well-being of a firm.

[2]M. L. Swink, R. Golecha, and T. Richardson, "Does Becoming a Top Supply Chain Company Really Pay Off? An Analysis of Top SCM Companies and Their Rivals," *Supply Chain Management Review*, March 2010, pp. 14–21.

concern), the type of service provided to customers (a marketing concern), and the training of employees (a human resource management concern). Managers of various functions cannot work in isolation if they hope to make decisions that are good for the overall success of the firm. Second, all activities, including marketing, finance, accounting, and so on, have operational elements to them. For example, think about the operational processes required to run a sales office. Managers in all functions need to understand the principles of operations management in order to keep their functional processes running effectively and efficiently.

Important Decisions in Supply Chain Operations Management

What?

- What types of activities and what types of goods or services are to be delivered by the system?
- What product features do our intended customers care about?
- What activities and resources are needed, and how should they be developed, allocated, and controlled?

How?

- How is the good or service to be designed, made, and delivered?
- How much should our transformation process be able to deliver (and under what conditions)?
- How should we measure and assess performance?

When?

- When should products be made, activities be carried out, services be delivered, or capacities/facilities come on line?

Where and Who?

- Where should certain activities be done, and who should do them: suppliers, partners, or the firm?

relationships

Operations managers answer these questions by defining both the structural and infrastructural aspects of the operations management system. Structural decisions affect physical resources such as capacity, facilities, technology, and the supply chain network. Once made, decisions in these areas determine what the operations management system can and cannot do well. Altering these decisions often requires significant investments and lots of time—often years. Infrastructural decisions affect the workforce, production planning and control, process innovation, and organization. Decisions in these areas determine what is done, when it is done, and who does it. Decisions in all of these areas are interrelated, making operations management a complex and cross-functional activity.

Differences in Goods and Services Operations

Operational activities exist in order to produce both tangible goods and intangible services. Books, cars, and televisions are all tangible goods. In contrast, services like health care, banking, and entertainment are largely experiential or informational. For example, at a hair salon, you *consume* the expertise and labor of the hair stylist as part of the experience of getting a haircut. The experiences and information you receive at school form a service called *education.* Table 1-1 summarizes some of the important differences between goods and services.

Some businesses are mostly about producing goods (e.g., production of gasoline), and some are mostly about delivering services (e.g., financial consulting). However, most businesses integrate a mix of goods-producing and service-producing operations activities.

TABLE 1-1   Characteristics of Goods and Services

Goods	Services
Tangible	Intangible
Can be inventoried	Cannot be inventoried
Little customer contact (consumption is often separate from production)	Extensive customer contact (simultaneous production and consumption)
Long lead times	Short lead times
Often capital-intensive	Often labor-intensive
Quality easily assessed	Quality more difficult to assess (more perceptual)
Material is transformed	Information or the customer is transformed

There are key structural differences in operational processes designed to provide mostly goods versus mostly services. Chapter 5 discusses these differences in depth, but we will highlight a few important ones here. First, goods can be produced in advance and stored in inventory until a customer buys or consumes them. Since services are intangible, they cannot be stored. The production and consumption of a service usually occur at the same time. While goods-manufacturing operations can use inventory to smooth out imbalances between production capacity and customer demand, a producer of services must maintain enough capacity to meet demand during peak periods; otherwise, it must postpone (backlog) the demand. For example, when you go into a restaurant during its busy time and the greeter asks you to wait in the lounge, you become part of a backlog of demand. Service operations managers often use reservation and appointment systems to help customers avoid long wait times.

In services, customers frequently can observe the operational processes directly. In fact, the customer may take part in producing and consuming the service at the same time (think of your roles as co-designer and quality inspector in getting a haircut). On the other hand, the production of goods may require little contact with the customer.

Finally, operations managers can easily establish measurable quality standards for tangible goods to evaluate whether they work adequately, how they appear, and so on. Quality control is more difficult for services, as it is not always easy to objectively measure a service product's attributes. Service operations managers often evaluate both methods of delivery and customer perceptions. For example, a quality control inspector for a movie theater might study how workers interact with customers as they sell tickets or food to customers. In addition, they may periodically survey customers to gauge their levels of satisfaction.

In reality, there are very few pure goods and pure services. Most manufactured products also include services. When you buy a new car,

activity

Think of the last time you visited an amusement park (like Disney World). How many different goods and services did you consume as part of your overall experience? How many of these products were "pure" goods and "pure" services? Which of these products was prepared before you ordered it (inventoried), versus being prepared at the very time that you ordered it?

for example, you may also buy financing, maintenance, and repair services. Many service products also include tangible items. A hospital, for example, provides medicines and bandages along with intangible diagnostic and treatment services.

Because most firms deliver products that involve both goods and services, operations managers recognize the importance of delivering a **total product experience**. This term refers to all of the outputs of an operation, both goods and services, that are combined to define a customer's complete consumption experience. The experience includes all aspects of purchasing, consuming, and disposing of the product.

total product experience All the goods and services that are combined to define a customer's complete consumption experience.

Processes and Process Thinking

process A system of activities that transforms inputs into valuable outputs.

LO1-3 Explain the role of processes and "process thinking" in operations management.

Operations management is a *process*-oriented discipline. What, then, is a process? It is a system of activities that *transforms* inputs into valuable outputs. Processes use resources (workers, machines, money, and knowledge) to transform inputs (such as materials, energy, money, people, and data) into outputs (goods and services). For example, one uses a grill (a resource) and heat (an input) to convert a raw hamburger patty (an input) into a cooked hamburger (an output).

Processes can also transform information, or even people (customers), from one condition into another. In decision making, for example, managers transform data into actionable information and decisions. Think about how you are "transformed" by going to a movie—this is a process in which you are both an input and an output! Other processes transform things by transporting them from one location to another, or by storing them (e.g., a warehouse stores finished goods). Finally, some activities check or inspect work to make sure that it meets standards for quality, quantity, or timeliness.

Every organization can be described as a bundle of processes that connect different organizational groups. For example, companies use *design processes* to develop new goods and services and *strategic planning processes* to determine how the firm should compete. They use *production processes* to plan and execute the supply, manufacture, and delivery of goods and services to customers. Finally, companies use *evaluation processes* to measure and report how well they are meeting their goals or using their resources.

It is valuable to think about operations as *sets of processes and subprocesses* with many interrelationships and linkages. Consider the operations of an airport. There are flight-scheduling processes, ticketing processes, facilities-management processes, security processes, vendor-management processes, and on and on. The structure governing how these processes work together determines the ability of the airport to serve its customers.

We all have experienced organizations with complex, bureaucratic processes that seem incapable of providing a desired service in a timely manner. The design of a process should reflect what customers want. If customers want quick response, for example, then the process should be designed to be fast and flexible. In this case operations managers must identify and eliminate unnecessary or redundant steps, reduce distances between steps or activities, and diminish the time needed to complete each step. This connection between the process design and customers' desires must be maintained. If customers' desires change, then processes may also have to change.

An airport operation contains dozens of interrelated processes.
© Gary Conner/Getty Images

FIGURE 1-1
Foundational Concepts
in Supply Chain
Operations Management

Process thinking is so important that we have dedicated an entire section of this book to topics related to it. Figure 1-1 shows the conceptual building blocks of process thinking that are essential to the management of any operation. A separate chapter in this book addresses each building block. The bottom three blocks represent the foundational principles that describe how operational processes work, how product and process characteristics are intertwined, and how certain process structures are related to operational objectives. In order to make good decisions, operations managers need to understand the "physics" that govern processes, as well as understand how they relate to product design and development.

Building upon this foundational knowledge, operations managers can better understand how to make good decisions regarding product quality and the use of inventory (the second row of blocks in Figure 1-1). Product quality is a result of how people and technologies work together to execute processes. Inventory management can make processes more or less efficient, depending on whether the inventory is used wisely or unwisely.

The top block in Figure 1-1, "Managing Lean Systems," represents the application of all the aforementioned process-related concepts in ways that maximize the overall productivity of the operation. A **lean operation** produces maximum levels of efficiency and effectiveness using a minimal amount of resources.

lean operation An operation that produces maximum levels of efficiency and effectiveness using a minimal amount of resources.

OPERATIONS MANAGEMENT YESTERDAY AND TODAY: GROWTH OF THE SUPPLY CHAIN MANAGEMENT PERSPECTIVE

Many of the formal practices and concepts of operations management have their origins in the Industrial Revolution, which took place in the latter half of the 18th century. As an activity, however, operations management is much older. Signs of organized operations have been found in all ancient civilizations including Greece, Rome, and Egypt. Building the great pyramids was undoubtedly accomplished by means of organized operations, even if we don't know the exact nature of those operations.

Table 1-2 provides a brief history of operations management. Since the Industrial Revolution, modern operations management has evolved at different rates throughout the world. In America, the early 20th century witnessed a huge growth in demand and the rise of mass production. The latter half of the century was marked by standardization of operations practices and by fierce global competition. Today, continued globalization, the Internet, and numerous other technologies are radically transforming business operations.

"Supply chain management" represents the latest technological shift in operations management. This now-dominant perspective is the result of certain forces in the marketplace, discussed below.

LO1-4 Explain what the supply chain is and what it means to view operations management using a "supply chain perspective."

TABLE 1-2   A Brief History of Operations Management

Operations Era		Technological Advances	Operations Management Span of Focus
1800–1850	Technical Capitalists	Improved manufacturing technology; interchangeable parts; locating factories on waterways and in industrial centers; emerging transportation network	Internal production
1850–1890	Mass Production	Emergence of local factory; movement to urban areas; introduction of steam and electrical power; new machines; economies of scale	Internal production
1890–1920	Scientific Management	More systematic approaches to operations management; moving assembly line; beginnings of process thinking	Internal production
1920–1960	Demand Growth	Increased automation; introduction of computers and quantitative analysis	Internal production
1960–1980	Global Competition	Just-in-time systems; emergence of statistical process control; early outsourcing	Internal production
1980–2000	World-Class Manufacturing	Increased computerization and information systems; world-class practices and benchmarks; greater global sourcing and need for supply chain coordination	Production, design, supply
2000–Present	E-commerce	Internet; enhanced communications and transportation technologies; integrated management across functions, including goods and services operations	Global supply chain

Operations management existed even in ancient times.
© Look and Learn/The Bridgeman Art Library

Advances in Technology and Infrastructure

Advances in communications, computers, and transportation technologies have enabled extensive connectivity and the growth of supply chain partnerships. With easier information transactions, there is less of a need to include all operations at one location or within one organizational boundary. Constant information sharing between supply chain partners improves efficiencies in planning, in material movements, and in the transfers of funds.

At the same time, growing transportation technologies and infrastructures have made the shipping of goods and the transport of people faster, more reliable, and more economical than in decades past. Transportation infrastructure (airports, train tracks, shipping docks, and highways) continues to be built in developing countries. This growing infrastructure improves the reliability of deliveries to remote places, thus opening opportunities to work with new suppliers and serve new markets.

Reduction in Governmental Barriers to Trade

global

In recent years we have witnessed incredible changes in governments and social systems around the world. More and more nations have moved away from centrally controlled economies to pursue free market systems. Russia, India, and China represent a few important examples. These falling political barriers have opened up new opportunities to develop global supply chains. While these global supply chains can offer improved product costs and quality, they can also be more complex and risky. Today, operations managers must often manage long pipelines of inventories that cross multiple country borders.

Focus on Core Capabilities

With new technologies and global sources of supply, firms are now able to focus attention on their core capabilities—that is, things they do well. A core capability is a unique set of skills that confers competitive advantages to a firm, because rival firms cannot easily duplicate them.

    A focus on core capabilities leads a firm to concentrate on those few skills and areas of knowledge that make the firm distinct and competitive. The firm would then likely outsource other, noncore activities to suppliers who have advantages due to better skills or higher scale of operations. For example, Honda was one of the first companies to outsource many non-core activities such as component manufacturing, logistics, and other services. This allowed Honda to concentrate on design and assembly of motors and engines, its core capabilities.

    The result of the core capabilities approach is supply chains in which each of the partnering organizations focuses on what it does best. The overall effect is to produce greater product value through higher quality and greater efficiencies. However, it also makes supply chain partners more interdependent.

core capability A unique set of skills that confers competitive advantages to a firm, because rival firms cannot easily duplicate them.

relationships

Collaborative Networks

As firms become more reliant on their suppliers, the greatest improvements in product value are usually achieved through better coordination with these partners. However, when firms concentrate only on their immediate relationships, they address only a small portion of the total opportunity to improve the overall effectiveness of the system. For example, uncertainties in the availability of raw materials at a *supplier's* supplier can severely limit a firm's ability to deliver products to its customers. Problems like this can be avoided when partners across a supply chain network share their plans and capabilities and work together to develop improvements. In addition, the creation of partnerships in integrated networks opens up opportunities to take advantage of complementary cost structures, the respective partners' technical expertise, market knowledge, and brand equities (reputations). By combining such assets, companies are able to make stronger product offerings together than they could individually.

VIEWING OPERATIONS MANAGEMENT FROM A SUPPLY CHAIN MANAGEMENT PERSPECTIVE

We began this chapter by noting that operations managers must coordinate a system of activities both inside and outside their firm's boundaries. The network of organizations that contains this system of activities is often referred to as a *supply chain.* So how then is "supply chain management" different from "operations management"?

    Supply chain management is the design and execution of relationships and flows that connect the parties and processes across a supply chain. Recall that our definition of *operations management* is the management of processes used to design, supply, produce, and deliver valuable goods and services to customers.

    As you can see, there is a substantial degree of overlap between the two definitions. Operations management focuses on managing *processes* (design, supply, production, delivery); supply chain management focuses on managing *relationships* and *flows* (flows of information, materials, energy, money, and people). Think of supply chain management as a way of viewing operations management. You can also think of the supply chain as a network of organizations in which operations activities are conducted.

supply chain management The design and execution of relationships and flows that connect the parties and processes across a supply chain.

LO1-5 Identify the partners and functional groups that work together in operations management.

Operations Management Partners Across the Supply Chain

Operations managers interact with three important groups that are external to the firm: (1) customers, (2) suppliers, and (3) stakeholders. Figure 1-2 illustrates how operations management links internal operational processes with the operational processes of customers and suppliers. The figure also identifies some of the points of interaction between operational groups and other business functional groups within the firm.

Customers

customers Parties that use or consume the products of operations management processes.

Customers include anyone (individuals or organizations) that uses or consumes the products of operations management processes. An organization cannot structure an effective or efficient operations management function unless it has clearly identified its customers. Types of customers include *internal* customers, *intermediate* customers, and *final* customers. For example, consider a car manufacturer. A company-owned distribution center might be considered an internal customer of the manufacturing group; a dealership is an intermediate customer; and people who buy the car and drive it off the dealer's lot are the final customers, or consumers.

While each of these customer groups is important, it is beneficial for operations managers to identify *key customers*. Key customers have the greatest impact on product

FIGURE 1-2   Partners and Operations Functional Activities in the Supply Chain

OM's internal functional partners at technology supply chain interfaces:
- Product engineering
- Process / facilities engineering
- Human resources management
- Supply management
- Finance
- Marketing

Resource and Technology Suppliers

The Business Enterprise

(Chapter 10)   Sourcing and Supply Mgmt

Product and Service Suppliers

Supply Mgmt

Internal Operations Mgmt

Customer Service Mgmt (Chapter 9)

Customers and Partners

Logistics Mgmt (Chapter 11)

OM's internal functional partners at upstream product supply chain interfaces:
- Supply management
- Finance
- Logistics management
- Warehousing/raw materials planning

OM's internal functional partners at downstream product supply chain interfaces:
- Marketing
- Sales and distribution
- Customer service/relationship management
- Logistics management
- Warehousing/finished goods materials planning

designs, sales, and future growth opportunities. Often, but not always, the consumer is the key customer. For example, you are the consumer of this book, yet another customer (your professor) has had greater impact on the product design, sales, and growth opportunities for this product.

Suppliers

Figure 1-2 identifies important types of suppliers in the supply chain. Suppliers provide inputs to operational processes. The horizontal dimension of Figure 1-2 illustrates the flow of materials, information, and money related to the sourcing, making, and delivery of products. The vertical dimension of Figure 1-2 depicts suppliers of technologies and support services. From a single firm's perspective, there are multiple types of suppliers:

suppliers Parties that provide inputs to operational processes.

relationships

- *Upstream product suppliers* typically provide raw materials, components, and services directly related to manufacturing or service production processes.
- *Downstream product suppliers* typically provide enhancements to finished goods such as assembly, packaging, storage, and transportation services.
- *Resource and technology suppliers* provide equipment, labor, product and process designs, and other resources needed to support a firm's processes.
- *Aftermarket suppliers* provide product service and support such as maintenance, repair, disposal, or recycling.

Not shown in Figure 1-2 are a host of other suppliers who make up a part of the total supply chain, including suppliers of indirect goods and services such as mail delivery, health care benefits, cleaning services, and so on. Since suppliers provide so many of a firm's needed resources, technologies, raw materials, and services, the total portfolio of a firm's suppliers affects its success to a great extent.

Stakeholders

In addition to customers and suppliers, other groups of people also have an interest in the well-being (financial and otherwise) of an operation. Stakeholders include employees and unions, the local community, social groups (such as animals' rights or environmental concerns), government, and financial investors.

stakeholders Groups of people who have a financial or other interest in the well-being of an operation.

sustainability

Why differentiate between customers, suppliers, and stakeholders? Stakeholders' demands often differ from the demands of customers or suppliers. For example, customers might care most about the price and quality of products, whereas some stakeholders might care most about environmental concerns. Like customers and suppliers, stakeholders can significantly affect how a firm operates.

Cross-Functional Relationships in Operations Management

We have already noted that operations managers must work closely with other functions in the firm. Managers making any operating decision should consider the decision's effects on other functions, including engineering, finance, marketing, human resources, and others. As shown in Figure 1-2, operations managers who work at the boundaries of the firm often work very closely with other functional groups. For example, an operations manager who works in supply management might work closely with finance managers to determine the most effective contract terms when purchasing equipment.

Some operations managers are primarily concerned with internal operations, such as manufacturing. These managers are always thinking about what operational capabilities are needed, and how to improve the cost, quality, and delivery of the products that the firm supplies to its customers. Other operations management groups work to integrate the internal operations of the firm with the external operations of supply chain partners. While Part 3 of this book specifically addresses these interfunctional relationships, we will provide a brief overview here.

relationships

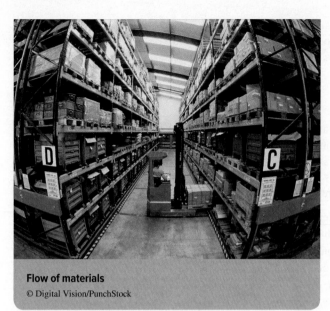

Flow of materials
© Digital Vision/PunchStock

customer management The management of the customer interface, including all aspects of order processing and fulfillment.

supply management The identification, acquisition, positioning, and management of resources and capabilities that a firm needs to attain its strategic objectives.

logistics management Management of the movement and storage of materials at lowest cost while still meeting customers' requirements.

Functional Activities That Connect Operations Managers

As shown in Figure 1-2, customer management, supply management, and logistics management activities serve to connect operational managers as they manage flows of materials and information throughout their firm and, ultimately, throughout the entire supply chain. Processes within each of these functional areas may be independent or highly integrated, yet because of the divisional organizational structure that most firms use, most business managers tend to think of operations management in these functional terms. Chapters 9, 10, and 11 in this book discuss each of these functional activities, respectively.

Customer management is the management of the customer interface, including all aspects of order processing and fulfillment. Functional groups directly concerned with customer management have names such as *distribution, sales, order fulfillment,* and *customer service.* Managers in these functions are always thinking about ways to improve customer satisfaction in efficient ways.

Supply management is the management of processes used to identify, acquire, and administer inputs to the firm. Related functional groups are called by names such as *purchasing, sourcing,* and *procurement.* Managers in these functions are always thinking about insourcing and outsourcing opportunities and ways to improve supply transactions and relationships.

Logistics management is the management of the movement of materials and information within, into, and out of the firm. Logistics functions go by names including *transportation/traffic management, warehousing, materials managers,* and so on. Managers in these functions are always thinking about ways to optimize these flows through better scheduling and the use of alternative transportation, storage, and information technologies.

An Example of Functional Relationships in a Supply Chain

Actual supply chains usually involve many processes, including planning, sourcing, making, servicing, delivering, and so on. For example, consider the supply chain of a movie production company depicted in Figure 1-3. Boxes in the figure represent organizations or individuals; arrows represent flows of material, information, or people. To keep things simple, the figure shows only some of the major parties in the supply chain. You can probably easily think of other ones that are not included.

A movie production company's operations managers interact with many suppliers of goods and services that can be considered as either product-related or resource-related inputs. Accordingly, Figure 1-3 indicates stages of a product supply chain in the horizontal dimension, and stages of a resource/technology supply chain in the vertical dimension. Whether a supplier is a "product" supplier or a "resource" supplier is not always clear. Often, a single supplier may fit in both categories. For example, the director of a movie could be considered a resource in the sense that she brings creativity and knowledge to the movie-making process. At the same time, her time and effort are consumed by the process of making the movie, and these could be considered to be product inputs. Usually, a product supplier provides an input that is fully consumed in the creation of a product or becomes part of the product (e.g., energy, raw materials, components). On the other hand, a resource or technology supplier provides an input that can be used again and again to create multiple products (e.g., information, product and process specifications, equipment, worker skills).

tier An upstream stage of supply.

In a supply chain, each upstream stage of supply is known as a **tier**. The tier number refers to how directly the supplier works with the firm. A *first-tier* supplier provides goods and services directly to the firm. For example, the stock film wholesaler is a first-tier supplier

FIGURE 1-3   Partial Supply Chain Network for a Movie Production Company

to the movie production company. A *second-tier* supplier provides inputs to the first-tier supplier, and so on. Each tier of the upstream supply chain could involve multiple suppliers for the same items or services. Also, a single supplier might provide inputs for multiple tiers of the

activity

student

Find a description of digital moviemaking technology on the Internet. Which of the stages and organizations depicted in Figure 1-3 are likely to be most affected by a shift to a completely digital process? How will the structure of the overall supply chain be changed?

supply chain. For example, the director in Figure 1-3 provides inputs to both the casting company and the movie production company.

Downstream stages of the supply chain are made up of layers of partners and customers commonly referred to as **echelons**. A single echelon might contain partners in locations all over the world. For example, there are usually many distributors for a given movie. These distributors can be thought of as suppliers of distribution services to the movie production company. The downstream supply chain can also be broken into different channels of distribution; theaters, direct/home delivery, and retail DVD/Blu-Ray sales are three channels shown in Figure 1-3.

Many different types of operations managers are needed in a movie production company. Supply managers help to identify and negotiate contracts with supply sources such as casting companies, directors, producers, equipment suppliers, film suppliers and so on.

echelon A downstream stage of supply or consumption.

Internal production managers are needed to schedule all movie-making activities such as casting, shooting, and editing. Sales and distribution managers identify and negotiate terms with worldwide distributors of the film. Other logistics managers work out the means for transporting actors and crew and storing film and equipment throughout the various locations involved in making the film.

Similar roles are filled by operations managers at all kinds of firms. The following Get Real box provides some examples of operations management job descriptions for undergraduate and graduate students. Operations managers' responsibilities can be quite exciting, as they are absolutely integral to the success of any organization.

GET REAL

Jobs in Operations Management

The following job descriptions provide examples of typical responsibilities of operations managers located in internal operations, customer management, supply management, and logistics management functions.

Typical job titles: Customer Program Manager, Enterprise Integration Leader, Commodity Manager, Procurement Specialist, Senior Global Commodity Specialist, Strategic Sourcing Commodity Leader, Project Manager for Supply Chain Information Systems, Production Team Leader, Materials Planning Manager, Logistics Specialist.

Typical job responsibilities:

- Choosing and developing suppliers.
- Designing and implementing systems and processes for improving the customer interface, reducing transaction costs, reducing inventories, and improving service levels.
- Sourcing materials, components, technologies, and services.
- Monitoring and managing inventory at all steps of the supply chain.
- Managing logistics, warehouses, distribution inventories, and service parts.
- Managing internal operations or service functions.
- Managing quality and Six Sigma projects throughout the supply chain.
- Strategically analyzing the supply chain to increase revenues, improve service, reduce cost, and ultimately improve profit.

Excerpts from actual job descriptions:

At a computer manufacturer: As part of the Americas Services Logistics team, Supply Chain Consultants design, develop, and improve processes throughout the company's industry leading logistics network as well as manage projects across multinational teams for the Americas region. The Supply Chain Consultant works on developing new concepts and strategies for the company's third-party logistics providers (3PLs) that enable greater product availability at lower costs and greater customer satisfaction. In addition to partnering with 3PLs, Supply Chain Consultants work closely with the company's world-renowned Enterprise Command Center in order to provide 24/7 critical logistics support and crisis resolution to millions of customers throughout the Americas. The general qualifications of a Supply Chain Consultant include:

- Strong analytical skills.
- Advanced verbal and written communication skills.
- Able to generate new and innovative solutions to complex problems.
- Strong knowledge of supply chain and service logistics concepts and practices, third-party logistics provider management experience preferred.
- Advanced understanding of processes and process improvement, Six Sigma experience preferred.
- Able to effectively negotiate with internal and external partners.
- Strong project management experience.
- Proven leadership skills.
- Unwavering customer focus.
- Bachelor's degree in Operations, Logistics, Engineering or Supply Chain Management with 3–4 years experience.

At a health care products company: Our Development Program in Operations is a fast-paced set of rotations that can turn you into a well-rounded, results-driven leader who is ready to move into a decision-making supervisory position. By gaining first-hand experience in our distribution centers and corporate/regional offices, you'll learn the necessary skills to manage our streamlined distribution process and help drive operational results and customer satisfaction. Our distribution centers across the country will offer you hands-on experience to help you develop your skills in project management, business process improvement, and labor management. We encourage and coach all participants to achieve outstanding results by giving them challenging and rewarding responsibilities. The Development Program in Operations lasts twenty-four months and offers rotations that concentrate on warehouse operations, inventory management, transportation, corporate operations and purchasing.

At a paper products company: Our co-op and internships will offer you a chance to explore the breadth of opportunities available

Continued

in the supply chain while working on real projects such as process improvements in flow planning for finished products, raw materials and finishing supplies, space utilization and optimization analysis, or warehouse operations systems analysis. You will be provided meaningful work experiences that contribute to the overall strategic business goals of the company. You'll be treated and respected as a valuable contributor and given your own responsibilities and accountabilities. Your intern experience will include performance evaluations that provide you with valuable professional feedback to gauge your strengths and measure areas of improvement.

At a not-for-profit organization: As director of donated goods operations you will help the organization provide people who have disabilities and other barriers to employment with opportunities to become independent, self-supporting citizens through training, work experience, and employment in the community. Position duties include:

- Develop short- and long-range plans for the donated goods operation to achieve service goals, budgeted revenue, and maximized contributed margin.

- Expand donated goods operation to new markets [and] new product lines [and] develop new sites and creative sales techniques to expand community and business donation base.
- Establish and monitor performance criteria for donated goods operation to enhance donated goods operations through increased efficiencies.
- Develop and manage inventory control system, a total quality improvement system, and e-commerce activities to assure customer satisfaction at all levels.
- Make recommendations to the President/CEO regarding the need for capital equipment additions or replacements.
- Contribute positively to the Executive Management Team. Promote positive image of the organization both internally and externally.
- Participate in and uphold the values and processes devoted to continuous quality improvement in all organizational operations.

You can find more operations management career information at:

www.careersinsupplychain.org
www.ism.ws/careercenter

The Changing Nature of Supply Chains

Supply chains are complex. Ultimately, all firms in an industry are connected to one another through links of sourcing, making, servicing, and delivery for different products in various markets. Adding to the complexity is the fact that the structures of supply chains are constantly changing in order to accommodate changes in the business environment. New suppliers emerge and old ones die out. Regulations, laws, and societal pressures change. Markets and technologies evolve. Consider, for example, the technological changes that are sweeping through the movie-making industry. One could argue that the resource-technology supply chain is really the most important one for movie-makers to manage. The importance of the upstream product supply chain, which provides the medium upon which the movie is delivered, is diminishing rapidly as digital movie production and distribution are rapidly replacing film-based media. In other businesses, where standardized products are produced many times over, the product supply chain plays a more prominent role in a company's strategy.

sustainability

Most of us are aware of the increasing concerns of societies and governments over environmental issues such as pollution, global warming, and hazardous wastes. Expectations are also rising for business firms to behave in more socially responsible ways regarding their labor practices, involvement in communities, and promotion of the general welfare. These increasing pressures act as tremendously important drivers of change in supply chains today. For example, some operations managers who formerly procured supplies from far away sources are now sourcing them locally in order to reduce the carbon dioxide pollution created by transportation of goods over long distances. This is such an important topic that we have dedicated an entire chapter to it (Chapter 16: Sustainable Operations Management). Additionally, you will encounter numerous examples addressing these issues throughout the book.

Levels of Operational Planning Across the Supply Chain

To keep up with changes in supply chains and the business environment, the functional groups in operations management must periodically work together to plan out their actions. These plans include forecasts and decisions about what the demands on the system will be, what resources and inputs will be needed, how to deploy those resources, and how to process those inputs.

strategic planning A type of planning that addresses long-term decisions that define the operations objectives and capabilities for the firm and its partners.

Figure 1-4 shows the different levels and types of planning in operations management. Chapters in Parts 1 and 2 of this book address **strategic planning**, which includes high-level product and resource design decisions that define the overall operations objectives and capabilities for the firm and its partners. For example, strategic planning decisions would include what new products to develop, where to locate new plants, and what new technologies to buy. These types of decisions take a long time to implement, and the choices made put limits on the capacities and capabilities governing operational processes.

tactical planning A type of planning that addresses intermediate-term decisions to target aggregate product demands and to establish how operational capacities will be used to meet them.

operational planning A type of planning that establishes short-term priorities and schedules to guide operational resource allocations.

Chapters in Part 4 of this book address tactical and operational planning. These types of planning occur more frequently than strategic planning does. **Tactical planning**, such as sales and operations planning, seeks to identify and target customer demands for aggregate product families and to establish the inventory and capacity plans needed to satisfy these overall demands. At the **operational planning** level, inventory and requirements planning activities address demands, materials, and capacities at the individual product level. Tactical planning usually spans months, whereas operational planning usually addresses weeks or days of activity. The chapters in Part 4 in this book also discuss planning approaches and technologies used in tactical and operational planning.

HOW THIS BOOK IS STRUCTURED

Table 1-3 provides a content overview of this book, indicating the chapters in which critical operations management issues are addressed. Collectively, the five major parts of this book provide an introduction to the principles, programs, and practices of operations management:

FIGURE 1-4 Operations Management: Planning Activities Across the Supply Chain

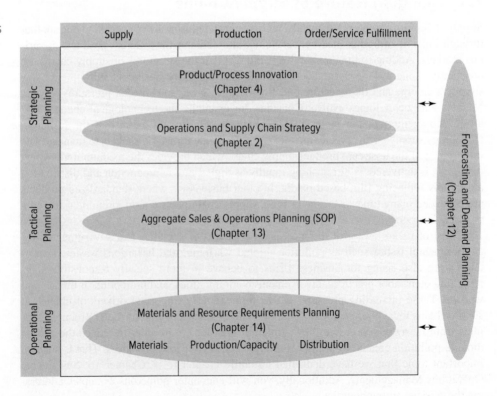

TABLE 1-3   A Content Map for This Book

Chapter	Relationships	Sustainability	Globalization
Part 1 Supply Chain: A Perspective for Operations Management			
1. Introduction to Managing Operations Across the Supply Chain	X	X	X
2. Operations and Supply Chain Strategy	X	X	X
Part 2 *Foundations of Operations Management*			
3. Managing Processes and Capacity	X	X	X
4. Product/Process Innovation	X	X	X
5. Manufacturing and Service Process Structures	X	X	X
6. Managing Quality	X	X	X
7. Managing Inventories	X	X	X
8. Lean Systems	X		X
Part 3 *Integrating Relationships Across the Supply Chain*			
9. Customer Service Management	X		
10. Sourcing and Supply Management	X	X	X
11. Logistics Management	X	X	X
Part 4 Planning for Integrated Operations Across the Supply Chain			
12. Demand Planning: Forecasting and Demand Management	X		X
13. Sales and Operations Planning	X		X
14. Materials and Resource Requirements Planning	X		X
Part 5 *Managing Change in Supply Chain Operations*			
15. Project Management	X	X	X
16. Sustainable Operations Management—Preparing for the Future	X	X	X

- Part 1 provides an overview of operations management as a field and describes its strategic role in a business from the perspective of supply chain management.
- Part 2 discusses foundational process-related concepts and principles that govern all operational processes.
- Part 3 deals with the primary functional relationships between internal operations management activities and other operational functions both inside and outside the firm.
- Part 4 discusses planning approaches and technologies used at different levels of operations decision making.
- Part 5 discusses how operations managers use projects, change programs, and technologies to shape the future of operations and supply chain management.

An overview and integration of the chapters contained in each part is provided at the beginning of each of the parts throughout this book.

CHAPTER SUMMARY

This chapter provides a broad overview and introduction to operations management. In discussing the scope and complexity of operations management, we have made the following points:

1. The goal of the modern firm is to develop and run an operations management system able to deliver superior product value to the firm's targeted consumers.

2. Operations management deals with the effective and efficient management of transformation processes. These processes include not only the making of products but also the design of products and related processes; sourcing of required materials and services; and delivery and management of relationships among customers, suppliers, and functions within the firm. As a system, operations management involves four major functional activities and their interactions: (1) customer relationships management, (2) internal operations (manufacturing and services) management, (3) supply management, and (4) logistics management.

3. The operations management system involves three major sets of partners outside the firm: (1) customers, (2) suppliers, and (3) stakeholders. Operations managers also work closely with other business functions within the firm.

4. The collective decisions made in areas of operations management determine the capabilities and success of the firm. In addition, the capabilities of a firm are heavily influenced by the capabilities of its suppliers.

5. For a number of reasons, the supply chain has grown to become a dominant way to look at operations management. Operations activities take place in various functional and geographic locations across a supply chain network. Whereas operations management is mainly about managing processes, supply chain management is mainly about managing flows and relationships.

6. Operations management is fundamentally dynamic; it is ever changing.

KEY TERMS

core capability 11

customer management 14

customers 12

echelon 15

lean operation 9

logistics management 14

operational planning 18

operations management 4

process 8

stakeholders 13

strategic planning 18

suppliers 13

supply chain 4

supply chain management 11

supply management 14

tactical planning 18

tier 14

total product experience 7

1. Review *Fortune* magazine's "Most Admired" American companies for 1959, 1979, 1999, and the most current year. (The issue normally appears in August each year.) Which companies have remained on the top throughout this period? Which ones have disappeared? What do you think led to the survival or demise of these companies?

2. Select two products that you have recently purchased; one should be a service and the other a manufactured good. Think about the process that you used to make the decision to purchase each item. What product characteristics were most important to you? What operational activities determine these characteristics?

3. What are the primary operations management decisions in each of the following corporations?
   a. Marriott Hotels and Resorts.
   b. A private golf and tennis club.
   c. Ben & Jerry's.
   d. ExxonMobil Corporation.

4. Consider the following processes that you frequently encounter as a college student:
   a. Enrolling in classes.
   b. Taking a class.
   c. Buying a ticket for a play, concert, or basketball game.

   Describe each process and its inputs, activities, and outputs. What is being converted or transformed in each process? Who are the customers, suppliers, and stakeholders for each process?

5. Recall the last time you went to a fast-food restaurant such as McDonald's. Describe all of the goods and services that make up your *total product experience*.

6. The following firms have long been seen as having strong competitive advantages:
   a. IBM
   b. Coca-Cola
   c. Xerox
   d. Walmart

   Read about one of these companies. Also draw from your experience as a customer to identify that company's competitive advantage. Discuss how operations management relates to the company's competitive advantage.

7. Why should a firm consider the position of stakeholders when evaluating operational alternatives? Consider the role of government and its impact. (*Hint:* Consider working conditions and pollution.)

8. Most people have worked as "operations managers" at some time. Describe a job or experience that you had that involved the management of a process.

CASE

Business Textbook Supply Chain

Dave Eisenhart, senior editor for Mountain Publishing, Inc., looked out his window as he considered the operational implications of the changes he had just heard discussed in the company's annual strategic planning meeting. The future looked to be both exciting and scary. As an editor for Mountain's business textbook division, Dave had recently witnessed major changes in his primary market. First, the body of knowledge in business school curricula had exploded over the past decade. It was getting harder and harder to cover all the content that any professor might want in a single textbook, while keeping the size of the book manageable. Second, Dave had noted that more and more schools were moving to modular course structures, including many shorter courses, sometimes as short as a week long. Third, a growing number of students preferred to buy their books from sources other than traditional bookstores, such as Amazon.com and other online sources.

At the same time, new technologies were changing the way that textbook content could be produced and delivered. Print technologies were improving the speed and quality of printing, so that it was easy to envision a day when books could be printed one copy at a time, "on demand." Some companies had already started to offer custom published books for professors who wanted to combine chapters and cases from several different publishers into a single readings packet for their students. While the quality of these "books" (packets) did not match that of traditional hardbound texts, many professors and students valued the flexibility associated with this option.

Finally, the demand for e-books was growing rapidly. While the percentage of books purchased in electronic form was currently small, the potential seemed to be very large. In addition, e-books provided a platform for many new ancillary and "interactive" learning tools. For example students using an e-book could immediately link to other, external sources of related material (including videos and Internet links), access online learning and assessment tools, and be provided with navigation links throughout the book. Dave thought about these possibilities, along with the implications that e-books would have for distribution, book re-use, revisions, and other existing strategies.

Dave began to think about the operational activities dispersed across Mountain's supply chain for textbooks. On the upstream (input) side, Mountain worked with authors (usually professors), text editors, graphic artists, commercial printers, and other suppliers to edit, design, and produce books. After typically large print runs (up to three years of forecasted demand) were produced, transportation suppliers delivered the books to Mountain's distribution centers located around the country. Orders from bookstores and online retailers were filled from these distribution centers. For traditional hardcopy textbooks, each of these players in the supply chain played a fairly clear role in creating value through the goods and services they provided. However, as Dave considered the market and technological changes currently under way, the operational value that each of these players provided became less clear.

Questions

1. Draw a diagram that illustrates the textbook supply chain from the publisher's point of view.

2. Who are the various customers for textbooks? What do these customers want in terms of goods and services related to textbooks? From the publisher's point of view, who is the *key* customer?

3. Who are the major players in the supply chain? What operational roles do they play in terms of creating value for the key customers?

4. Given the anticipated changes in the market and in product and process technologies, how do you envision each supply chain player's role changing in the future?

5. What advice would you give to Dave Eisenhart regarding long-term operational changes the firm should consider?

SELECTED READINGS & INTERNET SITES

Friedman, T. L. *The World Is Flat.* New York: Farrar, Straus and Giroux, 2006.

Goldratt, E. M., and J. Cox. *The Goal: A Process of Ongoing Improvement.* Great Barrington, MA: North River Press, 2004.

Journal of Operations Management. Amsterdam: Elsevier Science, B.V., 1980–current.

Manufacturing & Service Operations Management: M&SOM. Linthicum, MD: Institute for Operations Research and Management Sciences, 1999–current.

Production and Operations Management: An International Journal of the Production and Operations Management Society/POMS. Baltimore, MD: Production and Operations Management Society, 1992–current.

Swamidass, P. (ed). *Encyclopedia of Production and Manufacturing Management.* Norwell, MA: Kluwer Academic Publishing, 2000.

Womack, J. P.; D. T. Jones; and D. Roos. *The Machine That Changed the World.* New York: Rawson Associates, 1990.

Association of Operations Management **www.apics.org**

Council of Supply Chain Management Professionals **www.cscmp.org**

Institute for Supply Management **www.ism.ws**

2 Operations and Supply Chain Strategy

LEARNING OBJECTIVES

After studying this chapter, you should be able to:

LO2-1 Describe how operations strategy fits within a firm's overall strategic planning process.

LO2-2 Describe the need for "fit" between the key customers, value propositions, and operations capabilities—the essential elements that define an operations strategy.

LO2-3 Describe customer-desired outcomes in terms of order winners, order qualifiers, and order losers.

LO2-4 Explain what product-related and process-related operational competitive priorities are and how they are related to competitive advantage.

LO2-5 Explain how strategic performance can be assessed both operationally and financially by using the strategic profit model and the supply chain operational reference model.

REDBUBBLE

Credits for photos above appear at the end of this chapter.

Global

Today's customers, especially millennials (those born after 1980), are increasingly demanding. They want unique products and experiences that reflect their views and values. But they want them to be reasonably priced and delivered quickly. How do you satisfy this very strong demand? If you are Redbubble (www.redbubble.com), the answer is simple—you develop a supply chain that makes the "desired outcome" inevitable.

Redbubble's operations provide a great example of an Internet-based supply chain strategy built on two primary competencies: (1) a supply chain network of artist partners who create and share their designs; and (2) localized sources of production and delivery who apply designs to make end products close to customers. Redbubble began by recognizing that artists are creative people who are unlikely to willingly give up rights to their creations. Consequently, it understood the need to create a worldwide community of artists who find collaboration with

Redbubble both easy and profitable. The company offers artists free community membership, free promotion and other services, and retention of copyrights to their designs. It also allows the artists to regulate their own prices and to control which products will display their designs.

Redbubble understands that it has to "grow" new artists to keep this community fresh and dynamic—constantly offering new and different designs. To this end, Redbubble created an artist residency program in its Melbourne (Australia) office. The program develops new talent, while also encouraging new artists to work with other artists. To date, Redbubble has over 50,000 artists worldwide who have successfully sold their products (and the number keeps growing).

> Redbubble has introduced a new business model by developing a unique, global supply chain of artists and designers coupled with local product deliverers.

Creating the artist community, while critical, was not enough. Redbubble has designed a delivery system that makes products available quickly and at a reasonable price and also gives customers a rich set of choices for how designs are delivered. Designs can be put on t-shirts, tank tops, computer cases, stickers, wall art, home décor (e.g., throw pillows, duvets, mugs), stationary, and bags. Redbubble has created an extensive network of product suppliers, and it can add suppliers quickly in locations close to customers. The company makes its profits by placing charges on the products delivered by these suppliers.

Redbubble has seen phenomenal success so far. Its sales have seen exponential growth; every month over 8,000,000 unique viewers hit the company's website. The Redbubble example illustrates many of the themes and concepts introduced in this chapter. We see how Redbubble has designed a new approach to generating value for a key customer: the millennial who wants art made available in everyday life. To serve this customer, Redbubble has designed a set of capabilities intended to generate an ongoing flow of art and to make resulting designs available quickly. The result is a unique business model—one that matches the needs of key customers to the capabilities of the operations/supply chain (artists and deliverers). The company does this in a way that is consistent with Redbubble's promise—helping the customer bring art into everyday life.

---

operations strategy A set of *competitive priorities* coupled with supply chain structural and infrastructural design choices intended to create *capabilities* that support a set of *value propositions* targeted to address the needs of *critical customers.*

This chapter describes the decision processes and choices that make up an operations strategy, which is a set of *competitive priorities* coupled with supply chain structural and infrastructural design choices intended to create *capabilities* that support a set of *value propositions* targeted to address the needs of *critical customers.* Strategic decisions define the competitive objectives of an organization, establishing both the specific performance targets and the means by which the targets will be achieved.

To explain the process of strategic planning, this chapter will clarify the meanings of the terms *competitive priorities, capabilities, value propositions,* and *key customers.* We begin by providing a brief overview of different levels of strategic planning in firms and by describing how operations strategic choices create value. Then we describe a process of strategy development and deployment. The chapter concludes with a discussion of ways to communicate operations strategic choices and measure the performance of operational resources within the firm and across the supply chain.

LEVELS OF STRATEGIC PLANNING

Within most firms, planning processes take place at several different levels. Internally, there is a hierarchy of strategic plans consisting of (1) corporate planning, (2) strategic business unit (SBU) planning, and (3) functional planning. These three levels should be closely linked (as shown in Figure 2-1) so that they are mutually consistent and supportive.

Strategic plans made at all levels need to take into account the business environment, including economic conditions, competitor actions, market opportunities, regulatory changes, and so on. A firm's culture also typically influences the objectives it sets and the decisions it makes in strategic planning. For example, one firm might be more aggressive or more risk averse than another firm.

In this section, we examine the objectives and interactions of strategic planning at the three levels. The remainder of the chapter focuses on operations strategy, one of the areas of functional strategy development.

LO2-1 Describe how operations strategy fits within a firm's overall strategic planning process.

Corporate Strategic Planning

Many firms are involved in more than one business. For example, General Electric operates more than 20 diverse businesses, from aircraft engines to financial services.

FIGURE 2-1 Strategic Planning Hierarchy

Corporate strategic planning addresses the portfolio of businesses owned by a firm. Of the three levels of strategic planning, corporate strategic planning is the broadest in scope and the least constrained. Decisions made at this level limit the choices that can be made at lower strategic planning levels.

Essentially, a **corporate strategy** communicates the overall mission of the firm and identifies the types of businesses that the firm wants to be in. For a large, multidivisional firm, key decisions in corporate strategy address what businesses to acquire and what businesses to divest. Corporate strategy typically covers a long time horizon, setting the overall values, direction, and goals of the firm as a whole. It also establishes how business performance will be measured and how risks will be managed.

corporate strategy Determines the overall mission of the firm and the types of businesses that the firm wants to be in.

Business Unit Strategic Planning

Because products and markets differ across business divisions, a separate management team (usually headed by a president or vice president) is usually needed to run each of these semi-independent organizations, or **strategic business units (SBUs)**. An SBU can be organized along product, market, or geographic dimensions.

Business unit strategy essentially deals with the question, "How should our business unit compete?" To answer this question, managers make choices regarding what customers and market segments they will deem critical, what products they will offer, and specifically how they will create advantages over the business unit's competitors. These choices collectively form the business model that the unit will pursue. There are numerous types of **business models**. For example, long ago Gillette developed the "razor and blades" business model—give away the razor but make your money on the replacement blades. Many businesses follow this same type of model (printers, industrial equipment). Dell successfully applied the "direct sales" business model in computers—sell computers directly to the end consumer. A "loyalty" business model rewards customers for continuing to deal with the firm. This model has been widely implemented in the airline industry (through the frequent flier program) and in the retail trade (e.g., as in Best Buy's "Reward Zone" program). Changes in technologies, competitors, and markets can at the same time destroy the viability of an existing business model while giving rise to new ones. Consider, for example, how customers' growing concerns over sustainability issues have opened up the possibility of new business models that offer organic and eco-friendly products. These kinds of changes make it important for operations and business strategy managers to continually evaluate their existing business models and possible business model innovations.

strategic business unit (SBU) The semi-independent organizations used to manage different product and market segments.

business unit strategy Determines how a strategic business unit will compete.

business model The combination of the choices determining the customers an SBU will target, the value propositions it will offer, and the supply chain/operations management capabilities it will employ.

sustainability

SWOT A strategic planning technique to help firms identify opportunities where they can develop a sustainable competitive advantage and areas where the firm is significantly at risk.

functional strategy Determines how the function will support the overall business unit strategy.

A business unit's strategy and business model are both shaped by the corporate strategy, by the specific requirements of the SBU's products and markets, and by the SBU's operating capabilities. One technique that managers use to assess these attributes is SWOT analysis (short for Strengths-Weaknesses-Opportunities-Threats). A SWOT analysis helps managers match strategies with strengths and opportunities while also reducing risks associated with weaknesses and threats. SWOT can be used in various ways—to kick off strategic thinking or as a serious detailed strategic assessment/planning tool. Questions often considered in a typical SWOT analysis are summarized in Table 2-1.

Functional Strategic Planning

Every SBU consists of functional groups such as internal operations, marketing, accounting, engineering, supply management, logistics, and finance (to name a few). Each function has to generate a strategic plan—one that is coordinated with and supportive of the SBU plan. To that extent, the functional strategy must address certain critical questions:

- What specifically do we have to do to support the corporate and SBU strategies?
- What are the critical resources that we have to manage carefully if we are to achieve the corporate/SBU objectives?
- What metrics should we have in place to ensure we are making progress on these plans?
- What capabilities found in our function should be considered or recognized by the two higher stages of strategy?
- How should we coordinate our activities with those of the other functional areas within the firm to reduce friction and to enhance the ability of the firm/SBU to attain its overall objectives?

Of the three levels of strategic planning, the functional strategy is the most detailed, as well as the most constrained, as it must operate within a set of decisions made in the corporate and SBU strategic plans.

TABLE 2-1 SWOT Analysis—Example Questions

	Positive Factors	**Negative Factors**
Internal Factors	*Strengths* What advantages do we have? What do we do better than anyone else? What is our unique value proposition? What do our customers see as our strengths? What are our unique resources?	*Weaknesses* What could we improve? What should we avoid? What do our customers see as major weaknesses? What factors within our control prevent our ability to develop a competitive advantage? What limits our ability to pursue new strategies and opportunities?
External Factors	*Opportunities* What trends are we well positioned to take advantage of? What new technologies are we well positioned to exploit? What new markets are opening up? What changes in social patterns and population profiles might provide opportunities for us?	*Threats* What obstacles do we face? What are competitors doing that could adversely affect us? Are there any changes in technology that could hurt us? What new governmental regulations or standards pose difficulties for us?

DEVELOPING OPERATIONS STRATEGY: CREATING VALUE THROUGH STRATEGIC CHOICES

At the heart of operations strategy are choices made in three primary areas (see Figure 2-2):

- The *key customer* is the customer or customer segment receiving priority because it is highly important to the firm's current or future success.
- The *value proposition* is all of the tangible and intangible "benefits" that customers can expect to obtain by using the products offered by the firm.
- *Capabilities* are operational activities that the firm can perform well; these define the types of problems and solutions that operations can address proficiently.

These three elements operate in a setting that is the *environment*. The environment consists of those elements whose actions can and do influence the way managers think about and operationalize the three elements. Integral to the environment are elements such as the competition, the government, and technology.

Marketing managers often lead decision making regarding customers and products. However, decisions in all three areas listed above need to be jointly agreed upon by executives in the marketing, operations, and financial functions of the firm, because the decisions are so interdependent. For example, the types of customers that are chosen determine the value propositions that are relevant, which in turn determine the types of capabilities that will be required. As Figure 2-2 indicates, the objective of operations strategy development is to maximize the overlap among choices in these areas. The internal consistency of these choices is what ultimately creates value for the firm and for the marketplace.

To ensure that a high level of consistency is achieved, operations managers must develop a deep understanding of their key customers. First, this means understanding what these customers value in products. Second, the critical features of the value proposition need to be communicated in terms that make sense to operations managers. Third, strategic initiatives must be launched. If the required operational capabilities do not exist, then they must be developed, or different customers and value propositions should be targeted. The following sections discuss these decisions in more detail.

Key Customers

The starting and ending point for effective and efficient supply chain operations is the customer. As defined in Chapter 1, **customers** are parties that use or consume the products of operations management processes. A customer is not necessarily the end user. For example, a store manager or purchasing agent who buys products for resale is a kind of customer (as noted in the Get Real box about Huffy Bikes). Almost all firms deal with multiple customers having varied desires and needs that change over time. Hence, each firm has to identify its **key customers**.

relationships

LO2-2 Describe the need for "fit" between the key customers, value propositions, and operations capabilities—the essential elements that define an operations strategy.

customers Parties that use or consume the products of operations management processes.

key customer A customer that the firm has targeted as being important to its future success.

FIGURE 2-2 The Three Critical Elements of Operations Strategy

Huffy Bikes Targets Its Key Customer

Huffy Bikes markets a line of inexpensive, durable bicycles sold through mass merchandising channels (e.g., Toys R Us, Meijers, Walmart) to a wide range of customers (parents, students, young children). To succeed in this very crowded and competitive market, Huffy recognized that its key customer was not the end user—the person who bought the bike. Buyers of Huffy bikes are not particularly concerned with the Huffy brand; what they buy is determined more by availability and price. Two groups of managers determine availability—the store manager (who determines what products are stocked) and the purchasing manager (who determines what product lines will be bought). Consequently, Huffy has targeted these two groups as its key customers. It has tried to make the purchasing manager's job easier by reducing the transactions and effort required to buy from Huffy. In addition, it has focused on communicating to the store manager the financial benefits of selling Huffy bikes, including improved sales and profits, and fewer returns because of the ease with which Huffy

bikes are assembled. By focusing on these key customers, Huffy has strengthened its market position in a very competitive field.

© Roberts Publishing Services

Firms deem certain customers to be key or important for a number of reasons. For example, a key customer may be responsible for the largest current or future sales of the firm, or it may be the one with the highest prestige. In the automotive industry, Toyota is often such a customer because of its very high quality and performance standards; a supplier working with Toyota is often viewed as a top-rated supplier.

Assessing Customer Wants and Needs

LO2-3 Describe customer-desired outcomes in terms of order winners, order qualifiers, and order losers.

It is important for operations managers to know what product features and delivery terms key customers consider important, what they are willing to pay, and what they consider acceptable. These product-specific traits can be classified into one of three categories:[1]

order winners Product traits that cause a customer to select one product over its competitors.

- **Order winners.** These product traits cause customers to choose a product over a competitor's offering; for example, better performance or lower price. These are traits on which the operations management system must excel.

order qualifiers Product traits that must be met at a certain level for the product to be considered by the customer.

- **Order qualifiers.** These are product traits such as availability, price, or conformance quality that must meet a certain level in order for the product to even be considered by customers. The firm must perform acceptably on these traits (i.e., the products must meet certain threshold values of performance), usually at least as well as competitors' offerings.

order losers Product traits that, if not satisfied, cause the loss of either the current order or future orders.

- **Order losers.** Poor performance on these product traits can cause the loss of either current or future business. For example, when an online retailer fails to deliver an order in a timely manner, a customer might cancel the order and refuse to place orders in the future.

In reviewing these categories, there are several factors to remember. First, order winners and order qualifiers form the basis for customers' expectations. Order losers,

---

[1]Terry Hill, *Manufacturing Strategy: Text and Cases* (New York: McGraw-Hill/Irwin, 2000).

in contrast, result from customers' actual experiences with the firm and its operations management processes. They represent the gap between what the firm delivers and what customers expect. Second, order winners, order qualifiers, and order losers vary by customer. An order

winner to one customer may be an order qualifier to another. Third, these traits vary over time. An order winner at one time may become an order qualifier at another point in time. As can be seen in the Get Real box about the Bosch CS20 circular saw, being able to identify and act on order winners offers the firm a critical strategic advantage.

Value Propositions and Competitive Priorities

To attract key customers, the firm must formulate and implement a **value proposition**, a statement of product and service features that the firm offers to its customers. A value proposition needs to be both attractive to customers and different from what is offered by the firm's competitors. For example, Walmart's value proposition has been to offer everyday low prices on a wide variety of products. The value proposition is critical because it not only defines how the firm competes, it also determines the types of products that the firm will (and will not) offer.

A well-designed value proposition has four characteristics:

value proposition A collection of product and service features that is both attractive to customers and different than competitors' offerings.

1. It offers a combination of product features that customers find attractive and are willing to pay for.
2. It differentiates the firm from its competition in a way that is difficult to imitate.
3. It satisfies the financial and strategic objectives of the firm.
4. It can be reliably delivered given the operational capabilities of the firm and its supporting supply chain.

GET REAL

Bosch CS20: Finding a New Order Winner by Changing the Way Customers Cut Straight Lines

Managers at Bosch Power Tools faced a challenging problem—how to design and deliver a better circular saw. Such saws are found in nearly every handyman's workshop, and over the years their designs had become fairly standard. Consequently, there were few features except price to differentiate competing products. Bosch managers looked at circular saws from an outcome perspective. They saw that many of the circular saws on the market did a poor job of helping users attain a simple but critical outcome—cutting straight lines. Customers were frustrated because the lines were inevitably covered up by either sawdust or by the footplate of the saw itself. Bosch's solution? First, it installed a powerful fan to vacuum dust off of the cut line. Second, it replaced the steel footplate with an acrylic one that allowed users to see the line as they cut. The result: an award-winning product that customers want to buy.[2]

© Richard Hamilton Smith/Corbis

[2]For more information about this innovative product, see: www.newwoodworker.com /reviews/bcs20rvu.html.

The value proposition reflects the order winners, order qualifiers, and order losers for a key customer segment. Thus, the combination of traits contained in the value proposition greatly influences the competitive priorities for all the related operations across the supply chain. In order for operations managers to reliably deliver a given value proposition, they must appropriately align these product outcomes into operational competitive priorities. They need to clearly specify what the operations management system must do better than its rivals, what it must do at least as well as its rivals, and what it must avoid doing (because it will jeopardize customer satisfaction and orders). Competitive priorities, along with associated performance measures and targeted objectives, provide a language for managers to communicate the value proposition in operational terms.

Typically, competitive priorities address both product-related outcomes and process-related capabilities. Once these priorities are established, they form the basis for performance measurement.

Product-Related Competitive Priorities

LO2-4 Explain what product-related and process-related operational competitive priorities are and how they are related to competitive advantage.

Product-related priorities address the customer's problem to be "solved" and are communicated in terms of the quality, timeliness, and cost of the product "solution." As Table 2-2 shows, each of these three product-related competitive priorities involves various dimensions. There are many different aspects of quality that may be important to customers, for example. Each dimension potentially appeals to different types of customers; each also may require different capabilities of supply chain operations. Because it is difficult, if not impossible, to simultaneously deliver the highest levels of all of these product attributes, operations managers need to communicate which attributes are of highest priority and lowest priority, respectively, in accordance with the order winners and qualifiers of the targeted key customers. These priorities form the basis on which performance measures can be formulated and implemented.

Quality

quality A product's fitness for consumption in terms of meeting customers' needs and desires.

A product's **quality** is its fitness for consumption by the customer who bought it. It is an assessment of how well the customer's expectations are met. Some dimensions of quality are often viewed by customers as minimum requirements (order qualifiers) for most products. For example, poor conformance quality (many defects) is not tolerated in most markets. At the same time, superiority in other dimensions of quality

TABLE 2-2 Dimensions of Product-Related Competitive Priorities

Quality	Timeliness	Cost
Performance (superior attributes)	Reliability (on-time)	Purchase (price)
Features (unique attributes)	Speed (lead time)	Transaction (acquisition costs)
Conformance (no defects)	Availability (always on or in-stock)	Maintenance/repair
Reliability (long time to failure)		Operating (cost of consumables)
Durability (long useful life)		Salvage/disposal
Aesthetics (appeal)		
Service/support (ancillaries/intangibles)		
Perceived quality (image)		

can significantly differentiate a product. For example, a well-known brand can create a perception of quality that differentiates a product. Firms that produce high-quality products have many advantages, including improved company reputation and easier selling, the elimination of time-consuming activities and costly resources required to correct quality-related problems, and employees who are motivated by the knowledge that they produce great products.

Timeliness

Dimensions of product **timeliness**, the degree to which the product is delivered or available when the customer wants it, are a primary indicator of *customer service* in many businesses. These dimensions can serve as order winners or qualifiers, depending on the situation. On-time delivery of a product is in many cases an order qualifier (or order loser, if the product is late). Similarly, availability of a good or service is usually a qualifier. For example, grocery store customers expect products to be on the shelf. On the other hand, **lead time**, the amount of time that passes between the beginning and ending of a set of activities, is often an order winner, especially for nonstandardized products. There are two types of lead time that are typically important. The first, **time to market**, is the total time that a firm takes to conceive, design, test, produce, and deliver a new or revised product for the marketplace. This lead time is a once-in-product-life-cycle event. That is, a firm may spend 18 months designing a car and getting the supply chain ready for production, but once production has been ramped up and the cars begin rolling off the assembly line, there is no significant design product lead time needed to make subsequent copies of that car. Time to market can be an order winner if the new product offers features or performance that is not available in other products.

The other type of lead time is **order-to-delivery lead time** for an existing product. This encompasses the time interval starting at the moment that the customer places an order for a product, including the time required to place and fulfill an order, and ending at the moment that the customer takes delivery of the product. In services, customers often judge the value of a service largely on the operation's order-to-delivery performance. For example, a dining experience is marred by slow service, or it is irritating when a salesperson seems to have gotten lost in the back room. Order-to-delivery lead time is also important for highly customized, made-to-order products; a piece of customized jewelry, for example.

timeliness The degree to which a product is delivered or available when the customer wants it.

lead time The amount of time that passes between the beginning and ending of a set of activities.

time to market The total time that a firm takes to conceive, design, test, produce, and deliver a new or revised product for the marketplace.

order-to-delivery lead time The time that passes from the instant the customer places an order for a product until the instant that the customer receives the product.

Cost

It is well known that people like to get things cheaply but they do not like "cheap things." This statement describes both the attraction and the problem of emphasizing cost as the firm's major source of value. Customers typically want at least the same product performance for a lower cost, not simply less for less. A competitive priority placed on **cost** usually treats certain dimensions of quality and timeliness as givens and focuses on reducing cost.

Different types of costs may be more or less important to customers, depending on the product type. Purchase cost (price) is usually most important for consumer goods. However, maintenance and operating costs are often much more important for customers buying long-life items such as industrial machinery. Disposal costs are becoming more important considerations for durable goods (cars, washing machines) due to environmental concerns.

cost The expenses incurred in acquiring and using a product.

sustainability

LO2-4 Explain what product-related and process-related operational competitive priorities are and how they are related to competitive advantage.

Process-Related Competitive Priorities

While product-related competitive priorities focus on the outcomes that customers experience directly, process-related competitive priorities pertain to how supply chain operations are run over time. In addition to managing for cost, timeliness, and quality, operations managers place priorities on longer-term initiatives affecting areas such as flexibility, innovation, and sustainability. Capabilities developed in these areas contribute to supply chain operations' abilities to create new solutions and to respond effectively to changes in technology, competition, and the overall operating environment.

Innovation

innovation Both radical and incremental changes in processes and products.

Innovation refers to both radical and incremental changes in processes and products. Especially in highly industrialized countries, innovation is an important way to create new demand. Through the creation of new and improved products, firms can appeal to new market segments or take away business from competitors. Innovation may be a response to emerging customer needs, or it can even be a way to create new needs. For example, with the creation of the iPod, Apple combined existing technologies in a way that created a new business for selling online music and other content.

Traditional views of innovation tend to distinguish between product innovations and process innovations. In reality, product and process innovation are usually interrelated. Product innovations sometimes arise from process innovations, and process innovations (at least incremental ones) are usually required to support any new product innovation. Accordingly, operations managers located in various functions throughout the supply chain typically have two sets of innovation-related priorities: support product innovation and drive process innovation. In companies that pursue a low-cost strategy, most innovation tends to be incremental in nature, whereas technology-leading companies tend to pursue more radical product and process innovations.

It is important to realize that process innovations can be technological or organizational in nature. Operations managers are always looking for new technologies to enhance their capabilities. However, organizational innovations can also be effective in creating new efficiencies or new market opportunities. IKEA provides a good example of a company that has developed a strong value proposition by changing the organizational relationships in the supply chain that affect how its products are stocked and shipped (see the Get Real box below).

GET REAL

IKEA: Growth through Supply Chain Innovation[3]

IKEA is a franchise-based chain of household furnishing stores that does business in 31 countries. At the heart of IKEA's success is a simple but powerful value proposition: "We shall offer a wide range of well-designed, functional home furnishing products at prices so low that as many as possible will be able to afford them." To achieve this proposition, IKEA's designers have focused on delivering products that can be assembled by the customer; this is done by selling the products in "knocked-down" form, which is cheaper to store and ship. For example, an unassembled, knocked-down bookcase is more compact and cheaper to ship than a preassembled bookcase. In addition, by using flat-pack distribution methods, the products can be easily transported by either car or public transport (e.g., bus) from the store to the consumer's home. This innovation required changes in product designs, but it also required changes in suppliers, transportation modes, and scopes of responsibilities. Some of the supply chain responsibility has been shifted to the customer, for example.

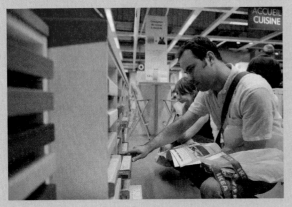

© Antoine Antonio/Bloomberg via Getty Images

[3]For more information, see www.ikea.com © INTER IKEA Systems B.V. 2003–2009.

Flexibility

Flexibility is generally defined as an operation's ability to respond efficiently to changes in products, processes (including supply chain relationships), and competitive environments. The words *respond efficiently* mean that an operation can cope with a wider range of changes faster or with less cost than competitors can.

With decreasing product life cycles, rapidly changing technologies, and growing pressure to meet localized, specific customer needs, flexibility has become an important priority for many companies today. Firms that have flexible operations have many opportunities to create value for their customers in unique ways. The potential for niche marketing is increased when operations can produce in small lots and deliver unique specifications quickly and inexpensively. Firms can command premium prices when their operations can be tailored to meet specific needs or when they can accommodate last-minute changes in demand.

There are many types of flexibility, including short-term, operational flexibilities such as labor flexibility, as well as longer-term, strategic flexibilities such as the ability to introduce new products quickly. Consequently, it is important for operations managers to clearly define and focus on the types of flexibility they want to develop.

flexibility An operation's ability to respond efficiently to changes in products, processes (including supply chain relationships), and competitive environments.

sustainability

Sustainability and Risk Management

In recent years, operations managers have begun to address *sustainability* and *risk-related* issues more explicitly as competitive priorities. With sustainability, the focus is on maintaining operations that are both profitable and nondamaging to society or the environment. A primary focus of risk management is to build operations that anticipate and deal with problems resulting from natural events (e.g., earthquakes), social factors (e.g., strikes), economic issues (e.g., the bankruptcy of a critical supplier), or technological issues (e.g., finding a major flaw in software). In addition to these operational types of risks, safety and security are growing key concerns, especially as supply chain operations become more global and dispersed. A famous example is provided by Mattel in 2007. The company recalled over nine million toys because of concerns over lead in the paint that was introduced by the actions of a lower-tier supplier located in China. In a more recent example, Volkswagen was ordered in 2015 to recall nearly a half million cars because these cars had software intentionally designed to circumvent environmental standards for reducing smog.

sustainability Maintaining operations that are both profitable and nondamaging to society or the environment.

risk management Developing operations that anticipate and deal with problems resulting from natural events, social factors, economic issues, or technological issues.

triple bottom line An approach to corporate performance measurement that focuses on a company's total impact measured in terms of profit, people (social responsibility), and the planet (environmental responsibility). Also referred to as **TBL,** the **3BL,** or the **3Ps.**

Governments, social groups, and consumers are placing increasing demands on companies to be more socially responsible. In response, operations managers must place priorities on preventing environmental or human damage as a result of operations. This means an increasing emphasis on the reduction of biohazards and the use of materials and processes that demand less energy, require less input, and generate less waste. Operations managers also want to ensure that workers are treated fairly and given a safe work environment. These priorities have serious implications for decisions affecting all aspects of operations, beginning with supplier selection and buying decisions and ending with product disposal.

The increasing importance of sustainability has caused many companies to adopt a "triple bottom line" approach to performance measurement. Using this approach, managers prepare three different measures of profit

Nancy Nord, commissioner of the U.S. Consumer Product Safety Commission, announces the Mattel toys recall. Mattel is the world's largest toy company.
© Shawn Thew/epa/Corbis

and loss. The first is the traditional measure of performance—monetary profit; the second is an assessment of its "people account"—how socially responsible the firm has been throughout its operations; and the third is the company's "planet account"—how environmentally responsible the firm has been. Together, these three Ps (Profit-People-Planet) capture the total impact of a firm's business.

Capabilities: Strengths and Limitations of Supply Chain Operations

capabilities Unique and superior operational abilities that stem from the routines, skills, and processes that the firm develops and uses.

The third element of delivering value, as identified in Figure 2-2, is capabilities. Capabilities are unique and superior operational abilities that stem from the routines, skills, and processes that the firm develops and uses. As we stated earlier, it is difficult for an operations system to simultaneously deliver high levels of performance on many different dimensions. Thus, it is important to develop capabilities in the few areas that are of greatest strategic value for the firm.

It is difficult to describe capabilities directly without describing them in terms of outcomes such as quality, flexibility, and so on. Usually, abilities to deliver superior performance come from investments and developmental efforts in one or more of the following areas:

- *Processes*—specialized routines, procedures, and performance measurement systems that guide operational activities.
- *Planning systems*—access and development of sources of information, and use of proprietary decision support systems and processes.
- *Technology*—proprietary usage of hardware or software that enables the firm to do things differently and/or better than competitors.
- *People and culture*—skills, associated training programs, and cultural norms for the company that produce better motivation and performance. The impact of culture must be recognized at both a corporate and at a national level.
- *Supply chain relationships*—unique and exclusive relationships with customers and suppliers that are unmatched by competitors.

core capabilities The skills, processes, and systems that are unique to the firm and that enable it to deliver products that are both valued by the customer and difficult for competitors to imitate.

The Seven Cycles operation discussed in the Get Real box presents a good example of how both company culture (philosophy) and special technologies can create unique capabilities.

Sometimes certain capabilities become so unique and valuable to a firm that they are considered to be "core," that is, central to the very existence of the firm. Core capabilities are the skills, processes, and systems that are unique to the firm and that enable it to deliver products that are both valued by the customer and difficult for competitors to imitate. These are strategically critical, and often the source of a stream of new products and market opportunities. For example, over the years Honda has developed successful products in a wide range of very different markets—motorcycles, power generators, cars, marine engines, lawn mowers, snow blowers, and now jet airplanes. In each market, Honda moved from being an outsider to become one of the major

Honda airplane powered by Honda jet engine.
© Kyodo/Landov

GET REAL

Seven Cycles: Building a Bicycle Your Way

"One bike. Yours." This isn't simply a slogan. It represents the heart of Seven Cycles' philosophy about who it is and what it does. And nowhere is this philosophy more apparent than in its manufacturing processes. At Seven Cycles, each craftsperson focuses on only one bike at a time. Unlike most bikes, which are produced on an assembly line or in batches—destined for a warehouse or a shop's inventory—a Seven Cycles bike is created specifically for a given customer: one machinist; one welder; one finisher; one bike.

Frame building at Seven Cycles is both an art and a science, requiring a special harmony between creative enthusiasm and manufacturing discipline. However, there's no room for interpretation when it comes to quality. Each stage in manufacturing—from materials selection to the application of the frame's finish—employs standards for precision unparalleled in the industry.

Seven Cycles owns several proprietary technologies that allow it to hold tolerances at much stricter levels than its competition. In addition, it has extremely rigorous quality inspection routines and supporting technologies. By developing these capabilities, Seven Cycles is delivering a riding experience that is different and unmatched by any competitor.

Source: www.sevencycles.com/home.php. Copyright © 2009 Seven Cycles, Inc.

players. Honda succeeded because its core capability is its ability to design and build high-efficiency, low-vibration motors and engines. Such engines are common to each of the markets that Honda has entered.

Other examples of core capabilities include Apple's focus on ease of use and system integration, 3M's specific knowledge of substrates, coatings, and adhesives, and Pixar's creativity in using visual technologies to tell interesting stories.

student activity

Investigate recent developments such as the Honda jet engine and the new Honda Insight. What is common about these developments? What is different?

Maintaining the Fit between Customer Outcomes, Value Propositions, and Capabilities

At the heart of operations strategy is the notion of fit. Fit exists when operational capabilities support the value proposition and the outcomes desired by key customers. If strategic planning processes are neglected, over time the dynamics of changing market trends, technologies, and competition can destroy the fit between customer-desired outcomes, value propositions, and capabilities. A company can find itself with capabilities and value propositions that no customers care about, either because it made improper investments, or because existing customers changed, or both. For example, a firm may find itself using technologies that have become obsolete. Under such conditions, management has three options: (1) live with the mismatch (which means reduced profits and potential opportunities for the competition); (2) change the key customers to those who value the solutions provided by the firm; or (3) change the operational capabilities. Each option requires top management involvement, resources, and time. Most often, changing operational capabilities is the hardest of the changes to make because the development of capabilities typically takes large investments made over long periods of time. Developing effective strategic planning processes that maintain fit is therefore imperative for a firm's survival over time.

The Get Real box below provides an excellent example of how Five Guys Burgers and Fries has maintained the fit between its capabilities, customers, and value proposition by refusing to offer products that are inconsistent with its core capabilities.

fit The extent to which there is alignment between the firm's operational capabilities, its value proposition, and the desires of its critical customers.

GET REAL

Don't Expect a Salad at Five Guys Burgers and Fries

Don't expect to have chicken, milk, or a salad at Five Guys Burgers and Fries—it won't happen. That is not what is at the heart of this fast-growing restaurant chain. Founded in 1986, Five Guys began franchising in 2002. By the end of 2014, Five Guys had grown to almost 1,200 stores and over $1.2 billion in sales. The secret to its success: Offer the customer a great hamburger truly done his/her way (with over 15 different toppings) and lots of fresh French fries. Also encourage employees to be personable and to avoid scripted greetings. Trust the cook to know when the burger is done, not some system. Finally, keep everything simple and stress the details. With a simple menu, errors or poor quality become obvious. Chicken and salad are considered distractions and not what Five Guys sells. Milk—well, when kids go out for a Five Guys burger, they want a treat. As the founder, Jerry Murrell, observed, Five Guys does not serve milk because kids don't actually like milk; kids like Five Guys because it is a pleasure.

DEPLOYING OPERATIONS STRATEGY: CREATING VALUE THROUGH EXECUTION

Once managers have established the objectives and goals of operations strategy, they must convert them into operating realities. Strategy deployment consists of two interrelated activities:

- *Execution*—to carry out plans and initiatives in order to deliver the realized value to customers.
- *Feedback/measurement*—to assess, communicate, and manage performance in ways that capture lessons learned and focus attention on areas needing improvement.

Operations strategy is ultimately defined by what is done over time, not by what is written down as plans. Managers have to assign resources to tasks, identify the relative priorities of competing orders, and monitor the progress of orders and work as they flow through the system. In addition, managers have to devise and implement strategic initiatives needed to make planned changes to supply chain operations a reality. For example, an operations strategy might depend heavily on making changes such as installing new equipment or systems, implementing a training program, adopting a new management approach, acquiring or divesting facilities, or downsizing the workforce.

relationships

Strategic initiatives typically address operations that are spread across internal functions as well as across organizations making up the supply chain. Initiatives need to be coordinated across internal supply management, logistics, marketing, sales, and engineering groups in order to ensure that consistent decisions are made. Similarly, including supply chain partners in strategic planning and execution creates opportunities to exploit the complementary skills and assets of the partnerships. However, this also increases the complexity of planning and reduces the amount of direct visibility and control that managers have over operational outcomes. Thus, decisions and strategic initiatives must be formed in ways that integrate the concerns of internal operational activities with the concerns of suppliers and customers, without creating too much dependence on external partners. Decisions must also address the physical, structural elements of operations as well as the intangible, infrastructural elements. Table 2-3 lists decision areas that define how an operations strategy is deployed. Taken together, these decisions define the operations management system of the firm, how it is structured, how it operates, and how it is evaluated. These decisions are discussed in more detail in various chapters throughout this book.

The first four decision categories presented in Table 2-3—*capacity, facilities, technology,* and *supply chain network*—are *structural* in nature. They affect strategy and the physical operations management system. Once made, decisions in these areas act as constraints, determining what the operations management system can and cannot do well. Altering these decisions often requires significant investments and lots of time—often years. The remaining four decision areas—*workforce, production planning and control, product/process innovation,* and *organization and management*—are *infrastructural* in nature. Decisions in these areas determine what is done, when it is done, and who does it. The decision areas are closely

TABLE 2-3   Strategic Decision Areas in Operations Management

Decision Domain	Operations Management Issues Considered	Other Functional Groups Involved
Capacity	Amount of capacity; timing of changes in capacity; type of capacity used	Finance, Marketing
Facilities	Size of facilities; location of facilities; specialization of what the facilities do	Finance, Marketing
Technology	Hardware: equipment types; automation; linkages Information systems and software: equipment; type; purpose of packages; interfaces/linkages	Finance, Engineering, Information Technology, Human Resources
Supply chain network	Supply network: sourcing policies; level of vertical integration/outsourcing; network structure and assignment of responsibilities; supplier relationships; segmentation of supply base Customer/distribution network: transportation modes; network structure and assignment of responsibilities; customer relationships; sales and delivery channels	Finance, Engineering, Marketing, Sales
Workforce	Skill level, training, and wage policies; employment security; incentives and reward systems	Human Resources
Production planning and control	Planning procedures and decision rules; controls on cost, workflow, and quality; performance measurement; market orientation (make-to-order, make-to-stock)	Finance, Human Resources
Product/process innovation	Improvement programs; problem-solving procedures; knowledge management; change management; new product launches; management of intellectual property	Engineering, Human Resources
Organization and management	Centralization, authority hierarchy, roles of staff people, intrafirm relationships, performance metrics	Human Resources, Marketing

interrelated. For example, decisions regarding the supply chain network also affect the type of information technology that must be in place, how activities are scheduled, and how people are recruited and evaluated. Because these areas are interrelated, managers who make a decision affecting one area must consider the impacts of the decision on the other areas. Equally important, decision makers must consider how operations decisions affect decisions in other areas such as marketing, finance, and human resources. Table 2-3 indicates some of the other functional areas likely to be affected by each of the decisions in operations management.

Feedback/Measurement: Communicating and Assessing Operations Strategy

Performance measurement plays very important roles in operations strategy. First, performance measures communicate strategic intentions to operations personnel. Second, performance measures control operations. By establishing metrics, managers can establish how performance is measured, the standard against which performance is to be compared, and the consequences of exceeding or not meeting the standard. These metrics tell workers what tasks to prioritize and how well they need to do them. In these ways, performance measures help to ensure alignment between the actions of operations managers and the objectives stated in corporate, SBU, and functional level strategies.

Different functional groups tend to measure performance in different ways. For example, finance managers look at performance using financial measures (e.g., return-on-sales, asset turnover); operations managers look at performance using operational measures (e.g., lead time, quality, cost). Consequently, performance measurement must include a mix of financial and operational measures. In the following sections, we examine two different measurement approaches frequently used in operations strategy.

LO2-5 Explain how strategic performance can be assessed both operationally and financially by using the strategic profit model and the supply chain operational reference model.

relationships

The Strategic Profit Model

strategic profit model
(SPM) A model that shows how
operational changes affect
the overall performance of a
business unit.

Also known as the DuPont Model, the **strategic profit model (SPM)** shows how income and balance sheet data are interrelated, and how operational changes affect the overall performance of a business unit. Thus, the SPM converts operational changes (often measured in time, defects, labor hours, etc.) into financial impacts (measured in dollars and returns).

As Figure 2-3 shows, the SPM focuses on return on assets (ROA), a metric that indicates how profitably a firm uses its assets. ROA is calculated by multiplying the net profit margin

FIGURE 2-3 Strategic Profit Model[4]

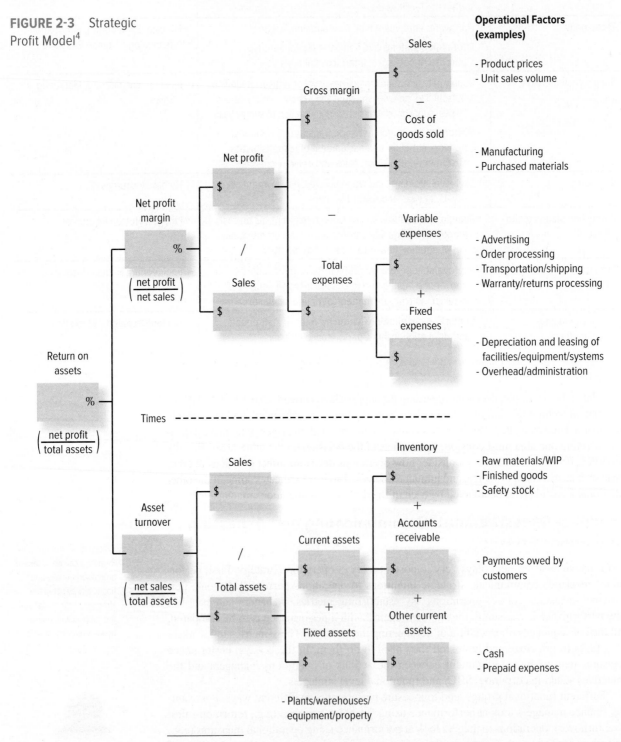

[4]Note that in the SPM, *cost of goods sold* refers to the actual costs incurred in procuring and making products and services, while *expenses* refers to the costs of supporting sales and business transactions.

(defined as a percentage) by asset turnover. The net profit margin measures the percentage of each dollar that is kept by the firm as net profit. The asset turnover measures how efficient management was in using its assets. For example, an asset turnover of 4 indicates that for every $4 of sales, management invested only $1 in assets. The net profit margin and asset turnover capture different aspects of performance. Net profit margin is influenced by issues such as sales volume, operating costs, and expenses. Asset turnover reflects issues such as the amount of inventory needed (a key concern of operations managers, and one of the major assets controlled by operations). In general, the higher the ROA, the better the level of performance.

The SPM is useful for evaluating both operational and marketing-based plans and actions and answering "what-if" questions such as: What if we reduced fixed expenses by 10 percent? What would be the overall impact on ROA? To answer this question, we would enter the dollar values of operational changes in the categories shown on the right side of the SPM. The calculations in the SPM then reflect the impacts of these changes on financial measures shown on the left side of the SPM (which are of interest to top managers). Consider the following example of this type of analysis.

EXAMPLE 2-1

Suppose that the director of marketing has approached you, as a member of the top management team, with a suggestion that appears very attractive. The proposal begins by noting that because demand is down, the firm (and its supply chain) has much unused capacity. Happily, the marketing group has identified a new potential customer segment. Unlike existing customers (who are price sensitive and who buy large quantities of fairly standard products), these new customers will likely order smaller quantities more frequently. The new customers are also likely to want to make last-minute changes to order sizes, due dates, and product mix. Your current operating system is not really set up to accommodate such changes. However, the marketing director feels that the prices these customers are willing to pay will provide gross margins (30 percent, as compared to the 10–15 percent currently being given by existing customers) that should be high enough to offset any operational problems. The chief financial officer has stated that, in order to enter any new market, it must be expected to generate at least a 25 percent return on assets (ROA).

Given the information provided below, would you recommend accepting the marketing director's proposal?

Category	Estimated First Year Impact	Comments
Sales	$420,000	
Cost of Goods Sold	$294,000	30% gross margin
Variable Expenses	$ 45,000	Need more for small batch shipping and expediting
Fixed Expenses	$ 40,000	More inspections needed
Inventory	$200,000	Need safety stock to ensure timely delivery
Accounts Receivable	$120,000	Customers tend to pay on longer cycles
Other Current Assets	$ 0	No change
Fixed Assets	$ 15,000	Need special fixtures and tooling

The strategic profit model is well suited for this type of analysis. A gross margin of 30 percent seems attractive. However, to make a good decision we need to factor in other required changes. By entering the data into the SPM (as can be seen in Figure 2-4), we find that expected ROA is 12.2 percent—less than the 25 percent hurdle rate. Consequently, we would recommend that the marketing request be rejected.

FIGURE 2-4 SPM
Analysis for Example 2-1

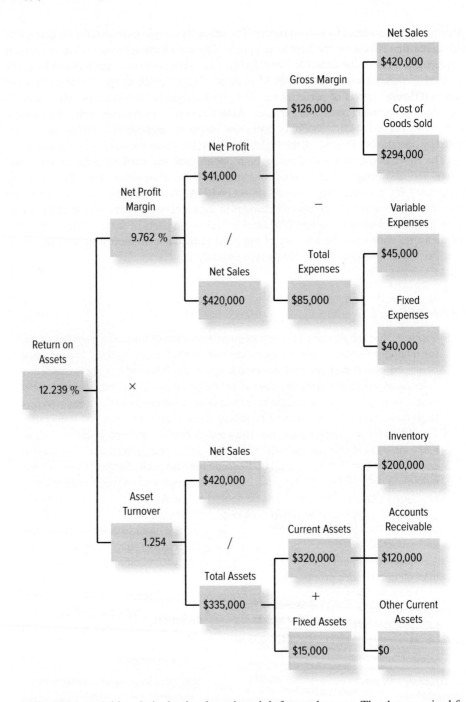

The SPM model is relatively simple and straightforward to use. The data required for the model are readily available in most firms with well-developed financial and accounting systems. The model reduces all aspects of performance into one number, ROA, making it simple to compare performance across different time periods and different divisions. It helps direct management's attention to those areas that represent opportunities or problems. Since the SPM is a system of metrics, it shows how performances in different areas of the firm are related. This helps managers avoid decisions that might improve performance in one area to the detriment of other areas.

The Supply Chain Operational Reference Model

With the advent of supply chain management, managers have increasingly sought to coordinate activities spanning customer and supplier organizations. In the late 1990s a group of industrialists from about 70 leading companies created an organization called the "supply chain council." Working together they developed the **supply chain operational reference model** (commonly known as the SCOR model).[5]

The SCOR model includes more than just metrics; it provides tools for charting and describing supply chain processes. It also describes supply chain management best practices and technology. However, we will focus only on the metrics portion of the model.

The SCOR model identifies basic management practices at different levels of operation. For example, "level 1" processes include plan, source, make, deliver, and return. One of the basic tenets of the SCOR model is that metrics should cascade hierarchically from one level to the next. At each of the levels addressing the supply chain, SCOR addresses five basic dimensions of performance. They are:

- *Delivery reliability:* The performance of the supply chain in delivering the correct product, to the correct place, at the correct time, in the correct condition and packaging, in the correct quantity, with the correct documentation, to the correct customer.
- *Responsiveness:* The velocity at which a supply chain provides products to the customer.
- *Flexibility:* The agility of a supply chain in responding to marketplace changes to gain or maintain competitive advantage.
- *Costs:* The costs associated with operating the supply chain.
- *Asset management efficiency:* The effectiveness of an organization in managing assets to support demand satisfaction. This includes the management of all assets: fixed and working capital.

The SCOR model identifies performance metrics for each of these dimensions. Figure 2-5 shows level 1 metrics along with examples of actual and desired levels of performance for a given supply chain. Note that Figure 2-5 also includes metrics addressing shareholder concerns such as profitability and return on assets.

One of the objectives of the SCOR model is to provide a framework for benchmarking and for deploying strategy. Figure 2-5 illustrates the results of a benchmarking analysis with the data provided in the right-hand columns. The data indicate the level of performance necessary to be on a par with the industry middle performers, as well as levels required to gain differential advantage. The data in the right-most column indicate the impact of improvement in a given performance metric, either on revenues, costs, or investments. This type of analysis could help partners in a supply chain to plan and prioritize operational improvement initiatives in accordance with an overall business strategy.

supply chain operational reference model (SCOR) A model for assessing, charting, and describing supply chain processes and their performance.

	Performance Attribute or Category	Level of Performance Metrics	Actual	Parity Median of Statistical Sample	Advantage Midpoint of Parity and Superior	Superior 90 Percentile of Population	Value from Improvements
EXTERNAL	Supply Chain Delivery Reliability	Delivery Performance to Commit Date	61%	85%	90%	95%	$30mm revenue
		Fill Rates	66%	94%	96%	98%	
		Perfect Order Fulfillment	51%	80%	85%	90%	
	Supply Chain Responsiveness	Order Fulfillment Lead Time	27 days	7 days	5 days	3 days	$30mm revenue
	Supply Chain Flexibility	Supply Chain Response Time	97 days	82 days	55 days	13 days	Key enabler to cost and asset improvements
		Production Flexibility	45 days	30 days	25 days	20 days	
INTERNAL	Supply Chain Cost	Cost of Goods	78%		63%	57%	$22m indirect cost
		Total Supply Chain Cost	19%	13%	8%	3%	
		SG&A Cost	20%	20%	17%	14%	
		Warranty / Returns Processing Costs	8%	4%	2%	1%	
		Value Added Employee Productivity	$122K	$156K	$306K	$460K	
	Supply Chain Asset Management Efficiency	Cash-to-Cash Cycle Time	196 days	80 days	46 days	28 days	$7m capital charge
		Inventory Days of Supply	77 days	55 days	38 days	22 days	
		Asset Turns	6.10	8.00	12.00	19.00	
SHAREHOLDER	Profitability	Gross Margin	26%	34%	43%	51%	
		Operating Income	11%	13%	17%	21%	
		Net Income	3%	6%	10%	14%	
	Effectiveness of Return	Return on Assets	9.6%	18%	22%	27%	

Performance Versus Competitive Population

FIGURE 2-5

Performance Metrics in the SCOR model

Source: Elaine Reichardt and Lindsay Jackson Nichols, "SCOR Your ISO Certification," *Quality* 42, no. 2 (February 2003), p. 44. Copyright © 2003 American Society for Quality. All rights reserved.

[5]See www.supply-chain.org for more information on the supply chain council and the SCOR model.

CHAPTER SUMMARY

This chapter has introduced the operations strategic planning process within the context of supply chain management. In discussing this process, the following points were made within this chapter:

1. Strategic planning defines the specific types of value that the firm will deliver to its customers. It takes place at three levels. Corporate strategy identifies the business units to be included in the firm. Business unit strategy defines how the business will compete. Operations strategy identifies the priorities, capabilities, and resource deployments needed to support the business strategy and associated value proposition. These three levels of strategic planning should be integrated, with planning taking place from the top down, while execution takes place from the bottom up.

2. Operations strategic planning is driven by the business model—an integrative, systematic view of how the SBU generates value. This planning process begins with the critical customer. It translates the demands of this customer into meaningful terms, using the concepts of order winners, order qualifiers, and order losers.

3. The business model and operations strategy bring together three critical elements: key customers, value propositions, and operations capabilities. The fit between these elements defines the effectiveness of the strategy.

4. Competitive priorities address product-related issues (quality, lead time, cost) and longer term process-related issues (innovation, flexibility, sustainability, and risk management).

5. In developing the future capabilities of the supply chain, operations managers must know what their firm's existing core competencies are (because these must be protected).

6. Extending strategy development to multiple functions and supply chain partners, operations managers must make critical strategic decisions about what is to be done, with what resources, when activities are to take place, and who is responsible.

7. Critical to strategic success is the ability of the firm to effectively integrate and maintain fit among the desires of key customers, the firm's value proposition, and its operational capabilities.

8. Strategic assessment tools like the strategic profit model (SPM) and supply chain operational reference model (SCOR) help link and integrate strategic plans, operations strategies, operational actions, and performance.

KEY TERMS

business model   27

business unit strategy   27

capabilities   36

core capabilities   36

corporate strategy   27

cost   33

customers   29

fit   37

flexibility   35

functional strategy   28

innovation   34

key customer   29

lead time   33

operations strategy   26

order losers   30

order qualifiers   30

order-to-delivery
  lead time   33

order winners   30

quality   32

risk management   35

strategic business unit
  (SBU)   27

strategic profit model
  (SPM)   40

DISCUSSION QUESTIONS

1. Why should the firm never outsource its core capabilities? What happens if the firm is approached by a supplier who is willing to supply goods and services based on these core capabilities at a significantly lower price? What should the firm do?

2. Apply the corporate/SBU/functional planning hierarchy introduced in this chapter to your university/college or business. What would be the equivalent to corporate planning? SBU planning? Functional planning?

3. How would you define capabilities within a school or business?

4. When can a consumer be a critical consumer? In other words, when does it make sense to focus on consumers such as retail stores, distributors, or buyers, rather than on the end consumer?

5. A critical concept introduced in this chapter was that of the value proposition. Explore two competing products (e.g., RIM's BlackBerry and Apple's iPhone). Identify the underlying value propositions present in these products and describe how these propositions are evident in the resulting products.

6. Core capabilities are critical issues in operations management. Are there any instances in which a firm's core capabilities can be a liability rather than an asset?

7. Fit is critical to the development and maintenance of a successful operations strategy. Suppose that we are faced with a firm in which there is a lack of fit between the outcomes desired by the critical customer, the value proposition, and the firm's capabilities. What options are available to the firm in the short term when dealing with this lack of fit? What is the impact of the lack of fit? What are the implications of the firm trying to improve the fit?

8. Suppose that you are the owner of a pizzeria that is located near a university or college. How could you use the concepts of order winners, order qualifiers, and order losers to help develop and implement an attractive business model?

9. Why should metrics be regarded as primarily methods of communication? Think about the relationship between a metric, the strategy, and the task being carried out by an operations person.

10. A metric consists of three elements: the measure, the standard (what is expected), and the reward. Why are all three elements critical? What happens to the effectiveness of a metric when one of these three elements is missing?

11. What is the impact of sustainability on the business model? How does it affect issues such as the order winners, order losers, and order qualifiers? How does it affect the identification of the critical customer? When addressing this question, look up such products as Chrome or Timbuk2 for bags or Teva or Timberland for shoes.

12. As North American firms increasingly turn to product innovation, the management and protection of intellectual property becomes an important issue. Discuss how intellectual property considerations can affect the following areas in supply chain strategy:
    a. Supplier relationships
    b. Supplier contracts
    c. Supplier location
    d. Attractiveness of vertical integration

13. In this chapter, you were introduced to Huffy Bicycles. You were also told that the key customers were store managers and purchasing managers. Now, assume that Huffy decided to target first parents and then children as its critical customers (using the information provided below). What impact would this shift in critical customer have on you—that is, how would you design the resulting operations management system (including the supplier base)?

Critical Customer	Order Winners	Order Qualifiers
Parent	Acquisition price Durability (has to be passed down) Ease of maintenance (does not cost much to maintain over the summer)	Safety Availability
Child	Style (colors) Can be easily customized Newness (I have the first one on the block) Imitation (it is what I see others having on television)	Availability Maintenance

14. Using a SWOT analysis, can the operations management system be a strength? Can the operations management system be a weakness? Provide examples.

SOLVED PROBLEM

Suppose you have been asked to determine the return on net worth for Great Northwest Canoe and Kayak, a small manufacturer of kayaks and canoes, located near Seattle, Washington. For this task, you have been given the following information:

Categories	Values
Sales	$32,000,000
Cost of goods sold	$20,000,000
Variable expenses	$ 4,000,000
Fixed expenses	$ 6,000,000
Inventory	$ 8,000,000
Accounts receivable	$ 4,000,000
Other current assets	$ 3,000,000
Fixed assets	$ 6,000,000

1. What is the return on assets for Great Northwest Canoe and Kayak?

Solution:

To address this question, we must first calculate net profit margin and the asset turnover. This can be done using the structure for the SPM found in Figure 2-3.

Gross Margin = $32,000,000 − $20,000,000 = $12,000,000

Total Expenses = $6,000,000 + $4,000,000 = $10,000,000

Net Profit = Gross Margin − Total Expenses = $2,000,000

Net Profit Margin = Net Profit / Sales 6.25%

Current Assets = Inventory + Accounts Receivable + Other Current Assets = $15,000,000

Total Assets = Current Assets + Fixed Assets = $21,000,000

Asset Turnover = Sales / Total Assets = 1.52

Return on Assets = Net Profit Margin × Asset Turnover = 6.25 × 1.52 = 9.5

2. What areas should we as operations managers focus on if our goal is to improve ROA?

Solution:

We can see that the largest asset under our control is inventory. By reducing inventory we can improve the ROA. (It is left up to the student to prove this. One way of doing this is to examine the impact on ROA of a $1 million reduction in inventory or a $1 million increase in inventory.)

PROBLEMS

1. Given the following information:

Categories	Values
Sales	$32,000,000
Cost of goods sold	$20,000,000
Variable expenses	$ 4,000,000
Fixed expenses	$ 6,000,000
Inventory	$ 8,000,000
Accounts receivable	$ 4,000,000
Other current assets	$ 3,000,000
Fixed assets	$ 6,000,000

   a. What is the net profit margin for this firm?
   b. What is the asset turnover?
   c. What is the return on assets?
   d. What is the size of the total assets used by the firm?

2. For the prior question, management wants to double the return on assets, without affecting sales, cost of goods sold, variable expenses, fixed expenses, or fixed assets. Rather it wants to focus on either inventory or accounts receivable.

   a. Can management focus on either inventory reductions or accounts receivable reductions alone?
   b. How can it achieve this objective?
   c. Do you see any downsides in pursuing this objective through a focus on inventory/accounts receivable reductions?

3. You are the operations manager for a small kayak and canoe manufacturer (Valley Kayaks) located on the Pacific Northwest (Oregon). Lately your company has experienced product quality problems. Simply put, the kayaks that you produce occasionally have defects and require rework. Consequently, you have decided to assess the impact of introducing a total quality management (TQM) program. After discussing the potential effects with representatives from marketing, finance, accounting, and quality, you arrive at a set of estimates (contained in the following table). Top management has told you that it will accept any proposal that you come up with, *provided*

that it improves the return on assets measure by at least 15 percent. Would you go forward with this proposal to improve quality?

Category	Current Values	Estimated Impact of TQM
Sales	$2,000,000	5% + (improvement)
Cost of goods sold	$1,500,000	0%
Variable expenses	$ 300,000	8.25% − (reduction)
Fixed expenses	$ 100,000	0%
Inventory	$ 300,000	25% −
Accounts receivable	$ 100,000	0%
Other current assets	$ 500,000	0%
Fixed assets	$ 400,000	0%

4. As the operations manager for Valley Kayaks (as described in the previous problem), you find yourself faced with an interesting situation. Marketing has informed you that they have lost a number of sales because of a lack of inventory. Kayaks, being seasonal in nature, have to be in stock at your dealers if they are to be sold (customers are not willing to wait). The director of marketing proposes that you increase inventories by 25 percent (a major investment to you). She has also given the information in the following table. How would you assess this proposal from marketing? Would the projected change in ROA justify the inventory investment?

Category	Current Values	Proposed Impact of Inventory Increase
Sales	$2,000,000	25% + (improvement)
Cost of goods sold	$1,500,000	0%
Variable expenses	$ 300,000	10% − reduction (why?)
Fixed expenses	$ 100,000	15% + (increase)
Inventory	$ 300,000	25% +
Accounts receivable	$ 100,000	0%
Other current assets	$ 500,000	0%
Fixed assets	$ 400,000	0%

5. Noble Bicycles of Glen Arbor, Michigan, is a small batch manufacturer of high-end bicycles. That is, it typically builds bicycles in batches of one to three units. Quality is high, only to be expected when the typical bicycle frame costs $2,500 and up. Yet, profits have not kept pace with top management's expectations. Management has set a goal of generating a minimum of 25 percent return on assets. As a result of a corporate SWOT analysis, management has identified one critical threat: the costs at Noble are simply too high—and one important opportunity: because of the flexibility of operations and the experience of the design team, many of whom are either professional or serious amateur bicyclists, Noble is well positioned to become an innovation leader. A top management team consisting of the marketing director, the finance director, the corporate vice president, the purchasing director, and the director of operations management has developed two alternative strategies: (1) focus on reducing costs through the application of lean systems and procedures (Chapter 8), and (2) focus on product innovation (Chapter 4). To assess the two approaches, the team has generated the following table.

Category	Current Values	Lean Proposal	Innovation Proposal
Sales	$12,500,000	$12,500,00	$16,000,000
Cost of goods sold	$10,625,000	$9,375,000	$12,000,000
Variable expenses	$ 750,000	$ 650,000	$ 800,000
Fixed expenses	$ 750,000	$ 600,000	$ 750,000
Inventory	$ 1,250,000	$ 900,000	$ 1,500,000
Accounts receivable	$ 600,000	$ 500,000	$ 600,000
Other current assets	$ 600,000	$ 600,000	$ 750,000
Fixed assets	$ 600,000	$ 600,000	$ 600,000

a. What is Noble Bicycles' current ROA?
b. How does the lean proposal affect operations at Noble Bicycles?
c. How does the innovation proposal affect Noble Bicycles (why)?
d. Which proposal would you recommend to top management? Why?
e. How much of a change in sales would be required in order to make the returns of the two proposals equivalent?
f. What are the strategic risks of these proposals?

CASE

Otis Toy Trains Explores the Supply Chain

Otis Toy Trains of Minneapolis, Minnesota, was a landmark company in the toy business. Since the 1900s, it had been responsible for building electrical and steam-driven toy trains. Since the 1950s, Otis trains had developed a major presence on children's television shows. Every person (especially boys) knew about Otis toy trains and nearly everyone wanted one. For many kids growing up in the 1960s to the 1980s, waking up on Christmas day and finding an Otis toy train set under the tree was a dream come true. However, the 1990s had not been good to Otis Toy Trains. The preferences of many children had changed. Instead of toys, what many children wanted was a game playing system (like Sony's PS2 or Microsoft Xbox or Nintendo's Game Boy Advance). After a lot of investigation and assessment, the management at Otis had decided to reorient the product and the market. Consequently, it decided to target the adult male customer in the 30- to 50-year age bracket. This market was selected for several reasons. First, they had grown up with Otis toy trains and, as a result, Otis had excellent brand recognition among these buyers. Second, since Otis had decided to maintain the bulk of its production facilities in the areas around Minneapolis (the major production facility was located in Rochester, Minnesota), it needed a buyer who was willing to pay the premium now demanded by Otis Toy Trains for its products. Adult males in the 30- to 50-year age bracket typically had the income necessary to support luxury buys such as Otis toy trains. Finally, the new target market was attractive because these buyers tended to buy more than one system and they tended to buy a large number of accessories with their toy train purchases.

To sell to this new market, Otis introduced in 1995 the Otis Premium Trains of the Past series. This was a line of highly detailed, highly accurate trains drawn from critical points in North American history. The first launch consisted of the De Witt Clinton Rocket (the first train operated in the United States), the Abraham Lincoln train (a train model based on the train coaches that were used to transport the body of assassinated President Lincoln from Washington, DC, to Springfield, IL, for final burial), the Zephyr (the famous streamlined train that ran between Chicago and Denver during the 1930s), and the Orange Blossom Special. Launched in limited numbers, this first series was an unqualified success. Subsequent launches were almost as successful. Over this time, the designers at Otis Toy Trains developed and refined the skill of identifying attractive train series and of designing products that were detailed, attractive, accurate, and highly evocative of past times.

By 2010, however, Otis Toy Trains found itself faced with the challenge of dealing with increasing labor costs. It was during this time period that the Joyous Luck Prosperity Toy Company (JLPTC) of China approached the management of the Otis Toy Train Company with a proposal that had already secured the support of Otis corporate accountants. They proposed to work closely with the designers of the Otis Toy Train Company with the goal of taking over the bulk of production of the Otis Premium Trains of the Past series. What JLPTC offered Otis was a landed price per unit that was between 40 and 60 percent lower than current manufacturing costs. This was a price that was too good to pass up.

Questions

1. Assume that you are hired as a consultant to help Otis Toy Trains. What recommendations would you give to the management of Otis regarding the attractiveness of this proposal?
2. Assume that Otis decided to accept this proposal. Identify and discuss the most appropriate relationship that you would recommend for Otis and JLPTC. What risks are present in this proposal? How could Otis protect itself from these risks?

CASE

Steinway & Sons Piano

Steinway pianos have long been the premier brand among serious pianists. Franz Liszt called his Steinway "a glorious masterpiece." Gioacchino Rossini, a 19th-century composer, described the Steinway sound as "great as thunder, sweet as the fluting of a nightingale." In short, Steinway's product is the piano of choice for the vast majority of concert artists.

From the beginning, Steinways were a work of art. José Feghali, a classical pianist, illustrated this point when he remarked, "With the best pianos, you can walk into a room with 10 pianos and it's like playing 10 different instruments." The prices of the 5,000 or so pianos that Steinway produces each year range from $10,000 for an upright to $62,000 for a special-order concert grand piano.

In the 1990s, Steinway & Sons encountered some problems. John and Robert Birmingham purchased the firm in a $53.5 million leveraged buyout deal. John's previous experience involved making plastic windows for envelopes. Robert's most recent experience was with a mail-order business selling products with bear themes. Robert Birmingham said that they were delighted with the purchase because they viewed Steinway as a "great opportunity" given the firm's "great name and great tradition."

Steinway's craft-driven organization had not fared too well under its previous owner, CBS. The turmoil resulting from frequent management changes had reduced the consistency of Steinway's cherished reputation. Dealers complained that Steinways weren't of the same quality any more—they were often badly tuned and had sloppy finishes. Finally, in 1978, CBS hired a long-time piano industry executive who helped restore much of Steinway's reputation.

Now, a new set of outsiders owned the company. That the owners liked classical music did not assure Steinway's 1,000 employees that they knew how to make classic quality pianos. To make matters worse, the Birmingham brothers were now talking about using their "extensive manufacturing experience" to streamline operations. One

commented that the operation was "too reliant on a few craftsmen."

Soon modern manufacturing methods crept into the Steinway operation. A computer control system was introduced to keep track of parts and inventory. Eight million dollars was invested in new equipment to make the quality of small parts, such as piano hammers, more consistent. The loose-leaf binders that specified how pianos were to be built were replaced with engineering drawings. By the late 1980s, Steinway had entered the 20th century. John Birmingham lamented: "The music industry is made up largely of people enamored of music and the instruments they make, but they don't necessarily have great management skills."

As Steinway became more scientific, some stakeholders began to be concerned. Many of the older craftsmen found the new work environment not to their liking, and they left. Equally important, some within the industry began to be concerned that Steinway pianos were losing their personality. Some dealers and their customers even began to question the quality of Steinway's latest pianos. One classical pianist fumed that he had to use a 30-year-old Steinway because he could not find a new one he liked. Another dealer hired a consultant to review the quality of the pianos he had purchased from Steinway. He claimed that the soundboard, a key contributor to a piano's quality, had developed cracks. The consultant reported that this problem "indicated inadequate or improper controls over wood moisture content during various stages of manufacture." Subsequent study indicated that Steinway's new production quotas might have caused workers to pull wood from the conditioning rooms before it was ready to be bent, say, into a piano.

Questions

Assume that you are hired as a consultant to help Steinway deal with these latest problems. How could you use a value-driven approach to help this firm address these problems? What would you recommend?

CASE

Trail Frames Chassis

Trail Frames Chassis (TFC) of Elkhart, Indiana, is a major manufacturer of chassis for the motor home and van markets. Since it was founded in 1976 by two unemployed truck-manufacturing engineers, TFC has grown into one of the major suppliers in this market. Success in the motor home and van markets is difficult because of the constant rate of change taking place. Increasingly, motor homes and vans are bought by people in their late 40s to 60s. What these people want is a motor home that rides like a car. They are willing to pay for innovations such as ABS (antilock breaking systems), assisted steering, GPS, voice-activated control, and computer-balanced suspension. TFC produces a pusher type of chassis. This is one powered by a diesel engine in which the engine is located in the rear. While expensive to build, this design offers the customer a large number of advantages (no tunnel for the transmission, reduced engine noise, better handling). However, these chassis are used in motor homes that are very expensive ($150,000 and up). TFC builds its chassis for the large manufacturers—companies such as Winnebago, Airstream, and Gulf Stream. In general, these companies place orders for small quantities (5 to 10 in a batch). Many of the units in a batch are customized to a specific customer's requirements.

TFC has become successful because of its ability to develop new lines of designs in a timely fashion. These designs build on TFC's extensive experience with motor home users. They also build on TFC's knowledge of new technological advances and its ability to incorporate these advances into its designs. As a result, TFC has become the technological leader in this market. It is generally recognized that no one in the industry can match TFC's design and marketing knowledge base.

TFC is proud of its ability to design and build highly customized chassis. As John Stickley, its young and aggressive chief operating officer, is proud of pointing out, "Trail Frames has never met a customized chassis it didn't like." Complementing this focus on customization and speed, TFC has developed a culture of doing anything necessary to meet the needs of the customer. Changes are often introduced on the fly with an engineer taking a change down to the assembly line. In many cases, the bills of materials (the recipes for what goes into a given chassis) that were generated initially in engineering do not agree with the components and parts actually put into the chassis.

This approach has served TFC well for a number of years. However, recently sales for TFC have begun to level off. After visiting numerous customers in the field, John Stickley identified what he thought was the reason for this leveling off—the market for high-end, customized motor home chassis had been effectively saturated. There were only just so many customized motor homes that people wanted. Several of the major customers for TFC had strongly hinted that there was another market that TFC could enter that was consistent with its design strengths and its reputation.

Many of TFC's customers had noticed that there was a significant gap between the high-end motor homes that TFC served and the low-end market. The high-end consisted primarily of "pushers," and it began at $150,000; the low-end consisted of "pullers," and these products sold for between $35,000 and $70,000. That is, a motor home manufacturer would take an existing truck body (which consisted of the front end and the cab) and mount on it a motor home body. Obviously, there was a significant gap between the two markets.

One of TFC's major customers, Gulf Stream, approached TFC with an interesting proposal. It wanted TFC to design and build a low-end pusher chassis for this market. This chassis would go into a motor home that would cost between $75,000 and $90,000. In contrast to the current line of products, this chassis would not be customized. Rather, once the chassis was designed, it would not be changed. Production runs would go up from batches of five to batch runs of 100. Critical to success in this market would be cost and conformance to the schedule. If TFC could be the first to produce such a chassis, it would own the market. The financials were very attractive. Theoretically, it seemed easy for TFC to enter this market. All that had to be done was to take an existing chassis and to take out the "costs" by using less-expensive components. While TFC had never built such a chassis, there was no reason why it should not work. The only danger that the people at TFC could identify was that once it entered this market, it would be potentially competing with such firms as Ford, GM, and Toyota (major suppliers of the existing chassis). However, these firms supplied pullers (a chassis with the engine in front)—not pushers, like the proposed TFC product. In light of these issues, John was not sure whether this was the right market for TFC.

1. Compare the order winners, order qualifiers, and order losers for the customized chassis and for the proposed TFC chassis. To what extent are these factors similar?

2. What type of strategic consistency would you expect to find in TFC for its existing customized chassis?

Would this be the same type of consistency that you would find with the proposed chassis?

3. Evaluate the proposal for this new line of chassis. Is this a business that TFC should get into? If yes, why? If no, why not?

4. What would you recommend to John Stickley that TFC should do to increase its sales and to stimulate demand?

CASE

Lil' Me Dolls Deals with the Millions of Toys (MOT) Proposal

It was late on Friday, and Lisa Jacobs, the CEO of Lil' Me Dolls, re-read the document before her. It was a proposal from the MOT (Millions of Toys) retail toy chain offering to carry the Lil' Me line of dolls. At first glance, this seemed to be too good to be true. If she agreed, the demand for Lil' Me dolls would increase threefold in one year, and Lil' Me Dolls would become a household name. Finally, if done right, this deal would provide financial security to Lisa Jacobs, Roberto Martinez, and the other founders of Lil' Me Dolls.

Lil' Me Dolls

Lil' Me Dolls was the brain child of Roberto Martinez, a pediatrician and surgeon located in Albuquerque, New Mexico. As Roberto worked with small children (ages 7 to 13), he noticed that they seemed to do better if they could hold a life-like doll. The dolls appeared to become friends and confidents– someone with whom the children could share their fears and pains. Consequently, he decided to design and make life-like dolls for his small patients. This led him to contacting Lisa Jacobs, an artist that he knew, to make the first doll. The resulting head, based on Lisa's own eight-year-old daughter, Sarah, was the origin of the Lil' Jill series. What quickly surprised Roberto was the demand for this doll! Parents and visitors visiting the ward wanted their own dolls as gifts for their daughters, nieces, and granddaughters. It quickly became apparent to Roberto that this was not something that he wanted to manage, since he liked being a doctor. He approached Lisa with a proposal that together they form a company to make and deliver such dolls.

Lisa quickly recognized that there were several keys to success. First, the company had to release new doll heads on a regular basis. These new heads had to reflect the diversity observed in society. Since Lisa was closely tied into the artistic community of Albuquerque, it made sense for her to secure the involvement of various local artists in designing such heads. Soon, Lil' Me Dolls was able to offer six new doll heads a year. These heads were unique; Lil' Me Dolls became the first company to offer doll heads that were African-American, Oriental, and Hispanic. Sold primarily on the Internet, Lil' Me dolls were offered in two sizes–18 inches (for $129 plus shipping) and 24 inches (for $179 plus shipping). By the end of the company's first year of business, sales were growing strongly, and the production of Lil' Me Dolls had moved from a rented loft to a small converted warehouse located on the outskirts of Albuquerque.

Lil' Me Dolls benefited from some unique advertising opportunities. For example, Lil' Me Dolls was approached by the "Make-a-Wish" Foundation with an interesting request. One of their candidates had asked specifically to visit the Lil' Me Dolls factory, because she loved its products. Lil' Me Dolls agreed, provided that it could get a picture of the girl. When the girl came to the plant, at the end of the tour, she was presented with her own unique Lil' Me doll–a doll that looked exactly like her (this became the Lil' Jenna line of dolls, which was one of the most popular ever sold by Lil' Me Dolls). This story was quickly picked up by the media. After the story appeared, everyone seemed to want their own Lil' Me doll.

From its beginnings, Lil' Me Dolls targeted parents or grandparents or relatives as key customers—people who wanted a unique, life-like gift for young girls. Furthermore, they wanted dolls that not only were life-like but that also could be dressed like their owners. As Lil' Me Dolls grew, a cottage industry grew up making matching clothes for both the dolls and the children. Since these dolls were primarily given at Christmas as gifts, reliably meeting the Christmas delivery date was essential to success—you could not miss a delivery to a young girl on Christmas. Meeting these delivery deadlines was made inherently more challenging by the very complexity of the product. One day, Lisa calculated that, given the number of head types, eye colors, skin colors, expressions, and sizes, Lil' Me Dolls could make over 60,000 different unique dolls. Because these dolls were often prized and used (or abused), Lil' Me Dolls soon began providing repair services.

By the time of the MOT proposal, Lil' Me Dolls had gotten to the point where it could grow no more given the current strategies and business model. It was profitable, but barely. Lisa knew better than anyone else that Christmas sales could literately make or break the company. Every year, she worried about the survival of the company; she wanted something more sustainable and that something appeared to be the MOT proposal.

Enter Millions of Toys

MOT was a major retailer of kids toys, clothing, and accessories in North America, with over 2,000 stores worldwide (along with a significant Internet presence). Soon after Lil' Me Dolls was established, MOT recognized that it needed to offer its customers something unique and prestigious. Lil' Me Dolls was identified as that something.

MOT made a proposal to offer Lil' Me Dolls through both its brick-and-mortar stores and its Internet site. However, MOT made some specific demands of Lil' Me Dolls. First, the price had to be reduced by at least 25 percent. Second, since its customers were primarily price sensitive, MOT wanted only a limited number of dolls–25 different types in total. Delivery and sales were expected to occur all year around. MOT would select the dolls, while Lil' Me Dolls would service all returns and repairs. Furthermore, MOT required that an initial order of 5,000 dolls be delivered by the start of November, with an additional 5,000 dolls delivered over the next two months. This was almost twice Lil' Me Dolls' annual production. As with all such contracts, there were penalties for failing to meeting obligations.

On paper, the deal looked good. If successfully carried out, it ensured Lil' Me Dolls' survival. Yet, something seemed to bother Lisa about this deal.

Questions

1. What recommendations would you give Lisa Jacobs regarding the MOT proposal? In preparing your answer, consider the following questions:
    a. What is your evaluation of the business model that is in place currently at Lil' Me Dolls?
    b. What would the business model look like if Lisa were to accept the MOT proposal?
    c. To what extent could the current business model service the needs of MOT?
    d. If there is a gap identified in question 3, what investments would have to be made to bring about alignment?
    e. Does Lil' Me Dolls have the time to make the changes required by the MOT proposal?

READINGS & INTERNET SITES

Fine, C. H. *Clockspeed.* New York: Perseus Books, 1998.

Hayes, R.; G. Pisano; and S. Wheelwright. *Operations, Strategy, and Technology: Pursuing the Competitive Edge.* Hoboken, NJ: John Wiley & Sons, 2005.

Hill, T. *Manufacturing Strategy: Text and Cases.* New York: McGraw-Hill/Irwin, 2000.

Mckeown, M. *The Truth About Innovation.* London: Frances Pinter, 2008.

Melnyk, S. A.; E. W. Davis; R. E. Spekman; and J. Sandor. "Outcome Driven Supply Chains." *Sloan Management Review* 51, no. 2 (2010): pp. 33–38.

Ulwick, A. W. *What Customers Want: Using Outcome-Driven Innovation to Create Breakthrough Products and Services.* New York: McGraw-Hill, 2005.

Apple Inc.
www.apple.com

General Electric Company
www.ge.com

Honda Motor Company, Inc.
www.honda.com

Honda Aircraft Company, Inc.
www.hondajet.com

Inter IKEA Systems B.V.
www.ikea.com

Seven Cycles, Inc.
www.sevencycles.com

2

FOUNDATIONS OF OPERATIONS MANAGEMENT

		relationships	sustainability	global
3	Managing Processes and Capacity	X	X	X
	Supplement: Process Mapping and Analysis	X		
4	Product/Process Innovation	X	X	X
5	Manufacturing and Service Process Structures	X	X	X
6	Managing Quality	X	X	X
	Supplement: Quality Improvement Tools			
7	Managing Inventories	X	X	X
8	Lean Systems	X		X

*J*ust how do organizations work? If you had to name the six things that every operations manager should know, what would they be? The chapters in Part 2, Foundations of Operations Management, explain the basic principles of how organizations operate. Each chapter addresses a fundamental building block of knowledge that describes how to design and manage operational processes.

A process is a system of structured activities that use resources to transform inputs (such as energy, materials, and information) into valuable outputs.

As the figure above indicates, the first three chapters in Part 2 of the book are about processes. **Chapter 3** discusses the principles that govern how processes work, and the accompanying supplement provides tools for analyzing any process. **Chapter 4** describes how product designs and supporting operational processes are invented and

developed. **Chapter 5** describes how resources and technologies are typically organized in different types of processes.

The other three chapters in Part 2 discuss fundamentals and ways to manage resources in operations so that objectives are achieved. The two overarching goals of operations management are to do things effectively and to do things efficiently. **Chapter 6** describes ways to ensure high product quality, a measure of effectiveness. The accompanying supplement shows tools and techniques for analyzing and improving product quality. **Chapters 7** and **8** describe ways to improve the efficiency of materials usage (inventories) and of process execution (systems). Together, these three chapters identify cutting-edge ways to make materials, people, and processes as effective and efficient as possible.

3

Managing Processes and Capacity

LEARNING OBJECTIVES *After studying this chapter, you should be able to:*

LO3-1 Understand the importance of processes and process thinking to operations and supply chain management.

LO3-2 Define the various components that make up processes, including types of inputs and outputs.

LO3-3 Distinguish between operational, tactical, and strategic capacity planning.

LO3-4 Estimate the capacity and utilization of a process.

LO3-5 Explain the impacts of bottlenecks, variance, and other factors on process performance.

LO3-6 Describe process improvement methodologies such as business process reengineering and Kaizen Events.

© Ed Zurga/Bloomberg via Getty Images

CLEANING UP DRY CLEANERS

For most customers, taking your clothes to be dry-cleaned is a time-consuming, unsatisfactory experience. You take your clothes to be dry cleaned; you get a ticket and date when to pick up your clothes; on that day, you go and pick them up. What happens to your clothes while they are at the dry cleaners—that's a mystery—a black box. This mystery takes place in a shops that are small, bland, and that strongly smell of chemicals. The smell is the result of a process that has not really greatly changed since the 1930s, when cleaners began using a cleaning agent called perchloroethylene or "perc." However, things are changing. In part this change is due to the major cleaning ingredient—perc. While perc is especially good at dissolving oil-based stains, it is unfortunately been classified by the Environmental Protection Agency (EPA) as a toxic air pollutant and potential human carcinogen. Furthermore, there is the dry cleaning process—that's something that happens in a black box. Finally, the EPA has mandated that all cleaning establishments located in residential areas eliminate their use of perc by 2020. Switching to safer cleaning approaches is expensive, requiring dry cleaners buy new equipment costing between $45,000 and $100,00.

This is not the only change taking place. Procter & Gamble research has found that many customers are unhappy with their experiences. For these customers, Procter & Gamble has developed a new approach built around a new process. The new approach—the Tide Dry Cleaners stores. What makes these stores so different is that they have reviewed and changed many of the processes encountered by customers. They offer valets to pick up and deliver clothes at the customers' cars; lockers with customized passwords allowing customers to pick up and drop off clothes after hours; bar codes to keep track of customers' data and dry cleaning preferences; and button reattachment and minor repairs are done free of charge. Most importantly, the Tide Dry Cleaners stores offer a new cleaning process that is not only more environmentally responsible, it is also highly visible to the customer. Gone are the smells and dinginess. Replacing the old process is one that is bright and open, with the equipment visible and the smells gone.

Tide's process changes encompass the entire consumer experience, from drop-off to pick-up.

A SHIRT'S JOURNEY

Dry cleaners are making changes to get rid of the solvent known as perc. Here's how the cleaning process generally works.

TICKETING, ID TAGGING: Items are checked in and ticketed with a tag designed to withstand the cleaning process. Some cleaners staple tags on, while others use plastic fasteners.

SORTING: Garments are arranged and sorted, generally by fabric type, color or stain.

PRE-TREATING: Some items undergo 'spot' cleaning by hand to treat stains.

RE-TAGGING: New ID tags are attached for customers. The items are hung on a conveyor and placed in garment bags for pickup.

SPOT CLEANING: Additional spot cleaning removes stains that didn't come out earlier.

IRONING Garments are pressed, typically with an industrial steam press. Certain items are pressed by hand with a small iron.

DRUM CLEANING: A dry-cleaning machine is much like a big washing machine, but solvents are used instead of water. Soaps are added to aid in stain removal. Some machines can hold 60 to 80 pounds of garments.

HEATING: At the end of the 40-to-50-minute cycle, high temperatures evaporate the solvents.

BUTTON CATCH, INSPECTION: A contraption in the rear of the machine catches buttons or embellishments that come off during cleaning. They are sewn on before the garment is returned.

Source: Adapted from Ray A. Smith, "The New Dirt on Dry Cleaners.," *Wall Street Journal*, July 28, 2011.

By improving the process from end to end, Tide Dry Cleaners wants to improve the overall experience for its customers, while also minimizing negative environmental impacts. The well-known Tide brand name instills trust, while the new processes ensure quality (all products are returned clean and fresh smelling) and service (24-hour drop-off and pick-up, pleasing store surroundings), all wrapped up in a process that does not pollute.

Revolutionary process changes in the dry cleaning industry offer an example of the importance of processes in operations management. Processes determine the specific types of products that an organization can offer to its customers, as well as the timeliness and quality of those products. When customers' requirements change or when a company wants to offer its customers something very different, then it must change its processes. In a supply chain, operations managers must recognize that they are fundamentally process managers. Consequently, they must understand the principles that govern processes and process thinking.

PROCESSES AND PROCESS THINKING

A **process** is a system of structured activities that use resources to transform inputs (such as energy, materials, and information) into valuable outputs. Every process has structural and resource constraints that limit the range of outputs it can produce. Each process has a structure that defines, orders, and links the activities included in the operation. Usually, it also has procedures, monitoring and control structures, and feedback mechanisms.

Process thinking is a way of viewing activities in an organization as a collection of processes (as opposed to departments or functional areas). This way of thinking focuses one's attention not only on an operation's outputs, but also on the processes responsible for these outputs. Outputs become viewed as the result of the process; if you don't like the outputs, then change the process.

Using process thinking, operations managers design, document, manage, and change business processes located throughout the supply chain, with the goal of ensuring that these processes make the desired results inevitable. Process thinking causes managers to address critical process elements, including activities, inputs, outputs, flows, structure, resources, and metrics.

At the heart of process thinking is **Juran's Law**. Joseph M. Juran (1904–2008) was one of the leading quality gurus of the 20th century. He once observed that *15 percent of operational problems are the result of human errors; the other 85 percent are due to systemic process errors.* Accordingly, to improve operations we should focus our attention on processes first.

Viewing supply chain operations as a collection of processes, rather than a collection of departments, functions, or companies is important because this perspective helps managers to break down organizational barriers that can impede operational performance. By focusing on managing processes, operations managers can better ensure that the operational capabilities and outcomes they create are more fully consistent with the firm's strategy. In addition, process thinking causes managers and workers to view operational activities from a customer's perspective. Processes are the means by which customers' needs are satisfied.

Note that the notion of a *process* is much more general than just *manufacturing processes*. As can be seen in Table 3-1, process thinking can be applied to any operation that involves the transformation of materials, information, currencies, or even people. These high-level processes consist of smaller and more focused subprocesses. Between every pair of subprocesses, an interface must be maintained. Often these interfaces cross

LO3-1 Understand the importance of processes and process thinking to operations and supply chain management.

process A system of activities that transforms inputs into valuable outputs.

process thinking A way of viewing activities in an organization as processes rather than as departments or functions.

Juran's Law A key premise of process thinking: 15% of operational problems are the result of human errors; the other 85% are due to systemic process errors.

TABLE 3-1   Major Types of Business Processes

Business Process	Inputs	Outputs
Strategic planning	Competitor data, market assessments, internal capability assessments, economic forecasts	Strategic vision, long-term objectives and plans
Innovation	Technological developments, customer needs, production capabilities	New products, new production technologies
Customer service	Customer orders and requests, complaints, demand forecasts, priorities	Entered orders, delivery commitments, resolved problems
Resource management	Strategic objectives, resource costs, availability of existing resources	Capacity plans, facilities plans
Human resource management	Strategic objectives, skill requirements, demand requirements by area, staffing requirements and shortfalls	Hiring plans, training programs (both at time of hire and subsequently), staffing plans, employee development plans
Supply management	Supplier capabilities, raw materials, customer orders, demand forecasts	Fulfilled orders, production schedules, goods and services
Performance measurement	Raw information, benchmarks, standards	Performance variances, trends

departmental boundaries. For example, a customer service process might involve personnel from sales, manufacturing, logistics, and other departments. In the same way, processes often span the organizational boundaries of different firms in a supply chain.

ANATOMY OF A PROCESS

Processes involve structured activities and resources that are guided by performance metrics. A particular process can be defined by its:

1. Activities
2. Inputs/outputs/flows
3. Process structure
4. Management policies

Activities of a Process

A process usually consists of many different activities. For example, at McDonald's the activity of moving hamburger patties to the cooking area is different from the activities of cooking the patties or assembling a sandwich. Activities usually fall into five distinct categories:

1. An **operation** is any activity that transforms an input. For example, operations occur when a part or person is physically transformed, when information is organized, when a transaction is made, or when planning and calculations take place. For the most part, operations are the major source of value creation in processes.
2. **Transportation** is any activity that moves an input from one place to another without transforming its other characteristics.
3. An **inspection** checks or verifies the results of another activity. For example, an inspector might examine a part to compare it against a standard. A planner might check the progress of a part to see if it is on track.
4. A **delay** occurs when the flow of an input is unintentionally stopped as a result of interference. You experience a delay when you wait in line to check into a hotel. Delays usually take place because of insufficient operating capacity, or because other needed inputs (information or materials) or resources are not available. For example, transportation delays occur when passengers are missing or when equipment breaks down. In practice, delays are unplanned, often difficult to predict, and sources of variance in process performance. Delays can also be a source of great frustration to customers (as described in the Get Real box below).
5. **Storage** is an activity where items are inventoried *under formal control.* Access to stored items requires authorization. For example, when you put money in a bank, you put money into storage. In manufacturing, inventory storage occurs in many places, including stockrooms, warehouses, and holding/receiving areas.

Inputs, Outputs, and Flows

Process activities create outputs from inputs through a series of flows. Most processes involve two basic types of flows: information flows and material flows. Information flows can include data communicated in many forms (e.g., speech, binary code, written words or pictures, currency). Material flows involve physical products, including people. Inputs are items that come from outside the process and are acted upon or consumed by the process. Even simple processes usually involve a wide range of inputs including materials, energy, information, capital, and even people (in the case of a service process). Resources such as facilities, equipment, and labor are also inputs to a process. For example, an inspection activity requires floor space for storing the items to be inspected, and it consumes either a machine or a person's time to actually do the inspection. Outputs include both intended and unintended products of the process, including physical goods, services, and information. Intended outputs usually have value for customers. Unintended outputs are often undesirable by-products. For example, an important part of process management is to minimize pollution and environmental waste.

LO3-2 Define the various components that make up processes, including types of inputs and outputs.

operation (change) An activity that changes an input.

transportation (move) An activity that moves an input from one place to another without changing any of its other characteristics.

inspection (check) An activity that checks or verifies the results of another activity.

delay (wait) An unintentional stoppage of the flow of work.

storage (inventory/store) An activity that intentionally stops the flow of work items and places them under formal control.

sustainability

GET REAL

States Reduce Waiting Times for Car License Renewals and Registrations

State officials across the United States are attempting to reduce the amount of time customers spend waiting for license renewals and car registrations. The horror stories of people waiting for hours to get their licenses renewed are the source of a great deal of voter frustration and anger. Officials in states such as Michigan, California, Virginia, New York, and Rhode Island (to name a few) are changing the process steps and technologies for renewing licenses and registering cars. For example, in Michigan, license renewals can now be done over the Internet or by fax. In Rhode Island, a study of the processes found that delays were caused by the lack of critical equipment. Some delays are avoided by providing better information to customers. For example, some states are using the Internet to post answers to frequently asked questions and to provide forms that can be downloaded and completed at home. State employees frequently act as greeters, welcoming incoming customers—and checking to see if they have the necessary forms and information. Operating hours have been extended to allow more customers to come in after or before work. The results: significant reductions in delays and waiting times. In Rhode Island, for example, the average waiting time in March was 81 minutes; by October, it had fallen to 23 minutes.

© Denver Post, Cyrus McCrimmon/AP Images

Structure

Structure deals with how inputs, activities, and outputs of a process are organized. Process managers define a process's structure by sequencing, physically positioning, and linking activities. Ideally, the sequencing, positioning, and linking of process activities should be closely tied to the priorities that process managers place on various performance outcomes. The structure limits the process capabilities—that is, the types of outputs that the process is able to produce, the specific types of problems that the process can best address, and the levels of performance the process is able to attain. For example, a process designed to minimize product delivery speed might be structured quite differently from a process that minimizes operating costs. Processes that have many parallel activities are typically faster and more flexible than more serial processes. On the other hand, because resources are often duplicated in parallel processes, they tend to be less completely utilized, thus making the process more costly.

> **process capabilities** The specific types of outputs and levels of performance that a process can generate.

How activities are positioned and linked is also important for process performance. Locating two activities closer to one another reduces the time needed to move materials and tools between them. Dedicated physical links such as conveyor belts can be used to reduce transfer time and variability, resulting in lower material handling costs. However, building physical links requires capital investment and fixed operating costs, and they can make it more costly to change the flows within a process. Specialized information links are subject to the same trade-offs.

Over the years, a number of typical process structures have evolved. Each of these structures (project, job shop, batch shop, assembly line, continuous flow) represents a scheme of supportive choices regarding the sequencing, positioning, and linking of activities in a process. Chapter 5, "Manufacturing and Service Process Structures," discusses these process types.

Management Policies

Any effective process has to be designed and managed so as to satisfy some customer requirement (e.g., to produce a product of a certain quality within a certain amount of time). How these requirements are specified, measured, and evaluated by managers can have great effects on the overall performance of the process. In addition, the policies that managers use to control resources, especially human resources, are very important. For example, worker compensation policies can have a huge effect on process outcomes. Paying a worker for a rate of output (pay by the piece) tends to motivate the worker to produce higher quantities. However, other aspects of performance may suffer, for example, quality, safety, and so on. Paying workers by the hour or paying them a straight salary has other advantages and disadvantages. It is important to design the management aspects of a process, including metrics, rewards, and controls, so that they are consistent with the overall mission.

PROCESS CAPACITY AND UTILIZATION

capacity The limit on the amount of output per period of time that a process can generate or store given a level of inputs and resources available.

Process **capacity** refers to the limit on the amount of output that a process can produce given an amount of inputs and resources made available to the process (i.e., machine hours, labor hours, tools, or square feet of floor space available). Process capacity is usually specified with respect to some unit of time, such as "this process can produce 100 units per hour." The term *capacity* is also used to denote size or storage limits. For example, a warehouse has a certain storage capacity limited by its square footage. Operations, transportation, and inspection activities are usually defined by output capacity, whereas delays and storage activities are defined by storage capacity.

The capacity of a process is determined by the limits of its resources. For example, the capacity of a circuit board assembly operation is limited by the types of tools, machines, and labor it employs; the capacity of a transportation activity is limited by the size of its equipment; and so on. Table 3-2 gives examples of the capacity-limiting resources associated with the five types of process activities.

LO3-3 Estimate the capacity and utilization of a process.

Operations managers usually express amounts of capacity in terms of either resource availability (e.g., available machine hours, labor hours, number of tools, or storage space) or potential output rate (e.g., number of parts that the process can produce in a day; dollars worth of products it can produce in an hour). Different types of business operations use different units of capacity measurement. Restaurants measure capacity in terms of the number of diners or meals that can be served during a day or specific mealtime. An amusement park assesses the number of patrons that can safely visit the park per day. A delivery company measures the number of packages that can be delivered per day. A manufacturing company may count the number of units (TVs, bicycles, tables, etc.) that it can make per day, or it might measure the amount of dollars of sales that it can support in a day. Capacity can also be measured in terms of inputs used. For example, a neighborhood bakery might measure the number of oven baking hours it has available, or it may simply measure the pounds of flour it can consume.

maximum capacity The highest level of output that a process can achieve under ideal conditions in the short term; also known as *design capacity*.

Capacity limits are often expressed in two different ways: *maximum capacity* and *effective capacity*. **Maximum capacity** is the highest output rate that an activity or a process can achieve under ideal conditions in the short term. This assumes that all equipment and workers are fully operational for the maximum amount of available time. For equipment this is also known as *rated* or *design capacity*; it is an engineering assessment of maximum output, assuming continuous operation except for normal maintenance and repair time. Usually, producing at a rate of maximum capacity can only be sustained for a relatively short time, because things do not always operate perfectly. When operations managers take into account the potential for disruptions in process flows, worker fatigue, machine

TABLE 3-2   Capacity and Process Activities

Process Activity	Associated Resources That Limit Capacity
Operation	Tools, labor, machine capacity, supplier capacity
Transportation	Pallets, carts, fork-lift trucks, trucks, trains, airplanes
Inspection	Inspectors, inspection stations, gauges, robots, or machine-vision equipment
Delay	Space on the shop floor, bins, carts, racks
Storage	Floor space, racks, bins, stockrooms, stockroom clerks

breakdowns, preventive maintenance, and so forth, they can estimate the **effective capacity** that the process can sustain. The sustainable effective capacity of a process may be only 70–80 percent of the maximum designed capacity, for instance. It is the effective capacity estimate that operations managers use when they make plans for how they will satisfy customer demand, though they may plan output that exceeds effective capacity levels for short periods of time (such as during periods of peak demand).

    Both design capacity and effective capacity are planning concepts (different types of planning are described in greater detail later on in this book). As a measure of performance, operations managers often compare planned capacities with what was actually produced. **Utilization** is defined as the percentage of process capacity that is actually used. Utilization can be calculated as the ratio of the actual output rate to the capacity. Alternatively, utilization is sometimes calculated as the percentage of available resource time that is actually used. Very low utilization rates suggest that equipment or employees are being underused, while extremely high utilization rates suggest overuse and a corresponding danger that problems may occur if demand continues to exceed available capacity. Example 3-1 shows how the various types of capacity are calculated.

> **effective capacity** The level of capacity or output that a process can be expected to produce under normal conditions; what management plans for under normal conditions.

> **utilization** The percent of process capacity that is actually used.

EXAMPLE 3-1

A distribution center for an Internet bookseller can handle a peak demand of 200,000 orders in a single day, under ideal conditions. However, the facility was designed to handle up to 120,000 orders per day during normal operating conditions. Orders processed for the first two weeks of December averaged 150,000 per day. Calculate the utilization of the distribution center relative to both maximum capacity and effective capacity.

SOLUTION

Maximum capacity = 200,000 orders per day
Effective capacity = 120,000 orders per day
Actual orders = 150,000 orders per day

Utilization of maximum capacity = (150,000/200,000) × 100% = 75%

Utilization of effective capacity = (150,000/120,000) × 100% = 125%

This example illustrates that the Internet bookseller can accommodate high periods of demand by utilizing maximum capacity (e.g., by using overtime work) in the short run. However, if this high demand continues for more than a few weeks, it should consider increasing its effective capacity by expanding its distribution center and/or hiring more workers.

Amazon distribution center.

Operations managers are usually concerned when effective capacity is greater than actual production (i.e., what we planned to make is greater than what we actually made, or the number of customers we planned to serve is less than the number we actually served). For either external or internal reasons processes are often not able to achieve desired levels of capacity utilization. External reasons include insufficient demand or supplied inputs. Internal reasons include lack of resource availability (machines break down or workers are absent), efficiency problems (workers are slowed by product changeovers, training, or unforeseen difficulties), and quality problems (some portion of the products do not meet requirements). In some contexts, there may be an insufficient yield rate. Yield rate is the percentage of good units produced as a percentage of total units begun. For example, a yield rate of 80 percent means that out of 100 units begun, only 80 were successfully completed; the remaining 20 units must be scrapped (thrown away) or reworked. It is the job of operations managers to minimize these sorts of difficulties in order to make the process as productive as possible.

yield rate　The percentage of units successfully produced as a percentage of inputs.

Operations managers are also concerned when actual production exceeds effective capacity for a long period of time. Most processes can exceed their effective capacities in the short run by working faster than normal, or by working longer than normal (overtime). Such overproduction is usually not sustainable, however. Typically, when workers are pushed beyond normal limits, errors and accidents become more frequent. People become fatigued and safety issues emerge. Similarly, machines that are utilized for too long will break down if they are not properly maintained. It is the job of operations managers to maintain the balance between making sure that capacity is fully utilized and avoiding unsustainable overutilization.

sustainability

Capacity Planning

LO3-4　Distinguish between operational, tactical, and strategic capacity planning.

Capacity decisions are important because demand, products, technology, and the competitive environment shift over time. Managers must consider these shifts to determine when and how much to change capacity. Typically, cross-functional teams make decisions about how much capacity is needed and when it should be added or removed. Too much capacity in a supply chain means that resources are underutilized, so costs increase. For example, after years of rapid expansion, Starbucks increased its capacity too much. In 2008, because of sagging sales, Starbucks announced it was closing 600 stores. Too little capacity in a supply chain can be a problem, too. When Nintendo first introduced its Wii© gaming console system, capacity problems at one of its suppliers led to empty store shelves, upset customers, and lost sales.

There are three general strategies for determining when to change capacity relative to demand. Some companies use a capacity lead strategy by adding capacity assuming that demand will grow. Apple used this strategy very effectively for its iPad© tablet computer, as described in the Get Real box below. A lead strategy ensures sales will not be lost and helps companies gain market share during the early stages of a product's life cycle. However, this strategy can result in costly underutilization if sales do not grow as expected. Other companies add or remove capacity to correspond to average demand. This approach balances the risks of having too much capacity and missing out on sales. A third approach, a capacity lag strategy, is to wait to add capacity until after demand is actually known. This strategy, often used as products mature, lowers the risk of overexpansion, but results in lost sales.

Capacity changes involve increasing or decreasing key resources such as facilities and space, equipment, and labor within the supply chain. Capacity changes can be strategic, tactical, or operational, as summarized in Table 3-3. Strategic capacity changes take a long time to implement and often include large increases or decreases in capacity, such as building a new retail mall or manufacturing plant or outsourcing customer service operations to a supplier. Tactical capacity decisions occur in the medium term (6 to 24 months) and may be medium-sized capacity changes, such as buying equipment and leasing space. Finding and qualifying an additional supplier or distributor is a tactical decision. Some tactical capacity decisions may be smaller changes, such as hiring specialized labor such

Capacity Planning Contributes to iPad's© Success

Although much of the credit for the iPad's© success goes to its innovative product design, effective capacity planning helped Apple to capture over 75 percent of the tablet computer market. Apple used a capacity lead strategy to tie up suppliers' capacities for key components such as the touch screen in anticipation of strong sales. In addition, Apple committed to use a large amount of the capacity of its contract manufacturer, Foxconn, which assembles the iPad in China. These moves helped Apple attain economies of scale, thus lowering costs, and left its competitors scrambling to purchase key tablet computer components.

TABLE 3-3   Capacity Decisions Addressing Different Time Frames

Time Frame (time required for changes)	Limiting Resource	Types of Capacity Change	Examples
Short term (0–6 months)	Low-skilled labor	Overtime, part-time, temporary labor, layoffs	Restaurant wait staff, bank tellers, production line workers
	Equipment, space	Rental, leasing	Landscaping equipment, temporary storage
Medium term (6–24 months)	Specialized labor	Hiring, firing, contract labor	Engineers, accountants, machine operators, physicians
	Equipment, space	Leasing, subcontracting, equipment installation and renovation	Distribution/ warehousing, fast-food restaurant rebuild, production line renovation
Long term (more than 2 years)	Physical plant	New building, outsourcing	Automotive plant open or closure, new office building

as physicians or engineers. Operational capacity decisions occur in the short term (zero to six months) and typically require small changes to low-skilled labor, equipment, and space. The use of temporary employees at retail stores and distribution centers for the holidays is an example of an operational capacity change.

Economies and Diseconomies of Scale

With the addition of capacity, some types of processes offer economies of scale. As production volumes increase with additions of capacity, the unit cost to produce a product decreases until some optimal level is reached. The left side of Figure 3-1 illustrates economies of scale. In some industries such as consumer electronics, operations managers install enough production capacity in a single manufacturing plant to meet global demand so that they can achieve economies of scale.

economies of scale As production volumes increase with additions of capacity, the unit cost to produce a product decreases to an optimal level.

global

FIGURE 3-1

Economies and
Diseconomies of Scale

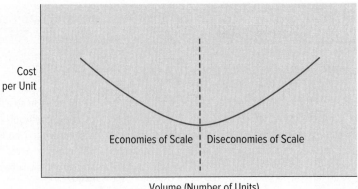

There are several reasons for economies of scale.

1. *Allocation of fixed costs,* which include things like depreciation of equipment, rent, taxes, insurance, utilities, and managers' salaries. Because fixed costs do not vary over a wide range of volumes, for accounting purposes they can be spread over more units as output grows, reducing the cost per unit.

2. *Equipment and construction costs* do not increase proportionally with size. For example, when the size of a storage tank in an oil refinery doubles, its cost only increases by about 1.5 times.

3. *Lower costs for purchases* because of higher volumes. When buying more, firms have more power to ask suppliers for lower prices. When volumes increase for suppliers, they gain their own economies of scale, and can pass some of the savings on to customers by lowering prices.

learning curve As the production volume doubles, the labor hours required decrease by a constant proportion.

4. As volume increases, *learning* occurs; this is a phenomenon called the learning curve. With practice, employees become more efficient at their jobs and find ways to improve processes. Learning is higher in assembly processes and for new products. Learning is lower in automated processes, and the rate of learning diminishes as employees gain experience making the product.

diseconomies of scale Occur when the cost per unit increases as an operation's size increases.

If the size of an operation increases beyond some point, costs per unit can increase and diseconomies of scale can occur, as shown on the right side of Figure 3-1. For example, hospital costs per patient decrease with the number of beds, up to a point; then costs begin to increase as more beds are added. A study in the U.K. suggested that the optimal size of a hospital was 400–600 beds, and beyond 600 beds, costs increased.[1] Several factors can cause diseconomies of scale. Overtime may be used more frequently and routine maintenance may be delayed, thereby increasing breakdowns. Use of overtime may not be sustainable in the long run. Too much overtime puts stress on employees and can cause safety problems.

sustainability

LO3-5 Explain the impacts of bottlenecks, variance, and other factors on process performance.

Theory of Constraints (TOC) The overall management system that strives to improve system performance by identifying, focusing on, and managing constraints.

PRINCIPLES OF PROCESS PERFORMANCE: THE THEORY OF CONSTRAINTS

Since processes are spread across the many organizations that make up a supply chain, it is important for all managers (even those in marketing and finance) to understand the basic operating principles of processes. One way of expressing these principles is through a management system known as the Theory of Constraints (TOC).[2] The principles offered by the Theory of Constraints apply universally, whether the processes are located in a manufacturing plant, a service facility, a sales office, or a financial planning office. The principles serve to

[1]J. Posnett, "The Hospital of the Future: Is Bigger Better? Concentration in the Provision of Secondary Care," *British Medical Journal* 319, no. 7216 (1999), pp. 1063–65.
[2]The theory of constraints was initially forwarded by Eli Goldratt. His popular book, *The Goal,* explains the basic principles in the context of a fictional story.

simplify process management by focusing managers' attentions on the important constraints that limit the performance of a process. There are five basic principles at the heart of TOC:

1. Every process has a constraint.
2. Every process contains variance that consumes capacity.
3. Every process must be managed as a system.
4. Performance measures are crucial to the process's success.
5. Every process must continually improve.

Principle 1: Every Process Has a Constraint

The overall operating capacity of a process is limited by one or more constraints. As indicated in Table 3-2, a constraint is a physical limitation applied by a person, by equipment, or by facilities. The constraining activity in the process that limits the overall output is called a **bottleneck**. Over time the output of a process can be no greater than the output of its bottleneck activity.

bottleneck An activity or resource that limits or constrains the output of a process.

Let's use the bottleneck principle to calculate the maximum capacity in a process. How we calculate capacity is strongly influenced by the structure of the process. A process can be serial/sequential or parallel. In a **serial/sequential structure**, the activities in the process occur one after the other; in a **parallel structure**, an activity is done by two or more resources simultaneously (e.g., two or more bank tellers serving customers). Example 3-2 describes a serial process while Example 3-3 describes a parallel process.

serial/sequential structure A process structure where the activities occur one after the other in sequence.

parallel structure A process where there are two or more resources doing the same task simultaneously.

EXAMPLE 3-2

Figure 3-2 below shows a circuit board assembly process with four serial operations. The maximum capacity for this process, 275 boards per hour, is based on the capacity of Operation C, which has the lowest capacity. Although Operation B can produce 400 boards per hour (125 more per hour than Operation C), the process cannot exploit this excess capacity because Operation C can accept only 275 boards an hour. Thus, Operation C is the bottleneck in this process.

Awareness of bottlenecks is critical. To improve the overall output of a process, operations managers must identify the bottleneck and ensure that it is always busy. An hour of lost output at the bottleneck equates to an hour of lost output for the entire process. For this reason, operations managers often keep an inventory of work waiting in front of the bottleneck activity so that it will never be "starved" for work. Managers also closely monitor and maintain the operation of the bottleneck to ensure that it is working correctly. Finally, awareness of bottlenecks is important because it affects investment strategies. Investing money or effort to improve the capacity of a nonbottleneck activity is actually a waste of time and money, since it has no effect on overall output.

The notion of bottlenecks is simple to understand. In practice, however, bad decisions are often made simply because operations managers do not have a clear view of how bottlenecks constrain their operating processes. The same situation applies in a supply chain context. Take another look at Figure 3-2, but this time imagine suppliers and customers in

A Process for Manufacturing Circuit Boards
(all capacities listed are maximum)

A → B → C → D → Finished Circuit Board

325 boards per hour / 400 boards per hour / 275 boards per hour / 375 boards per hour

FIGURE 3-2

Maximum Capacity in a Serial Process

EXAMPLE 3-3

If a process contains parallel resources that do the same type of activity, then the total capacity of the set of parallel activities simply equals the sum of the individual resource capacities. Figure 3-3 revises the circuit board assembly process to show a second operational stage made up of three parallel operations, each performing the same type of task. The total capacity for this second stage is not 90 boards (the single-operation minimum) but 400 boards (the sum of the capacities of Operations E, F, and B). The maximum capacity for the overall process remains at 275 boards per hour, however, because the work must still flow through Operation C.

FIGURE 3-3

Maximum Capacity in a Parallel Process

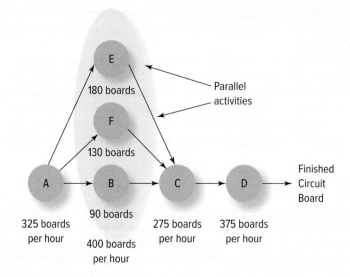

place of the four serial activities shown in the process. Ultimately, if Supplier B adds to its capacity, it does not help the overall supply chain, as it will always be limited by the capacity of Supplier C. Because various suppliers and partners in a supply chain are often unaware of capacity differences and have little control over them, isolated investments in capacity can be ineffective as far as the overall supply chain is concerned.

A bottleneck affects more than capacity in a process. It also impacts the timeliness of outputs produced, as well as cost and quality. The bottleneck determines the time that an input unit spends in a process because the bottleneck ultimately determines the rate at which units are processed. Little's Law[3] helps us to understand this relationship. Little's Law shows how flow time (F) is related to the inventory (I) and throughput rate (TH) of a process.

Little's Law An empirically proven relationship that exists between flow time, inventory, and throughput.

(3.1) $$F = I/TH$$

flow time The time it takes one unit to get through a process.

Flow time is the total time it takes one unit to get through a process; that is, the time that a unit spends being processed plus the time that unit spends waiting to be processed. The time that a unit spends being processed at a given operation in the overall process is called the cycle time. The throughput rate, or capacity, of a process is simply the reciprocal of the cycle time at the bottleneck operation. For example, if it takes 10 minutes for an operation to process a unit (the cycle time), then the throughput rate is one unit every 10 minutes, or six units per hour.

cycle time The time that it takes to process one unit at an operation in the overall process.

Little's Law indicates that the flow time for a given unit is dependent on the inventory that is in front of the unit, and the rate at which that inventory is processed (throughput

---

[3]John D.C. Little, "A Proof for the Queuing Formula: L = λW," *Operations Research* 9, no.3 (1992): 383–87.

rate or capacity). Recall from the preceding examples that the throughput rate for a given process is determined by the throughput rate of the bottleneck operation in that process. Because in most processes the time a unit spends waiting far exceeds the time it spends being processed, identifying the causes of waiting and reducing or eliminating them can create fundamental improvement in the process. In most processes, a bottleneck is ultimately the cause of waiting time and the attendant costs and quality problems. Example 3-4 shows how Little's Law can be used to set process times for a theme park ride.

Inventory due to bottlenecks creates requirements for longer total operating time and for more space to store inventoried items. Labor is needed to track and control this inventory.

EXAMPLE 3-4

A theme park (like Disney World in Orlando, FL; Cedar Point in Sandusky, OH; or Canada's Wonderland in Toronto, ON) plans to introduce a new thrill ride. At present, about 18,000 people come to the park every day, and the park is open for 12 hours. If managers want everyone in the park to have at least one chance to experience the ride, what should the maximum cycle time for the ride be? To process all 18,000 people (*I*) in 12 hours (*F*), the ride would need to "process" them at a throughput rate (*TH*) of 18,000/12 = 1,500 per hour. If the ride holds 100 people each time it runs, then it must run at a rate of 15 times an hour, or once every four minutes. The cycle time must be no more than four minutes. That is, the time needed to load the ride (get the people on the ride), provide proper safety instructions, let the ride experience occur, and then unload the ride, can take no longer than four minutes.

All of these factors increase costs. Quality also suffers. As inventory grows, more units are susceptible to damage, and problems in production are not as easily detected. In addition, insufficient capacity tends to encourage process workers to hurry, which in turn leads to mistakes. As one manager said, "Quality is the first victim of insufficient capacity."

activity

student

What symptoms would you look for that would indicate the presence of a bottleneck? Go to a fast-food restaurant and see if you can identify the bottleneck resource or operation.

The supplement to this chapter gives steps for diagramming a process and analyzing its capacity, lead time, and cost.

Estimating Capacity Requirements

Operations managers use their understanding of bottlenecks in capacity planning. They estimate capacity requirements for a process by using a forecast of each product's demand, its processing requirements, and any setup time that is needed when switching between products. The capacity requirements are determined by dividing the sum of the total time needed to make the products and the total time needed for setup by the operating time that is available. Example 3-5 gives us an example of how a manager might go about the task of estimating capacity requirements.

Principle 2: Every Process Contains Variance That Consumes Capacity

The second principle governing all processes is that every process has variance. Variance, or variability, exists in outputs, inputs, or in the process activities themselves.[4]

---

[4]The impact of variability on process performance is also discussed in the Lean Systems chapter.

EXAMPLE 3-5

Table 3-4, shows the annual demand forecast and the processing time for four different styles of desk chairs that can be assembled on the same assembly line. Assume that there is no time required to set up when changing over from making one type of chair to another. Multiply the annual demand for each chair by its processing time to estimate the processing time per year for each type of chair. Then, add these times together to get the total processing time for all four chairs. In this example the total processing time is 468,500 minutes.

The total processing time required for all chairs is divided by the total operating time that is available to determine the number of assembly lines needed. To ensure there is enough capacity, always round up to the next unit of capacity. In this example, the firm operates one eight-hour shift 250 days per year.

$$\text{Total operating time available (minutes/year)} = 250 \text{ days/year} \times 8 \text{ hours/day}$$
$$\times 60 \text{ minutes/hour}$$
$$= 120,000 \text{ minutes/year}$$

$$\text{Number of assembly lines} = \text{(Total processing time required)/(Total operating time available)}$$
$$(468,500 \text{ (minutes/year)})/(120,000 \text{ (minutes/year)})$$
$$= 3.9 \text{ assembly line, so round up to 4 assembly lines.}$$

If time is required to set up, this must be considered when determining capacity requirements. Let's recalculate the capacity requirements for the desk chair assembly assuming that setup time is needed. Table 3-5 shows the setup time and lot size for each chair. The number of setups per year is determined by dividing the annual demand for each chair by its lot size. Multiply the number of setups for each chair type by its setup time to get the total annual setup time per chair. The annual setup times are summed together to get the total setup time required per year.

The setup time is added to the total processing time, and this value is divided by the total operating time available to determine the capacity required.

$$\text{Number of assembly lines} = \text{(Total processing time required + Total setup time required)/(Total operating time available)}$$
$$(468,500 \text{ (minutes/year)} + 6,500 \text{ (minutes/year)})/$$
$$(120,000 \text{ (minutes/year)})$$
$$= 3.96 \text{ assembly lines rounded-up to 4 assembly lines}$$

In this example, the setup time did not increase the overall number of assembly lines needed. However, in some cases, setup time consumes a large amount of capacity. By reducing setup time, the capacity requirements and an organization's resource requirements and costs can be reduced.

TABLE 3-4 Estimating Capacity Requirements for Chairs

Chairs	Demand Forecast (chairs/year)	Processing Time (minutes/chair)	Processing Time Required (minutes/year)
A	2,000	20	40,000
B	3,800	45	171,000
C	2,500	33	82,500
D	5,000	35	175,000
		Total Processing Time (minutes/year)	468,500

TABLE 3-5 Estimating Capacity Requirements for Chairs with Setup Time

Chairs	Demand Forecast (chairs/year)	Lot Size (number of chairs)	Number of Setups/Year	Setup Time (minutes/setup)	Setup Time/Chair (minutes/year)
A	2,000	10	200	5	1,000
B	3,800	19	200	8	1,600
C	2,500	10	250	10	2,500
D	5,000	25	200	7	1,400
				Total Setup Time (minutes/year)	6,500

Table 3-6 summarizes the effects that different types of variability have on process capacity. Essentially, variability of different sorts introduces complexity and uncertainty into processes, which in turn increase the difficulty of efficiently and fully utilizing resources. In addition, resources must be dedicated to managing complexity and uncertainty. For example, more support personnel are needed to plan and control activities that often do not contribute directly to producing outputs (inspection and storage, for example). These activities take away from the total productive capacity of the process.

In addition to consuming capacity, variance increases process congestion and increases flow times because jobs must sit in queues and wait. This phenomenon is specified by equation (3.2). For a single operation, this equation quantifies the effects on a unit's **wait time** that result from both the level of variance and the level of utilization. This formula, developed from queuing theory, can be used to examine the interaction of utilization and variance.

wait time The amount of time that an item spends waiting.

TABLE 3-6 Types and Effects of Process Variability

Type of Variability	Example of Effects on Capacity
Output—product variety	As one facility is used to produce a wider range of products, more process changeovers are required. Each changeover requires time that could otherwise be used to create output.
Output—variable schedule	As demand and production schedules vary, they become more complex and coordination becomes more difficult. Different activities become bottlenecks at different times (especially if product variety is large and if production batches are large). This increases the potential for bottleneck activities to be poorly scheduled and left idle.
Process—quality variance	Defective product subtracts from the effective capacity of the process. In addition, productive resources are consumed by quality control and rework activities.
Process—resource availability variance	Absent employees and broken-down machines hold up production.
Process—variance in processing speed	As processing speed at an activity becomes more variable, upstream activities are blocked from clearing work from their areas and downstream activities are starved for needed inputs more frequently. This increases idle time, thereby reducing output.
Input—variance in quality	Poor quality results in unexpectedly insufficient quantities of needed inputs (e.g., materials, energy, information). It also introduces variance into the process that may result in poor final product quality.
Input—variance in delivery	As delivery variability increases, there is greater potential for process activities to be halted because they are missing needed components.

FIGURE 3-4

Effects of Process Variability on Wait Time

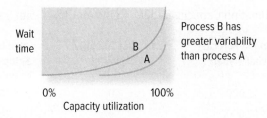

Wait time

Process B has greater variability than process A

B
A

0%   100%

Capacity utilization

(3.2)

$$Wait\ time = \left(\frac{c_a^2 + c_p^2}{2} \right) \left(\frac{u}{1-u} \right) t_p$$

c_a = coefficient of variation (standard deviation divided by the average) of job arrival times

c_p = coefficient of variation of job processing times

u = utilization of the work center

t_p = average processing time (cycle time) for jobs

In equation (3.2), the terms c_a and c_p represent variability in the arrivals and in the processing of jobs in the work center. Figure 3-4 illustrates the relationships specified in equation (3.2). As one can see, the effect of variance on wait time is nonlinear; it increases at an increasing rate. In addition, the impact of variability on wait time is worsened as utilization levels are increased. The use of the wait time calculation is illustrated in Example 3-6.

EXAMPLE 3-6

Suppose you are the manager of the Accounts Receivable department in your university. Recently, you have been hearing complaints from the students about having to wait too long in line before they can discuss their bills with one of the counselors. After discussing the situation with your boss, you decide that students should expect an average wait time of 20 minutes. With this standard in mind, you collect the following information during periods of high demand (i.e., the start of term).

Average arrival rate = 5 minutes
Standard deviation of arrivals = 10 minutes
Average time to discuss bill = 3 minutes
Standard deviation of discussion time = 4.5 minutes
Utilization = 85 percent

Based on this information, you can use equation (3.2) to determine that the expected average wait time is as follows:

Wait time = $(((10/5)^2 + (4.5/3)^2)/2) \times (.85/(1 - .85)) \times 3 = 53.125$ minutes

You now understand why students are so upset about having to wait so long. To improve this situation, you are left with a number of options:

- Reduce the variance in student arrival times (this can be done by telling students when the busiest and least busy times are so that they can decide to arrive during the least busy periods).
- Reduce utilization by having more staff.
- Reduce the processing times by improving the efficiency of the current processes.

For example, the target wait times can be achieved if the average utilization can be reduced from 85 percent to 68 percent (by having more counselors available during peak periods). Use equation (3.2) to verify this result.

GET REAL

Storyboarding: The Key to Success at Pixar

Few people can deny the success of Pixar. This company has the enviable record of a string of hit movies, including *Toy Story, A Bug's Life, Finding Nemo, The Incredibles, Cars, Toy Story 2, WALL-E, Up, Brave*—and Pixar's latest hit—*Inside Out.* Critical to this success is the practice of storyboarding. Storyboarding was first developed at the Walt Disney studio during the early 1930s. It involves developing a series of illustrations displayed in sequence for the purposes of previsualizing a motion graphic or media sequence. It allows users to experiment with changes in storylines to evoke stronger reactions or interest. It also facilitates brainstorming. Pixar has adapted this process to fit with computer animation. A storyboard is the blueprint of the movie, beginning with the concept and ending with the finished product. One of the reasons that Pixar has been so successful is that it focuses intensely on this practice. About three-quarters of a film's development at Pixar is spent in the story and in the storyboard. To better understand this process, see www.pixar.com/howwedoit/index.html.

© Buena Vista Pictures/Photofest

© Jim Sugar/Corbis

Because variability can create severe problems for a process, managers spend a great deal of time and effort in managing and responding to variability. There are three basic ways to deal with variability in a process. The first is to *reduce it.* This means finding sources of variability in process activities and eliminating or controlling them. For example, experimentation with the settings of a production machine might uncover ways to reduce its inherent variability. The second way to deal with variation is to *buffer it.* By placing safety stock (buffer inventories) before and after highly variable activities, one can reduce some of the bad effects on resource utilization. Finally, managers deal with variation by designing processes that *flexibly respond to it.* By investing in flexible technologies and cross-training of labor, managers can create processes that quickly react to unplanned situations so that, once again, the detrimental effects of variation are minimized.

Principle 3: Every Process Must Be Managed as a System

Operations management is by its very nature a system management activity. As discussed earlier, the elements of the "system" include process activities, input and output flows, structure, and management policies. All of these elements need to be aligned to the needs of the customers that the process serves. Activities within a process are connected, so that what happens in one area of a process can affect what happens elsewhere. This is very much the case when dealing with variance and bottlenecks. Because of interdependencies in the system, variances tend to be amplified throughout the system. If activity B is dependent on activity A, then B cannot work faster than A works. In addition, delays due to variability in activity A are passed on to activity B.

Changing one element of a process in isolation can lead to unpredictable results. Every change made to a given activity needs to be evaluated in light of how it relates to other

relationships

activities in the process. The application of this principle has contributed to the success of entertainment companies such as Pixar (see the Get Real box above). As we noted earlier, adding capacity to an activity will have different effects on the overall process performance depending on that activity's role in the overall process (i.e., whether or not it is a bottleneck). Similarly, changes to one management element of a process will have effects on many other elements. For example, changing the way that employees are evaluated and rewarded will affect behaviors and process outcomes.

Principle 4: Performance Measures Are Crucial to the Process's Success

metric A measure, a standard, and a consequence that work together to close the gap between what is valued by the customer and what is intended by the organization.

relationships

Because almost all processes involve human beings, performance measures are important drivers of process success. Process performance measures, or metrics, need to address the aspects that are important to the customer as well as the organization. Simply stated, a metric consists of three important elements: the measure, the standard against which the measure is compared, and the consequence associated with the measure's meeting or not meeting the standard. A metric should be designed to close the gap between what is valued by the customer and what is intended by the organization. Metrics should be *verifiable* and *quantitative* and they should be computed using a clearly specified method that uses objectively gathered data.

Equally important are the standards and rewards associated with metrics. The standard defines what an acceptable level of process performance is. The reward, which can be either positive or negative, serves to motivate behaviors. Metrics (measures, standards, and consequences) communicate a firm's strategy and priorities related to the process. These aspects of management provide a language for communicating process performance to workers, customers, and top managers. They also provide the basis by which managers can monitor, control, and improve process performance by directing everyone's efforts and all decisions toward the same set of corporate objectives.

Several steps can be taken to insure that metrics motivate process behaviors in ways that increase customer value. The first is to identify and prioritize the customers served by the process. Processes typically serve many potential customers, some of whom may be internal to the operation. For example, a school serves its students as "customers" who consume education. At the same time, the school serves many other customers including the students' parents, recruiters who hire the students, and even the community as a whole. Different customer groups rarely have identical wishes, and it is rarely possible to completely satisfy all customers. Consequently, managers must identify the critical (most important) customers. Second, they have to prioritize the requirements of these critical customers, while not losing sight of less critical groups. Third, they must pick a limited number of critical requirements and provide meaningful operational definitions (metrics) for them. These metrics should be consistent with the specific types of value that the firm provides within the marketplace and with the ways that the firm differentiates itself from its competitors. Having established metrics, managers can then assess the adequacy of the current process and establish objectives for a redesigned process as needed.

Principle 5: Every Process Must Continuously Improve

LO3-6 Describe process improvement methodologies such as business process reengineering and Kaizen Events.

Operations managers do not work in a static world. Technology is always changing, the competition is changing, and customers (and their expectations) are changing. Consequently, processes (especially the critical processes identified in Table 3-7) should also be changing. They must be evaluated and changed when the level of value that they provide is no longer acceptable to customers.

TABLE 3-7 Six Types of Critical Processes

Process Type	Why Critical?
Bottleneck	Limits output; increases lead time; adversely affects cost, quality, and flexibility.
Visible to the customer	Affects how the customer views not only the process but also the firm.
Core capability	A process that incorporates a critical strategic skill set that is difficult for the competition to copy. Must be guarded, managed, and improved continuously because it is the major source of the firm's value.
Feeder process	A process that feeds a number of alternative processes coming out of it. A problem in this process (e.g., delay) can affect many downstream outcomes.
Greatest variance	Variances are amplified by sequential steps in processes. To reduce variance, managers should identify those steps that are sources of greatest variance.
Most resources consumed	We focus on these processes because they offer the "biggest bang for the buck."

There are a number of specific tools that can be used to aid process improvement efforts, including process flow analysis (covered in detail in the supplement to this chapter) and Kaizen Events.

Kaizen Events: Small Process Changes Made Quickly

One approach for continually improving processes makes use of Kaizen Events. A Kaizen Event is a short-term project aimed at improving an existing process, or an activity within a process. It is characterized by the following traits:

Kaizen Event A short-term (i.e., lasting one week or less) approach to enhancing efficiency that focuses on improving an existing process or an activity within a process.

- *Team-oriented:* The responsibility for an event is placed in the hands of a cross-functional team consisting of employees from the process being studied, employees outside of the process, management, and in some cases, supplier representatives. The entire team is responsible for all the Kaizen steps. As a result, the team members develop greater ownership of the changes.

- *Short-term and focused:* Kaizen Events usually take between one and four days from start to finish and focus on a tightly bounded process or activity. During this period, team members are introduced to the process analysis tools that they will use. They then study the process, identify opportunities for improvement, implement them, assess the impact, redo the cycle, and present their results to management.

- *Action-oriented:* An interesting feature of Kaizen Events is the immediacy of action. Any change that is identified and approved by the team is immediately implemented. The only major constraint is that the changes not require any major funding or capital requests. After the changes have been implemented, the new system is run and the resulting performance is documented and compared with the old system. As one American manager put it, the motto of a Kaizen Event is, "Ready, Fire, Aim."

- *Repetitive:* Once begun, Kaizen Events are regularly repeated. Each event generates an action list or a list of opportunities for improvement identified by the team in areas that they could not address within their event. These items, in turn, become the focal point for future Kaizen Events.

relationships

To understand both the attraction of Kaizen Events and their impact on operations performance, consider the experience of Delta Faucet . Its personnel applied the Kaizen Event approach to resolve a quality/scrap problem (as described in the Get Real box above).

Along with Kaizen Events, operations managers may occasionally use more radical approaches for improving processes. Managers typically decide what types of approaches to use depending on the size of the gaps between the current process capabilities, competitors' capabilities, and customers' requirements. Substantial gaps justify major process renovations, whereas small gaps encourage incremental improvements through Kaizen Events.

Delta Faucet Uses a Kaizen Event to Improve Quality and Reduce Scrap

Delta Faucet designs and builds premium faucets. Managers determined that during a cooling process in one of the plants, the faucets seemed to develop surface defects that resulted in either increased rework or scrap. They decided to set up a Kaizen Event team to focus on this process-related problem. To execute this Kaizen Event successfully, the management team followed these steps:

1. *Define the desired outcome and associated metrics.* The desired outcome was to reduce rework and rejects due to process problems. Their metric was "to maximize the percent of faucets acceptably finished the first time." Management was convinced that an acceptable standard was a minimum of 95 percent of all the faucets finished correctly the first time.

2. *Establish the Kaizen Event team.* Management assigned a team consisting of one facilitator, two people who were experts with the process, one customer representative, one supplier representative, and one person who was completely unfamiliar with the process (that person's role is to question everything about the process).

3. *Set the contract of the Kaizen Event.* The time period for the Kaizen Event and the goals of the event were reviewed with the facilitator. The event was targeted for four days.

4. *Implement the Kaizen Event.* The facilitator introduced the team to the problem, the desired outcome, and the metrics. Next, the members of the team were introduced to the necessary tools: value stream mapping, cause and effect diagramming, and Pareto analysis. They then studied the process to understand why the problems were occurring. As opportunities for improvement were identified, they were implemented immediately to see if these "solutions" worked. At the end of four days a new process emerged.

5. *Present the results.* In the presentation of the results, the team described what the problem was, discussed the underlying causes of the problems, the solutions evaluated, and the new, "improved" process. Finally, the team presented management with the *action list*—a list of opportunities for improvement that were identified over the course of the event but that could not be explored because they fell outside of the scope of the event. These actions became the basis for future events.

© The Indianapolis Star, Matt Detrich/AP Images

CHAPTER SUMMARY

Processes are the critical building blocks of operations across the supply chain. The importance of processes is emphasized in the following critical lessons:

1. Every business is defined by its various processes. These processes determine capabilities, including what the organization can and cannot do regarding the types of product value delivered to customers.

2. A process is a collection of activities that uses resources to convert various inputs into outputs that customers value. Inputs used by processes include materials, energy, information, management, technology, and labor. Outputs consist of products, information, and experiences.

3. Processes are characterized by activities (i.e., operations, decisions, storage, transportation, delays, and inspections), flows (inputs and outputs), structures (organization schemes of activities), resources, and metrics.

4. Capacity within the supply chain should be managed strategically. Key decisions include when capacity should be added or deleted, which supply chain member should have capacity, and how much capacity is needed.

5. In many situations, as output volume increases, economies of scale and reductions in cost per unit are encountered until an optimal level is reached. If volume increases too much, the cost per unit can increase because of diseconomies of scale.

6. The maximum level of output from any process is determined by the activity with the lowest capacity, known as the *bottleneck*. Attempts to increase output and decrease lead time must focus on bottleneck activities.

7. Capacity requirements are estimated by considering the sum of total processing time and the total setup time for products divided by the total operating time available.

8. Variability in processes also consumes capacity, cost, and lead times.

9. Processes need to be continuously improved and, sometimes, entirely renovated or replaced. Kaizen Events are appropriate when intensive, focused modifications in the current process are desired.

KEY TERMS

bottleneck 67	Kaizen Event 75	serial/sequential structure 67
capacity 62	learning curve 66	
cycle time 68	Little's Law 68	storage (inventory/store) 60
delay (wait) 60	maximum capacity 62	
diseconomies of scale 66	metrics 74	Theory of Constraints (TOC) 66
economies of scale 65	operation (change) 60	transportation (move) 60
effective capacity 63	parallel structure 67	utilization 63
flow time 68	process 59	wait time 71
inspection (check) 60	process capabilities 61	yield rate 64
Juran's Law 59	process thinking 59	

DISCUSSION QUESTIONS

1. Describe the various operations within an amusement park that are most likely to become a bottleneck. How might an amusement park influence demand to better fit available capacity?

2. What are the primary resources that determine the capacity of each of the following?
   a. A grocery store.
   b. A hospital emergency room.
   c. A company that assembles appliances.

3. How can a university attain economies of scale? What impact might this have on quality and flexibility?

4. How would you define the maximum capacity for the front desk of a hotel? What is meant by the effective capacity? Define the difference in these two terms relative to the number of customers that can be checked into the hotel in a given period.

5. Which would require a larger amount of excess capacity, a hospital emergency room or a doctor's office? Why?

6. Discuss the challenges that an operations manager can expect to encounter when applying the principles of process performance to the upstream (supply-based) section of a supply chain.

7. Which of the five activity categories is represented by each of the following actions?

   a. A person taking an order from you at a restaurant.
   b. A conveyor belt carrying your order to you at a store.
   c. Work waiting at a workstation.
   d. Parts in a bin that an operator is working on.
   e. The safe at your bank.
   f. A person setting up a workstation to process parts.
   g. The advisor at your college checking your transcripts over to make sure that you have enough credits to graduate.

8. Under what conditions could inspection, storage, and transport be considered value-adding?

9. How would you define the capacity of your school? In what way does capacity influence the value of your college experience?

10. Under what conditions would you use a Kaizen Event?

11. Why is it important to begin with the metrics rather than to start by looking at the process?

12. Interpret Juran's Law from a process thinking perspective. How would this change your approach to problem solving?

13. If your goal is to reduce variance within a supply chain (especially if the variance is most evident in your supply), under what conditions does it make sense to focus first on the customer side of the supply chain?

SOLVED PROBLEMS

1. **Process Capacity at Zug Island Steel**

   Zug Island operates a mill that makes steel for a variety of uses. You have been hired as a consultant to evaluate the current state of operations of the coking oven, blast furnace, and basic oxygen furnace (BOF) departments. In the first stage of the process, a coking oven changes coal from a nearby coal dump into coke. The coke is left to cool in a heap and then moved to a pile near the blast furnace. Currently, the coke oven has a design capacity of 71,000 tons of coke per year.

   The blast furnace converts coke from the pile and iron pellets, also from a nearby pile, into pig iron. The pig iron is moved to a staging area to cool. The blast furnace uses 1.5 tons of coke and 2.3 tons of iron pellets to make every ton of pig iron, with a design capacity of 55,000 tons of pig iron per year.

   In the next step, the BOFs convert pig iron into steel, which is taken to a soaking pit to await the next stage of processing. The BOFs require 0.8 tons of pig iron and 1.2 tons of scrap and chemicals to produce a ton of steel. They have a design capacity of 68,000 tons of steel per year.

   Over the last year, the plant produced 60,000 tons of steel. You have been asked to calculate the capacity of the production process at Zug Island, stating results in tons of finished product (i.e., tons of steel). Also, the company is considering increasing the capacity of the blast furnace from 55,000 tons to 70,000 tons of pig iron per year, citing two major reasons. First, managers see a need to balance capacity across processes. Second, the change seems very attractive economically, with a return on investment significantly above the firm's requirement. What is your evaluation of this proposed change?

Solution:

Initially, this problem seems complex with many different activities and capacities stated in varying units such as pig iron tons, steel tons, and coke tons. The following four steps show how the problem can be analyzed.

1. Figure 3-5 lays out three operations (the coking oven, the blast furnace, and the basic oxygen furnaces) and six storage activities within the steel-making process. The process is organized sequentially, as the coking oven feeds the blast furnace that feeds the basic oxygen furnaces. Therefore, the overall capacity for this process depends on that of the lowest-capacity activity.
2. The most appropriate time period for the capacity calculation is one year because all data are stated in annual units.
3. To establish a common unit of measure, the calculation must convert the first two units—coke tons and pig iron tons—to steel tons to satisfy the company's requirements for the capacity data. As Table 3-8 shows, to convert the output of the coke oven (measured in coke tons) into pig iron tons, divide the number of

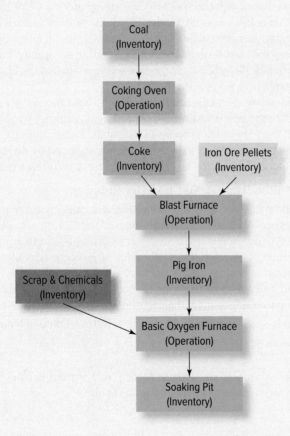

FIGURE 3-5 Process Flow for Zug Island Steel

TABLE 3-8 Converting between Different Units of Capacity Measurement

Unit of Capacity	To Convert to Coke Tons	To Convert to Pig Iron Tons	To Convert to Steel Tons
Output of coke oven (CO)	No conversion	(CO output)/1.5	(CO output)/(1.5 * .8)
Output of blast furnace (BF)	BF output * 1.5	No conversion	BF output/.8
Output of basic oxygen furnace (BOF)	BOF output * 1.5 * .8	BOF output * .8	No conversion

TABLE 3-9   Calculating Maximum Capacity

Unit of Capacity	Maximum Coke Tons	Maximum Pig Iron Tons	Maximum Steel Tons
Output of coke oven (CO)	71,000	47,333.33	59,166.67
Output of blast furnace (BF)	82,500	55,000	68,750
Output of basic oxygen furnace (BOF)	81,600	54,400	68,000

coke tons by 1.5 because the blast furnace needs 1.5 tons of coke to create a ton of pig iron. Similarly, to convert steel tons to coke tons, multiply the output of the BOF (in steel tons) by 0.8 (because it takes 0.8 tons of pig iron to make a ton of steel) and that result by 1.5 (because it takes 1.5 tons of coke to make a ton of pig iron).

4. Finally, Table 3-9 calculates the maximum capacity for each operation. This shows a maximum capacity for the steel-making process of 59,166.67 steel tons per year. The coke oven is the bottleneck for the process, since it generates the lowest output, measured in any units. The coke oven cannot produce enough coke to keep the blast furnace and BOFs operating at capacity, constraining the overall output of the process. The maximum capacities of the blast furnace and the BOFs are fairly well-balanced.

   This capacity calculation indicates that the blast furnace is not the bottleneck, so the proposed investment in expanding its capacity would not improve the overall capacity of the process. In fact, at the higher capacity, the blast furnace would be used only 67.6 percent of the time, found by dividing the coking oven's output of 59,166.76 steel tons by the new blast furnace output of 87,500.

2. **Addressing Waiting Time at Nu-Clean Dry Cleaners.**

   Terry Ilgen, the owner of Nu-Clean Dry Cleaners, was concerned about customer waiting time, especially during peak/rush times. After talking with several of her target customers (young professionals who were starting out in their careers and were more likely to invest in high-quality clothes that often needed dry cleaning), she came to the conclusion that waiting time at the front counter was a major issue. Her customers were willing to wait up to five minutes before they started to become upset; they were not willing to wait any more than 10 minutes.

   Peak periods were from 8 a.m. to 10 a.m. and from 4 p.m. to 6 p.m.

   Solution:

   Terry undertook a process study with the help of her front counter staff. They collected data for two weeks and obtained the following:

Average arrival rate at peak	1 arrival every two minutes
Standard deviation of arrivals	1 minute
Average time to process an order	2 minutes
Standard deviation of process time	3 minutes
Total amount of time for peak	56 hours
Time that clerks were busy	36 hours

   Given this information, what is the expected waiting time for a customer during the peak period?

To answer this question, we have to get the information needed in the equation for wait time [equation (3.2)]:

$$Wait\ time = \left(\frac{c_a^2 + c_p^2}{2}\right)\left(\frac{u}{1-u}\right)t_p$$

Coefficient of variation of job arrivals (arrival time at peak and standard deviation of arrivals) (c_a^2) is $1/.5 = 2$

Coefficient of variation for procession (c_p^2) is 3 (standard deviation of processing time) / (average time to take an order) = 1.5

Utilization (u) is $36/56 = .64$

Average processing time $(t_p) = 2$

Plugging these numbers into the equation, we get:

$$Wait\ time = \left(\frac{2^2 + 1.5^2}{2}\right)\left(\frac{.65}{.38}\right)2$$

$$= 11.11\ minutes$$

We can see that the average expected waiting time is greater than the 10-minute maximum desired by customers. In reviewing this analysis, one of Terry's employees suggested, why not use bar code tags for frequent customers? Terry estimated that this change would reduce the average processing time from 2 minutes to 1.5 and the standard deviation from 3 to 2. Further analysis also indicated that the total time that the clerks would spend working should fall from 36 hours to 25 hours. Should Terry consider this suggestion?

The suggestion changes c_p^2 u, and t_p.

$$u = 25/56 = .45$$

$$c_p^2 = \left(\frac{2}{1.5}\right)^2 = 1.78$$

$$Wait\ time = \left(\frac{2^2 + 1.33^2}{2}\right)\left(\frac{.45}{.55}\right)1.5$$

$$= 3.54\ minutes$$

This is a good suggestion since it not only reduces the average waiting time, it also helps Terry to keep the average waiting time in a range that is acceptable to her critical customers.

3. **Capacity Planning at X-Games Skateboard Company.**

The X-Games Skateboard Company is planning to introduce three new skateboards: the Pro, the Trickster, and the Traverse. The boards can all be made in the same type of work cell. The manufacturing plant operates two 8-hour shifts, 250 days per year. Given the demand forecast, processing time for each skateboard type, and setup time information shown in Table 3-10, how many skateboard work cells are needed?

Solution:

First, determine the total processing time for the skateboards. Multiply the annual demand for each skateboard by its processing time to estimate the processing time per year per skateboard. Then, sum these times to get the total processing time for all three skateboards.

TABLE 3-10   Skateboard Demand, Processing Time and Setup Time

Skateboard	Demand Forecast (units/year)	Processing Time (minutes/unit)	Lot Size (# of boards)	Setup Time (minutes/setup)
Pro	5,000	90	10	15
Trickster	8,000	75	10	25
Traverse	12,000	45	25	10

Skateboard	Demand Forecast (units/year)	Processing Time (minutes/unit)	Processing Time Required (minutes/year)
Pro	5,000	90	450,000
Trickster	8,000	75	600,000
Traverse	12,000	45	540,000
Total Processing Time (minutes/year)			1,590,000

Next, determine the number of setups required by dividing the annual demand for each skateboard by its lot size. Multiply the number of setups for each skateboard type by its setup time to get the annual setup time per skateboard. The annual setup times are summed to get the total setup time required per year.

Skateboard	Demand Forecast (units/year)	Lot Size (# of boards)	Number of Setups/Year	Setup Time (minutes/ setup)	Setup Time/ Board (minutes/year)
Pro	5,000	10	500	15	7,500
Trickster	8,000	10	800	25	20,000
Traverse	12,000	25	480	10	4,800
Total Setup Time (minutes/year)					32,300

Determine the total operating time available.

$$\text{Total operating time (minutes/year)} = 250 \text{ days/year} \times 2 \text{ shifts/day} \times 8 \text{ hours/days} \times 60 \text{ minutes/hour)}$$
$$= 240,000 \text{ minutes/year}$$

To determine the number of work cells, the total setup time is added to the total processing time, and this value is divided by the total operating time available.

$$\text{Number of work cells} = (\text{Total processing time required} + \text{Total setup time required})/\text{Total operating time available}$$
$$(1,590,000 \text{ (minutes/year)} + 32,300 \text{ (minutes/year)})/ (240,000 \text{ (minutes/year)})$$
$$= 6.7 \text{ work cells, so round up to 7 work cells.}$$

PROBLEMS

1.

Operation	No. Equipment	Design Capacity (by equipment)	Planned Utilization (overall)
A	1	400 units/hr	80%
B	4	100, 80, 150, 125	77%
C	1	350 units/hr	95%
D	2	190, 235	72.5%

With the process information provided in the preceding table, when the sequence of flow is A → B (any machine can be used if available)→ C → D (any machine can be used if available), calculate the overall flow rate for:

a. Maximum capacity
b. Effective capacity

2. You are given the following information. Which of the statements below can you support with this information?

Maximum capacity (labor hours): 480 hours per week

Effective capacity ratio: 85%

Actual time worked: 380 hours per week over the last two weeks

On-time delivery %: 75 percent of the jobs are being completed on time

   a. More capacity needs to be added in the short term to improve performance in the system.
   b. We need to look at variability in the rate at which jobs enter the shop.
   c. Our workforce is not working hard enough.
   d. Our workforce may be waiting on delayed arrivals of inputs needed to do the work.

Describe the reasons why you selected the specific option(s) that you did.

3. Electronics Assembly Inc. is a contract manufacturer that assembles consumer electronics for a number of companies. Currently, the operations manager is assessing the capacity requirements as input into a bid for a job to assemble cell phones for a major global company. The company would assemble three models of cell phones in the same assembly cell. Setup time between the phones is negligible. Electronics Assembly Inc. operates two 8-hour shifts for 275 days per year. Use the information in the table to determine the capacity requirements.

Cell Phone	Demand Forecast (phones/year)	Processing Time (minutes/phone)
Mars	15,000	15
Saturn	8,000	18
Neptune	12,000	16

4. Penny's Pies is a small specialty supplier to a national coffee-house chain. Penny's makes three types of pies (apple, cherry, and pecan). Penny's operates 250 days per year with a single eight-hour shift. Capacity is controlled by the number of production lines within the bakery (a line consists of mixing equipment, rolling and cutting equipment, an oven, and packaging equipment). Based on the information provided in the table, determine the number of production lines Penny's should have.

Pie	Demand Forecast (pies/year)	Processing Time (minutes/pie)	Lot Size (# of pies)	Setup Time (minutes/setup)
Apple	60,000	2	600	10
Cherry	30,000	4	200	15
Pecan	20,000	3	200	30

5. Best Bicycles manufactures three different types of bikes: the Tiny Tike, the Adult Aero, and the Mountain Monger. Given the information in the table, calculate the required capacity for this year's production. Note that the times are given for assembly lines, so capacity calculations should be in terms of the number of lines necessary. Assume that Best Bicycles operates two shifts, each with 2,000 hours per year.

Bike	Demand Forecast (units/year)	Processing Time (minutes/unit)	Lot Size (# of bikes)	Setup Time (minutes/setup)
Tiny Tike	14,000	8	10	50
Adult Aero	16,000	10	10	80
Mountain Monger	19,000	12	25	40

6. Doog's Donuts produces five varieties of pastries, which are sold to a national grocery chain: muffins, donuts, cookies, cream puffs, and fritters. Assuming that Doog's operates a single shift for 1,800 hours per year, calculate the required capacity. The processing time per unit, setup time per lot, the annual demand, and lot size are given in the table. Assume that the times given are for a work cell of four workers each, so required capacity should be in terms of the number of work cells needed.

Pastry	Demand Forecast (units/year)	Processing Time (minutes/unit)	Lot Size (# of pastries)	Setup Time (minutes/setup)
Muffins	440,000	0.1	400	20
Donuts	600,000	0.1	300	5
Cookies	1,000,000	0.05	1,000	10
Cream Puffs	240,000	0.2	200	20
Fritters	180,000	0.2	300	15

7. Spartan Redi-Care is a small urgent care facility located near the university. Because of the high competition for student business, the manager of Spartan has decided that the most effective way of competing is to emphasize short wait times. Spartan Redi-Care has even gone so far as to adopt the slogan, "Get in, Get better, Get out." As the facility manager, you have decided that this slogan translates into an average customer wait time of 30 minutes. You have collected the following data taken from a three-week period of typical demand:

$c_a = 3$

$c_p = 1$

$u = 70$ percent

$t_p = 6$ minutes

   a. What is the expected average wait time for Spartan Redi-Care?
   b. If the expected average wait time is greater than what you have promised, what are some actions that you could introduce to correct this imbalance (be specific)?

8. New Time Videos (NTV) is a new online video rental service. In the field, it is trying to compete by offering its customers access to all of the major new video releases in one business day. That is, if you order a video from NTV, you can expect it in one business day from the time when you placed the order. When you are done with the video, you simply drop it in the prepaid mailing envelope and return it. All videos arrive in a sorting facility located in the Midwest where envelopes with the videos are opened, checked (right video with the right sleeve, no scratches, no cracks, no dirt on the videos), and made ready to be sent out again. As the manager of this facility, your goal is to turn the returned videos around in 6 hours (a shift is 8 hours long). You have the following information:

   Inventory of videos: 450,000 per shift
   Throughput: 325,000 per shift

   a. Calculate the expected average flow time. (*Hint*: Use Little's Law.)
   b. What changes would you recommend to meet the goal of processing a returned video within 6 hours?

9. PizzaTime Restaurants is building a new pizza place and needs to determine how big to make the various parts of its facility. It wants to be able to accommodate a maximum of 500 customers per hour at its peak times. PizzaTime has collected the following information: the average time to place and receive an order is 1.1 minutes, 20 percent of the customers have cars and require parking spots, and the average length

of time at the restaurant is 20 minutes per customer. Assuming a capacity cushion of 20 percent, find:

a. The number of cash registers required (assume an average of 4 customers per group).
b. The number of parking spaces needed.
c. The number of seats/tables needed (assume 4 seats per table).
d. Which of these operations are likely to be bottlenecks?

10. Mike operates a hair-cutting salon that specializes in providing quick walk-in service for just about any type of haircut. He deals with customers as they walk in the door. This includes writing down the customer's name and what they desire in terms of haircut, wash, dry, and so on. This process usually takes two minutes. If no hair stylist is available, the customer then goes to the waiting area, where he/she is processed on a first-come, first-serve basis. The salon has five hair stylists who work eight hours each day. It takes, on average, 25 minutes for a stylist to greet the customer, wash and/or cut his hair, and wish him a fond farewell. Then Mike completes the process by taking the customer's money and telling him about the satisfaction guarantee offered by the shop. This final set of steps takes two minutes on average.

a. Assuming that the waiting area always has at least one customer in it, how many customers on average can Mike's salon process in a day (assuming no problems in utilization, quality, or efficiency)?
b. Suppose that you need an "average" haircut, and as you walk into the salon you see three people sitting in the waiting area. You notice that another person is just sitting down in one of the stylists' empty chair, and the other stylists are all busy with customers. Assuming you choose to wait, how long would you expect it to be before you are ready to leave the salon?

11. Cooper's Copy Shop is considering two different processes for completing copying jobs brought in by customers. Process A uses one person to set up the job and do the copying. If this approach is used, an experienced person can complete an average of 20 jobs per day. Process B uses two people. One person does the setup and the second person does the actual copying. Setup on one job can be done while copying is being completed on another but copying must be completed on a job before the copying machine can start copying the next. After some practice, this second process can be completed with a standard time of 10 minutes for setup and 15 minutes for actual copying. In either case, assume an 8-hour day, 5 days per week, 250 days per year.

a. Assuming ideal conditions, what is the maximum capacity of process B?
b. How long would it take to process 200 jobs using process A (assume only one worker and one machine)?
c. How long would it take to process 200 jobs using process B (assume only one "production line")?
d. If Cooper is primarily interested in providing low cost to customers, which process should he put in place?
e. If Cooper is primarily interested in providing quick service to customers, which process should he put in place?

12. Metal Hoses Inc. (MHI) is a major manufacturer of metal braided hoses for industry. These products are used in everything from cars to tanks to motorcycles. MHI's products can even be found on the Space Shuttle. At first glance, it may seem that MHI's products are mature and compete on the basis of cost alone. However, recently, management at MHI has identified that there is a market segment that demands (and is willing to pay for) speed in delivery. That is, these customers are willing to pay if MHI can receive, process, and deliver orders quickly. From talking with its customers, the management at MHI has determined that the customers are most sensitive to order lead times of one week or less (from time of receipt to time of delivery). In studying their processes, management has determined that order entry is the major bottleneck. This process consists of the following steps: (1) the order is received from the customer; (2) it is moved to accounting where it is checked and entered; (3) it next goes to engineering for evaluation and acceptance; (4) purchasing is next for material

assessment; and (5) it is scheduled by operations. These five steps are separated physically since the order has to move to the departments where these activities are carried out. Analysis of the situation has indicated that under the current process it takes an order two weeks to complete this process. However, when errors are uncovered, the process can take up to five weeks (since the problem order has to return to the steps where the problem was first created). Management has determined that order entry should take no more than four hours.

    a. Identify appropriate metrics for both the order entry process and the overall order fulfillment process for MHI.

    b. Use process thinking to reengineer the order entry process
- With technology.
- Without technology (management has determined that MHI should not spend its way out of this problem).

13. "This should be a simple issue. You know that our average weekly sales are $2,000 and the flow time is one day. Surely with this information, you should have no problem maintaining an inventory level of $200 to serve the sales."

    With these words, the director of finance leaves your office. Now, you have a challenge before you—that of determining whether the analysis carried out by the director makes sense.

    a. Using Little's Law, determine anticipated flow time and compare it with the expected flow time. (*Hint:* The flow time is in days, the sales in weeks; use a common unit of measure.)

    b. Keeping the flow times and throughputs constant, determine if the process as currently described can be supported by $200 of inventory. If not, what options should you consider?

14. You have been asked to determine the average wait time for a process that has caused problems for the management of your company. From data you collected over a two-week period (which you feel are representative), you have determined the following:

Average processing time:	10 minutes
Average job arrival rate:	10 minutes
Processing time, standard deviation:	50 minutes
Arrival rates, standard deviation:	100 minutes

    a. What is the average wait time?

    b. If management wants to promise its customers an average wait time in the system of no more than 24 hours, what recommendations would you provide management on how to change the operation of the process of concern?

15. You have been approached by one of the staff who works testing equipment that passes through your facility. Every day, you receive computers from the university that have been repaired but now need to be tested to ensure that they can work under high stress. This means running them in your test labs. Because the test labs are as stressful on the test equipment as they are on the computers, you have planned for downtime in the past. To get this downtime, you have tried to ensure that effective capacity utilization is about 65 percent. Yet, the staff person has informed you that a backlog of yet-to-be tested equipment is building up. Furthermore, the test equipment is now starting to break at a rate faster than anticipated. To address this issue, you know that the design or maximum capacity is 720 hours and that over the last three weeks, you have spent 600 hours per week testing equipment.

    a. Based on these data, what is your effective capacity utilization?

    b. What do the data tell you about why the loads are building up and why the test equipment is breaking down?

16. Something seems to be wrong in your department. You have been given the following data:
    - Design capacity: 1,060 hours
    - Effective capacity ratio: 85%
    - Demonstrated (actual) capacity: 839 hours
    - On-time delivery percentage: 75 percent of the jobs are being completed on time
    a. Using these data, what can we say about the relationship between what you planned to deliver and what you actually delivered?
    b. What areas would you look at if you wanted to improve performance?

17. You are the manager of Spartan Care–a local Redi-Care facility. While this facility serves a range of clients, everyone agrees that quick service is very important (defined as the difference from the time that clients arrive and are registered at the front desk until they are seen either by a nurse or a doctor). Currently, you have been receiving numerous complaints from the clients that the time spent waiting to see someone is simply too long. To assess the situation, you collect the following information from a two-week period:
    - Average process utilization: 70 percent
    - Average processing time: 15 minutes
    - Average arrival time: 10 minutes
    - Processing time, standard deviation: 22.5 minutes
    - Arrival rates, standard deviation: 20 minutes
    a. What is the average wait time?
    b. If your goal is to ensure no patient waits more than 40 minutes on average, what options are available to you and how would these options affect wait time?
    c. How could you use technology to manage wait time?

CASE

Evergreen Products

The top managers of Evergreen Products of East Lansing, MI, have asked you to act as a consultant on a problem plaguing the entire company. Evergreen Products manufactures decorated containers and care tags for a market consisting primarily of small- to medium-sized florists and grocery stores. The containers are relatively inexpensive to make, but they are sold at a high markup (60 percent). The same is true for the tags. Because of the targeted market segment, management feels that it must be able to provide its customers with quick delivery and quality. However, this has not been happening lately.

To understand what happens, it is useful to first follow the course of an order received from the customer. Orders are placed in one of two ways at Evergreen. First, customers may notice that their stocks are getting low. They call the Evergreen sales department with an order, which is received by one of three clerks. The clerk records on a sheet the customer number, the type of product, and the quantity needed. At this point, a customer due date is set based on the customer's needs. However, the clerks try to encourage a due date that is about five working days out (there is no hard-and-fast rule for this procedure).

Once a day, the sales account manager picks up all sales orders. He is responsible for ensuring that all orders are complete and accurately entered and that the customer's credit rating is OK. If it is, the order is put into another pile where it is picked up once every morning. If the order is not acceptable or if there are errors, the order is returned to the person who took the order. That person is then responsible for correcting the problem within a reasonable period of time. When the order has been corrected, the process is repeated. It takes about half a day to move from phone order to sales account manager and about an hour to clear the sales account manager. Forty percent of the orders experience some form of error.

The second way that an order can be placed is through the company's own traveling salespersons that stop in on accounts and check their inventory stocks. When they see that an item is low, they fill out an order. They then phone the order into the plant (about once every day—this varies depending on how busy they are). Since each salesperson is rated on the total dollar sales he generates, there is a built-in incentive to be very concerned about clients' inventory stocks. When the order is turned over to the sales account manager, the process is identical to the one previously described. On average, the delay for entering orders through the salesperson is about half a day (but it can range up to two days).

Once the order clears the sales account manager, it goes to accounting, where it first is put into the day's pile. It is then entered into the accounting system. This step marks the beginning of the billing process. It takes an average of half a day to clear accounting (but this can range up to two days). From here, it goes to the shop floor scheduler.

The shop floor scheduler reviews all orders for accuracy and completeness. Any problem orders are set aside and returned to the sales account manager for correction. About 15 percent of the orders are typically set aside each day. The rest of the orders are released to the shop floor. It typically takes one day to clear the shop floor. The time can vary depending on the time of year. Christmas, Valentine's Day, Easter, Mother's Day, and other similar holidays put a great deal of pressure on the shop floor (which runs on average at 80 percent utilization). The shop floor is held accountable for meeting all quoted customer due dates.

Top management is concerned over the poor performance of the shop floor. Inventories are high and growing; overtime is excessive; on-time delivery performance is poor; and customer dissatisfaction is growing. The top manager has asked you if he should replace the current shop floor scheduler.

Questions

1. What are the desired outcomes for Evergreen? What should Evergreen wish to accomplish with its order entry system? How do we know if the order entry system is working well or poorly? How is it doing now?

2. What do the customers want from Evergreen? What types of problems do the existing customers pose for Evergreen? Why?

3. Apply the process for incorporating value through process thinking to this problem. What metrics would you apply to this process? What insights into the process did you obtain?

4. How would you improve the operation of the current order entry process at Evergreen? Be specific.

Hints

1. Make sure that you identify and understand the various customers. To simplify the analysis, focus on the florists as the critical customer.

2. Bound the process by focusing only on the orders that come into the system by telephone.

3. Make sure that you establish metrics at the outset.

4. Assume no errors in the process.

CASE

Midas Gold Juice Company

You are the purchasing director for Midas Gold Juice Company, a small Midwestern fruit-juice company that produces a line of premium, limited-run fruit juice (Slogan: Midas Juice—You'll be touched by the Gold). As one of your responsibilities, you review all requests for capital equipment that costs $10,000 or more. Recently, you have received a request from the production department to purchase an additional stamping machine. This machine will double the capacity of the tin shop from its current level of 80,000 lids (design capacity) to 160,000 lids. Every can needs two lids. Production managers also claim that the new machine will balance the line and improve output dramatically.

In reviewing the request, you decide to examine the production process. You find a fairly straightforward process that starts by squeezing the juice from the fruit and storing it in tanks. On average, these tanks hold 4,000 gallons available at any time. Under ideal circumstances, this amount fills 40,000 cans per month.

The can-making process has two stages. In the first, the cans are made in two steps involving two departments.

The tin department makes lids with a current capacity of 80,000. The stamping department converts sheets of tin into the can bodies. The tin department uses 4,000 sheets of tin per month, and each sheet produces 12 can bodies. The bodies and lids are assembled in the filling department where they are filled and sealed. The design capacity of the filling department is 50,000 cans per month.

Questions

1. What is your response to the request for the new machine?

2. Identify any concerns that you have. (*Hint:* Think about the process and its design capacities when answering this question.)

Hints

1. Make sure that you express all the capacity in the same units.

2. You may want to use the process mapping and analysis techniques described in the supplement to this chapter.

CASE

American Vinyl Products

To: Brad Hadley, President, American Vinyl
Products (AVP)

From: Bev Trudeau, Director of Purchasing,
American Performance Car, CA

Subject: Customer Service at American Vinyl Products

Our two companies have basically had a good relationship over the last two years. We have generally been pleased with both the quality of the products as well as the price offered. These features, while important, are not critical. What is critical to our future relations is customer service. This is one area where you have recently fallen down. Our staff has persistently experienced delays in getting through to your staff by phone. When we do, we experience further delays in getting answers. Our needs are few but simple. We want to contact American Vinyl quickly. We want to get through to a person quickly. We want to place orders, confirm status, and change requirements quickly. Three days ago, Brad Allenby from our purchasing department spent 20 minutes waiting to get through. He had a critical problem that had to be resolved. He kept waiting. All the time, all he heard was how it was important that he remain on the line and that he would be answered in the order in which he was received. He finally gave up and called Joan in your marketing department. Even then, it took 24 hours before he got an answer. This is unacceptable. Unless you adequately resolve the problems with your phone system, we will take our business elsewhere. As you are aware, your contract with American Performance Car is going to be up for review in six months. Your product is not so unique that we cannot quickly find an alternative supplier. I am sorry for the angry tenor of this letter. However, this note reflects the frustration that we have experienced. It is totally unacceptable that we cannot even get hold of anyone at American Vinyl after 3 p.m. our time here in California. Your company must become more customer-oriented. Or

else. You have 90 days to provide us with an acceptable resolution to the current situation.

As Tom Adamson, the vice president for operations at American Vinyl Products, put down the fax and looked at Brad, the president, Tom knew that things were not good. The phone system had been a persistent source of problems for American Vinyl Products (AVP). Tom knew that this complaint was not an isolated event. He also knew that Brad had commissioned a local telecommunications company to do a study on AVP's phone system. Their recommendation was that a new system be put in that offered more lines and more staff capacity. Brad thought that this might be the answer. Tom also knew that he would be asked to come up with recommendations for improving the current system.

As Tom got up and left the office, he reviewed the information that he had recently gathered. AVP was a small manufacturer of vinyl and plastic products, including vinyl car products (e.g., decals and pin striping for cars), plastic after-market products (e.g., new brake lenses for cars designed to make the car look more sporty), and decals for the recreational market (AVP sold name decals to FourWinns in the boating marketing and to Bombardier in the ski-doo and sea-doo markets). Located in Charlotte, Michigan, this company had experienced a great deal of recent growth. Part of the reason for this growth could be traced to the excellent customer service that AVP gave its customers.

AVP sold primarily to three groups of customers. The first were the do-it-yourselfers (DIY). These typically bought vinyl striping from a local retail or car accessory store. As a rule, their purchases were very small yet they needed a great deal of information. Often, they would call AVP asking for a catalog of products, information on how to use AVP's products (or information on how to correct a problem with an AVP product), or information on where they could get AVP products. As a rule, DIYs

Customer Type	Average Calls per Day	Average Time per Call (min.) Range in ()	Average Revenue per Call
DIYs	200	20 (min of 5, max of 35)	$5.00 per call (estimated)
Professional users	40	10 (min of 5, max of 20)	$40.00
Large corporate accounts	20	5 (min of 1, max of 10)	$400

were very price sensitive. The second market consisted of professional users. These were the people who used AVP products as part of their business (e.g., in a body shop). While buying a moderate amount of product, they were often more interested in getting very technical information pertaining to the use of an AVP product. They were often considered to be very demanding with the result that only the most experienced sales staff worked with them. Finally, there were large corporate accounts, accounts such as American Performance Car. These accounts would call AVP typically to place orders, to determine the status of current orders, and to see if they could change the status of current orders (i.e., change the due date, the order quantities, or the product mix). Typically, their calls were short and to the point. The differences between the three groups are summarized in the table below.

The same phone process served all three customers. All three customers called into the same 1-800 number. Once they called, their calls went into a queue area where they waited until a service representative was available. The calls were answered on a first-come, first-served basis. In this phone-bank area, the current system would periodically remind them that: (1) their call was important, and (2) their calls would be answered in the order received. When the calls were answered, a representative would try to determine the type of customer and then determine what was needed to answer the call. Typically, the representatives would fill in a form (in the case of a catalog request), look up locations of outlets selling their products

(done using a large book centrally located), and look up possible solutions from a tips file or generate a follow-up form (in the case of a customer-requested change or status query). When completed, the information would be placed in a large basket for processing. Finally, the representatives would then give the customer a best guess of when they could expect an answer (if further information was needed). Because of the great diversity in the types of calls and the demands of the callers, training and staffing was considered a major obstacle. At present, the line was staffed with 10 representatives on average over an 11-hour period (however, over the two-hour staggered lunch, there were fewer representatives). The department was open from 7:00 a.m. until 6:00 p.m. The rate at which the calls came in was difficult to predict. However, past experience was that it was never level. Finally, since 1995, 40 percent (and growing) of the sales came from California, Washington, Nevada, and Oregon. Unlike Michigan, which is in the Eastern time zone, these states were located three time zones away.

Questions

1. You have been asked to help Tom. What recommendations would you give him about how to improve the operation of the phone system?

2. Tom has a recommendation for increasing the capacity of the phone system. Is this recommendation adequate to help address the problems facing AVP? Make sure that your answer is supported by the appropriate analysis.

SELECTED READINGS

Andrews, D. C., and S. K. Stalick. *Business Reengineering: The Survival Guide.* Englewood Cliffs, NJ: Yourdon Press, 1994.

Imai, M. *Gemba Kaizen.* New York: McGraw-Hill, 1997.

Madison, D. *Process Mapping, Process Improvement, and Process Management.* Chico, CA: Paton Press, 2005.

Melan, E. H. *Process Management: Methods for Improving Products and Service.* New York: McGraw-Hill, 1993.

Miller, H. "Apple Has Edge on Tablet Rivals with iPad Costs, Report Says." BusinessWeek.com, March 2, 2011.

Rummler, G. A., and A. P. Brache. *Improving Performance: How to Manage the White Space on the Organization Chart.* San Francisco, CA: Jossey-Bass Publishers, 1990.

Sengupta, S. "A Plan for Building a New Supply Chain." *Supply Chain Management Review* 12, no. 1 (January/February 2008), pp. 46–52.

Shapiro, B. P.; V. K. Rangan; and J. J. Sviokla. "Staple Yourself to an Order." *Harvard Business Review* 70, no. 4 (July/August 1992), pp. 113–22.

Smith, H., and P. Fingar. *Business Process Management: The Third Wave.* Tampa, FL: Meghan Kiffer Press, 2006.

Womack, J. P., and D. T. Jones. *Lean Thinking: Banish Waste and Create Wealth in Your Corporation.* New York: Simon and Schuster, 1996.

3

Chapter Supplement: Process Mapping and Analysis

LEARNING OBJECTIVES

After studying this supplement, you should be able to:

LO3S-1 Work through the various steps in process mapping and analysis.

LO3S-2 Assess a process to determine how effective it is in achieving its desired outcome(s).

LO3S-3 Determine to what type of activity each step in a process belongs.

LO3S-4 Understand when and how to apply the various tools of process mapping.

LO3S-5 Change a process to make it more effective and efficient by either refining the current process or designing a new replacement process.

Process mapping and analysis is a technique for documenting activities in a detailed, compact, and graphic form to help managers understand processes and highlight areas for potential improvements. The technique generates a process blueprint that supplies nearly all of the information needed to effectively evaluate a process. As the name implies, process mapping and analysis helps managers improve the effectiveness and efficiency of processes by first mapping (diagramming) the process, and then analyzing it to identify and eliminate sources of waste or inefficiency.

process mapping and analysis
A technique for graphically documenting the activities in a process with the goal of identifying opportunities for improvement.

THE "PROCESS" OF PROCESS MAPPING AND ANALYSIS

LO3S-1 Work through the various steps in process mapping and analysis.

Process mapping and analysis consists of six steps:

1. Determine the desired outcome for the process and the associated metrics needed to evaluate its performance.
2. Identify and bound the critical process.
3. Document the existing process (the "current state" map).
4. Analyze the process and prioritize opportunities for improvement.
5. Recommend appropriate changes to the process (the "future state" map).
6. Implement the changes and monitor improvements.

The remainder of this supplement describes the steps by way of an example. The example illustrates how process mapping and analysis can be used to uncover problems and improve the efficiency and effectiveness of the affected processes.

AMERICAN HEALTH AND MEDICAL PRODUCTS (AHMP)

American Health and Medical Products (AHMP) is a major designer, innovator, manufacturer, and supplier of medical and health supplies for hospitals, nursing homes, medical facilities, and doctor/dentist offices. One of AHMP's major product lines consists of sterilizers, more commonly known as autoclaves. AHMP is the market leader in autoclaves; its products are viewed as the most sophisticated among all of its competitors. Customers buy AHMP autoclaves expecting to receive a well-designed, quality product, quickly delivered. In fact, order-to-delivery lead time is very important to the customers. Typically, AHMP promises its customers that they will receive delivery of an ordered autoclave within 16 weeks. Allowing one week for shipping, this means that AHMP has 15 weeks for order entry, material acquisition and delivery, and manufacturing. Recently, a competitor advertised that it would deliver a standard autoclave in as little as 10 weeks. Managers at AHMP felt that they had to respond.

The managers carried out a series of process studies with the goal of determining whether the existing process could be reduced from 16 weeks to 6 weeks, including shipping. If successful, they felt that this significant reduction in lead time would meet the competitive threat. An initial study indicated that the internal manufacturing process could be accomplished in two to four days *provided* that the necessary orders, capacity, and materials were in place. A second, purchasing-oriented study determined that components could be procured within two weeks of order placement. Thus, allowing two weeks for procurement, one week for manufacturing, and one week for shipping, the remaining question was whether

© BSIP/UIG Via Getty Images

or not the order entry and approval process could be completed in two weeks. Order entry managers estimated that the average actual lead time for order entry was four weeks, with a range of one to six weeks. This is the process element that we will study as our example.

Step 1: Identify the Desired Outcomes in Advance

LO3S-2 Assess a process to determine how effective it is in achieving its desired outcome(s).

Before making any change to a process, it is important to clarify what the process should achieve. These are the key customers' desired outcomes, as discussed in Chapter 2. Objectives may include lowered costs, decreased lead times, improved quality, more reliable deliveries, or other outcomes. Metrics are critical in making these desired outcomes meaningful to those involved with the process. Table 3S-1 contains some of the more commonly

TABLE 3S-1 Examples of Commonly Used Measures

Desired Outcomes	Output Measures	Process Measures
Cost	Actual cost per unit Actual cost vs. standard cost Target prices—relation of actual costs to target or desired costs Percentage cost savings achieved Reduction of administrative/overhead costs	Number of steps in the process (more steps should lead to higher costs) Number of people involved in the process (more people involved, the higher the costs) Average setup costs (higher setup costs should lead to larger batch quantities, which should increase costs) Percentage of unique components (the more unique items, the higher the costs)
Quality	Total Cost of Quality (discussed in Chapter 6) Percentage of products done right the first time Actual yield rates vs. standard yield rate Percentage of work reworked or rejected or held for further inspection Defective parts per million (PPM) Customer quality incidents Factory quality incidents Percentage and number of defect-free shipments	Number of times an item is handled (more handling creates more opportunities for quality problems) Number of steps in the process Number of times that the item is allowed to stop or go into inventory (more times, more opportunities for quality problems) Number of inspections (more inspections is an indication of quality concerns) Number of steps in the process (more steps increase the probability of more quality defects)
Availability	Amount of inventory Order fill-rates Fill-rate by line On-time arrivals Number of lines/customers shut down because of supply shortages	Number of delays in the process (more delays create more unanticipated stoppages) Number of inter-departmental hand-offs (more hand-offs usually mean more delays)
Lead time	Actual lead time to build a unit Actual lead time vs. standard lead time Percentage reduction in lead time	Number of steps (the more steps, the longer the lead time) Average setup time (as setup times increase, order quantities go up, and total lead times are increased) Distance covered by the process (the greater the distance, the longer the transport time) The number of people who touch the order (more touches create more costs, time, and potential errors

used output metrics (measured at the end of the process) and process metrics (traits of the process that affect the outcomes being pursued).

Applying Step 1 to AHMP

AHMP's goal was to deliver a standard autoclave to the customer in no more than six weeks. Further discussion led managers at AHMP to determine that they would like 95 percent of all standard autoclave orders to be entered and approved within one week, with no order taking more than two weeks. Thus, the desired outcome for the process is to *maximize the percentage of orders going through order entry that are completed within one week from the time that they are received, with 95 percent being an acceptable level of performance.*

In process improvement efforts, it is important to consider how progress can be quickly communicated. Figure 3S-1 shows a useful way to visually communicate performance against the desired outcome, where performance is color coded using three colors: green if the order entry is completed within one week; yellow if order entry takes more than one week but not more than two weeks; and red if order entry takes more than two weeks. The figure quickly shows how well the process is meeting or failing to meet the standard of 95 percent.

Step 2: Identify and Bound the Critical Process

The second step involves identifying and bounding the process that is most important to our desired outcome. As noted in Chapter 3, a critical process typically exhibits at least one of the following traits:

1. It is a bottleneck process—one that limits capacity for the overall system.
2. It is visible to the customer—one that directly affects customers' perceptions of value.
3. It consumes the largest amount of resources—one that offers the greatest potential for cost savings.
4. It is a shared process—one that feeds multiple downstream processes.
5. It exhibits the greatest level of variance—one that offers potential for improved reliability and capacity gains.
6. It is a process that is related to a unique skill or core competency—one that serves to differentiate us from competitors.

It is important to clearly define the limits of the process that is to be improved. Without bounds, a process study runs a real risk of never being completed. Bounding includes defining the physical starting and ending points for process analysis, as well as defining the operating conditions or demands to be considered in the analysis. A manager has to decide

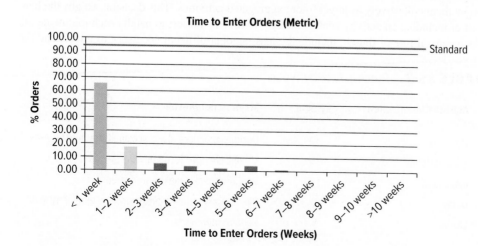

FIGURE 3S-1 Using a Metric for Time to Enter Orders

whether to study the process under low demand, average demand, or peak (highest) demand conditions. For example, if the process involves a perishable product such as a service, then it makes sense to focus on the performance of the process under peak demand. Process bounding also includes defining the error conditions that will be studied. When things do not go as planned, there are often certain rework or recovery processes that take place. Managers must decide whether or not these rework processes should be included in the analysis.

Applying Step 2 to AHMP

In AHMP's case, the critical process is order entry. The order entry process is a *shared* process. All orders (both standard and special) go through this process. The physical/spatial bound of the order entry process is also relatively easy to establish. The process starts with the receipt of the order and it ends when the order has entered production scheduling. Because demand does not vary much over the year, we will use average demand as the demand setting. AHMP has to deal with both standard and nonstandard orders (typically nonstandard orders have unique features or finishes—an autoclave done completely in stainless steel is a nonstandard order). In this case we will limit the process mapping exercise to standard orders. Finally, to keep things simple we will deal with the "best-case" scenario (no problems with the order).

Step 3: Document the Existing Process (the "Current State" Map)

current state The state of the process in its current or "as is" state.

Describing the current state of a process can be difficult. Inefficiencies and poor designs in the process may reflect poorly on particular managers or workers, so they may be reluctant to offer process information. It is important for the analyst to speak directly with the people who actually perform the process, not just those who manage the workers. Otherwise, the analyst might develop a distorted view of the "actual" process. Finally, the analyst must be aware that his or her presence near the workers can alter the way in which work is performed (for various reasons), thus making it difficult to develop an accurate picture of the process.

LO3S-3 Determine to what type of activity each step in a process belongs.

An effective way to document and communicate the current state of a process is to develop a process map, or diagram. By using a set of symbols in such a map, the analyst can graphically present how the inputs, outputs, flows, and activities of a process are linked together. Table 3S-2 lists five types of process activities that were defined in Chapter 3, along with each activity type's symbol. These categories can be used to classify nearly all activities in a process.

Process mapping and analysis can be complex and time-consuming, but there are some general guidelines that can make this task simpler and easier to manage.

Identify Minimum Acceptable Levels of Detail

A process analyst must decide whether to show small activities separately in a map or to show them collectively as larger, more aggregated activities. This decision weighs the benefit of including an activity against the cost in time and effort to handle such minute detail. As a general rule of thumb, include the least amount of detail necessary to understand the

TABLE 3S-2 Process Activity Types

Activity Classification	Symbol	Major Action/Result
Operation	O	Decides, produces, does, accomplishes, makes, uses
Transportation	⇒	Moves, changes location
Inspection	□	Verifies, checks, makes sure, measures
Delay	D	Blocks, starves, interferes, imposes a temporary stop
Storage	∇	Keeps, safeguards

process. As problems in one specific part of the process are identified, that section can be documented in greater detail. The documentation of a process is similar to the act of peeling an onion—begin with a very general picture of the process and then peel away successive layers of detail if necessary until you reach a sufficient level of understanding of the process.

Use Different Process Mapping and Analysis Techniques

Use as many different display formats as necessary to provide a complete picture of what is taking place within the process. Pictures, physical layouts or blueprints, work routing sheets, and other documents might be needed to give a better overall description of the process. If interdepartmental coordination issues are critical, it is sometimes useful to enhance a process map by color coding or repositioning front office and back office activities, or activities that are the responsibility of different departments.

Watch Out for Hidden Steps in a Process

It is often easy to overlook certain types of activities, especially delays. Sometimes there might be confusion or disagreement about the sequence of activities. One useful approach to make sure that all activities are correctly identified is to "Staple Yourself to an Order."[1] In this useful (and sometimes fun) approach, you pretend that you are the workpiece (e.g., an order, a part, a piece of information) moving through a process. As you go from activity to activity, you record what happens to you (taking pictures is a good idea) and you ask questions of the workers performing the activities (e.g., what are you doing? how often do you do this task?). This approach frequently provides insights into the process that don't normally arise from simple descriptions given by process workers.[2] Keep in mind, however, that your presence might influence the ways that people working in the process behave.

activity

student

"Staple Yourself to an Order." Pick a process and *become* the order within it. What steps were involved? How long did it take for the process to complete operations? What did you learn? What surprises did you uncover?

When documenting the current state of a process, the analyst should try to capture all the relevant aspects, including the following attributes:

1. Number of steps in the process (broken down by category).
2. Distance covered by workpieces in the process (both vertically and horizontally).
3. Time required for activities (minimum, maximum, average, variance).
4. Value orientation of the activities (value-adding or not).[3]
5. Number of departmental boundaries crossed by workpieces.
6. Number of departments involved in each activity.
7. Number of people who touch or come into contact with the workpiece or activity.

After the existing process (the current state) has been mapped, it should be verified by reviewing it with the people involved.

To help meaningfully map a process, analysts often make use of three basic charting and analysis tools:

1. Process flow table
2. Physical layout diagram
3. Process summary table

---

[1] For a deeper look at tracing and analyzing order management cycles, see B. P. Shapiro; V. K. Rangan; and J. J. Sviokla, "Staple Yourself to an Order," *Harvard Business Review* 70, no. 3 (July/August 1992), pp. 113–22.

[2] As Chapter 8, Lean Systems, points out, the approach of studying the process as it takes place in its actual environment is referred to as "Gemba." Gemba often means "the actual place" or "the real place."

[3] This aspect of process mapping is discussed in greater detail later on in this supplement.

Applying Step 3 to AHMP

The order process for AHMP is currently carried out as follows. The order is received by an order entry person via fax, mail, or phone. An order form is placed into a pile where it waits until the orders are moved by a person to the engineering department. This is done twice a day. There, all of the orders are checked to determine what type of engineering work is required. For a standard autoclave, one of the engineers checks the order and its specifications (verification only) and then signs off on it (this takes no more than 10 minutes). The standard order is then put in another pile to wait until it is moved to the marketing office. Once it arrives there, it goes into a pile to wait for the marketing accounts manager to review and approve it. It usually takes no more than five minutes to process an individual order. Once it is approved, it goes next to accounting for entry (five minutes per order) and from accounting it goes to production scheduling.

process flow table A technique that records process activities, their key attributes, and their sequence.

A **process flow table** systematically records process activities, their key attributes, and their sequence (see the five types of process activities presented in Table 3S-2). The user fills in the required information and designates the appropriate symbol for each activity on one line of the table and then connects the symbols to show the flow through the process. The completed chart also records several important pieces of information for each activity:

- *Distance and time:* The chart reports the physical distance a workpiece covers in each activity and the amount of time it takes measured as a standard time, mean observed time, or range or standard deviation of observed times. These statistics indicate the reliability or predictability of the activity. Users could also record setup or changeover times associated with activities.
- *Activity symbol:* One simply circles or marks the appropriate symbol.
- *Number of people:* Staffing needs for an activity can indicate overall costs. Sometimes analysts indicate the numbers of direct workers and indirect (overhead) workers.
- *Value code:* Analysts classify each activity as one that (1) adds value (V), (2) generates waste (W), (3) adds no value but remains necessary (N) (e.g., equipment setup or an inspection required by a customer), or (4) is uncertain in terms of its impact on value (indicated by a question mark). We discuss the rules for determining the value content of an activity in greater detail later.
- *Activity description:* Along with the activity description, the table might indicate the analyst's recommendation to keep the activity as is, eliminate it entirely, combine it with another similar activity, or rethink it.

The process flow table is handy for identifying activities, describing their organization and sequence, and categorizing them for detailed study. It gives less information regarding spatial relationships, however. Physical layouts can be important to consider when evaluating the distance that each workpiece must cover and its lead time, handling requirements, costs, and quality.

physical layout diagram A technique that documents both the horizontal and vertical movements of work within the process.

The **physical layout diagram** documents both the horizontal and vertical movements of workpieces from one area to another, recording process performance in units of time and distance. Labels on the physical layout diagram indicate areas or activities that correspond to the list on the process flow table, creating a strong, complementary relationship between these tools.

Figure 3S-2 presents an example physical layout diagram for the office complex at AHMP. This diagram shows the physical flows across offices involved in the order entry process. As can be seen from this diagram, one of the challenges facing AHMP is a series of long moves (the moves are identified as 1, 2, 3, and 4 and correspond to the four moves in the order in which they are noted in Table 3S-3). A manager looking at this figure would see that there is an opportunity to reduce time by locating the office areas closer together (thus reducing the physical distance covered by the order while also improving the quality and frequency of communication between the groups).

Analysis of a physical layout diagram looks for excessive and unnecessary movements, such as long moves between activities, crossed paths, repeated movements or activities,

FIGURE 3S-2   Physical Layout Diagram

or illogical or convoluted flows. An effective, efficient process eliminates crisscrosses and locates sequential, high-volume activities close together to minimize move times and improve communication.

Step 4: Analyze the Process and Identify Opportunities for Improvement

In this step, we are interested in determining if the process requires minor or radical changes to it. If the current process is basically acceptable in its structure and operation, all that may be needed are repositioning and alterations of existing activities (i.e., minor changes). Alternatively, if managers decide that the process requires major changes, it is sometimes better to throw out the current process and to design a new one starting with a clean slate (i.e., a radical change is required). Whether minor or radical process changes are anticipated, it is always a good idea to keep in mind the goal of improving the value that a process delivers to its customers. The following paragraphs describe a three-stage analysis for generating improvement ideas: assessment, dispositioning, and repositioning.

LO3S-4 Understand when and how to apply the various tools of process mapping.

Assessment—Mapping Value

Ideally, every activity in a process should create value as it is defined from the customer's perspective. Hence, we must assess every step in the process in terms of the extent to which it adds value or adds waste. In this type of assessment, an analyst can classify each activity into one of four different categories: *value-adding, necessary but not value-adding, waste-generating,* and *question mark.*

A **value-adding activity** moves the product (be it a good or a service) closer to the form or location that the customer desires. In general, operations and transportation activities tend to most often contribute to value, but not all do. For example, an operation that creates scrap is not value-adding. Similarly, a transportation activity that temporarily moves a workpiece to storage only to later move it back again does not add value. Other activities may create value only under certain conditions.

An inspection only creates value for a customer when the customer demands it, or when it somehow differentiates the product. For example, at Steinway, a pianist plays the piano coming out of manufacturing to determine its tone and "voice," because different tones are best suited for playing different types of music. In this case, "inspection" adds value. One simple way to assess the value-adding extent of an activity is to ask, "Would a fair-minded customer be willing to pay for this activity?"

value-adding activity Any activity that moves the product closer to the form or location desired by the customer.

TABLE 3S-3   Process Flow Table for AHMP Order Entry Process

Process Flow Table

Page __1__ of __1__

Overall Description of Process Charted:

Date Charted: _____   Charted by: _____

Check appropriate box: Current Process: (X)   Proposed Process: ( )

Dist Meters	Average Time (range)	Symbol	Pers Invol.	Value Code V/W/N/?	Description of Activity (indicate outcome)
	15 min	● ⇒ D □ ∇	1	V	Order received by operator.
	120 min (1-240)	O ⇒ ▌ □ ∇		W	Order placed in pile, waiting to be moved. Orders picked once in the morning, once in the afternoon.
200	60 min	O ➡ D □ ∇	1	?	Order moved to engineering.
	45 min 1-180	O ⇒ ▌ □ ∇		W	Order waits in pile until an engineer can check it.
	5 min	● ⇒ D □ ∇	1	N	Engineer decides whether the order is standard or special.
	10 min	O ⇒ D ■ ∇	1	?	Engineer verifies the technical specifications for the standard autoclave order.
	120 min 1-240	O ⇒ ▌ □ ∇		W	Wait in pile waiting to be picked up for Marketing. Two pickups per day.
300	30 min	O ➡ D □ ∇	1	?	Move to Marketing.
	7 days 1–15	O ⇒ ▌ □ ∇		W	Wait until the Marketing Accounts Manager has a chance to review the order.
	5 min	O ⇒ D ■ ∇	1	N	Review the order.
	120 min 1-240 min	O ⇒ ▌ □ ∇	1	W	Wait to be picked up. Two pickups per day.
200	30 min	O ➡ D □ ∇	1	?	Move to accounting.
	5 min	● ⇒ D □ ∇	1	N	Enter order into accounting system.
	120 min 1-240 min	O ⇒ ▌ □ ∇		W	Wait to move to scheduling.
250	30 min	O ➡ D □ ∇	1	?	Move to scheduling.
	30 min	O ⇒ ▌ □ ∇		?	Wait in pile.
	5 min	● ⇒ D □ ∇	1	N	Schedule autoclave order.
Totals: 950 m	8.54 days[4]	4 4 7 2 0	11	1 (V); 4 (N) 6 (W); 6(?)	

---

[4]Order entry at AHMP is done during the day shift, Monday to Friday. Consequently, it is assumed that 8 hours or 480 minutes equals one day.

Some activities are necessary but not value-adding activities; that is, some activities do not add value directly, yet they are necessary to enable a value-adding activity. For example, consider a process setup that prepares equipment for a task. Measuring performance, entering data into the accounting system, and generating reports for managers may also be non–value-adding but necessary activities.

A waste-generating activity consumes resources and time without returning some form of value. Inspection and transportation activities are often waste-generating activities. One can view an inspection activity as an admission that there are problems within the process that we have not been able to eliminate or control. Similarly, transportation can be considered wasteful if it is redundant or a result of problems in the physical layout of the operations management system. Waste-generating activities offer prime opportunities for process improvement.

Sometimes it is not easy to identify the extent to which an activity contributes to waste or value. At that point, it is essentially an unknown and can be categorized as a question mark activity, at least temporarily. One procedure that often helps analysts move an activity from a question mark activity to one of the other categories is to ask "Why" until the root cause for the activity is uncovered. For example:

1. Why are we inspecting part #4567? Answer: To see if it conforms to spec.
2. Why are we checking to see if it conforms to spec? Answer: To see if the machine is under control.
3. Why are we seeing if the machine is under control? Answer: Because the machine output is highly variable.
4. Why is the machine output highly variable? Answer: Because its operating procedures are not adequately specified and the operator is not well trained.

In this case, we can label the inspection as a wasteful activity that could be eliminated after giving adequate training to the machine operator.

Dispositioning

Dispositioning involves deciding what to do with each specific activity at the time of analysis. In general, there are four disposition options available: *keep, combine, rethink,* and *eliminate.*
- Keep—Leave the activity intact.
- Combine—Join an activity with others that do the same or similar things to improve the efficiency of the process.
- Rethink—Reevaluate an activity that produces a favorable outcome (value-adding or necessary but not value-adding), but does so inefficiently.
- Eliminate—Drop the activity because it generates waste.

Repositioning

Repositioning looks at where (i.e., on which path) an activity should be positioned within the overall process. Within every process there are two types of paths: critical paths and noncritical paths. The critical path is the set of sequential activities with the largest total activity time. This path is critical because it determines the overall lead time of the process. By moving activities from critical to noncritical paths one can shorten the total order lead time for the process.

Another potential improvement comes from shifting work or resources from one activity to another activity so that bottleneck constraints are broken and the workload is better balanced. Yet another way to improve process performance is to break a single path of activities into two parallel paths. Many times these types of changes are not possible because of technical constraints (e.g., one activity must precede another) or resource constraints (e.g., making parallel paths would increase the number of workers required). Nevertheless, it is important to question why each activity is positioned where it is, and whether moving it could improve process performance.

---

necessary but not value-adding activity Any activity that does not add value directly but is necessary before a value-adding activity can take place.

waste-generating activity Any activity that consumes resources and time without returning any form of value.

question mark activity Any activity that cannot be easily categorized into one of the prior categories (value, necessary but not value-adding, waste).

dispositioning A decision regarding what to do with each specific activity at the time of analysis.

Keep A disposition decision where we agree to the keep the process as is for the time being.

combine A disposition decision to join the activity with others that do the same or similar thing.

rethink A disposition decision to reevaluate the activity with the goal of improving its efficiency.

eliminate A disposition decision to drop the activity because it generates waste.

repositioning Deciding where to position an activity in the overall process—either on the critical path or off the critical path.

TABLE 3S-4   Principles of Process Improvement

1. Design the process to produce at the rate of customer demand.

2. Produce each product in a mix of products at a rate proportional to the customer demand.

3. Eliminate or reduce process interruptions, uncertainties, variability, or any other instabilities that lead to delays or storage.

4. Break a series of activities into parallel paths if you can do so without increasing resources.

5. Process workpieces on a first-in, first-out (FIFO) basis.

6. For each resource, sequence activities to minimize setups, distance, or other activity transition costs.

7. Add resources only to bottleneck (least capacity) activities on critical paths.

8. Use redundant resources and parallel copies of activities to reduce throughput time and increase route flexibility. Use single resources and serial activities to minimize cost.

9. Minimize cross-departmental hand-offs.

10. Keep non–value-adding but necessary activities (e.g., measurement) off the critical path.

11. Co-locate activities that share resources or information.

12. Try to limit the number of entry points of workpieces into the process.

13. Develop the ability to economically make every part every day (i.e., make setup times as minimal as possible).

14. When processing a variety of different items, group them into "families" of items with similar processing requirements and dedicate resources to each family (i.e., create work "cells").

15. Capture data at its source. Minimize translations of data.

16. Change the product design to facilitate process improvements.

Principles of Process Improvement

Improvement opportunities are unique to each process, but there are certain principles that one can draw upon when making the process evaluation. Typically, managers get better at identifying improvement opportunities as they gain experience in multiple process mapping and analysis projects. Table 3S-4 lists some important principles of process improvement.

Applying Step 4 to AHMP

As previously noted, the overall order fulfillment standard was to be six weeks, with 95 percent of order entries taking no more than one week. In reviewing the current state, the team came up with the following observations:

- The current process could not meet the standard set by management on a regular, consistent basis. The average lead time for order entry was 4 weeks. The best-case scenario of one-week order entry was not very likely to occur regularly.

- The order entry process consisted of 17 steps: 4 operations, 4 transportations, 2 inspections, and 7 delays. Several of the activities were especially bothersome since they exhibited a very high level of variance. Furthermore, the process included only one value-adding activity, with 6 wasteful activities, 4 necessary-but-not-value-adding activities, and 6 question marks. The process appeared to be confused, highly variable, and not effective.

- What bothered the team was the nature of the delays. How long the order stayed in a delay appeared to be dictated by various informal scheduling practices. For example, the reason for the relatively short delay in moving orders from accounting to scheduling was the accounting practice of running the orders down to scheduling once an hour. In contrast, the marketing manager wanted to build up enough orders so that he could spend the entire morning (or afternoon) reviewing them. It was his view that checking the orders was time-consuming and compromised his ability to do other more "valuable" activities.

- The marketing review was really only necessary for new customers or customers who had some special problem.
- There was no real need for engineering to review the technical specifications of standard autoclaves. This review requirement was a carryover from the time when all orders in AHMP were engineered to order.

Step 5: Recommend Appropriate Changes to the Process (the "Future State" Map)

Once a list of possible changes for improvement has been made, it is important to bring together representatives from the various stakeholder groups to evaluate and prioritize the changes. Stakeholders in a process include the suppliers to and customers of the process, workers and support personnel involved in the process, and various functional managers. The prioritization of possible improvements to the process often classifies them into one of three basic categories:

1. Make the change immediately.
2. Postpone the change until sufficient resources or capabilities become available.
3. Determine that the change is not ultimately desirable or feasible.

Many times desirable process changes are not implemented (category 2 above) because resources such as capital, skills, or machinery are not currently available. All too often changes are not implemented because the organization's internal culture or politics will not support the change. In any event, it is important to document the potential benefits of such changes and to schedule reevaluations when future conditions are likely to be more conducive to the change.

An effective way to communicate the impacts of a potential process change is to represent the changes in a new process flow table, or a new process map, called the **future state** map. By comparing and contrasting the future state map with the current state map, decision makers can more easily identify the impacts on resources, flows, and other process elements.

Applying Step 5 to AHMP

The process analysis team at AHMP proposed a process redesign as specified in the new future state process flow table shown in Table 3S-5. First, standard autoclave orders for existing customers in good standing would be quickly identified and separated out. Second, accounting and scheduling representatives would be moved and co-located in the same office so that orders would be quickly transferred (it was recognized that in the near future this manual system could be replaced by a computerized, online system). These changes reduced the expected order entry lead time from about seven days to only 24 minutes for standard orders. Since most orders were for standard autoclaves, the new process made the strategic objectives for AHMP now possible. The team recognized that more work could be done to streamline the order entry for nonstandard orders.

To communicate these changes effectively, the team developed a **process summary table**. This type of table summarizes the current process, the proposed new process, and expected improvements from the proposed changes (see Table 3S-6). It indicates at a single glance the major problems in the existing process, measured in activity time, frequency of occurrence, or total time. Improvements are indicated by the presence of fewer activities, less distance, fewer people, and/or less time.

Step 6: Implement the Changes and Monitor Improvements

Process improvement is usually an iterative, trial and error activity. Consequently, feedback mechanisms should be put into place whenever a significant process change is implemented so that managers can evaluate its impacts and make adjustments as needed.

relationships

LO3S-5 Change a process to make it more effective and efficient by either refining the current process or designing a new replacement process.

future state The new or proposed process that the changes in the existing processes are intended to achieve.

process summary table A table that summarizes the current process and the proposed new process and identifies the expected improvements offered by the proposed process.

relationships

TABLE 3S-5 Future State Process Flow Table for AHMP

Process Flow Table

Page ___1__ of __1___

Overall Description of Process Charted:

Date Charted: _____ Charted by: _____

Check appropriate box: Current Process: ( ) Proposed Process: (X)

Dist Meters	Average Time (range)	Symbol	Pers Invol.	Value Code V/W/N/?	Description of Activity (indicate outcome)
	15 min	●⇒D□▽	1	V	Order received by telephone operator.
	1 min	●⇒D□▽	1	N	Order reviewed to see if it is standard or special.
	1 min	●⇒D□▽	1	N	Order reviewed to see if customer is existing customer in good standing.
2	1 min	O⇒D□▽	1	?	Order moved within same room to the accounting representative.
3	1 min	O⇒D□▽	1	?	Move to scheduling representative (located in same room).
	5 min	●⇒D□▽	1	N	Schedule autoclave order.
Totals: 5 m	24 min	4 2 0 0 0			

TABLE 3S-6 Process Summary Table for AHMP

Activities	Current		Proposed		Difference	
	#	Total Time	#	Total Time	#	Total Time
Operations (O)	4	30	4	22	0	8
Inspections (□)	2	15	0	0	2	15
Transportations (⇒)	4	150	2	2	2	148
Storages (▽)	0	0	0	0	0	0
Delays (D)	7	3915	0	0	7	3915
Distance (feet/meters)	950		<15		935	

In some cases a pilot study might be done to verify the benefits of a process change. In others, a wholesale, radical change might be attempted very quickly to shake up existing infrastructures and to overcome barriers to change that often arise. It is important to get agreement from all important stakeholders and to make sure that all important resources needed to support the change are identified and secured.

OTHER PROCESS MAPPING TOOLS

In addition to the techniques introduced in this supplement, there are several other approaches that can be used.

Process flow diagramming is commonly used to indicate the general flow of plant processes and equipment. This procedure shows the relationship between major equipment but not the minor detail such as piping and such. An example of this technique being used to diagram the process of converting corn to fuel-grade ethanol is shown in Figure 3S-3.

Value stream mapping is a mapping technique that analyzes the flow of material and information currently needed to bring a product to a customer. Value stream mapping is used to assess the extent to which the current process adds value (as a percentage of the total time) and to identify opportunities for reducing lead time. It is more comprehensive and complex when compared to the process mapping approach introduced in this supplement. In some implementations, value stream mapping requires the use of over 25 different symbols (as compared to the five discussed in this supplement).

Service blueprinting (discussed in Chapter 5) is used to map an entire service system, so that the process can be analyzed, monitored, and improved in terms of its ability to satisfy the needs of the customer. It maps out and assesses all of the various interactions and actions that occur when the customer and the company (and its process) meet.

Swim lanes is a visual element used in process flow diagrams or flowcharts that organizes the activities into groups based on the major types of tasks being carried out or the departments responsible for those activities. The major attraction of swim lanes

process flow diagramming A technique used to indicate the general flow of plant processes and equipment.

value stream mapping A mapping technique that analyzes the flow of material and information needed to bring a product to the customer.

service blueprinting A technique for mapping an entire service system, so that the process can be analyzed, monitored, and improved in its ability to satisfy the needs of the customer.

swim lanes A visual element used in process flow diagrams or flowcharts that organizes the activities into groups based on the major types of tasks being carried out or the departments responsible for those activities.

FIGURE 3S-3   Process Flow Diagram: Dry-Mill Ethanol Process for Converting Corn to Fuel-Grade Ethanol[5]

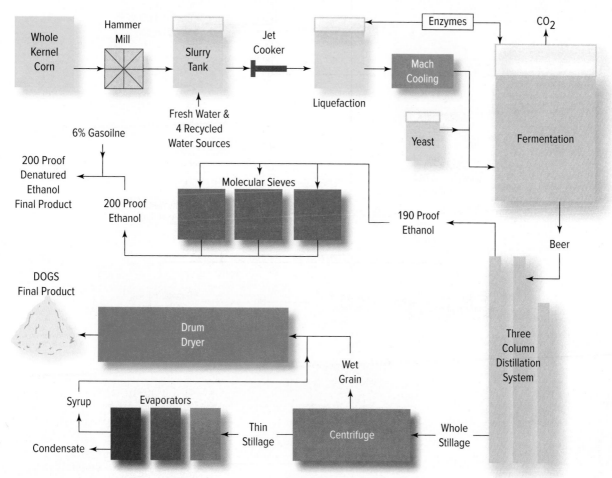

(also known as *functional bands*) is that this technique helps organize the processes into functional or organizational blocks (and responsibilities). Figure 3S-4 provides an example of swim lanes. Here we can see that the overall process consists of five major activities: order entry, division, warehouse, credit, and customer—each potentially managed by a different group. This means that if we want to improve or change the process presented in Figure 3S-4, we have to coordinate our activities with up to five different groups.

FIGURE 3S-4 Swim Lanes for an Order Fulfillment Process[6]

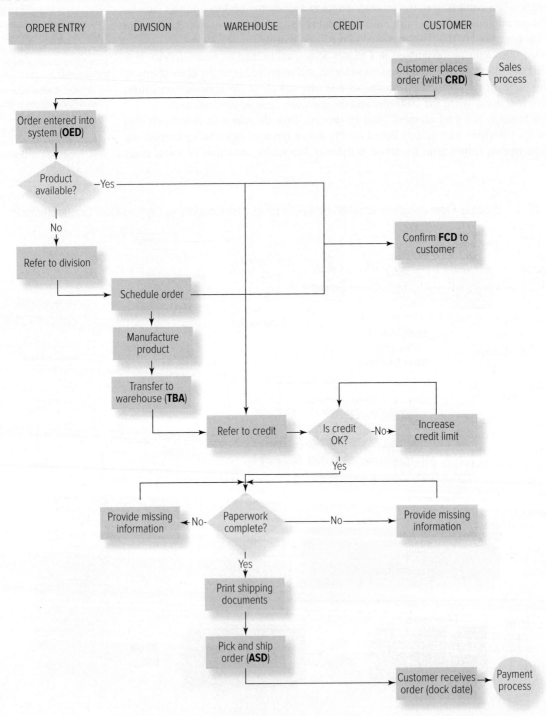

[6]A. M. Schneiderman, 1996, "Metrics for the Order Fulfillment Process (Part 1)." *Journal of Cost Management* 10, no. 2 (Summer 1996), pp. 30–42.

SUMMARY

Process mapping and analysis tools provide the means for process improvements that can have great performance impacts. This supplement illustrates the process mapping and analysis method, including the following important points:

1. Process mapping and analysis involves six major steps: (1) determine the desired outcome for the process and the associated metrics needed to evaluate its performance; (2) identify and bound the critical process; (3) document the existing process (the "current state" map); (4) analyze the process and prioritize opportunities for improvement; (5) recommend appropriate changes to the process (the "future state" map); and (6) implement the changes and monitor improvements.

2. Processes are characterized by six basic types of activities (i.e., operations, decisions, storage activities, transportation activities, delays, and inspections).

3. Process mapping and analysis is a graphic technique to study and improve processes using symbols, diagrams, and tables to map process flows. Process analysis tools include the process flow table, physical layout diagram, process map, and process summary table. These tables and charts describe the number and types of activities in a process, their organization, the time they require, and the distance they cover.

TERMS

PROBLEMS

1. You are making your weekly trip to your local grocery story. Use a process flow diagram chart to describe your decision-making process about what to buy and where to buy it. What inputs did you use in helping you make these weekly decisions? How could an advanced consumer information system have made your process easier?

2. Your eyeglass frame-making firm is considering one of two distribution alternatives. The first is to make all shipments from your Chicago plant to one of three regional warehouses located in Philadelphia, Chicago, and Reno. All orders from eyeglass

retailers would be shipped from these sites. The second alternative is to create one warehouse in Memphis, Tennessee, and ship all orders via Federal Express.

    a.   Prepare a process flow diagram of each alternative.

    b.   What additional information would you need to ascertain which alternative will provide the best value to your customers?

    c.   Is this different from a lower cost solution? Why?

3.   Murphy's Bagel Shops (MBS) is a chain of bagel eateries supported by a central bakery. Most raw materials are delivered to MBS's bakery where the ingredients are inspected for quality and then stored in the raw materials warehouse, which is located on the bakery's second floor. The second floor is also where the ingredients are measured into batch quantities before being inserted into the bagel dough blender. Two hundred–pound batches of each bagel blend are mixed for about one hour. The mixed dough is then extruded into bagel shapes and placed on flat baking pans. The full pans are placed in "shipping racks," which are then sent about 50 yards to the shipping area.

    Each day, the shops order raw pre-cooked bagels in increments of the number on each flat baking pan. The shipping department rearranges the number of each type of bagel on each shipping rack to assure that the number shipped to a given bagel shop matches the number ordered. Each shop's filled shipping racks are segregated by the delivery department to assure that the incoming trucks can be accurately and quickly loaded. Loading a truck requires approximately 20 minutes.

    The bagel dough rises during the transportation process for about 40 minutes. The trucks are scheduled to arrive at each bagel shop at 5 o'clock in the morning. There the bagel shop crew unloads each shipping rack, places any surface ingredients (i.e., poppy seeds) on the bagel trays as needed, and then places them either into the shop's ovens or the raw bagel storage area. It takes approximately 40 minutes to cook most bagels. Trays of cooked bagels are removed from the ovens and placed in the bagel cooling area.

    Once sufficiently cooled, the fresh bagels are placed into the retail area displays that are designed to send bagel-scented air in the direction of the customer-seating area. Fresh bagels are cooked each morning as needed. Unsold bagels are packaged into six-pack bags and sold at a discount after 2 p.m.

    a.   Prepare a process flow diagram of the above business.

    b.   Indicate the operations in which value is being added.

4.   Using Evergreen Products (the case found in Chapter 3), carry out the first step in the process of process mapping and analysis, as presented in this supplement, for the two different key customers:

- Florists
- Grocery stores

    1.   What differences did you note in terms of the desired outcomes for the processes and in the measures and metrics used?

    2.   To what extent can the same process effectively serve both key customers equally well?

    3.   What is the implication of your analysis for how firms should think about key customers and the processes that serve them?

5.   This problem uses Evergreen Products (the case found in Chapter 3).

    Management is not happy with the current process that is present at Evergreen Products. You have been called into the office of the CEO and given the following task.

    Beginning with a blank sheet of paper, you are to reengineer the entire order fulfillment process so that it can achieve the following performance metric: Irrespective of however the order is placed (by phone or by a salesperson), the time from when an order is placed to when the customer receives the order must be no longer than four hours. This new system must even provide delivery of orders on holidays (e.g., Valentine's Day).

You are allowed to challenge any of the current practices in place. In doing your analysis, please recognize the following assumptions and constraints:

- Time is measured from the moment that the order is placed by the customer until the order is in the hands of the customer.
- It takes about 90 minutes to build a load and to fill a truck for shipments.
- No less-than-truckload quantities will be allowed.
- It takes, on average, about 60 minutes to go from the plant to the specific florist.
- Assume that it takes about 60 minutes from the time that a call is received until enough orders are consolidated for a full truckload to be planned.
- Truck drivers/salespeople have cellphones and are in contact with the plant.

(*Hint:* There is a feasible solution to this problem, but only if you are willing to challenge any and all assumptions and practices found in the current process!)

CASE

Midwestern Lighting[7]

"I can't see why you have to spend so much time looking at our processes. Hey, we have everything under control. It has been over five years since we got our last EPA inspection and nearly six years since we got our last major citation and fine. Things are going really smoothly and I really don't see why you have to look at the process. Now, why don't you go out and get me some cost savings? Every time I can save a penny per finished lighting assembly, I get that much better a chance to keep my business with the big boys."

With those words, Barry Jamieson, the plant manager of Midwestern Lighting's Light Fixture Plant (LFP) dismissed Tim Bryant. Tim had been hired some six months ago to help improve overall operations at LFP. Initially, he had been brought in by corporate to identify opportunities for cost reduction and for reducing scrap and landfill related costs. When he arrived at LFP, located in New Hudson, Michigan, Tim found a plant that was operating under a siege mentality. Everyone knew that they had to reduce costs and improve operating efficiencies if they hoped to win another contract from LFP's three major customers. LFP was unique in that it was one of the few plants in the automotive industry that built light fixtures for GM, Ford, and Daimler-Chrysler. While LFP was noted for its superb quality, it was also recognized as not being very cost efficient. The managers of Midwestern Lighting had tried to convince the plant manager at LFP to consider QS9000 certification. That effort was a disaster and ultimately resulted in the dismissal of the plant manager. It was that dismissal that gave rise to the hiring of Barry

Jamieson. Since arriving at LFP, Barry had developed a reputation for being a hard-nosed manager. To Barry, if you couldn't reduce cost, then you didn't have anything to say of importance. Barry was not really excited by Tim's presence. To Barry, Tim represented nothing more than increased overhead.

The Production Process Described

Since arriving at LFP, Tim could not help but feel that there were too many "diamonds in the rough" to ignore. Typical was the process for making the tail light assemblies for the Dodge Ram, one of the best-selling trucks in the market. The process began with the back plate. This was long black piece of extruded ABS plastic (produced in another part of the plant) that contained two concave depressions–one for the turn light and one for the backup light. These were withdrawn from a temporary storage location found near the assembly line. Each back plate was first checked for cosmetic defects. Those that failed this step were placed in a bin where they were eventually used as a source of raw material for regrinds. Any plate passing this test was placed in a metalization chamber, where nickel metal particles were sprayed on using a high-pressure water-based system. Because of the nature of the process, only half of the material ever reached the back plate. The rest either fell to the bottom of the chamber or was vented out. Periodically, the chamber had to be taken off line and cleaned out. This process took 1 to 2 days and effectively shut down production of the tail light.

[7]This case is prepared for the purpose of class discussion rather than to illustrate either effective or ineffective handling of an administrative situation. Ford Motor Company supplied the data. Some of the data have been modified to protect proprietary information. The writers of the case are fully responsible for the information within the case.

After the parts were metalized, they were removed from the chamber and checked for completeness and evenness of the coverage. Any rejected parts were placed in a bin. Because of the presence of the metal coating, the back plate could not be recycled, so it had to be landfilled. The accepted parts went into a rack where they waited for the arrival of lenses from a supplier. A plastic-wrapped film covered the lenses. Each lens, as it arrived from the supplier, was checked for surface flaws. Any rejected lenses were then put into a recycle bin, where they were used as inputs for any parts requiring low-grade black plastic.

The next step in the process was mating. At this stage, each lens was mated to a back plate. This was accomplished by placing the back plate and the lens into two fixtures. These fixtures were then fed into an automated gluing machine. The machine placed a bead of glue on the lens, waited for 10 seconds and then placed the lens onto the back plate. Periodically, the gluing machine had to be purged and cleaned. This was typically done twice a shift; each instance required 30 minutes. This process was fairly messy and required several globs of glue to be expressed through the nozzle. After this was done, the last glob of glue was then expressed and the nozzle was removed. The machine had four nozzles. The residual glue and nozzles were then thrown into an old 55-gallon barrel. Because this barrel was used as a receptacle for all sorts of scrap (including floor sweepings and cigarette butts), the only disposal option was a landfill.

After mating, the back light assembly was next tested for leaks. Placing the body into a tank of water and then shooting a burst of air through it completed the testing. Again, any assemblies that failed this test were put into a bin for eventual disposal in a landfill site. Those that passed this stage next proceeded to the finishing assembly. It was here that two light bulb assemblies were first made. These assemblies required one receiver and one light bulb each. Both the receiver and the light bulbs were provided by outside suppliers. After they were assembled, the assemblies were inserted into the appropriate holes in the car body. The light assembly was then inspected for performance and surface blemishes. Any problem assemblies were put aside for rework. Those that could not be reworked were set aside for disposal (again landfilled). The remaining "good" assemblies were packed into a cardboard box and shipped out to the Dodge Ram assembly plant.

The current practice at LFP was to allocate the total production cost to the number of good assemblies produced. By working with the material requirements planning system at LFP, Tim and others were able to track the following costs associated with waste in the process. For the tail light assemblies, the line produced 3,600 lot size/shift. Labor and overhead costs were considered to be fixed.

Current Process	Molding	Metalization	Inspection
Direct materials waste	.05	.001	.000
Other waste (materials and labor)	.058	.023	.048
Production cost/piece	.093	.042	.023
Total cost/piece	1.15	1.216	10.727

Questions

1. Assess the production process for the Dodge Ram tail light assembly. How efficient is it?

2. Develop a process map for this operation.

3. Where are the largest opportunities to reduce waste and associated costs?

4. What strategy/approach would you use for making recommendations to Barry Jamieson?

Jacka, J. M. *Business Process Mapping: Improving Customer Satisfaction.* New York, NY: Wiley, 2002.

Lovelle, J. "Mapping the Value Stream." *IIE Solutions* 33, no. 2 (February 2001), pp. 26–33.

Melan, E. H. *Process Management: Methods for Improving Products and Service.* New York: McGraw-Hill, 1993.

Rother, M., and J. Shook. *Learning to See: Value Stream Mapping to Create Value and Eliminate Muda.* Brookline, MA: The Lean Enterprise Institute, Inc., 1999.

Rummler, G. A., and A. P. Brache. *Improving Performance: How to Manage the White Space on the Organization Chart.* San Francisco, CA: Jossey-Bass Publishers, 1990.

4

Product/Process Innovation

LO4-1 Explain why product/process innovation is an important contributor to a firm's performance.

LO4-2 Contrast different types of innovation strategies and projects.

LO4-3 Describe new product/process design and development objectives and project phases.

LO4-4 Explain why cross-functional integration is needed in product and process design.

LO4-5 Apply tools and techniques for integrating customer needs and supply chain considerations into product/process design and development.

Want a Coke? We've Got 100 Different Kinds.

Ever had one of those moments where all you wanted was a Diet Black Cherry Vanilla Coke, but all that the fountain could offer you was regular old diet? Coca-Cola solved that problem by introducing the Coca-Cola Freestyle. A single machine can dispense more than 100 regular and low-calorie branded beverages. Pick what you want, and the Freestyle mixes it on the spot—including many varieties of waters, sports drinks, lemonades, energy drinks, and sparkling beverages that previously were not widely available. Even with all these options, the machine uses the same amount of space as typical six- or eight-valve fountains.

The Freestyle offers a great example of an innovation that creates an exciting new customer experience while also providing tremendous operational advantages. Coca-Cola succeeded in bringing this product to market by working with new partners to combine previously unlinked technologies in a novel way. The fountain has an intuitive and easy-to-use touchscreen developed by BSQUARE. "We worked closely with the Coca-Cola Company and studied consumer feedback to provide the software that would ultimately power Coca-Cola Freestyle," says BSQUARE CEO Brian Crowley. The flavors are mixed by "Pure-Pour" technology, which was originally developed to measure extremely precise amounts of dialysis and cancer drugs. Radio-frequency-identification (RFID) scanners are used to match cartridges to dispensers and to track inventory levels of each flavor, and the onboard computer powered by Windows Embedded confirms that everything is in place.

The Freestyle dispensers are certainly more expensive to produce than old-style fountains, but Coca-Cola managers expect operational savings to far exceed added costs. Existing soda fountains use five-gallon concentrate bags and require lots of backroom space and labor. Now all that is required is a highly concentrated 46-ounce cartridge inside a self-contained machine. The built-in communications software provides other important supply chain management capabilities. It sends business data back to Coke's headquarters in Atlanta, continuously providing details on beverage consumption, peak times, and popular locations. In addition to providing valuable insight into consumer behavior, these data make it easy to track and efficiently restock inventory levels within each fountain dispenser. Each Freestyle also notifies maintenance personnel as to when and how it needs to be serviced. Coke can also talk back to the machine, letting it know if a particular flavor needs to be discontinued or recalled, and causing it to stop serving the drink immediately.

According to Gene Farrell, Coca-Cola Freestyle vice president and general manager, the Freestyle creates "... an unprecedented beverage experience for consumers." The system also creates fantastic operational efficiencies. In these ways, Coca-Cola's innovation creates a winning advantage for itself and its retail partners.

This chapter is about managing product and process innovations. The Coca-Cola Freestyle story illustrates some of the unique opportunities associated with bringing a new product to market. When a business succeeds in closely linking new product innovations to its supply chain's operational capabilities, it often sees dramatic benefits in terms of profits, growth, and competitive advantages.

Innovative changes made to products and processes can be large or small. Continuous improvements to existing operational processes happen in all areas of the supply chain, and these types of innovations are discussed throughout the chapters of this book. In this chapter, however, we focus on operational approaches for developing new products and processes. In addition, the chapter describes tools used to integrate product design and supply chain process design decisions.

THE ROLE OF PRODUCT/PROCESS INNOVATION IN SUPPLY CHAIN OPERATIONS MANAGEMENT

LO4-1 Explain why product/process innovation is an important contributor to a firm's performance.

In today's rapidly changing world, managers throughout the supply chain are continually thinking about how to exploit new technologies to improve their products and processes. Most of the time, these development efforts are accomplished through projects.

New product design and development projects transform a new market opportunity and/or new product technology into a set of specifications that define a product. Coca-Cola's introduction of the Freestyle was the culmination of a new product design and development project.

New process design and development projects transform product specifications and new process technology into a new or revised production system.[1] Examples are the design and installation of a new production line in a factory or a new information system in a bank.

new product design and development projects The transformation of a new market opportunity and/or new product technology into a set of specifications that define a product.

new process design and development projects The transformation of product specifications and new process technology into a new or revised production system.

You might think that product development is mainly a marketing and engineering activity, while process development is more of an operations management activity. Actually, operations managers get involved in both types of development projects in at least two different ways.

First, all development projects are actually operational processes. Operations managers bring their project management skills to bear as a business seeks to improve the speed, quality, and productivity of its innovation development efforts. This chapter explains operational approaches that can be used to improve development projects.

Second, in most settings new product and new process development activities are closely linked together. For example, in the steel industry, new grades of steel often result from newly designed or refined production processes. In services, such as a hospital or a hotel, the process *is* the product, so product development and process development are essentially the same thing. Even when a product is mostly a tangible good, product design decisions usually have huge impacts on all aspects of internal operations (facilities, equipment, layout, and workforce) as well as on suppliers' roles and logistical requirements. For this reason, operations managers located throughout the supply chain have a large stake in how product design decisions are made, and they usually play important roles in supporting product development tasks.

Ultimately, product/process design and development can be viewed as part of the resource/technology supply chain. These activities *supply* performance requirements and technology

---

[1]Types of goods and service production systems are described in Chapter 5, "Manufacturing and Service Process Structures."

specifications as inputs to operations managers located throughout the supply chain; operations managers then turn these specifications into goods and services for customers.

The Product Life Cycle

Most products go through periods of sales growth and decline that necessitate changes in a firm's operational capabilities. For a given product, this pattern of changes is known as the product life cycle. Figure 4-1 illustrates the role of innovation throughout a product's life cycle.

product life cycle A pattern of sales growth and decline over the period in which a product is offered.

The product life cycle has four phases: launch, growth, maturity, and decline.

- *Launch*—A new product launch is usually the culmination of an intense product design and development effort. Supply chain process innovation may be required too if the product does not make use of existing process technologies and capacities.

- *Growth*—As sales begin to grow, customer responses give the firm information about how to refine the product specifications. Product modifications continue until standardized forms of the product begin to emerge. During this growth stage, major investments in process innovation are usually postponed. Operating processes in the supply chain must be flexible in accommodating a high mix of low-volume product orders, and they must be able to rapidly increase capacity in order to avoid losing sales.

- *Maturity*—Once demand stabilizes and product refinements become less frequent, costs become more critical because low-cost competitors often enter the market. Process innovation is usually needed in this stage to increase supply chain efficiencies. Process innovation is justified because the product specifications are fairly stabilized, and early profits have generated funding for process investments.

- *Decline*—Product maturity may last for many years, yet eventually products enter a decline stage as customer needs change or as new technologies supplant existing ones. As demand declines, operations process managers across the supply chain face intense pressures to reduce cost and to efficiently decrease capacity. Firms often try to avoid the decline phase by using incremental product design and development projects to revitalize products with new or better features or replace them with next generation products (e.g., new versions of iPads, new types of credit cards, added sites to guided tours).

Product life cycles can be very short (months) or very long (many years). For example, sales for a trendy new toy might grow and decline very quickly, whereas products like certain breakfast cereals have been in the maturity stage for decades. Operations managers use the product life cycle concept to plan the initial design and periodic changes to supply chain processes.

FIGURE 4-1

Innovation Across a Product's Life Cycle

How Product/Process Innovation Affects Firm Performance

relationships

Throughout a product's life cycle, product and process innovation affect a company's growth, as well as its profitability. Excellent innovation projects translate customer desires and technology-based opportunities into product and process designs that operations managers can deliver reliably and efficiently. It is widely believed that 80 percent of a product's total supply chain costs are determined by decisions made in product design. To make good product design decisions, managers need to integrate inputs from many different functions and groups located within a firm and across its supply chain. In particular, these groups play important roles in new product development:

- Customers communicate their needs and desires.
- Financial managers help evaluate and select the most promising innovation opportunities.
- Marketing managers understand and communicate customers' needs, competitive opportunities, and marketing strategies.
- Engineers and designers use technological knowledge and creativity to turn needs into product and process specifications.
- Various operations managers located across the supply chain determine how to best source, produce, and deliver the product to meet the firm's objectives based on their operational capabilities.

The best innovative firms have well-defined processes that integrate the inputs of these groups at appropriate times throughout design and development projects. A later section of this chapter discusses integrated design and development approaches in detail.

LO4-2 Contrast different types of innovation strategies and projects.

Numerous studies have shown that more-innovative firms consistently outperform their rivals. Firms that have developed strong innovation competencies grow at rates that are three to six times the rate of their competitors, and they typically create profits that are 20 to 150 percent greater than the profits of their competitors. Why are innovative firms so successful? They gain the following advantages from being faster, better, and more efficient innovators.

Fast innovators:

- Capture additional sales by getting their new products to market more quickly than their competitors do.
- Are able to react quickly to competitors' product introductions, thus capitalizing on the development and promotional efforts of their competitors.
- Produce a more continuous stream of new product introductions that create a greater and more constant market awareness of their brands.

High-quality innovators:

- Have fewer problems in launching new products and fewer failures in the marketplace.
- Satisfy customers more effectively, building strong brand image and customer loyalty.

Efficient innovators:

- Are able to fund more new design and development projects than other firms.
- Can sell at lower prices or lower the total sales needed for a new product to pay back its initial development costs.

Finally, product/process innovation projects also contribute to a firm's competitiveness in ways that go beyond the immediate creation of new products or processes. Every innovation project, successful or not, involves learning—learning about new markets, new technologies, new methods, new suppliers, and even new personnel. These lessons learned often lead to new innovation opportunities that create competitive advantages.

INNOVATION COMPETENCIES

To effectively coordinate all of the inputs from the various functional contributors to innovation processes located across the supply chain, a firm has to have a strong overarching innovation strategy, as well as operational competencies in the areas of idea development, project selection, project management, and organizational learning. As Figure 4-2 shows, one can view innovation as a "funnel." While many new product and process ideas may be initially considered, the best innovators are good at pursuing a portfolio of ideas that have high potential impacts and also fit well with the firm's strategy and capabilities. Strong innovators are also good at managing projects needed to bring new product and process ideas to fruition. Finally, they are good at launching new products and then learning from successes and failures. Note that firms often involve customers and suppliers as innovation partners. Operations managers play key roles in establishing these partnerships and in making decisions at each stage of the funnel.

Idea and Opportunity Development

Some firms are better than others at finding and developing new ideas and opportunities for innovation. Excellent firms have a culture that motivates workers in all areas of the firm's operations to constantly look for new ways to improve processes and to please customers. Firms foster an innovative culture through the following practices:

- *Hiring the best and the brightest.* Innovation ultimately depends on people!
- *Creating effective rewards.* Many firms create efficient and fun ways for employees and partners to submit ideas, along with payments for ideas based on their merits.
- *Providing adequate resources.* Firms that are dedicated to innovation typically set aside significant amounts of money and worker time to the development of new ideas. Most large firms have separate R&D organizations dedicated to innovation. Where the average U.S. firm allocates about 2 percent of its revenues to R&D, innovative firms may allocate as much as 10 percent, or more, to this purpose.

In addition to developing ideas internally, some firms have taken extraordinary steps to solicit new product and process ideas from external networks including customers, suppliers, universities, and even competitors. This approach is known as **open innovation**. Pharmaceutical companies such as Eli Lilly, for example, have created websites where scientists from around the world can quickly enter new product formulation ideas, and where the

relationships

open innovation An organizational effort to capture ideas and resources from sources outside the firm for use in innovation efforts.

FIGURE 4-2

Competencies for Product/Process Innovation Management

company can publish requests for help in solving certain medical problems. Firms that are good at idea and opportunity development typically have many such systems in place that scan various environments for useful market, technological, and competitor intelligence.

A particular application of open innovation is known as crowdsourcing. In this approach, firms or individuals can search for needed services or ideas by soliciting contributions from large populations of people. The Internet enables mass solicitations and the ability to build online communities. The Get Real box below describes how LEGO uses crowdsourcing to gather and evaluate new product ideas.

crowdsourcing The process of obtaining ideas or services by soliciting contributions from a large group of people, especially from an online community.

GET REAL

LEGO: Crowdsourcing for Product Ideas and Customer Engagement

In the past decade, LEGO has grown from a basic children's toy manufacturer to a truly global brand. It has grown its presence in the social psyche through direct retail operations, a highly successful feature-length movie, and the development of a huge online community. LEGO draws upon the expertise and imagination of its customers (young and old alike) through its LEGO IDEAS social medium. At the LEGO website (ideas.lego.com), community members can review and submit ideas for new LEGO sets. New set ideas typically reflect famous or historical characters, sites, monuments, architecture, or vehicles, as well as trendy movies or events.

Community members review and vote for the ideas that they like. An idea that receives at least 10,000 votes is evaluated and possibly approved by a board of LEGO product managers. Once an idea is approved, it is produced and sold. Contributors of approved projects are recognized on the community website.

At the time of this writing, the LEGO community site had more than 14,000 project ideas under review. Using this crowdsourcing form of open innovation, LEGO involves its customers in the process of developing and testing new product ideas. Perhaps even more important, by engaging current and prospective consumers in this way, LEGO builds loyalty, interest, commitment, and a sense of ownership in the brand and in the success of the firm.

Wall-E:

© McGraw-Hill Education/Editorial Image, LLC, photographer

Lovelace & Babbage build the first computer:

© Stewart Lamb Cromar

Big Bang Theory:

© McGraw-Hill Education/Editorial Image, LLC, photographer

Innovation Portfolio Planning[2]

Most firms have more innovation ideas than they have the resources to pursue. It is important for new ideas to be formally screened to identify those that are most promising and most consistent with the firm's business strategy and development capacity. The screening process, known as innovation portfolio planning, analyzes estimated market share (by customer segment and channel), revenues, profits, investment, and development time requirements. These factors must be compared with the firm's marketing and technology strategies in order to ensure that design and development projects move the firm in the right direction. The screening must also compare the resource needs of a potential development project to the resources available, while considering the needs of other ongoing and planned projects. This type of aggregate innovation planning helps establish the priority and role of every project within the overall business strategy.

Figure 4-3 compares four primary types of innovation projects:

- *Research and advanced development projects* are aimed at finding new core products or processes; for example, a project by an auto company to develop a hydrogen fuel cell vehicle.

- *Radical breakthrough development projects* develop products or processes that will employ some entirely new technology, perhaps one developed through an advanced development project; for example, the initial development of digital cameras employed a new core technology.

- *Next generation or platform development projects* develop new product platforms using mostly existing technologies. Apple's iPod provides a good example of a new platform product, as it essentially brought together some existing technologies under a new overall architecture. If successful, platform innovations provide starting points for follow-on derivative products.

- *Enhancements, hybrid, and derivative development projects* refine and improve selected features of existing products. Adding a peanut butter flavor or a new color to M&Ms candy amounts to a derivative project. The scope of such a project is much narrower than the other, more ambitious innovations.

Operations managers can play different kinds of roles in each of these project types. A new supplier or technology vendor may play a very central role in advanced development and radical product development projects, especially if product and process technologies are highly interrelated. For example, Gillette employed the services of equipment vendors to develop

LO4-2 Contrast different types of innovation strategies and projects.

innovation portfolio planning
The process of selecting and prioritizing innovation projects to ensure that they are consistent with the firm's strategy and development capacity.

FIGURE 4-3
Types of Development Projects
Source: S. C. Wheelwright and K. B. Clark, *Revolutionizing Product Development* (New York: Free Press, 1992).

---

[2]Methods for project evaluation and selection are discussed in Chapter 15, "Project Management."

a radical new welding technology for production of the first flexible, moving head shaving razors. Platform and derivative development projects tend to rely more upon existing process technologies. In these projects, supply chain operations managers typically play consulting roles by clearly communicating the existing capabilities of processes to product designers.

Innovation Project Management

In innovative firms, product/process design and development projects are marked by two key competencies: discipline and flexibility. Innovation projects often involve uncertainty relating to customers' responses, competition, technology, and resource availability. Good innovation project teams clarify and reduce uncertainty as much as possible and build flexibility for situations in which uncertainties persist.

- A *disciplined* innovation project has well-defined process steps, consideration and inclusion of all relevant stakeholders and decision makers, and well-thought-out metrics and incentives.
- A *flexible* innovation project includes rigorous risk analysis and contingency plans; planned evaluation and decision points where the project may be killed, redirected, or continued; and extra resources (funds, people, equipment) that can be quickly redeployed.

Operations managers are usually directly responsible for planning and executing product/process innovation projects. Because this is such an important task, most of the remainder of this chapter is dedicated to the discussion of approaches and tools that can be used to make innovation projects more disciplined, flexible, and ultimately more successful.[3]

New Product/Process Launch and Learning

Beyond the management of each individual project, the *progression* of innovation projects needs to be managed. After a new product is launched or a new process is brought online, it is important to capture the lessons learned from the project. A continual chain of innovation projects adds to a firm's overall capabilities when the knowledge gained in one project is captured and exploited in the next project.

Codevelopment

relationships

early supplier involvement (ESI)
A codevelopment approach in which suppliers participate directly in product design activities.

A single firm rarely possesses all of the knowledge and resources it needs to bring a major new product to market or to bring a major new process online. Consequently, firms often partner with other firms to codevelop the new product or process. A codevelopment relationship may involve joint ownership of the new product design, or the development partner may participate strictly on a contract basis.

Operations and supply managers play important roles in helping to identify partners with high potential. Many firms ask production suppliers to participate directly in their product development processes. This practice is referred to as **early supplier involvement (ESI)**. By being involved early, suppliers of all kinds of services can influence design decisions so that products can be produced and delivered more efficiently. They also can plan for changes that they need to make in their own production processes and supply chain networks. In fact, suppliers often develop parts and even complete systems for their customers' products. On the Boeing 787, for example, a supplier developed the fuselage using carbon fibers rather than a metal exterior, a radically different approach from that of other passenger planes. Supplier involvement allows the buying firm to focus on overall systems integration and product functionality, rather than getting lost in the detailed technical designs of multiple complex systems.

Codevelopment produces several benefits, as well as some risks. The benefits:

- By opening up its innovation processes, the firm increases the number of sources for new and better ideas, leading to higher-quality products.

---

[3]In addition, Chapter 15 discusses tools and techniques that can be applied to any type of project.

- By leveraging the expertise and resources of suppliers, research firms, universities, and other partners, companies can increase the number of products they successfully launch and reduce the time it takes to bring new products and processes online.
- When companies work together to codevelop new products, they often share the financial and legal risks of development.

Some of the risks of codevelopment include:

- By including more partners, a firm risks losing control over intellectual property. Either intentionally or accidentally, a codevelopment partner may leak secret plans or technical knowledge to competitors or other parties who might use this information against the firm.
- The firm can lose control over the goals and timing of the innovation project if it becomes too dependent on partners.

Managers have to weigh these pros and cons as a part of their overall innovation strategy. As more and more firms increase their levels of open innovation and codevelopment activities, the roles of internal operations managers and external supply managers become more and more important. Operations and supply managers must work together with other functional groups to evaluate the benefits and risks associated with innovation partnership opportunities and to comprehend the technical capabilities and innovation competencies of their potential partners.

GET REAL

Codeveloping with a Competitor: Clorox Aligns Its Business Model with P&G

A few years ago, Clorox (famous for its Clorox brand bleach) acquired the Glad brand from SC Johnson. The Glad product line includes baggies, food wrap, and trash bags. It is a strong brand, but Clorox managers soon realized that they lacked the technological advantage needed to create follow-on products in this category. Thus, they feared that the Glad products would eventually become commodities. Clorox eventually learned that scientists at Procter & Gamble were developing and market testing two important technologies: Press'n Seal and Force Flex. Both developments looked very promising, but at the time P&G lacked the financial resources needed to launch and distribute a new brand highlighting these technologies.

At first glance, this looked like a match made in heaven. P&G had innovative technologies; Clorox had an existing brand and financial wherewithal. However, Clorox and P&G had also been long-time competitors. Both companies saw big risks in a partnership in which P&G licensed the technologies to Clorox. Clorox could simply sit on the technologies (not use them), thus killing the potential gains for P&G. P&G could license the technologies to Clorox, but withhold important information that Clorox would need in order to embed the technologies into its products and manufacturing processes.

global

The two companies eventually agreed upon a joint venture arrangement in which both companies held a significant stake in the success of new products using the technologies.

The venture has been a huge success. In fact, Clorox subsequently approached P&G for another deal in which P&G would take some of Clorox's other brands into Asian markets, where P&G has strong distribution channels and Clorox does not. This new option would never have emerged had either Clorox or P&G been unwilling to take on the risks of their initial deal. This story clearly shows how codevelopment benefits can extend far beyond the profits associated with a single joint product development effort.

© Roberts Publishing Services

Source: Henry Chesbrough and Kevin Schwartz, "Innovating Business Models with Co-development Partnerships," *Research-Technology Management* 50, no. 1 (January/ February 2007), pp. 55–59.

PRODUCT/PROCESS DESIGN AND DEVELOPMENT

There are many ways to describe the activities included in an innovation project. The most common approach is to think of stages through which the project must progress. Table 4-1 describes six major stages in product design and development. These stages can be collapsed into fewer phases or expanded into more detailed steps depending on the nature of the product and market environments and the planning needs of the company. Service innovation projects follow similar stages.

The Stage-Gate Process

stage-gate™ process A disciplined approach that defines specific criteria for each project stage that must be completed before proceeding to the next stage.

LO4-3 Describe new product/ process design and development objectives and project phases.

Some firms use a disciplined **stage-gate™ process** developed by Robert G. Cooper[4] to manage costs and risks in product/process innovation projects. Resources are committed to the project only on a stage-by-stage basis. Near the completion of each stage, the project is reviewed by senior managers and a go/no-go decision is made to determine if the project should be continued. If the decision is go, then resources are provided to allow the project to continue into the next stage until the next gate is reached. At the next gate, the project is

TABLE 4-1   Stages of Product/Process Innovation

Stage	Activities and Decisions
Concept Development	• Identify core product concept
	• Conduct market, technical, and financial assessments
	• Identify the target values of the product attributes, volume, and price
	• Determine the primary product architecture, including product variants and components sharing plan
	• Propose and investigate production process concepts
Product and Process Planning	• Decide which components will be designed versus off-the-shelf
	• Identify who will design, produce, and assemble the components
	• Specify the types of processes to be used to produce the product and the structure of the supply chain
	• Identify who will develop and supply needed process technologies
	• Develop early prototypes and system-level simulations
Detailed Design and Development	• Determine the values of the key design parameters
	• Perform detailed design of the components, including material and process selection, assembly precedence, and tooling requirements
	• Build full-scale prototypes and detailed simulations
Product and Market Testing	• Conduct full-scale product performance tests and simulations
	• Conduct customer tests
	• Design and test critical tools and production procedures
	• Refine details of product design
Commercialization	• Evaluate pilot production units
	• Establish market channels and an order fulfillment system
	• Train sales force and field service personnel
Market Introduction	• Ramp-up production volume
	• Fill distribution channels
	• Launch promotion and advertising campaigns
	• Evaluate field experience with product

---

[4]http://www.stage-gate.com/index.php

reviewed again and another go/no-go decision is made. If the decision is no-go then the project may repeat the stage, or it may be terminated and its resources reassigned to other projects. The discipline imposed by the stage-gate approach has been shown to increase teamwork, reduce product development time and cost, and identify problems earlier. This approach also helps to identify and reduce risks, as it allows managers to give more scrutiny to the project's progress before additional resources are committed.

Integrated Product/Process Design and Development: Concurrent Engineering

Some stages of product/process design and development naturally follow other stages, yet the stages do not have to be executed in a purely sequential way. For example, when developing a new laundry detergent using a sequential approach, the formula would be developed, then the production process would be designed, then the product packaging would be designed, and then the sales and advertising plans would be developed. Each development step would be performed by a different functional group that knows the most about doing that step. In reality, however, many activities in each of these steps can be overlapped using an approach known as **concurrent engineering** (see Figure 4-4). Concurrent engineering (CE) is defined as the simultaneous design and development of all the processes and information needed to produce, sell, distribute, and service a product. Other terms sometimes used in place of CE include *simultaneous engineering* and *integrated product development.* By getting different groups to work together, concurrent engineering integrates and facilitates cross-functional communication, leading to better decision making and faster development.

Operations managers located across the supply chain play very important roles in concurrent engineering product development projects because they get involved in design and development activities much earlier than in conventional projects. Consider the two product development projects depicted in Figure 4-5. The overall resources spent in new product/process development can be split into three categories:

- Development costs—spent to fund the design, development, and testing activities in the development project.

- Sustaining and warranty costs—spent to make changes to the product design and to production processes needed to solve problems uncovered both in production and in the field. This includes costs to repair and replace defective products for customers.

- Production and sales support costs—spent to promote, sell, produce, and distribute the product.

In the functional/sequential development project shown in Figure 4-5, the design and development stages are pursued sequentially, without much interaction among various functional groups. This approach can lower the development costs because each functional group focuses only on its specific development tasks. However, interdependencies in design decisions at different stages are often not fully considered. For example, what if a small change in laundry detergent formulation could have a large impact on manufacturing

relationships

concurrent engineering The simultaneous design and development of all the processes and information needed to produce, sell, distribute, and service a product.

LO4-4 Explain why cross-functional integration is needed in product and process design.

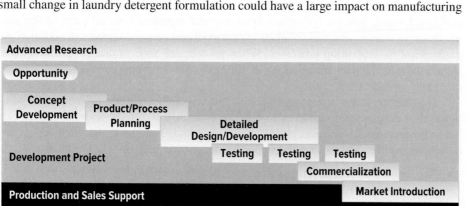

FIGURE 4-4
Overlapped Product Development Activities: Concurrent Engineering

FIGURE 4-5
Comparing Resource Expenditures in Functional and Integrated Product Development Projects

Functional/sequential product development project

Fewer development dollars ($)

More production & sales support dollars ($)

Dollars ($) spent

Sequential design and testing managed by one functional group at a time

Project launch

Market introduction

Time

More sustaining engineering & warranty dollars ($)

Integrated/concurrent engineering product development project

Cross–functional design and testing
• Design for customer
• Design for supply chain

More development dollars ($)

Fewer production & sales support dollars ($)

Dollars ($) spent

Project launch

Time

Market introduction

Earlier market introduction

Fewer sustaining engineering & warranty dollars ($)

cost without affecting its washing performance? Product designers involved in a sequential development project may never be prompted to consider such a change because they are focused only on product performance.

In contrast, the integrated/concurrent engineering approach overlaps the development activities (as shown in Figure 4-4), and many functional representatives work together in collocated teams. Internal operations managers and suppliers from all parts of the supply chain participate alongside marketing personnel and design engineers to codesign the product and its supporting processes. When product and process designs are developed simultaneously, the interdependencies in design decisions become more apparent and are more fully considered.

The integrated/concurrent engineering approach often requires a more up-front commitment of development resources in order to evaluate a larger set of design issues earlier in the product development project. This concentrated and more thorough design and development effort provides several important benefits, as illustrated in Figure 4-5:

- First, by overlapping development phases, managers are usually able to complete the project faster and introduce the product sooner. Speed to market can be especially valuable if there are many competitors or if the market window of opportunity is limited.

- Second, by identifying and solving more product- and process-related problems before market introduction, product sustaining and warranty costs can be drastically reduced. It is usually much cheaper to solve problems in design before expensive commitments to tooling, production, and other commercialization processes have been made.

- Finally, by considering product performance specifications and process design alternatives simultaneously, concurrent engineering teams are usually able to design supply chain processes that are more cost effective. Thus, the production and sales support costs can be lowered over the life of the product.

The following sections describe procedures that make concurrent development activities most effective. Some are aimed at ensuring that designs meet customers' needs, and others are more concerned with the constraints and capabilities of supply chain operations. All of these approaches involve cross-functional teams made up of marketing, engineering, and supply chain operations personnel.

Design for the Customer

LO4-5 Apply tools and techniques for integrating customer needs and supply chain considerations into product/process design and development.

To be successful, a product must meet the targeted customer's needs. There are several techniques that are used to ensure that the product has the right product features and performance at the right price.

Voice of the Customer

The voice of the customer (VOC) is a term used to describe a research effort that typically takes place in the early phases of a new product or process concept development. The effort uses customer interviews, focus groups, surveys, and other means to gather detailed data describing customers' wishes, needs, likes, and dislikes regarding specific product features and functionalities. In addition to working directly with key customer representatives, many companies use the Internet to understand what product features customers like by allowing them to create customized virtual products. For example, the websites of most major car companies allow you to select and view the features and colors you want in a customized car. In industries such as software development, lead customers use prototype versions of the software and provide feedback to developers, a process known as beta testing.

All of these approaches are aimed at acquiring and implementing the best new ideas and technologies as quickly as possible. Both qualitative and quantitative data are organized and prioritized so that product feature alternatives can be assessed by cross-functional teams who evaluate their benefits and costs. The information developed in a VOC process provides the key input for setting the detailed design specifications using a process such as quality function deployment.

voice of the customer (VOC) Research efforts that gather detailed data describing customers' wishes, needs, likes, and dislikes regarding specific product features and functionalities.

beta testing An approach in which customers use product prototype versions and provide feedback to developers.

Quality Function Deployment

Quality function deployment (QFD) is widely regarded as a useful tool for translating ordinary language used to describe customer needs into engineering language used to set product and process design parameters. Using QFD, a cross-functional team identifies all of the major customer requirements for a given product (possibly through a VOC effort) and evaluates how well the current product and process designs meet or exceed those requirements. A diagram know as the customer requirements planning matrix, also known as the House of Quality, guides the process.

QFD has proved useful in both manufacturing and service firms. For example, Ritz-Carlton Hotels coupled QFD with process analysis to improve its housekeeping operations. It cut the average time to clean a room in half, reduced interruptions by one-third, and improved productivity by 14 rooms per worker. Law offices, hospitals, and even not-for-profit institutions such as higher education have also benefited from QFD.

quality function deployment (QFD) A method for translating ordinary language used to describe customer needs into engineering language used to set product and process design parameters.

customer requirements planning matrix A template that guides identification and translation of customer requirements into product features.

House of Quality A template that guides identification and translation of customer requirements into product features.

EXAMPLE 4-1

Quality Function Deployment

We can use a hotel example (shown in Figure 4-6) to understand how a customer requirements planning matrix (House of Quality) is constructed:

Customer desired traits. The information filling the rows of the matrix under "Customer Desired Traits" defines what the hotel needs to do well in order to satisfy customers. This information is usually developed from research including surveys, focus groups, and other efforts to acquire the voice of the customer. In our example, customers have communicated that they want their valuables to be secure (the trait receiving the highest importance rating), they don't like to wait for their rooms, they want consistent service, and so on. Note that management has also added "Reduce housekeeping cost/labor" as a desired trait. While customers might not identify this trait directly, management realizes that it is an important goal that interacts with the other traits.

Assessment of competition. Data on the right-hand side of the matrix provide a comparison of how well the hotel is doing on each customer desired trait, relative to its competitors. This information might come from the hotel's own survey combined with intelligence gathering efforts—hotel employees might even visit competitors' facilities to gather such intelligence. These data give an indication of the traits in which the hotel has an advantage, and where it needs to improve. The hotel appears to do quite well in having rooms ready when customers arrive. It needs to improve the consistency of service, however.

Technical features and target values. The top and bottom columns of the matrix define the "hows" related to delivering the customer desired traits. In the design of a tangible product, these columns would contain engineering characteristics that are related to the delivery of various product functions. For example, the number of gears on a bike (a technical feature) determines how easy the bike is to pedal (a customer desired trait). In the hotel example, the technical features are service process characteristics that define how housekeeping services might be delivered and controlled. The data at the bottom of the matrix give target performance ranges for each service technical feature. For example, the target time to complete room cleaning is less than 20 minutes.

Interrelationships. The symbols in the remainder of the matrix define relationships. First, the symbols in the body of the matrix show how customer traits are related to technical features. For each desired trait, these relationships indicate the specific, directly observable measures of technical features that are good indicators of customer satisfaction. For example, room cycle time is at least weakly related to five of the customer desired traits. The second set of symbols, found in the "roof" of the matrix, shows the relationships among the various technical features. These data help identify trade-offs among various dimensions of performance. For example, there appears to be a strong trade-off making it difficult to maintain high housekeeping productivity while maintaining a low defect rate. Establishing all of the interrelationships shown in the matrix is the heart of the product/process design activity.

Process plans and instructions. The next step for operations managers would be to translate the performance targets into process specifications. For example, hotel operations managers would use the 20-minute room cleaning target and quality requirements to develop procedures defining the cleaning and inspection steps, cleaning tools to be used, employee training programs, and so on.

In order to complete a House of Quality analysis, marketing, engineering, and operational personnel typically must have many discussions regarding the interpretations of customer inputs and the pros and cons of various technical options for meeting customer desired traits. These discussions ultimately produce better product design, as they facilitate a more thorough design analysis, with richer cross-functional interactions.

FIGURE 4-6 House of Quality for Housekeeping Services

Failure Modes and Effects Analysis

One of the important goals of innovation is to identify and eliminate potential quality problems early during design. These problems can affect both product performance and process reliability; that is, the ability to consistently produce a good or deliver a service that conforms to design specifications. **Failure modes and effects analysis (FMEA)** is a procedure for identifying and correcting potential quality problems inherent to product or process designs. FMEA is team-based; it brings together representatives from such groups as engineering, manufacturing, purchasing, quality, research and development, and field service. The FMEA team is tasked with answering two basic questions:

failure modes and effects analysis (FMEA) A procedure for identifying and correcting potential quality problems inherent to product or process designs.

- How can this product design (or process design) fail to do what it is supposed to do?
- What should we do to prevent these potential failures?

Answering these questions involves five major steps from problem identification to resolution:

1. *Determine what portions of the product or the process are to be analyzed.*
2. *Identify types of potential failures, modes for each failure type, and causes and effects of each failure mode.* For example, a failure for a coffeemaker could be that

the coffee is the wrong temperature. This failure has two modes: the coffee could be too hot or too cold. Each of these failure modes has potentially different causes and different effects on customer satisfaction.

3. *Prioritize the failure modes.* For each failure mode, rate the frequency or probability of its occurrence, the severity of its effects, and the inability to detect the problem early. Then prioritize failure mode causes and identify the critical ones requiring action. To simplify the process of prioritizing, a **risk priority number (RPN)** is calculated as:

$$\text{RPN} = \text{Occurrence Rating} \times \text{Severity Rating} \times \text{Undetectability Rating}$$

risk priority number (RPN) A rating used in FMEA to indicate the combined probability, severity, and undetectability of a failure mode.

4. *Create plans to deal with each critical failure mode.* The consequences of a failure mode can be alleviated by eliminating it, reducing its severity, reducing its occurrence, and/or increasing its detection in advance.

5. *Implement the plans, measure their impact, and repeat the analysis as needed.* Like other design tools, FMEA is very much an iterative procedure. As critical failure modes are eliminated or reduced, other failure modes may be targeted for action. This process continues until the design is viewed as being sufficiently reliable.

relationships

EXAMPLE 4-2

FMEA

In examining a proposed design for a new coffeemaker, the heating element (that part of the coffeemaker that keeps the coffee warm and at a constant temperature) is a potential area of concern. After studying the problem, a cross-functional team developed the FMEA found in Table 4-2. The table indicates two possible failures pertaining to the heating element. Of these, the more serious is the problem of a malfunctioning regulator causing the coffee to be too hot. Its high severity and undetectability gave it the highest RPN. Having burned hands or a burned mouth is a much greater consequence than having to throw away a pot of coffee because it is too cold. The last column in Table 4-2 shows the team's recommended actions. The goal here is to find the most cost-effective way to minimize the overall risk (RPN) by lowering either the severity, occurrence, or undetectability of the failure mode. The team decided to take no action regarding the potential for a broken heating element. They believed that the consequences of this cause of failure were small enough to be acceptable, given the cost of dealing with this problem.

TABLE 4-2   FMEA for Coffee Heating Element

Name	Function	Failure Mode	Effect	Cause	Severity (S)	Occurrence (O)	Undetect-ability (U)	RPN = S × O × U	Recommen-dation
Heating Element	Keep coffee at constant temperature	Coffee cold	Coffee thrown out	Broken connection	3	6	6	108	Reinforce connection guides for protection
				Broken heating element	3	4	3	36	No action
		Coffee too hot	Mouth or hands burned	Malfunc-tioning regulator	8	4	8	256	Swap current regulator for new, redesigned one provided by supplier

In addition to improvements to product reliability and safety, FMEA has been found to reduce development costs and time, provide insights for product testing and maintenance, and serve as a means for tracking and communicating design activities throughout the organization.

Value Engineering/Value Analysis

Another process for developing improvements in product and process designs is known as **value engineering/value analysis**. In a typical value engineering project suppliers meet with internal cross-functional teams, bringing together critical information about a new product concept, its function, its marketing appeal, and its production methods. Value analysis uses the same approach for existing products, including the following steps:

> **value engineering/value analysis**
> A method to improve the benefits and costs of a product through a detailed examination of its function.

1. *Identify the functional purposes of a product or component.* Describe what the product does, not what it is. Describe each function using a two-word phrase (one verb and one noun). For example, a function of a pencil is to "make marks."
2. *Separate the various functions into two categories, those that make the product work, and those that make it sell.* For example, a drill motor's housing protects the user from the motor and gears; this helps to make it work. A housing with an especially comfortable handle makes the drill easier to use; this helps to sell the product.
3. *Estimate the value (benefits and costs) of each function.* Rate each function (high, medium, low) according to a typical customer's assessment of the importance of the function and the cost of providing that function.
4. *Compare the importance of each function with its cost.* Asking certain questions can improve the analysis; questions such as: Can the function be eliminated entirely? Can the function be provided in some other way? Can the product be simplified or standardized? What changes will reduce costs or speed up production?
5. *Implement changes to the product design that maximize the value of the product.* Verify the team's conclusions by gathering information from customers and suppliers, whoever has a stake in the success of the product. Then make the changes and measure the results.

A value analysis of electric drill motors prompted a redesign of the housing, replacing cast steel housings with plastic ones. While plastic proved less durable than steel, it was cheaper and faster to make. A plastic housing also made the drill motor lighter and more comfortable to hold, reducing user fatigue. Also, plastic does not conduct electricity, so it reduced the safety risk of electrical shock as compared to steel housings and eliminated the need for grounding.

Design for Supply Chain Operations

The foregoing approaches focus on the value and performance quality of goods and service designs. Other product design improvement programs focus squarely on attributes that affect the efficiency or effectiveness of supply chain operational processes. Each of the following "design for" methods focuses on a specific area of supply chain management. By matching the design of products to the operational capabilities that exist throughout the supply chain, products can be made and delivered faster, cheaper, and with better quality.

Design for Manufacture

Design for manufacture (DFM) is an umbrella term that describes any of a host of methods and tools that focus design activities on improving product **producibility**. Producibility is a measure of the speed, ease, cost efficiency, and reliability with which a product can be produced. DFM efforts make use of many tactics for communicating and highlighting the needs and limitations that process capabilities impose on the product design. One tactic is to publish design rules such as:

> **design for manufacture (DFM)**
> An umbrella term that describes methods and tools that focus design activities on improving the ease with which products can be produced.
>
> **producibility** A measure of the speed, ease, cost efficiency, and reliability with which a product can be produced.

- Reduce the total number of unique parts in the product.
- Reduce the number of fasteners used.

- Eliminate the need for specialized tools.
- Design all assembly tasks to come from one direction.

While DFM often focuses on aspects of product fabrication, this type of analysis can address many processes throughout the supply chain such as:

design for assembly Focus on minimizing the number of parts in a product and easing the assembly processes.

- **Design for assembly**—designers focus on minimizing the number of parts in a product and on easing assembly processes.

design for product serviceability Focus on easing product disassembly and reusing product components.

- **Design for product serviceability**—designers focus on easing product disassembly and maintenance, and on the reuse of product components. For example, cars, computers, and other equipment usually have modules that can be easily swapped out and recycled.

Design for Six Sigma Focus on systematically evaluating the consistency with which a good or service can be produced or delivered given the capabilities of the processes used.

- **Design for Six Sigma**[5]—designers systematically evaluate the consistency with which a good or service can be produced or delivered given the capabilities of the processes used.

robust design Focus on designing products that can be made consistently even with varying inputs and operating conditions.

- **Robust design**—designers use experiments and simulation models to design products that can be produced consistently, even when production processes vary greatly. For example, designers of corn flakes cereal develop a recipe that yields the same consistency of product, regardless of the source of the corn, the humidity or temperature in the production plant, and so on.

DFM involves design review meetings between product engineers and manufacturing workers. Meetings in early phases of design and development typically focus on product architectural decisions such as the number of product variants envisioned, the potential for reusing existing or standardized parts across different products, and the role of modularity in the product design. As the product design becomes more detailed and prototypes become available, design review meetings focus more on specific component and feature issues such as dimensional tolerances, use of fasteners or other means of assembly, and part geometry issues (e.g., shape and symmetry).

DFM efforts have been credited with improving the quality of products while saving firms thousands or even millions of dollars. For example, Mattel Toys saved over $40 million in production costs in a single year due to the implementation of DFM (see the Get Real box describing the impact of DFM on a Mattel product).

Components Standardization

components standardization Reusing part designs across multiple products in order to reduce development and production costs.

A way to reduce development and production costs and to increase product quality is to standardize the parts and components used across various product designs in a product family. Instead of designing a new part for each product, designers reuse parts from existing products. **Components standardization** produces several advantages. Fewer new designs must be created, reducing development cost and time. Fewer unique parts in an operations system also simplifies inventory management because there are fewer parts to order, warehouse, and control. This produces savings in overhead, personnel, and storage space. With fewer parts, purchasing leverage can be increased because the volume per part is increased, lowering prices per unit (through quantity discounts). Supply management is also made less complex because fewer parts must be ordered.

Environmental management is simplified as well. Until recently, for example, Chrysler used over 40 different plastic films for protecting, wrapping, and storing items. This meant that the company had to have a different set of environmental procedures for each plastic film, and frequent problems were encountered when it came time to separate the films for recycling. Chrysler reduced these 40 films to one standard film, which enabled the

sustainability

---

[5]Design for Six Sigma is described in Chapter 6, "Managing Quality."

GET REAL

Mattel's Serious Approach to DFM for Toys

The creator of Barbie dolls and other children's toys should be in a fun business. In reality, it's a cutthroat, mature business that requires a cost minimization strategy to remain competitive. Hence, Mattel manufactures in many low-labor-cost countries.

Because there are limits to the benefits of cheap labor, Mattel created a "Design for Competitive Advantage" program to streamline costs. It started off right by setting up a training program to teach DFM principles to its engineers. To begin, Mattel created a computerized data bank to help identify similar or redundant parts. This system also helped to establish standardized part tolerances. The result? Lower costs and a shorter product design cycle.

To illustrate its new approach, Mattel selected Color Spin, an existing product that helps a toddler develop "visual awareness and action–reaction motor skills." The product retails for about $13 and is designed for babies six months and older. The existing product design called for 55 parts to be made, purchased, and assembled. The schematic of the parts and their location in the final product is shown below. After applying simple DFM principles,

the Mattel team reduced the number of parts by 50 percent while increasing quality and performance. The improved product also appears below. How did they do it? Mostly by redesigning parts to snap together. In other cases, plastic welding replaced fasteners. An in-house software system analyzed the cost effectiveness of design alternatives.

Mattel was able to shave 38 percent from the cost of Color Spin—an annual savings of $700,000. When asked what advice they would give to others, team members responded:

- Make sure it's a team effort, with designers aboard as allies.
- Choose a leader who has experience on both sides, design and manufacturing.
- Get support from as high up in the company as possible.
- Assure recognition for DFM achievements and stimulate continued interest.
- Maintain an understanding of what the customer wants, and exceed those expectations.

Mattel's Color Spin Toy

Color Spin Before DFM
55 Parts

Color Spin After DFM
27 Parts

The DFM team reduced the Color Spin's parts count by 49 percent, while increasing the toy's quality and performance. Creative plastic molding, ultrasonic welding, and combining moving parts aided the effort.

Source: D. Gardner, "DFM Adds Sparkle to Toy Line," *Design News*, July 7, 1991, pp. 62–64. Used by permission.

PowerShot: SX200, ELPH, A-Series, E-Series (in various colors)

EOS: XTI, EOS 50D, Rebel XT (silver), Rebel XSI

Four platforms for Canon cameras. Each row represents a separate platform.
© Roberts Publishing Services

modular product design Using combinations of components with standardized product interfaces to create different product variations.

company to reduce the number of suppliers from eight to two. Other benefits included the elimination of floor space needed for storing and sorting the various plastics, a reduction in environmental management procedures, the elimination of charges made by recyclers who had to re-sort incorrectly sorted plastic films, and a reduction in the purchase price.

Modular Product Designs

For some products, customers demand a wide array of features. Take digital cameras, for example. A company like Canon designs cameras for many different customer groups, each of which wants a different combination of camera features. Some customers want a simple "point and shoot" camera while others want advanced features. Rather than design an entirely new product variant for each customer group, it is much more efficient for a company like Canon to design a few basic product platforms and then design modules that can be added or subtracted from those platforms to create different combinations of product features.

This approach, designing products as combinations of standardized components and processes, is known as modular product design. Canon can switch out different lens assemblies and digital logic control systems in a common camera platform (the camera body) to produce many different product variants with various levels of functionality and cost. This modular approach is used in hundreds of different products, both goods and services. For example, a company that provides guided tours might design basic packages that can be supplemented with special events to tailor the experiences to the desires of particular tour groups. By using modular product designs, operations managers can create all kinds of efficiencies in supply chain processes, while at the same time satisfying a wide variety of customer needs.

Design for logistics

design for logistics Focus on minimizing packaging, handling, and shipping costs for products.

Design for logistics focuses on minimizing the packaging, handling, and shipping costs for products. Logistical operations managers, both internal and from supply partners, work with designers to reduce product size and weight, as both factors tend to drive logistics costs. In addition, by redesigning the product's packaging orientation, managers can sometimes increase the amount of product that can be stored in a given facility or transportation vehicle. For example, the packaging for recent versions of the iPhone is half the size that it was for the original iPhone shipped in 2007. Thus, almost twice as many product boxes fit on each shipping pallet. Yet another typical analysis addresses the taxes and duties associated with procurement, storage, and distribution alternatives for a product. For example, if a product is designed to be more modular, then this might create more options for the sourcing and assembly of its components. By sourcing from low-tax regions, and by importing components rather than finished assemblies, import taxes and duties might be decreased. Finally, design for *reverse-logistics* is becoming more and more important. The concern here is to design products so that they can be easily returned and refurbished or recycled after use. For example, makers of ink cartridges for printers often include return envelopes in product boxes, and they design the cartridges to be easily cleaned and refilled.

Design for Environment

design for environment Focus on minimizing the detrimental environmental impacts of product and process designs across all stages of a product's life.

Design for environment seeks to minimize the detrimental environmental impacts of product and process designs across all stages of a product's life. Typical design-for-environment analyses evaluate product material and packaging choices to minimize the use of energy and hazardous materials and maximize the potential for product reuse and recycling. Analyzing the carbon dioxide impact of products is of special and growing importance as

GET REAL

TI Builds a Green Wafer Factory

While other semiconductor manufacturing companies are moving their factories to China and Taiwan, Texas Instruments (TI) recently built a completely new silicon wafer manufacturing plant near its headquarters in Richardson, Texas. Its goal was to build a plant for $180 million less than the cost of its most recent plant built seven years earlier and six miles away. Even more stunning was TI's aggressive goal to lower the operating costs of the plant while making it as energy efficient and environmentally friendly as possible. A typical wafer fabrication plant uses the same energy as 10,000 homes.

Through intense cross-functional efforts with Rocky Mountain Institute, its design partner, TI achieved its goals, ultimately spending 30 percent less capital on plant construction . . . and lowering projected production costs more than $4 million per year—due to a 20 percent energy reduction, 35 percent water-use reduction, and 50 percent emissions reduction. TI started with a radical innovation in architectural design. Conventional wafer factories have at least three floors because of the need to surround the manufacturing process with cooling and other support systems. The design team developed a plan with only two floors, saving all the associated infrastructure and energy costs. Numerous other innovations included:

- A reduction in the number of elbows in water pipes and air ducts, thus reducing friction and enabling the use of smaller pumps.
- Use of passive solar technologies, including reflective concrete and a plastic roof covering that reflects 85 percent of the sun's radiation.
- Design of windows and reflection systems to maximize natural lighting.
- Use of native plants for landscaping and recycled water for irrigation and cooling.
- Recycling of almost 90 percent of construction waste.

Operations managers sometimes believe that it costs more to build and operate green (environmentally friendly) processes, but TI showed that this isn't necessarily so. Well-designed processes can be both *green* and *lean*.

Silicon wafer.
© Flirt/Alamy Stock Photo

---

more and more countries impose pollution taxes or caps on a company's outputs of carbon dioxide and other greenhouse gases. The Get Real box below tells how Texas Instruments redesigned a manufacturing plant to minimize its environmental impacts.

sustainability

ENABLING TECHNOLOGIES FOR PRODUCT/ PROCESS INNOVATION

Information technology and computerization have greatly enhanced innovation processes by speeding up design activities, improving computational power, and enhancing communications among design partners. Here we very briefly describe some of the more important technological developments that are improving the speed and quality of design and development activities.

Computer-aided design (CAD) systems automate many aspects of the design process, especially the development of drawings and technical specifications. Design rules (DFM rules, for example) and best-practices can be embedded into CAD systems. Data captured in these systems can be accessed by persons located around the world for use in product design, process planning, and computer-aided manufacturing.

computer-aided design (CAD)
Systems that automate the development of drawings and technical specifications.

3-D CAD model of the BMW 645i.
© Joe Polimeni/EPA/Newscom

© Fabrizio Bensch/Reuters/Corbis

computer-aided engineering (CAE) Systems that create and analyze three-dimensional product models, reducing the need to build physical prototypes.

3D printing Also called additive manufacturing, this process makes products by putting down successive layers of thin material such as plastic, metal, ceramics, or food.

group technology An approach to work layout and scheduling that gathers in one location all of the equipment and work skills necessary to complete production of a family of similar products.

product life cycle management (PLM) A software-facilitated process used to capture and share all the information needed to define products throughout their life.

Computer-aided engineering (CAE) tools are frequently linked to CAD systems in ways that reinforce good design practices. These sophisticated systems create and analyze three-dimensional models of parts and assemblies, reducing the need to build expensive and time-consuming physical prototypes. For example, linked CAD/CAE systems can automatically analyze assembly designs to identify areas of potential interference between parts. Further, many CAD systems embed process information and design rules directly into the design software so that it may be linked to certain design features. For example, when a designer draws a hole, she can then select a pull-down window of information providing a list of processes that could create the hole, typical dimensional tolerances, defect rates associated with each process, and any other design rules related to the feature.

Some companies have developed CAE systems that aid the evaluation of design choices using virtual prototypes of products. These systems can analyze both product and process functionalities, including physical stresses and thermal patterns, mechanical assembly steps, printed circuit board design, and so on. The technology for developing virtual prototypes is still emerging, but as it is refined it is expected to play a major role in design and development.

Even with the growth of virtual prototyping, product designers usually need physical prototypes for evaluation and demonstration purposes and for display to potential customers. **3D printing** (also know as *additive manufacturing*) has emerged as technology that makes the production of physical prototypes much faster and less expensive. Essentially, 3D printers are machines that add layers of material (e.g., plastics, metal) to a platform in order to build up a component or assembly according to the designs embedded in CAD software. This process has become very precise and can produce product prototypes without the need for expensive production equipment.

In large organizations, designers often waste time and resources by unknowingly re-creating existing designs. CAD systems can be linked with product databases that contain information on preferred components, existing designs from other products, and suppliers of purchased items. Classification and coding systems enable designers to easily search design databases for existing designs that meet their current needs. Similarly, databases that list preferred components and vendors can speed up a designer's search for suitable parts. These databases frequently make use of **group technology**, a coding system that allows designers and manufacturing planners to identify "families" of parts that have similar design or processing characteristics. These approaches reduce design time and reap enormous benefits in manufacturing because fewer unique parts must be fabricated and inventoried, less special tooling is needed, production scheduling is simplified, and less disruption is experienced.

Product life cycle management (PLM) is a process, facilitated by computer software and databases, used to capture and share all the information needed to define products throughout their life. PLM is used during all phases of development, product launch, production, and disposal. By capturing development information, development of next generation and derivative products that reuse much of the design of current or former products can be accomplished much faster. The benefits include increased collaboration, because all groups involved in design and development can access and share the same information. Learning within the organization is facilitated since the information is captured in the organization rather than staying with an individual.

CHAPTER SUMMARY

New product/process innovation activities define the products and markets that a firm will pursue. Operations managers in the supply chain play critical roles in bringing product and process innovations to reality. They also help their firms find competitive advantages by developing codevelopment partnerships, fast time-to-market capabilities, high development efficiency, and design creativity. The following points offer important considerations and tools for managing innovation projects:

1. Innovative firms gain advantages over their competitors by virtue of their innovation competencies in areas including idea and opportunity development, project portfolio planning, project management, and postproject learning.

2. More and more, innovation is a supply chain activity in which a firm involves its customers, key suppliers, and other partners. This process of open innovation and codevelopment leads to higher quality products developed faster and more efficiently.

3. A typical innovation project has stages of development including concept development, product and process planning, detailed design and development, product and market testing, commercialization, and market introduction.

4. Innovation project stages can be executed sequentially or concurrently, using an approach called concurrent engineering, depending upon the requirements of the particular project.

5. A key challenge in managing an innovation project is the integration of the many interrelated product/process design issues. A number of methods and tools are useful for managers who want to encourage teamwork and cross-functional communication among project workers. These methods include voice of the customer, early supplier involvement, quality function deployment, failure modes and effects analysis, value analysis, design for manufacture, components standardization, and modular design.

KEY TERMS

beta testing   125

components standardization   130

computer-aided design (CAD)   133

computer-aided engineering (CAE)   134

concurrent engineering   123

crowdsourcing   118

customer requirements planning matrix   125

design for assembly   130

design for environment   132

design for logistics   132

design for manufacture (DFM)   129

design for product serviceability   130

design for Six Sigma   130

early supplier involvement (ESI)   120

failure modes and effects analysis (FMEA)   127

group technology   134

House of Quality   125

innovation portfolio planning   119

modular product design   132

new process design and development projects   114

new product design and development projects   114

open innovation   117

producibility   129

DISCUSSION QUESTIONS

1. Describe a situation where the functional/sequential approach to product development might be more appropriate than the integrated/concurrent engineering approach.

2. Operations personnel tend to favor product component standardization while design and marketing personnel tend to resist it. Why is this true? What are the potential disadvantages to standardization?

3. Why are discipline and flexibility both needed in new product/process innovation? Are these two capabilities in conflict with each other?

4. What major differences would you expect to find in the management approaches used for breakthrough innovation projects versus those used for derivative or enhancement projects?

5. Discuss the pros and cons of open innovation.

6. Under what circumstances might concurrent engineering (overlapping the stages of design and development) be a bad idea?

7. Discuss the roles that personnel from warranty/field service and the manufacturing shop floor might play when conducting a FMEA.

8. In which stages of a new product design and development project are supply chain operations managers most likely to have the greatest impact? Why?

PROBLEMS

1. Refer back to the QFD for housekeeping services shown in Figure 4-6.
   a. What seem to be the biggest opportunities for improvement, relative to competitors' levels of performance?
   b. Which technical feature is most strongly related to the goal of protecting the safety and security of guests' possessions?
   c. Why would room cycle time and defect rate be negatively correlated?
   d. Which technical feature has the strongest associations with the largest number of guest requirements?

2. Given the FMEA data provided in the table below:
   a. What is the RPN for each failure cause?
   b. Which failure cause would be of least concern?
   c. Which failure cause would be of greatest concern?
   d. For the failure of greatest concern, would your recommended action be aimed at reducing failure severity, occurrence, or undetectability? On what other information would your answer depend?

Failure Cause	Severity	Occurrence	Undetectability
M	5	2	1
N	3	4	9
X	2	2	3
Y	7	3	2
Z	9	1	5

3. Identify three or four important failure modes for a cellular phone.

4. Conduct a FMEA for a simple service or tangible product with which you are familiar. Identify a few failure modes, estimate the RPNs, and recommend possible improvements.

5. Complete a value analysis for the following products:
   a. Paper clip
   b. Textbook

6. Make a list of customer desired traits for a pencil.

7. Document the steps that someone using the House of Quality procedure might follow in developing:
   a. A new mountain bicycle.
   b. An introductory operations management course.
   c. A new candy bar.

8. Patients at an emergency department located in a large, urban hospital frequently experience long wait times before they actually see a physician. The hospital has decided to use FMEA to determine an action plan for addressing the problem, defining a "failure" as a wait time of 30 minutes or longer. A group study has produced the following data:

Cause	Severity	Occurrence	Undetectability
Peak demand exceeds staff capacity	5	5	8
Patient fails to register correctly	5	2	1
Patient is placed behind more urgent cases	5	3	4

   a. Which failure mode has the largest RPN?
   b. Provide a suggestion on how to lower the probability of occurrence or impact for each of the three failure modes (causes).

CASE

The ALPHA Timer Development Project (A)

Roger Terry hurried down the hallway toward the planning meeting for the ALPHA timer product development project. Terry had served as project manager for the initial stage of the ALPHA single-block product development, and he was now preparing to start the follow-on development activities.

The ALPHA timer development project was a major effort for Doorley Controls, Inc., to develop a new platform design for its washing machine timer control mechanism. The project was started with a conscious strategy to gain market position with Doorley's key customers: Whirlpool, Maytag, and Frigidaire. The idea was to create a new core product design to increase sales to Whirlpool. Doorley planned to replace multiple existing timers with a lower cost, single product platform with enhancements. While existing timers were made with numerous plastic and metal parts requiring a lot of hand assembly, the ALPHA would be made mostly of molded plastic parts, assembled by automation. The product concept also included a unique feature called *quiet cycle-select,* which allowed the user to index the control shaft quietly. The idea for it came out of Doorley's internal quality function deployment (QFD) analysis. The results of the ALPHA QFD analysis are shown below.

Questions

1. What features of the timer design appear to offer Doorley the strongest advantages over its competitors' products? What features are apparent weaknesses?

2. Which manufacturing methods are most strongly related to the goal of producing a flexible drive system? Do any of these methods conflict with each other?

3. Which design parameter has the strongest dependence on any of the manufacturing methods?

4. What evidence is there that the ALPHA team has used a DFM approach?

CASE

The ALPHA Timer Development Project (B)

The ALPHA single-block timer development project had not gone exactly as planned. The product development time-to-market was 48 months instead of the planned 30 months, and capital expenditures for the project were at least 30 percent over budget. On the other hand, quality levels for the timer were much better than before, and assembly labor costs were reduced by 25 percent.

Near the end of the first year of the project, difficulties began to arise. Changes in the appliance industry occurred as governmental pressures for more energy-efficient washers favored horizontal-axis machines, which required more complex timing devices. A marketing manager complained, "Even if we would have gone to our customers and asked them what they wanted in a new timer, I doubt that they could have told us at that time." It also soon became clear that a more complex, double-block version of the timer would be needed for top-of-the-line washers. This surprised the project team. As a team member explained, "We expected that customers would use more electronics or hybrids in the top-of-the-line appliances. We didn't really realize at the time that our customers still considered mechanical timers to be very important for the top end of the line. The *quiet cycle-select* was a very nice feature that they wanted to have in the top of the line, and if we couldn't provide that feature in double-block designs, they didn't want to use it anywhere."

An engineer from the program recalled other problems in the development process: "We were testing a new rigid material for the timer housing, which Whirlpool had approved. However, our initial testing showed that it could not be molded at the wall thickness that our supplier told us we could produce. We lost several months in development as a result. The alternative material we finally selected required some major production tool changes that also took more time. Manufacturability problems with the combsets in the timer also caused delays, requiring another four-month redesign."

Finally, the first timer samples were delivered to Whirlpool for evaluation. They were rejected. An engineer explained, "We knew all along that Whirlpool was concerned about the damaging effects of SPRAY'n WASH on some plastics. We did SPRAY'n WASH testing here and had all our plastic suppliers do SPRAY'n WASH testing. Unfortunately, we tested the parts using the manual pump version of SPRAY'n WASH, not the aerosol version, which is the problem product. We lost a good six months in development figuring out a new material to use."

Project manager Roger Terry had mixed feelings as he walked back to his office after the double-block planning meeting had ended. The meeting had gone well, and it seemed that everyone was enthusiastic about the program. Terry knew that the success of the new double-block platform project depended on his ability to analyze the single-block experience and apply the lessons they had learned.

Questions

1. Assess the outcomes of the ALPHA project. Was the project a success?

2. Were the problems encountered in the development project typical, or could they have been avoided?

CASE

The ALPHA Timer Development Project (C)

As he stopped to refill his coffee mug, Roger Terry began to recall some of the comments he had heard from various members of the single-block product development team (see the comments reproduced below).

The following comments were gathered from informal conversations with ALPHA program team members after the project's completion:

"Very large portions of time were lost because of having to go back and reinvent the wheel and make ALPHA something it was never proposed to be."

"We struggled with the project because of our relationship with Whirlpool. They wanted exclusivity. We were trying to maintain secrecy, working only with them, when we really needed the whole market to speak out. We don't have any real marketing department, we have a sales department that takes care of the ongoing business."

"Part of the problem is that you end up with two masters here. You've got the engineering guy who is always worried about the material content and uniqueness of design, and you've got an operations guy who's only worried about the automation and the labor content. The structure and incentives in the organization sometimes pit functions against one another."

"The design for manufacture efforts in the beginning included quality and tooling people from operations at headquarters, but plant manufacturing people only first heard of the ALPHA concept after parts had been designed and tooling orders were about to be released."

"I don't know what we could have done to try harder—I mean, we made people available, and tried to schedule sessions with all the appropriate functional areas and people who where in the know, and participate and critique and give us their feedback. Even though we made all those efforts to get input, as time goes on and people change, and the complexity of it unfolds, and you've got people at Whirlpool saying we didn't do our homework—we did not ask them what they wanted. But we came and asked and asked and asked!"

"There is a culture within the company of limited information sharing. When things went wrong, instead of dealing with facts, things were rearranged to make it seem a little bit better for whatever reason. A lot of doubt was generated within the company and then a lot of doubt was generated in 'customer-land.' It just started building—this great big wall of doubt. Our customers asked us if we were having design problems, and we said 'No.' They knew better."

"No one person was responsible for the entire project. Operations did their thing, engineering did their thing, but early on no one coordinated things. When push came to shove, when a decision had to be made quickly, then one person needed the authority to get the plant people, operations people, quality people, engineering people, and sales people together to decide once and for all what to do."

"We really didn't have the kind of input into equipment design and manufacturer choices that we needed to have. The headquarters group always had the final say. Consequently, there are several changes that we will make to get further cost reductions and quality improvements in the next few years that we could have had right off the bat."

Questions

1. How would you describe the team members' morale at this point? What are their primary concerns?

2. Given the team members' comments, what advice would you give Roger Terry regarding the forthcoming double-block timer development effort?

Cargille, B., and C. Fry. "Design for Supply Chain: Spreading the Word Across HP." *Supply Chain Management Review,* July/August 2006, pp. 34–41.

Chesbrough, H. W. *Open Innovation: The New Imperative for Creating and Profiting from Technology.* Boston: Harvard Business School Press, 2003.

Cooper, R. G., and E. J. Kleinschmidt. "Stage-Gate Systems for New Product Success." *Marketing Management* 1, no. 4 (1993), pp. 20–29.

Dodgson, M.; D. Gann; and A. Salter. "The Role of Technology in the Shift Towards Open Innovation: The Case of Procter & Gamble." *R&D Management* 36, no. 3 (June 2006), pp. 333–46.

Huston, L., and N. Sakkab. "Connect and Develop." *Harvard Business Review* 84, no. 3 (March 2006), pp. 58–66.

Petersen, K. J.; R. B. Handfield; and G. L. Ragatz. "Supplier Integration into New Product Development: Coordinating Product, Process, and Supply Chain Design." *Journal of Operations Management* 23, no. 3/4 (April 2005), pp. 371–88.

Swink, M. "Building Collaborative Innovation Capability." *Research-Technology Management,* March–April 2006, pp. 37–47.

Swink, M. "Product Development—Faster, On Time." *Research-Technology Management,* July–August 2002, pp. 50–58.

Swink, M., and V. Mabert. "Product Development Partnerships: Balancing Manufacturers' and Suppliers' Needs." *Business Horizons* 43, no. 3 (May–June 2000), pp. 59–68.

Ulrich, K. T., and S. D. Eppinger. *Product Design and Development.* 2nd ed. New York: McGraw-Hill, 2000.

Wheelwright, S. C., and K. B. Clark. *Revolutionizing New Product Development.* New York: Free Press, 1992.

Product Development Management Association
www.pdma.org

Quality Function Deployment Institute
www.qfdi.org

5 Manufacturing and Service Process Structures

LEARNING OBJECTIVES

After studying this chapter, you should be able to:

LO5-1 Compare and contrast the seven process structures: project, job shop, batch, repetitive process, continuous process, mass customization, and cellular manufacturing.

LO5-2 Compare and contrast the goals and challenges associated with a service factory, a mass service, a service shop, and a professional service.

LO5-3 Describe how each of the operations layouts—fixed-position, functional, product, and cellular—is designed to meet the demands placed upon it.

LO5-4 Analyze a product layout using line balancing.

LO5-5 Explain how technology is used in the supply chain and the benefits and drawbacks of process automation.

Process Design and
Process Technologies
Are the Key to Success
for Invisalign.®

Process design and new process technologies are enabling companies to make customized products quickly and cost effectively, sometimes dramatically changing an industry. One example of how process design created radical change is in the field of orthodontics. If you had metal bracket and wire braces you may recall frequent trips to the orthodontist for wire tightening, giving up foods such as popcorn and apples, and feeling self-conscious when smiling.

This all changed when Align Technology, Inc., developed and introduced the Invisalign® system. This system uses a series of factory-produced clear plastic, removable "aligners" that are custom designed for each patient's needs. The Invisalign® system, made possible by advances in information technology and manufacturing technologies such as 3D printing and robotics, may make metal braces a thing of the past.

The Invisalign® process begins when the dentist takes a digital scan of the patient's teeth. The scan is then electronically transmitted to Align Technology's technicians who use proprietary software to create an individualized treatment plan. After the dentist approves the plan, the digital scans are used to "3D print" molds that are used to form the correct shapes for the plastic aligners. Up to 80,000 custom designed aligners are made per day using a highly automated assembly line. Robots complete tasks with precision and accuracy. Radio frequency identification (RFID) tracking ensures that each patient receives the correct aligners. Even the packaging process is totally automated. The design of each step from the dentist's office through manufacturing guarantees that each patient receives a high quality, cost-effective treatment to create a perfect smile.

Whether an operation is manufacturing-oriented, service-oriented, or some combination of the two, the capabilities contained within its supply chain drive its ability to compete on quality, time, cost, or flexibility. This chapter describes some of the key decisions about manufacturing and service structures that determine an organization's operations and supply chain capabilities. For example, the Invisalign® process is designed for high quality, flexibility, and efficiency. This chapter focuses on three process structure decision areas—process selection, operations layout, and technology selection—that are key to achieving these goals.

PROCESS STRUCTURES

Managers must design processes based on *what kind* of work needs to be done. Different process structures provide different capabilities. Process structure determines how inputs, activities, flows, and outputs of a process are organized. Within a supply chain, each organization must select the process structures that are appropriate considering its competitive priorities of quality, timeliness, cost, flexibility, and innovation.

Product-Process Matrix

LO5-1 Compare and contrast the seven process structures: project, job shop, batch, repetitive process, continuous process, mass customization, and cellular manufacturing.

To better link a product's life cycle and marketing decisions with operations capabilities, Hayes and Wheelwright developed the product-process matrix. They observed that processes progress through a life cycle just as products do. Although developed for manufacturing, the product-process matrix also describes many service processes. To achieve high performance, a firm's process structure must be aligned with its competitive priorities and marketing strategies.

The matrix shows five process structures along the diagonal based on output volume and variety: project, job shop, batch, repetitive process, and continuous process (see Figure 5-1). Often within a single company, different process structures are used for different products. An entire supply chain typically has each of these process structures. For example, the glass for a car's windshield is made using a continuous process, seats are made using a batch process, and the car is made using a repetitive process. Let's examine the characteristics of each of the process structures, as summarized in Table 5-1.

product-process matrix
Categorizes processes into structures based on output volume and variety.

FIGURE 5-1 Product-Process Matrix

Source: Adapted from R. Hayes and S. Wheelwright, *Restoring Our Competitive Edge: Competing Through Manufacturing* (New York: John Wiley & Sons, 1984).

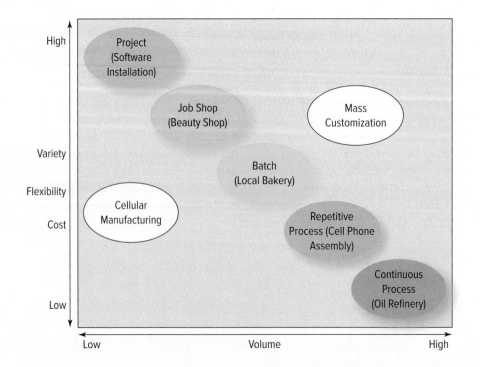

TABLE 5-1   Comparison of Process Types

Process Type	Output Characteristics	Example	Process Characteristics
Project	Unique One of a kind	Custom home Designing a video game	Unique sequencing High complexity Employees and equipment must be flexible Activities are often outsourced to specialists
Job shop	Customized, low volume	Auto repair Beauty salon	High variety of inputs and process flows Job sequencing is challenging High work-in-process inventory Highly skilled, flexible workers General-purpose equipment
Batch	Moderate volume and variety	Bakery Automotive parts Cinema	Dominant flow patterns Some common inputs Setup time can be high Moderately flexible employees and equipment
Repetitive process	Standard products with a range of options	Appliances Automobiles Buffet restaurant	All products follow the same sequence Standard methods and materials are used Low-skilled workers specialize in completing a limited number of activities
Continuous process	Commodities with high volume, little variety	Aluminum cans Laundry detergent Gasoline	Products follow sequence Operations often run 24/7 Line stoppages are very costly Highly specialized equipment Low-skilled operators

Project

A **project** produces a unique, "one of a kind" output. Examples of projects include building a custom home, designing a video game, or planning a wedding. Because the outputs are customized, the customer is highly involved in the design process. The type, sequencing, and complexity of activities change from project to project, so employees and equipment must be flexible. To maximize flexibility, a project manager plans and organizes the project, and activities are often outsourced to suppliers. For example, a wedding planner consults with a bride and groom to determine their preferences for flowers, music, photography, and food. The planner then hires and manages the florist, musicians, photographers, and caterers.

project A one-time or infrequently occurring set of activities that create outputs within prespecified time and cost schedules.

relationships

Job Shop

Automobile dealers' service shops, beauty salons, and department stores use **job shop** process structures, in which outputs are customized and produced in low volumes. Products are typically made to order for a specific customer. Each order or "job" can involve different inputs and a different sequencing of activities and thus have different flows through the process.

job shop A flexible process structure for products that require different inputs and have different flows through the process.

Because of the high variety of inputs and activities, planning and scheduling jobs can be challenging. Products can spend a lot of time waiting to be worked on, resulting in high work-in-process inventory and the need for expediting.

Because of the differences from order to order, the equipment used in a job shop is general purpose, and employees must be skilled and flexible enough to handle a wide range of tasks. Job shops are typically more labor-than capital-intensive. Equipment and employees capable of doing similar activities are typically located together in departments or groups.

Batch Process

batch process A process in which goods or services are produced in groups (batches) and not in a continuous stream.

A local bakery that produces cookies, cakes, and pies uses a batch process structure. Many interior parts for automobiles such as the center console are made using batch processes. Cinemas offer movies in batches. A batch process structure works well when products have moderate levels of volume and variety. A batch structure is a good choice for products that have basic models with several different options.

Although there may be some differences between the flow patterns of each batch, there are dominant flow patterns. Equipment and employee flexibility are important, but the range of flexibility needed is less than with projects or job shops. Cleaning and setup are usually required between each batch, reducing the available capacity and increasing costs. However, some companies have found creative ways to eliminate cleaning and setup. The "mystery" flavor of Spangler Candy Co.'s Dum Dum Pops is created by the mixing of flavors between batches. By eliminating the need to clean the equipment between batches, Spangler effectively reduces costs and increases productive time.

Repetitive Process

repetitive process A process in which discrete products flow through the same sequence of activities.

When there are many customers who want a similar product, such as automobiles, appliances, cell phones, or lunch at a buffet restaurant, a repetitive process structure is used. Some standard options such as a range of colors, features, or menu items are offered, but the range of choices is limited and determined by marketing in advance of the customer's order.

Products made using a repetitive process are typically made to stock. Discrete products flow through the same sequence of activities, and equipment can be specialized to each specific task. Operations managers usually focus on developing standard methods and procedures to continuously improve quality and reduce costs.

Employees who work on the line may not be highly skilled, but they become very efficient in completing one small task. For example, in assembling a car, one employee may install the front seats. Because employees can become bored preforming the same activity repeatedly, job rotation is often used to lessen this problem.

Continuous Process

continuous process A single-flow process used for high-volume nondiscrete, standardized products.

Standard, nondiscrete products such as gasoline, chemicals, laundry detergent, aluminum cans, and cereal are produced using continuous processes, in which products always flow through the same sequence of production steps. Check and mail processing are examples of continuous processes. These made-to-stock products offer customers very little variety and are considered as commodities. Differentiation typically occurs at the end of the production process. For example, laundry detergent comes in different sizes or aluminum cans are printed with different labels.

These processes use highly specialized, automated equipment, which often runs 24 hours a day, seven days a week. Economies of scale reduce unit cost, but it is very costly to stop or change the product because the specialized equipment

activity

student

Companies focusing on different competitive priorities can use different process structures for the same type of product. For example, a company that produces off-the-rack clothing uses a different process structure than a company that produces custom-tailored clothing. Identify a product and competitors who are using different competitive priorities. What position on the product-process matrix would you expect for each?

is expensive. Low-skilled employees monitor equipment while highly skilled engineers and maintenance employees work to minimize downtime and improve processes.

Mass Customization

When the product-process matrix was developed in the 1970s, the processes on the diagonal were thought to lead to the best performance. Today, changes in management practices and technologies have created more options. One way to get the cost advantages of high-volume continuous and repetitive processes while increasing variety is mass customization. The process used for the Invisalign® system is an example of mass customization. In other cases customers "design" products by choosing from a range of options. For example, using the NIKEiD website, customers can choose the style, color, and material for shoes with delivery in four weeks or less.

© Cultura Creative (RF)/Alamy Stock Photo

Process flexibility is essential for mass customization. Different approaches can be used to create flexibility. Mass customization can occur when products are assembled from standard modules that are stored in inventory, reducing the elapsed time from order to delivery. The exact product configuration is postponed until a customer order is received. Companies also use technologies such as 3D printing (or *additive manufacturing*) or flexible manufacturing systems (FMS) to produce a wider range of products in a wider range of volumes than is economically feasible using conventional equipment.

The Internet and other technologies facilitate mass customization. For example, customers can design their own high school or college class rings at Jostens by choosing band style, metal, stone, and carvings. In doing so, each customer can trade off features and price. Mars Inc. used the Internet and new printing technology to mass customize M&Ms and create a whole new market segment, as discussed in Get Real: "Personalized M&Ms".

3D printing has the potential to increase the use of mass customization and radically change what we know about process structures. 3D printing creates objects by laying down successive thin layers of a material to build the product based on 3D modeling software. Objects can be made from a wide range of materials, including plastics, metals, ceramics, and even chocolate. Products such as jet engine parts, hearing aids, and pasta are being made using 3D printing. Advances in technology, especially in the types of materials that can be printed, will expand use of this technology. Compared to traditional manufacturing processes, 3D printing:

- Is highly flexible.
- Can eliminate the need for producing parts and assembly by printing products in one piece.
- Uses relatively low-cost equipment.
- Can be made close to the customer, reducing inventory and transportation.

mass customization Uses advanced technologies to customize products quickly and at a low cost.

3D printing Also called *additive manufacturing*, this process makes products by putting down successive layers of thin material such as plastic, metal, ceramics, or food.

Flexible manufacturing systems (FMS) Combine automated machines, robots, and material handling systems that are all controlled by a single computer.

activity

student

Do some research to identify a product that is made using 3D printing. How have the operations and supply chain changed as a result of moving to the new manufacturing process?

Cellular Manufacturing

At the other end of the product-process matrix, the flexibility of job shop and batch production is retained but costs are lowered through use of cellular manufacturing. The complexity of job shop and small batch production environments can be reduced and efficiency increased by producing products that have similar processing characteristics using small assembly lines referred to as *cells*. The cellular approach also works well in

cellular manufacturing The production of products with similar process characteristics on small assembly lines called *cells*.

services where information or customer needs can be grouped by their similar processing characteristics. The cellular process structure will be discussed in more detail later in this chapter, in the section titled "Operations Layout."

Aligning Process Structure and Market Orientation

Different process structures involve different decisions about whether a product should be designed and produced *before* a customer order is placed or *after* the order is placed. This decision determines how the firm competes in the marketplace. There are four different marketing orientations; each delivers a different level of service in terms of lead time and customization. To be effective, an organization's process structure must fit with its marketing orientation.

engineer to order (ETO) Unique, customized products.

Products that firms **engineer to order (ETO)** are designed for individual customers and generally have long lead times. Examples include a custom-built house, a cruise ship, specialized industrial equipment, and a customized employee training program. Because each ETO product requires an entirely new design, a customer must place an order before work begins. Firms that anticipate orders often carry raw materials inventory to reduce lead times. Products that are ETO typically use either project or job shop process structures.

make to order (MTO) Products that have similar designs but are customized during production.

The basic design of **make to order (MTO)** products covers the needs of broad groups of customers but allows for some customization during production. Like ETO, a customer order triggers activities at the very early stages of production. Because the design does not start from scratch, the lead time for MTO is less than for ETO. A jet airplane, a meal at an elegant restaurant, a haircut, and a trip to the emergency room are examples of MTO operations. MTO products typically use job shop, batch, and cellular process structures.

assemble to order (ATO) Products that are produced from standard components and modules.

The designs of the components and modules in **assemble to order (ATO)** products are standardized and do not change with customer orders. However, the components and modules can be assembled in different ways to create end product configurations that meet individual customer needs. Raw materials and components are produced and stored in inventory, but final assembly is postponed until the customer places an order. For example, paint stores mix coloring agents with a white base paint after the customer places an order, to provide many color options. Subway Restaurants assemble sandwiches to order from

GET REAL

Personalized M&Ms

Who would have thought that a mature candy brand introduced in 1941 would be a candidate for mass customization? Standard M&Ms are produced using a continuous process and are packaged for distribution through grocery stores and other retail outlets all over the world.

Engineers at Mars developed a breakthrough in printing technology that enabled the introduction of personalized M&Ms in 2005. Now, customers can even put their own faces on M&Ms after uploading their own images at my.m&ms.com.

Personalized M&Ms follow the same continuous process as standard M&Ms, until the printing process. Then, the customer's choice of M&M colors are printed using the images provided by the customer. The M&Ms are then filled into packages selected by the customer and sent directly to the customer's home or business address. However, based on the price per ounce, you may not want to have these for an everyday snack.

© McGraw-Hill Education/Editorial Image, LLC, photographer

prepared ingredients, including freshly baked bread. Repetitive processes are used for ATO products, and many firms have developed mass customization processes for their ATO products.

Groceries, retail clothing, electronics, and cars are examples of make to stock (MTS) products. So that products are immediately available, finished products are made in advance of customer orders and held in inventory. Thus, firms must make products based on forecasts of customer demand. MTS items are typically standardized, mature products. Repetitive assembly lines and continuous processes are typically used for MTS products.

> **make to stock (MTS)** Finished goods that are held in inventory in advance of customer orders.

UNIQUE ASPECTS OF SERVICE PROCESSES

Although the product-process matrix can be used to describe services, it does not address the fact that customers often participate in service processes. Customer contact refers to the presence of the customer in a service process. Services range from those with high customer contact, such as a haircut, to those with low customer contact, such as package delivery. Contact with the customer creates unique challenges in designing, controlling, and operating service processes. Thinking back to the opening vignette, customer contact occurs at the dentist's office and is a critical step in the Invisalign® process. However, because Invisalign® aligners are made at a factory, customer contact is lower than for traditional braces, which are fitted and adjusted at the dentist's office.

> **customer contact** The presence of the customer in a process.

Service Process Matrix

Building on the concept of the product-process matrix, Schmenner developed the service process matrix shown in Figure 5-2 that categorizes services based upon the degree of customization/customer interaction and labor/capital intensity involved. Services in the same industry can compete in different ways by adopting process structures specified in this matrix.

> **service process matrix** Categorizes service processes based upon the degree of customization/customer interaction and labor/capital intensity.

Professional Services.

Lawyers, doctors, consultants, and accountants interact closely with clients to deliver customized services. Professional services tend to be time-consuming and costly because providers are highly skilled and educated. However, by reducing the degree of customization, some firms have reduced time and costs. Retailers such as Target, Walmart, and CVS have in-store medical clinics staffed with nurse practitioners. These clinics treat minor ailments quickly and at a much lower cost than a traditional family doctor.

> **LO5-2** Compare and contrast the goals and challenges associated with a service factory, a mass service, a service shop, and a professional service.

Service Factory.

Trucking companies, airlines, and hotels are examples of service factories. Customer contact, customization, and labor intensity are low while investment in facilities and equipment

FIGURE 5-2   Service Process Matrix

Source: Adapted from R. W. Schmenner, "How Can Service Businesses Survive and Prosper?" *Sloan Management Review* 27, no. 3 (1986), pp. 21–32.

is high. A range of standard services is offered to customers who tend to value low price above all else. Operations managers in service factories are mainly concerned with utilizing equipment and facilities to a maximum extent, because these fixed assets account for the majority of operating costs. Matching capacity and demand to keep equipment and facilities busy is important to both competitiveness and profitability.

Service Shops.

Automobile repair shops and hospitals are examples of service shops, which have a high degree of capital intensity and high customer interaction/customization. Keeping up-to-date on new technology and scheduling to ensure effective utilization of technology are key operations issues. For example, auto repair shop operations typically have large spikes in demand on Mondays, making scheduling a challenge. Some organizations have specialized to reduce the variety of services offered, thus moving from service shops to mass services (described next). For example, muffler replacement and oil changes are mass services.

activity

student

Think of the last service you purchased. What category of service was it? Can you suggest changes in product features or delivery technologies that would move the service to another category? What could be the advantages of such a change?

Mass Services. Mass services, such as retail banks, gas stations, and other retail outlets, meet the standard needs of a large volume of customers. These services have low customer interaction/customization and high labor intensity. Through automation, some mass services have reduced costs and improved customer service availability. Using ATMs, the Internet, or mobile apps, customers can do routine banking activities 24/7. Using the self-checkout at a grocery or superstore reduces the wait time for customers and requires fewer cashiers. Many mass services have been automated through Internet technologies.

Managing Front-Office and Back-Office Processes

front-office processes Processes that have contact with the customer.

back-office processes Processes that are not seen by the customer.

While some processes within a company require customer involvement and interaction, others do not. Processes involving customer contact are referred to as the **front-office processes**. Those that are behind the scenes are called **back-office processes**. In a formal restaurant, the front office is the dining room where the host and servers interact with the customer, and the back office is the kitchen. Clearly, front-office and back-office processes require different employee skill sets, equipment, and physical layouts.

Depending upon the nature of the service, front-office and back-office processes can be decoupled or separated from each other. With decoupling, each process can be managed separately, creating opportunities for efficiency gains. For example, consistent quality and economies of scale occur when back-office operations from different locations are combined. Fast-food chains prepare ingredients at a centralized location, with final preparation taking place in each individual restaurant's kitchen.

global

The ability to decouple services allows different processes to be done by different supply chain members who are dispersed globally. Decoupling through use of the Internet allows a physician in India to analyze an MRI to diagnose the illness of a patient in the United States. These approaches do not always work out as planned, however. For example, the outsourcing of activities such as call centers has resulted in complaints about customer service. The decision of what and how to decouple service operations should be driven by competitive priorities and customer needs.

Service Blueprinting

service blueprinting An approach similar to process mapping that analyzes the interface between customers and service processes.

Service blueprinting is a tool that focuses on understanding the interfaces between customers and service providers, technology, and other key aspects of the process. The approach is similar to process mapping, which we described in the supplement to Chapter 3. A cross-functional team identifies the service process to be blueprinted, documents the process step-by-step, analyzes process enhancements or causes of problems, implements improvements, and monitors the results. However, service blueprinting differs from process mapping in that it focuses on the following elements that are particular to services:

- *Customer actions* include all of the steps that customers take as part of the service delivery process.
- *Front-office/visible contact employee actions* are the actions of frontline contact employees that occur as part of a face-to-face encounter with customers.
- *Back-office/invisible contact employee actions* are nonvisible interactions with customers, such as telephone calls, as well as other activities employees undertake to prepare to serve customers.
- *Support processes* are all activities carried out by employees who do not have direct contact with customers, but whose functions are crucial to the service.
- *Physical evidence* represents all of the tangibles that customers see or collect during their contact with a company.

For example, at a retail clothing store, customer actions include looking at clothing, selecting clothing, trying on clothing, and making a purchase. The visible part of the store includes the clothing displays and dressing rooms. Behind the scenes would be receiving and storage. Physical evidence would include the store décor, the displays, and the merchandise.

In addition to evaluating existing services, blueprinting can help a new service design team identify the critical aspects of the process and find opportunities for inno-vation. The service blueprint itself is a tangible, visual document that lays out where and how custom-ers and companies interact. Good blueprints require inputs from all supply chain members, including customers. Figure 5-3 shows a ser-vice blueprint for a hotel stay.

activity

student

Select a service on campus and create a service blueprint for this service. How did the service blueprint help you to understand the process? What process improvements do you recommend?

FIGURE 5-3 Service Blueprint for a Hotel Stay

Sources: http://knowledge.wpcarey.asu.edu/article.cfm?articleid=1546; and M. J. Bitner, A. L. Ostrom, and F. N. Morgan, "Service Blueprinting: A Practical Technique for Service Innovation," *California Management Review* 50, no.3 (Spring 2008), p. 66.

Service blueprinting of a houseboat resort in Lake Powell, Arizona, showed key reasons why guests were not returning: they were doing a lot of work during their vacations. Guests had to shop for groceries and supplies and then carry these items, along with luggage, onto their boats. To remedy these problems, resort managers added a series of new services, including grocery buying and onboard chefs. As a result, the company experienced a 50 percent drop in complaints, while repeat business jumped 12 percent.

OPERATIONS LAYOUT

LO5-3 Describe how each of the operations layouts—fixed-position, functional, product, and cellular—is designed to meet the demands placed upon it.

The type of process structure selected influences the physical layout of the operation, including arrangement of the equipment, employees, inventory, and aisles for movement. When managers decide to build a new facility, develop a new product, implement new process technology, or modify processes to accommodate changes in demand, they must make layout decisions. Layout has a major impact on performance, especially cost, time, and flexibility. There are four basic types of layouts: fixed-position, functional, product, and cellular.

Fixed-Position Layout

fixed-position layout The layout used when the product cannot be moved during production.

When a product cannot be moved during its production, a fixed-position layout is used. Fixed-position layouts are typically used for projects involving large products such as homes, buildings, bridges, large ships, airplanes, and spacecraft.

With a fixed-position layout, all of the resources and inputs must come together at the product's location. During a visit to your family physician, a fixed-position layout is used because the nurse, doctor, and any needed treatments are brought to you.

One of the supply chain challenges associated with a fixed-position layout is ensuring that the right people, equipment, and materials all arrive at the work site at the right time. Scheduling is very complex, and project management software tools are often used to manage the process.

Functional Layout

functional layout A layout that groups together similar resources.

Multiple copies of similar resources are grouped together in a functional layout (sometimes called a *departmental* layout). Fitness centers and beauty salons use a functional layout. Retailers such as Macy's use a functional layout with different departments for shoes, jewelry, women's clothing, men's clothing, and cosmetics. In manufacturing, one area of

In a functional layout, workers weld parts on a door frame at the Volvo truck assembly line in Dublin, Virginia.
© Steve Helber/AP Images

a plant may do stamping, another welding, and a third assembly. Job shops and batch processes often use a functional layout where work centers using the same types of equipment are grouped together. For example, in a salon the bowls for hair washing are grouped together as are the workstations for doing nails.

There are several benefits to using a functional layout. By grouping general-purpose equipment together, a functional layout offers many different routes for a given job or customer so each has a unique flow through the process. A problem occurring at a single workstation does not usually stop production, because other similar workstations are located nearby. Learning and collaboration increases because employees with similar skills work together.

The functional layout also has several drawbacks. Because each job or customer takes a unique route through the process, scheduling, planning, and control are difficult. Processing times and work-in-process inventory tend to be high as jobs or customers wait to be processed in different departments. Consider the time you spend traveling and waiting when shopping at multiple stores within a shopping mall. Also, a significant amount of time is usually needed to clean and set up workstations when changing from one job or customer to another. In manufacturing, materials handling costs are high when jobs are moved from department to department.

In designing functional layouts, a common goal is to arrange the departments so that the time and cost of moving materials and people are minimized. To select a low-cost layout, managers compare the estimated number and cost of interdepartmental movements for all possible layouts. The complexity of this calculation increases rapidly with the number of departments involved in the decision, so facility layout software is typically used to determine functional layouts.

In retail layouts, an additional goal is usually to increase sales. Big box retailers look for ways to overcome the drawbacks of functional layouts. In large stores, customers grow tired of going from department to department looking for the items they need. Some retailers such as Target have rearranged merchandise by purchase type rather than by item type. For example, all the key items that new parents might need, such as baby clothes, diapers, and strollers, are located in the same department.

Product Layout

A **product layout** arranges resources according to a regularly occurring sequence of activities in the process. An automotive assembly line, Invisalign®, a Taco Bell kitchen, a buffet line, and an insurance claims office all use product layouts. Repetitive processes and continuous processes typically use a product layout. Product layouts minimize processing times and

product layout A layout where resources are arranged according to a regularly occurring sequence of activities.

simplify planning, scheduling, and control because work centers are positioned in a sequence that mirrors the steps needed to assemble the product or serve the customer.

In a product layout, the flow of products or customers is visible and easy to trace. Operations managers sometimes use kanban systems, which are lean tools, to pull material from one workstation to the next just when it is needed. This approach minimizes the inventory of parts and components needed to support the process. In high volume situations, workstations are often linked by conveyors so that products can be automatically transported from one workstation to the next.

Lack of flexibility and low work variety for employees are drawbacks to product layouts. Because activities are linked, a problem at any single workstation can cause the entire line to stop. Think about your frustration when you are behind an indecisive person in a buffet line. This is one reason why automotive assemblers demand on-time

Automobile assembly lines use a product layout.
© Ralph Orlowski/Getty Images

delivery and high quality from their suppliers. A quality problem with any supplied part can shut the entire assembly line down. At an automobile assembly plant, this can cost tens of thousands of dollars per minute.

LO5-4 Analyze a product layout using line balancing.

line balancing Used to assign tasks so that idle time and the number of workstations are minimized.

precedence relationships Presents the order in which tasks must be completed.

takt time The maximum allowable cycle time at each workstation based on customer demand.

cycle time The time that it takes to process one unit at an operation in the overall process.

Line Balancing in Product Layouts

In designing a product layout, the goal is to have a smooth, continuous flow through the process. Line balancing is used to assign individual tasks to workstations for a desired output rate. Idle time and the number of workstations are minimized to increase efficiency. In Example 1 below, we review a simple example of line balancing that involves assembling a sausage and pepperoni pizza. In manufacturing, most line balancing problems will be much more complex than this example.

Example 1

First, identify the time required to complete each task and the order in which the tasks must be done—the precedence relationships (Table 5-2). Some tasks physically cannot be done until others are completed. For example, the dough must be formed before it is topped with sauce. However, either sausage or pepperoni can be added after the cheese. Both sausage and pepperoni must be added before the pizza is packaged. Visually, Figure 5-4 shows the precedence relationships.

Next, determine the maximum total task time allowable at each workstation based on customer demand, referred to as takt time. The time that it takes to process a unit at a workstation is the workstation's cycle time. To ensure that a process can meet customer demand, the cycle time at each workstation in a process cannot exceed the takt time. If customer demand changes, the takt time should be recalculated and the assembly line rebalanced as necessary.

(5.1) Takt time (T) = (Available production time in a time period)/(Output needed in that time period to meet customer demand)

In our example, the time period is one 8-hour shift per day, so 480 minutes of production time are available. The customer demand for sausage and pepperoni pizzas is 200 pizzas per day. Thus, the cycle time for each workstation must be less than or equal to 2.4 minutes.

Takt time (T) = (8 hours/shift × 60 minutes/hour)/200 pizzas = 2.4 minutes per workstation

FIGURE 5-4 Precedence Diagram for Sausage and Pepperoni Pizza Assembly

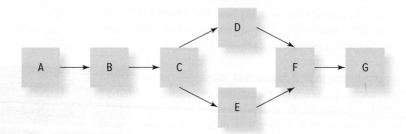

TABLE 5-2 Precedence Relationships for Sausage and Pepperoni Pizza Assembly

Task		Predecessors	Time (minutes)
A	Shape the dough to form the crust	None	2
B	Add the pizza sauce	A	1
C	Add the cheese	B	2
D	Add the sausage	C	0.75
E	Add the pepperoni	C	1
F	Package the pizza	D, E	1.5
G	Label the package	F	0.5
		Total Time	8.75

The next step is to determine the theoretical minimum number of workstations. This would be the minimum possible number of stations; the balanced line may have more stations. When determining the number of stations, *round up* to the next whole number, otherwise there will not be enough time to make all the products to meet customer demand.

(5.2)   Theoretical number of stations (N) = (Total of all task times)/(Takt time)

For the pizza example:

N = (2 min. + 1 min. + 2 min. + .75 min. + 1 min. + 1.5 min. + .5 min.)/(2.4 min. per station)

= 3.7, so round up to 4 workstations

Assign as many tasks as possible to each workstation such that the sum of the task times is not greater than the takt time, which is 2.4 minutes in our example. Remember, when assigning tasks to workstations, you cannot violate the precedence relationships. For example, A must be completed before you can begin work on B.

When balancing a line, sometimes more than one task can be assigned, so you must decide which task to assign first. For example, once the pizza is topped with cheese, you can next add either sausage or pepperoni. To make this decision, you can use rules or guidelines that lead to a good, but not necessarily the best, solution. Two commonly used rules are to first enter:

1. The task with the longest operating (task) time.
2. The task with the most number of followers.

In our example, we use the longest operating time rule to assign tasks. Because both tasks D and E can be assigned after C, using the longest operating time rule, we add the pepperoni first (Task E) (see Table 5-3). If one rule results in a tie between two tasks, the other rule is typically used to decide which task to assign.

With a complex process there may be several different ways to balance the line, so select the alternative that provides the highest efficiency.

(5.3)   Efficiency = [Sum of all task times/(Actual work stations × takt time)] × 100

Efficiency = [(2 min. + 1 min. + 2 min. + .75 min. + 1 min. + 1.5 min. + .5 min.)/(5 stations × 2.4 min./station)] × 100 = 73%

As with the functional layout, as the number of tasks increases so does the complexity of the line balancing problem. Bottlenecks, as described in Chapter 3, are constraints that have lower output than other workstations on the line, slow the process, and reduce efficiency. To improve efficiency, reduce time at the bottleneck workstation. For example, perhaps split tasks into smaller work elements, change technology to reduce the time required, or deploy more workers at the bottleneck.

TABLE 5-3   Workstation Assignments for Pizza: Balanced Using the Longest Task Time

Workstation	Tasks in Order	Workstation Time (minutes)	Idle Time (minutes)
1	A	2	0.4
2	B	1	1.4
3	C	2	0.4
4	E, D	1.75	0.65
5	F, G	2	0.4

Cellular Layout

In situations with mid-range volume and variety, a cellular layout combines the flexibility of a small, focused job shop with the efficiency of a repetitive line. A cellular layout arranges workstations to form a number of small assembly lines called *work cells*. Workstations within each individual work cell are arranged using product layout principles. The first step in designing a cellular layout is to use group technology to identify products that have similar processing requirements, called **product families**. Product families may have similar shapes, sizes, process flows, or demand. Each work cell can be dedicated to make a product family.

Workers are typically dedicated to a cell and are trained in all of the activities within a cell, increasing process flexibility. As they become intimately familiar with the product and demand requirements of the cell, the workers as a team identify opportunities for improvement and take on larger roles, including planning, maintenance, and quality inspection.

Cells can make job shops or batch processes more efficient or increase the flexibility of repetitive processes. Processing time, inventory, material flow distance, and setup times are reduced, and scheduling is less complex than with functional layouts. For example, cellular manufacturing and other lean practices helped the La-Z-Boy furniture plant in Dayton, Tennessee, drastically reduce the time needed to produce and deliver a custom order. Similarly, insurance firms and banks have increased efficiencies by grouping together workers and activities that were formerly isolated into different departments.

Converting a product layout into cells creates more options in how products might be routed from cell to cell, increasing flexibility. When converting a product layout to a cellular layout, managers must determine where customization will be added to the product line. This indicates where the line should be broken, what activities should be included in each cell, and how the cells should relate to each other. Product, functional, and cellular layouts are shown in Figure 5-5. Each shape represents a different type of activity.

product families Groups of products that have similar processing requirements.

FIGURE 5-5 Product, Functional, and Cellular Layouts

Functional Layout

Cellular Layout

Product Layout

CAPABILITY ENABLING TECHNOLOGIES

Technology has a major impact on operations and supply chains, so deciding how to use technology to enhance value for customers is an important managerial decision. Table 5-4 shows some of the technologies that are used in operations and supply chain management. Technology can reduce variation, increase efficiency, and improve safety by replacing human involvement and decision making with process automation. Advances in information technology and communications have dramatically improved operational processing, data management, visibility, and coordination across global supply chain networks. New capabilities can also be created through the use of technology, with opportunities to increase customer satisfaction or create entirely new business models—as was the case for Instagram, Uber, and Airbnb.

LO5-5 Explain how technology is used in the supply chain and the benefits and drawbacks of process automation.

Information Sharing

Quickly and accurately sharing information within the supply chain is essential for making good business decisions. Processing, communication, decision-making and integrative technologies provide the capabilities needed for information sharing. In the planning

TABLE 5-4   Types of Supply Chain Operational Technologies

Type of Technology	Capabilities	Examples
Decision support systems	Provide computing power and data management to make higher-quality decisions faster.	• Advanced planning systems • Supply chain network design • Transportation management systems (TMS) • Warehouse management systems (WMS) • Manufacturing execution systems (MES)
Processing technologies	Automate material and data processing to provide 24/7 resource availability, faster processing, greater consistency, and lower cost.	• Computer-aided design • 3D printing • Industrial robots • Drones • Flexible manufacturing systems (FMS) • Automated storage and retrieval systems (AS/RS) • Point of sale (POS) bar code scanners • Radio frequency identification (RFID) • E-procurement
Communications technologies	Create greater connectivity and speed flow of richer forms of information.	• The Internet • Mobile apps and wearables • Communication satellites • Fiber optic cables • Radio frequency data communications (RFDC)
Integrative technologies	Combine data management, communications, decision support, and processing capabilities.	• Cloud computing • Internet of Things (IoT) • Enterprise resource planning (ERP) • Product life cycle management (PLM) • Customer relationship management (CRM) • Supplier relationship management (SRM) • Collaborative planning, forecasting, and replenishment (CPFR)

phase, companies work with key customers and suppliers using collaborative planning, forecasting, and replenishment (CPFR) to ensure that they understand what products need to be made and when.

As sales are made in retail stores, sales and inventory information is automatically captured by point of sale (POS) bar codes, RFID scanners, or sensors. The data are then conveyed through the Internet to the company's enterprise resource planning system (ERP), which may be in the cloud. Inventory records are updated and, when needed, replenishment orders are generated and communicated to suppliers. The company and its suppliers may use manufacturing execution systems (MES) for their internal operations. Inventory replenishment orders that are sent from warehouses to the retail stores are scheduled and monitored using warehouse management systems (WMS) and transportation management systems (TMS). These decision support systems optimize the sequencing and routing of material flows throughout the distribution network.

Process Automation

Using technology to automate processes can increase productivity, reduce direct labor costs, and reduce variation, thereby improving quality, increasing worker safety, and improving customer service. Example automation technologies include mobile apps, robots, drones, and the Internet of Things (IoT).

Mobile apps increase convenience for customers and automate customer contact for many services. When you use an app to order a pizza, schedule a service appointment for your car, or check in for a flight, you do not have to wait for a person to assist you. This increases flexibility for you and reduces the number of customer contact employees needed by the company. In some cases, mobile apps are changing and replacing entire processes. When checking in to a Hilton hotel, for example, customers select their room and get an electronic "key" with a mobile app, allowing them to bypass the registration desk altogether.

For years robots have helped manufacturing plants to be safer and more efficient and produce higher quality products. For example, Ford Motor Company has over 20,000 robots in its factories worldwide doing everything from hazardous jobs like welding and painting, to lifting and moving heavy parts, installing windshields, and even performing quality inspections. Distribution centers also use robots extensively to pick and move products. Advances in technology are allowing "collaborative" robots to safely work side-by-side with humans. As the technology improves and the costs of robots decrease, we are likely to see more applications across a range of industries, as shown in the Get Real: Robots box below.

Drones, or unmanned aerial vehicles (UAV), are likely to bring new delivery capabilities to the supply chain. The flexibility and low cost of drone delivery make it attractive to postal services and carriers such as UPS, FedEx, and DHL. In 2015, Amazon filed a patent application for a drone delivery process in which customers can place orders using mobile devices, with order fulfillment and delivery within 30 minutes. Although there are still many regulatory, safety, and technical hurdles to overcome prior to full commercialization, drones will certainly have an impact on operations and supply chains.

The Internet of Things (IoT) allows products and machines to connect to the Internet and share data with other devices. A simple example is a washing machine that sends a text to your phone when the clothes are ready for the dryer. A more complex example is a self-driving car.

In operations and supply chains, the IoT is allowing manufacturers to gather data on product performance and make automatic changes in the process. Data can be used to optimize current products and processes, design new products, and improve customer service. For example, Diebold uses the IoT to monitor ATMs and provide maintenance before an ATM stops working, thus reducing downtime for its banking customers. Applications of the

©Andreas Rentz/Getty Images

GET REAL

Robots: Coming to a Pharmacy Near You?

Although robots have long been used in manufacturing, we are starting to see some surprising new applications in services. Large hospitals and pharmacies are starting to invest in robots that can fill prescriptions to increase patient safety, fill speed, and efficiency.

The University of California San Francisco Medical Center invested $15 million in a robotic system that fills prescriptions based on a doctor's electronic prescription. Compared with the traditional process previously used by the University, which had error rates of almost 3 percent, the robot fills prescriptions with remarkable accuracy. So far, it has made only one error in the six million prescriptions filled. Given that drug errors can cause injury or death, improved accuracy can be life-saving. An added benefit to the hospital is that pharmacists can now spend their time working more effectively with patients and doctors to develop treatment plans. To see the robot in action, access the following link and check out the video:

http://www.npr.org/sections/money/2015/05/27/407737439/watch-robots-transform-a-california-hospital

© 67photo/Alamy Stock Photo

IoT are currently in their infancy, but the potential for operations and supply chain management seems endless.

Despite the many benefits, there are also drawbacks to process automation. Purchasing, installing, and maintaining automation technology usually requires a high capital investment, increasing an organization's fixed costs. Limits on an organization's ability to obtain credit to finance these investments may impact its ability to automate processes. Because of the high investment, companies are sometimes reluctant to change technologies, even though they should to stay competitive.

The impact of process automation on labor should also be considered. Low wage jobs are often eliminated, but managing and maintaining automated systems requires highly skilled IT professionals, process engineers, and maintenance employees, increasing indirect labor or outsourcing costs. In some cases, customers may have concerns with the quality of a more highly automated process. For example, consider when you have to talk to an automated call center system rather than a person. When deciding to automate processes, the benefits need to be balanced against the drawbacks.

CHAPTER SUMMARY

This chapter describes some of the key decisions relating to manufacturing and service process structures and how they impact an organization's capabilities.

1. The product-process matrix classifies processes based on output volume and variety. The process types are: project, job shop, batch, repetitive process, and continuous process. Two contemporary process structures are mass customization and cellular manufacturing.

2. Services can be categorized based on customization/customer interaction and labor/capital intensity. A framework shows four classifications: professional service, service factory, service shop, and mass service.

3. The front office of a service process that is in contact with the customer has different requirements than the back office of a process that is not visible to the customer. Decoupling often increases efficiency in both the front-office and the back-office processes.

4. Layout is the physical arrangement of resources in a process. The type of layout is closely related to the type of process. Layout types are product, functional, cellular, and fixed-position.

5. Advances in technologies have enabled new business models and supply chain improvements. Process automation can reduce variation, increase efficiency, increase safety, reduce direct labor costs, and increase customer satisfaction. However, automation requires a high capital investment and highly skilled technical support, may not be able to adapt to major product changes, and in some cases may reduce customer satisfaction.

KEY TERMS

assemble to order (ATO)   148

back-office processes   150

batch process   146

cellular manufacturing   147

continuous process   146

customer contact   149

cycle time   154

engineer to order (ETO)   148

fixed-position layout   152

flexible manufacturing system (FMS)   147

front-office processes   150

functional layout   152

job shop   145

line balancing   154

make to order (MTO)   148

make to stock (MTS)   149

mass customization   147

precedence relationships   154

product families   156

product layout   153

product-process matrix   144

project   145

repetitive process   146

service blueprinting   150

service process matrix   149

takt time   154

3D printing (additive manufacturing)   147

DISCUSSION QUESTIONS

1. Airlines allow customers to purchase tickets, select seats, and check in using mobile apps. How does this process differ from a check-in process at an airline ticket counter?

2. Think of two companies in the same industry that use different process structures. Why is this the case? Is one process structure a better choice than the other? Why, or why not?

3. Consider several members of the supply chain of a company that makes plastic toy cars and trucks. Which of the processes described in the product-process matrix is likely to be used by the following supply chain members? Why?

   a. The company that assembles the toys.

   b. The company that produces the parts that go into the toys.

   c. The company that produces the plastic.

4. Provide an example of how technology has made it possible to use processes that are not on the diagonal of the product-process matrix.

5. Are some process structures inherently safer or more environmentally friendly than others?

6. In which of the service categories would you put a large state university? Why? Would a small private university be in the same category? Why, or why not?

7. Some upscale restaurants have their kitchens visible to their customers, changing the traditional view of front-office and back-office processes. What are the benefits and drawbacks to this approach?

8. Think about three of your favorite fast-food restaurants. What type of layout is used in the food preparation area of each? Are these layouts a good fit with the organization? Why, or why not? Should the layout be changed and, if so, how?

9. Provide an example of a type of technology that enhances customer service and a type of technology that reduces customer service. Why is this the case?

10. Postal services and logistics companies are experimenting with delivery using drones. What are the benefits and drawbacks of this application of technology?

SOLVED PROBLEMS

1. Using the information in Table 5-5, balance the assembly line for the Tourist T-Shirt Company. The operations run continuously for eight hours per day. Each day, 80 t-shirts must be produced to meet customer demand.
   a. Draw the precedence diagram.
   b. What is the takt time?
   c. What are the theoretical number of workstations?
   d. Assign tasks to workstations using the longest operating time rule.
   e. What is the efficiency of the balanced line?

TABLE 5-5 Precedence Relationships for Making a T-Shirt

Task		Predecessors	Time (minutes)
A	Put the pattern on the material	None	5
B	Cut out the pattern	A	3
C	Hem the neck slit opening	B	2
D	Sew the sleeve seams	B	1
E	Hem the sleeves	D	2
F	Sew the side seams of the tunic	C	3
G	Sew the sleeves to the tunic	E, F	4
H	Hem the bottom of the shirt	F	5
		Total Time	25

Solution:

a. Precedence diagram.

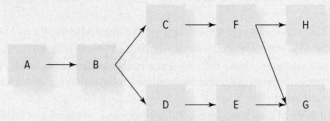

b. Takt time (T) = Production time per day/Output needed per day

Takt time (T) = (8 hours/shift × 60 minutes/hour)/(80 T-shirts/day) = 6 minutes/workstation

c. Theoretical minimum number of stations (N) = Total of all task times/Takt time.

N = (25 minutes)/(6 min./station) = 4.2, so 5 stations

d. The tasks are assigned to each station in order of precedence, assigning as many tasks as possible to each station. When you can choose among multiple tasks, for example, C or D, choose the task with the longest operating time.

Workstation	Tasks in Order	Workstation Time (Min.)	Idle Time (Min.)
1	A	5	1
2	B, C, D	6	0
3	F, E	5	1
4	H	5	1
5	G	4	2

e. Efficiency = [Sum of all task times/(Actual workstations × Takt time)] × 100

Efficiency = [(25 minutes)/(5 stations × 6 min./station)] × 100 = 83%

PROBLEMS

1. An assembly line currently has five workstations, and the time required for each is shown below.

1 45 sec.	→	2 32 sec.	→	3 38 sec.	→	4 50 sec.	→	5 42 sec.

 a. What is the current cycle time?
 b. What is the efficiency of the process?
 c. Customer demand is 80 units per hour. What is the hourly production rate of the current process?
 d. What does the cycle time need to be to be able to meet demand (i.e., what is the takt time)?
 e. What changes to the process are needed?

2. An insurance company uses the following tasks to process paperwork. Forty claims need to be processed in an *eight-hour workday*.

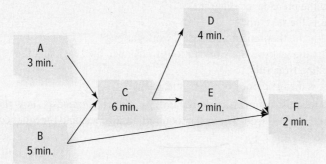

 a. What is the takt time?
 b. What is the theoretical number of workstations?
 c. Assign the tasks to the workstations to balance the line using the longest operating time rule.
 d. What is the efficiency of the balanced line?

3. Swoosh Snowboard Company must set up an assembly line for snowboards. Forecasts show that 600 units per day should be produced. The plant operates *two eight-hour shifts each day* and runs the line continuously during both shifts. The tasks required, task times, and precedence relationships are as follows:

Task	Time (seconds)	Predecessors
A	40	–
B	27	A
C	30	A
D	35	–
E	30	B
F	40	D
G	55	C, E, F
H	39	G

 a. Draw the precedence diagram.
 b. What is the takt time?

c. What is the theoretical number of workstations?
d. Assign the tasks to the workstations to balance the line using the longest operating time rule.
e. What is the efficiency of the balanced line?

4. The Carry-on Luggage Company must set up an assembly line for a wheeled carry-on bag. Forecasts show that 60 units per hour should be produced. The tasks required, task times, and precedence relationships are as follows:

Task	Time (seconds)	Predecessors
A	30	–
B	50	A
C	25	A
D	10	B
E	25	B
F	15	B
G	10	C, E, F
H	30	D, G

a. Draw the precedence diagram.
b. What is the takt time?
c. What is the theoretical number of workstations?
d. Assign the tasks to the workstations to balance the line using the longest operating time rule.
e. What is the efficiency of the balanced line?

5. Wild Widget must set up an assembly line for widgets. Forecasts show that 50 units per hour should be produced. The tasks required, task times, and precedence relationships are as follows:

Task	Time (seconds)	Predecessors
A	10	–
B	30	A
C	15	A
D	35	C, B
E	25	D
F	10	D
G	35	E, F

a. Draw the precedence diagram.
b. What is the takt time?
c. What is the theoretical number of workstations?
d. Assign the tasks to the workstations to balance the line using the longest operating time rule.
e. What is the efficiency of the balanced line?
f. If demand decreased to 40 units per day, what changes would be needed, if any?

6. Golf Carts Inc. must set up an assembly line for golf carts. Forecasts show that 10 units per day should be produced. The plant operates *one eight-hour shift each day* and runs the line continuously during the shift. The tasks required, task times, and precedence relationships are as follows:

Task	Time (minutes)	Predecessors
A	12	–
B	10	–
C	16	–
D	24	A, B
E	14	C
F	30	D
G	15	E, F

a. Draw the precedence diagram.
b. What is the takt time?
c. What is the theoretical number of workstations?
d. Assign the tasks to the workstations to balance the line using the longest operating time rule.
e. What is the efficiency of the balanced line?
f. If demand increased to 12 units per day, what changes would be needed, if any?

7. Williams Motor Manufacturing assembles small motors for sale to major appliance manufacturers around the world. Average demand for its best-selling motor is 600 units per day. The assembly line operates continuously during a *single eight-hour shift*. The tasks required, task times, and precedence relationships are:

Task	Time (seconds)	Predecessor
A	12	–
B	22	–
C	20	–
D	20	A
E	18	C
F	30	B, D
G	17	E
H	25	F, G
I	20	H

a. Draw the precedence diagram.
b. What is the takt time?
c. What is the theoretical number of workstations?
d. Assign the tasks to the workstations to balance the line using the longest operating time rule.
e. What is the efficiency of the balanced line?
f. If demand increased to 650 motors per day, what changes would be needed, if any?

8. A company that assembles high fidelity headphones needs to design an assembly line for one of its new products. The tasks needed and their relationships are shown in the following figure. To meet demand, the company must produce 80 headphones an hour.

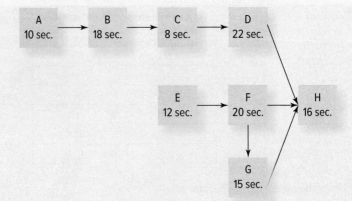

a. What is the takt time?
b. Design the line by assigning the tasks to the workstations to balance the line using the longest operating time rule.
c. Redesign the assembly line by assigning the tasks to the workstations to balance the line using the most number of followers rule. If a tie is encountered, use the longest operating time rule to decide which task to enter.
d. Which approach to line balancing results in the most efficient assembly line?

9. The Office Interiors Company has developed a new, modern office chair. Initial sales forecasts are for 50 chairs per day. The assembly operations will run for *two eight-hour shifts*. The process engineer and operations manager are working together to balance the line to make the new chair as efficiently as possible. The process engineer suggests using the longest operating time rule while the operations manager suggests using the most number of followers rule to design the line. If there is a tie, use the other rule to break the tie. Based on the processing information, which approach do you recommend? Why?

Task	Time (Minutes)	Predecessor
A	7	–
B	12	A
C	6	B
D	13	–
E	8	C, D
F	10	–
G	4	F
H	10	E, G

CASE

Coffee Roasters

Once considered a commodity product, many small boutique coffee companies are luring customers with promises of high quality and unique flavors. How do the processes used by the small companies compare with those of the major coffee processors? Coffee producers purchase green coffee beans, which have been processed through several steps. At the manufacturer, green coffee beans are screened to remove debris, and then roasted for up to 30 minutes. A roaster is typically a rotating drum in which the beans are heated. The length of time spent in the roaster impacts coffee flavor. The longer the time spent in the roaster, the richer the coffee flavor. Following roasting, beans are sprayed with water, cooled, and screened to remove any remaining debris. Once roasted, coffee is ground to the size required for the brewing process and packaged.

Ohori's Coffee is an example of a boutique coffee company. Established in 1984, Ohori's Coffee is located in Santa Fe, New Mexico. This privately owned business microroasts 32 types of coffee from Africa, the Saudi peninsula, Indonesia, the Pacific Rim, and North and South America. In batch sizes of 30 pounds or less, coffee beans are roasted in natural gas-fired rotating drum roasters carefully monitored by highly skilled "master roasters." To maintain quality, Ohori's depends on humans, not computer controls in the roasting process. Online and in its Santa Fe location, Ohori's sells whole beans and 10 different grinds ranging from Percolator to Turkish style. (Source: http://ohoriscoffee.com.)

Folgers Coffee was purchased from Procter & Gamble in 2008 by the J. M. Smucker Company in a deal reportedly worth $3.3 billion. Folgers Coffee accounts for over 30 percent of the U.S. packaged coffee market, with over $2 billion in sales. Sales growth is estimated to be 2–3 percent per year.

Folgers's largest roasting and blending facility is in New Orleans, with 550 employees. It also has manufacturing operations in Kansas City, Missouri, and Sherman, Texas. The distribution center for Folgers is near New Orleans in Lacombe, Louisiana. Its coffee is sold in a single grind type. The company sells three Classic blends, seven blends in its Coffee House product line, five types of flavored ground coffee, and 10 flavors of Folgers Gourmet Selections.

Folgers has introduced an enhanced roasting process for its Classic products. The coffee beans are preconditioned to reduce moisture and improve consistency before the final roasting. (Source: www.folgers.com.)

Think about the production processes used by Ohori's and Folgers.

Questions

1. Using the product-process matrix, which processes are likely to be used by Ohori's and Folgers? Why?

2. Explain how the choice of process supports each organization's competitive priorities.

3. Is the operations layout likely to be the same or different at Ohori's and Folgers? Why?

4. What changes would Folgers need to make to compete directly with Ohori's? Why?

CASE

Sonnie's Gourmet Sandwich Café

Sonnie's Gourmet Sandwich Café, a popular new fast casual restaurant, serves high-quality, made-to-order sandwiches. Located in a local outdoor shopping center, parking in front of Sonnie's is limited. However, there are many parking spaces available behind the café within a five-minute walk. The café has an inviting, bright, and open interior with deli cases, blackboards listing specials, and oak tables and chairs.

The café's popularity at lunch is a concern for Sonnie. During the prime lunch time between 11:30 a.m. and 1:30 p.m. Monday through Friday, the waiting line is often out the door. On average Sonnie would like to serve 40 customers per hour at lunch. Working professionals, who typically spend more than other customers at lunch, are on busy schedules and do not have time to wait in line. Sonnie estimates that currently some customers go to other restaurants because of the line.

The menu at Sonnie's includes nine standard sandwiches such as roast beef, pastrami and rye, and a BLT. Many customers choose to build their own sandwiches, selecting from eight types of bread, 25 meats, 12 cheeses, and 20 different vegetables. Sandwiches are served with chips or a choice of four types of salad.

Order Placement

When customers enter the café, they walk past a large deli counter displaying meats and cheese on their left and stop in front of a counter to place their orders. An employee greets the customer, asks for each customer's name, then takes his or her order by filling out a two-part paper form. Because of the number of choices, customers take, on average, 1 minute and 20 seconds to place their orders. However, those ordering standard sandwiches complete the order in about 1 minute. The employee gives the top part of the order form to the customer (10 seconds) to take to the cashier and the other is handed to the next employee in line, who starts working on the order. The employee who took the order then fills the customer's beverage order and hands it to the customer (30 seconds). The customer then walks about 15 feet to the cashier and pays, which on average takes 1 minute and 30 seconds. Then the customer selects a table and waits for his or her name to be called when the order is complete.

Order Fulfillment Process

Three employees work in the food preparation area, which uses a product layout. The first employee in the food preparation line puts the choice of side on a plate (35 seconds) and then assembles the sandwich from presliced bread, meat, and cheese, a task that takes about 1 minute and 20 seconds. The sandwich is handed off to the next employee, who adds toppings and sauces (45 seconds) and slices the sandwich (10 seconds). The last employee checks the order for accuracy (15 seconds), moves the sandwich to the pick-up area, and calls the customer by name (20 seconds).

Questions

1. Compared to a fast-food restaurant such as McDonald's, where would Sonnie's sandwich shop be placed on the service process matrix? What challenges and opportunities does this position create relative to McDonald's? Why?

2. How many customers is the current process able to accommodate per hour?

3. Use line balancing and service blueprinting to redesign the process at Sonnie's. What changes do you recommend? Why?

Berman, B. "Should Your Firm Adopt a Mass Customization Strategy?" *Business Horizons* 45, no. 4 (2002), pp. 51–61.

Bitner, M.; A. Ostrom; and F. Morgan. "Service Blueprinting: A Practical Technique for Service Innovation." *California Management Review* 50, no. 3 (2008), pp. 66–94.

Chase, R. B., and D. A. Tansik. "The Customer Contact Model for Organizational Design." *Management Science* 29, no. 9 (1983), pp. 1037–50.

D'Aveni, R. "The 3D Printing Revolution." *Harvard Business Review* 93, no. 5 (2015), pp. 40–48.

Hayes, R., and S. Wheelwright. "Link Manufacturing Process and Product Life Cycles." *Harvard Business Review* 57, no. 1 (1979), pp. 133–40.

Hayes, R., and S. Wheelwright. *Restoring Our Competitive Edge: Competing Through Manufacturing.* New York: John Wiley & Sons, 1984.

Lummus, R.; R. Vokurka; and L. Duclos. "The Product-Process Matrix Revisited: Integrating Supply Chain Trade-offs." *SAM Advanced Management Journal* 71, no. 2 (2006), pp. 4–10, 20, 45.

Marsh, R. "Amazon Drone Patent Application that Comes to You with One Click." CNN Politics, May 12, (2015), http://www.cnn.com/2015/05/12/politics/amazon-patent-drone-delivery/

McKenzie, S. "Rise of Robots: The Evolution of Ford's Assembly Line."(2015) http://money.cnn.com/gallery/technology/2015/04/29/ford-factory-assembly-line-robots/index.html

Minter, S. "2012 IW Best Plants Winners: La-Z-Boy Never Rests on Continuous Improvement." *Industry-Week,*" (Jan. 17, 2013) http://www.industryweek.com/iw-best-plants/2012-iw-best-plants-winner-la-z-boy-never-rests-continuous-improvement

Porter, M. E. and J. E. Heppelmann. "How Smart, Connected Products Are Transforming Competition." *Harvard Business Review* 92, no. 11 (2014), pp. 64–88.

Safizadeh, M., and L. Ritzman. "An Empirical Analysis of the Product-Process Matrix." *Management Science* 42, no. 11 (1996), pp. 1576–95.

Sampson, S., and C. Froehle. "Foundations and Implications of a Proposed Unified Services Theory." *Production and Operations Management* 15, no. 2 (2006), pp. 329–43.

Schmenner, R. "How Can Service Business Survive and Prosper?" *Sloan Management Review* 27, no. 3 (1986), pp. 21–32.

Schmenner, R. "Service Businesses and Productivity." *Decision Sciences* 35, no. 3 (2004), pp. 333–47.

Selladurai, R. "Mass Customization in Operations Management: Oxymoron or Reality?" *Omega* 32, no. 4 (2004), pp. 295–301.

Sohel, A., and R. Schroeder. "Refining the Product-Process Matrix." *International Journal of Operations and Production Management* 22, no. 1 (2002), pp. 103–25.

Solomon, M. "Your iPhone as Hotel Room Key: Hilton Shakes up Hospitality Industry." *Forbes* (July 31, 2014), http://www.forbes.com/sites/micahsolomon/2014/07/31/hilton-shakes-hospitality-industry/

Verma, R. "An Empirical Analysis of Management Challenges in Service Factories, Service Shops, Mass Services, and Professional Services." *International Journal of Service Industry Management* 11, no. 1 (2000), pp. 8–25.

Verma, R., and K. Boyer. "Service Classification and Management Challenges." *Journal of Business Strategies* 17, no. 1 (2000), pp. 5–24.

Hilton Worldwide http://news.hiltonworldwide.com/index.cfm/news/hilton-worldwide-truly-opens-doors-company-to-roll-out-mobile-room-keys-in-2015-at-hundreds-of-us-hotels-across-four-brands

Invisalign
www.invisalign.com

Jostens
www.jostens.com

Martha Stewart
www.marthastewart.com/article/mandm-factory-tour

My M&Ms
www.mymms.com

NPR news article
http://www.npr.org/sections/money/2015/05/27/407737439/watch-robots-transform-a-california-hospital

Spangler Candy
www.spanglercandy.com

6 Managing Quality

LEARNING OBJECTIVES

After studying this chapter, you should be able to:

LO6-1 Explain what the concepts of *product quality* and *quality management* entail.

LO6-2 Explain the roles that operations and other functional managers play in determining product quality.

LO6-3 Apply the core values and typical practices associated with quality management.

LO6-4 Perform a cost of quality analysis.

LO6-5 Apply the Six Sigma DMAIC approach to quality improvement.

LO6-6 Compare and contrast various quality standards and certification programs.

© Yonhap, Lee Sang-hyun/AP Images

For much of its history, Hyundai cars were widely considered to be of low quality. This Korean manufacturer achieved sales growth mainly by offering low prices. In 1999, Chairman Chung Mong Koo decided to refocus the company on catching Japanese rival Toyota in quality. Toyota's reputation for quality had given it levels of customer retention that few companies could match while also lending cachet to its luxury nameplates. Consistent with this change in focus, Hyundai made the following changes to improve quality:

- Increased the number of workers on the quality control team from 100 to more than 850.

- Instituted mandatory seminars for all workers on the importance of quality.

- Invoked the direct involvement of its CEO in twice-monthly meetings comparing Hyundai quality with that of its rivals.

- Made capital investments in problem areas, including $30 million invested in a computer center to test electronic systems.

By 2015, Hyundai had compiled an impressive track record of quality:

- According to Kelley Blue Book, brand loyalty for Hyundai surpassed that of Honda and Toyota to take the No. 1 spot.

- Cars.com recently ranked five Hyundai cars among its "Best Bets" for safety, reliability, and fuel efficiency.

- By introducing its Sonata and Genesis models, Hyundai has become a strong competitor in the luxury market, where excellent quality is imperative.

- In 2014 Hyundai placed first in the J.D. Power Initial Quality Study (the industry's most prestigious award).

- In 2015 Hyundai and its sister company Kia averaged 90 problems per 100 vehicles, 20 percent fewer problems than those found in European, Japanese, and American cars, on average.

In recent years, Hyundai models have consistently provided strong levels of quality and dependability. However, initial negative quality perceptions are difficult to change. Given that quality is a primary consideration for car buyers, Hyundai will have to continue to provide excellence in the dimensions of product quality that consumers care most about.

Quality is an integral focus of operations management. As we can see from the experiences of Hyundai, quality offers firms a way of enhancing their competitiveness and strategic position in the marketplace. The reality in today's competitive world is that no firm can afford to forget quality; no firm can afford to compromise on quality. Quality is expected and must be delivered. To be delivered, it must be understood, and that is the focus of this chapter.

This chapter describes how operations managers and their supply chain partners improve and ensure the quality of products that the company delivers. First, we define the dimensions of product quality and the roles that different functional groups across the supply chain play in delivering quality. Next, the chapter explores the core values of quality management to help you understand why quality is so important, as well as how companies are continually improving all processes involved in the design and delivery of products. The final sections of the chapter describe international quality standards and the Six Sigma approach to quality management which apply many of the core values and practices associated with quality management. The supplement to this chapter provides an explanation of many of the data analysis and statistical tools used in quality management programs.

DEFINING THE DIMENSIONS OF QUALITY

LO6-1 Explain what the concepts of *product quality* and *quality management* entail.

Quality management can dramatically impact business success. Over a decade ago, for example, Hewlett-Packard found defects in 4 of every 1,000 soldered computer components. Through better quality management, the company originally hoped to cut defects in half; it was ultimately able to reduce the defect rate to 2 defects per 1 million soldered components! The impact of this improvement was significant and widespread—fewer product returns in the field, less internal rework, fewer inspections, improved reputation with customers, less inventory, reduced lead times, less floor space needed for inspections and rework, and ultimately, lower costs. Quality management programs can create equally dramatic improvements in all types of service industries. Some services, such as McDonald's restaurants, offer outstanding consistency in their quality of service. Others, such as Ritz-Carlton Hotels (see the accompanying Get Real box), offer premium quality experiences.

As we discussed in Chapter 2, product quality can be broadly defined by the following terms:

product quality A product's fitness for consumption in terms of meeting customers' needs and desires.

design quality A measure of how well a product's designed features match up to the requirements of a given customer group.

Product quality is a product's fitness for consumption—how well it meets customers' needs and desires. Fitness for consumption is determined by both a product's design quality and its conformance quality.

Design quality is a measure of how well a product's designed features match up to the requirements of a given customer group.

GET REAL

Ritz-Carlton: Where Quality Is First and Foremost

The Ritz-Carlton is a hotel chain that prides itself on offering its guests an extraordinary experience during their stay. The Ritz's goal is to exceed customers' expectations, rather than simply meeting them. Its commitment to quality has made the hotel chain highly successful in achieving this goal. The Ritz-Carlton is one of only two American companies to have won the Malcolm Baldrige Quality Award twice (the Malcolm Baldrige Award is the "Oscar" of quality).

Management at the Ritz-Carlton has integrated quality into every activity. Every morning, the performance of every department in every hotel is compared to metrics in the Ritz's Service Quality Index (SQI). Every one of the 14,000 employees of the Ritz-Carlton knows the Ritz's "Gold Standards" of customer service, consisting of the Credo, the Three Steps of Services, the Motto, and the Twenty Basics. All employees carry laminated pocket versions of the Gold Standards with them.

Information regarding The Ritz-Carlton and its Gold Standards is available for review at the corporate site of the Ritz-Carlton website (www.ritzcarlton.com).

Conformance quality is a measure of whether or not a delivered product meets its design specifications.

Quality management is a management approach that establishes an organization-wide focus on quality, merging the development of a quality-oriented corporate culture with intensive use of managerial and statistical tools.

Fitness for consumption is a very broad definition of quality. Operations managers must define quality in more specific terms that are relevant for their products and intended customers. In Chapter 2 we noted various aspects of product quality, addressing product design and conformance. Aspects of design quality address product functions, features, and characteristics. This includes how well the product does what the consumer needs, but it also includes ancillary aspects such as how environmentally friendly the product is, or how socially responsible the providing company is. Conformance quality is measured by how well an actual delivered product matches the dimensions and traits specified in its design.

These quality traits were originally developed with tangible goods in mind. However, they apply equally well to services. In addition, face-to-face services require an expanded notion of product quality that considers interpersonal interactions and customers' perceptions throughout the service experience. Table 6-1 provides a summary of dimensions of product quality that have been identified for goods and services, respectively. Note that the service quality dimensions go beyond the specifics of the service task. Service quality is affected by the environment surrounding the service as well as by the interpersonal communications and experiences involved. These aspects can have huge effects on customers' perceptions of service quality.

It is easy to draw parallels between the quality dimensions for tangible products and those for service products. Notions of performance, features, reliability, durability, and conformance can be applied to the task portion of the service quality dimension.

conformance quality A measure of whether or not a delivered product meets its design specifications.

quality management A management approach that establishes an organizationwide focus on quality.

sustainability

TABLE 6-1   Dimensions of Quality for Goods and Services

Dimension of Product Quality	Description for a Tangible Good	Description for an Intangible Service
Performance	The degree to which the product meets or exceeds certain operating characteristics	
Features	Presence of unique product characteristics that supplement basic functions	
Reliability	Length of time a product performs before it must be repaired	Ability to perform the promised service dependably and accurately
Durability	Length of product life or the amount of use one gets before a product deteriorates	
Conformance	The degree to which a product meets its design specifications	
Aesthetics	Subjective assessment of a product's look, feel, sound, taste, or smell	Appearance of physical facilities, equipment, personnel, and communication materials
Support/Responsiveness	Competence of product support in terms of installation, information, maintenance, or repair	Willingness to help customers and provide prompt service
Perceived Quality (Reputation/Assurance/ Empathy)	Subjective assessment based on image, advertising, brand names, reputation, or other information indirectly associated with the product's attributes	Subjective assessment of the knowledge and courtesy of employees and their ability to convey trust and confidence Subjective assessment of the caring, individualized attention paid to customers

Source: Adapted from A. Parasuraman, V. A. Zeithaml, and L. L. Berry, "SERVQUAL: A Multiple Item Scale for Measuring Customer Perceptions of Service Quality," *Journal of Retailing,* April 1992, pp. 57–71; R. B. Chase and D. M. Stewart, "Making Your Service Fail-Safe," *Sloan Management Review* 35, no. 3 (Spring 1994), pp. 35–45; and D. A. Garvin, *Managing Quality.* New York: Free Press, 1988.

For example, the durability of a service might be associated with how well a service is performed (how often do you have to get your hair "permed"?). Both tangible good and service quality dimensions contain some aspects that are fairly easy to measure objectively and other aspects that are mostly subjective and very difficult to assess. For example, aesthetics and perceived quality dimensions are both difficult to quantify, mainly because judgments vary widely from customer to customer and from situation to situation.

Surprisingly, quality is poorly understood and weakly defined in some firms. Managers in different functions sometimes emphasize different dimensions of quality. Marketing managers tend to care a lot about product aesthetics and perceptual aspects such as brand image. Design engineers tend to focus on aspects such as performance, reliability, and durability. Operations personnel, on the other hand, often focus on conformance quality. While each functional group has its primary area of focus, it is important for all managers in a given firm to understand all of the dimensions of quality that are important to customers.

Functional Roles in Quality Management

LO6-2 Explain the roles that operations and other functional managers play in determining product quality.

Quality management is fundamentally a *business* management approach, in that it encompasses many functional areas and activities both within and across companies in the supply chain. Table 6-2 provides examples of some of the ways that decisions made by managers in various functions might impact product quality. Note that some of these decisions might be made in places and times that are far away from actual production and delivery operations. Sometimes it is difficult to anticipate how decisions about markets or facilities, for example, might affect product quality outcomes in the future. Managers who are far removed from operations activities might not even be aware of how their decisions impact product quality. This is why the development of a culture of quality awareness is such a fundamentally important beginning to quality improvement programs within a business.

It is not enough that managers within a given firm practice quality management principles; those principles need to permeate throughout the supply chain (for example, see the Get Real box in the next section on tracing quality in food supply chains). Quality is an important consideration when selecting suppliers. Practices such as single sourcing and full partnerships with suppliers can be used to extend quality management practices upstream and downstream. Some large companies help their suppliers understand and implement quality management practices. Similarly, companies work closely with their customers in order to clearly define customers' specifications of quality. Ultimately, the customer decides whether a "quality" product has been delivered.

relationships

Core Values and Concepts of Quality Management

LO6-3 Apply the core values and typical practices associated with quality management.

Some of the philosophical elements of quality management have been around since the industrial revolution. However, events in Japan made that country a fertile ground for the development and refinement of these elements. World War II devastated the Japanese economy. Japan had such a reputation for building inferior products that the phrase "Made in Japan" was synonymous with shoddy workmanship. After World War II, Japanese managers searched for ways to restructure their firms and the country's economy as a whole. Thought leaders like W. Edwards Deming, Joseph Juran, and others brought the seeds of a management philosophy to Japan as they worked as part of the American Occupation Force. W. Edwards Deming and Joseph Juran complemented each other as they worked to spread the word of quality: Deming focused his message on the role of top management,

global

TABLE 6-2 Functional Influences on Product Quality

Functional Personnel	Decisions and Activities with Potential Impacts on Product Quality
Marketing Managers	Choices of markets to pursue and product features to offer
	Design of advertising and other programs that communicate product attributes to customers
	Development of new product testing programs
Sales Managers	Setting of sales targets
	Interactions with customers
	Interpretations of customers' needs and desires
Product Engineers	Design of product specifications, service elements, dimensional tolerances, etc.
	Design of product prototyping procedures
Process Engineers	Design of manufacturing and service processes
	Choices of technology and associated capabilities and capacity limits
	Design of quality assurance tests and procedures
Finance and Accounting Managers	Setting of restrictions for equipment purchases
	Establishing goals for utilization of facilities and working capital
	Design of measures used to assess efficiency and productivity
Human Resources Managers	Design of hiring criteria and training and development programs
	Setting of compensation schemes and incentives
Manufacturing and Service Operations Managers	Design and execution of processing procedures
	Design of work policies
	Interactions with customers
	Management of facilities and equipment
	Scheduling of work
Supply Managers	Description of purchase requirements
	Selection of suppliers
	Establishment of contracts and associated incentives and penalties
	Management of and interactions with suppliers
Logistics Managers	Selection of transportation providers
	Development of tracking and other information systems
	Design of packaging, storage, and material handling processes
	Management of and interactions with transportation providers

while Juran emphasized the tactical/operational side of quality. These leaders advocated merging certain core management values with statistical techniques and other management tools. The resulting "total quality management," or TQM, approach helped to transform Japan's economy, making it an industrial powerhouse. Since then, this approach has spread

GET REAL

Food Safety in Global Supply Chains—A Real Challenge

sustainability   global

The Centers for Disease Control and Prevention estimate that one in six U.S. residents suffer from food poisoning each year. Quality problems in our food supply are often in the news. Rather than becoming less frequent, recent trends suggest that food safety problems are occurring even more often. In fact, many of the largest food recalls in history have occurred since 2007:

Menu Foods Pet Food—In 2007 Menu Foods Inc. recalled several brands of dog and cat food because they contained melamine, an industrial chemical used in the making of plastics.

Hallmark/Westland Meat Packing—In 2008, an investigation into slaughter practices resulted in the recall of 143 million pounds of beef, much of it destined for school lunch programs.

Peanut Corporation—This company shipped products containing salmonella a dozen times between 2007 and 2008. The shipments were later linked to eight deaths, and they sickened over 600 people in 46 states and in Canada.

Wright County/Hillandale Farms—Salmonella was the cause of a 2010 recall of over a half billion fresh eggs. The Centers for Disease Control noted over 1,900 reports of illness connected with the outbreak.

Cargill—In 2011 Cargill recalled over 35 million pounds of ground turkey due to contamination. The contaminated meat was responsible for one death and the sickening of over 75 people.

Blue Bell—In 2015 Blue Bell Ice Cream recalled over 8 million gallons of ice cream because of listeria contamination linked to at least 3 deaths and the reported illness of hundreds.

Chipotle Mexican Grill—In 2015 an E. coli outbreak sickened dozens of customers across six U.S. states. The quality failure led to the closure of 43 restaurants for almost two weeks and caused Chipotle managers to decrease sourcing from local producers. This approach had been an important selling point for the chain.

While there are likely many root causes to these quality failures, a growing concern is the lack of traceability of products as food manufacturers in industrialized countries increasingly source their ingredients from distant, low-cost countries. Many of these countries do not have the same sanitary standards for production, especially in the case of seafood and fresh produce. Sourcing products and ingredients internationally provides cost savings and the ability to source products all year long. On the other hand, the global supply chain adds complexity to an already complex system of food safety, quality, and logistics.

---

to the United States and the rest of the world. Table 6-3 summarizes the contributions of the major quality gurus. Note the similarities and differences in the core values of these leaders.

TQM: A "TOTAL" VIEW OF QUALITY

total quality management (TQM) An integrated business management strategy aimed at embedding awareness of quality in all organizational processes.

Total quality management (TQM) is an integrated business management strategy aimed at embedding awareness of quality in all organizational processes. The word *total* in total quality management has several important connotations. First, a product's quality is ultimately determined by the customer's acceptance and use of the product. Accordingly, any discussion of product quality issues should always start with a focus on all of the attributes, the total package that targeted customers will care most about. Second, quality management is a total, organizationwide activity, rather than a technical task. Quality assurance is not simply the responsibility of product inspectors. Every employee in a company has a stake in product quality, and almost everyone has some direct or indirect influence on it. Third, quality improvement requires a total commitment from all employees. A quality product results from good design combined with effective production and delivery methods. Because almost everyone in a company has some role either directly or indirectly related to design, production, or delivery, commitment to high quality is required of everyone in the firm. To make good decisions, people from all affected functions should be involved. Consequently, TQM has a heavy emphasis on decision making in cross-functional teams.

TABLE 6-3 Contributions of Quality Management Thought Leaders

Deming	Juran	Crosby	Imai
All employees are responsible for quality	Quality has many dimensions	Quality is free; zero defects is an appropriate goal	Kaizen system of continuous improvement
Variability is the source of most problems	Quality management is change management	Focus on incremental and continuous change	Need a process-oriented view
The customer is the final arbiter of quality	Cost of quality analysis highlights need for change		Frontline workers have important insights
			Worker training and development are key
Deming's 14 Points	**Juran's Universal Breakthrough Sequence**	**Crosby's 14 Steps for Quality Improvement**	**Imai's Kaizen Steps**
1. Create consistency of purpose for continual improvement of goods and services.	1. Proof of Need. Create awareness by showing the costs of not changing.	1. Management commitment. Make quality a high priority for the firm.	1. Standardize an operation.
2. Adopt the new philosophy for economic stability.	2. Project Identification. Pick an initial project that has the highest, most visible payoffs.	2. Quality improvement teams. Cross-functional teams guide and achieve improvements.	2. Measure the standardized operation.
3. Cease dependency on inspection to achieve quality.	3. Organize for Improvement. Put in place the resources, top management, employees, and work policies needed to ensure success.	3. Quality measurement. Clear measures that relate to individual activities.	3. Gauge measurements against requirements.
4. End the practice of awarding business on price tag alone.	4. Diagnostic Journey. Identify and understand the critical few problems and their causes.	4. Cost of quality evaluation. Assess prevention, appraisal, and failure costs.	4. Innovate to meet requirements and increase productivity.
5. Improve constantly and forever the system of production and service.	5. Remedial Action. Identify and implement necessary corrective actions.	5. Quality awareness. Formal programs for creating awareness.	5. Standardize the new, improved operations.
6. Institute training on the job.	6. Resistance to Change. Overcome resistance by encouraging wide participation and by giving people sufficient time to understand and accept the changes.	6. Corrective action. Teams identify, study, and resolve problems.	6. Continue cycle *ad infinitum*.
7. Adopt and institute modern methods of supervision and leadership.	7. Holding Onto the Gains. Prevent a return to the "old" ways of doing things by establishing new standards, increasing training, and developing new control systems.	7. Zero defects planning. Move from correcting problems to totally eliminating them.	
8. Drive out fear.		8. Employee education. Employees at all levels trained to fulfill their proper roles.	
9. Break down barriers between departments and individuals.		9. Zero defects day. Event to signal a new, higher standard of performance.	
10. Eliminate the use of slogans, posters, and exhortations.		10. Goal setting. New goals to guide performance and to keep quality in the forefront.	
11. Eliminate work standards and numerical quotas.		11. Error cause removal. Moves from correcting problems to removing the underlying causes.	
12. Remove barriers that rob the hourly worker of the right to pride in workmanship.		12. Recognition. Appreciation of employees whose actions have helped the firm achieve its quality objectives.	
13. Institute a vigorous program of education and retraining.		13. Quality council. Team leaders meet regularly to share experiences and plans.	
14. Define top management's permanent commitment to ever-improving quality and productivity.		14. Do it all over again! Repeat the steps at a higher level.	

Recognizing the Total Impacts of Quality Performance

LO6-4 Perform a cost of quality analysis.

cost of quality (COQ) A framework for quantifying the total cost of quality-related efforts and deficiencies.

prevention costs Costs associated with efforts to prevent product defects and associated failure and appraisal costs.

appraisal costs Costs resulting from inspections used to assess quality levels.

internal failure costs Costs associated with quality failures uncovered before products are delivered to customers.

external failure costs Costs associated with quality failures uncovered after products reach customers.

In addition to affecting sales and other direct measures of business performance, poor product quality can have hidden or indirect effects. For example, poor quality can affect inspection, rework, and warranty costs—elements often buried in a company's overhead expenses. A focus on quality management demands that the total costs and benefits of quality performance be first understood by everyone in the organization. This usually requires a quite involved and far-reaching analysis, known as a cost of quality (COQ) analysis, to help clarify the cost impacts of poor conformance quality. COQ identifies and assesses four major cost categories:

- **Prevention costs** result from efforts to prevent product defects (nonconforming products) and from efforts needed to limit both failure and appraisal costs. Such costs include resources spent on planning, new-product reviews, investments in more capable processing equipment, training, process control, and quality improvement projects.

- **Appraisal costs** result from inspections used to assess products' quality levels. Such costs include resources spent on incoming material inspections, product and process inspections, inspection staff salaries, test equipment, and development of test procedures.

- **Internal failure costs** result from defects that are found in products prior to their shipment to customers. These costs include scrapped materials, salvage and rework, excess material inventories, and other costs of correction.

- **External failure costs** result from defects that are found only after products reach customers. These costs include complaint settlements, loss of customer goodwill and future sales, returned materials, warranty work, and field service or repairs.

Fill level tolerances, by law, are very narrow when it comes to permissible underfilling. However, business profitability demands that overfill be kept to a minimum, too. Machine vision systems can check fill level to verify minimum product requirements and alert lineworkers when overfill results in excessive product giveaway.

Courtesy of Omron

Prevention costs are the costs of activities aimed at eliminating the potential causes of product defects, or failures, while appraisal costs are the costs of activities aimed at ensuring that defective products are identified and not delivered to customers. Failure costs include both the internal costs of defects found inside the company and the external costs of defects found by customers.

It is important to note that, as a product progresses from one stage to the next in the supply chain, a defect found in later stages is much more costly than a defect found in earlier stages. In later stages more resources have been invested in the product, and there is sometimes less ability to rework the product. Costs are highest when a defect is uncovered by the customer. Repair costs are relatively large, but often, and more importantly, the costs of lost sales and tarnished product image can be very large.

Some of the costs contained in these four categories are identifiable in expense reports, yet others are hidden in overhead and other administrative accounts. For example, it may be difficult to establish the percentage of production engineering and management salaries (an overhead expense) that is attributable to solving quality problems. Similarly, some percentage of safety stock inventories may be needed to cover quality problems, but this is rarely explicitly identified.

A thorough COQ analysis usually requires quite a bit of digging, in addition to the cooperation of accounting and operations personnel. They often find that the cost

GET REAL

Cost of Quality Analysis Applies to Both Services and Manufacturing

The following table provides recent cost of quality data for two different companies. The left side of the table provides costs as a percentage of revenues for a hotel restaurant; the right side shows average costs of quality across 11 manufacturing plants owned by a single large company.

Comparing these two analyses points out some interesting differences in how services and manufacturing firms may apply the cost of quality approach. First, note that total costs of quality range from about 7 percent to 16 percent of revenues. These are fairly typical values. For a large company, costs of quality at this level could amount to hundreds of millions or even billions of dollars! In both cases, the total costs of quality went down from year 1 to year 2, especially for the restaurant, where total costs decreased from 16 percent of revenues to 12 percent of revenues.

Comparing Costs of Quality for a Hotel Restaurant and Manufacturing Plants

Hotel Restaurant	Percentage of Revenues		Manufacturing Plant	Percentage of Revenues	
	Year 1	Year 2		Year 1	Year 2
Prevention costs:			*Prevention costs:*		
Design menu	0.70%	1.12%	Design engineering	0.38%	0.27%
Equipment maintenance	0.30%	0.70%	Preventive repair / maintenance	0.43%	0.31%
Training	0.75%	1.76%	Training	0.13%	0.14%
Vendor evaluation	0.25%	0.42%	Process engineering	0.32%	0.38%
			Quality engineering	0.70%	0.91%
Total prevention costs	2.00%	4.00%	Total prevention costs	2.00%	2.00%
Appraisal costs:			*Appraisal costs:*		
Inspection of production	0.90%	0.65%	Manufacturing inspection	0.41%	0.32%
Product-testing (equipment)	1.15%	0.56%	Design analysis	0.24%	0.17%
Product-testing (labor and material)	1.70%	0.63%	Product acceptance	0.77%	0.63%
Incoming products inspection	0.25%	0.40%	Receiving inspection	0.24%	0.22%
			Lab audit	0.42%	0.40%
Total appraisal costs	4.00%	2.00%	Total appraisal costs	2.00%	1.70%
Internal failure costs:			*Internal failure costs:*		
Scrap	2.20%	1.30%	Scrap	2.84%	2.43%
Rework	1.50%	0.85%	Rework	0.58%	0.42%
Breakdown maintenance	0.80%	0.35%	Process engineering	0.15%	0.18%
Total internal failure costs	4.50%	2.50%	Total internal failure costs	3.57%	3.03%
External failure costs:			*External failure costs:*		
Returned meals (room service)	0.70%	1.10%	Returned material	0.20%	0.29%
Customer support	0.50%	0.20%	Marketing	0.05%	0.05%
Discount due to defects	1.80%	0.70%	Process engineering	0.07%	0.08%
Lost sales	2.50%	1.50%	Repair	0.02%	0.01%
			Travel	0.03%	0.03%
Total external failure costs	5.50%	3.50%	Total external failure costs	0.37%	0.46%
Total cost of quality	16.00%	12.00%	Total cost of quality	7.98%	7.24%
			Defect rate (per million units)	3.307	1,332

Sources: C. Ramdeen; J. Santos; and H. K. Chatfield, "Measuring the Cost of Quality in a Hotel Restaurant Operation," *International Journal of Contemporary Hospitality Management* 19, no. 4 (2007), pp. 286–95; and Venky Nagar and Madhav V. Rajan, "The Revenue Implications of Financial and Operational Measures of Product Quality," *The Accounting Review* 76, no. 4 (2001), pp. 495–513.

Continued

Restaurant managers attributed this improvement to the increased investments that they made in prevention—note that they spent twice as much on prevention in year 2. This supports the quality management principle that prevention is better than cure.

A second difference is in the kinds of costs tracked by the restaurant versus the manufacturing plants. While the four cost of quality categories are used by just about everyone in business, most companies need to include or exclude specific costs in accordance with the nature of their business. For example, the manufacturing plants include more engineering-related costs. Also note the differences in drivers of total costs. External failure costs make up a much larger share of the total costs of quality in the restaurant than they do in the manufacturing plants. This attests to the fact that it is much more difficult to provide remedies for service failures than for failures in tangible goods—it is hard to "repair" bad service! External failure costs can vary a great deal across different manufactured products too, depending on their durability and warranty policies.

relationships

of poor quality is surprisingly large! Once a COQ analysis has been used to quantify the monetary impact of quality on their company's performance, managers are typically highly motivated. The COQ analysis points out the magnitude of the opportunity and gives managers a stronger basis for financially justifying investments in quality improvement initiatives.

An Inverted View of Management

A focus on quality management turns a conventional view of management on its head. Traditional management views make sharp distinctions between managers and workers, often elevating the importance of managers. That is, the workers are present to support the activities of management. This view is illustrated by the pyramid shown on the left-hand side of Figure 6-1. The base of the pyramid consists of frontline workers who interact routinely with customers and operational processes, so they deal with the daily problems and difficulties of running the business. In doing so, frontline workers can be seen as supporters of smaller and smaller layers of management. In this view of the organization, managers are thought to be the decision makers and "owners" of operating processes and, therefore, they are seen to have primary responsibility for product quality.

A progressive quality management approach challenges this view, arguing that it is the workers on the front lines of business who should actually have primary "ownership" of operating processes. Further, managers should support workers, not the other way around. Frontline workers have the closest contact with customers and operational processes; therefore, they ultimately determine the quality level that the firm offers and how customers view the firm. In addition, they know more than anyone about the firm's problems and the best ways to solve them. Total quality management advocates believe that the entire organization should support the frontline workers, as the right-hand side of Figure 6-1 illustrates. This idea of elevating and empowering frontline workers is a core value of total quality management.

What does employee *empowerment* actually mean? Several elements are required. First, frontline workers must be given both the responsibility and authority to make decisions. This is sometimes the hardest change for both managers and frontline workers to accept. Both groups have to clearly define and recognize the enlarged scope of decisions for which frontline workers are responsible, and then managers have to relinquish control and actively encourage these frontline workers to take charge. Measurement and incentive systems may also need to be changed to motivate frontline worker involvement.

Second, frontline workers need to have the knowledge required to make good decisions. Empowerment usually requires education and cross-training (job rotation) of employees on all technical issues related to their job environments. Equally important, employees need training on quality management concepts and in the use of problem-solving tools. If frontline workers are to set appropriate priorities and make good business decisions, they also need an understanding of the organizational strategy and current objectives.

Finally, frontline workers must have the resources required to make quality improvements. Such resources usually include data, tools and systems, money for investments, and time.

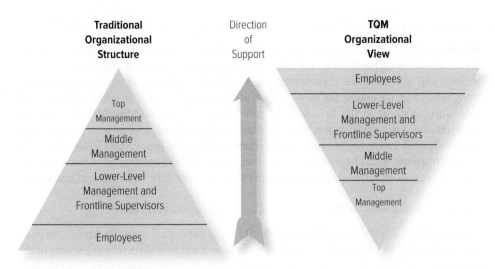

Process-Oriented Focus on Prevention and Problem Solving

Quality management is based on the idea that products are outcomes of processes. All organizations, functions, and activities involved in the design, production, and delivery of a product, good, or service should be viewed collectively as parts of a process. This extended process view includes suppliers and customers, making quality management principles very consistent with the overall supply chain management perspective. Quality problems are often only solvable through the involvement of suppliers, because their inputs may be related to problem causes. Suppliers can also help determine the costs and feasibility of changes required to address quality problems. As stated above, it is almost always more efficient to solve problems at the earliest stage possible in the supply chain, rather than trying to find a remedy or workaround at some later stage. Involving customers can clarify requirements needed to define acceptable levels of quality.

In TQM, problem prevention is emphasized, as opposed to fixing problems after they occur. It is better to eliminate the causes of problems than it is to find and sort out defective products before they go to customers. In the long term, prevention is almost always cheaper than correction. Sometimes managers refer to this prevention-oriented approach as *quality at the source* as opposed to *quality through inspection.* Furthermore, problem solving is most effective when decisions are based on the analysis of actual data, as opposed to conjectures or opinions. The supplement to this chapter illustrates a number of analytical tools that have been developed to collect and analyze data. Use of these tools along with a data-led, or fact-based, approach helps managers to detect and solve problems in processes.

Variability in repeated activities is often the major source of problems in operations processes. For example:

- Variability in the time it takes to complete a task often disrupts work flows.
- Variations in a purchased material characteristic, such as in the diameter of a ball bearing, can cause unreliability in product performance.
- Variations in marketing promotions can cause large swings in product demand, which make production processes less stable.

Variability causes unpredictability, which increases uncertainty and reduces control over processes and outputs. Thus, an important task in quality management is to continually find and eliminate sources of unwanted and uncontrolled variability. Later in this chapter we will discuss the Six Sigma program for quality management, an approach that builds upon this idea.

Viewing Quality Management as a Never-Ending Quest

Because products and processes are continually changing, and because perfection (zero defects) is deemed to be an appropriate goal, continuous process improvement should be a part of every person's job. A widely used improvement process known as Kaizen, or Continuous Improvement, is based on the notion that the long-term survival and success of any organization occurs only when everyone in the firm actively pursues opportunities to identify and implement improvements every day. Chapter 3 discussed the practice of Kaizen for process improvement. Pursuit of small improvements keeps people thinking about the process and its current operation. Furthermore, small improvements are often gained without needing large investments of capital. In many cases, these improvements can be gained with little or no required investment.

Building an Organizational Culture around Quality

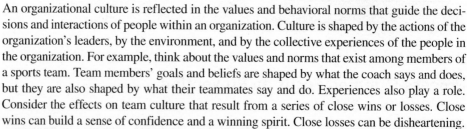

relationships

An organizational culture is reflected in the values and behavioral norms that guide the decisions and interactions of people within an organization. Culture is shaped by the actions of the organization's leaders, by the environment, and by the collective experiences of the people in the organization. For example, think about the values and norms that exist among members of a sports team. Team members' goals and beliefs are shaped by what the coach says and does, but they are also shaped by what their teammates say and do. Experiences also play a role. Consider the effects on team culture that result from a series of close wins or losses. Close wins can build a sense of confidence and a winning spirit. Close losses can be disheartening.

Managers have to recognize that their actions, more than their words, help to shape culture. At the same time they have to recognize that they are not completely in control of the firm's culture. Both past experiences and external forces, such as the economic environment, labor union influences, and governmental controls, can have big impacts.

The culture within an organization can have tremendous effects on the success or failure of quality improvement initiatives. History contains many cases of companies whose quality initiatives were rendered ineffective by an incompatible culture. Most often cultural barriers to change are created by perceived inequities that have created a mistrust of management, or by incentive systems that motivate behaviors at odds with the values of quality management (e.g., when management pays for output irrespective of its quality).

It is critical for managers to continually assess their organizations and identify the dynamics of culture that may be creating values and norms of behavior that are supportive, or damaging, for quality management initiatives. Through communications, actions, measures, rewards, and incentives, managers should seek to build the values of total quality management into their corporate culture. Table 6-4 lists the values we have discussed in this section, along with some

TABLE 6-4   TQM Values and Success Factors

Values that Characterize TQM	Factors Affecting the Success of TQM
• Holistic view of product quality and its impacts	• Strong, charismatic leadership
• Emphasis on customer requirements	• Trust between labor and management
• Extended process view of operations	• Crisis situation or compelling reason for change
• Emphasis on prevention rather than inspection	• Adequate resourcing of training and improvement projects
• Disdain for variability	• Clear, well-communicated, uncomplicated change process
• Data-based decision making (vs. opinion-based)	• Unquestionable success of early efforts
• Employee empowerment	
• Top management support	
• Supplier involvement	
• Continuous improvement	

of the factors that have contributed to the creation of a TQM culture. Note that the success factors are not guarantees of success, but their absence will hinder successful implementation.

The core values of quality management are fleshed out in various quality improvement methodologies, certification standards, and awards criteria. In the following sections, we describe several methodologies and standards that you are likely to encounter, namely:

- Plan-Do-Check-Act Cycle
- Six Sigma Approach to Quality Improvement
- ISO 9000 Series: An International Quality Standard

GUIDING METHODOLOGIES FOR QUALITY MANAGEMENT

Plan-Do-Check-Act Cycles (Deming Wheel)

A popular methodology used to guide problem identification and solution is the **plan-do-check-act cycle (PDCA)**, also known as the *Deming Wheel* or *Deming Cycle* (in honor of W. Edwards Deming). The PDCA cycle (see Figure 6-2) describes the sequence used to solve problems and improve quality continuously over time.

The PDCA cycle consists of four separate but linked activities:

- *Plan.* Identify a problem by studying the current situation to detect a gap between it and the desired future situation. Identify actions to improve the situation (i.e., close the gap). Formulate a plan for closing the gap (e.g., a plan for reducing the number of defects coming from a specific process).
- *Do.* Having formulated a plan, implement it.
- *Check.* Use performance metrics to monitor and inspect the results. Identify unplanned problems elsewhere in the system or previously hidden problems uncovered by the changes.
- *Act.* Review information collected in the check step and take corrective actions to prevent reoccurrence of problems. Institutionalize changes (through revised procedures and associated training) as a starting point for the next PDCA cycle.
- The PDCA method is simple, giving all employees the impetus and guiding structure for attacking problems on a daily basis. Workers at all levels can be trained in the PDCA process and in the use of the quality tools referenced above.

Six Sigma: A Systematic Approach to Quality Management

In addition to general methods for quality improvement that can be applied by all workers, companies often need to organize specific quality improvement projects. The **Six Sigma**

plan-do-check-act cycle (PDCA) A process for improving quality that describes the sequence used to solve problems and improve quality continuously over time; also known as the *Deming Wheel* or *Deming Cycle*.

Six Sigma A management program that seeks to improve the quality of process outputs by identifying and removing the causes of defects and variation in the various processes.

FIGURE 6-2
PDCA in Action

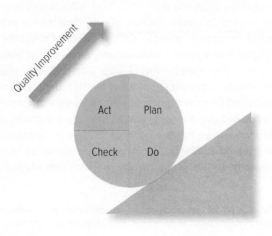

program for quality and process improvements has been adopted by many of the larger firms around the world. Six Sigma is a management approach that seeks to improve the quality of process outputs by using projects to identify and remove the causes of defects and variation in the various processes.

The term *sigma* refers to the Greek symbol, σ, that represents the standard deviation of values for the output of a process. The standard deviation is an indicator of process variability (inconsistency). In statistics, standard deviation is a measure of the variability or dispersion of a population, a data set, or a probability distribution. A low standard deviation indicates that the data points tend to be very close to the same value, typically the mean, while high standard deviation indicates that the data are spread out over a large range of values. As standard deviation increases, there is greater uncertainty about the exact outcome. As previously noted in this chapter, variability is regarded as a source of quality failures. A primary objective of the Six Sigma method is to design and improve products and processes so that sources of variability are reduced.

That explains the *sigma* in Six Sigma, but what about the *six?* One of the issues in quality improvement is deciding how far variability reduction efforts should go. In a Six Sigma approach, the goal is to achieve a process standard deviation that is 12 times smaller than the range of outputs allowed by the product's design specification. In this case, the design specification encompasses *six* process output standard deviations on each side of its center point.[1] Consider Example 6-1 below.

Curious students often ask, "Why is *six* sigma the goal? Why not *five* sigma, or *seven* sigma?" Good question. Early developers of the Six Sigma approach at Motorola originally chose six sigma as an appropriate goal because of the nature of their products and manufacturing processes. A six sigma rated process, where upper and lower product specifications are set 12 standard deviations apart, will produce at most only 3.4 product defects per million outputs. Is this goal suitable for other products? It all depends on the costs of quality. If the costs of failure outweigh the costs of prevention and appraisal, then pursuing greater levels of conformance (more "sigmas") is probably justified. However, for some products there is a point at which the size of potential failure cost savings does not justify the investments required to achieve them. For example, Six Sigma quality is arguably not justified for a product such as an inexpensive ballpoint pen, because the internal and external failure costs are low once a reasonable level of quality has been achieved. On the other hand, Six Sigma quality may be too low a goal for products such as drugs and medical devices, where the cost of a single failure can be very high (someone's life!).

standard deviation A measure of the variability or dispersion of a population, data set, or distribution.

EXAMPLE 6-1

You operate a trucking company that delivers products to distribution centers for a large retailer such as Walmart. Distribution centers are very busy places. Consequently, they schedule deliveries in very tight windows of time. Walmart often requires that deliveries arrive within a 15-minute window, that is, no more than 7.5 minutes before or after a scheduled time. A Six Sigma approach would seek to make truck arrivals so consistent that the standard deviation of arrival times is no more than 1.25 minutes (15 minutes/12). If this level of consistency were achieved, it would be highly unlikely that a truck would ever arrive too early or too late.

How would you reduce driving time variability this much? The Six Sigma approach provides a systematic process for first identifying sources of variability and then reducing them. For example, you might start by thinking of all the possible causes of early and late arrivals (weather, traffic, breakdowns, and so on). Then you would brainstorm ways to prevent these causes or overcome them. If variability cannot be reduced sufficiently, another option would be to widen the specifications; that is, to negotiate wider delivery windows with Walmart.

---

[1]This relationship between product specification and process variation is illustrated in the supplement to this chapter, "Quality Improvement Tools," in the section describing process capability.

TABLE 6-5   How Quality Relates to Sigma

Sigma Level	Defects per Million Units
2 σ	308,770
3 σ	66,810
4 σ	6,209
5 σ	233
6 σ	3.4

The Classical View of Quality "99.9% Good" (4.6σ)	The Six Sigma View of Quality "99.99966% Good" (6σ)
• 20,000 lost articles of mail per hour.	• Seven lost articles of mail per hour.
• Unsafe drinking water almost 15 minutes each day.	• One minute of unsafe drinking water every seven months.
• 5,000 incorrect surgical operations per week.	• 1.7 incorrect surgical operations per week.
• 2 short or long landings at most major airports daily.	• One short or long landing at most major airports every five years.
• 200,000 wrong drug prescriptions each year.	• 68 wrong drug prescriptions each year.
• No electricity for almost 7 hours each month.	• One hour without electricity every 34 years.

Table 6-5 shows the levels of quality associated with other sigma levels, along with some of the quality levels seen in our everyday lives. In truth, very few business operations ever attain a Six Sigma level of quality. More important than the absolute goal are the quality improvement processes that comprise a Six Sigma program.

DMAIC: The Six Sigma Process

At the heart of the Six Sigma approach is a five-step process: define, measure, analyze, improve, and control (DMAIC). Figure 6-3 describes the DMAIC process. For any given good or service, members of a cross-functional team usually work through these

> **activity**
>
> **student**
>
> For a candy such as M&Ms, identify the important critical-to-quality characteristics. How would you measure these characteristics objectively? Which of these measures pertain to the physical product itself? Which of these measures relate to the packaging or the services surrounding the good?

steps together to complete a quality improvement project. The focus of the DMAIC improvement process is initially on the product outcome; then it shifts to the underlying processes needed to produce and deliver the product.

As project teams work through the DMAIC process, they focus on several objectives:

1. Each *critical-to-quality* (CTQ) characteristic should be defined from a customer's perspective and in a way in which it can be measured as objectively as possible.
2. It is important to determine and consider the future market and technology strategies for the product, as well as the strategies for the processes that are involved in delivery of the CTQ characteristics.
3. The quality improvement tools described in the supplement to this chapter are especially useful in the analyze, improve, and control steps of the process.
4. If the data do not already exist, the project team needs to develop a way to measure important outcomes on a frequent and regular basis.

DMAIC An acronym for the five steps at the heart of the Six Sigma process: define, measure, analyze, improve, and control.

 LO6-5 Apply the Six Sigma DMAIC approach to quality improvement.

FIGURE 6-3 The DMAIC Process

Source: Dynamic Diagrams, 2009.

How does
Six Sigma
work?

BEFORE SIX SIGMA

Business process towards desired end product requirements

1. DEFINE
A cross-functional team uses inputs describing customer's needs and product functionality requirements to define Critical-to-Quality (CTQ) characteristics of the product or service. CTQs represent the few characteristics that have the greatest impacts on customers' perceptions of quality, thus requiring priority and focus for related operational processes.

2. MEASURE
The team identifies specific processes that create or influence CTQs, and measures current levels of quality (defects) for each CTQ, considering allowable tolerances for variation in each CTQ outcome.

process range

acceptable range

3. ANALYZE
The team performs data-based analyses to uncover important root causes of process variations that lead to CTQ defects.

Key process variable introducing highest likelihood of variation

4. IMPROVE
The team designs and implements process improvements that reduce variabilities, thereby increasing the probability that CTQs will be delivered within allowable ranges.

5. CONTROL
The team installs monitoring and adjustment systems or procedures to insure that process variations remain minimized, and that CTQ variables remain within allowable output ranges.

AFTER SIX SIGMA – Less Variation

Business process towards desired end product requirements

5. The lessons learned from the process should be documented, and the final problem solution should be implemented in all applicable areas.

The nearby Get Real box provides an example of how DMAIC can be successfully used to resolve quality problems.

Design for Six Sigma

Design for Six Sigma (DFSS)
A design approach that balances customer requirements with the constraints and capabilities of the supporting manufacturing and service processes.

The DMAIC process is usually aimed at improving existing products and their supporting operational processes. A similar approach has been developed to guide design decisions made in the creation of new products. Design for Six Sigma (DFSS) is an approach in which a cross-functional team designs products and processes in a way that balances customer requirements with the constraints and capabilities of the supporting manufacturing and service processes. The primary difference between DFSS and DMAIC is that DFSS takes place in the development phase, whereas DMAIC usually takes place after a new product has been launched. DFSS makes use of design engineering tools that may be used to simulate and evaluate different product/process design scenarios, whereas DMAIC ideally works with actual product and operational data. Other "design-for" processes and tools similar to DFSS are described in Chapter 4.

GET REAL

Applying DMAIC to Cough Drops

A British food company used DMAIC to improve operations in its cough drop production line, which suffered high rates of machine downtime, scrap and rework, and chronically late order deliveries.

- *Define:* The project team mapped out the production process, identified a probable cause of their defined problem—variability in the size of the cough drops—and calculated the costs associated with this problem. Too much variance in the size of a cough drop may seem incidental, but larger tablets were more likely to chip and introduce abrasive sugar dust into the machinery, causing breakdowns. That problem, along with slowdowns in packaging and the added maintenance, was estimated to cost £485,000 (783,000 USD) per year.
- *Measure:* The cough drop team found that the existing measuring techniques were not precise enough, so they did their own process measurements. They found that the process was not within specifications: Almost 20 percent of the cough drops were too large, while almost none were too small.
- *Analyze:* The team measured the accuracy of the syrup base extrusion system and found it to be accurate. They then determined that air bubbles forming in the tablets somewhere in the process were the culprit. The team investigated possible process steps where air could enter the product, finally settling on three possible steps.
- *Improve:* The team experimented with changes in product temperature, machine lubrication, and other factors to prevent air bubbles from forming. Implementing these changes caused cough drop variability to fall within

process specifications. Even so, the team noted that the process was still fairly low in capability. They suggested adding an additional wrapping line with wider tolerances for larger tablets.
- *Control:* The process changes included training for personnel and the installation of new monitoring systems to ensure that the variability improvements were maintained.

The financial impact of this project was dramatic. By decreasing the variability and increasing the wrapping tolerance for larger sizes, the company was able to save £290,000 (470,000 USD) per year in waste, maintenance, downtime, and late orders. The cost of the DMAIC project team was only £13,000 (21,000 USD), while the return on investment was 2,230.8 percent!

© Stockbyte/Punchstock

Implementing Six Sigma

Organizations often view Six Sigma as an improvement program aimed at gaining greater consistency and efficiency throughout the organization. The most common approach for implementing Six Sigma is to start by training key leaders in the organization in quality management philosophies and tools. Then these initial leaders train others, who then train others, and so on. Usually there are two to three levels of training targeted for various employees in the organization. Persons completing the levels of training are given names taken from the Asian martial arts tradition. For example, persons who complete the highest levels of training are called Black Belts, or even higher-level Master Black Belts. Black Belt personnel have usually completed at least several quality improvement projects. Master Black Belts may even work full-time in training others in Six Sigma processes. Employees who complete the basic level of training are often called Green Belts.

To achieve Green Belt status, employees usually must complete a project that applies the Six Sigma process to a product in their own area of work. These projects often must satisfy certain operational or financial performance goals (e.g., the project will achieve a 25 percent reduction in lead times, or the project will generate a minimum 25 percent return on investment). The cost savings from such projects can be used to pay back the costs of training for the Six Sigma program. Numerous companies have shown tremendous benefits from implementing Six Sigma. A recent study showed that a medium-sized firm that adopts Six Sigma should expect to add \$35 – \$40 million in profit each year![2]

CERTIFYING PROGRESS IN QUALITY MANAGEMENT

LO6-6 Compare and contrast various quality standards and certification programs.

The TQM and quality initiatives we have discussed up to this point are company specific; process improvements vary from company to company. Operations managers often want to know how their operational quality processes compare to others. In addition, prospective customers often want assurances that a given supplier has achieved a high level of quality performance. Certifications such as the ISO 9000 help to provide universal standards that managers and customers can use to gauge a company's quality progress.

ISO 9000: An International Quality Standard

ISO 9000 A set of internationally accepted standards for business quality management systems.

ISO 9000 defines a set of internationally accepted standards for business quality management systems. It was initially developed by the International Organization for Standardization to facilitate international trade. Since its inception in 1987, the standard has been revised several times. The newest version is referred to as the ISO 9000:2015 standard. National bodies from over 120 countries support this standard.

As a standard, ISO 9000 is applicable to all forms of organizations, irrespective of size or product offerings. Certifications have been attained by banks, consulting operations, manufacturing plants, software development firms, tourism operations, and even universities. The essential purpose of ISO 9000 is to ensure that operating processes are well documented, consistently executed, monitored, and improved. ISO 9000 certification provides essentially the same function for business processes as financial accountants provide when they audit a company's financial transactions.

Attaining ISO 9000 Certification

Over one million organizations have been independently certified to ISO 9000. To attain certification, an organization must be audited by an external, authorized party. Certification states that the firm's processes meet the requirements in the ISO 9000 standards. Typically, an organization first conducts an internal audit to determine whether its processes are consistent with the standards. Then, it contracts with a registrar (an external and independent body)[3] to perform a formal audit. Attaining ISO 9000 certification is usually quite demanding and time-consuming. The process can take anywhere from three months to two years, depending on the initial level of compliance of the firm's systems. If the organization passes the audit, its certification is recorded by the registrar.

The standard itself consists of five sections. Table 6-6 provides a brief description of each section. The standard emphasizes many of quality management's core values.

- First, it is customer-oriented, with a great emphasis placed on defining, meeting, and achieving customer satisfaction.
- Second, it emphasizes the role of leadership in engaging people to make improvements on a regular basis.
- Third, it recognizes the importance of a process-oriented approach, including the definition, measurement, and documentation of processes.

---

[2]M. Swink and B. Jacobs, "Six Sigma Adoption: Operating Performance Impacts and Contextual Drivers of Success," Journal of Operations Management 30, no. 6 (2012), pp. 437–53.
[3]It is possible to self-certify a system to be ISO 9000 compliant. However, such an action does not carry the weight and credibility of external certification.

TABLE 6-6   The ISO 9001: 2015 Certification Structure

Section		Focus/Description
4		**Context of the organization**
	4.1	Understanding the organization and its context.
	4.2	Understanding the needs and expectations of interested parties.
	4.3	Determining the scope of the quality management system.
	4.4	Quality management system and its processes.
5		**Leadership**
	5.1	Leadership and commitment.
	5.2	Policy.
	5.3	Organizational roles, responsibilities, and authorities.
6		**Planning**
	6.1	Actions to address risks and opportunities.
	6.2	Quality objectives and planning to achieve them.
	6.3	Planning of changes.
7		**Support**
	7.1	Resources.
	7.2	Competence.
	7.3	Awareness.
	7.4	Communication.
	7.5	Documented information.
8		**Operation**
	8.1	Operational planning and control.
	8.2	Requirements for products and services.
	8.3	Design and development of products and services.
	8.4	Control of externally provided processes, products, and services.
	8.5	Production and service provision.
	8.6	Release of products and services.
	8.7	Control nonconforming outputs.
9		**Performance evaluation**
	9.1	Monitoring, measurement analysis, and evaluation.
	9.2	Internal audit.
	9.3	Management review.
10		**Improvement**
	10.1	General
	10.2	Nonconformity and corrective action.
	10.3	Continual improvement.

- Fourth, it places a high priority on evidence-based decision making.
- Finally, the standard emphasizes the importance of managing inter- and intraorganizational relationships.

In general, the standard is fairly flexible in that it tells management *what* to do, but not necessarily *how* to do it.

Businesses are motivated to seek ISO 9000 certification for several reasons. Increasingly, firms are required to be certified to sell products in most major markets. Virtually every major industrial nation in the world has accepted these standards. Certification at least gives the appearance that a company will be a reliable supplier. Beyond appearances, ISO 9000-certified firms benefit from internal improvements as a result of the certification. To pass the audit, employees usually must reexamine and critically challenge their practices. The certification process can also improve communication links between functional areas within the firm. It forces people to forge agreements on important issues such as the firm's definition of quality and its identification of its target market. The success with ISO 9000 has caused the ISO organization to extend the focus of business issues covered by such standards. For example, in 1996 ISO introduced the ISO 14000 standard for environmental systems. This standard is discussed in greater detail in Chapter 16.

Industry Interpretations of ISO 9000

While the guidelines in ISO 9000 can be applied just about anywhere, each organization needs to carefully interpret them for their context. In some cases industry groups have created interpretations for their specific requirements. Table 6-7 shows some examples of common interpretations of ISO 9000.

TABLE 6-7   Industry-Specific Interpretations of ISO 9000

Standard	Industry
TickIT	Information technology industry (specifically software development)
AS9000	Aerospace manufacturers (e.g., AlliedSignal, Allison Engine, Rockwell-Collins, Boeing, Lockheed-Martin)
ISO/TS 16949	American and European automotive manufacturers
TL 9000	Telecom consortium (QuEST forum)
ISO 13485	Medical industry
ISO/IED 90003	Computer software
ISO/TS 29001	Petroleum, petrochemical, and natural gas industries.

CHAPTER SUMMARY

In this chapter we have explored the concept of quality management by tracing its origins and philosophical elements and describing how its core values have been fleshed out in quality standards and improvement programs today. We can summarize the important points of this chapter as follows:

1. Quality management strives to achieve a sustainable competitive advantage by focusing company actions on customer satisfaction, employee empowerment, and powerful management and statistical tools to achieve superior quality.

2. It is important to integrate quality management into the firm's strategic activities by ensuring that the voice of the customer is heard. The Six Sigma approach to quality is a corporatewide system to integrate the elements of the customer, strategy, value, processes, statistical tools, and metrics. This approach has been successfully implemented in many firms.

3. Formal certification to quality standards such as ISO 9000 indicates that a firm has passed a rigorous audit to confirm that its major processes have been documented, that everyone associated with those processes understands correct procedures, and that people routinely follow these procedures. ISO 9000 seems likely to make certification a near-universal order qualifier in important markets around the world.

4. Quality management in face-to-face services must take into consideration the interpersonal interactions of service providers and customers. Sometimes customers' perceptions of quality vary widely as they are potentially influenced by many different aspects of the operating system.

5. Regardless of the form of quality improvement program that a firm pursues, the core values of total commitment, cross-functional decision making, continuous improvement, and data-based decision making are the critical aspects to making quality improvement a success.

KEY TERMS

appraisal costs 178	external failure costs 178	quality management 173
conformance quality 173	internal failure costs 178	Six Sigma 183
cost of quality (COQ) 178	ISO 9000 188	standard deviation 184
design for Six Sigma (DFSS) 186	plan-do-check-act cycle (PDCA) 183	total quality management (TQM) 176
design quality 172	prevention costs 178	
DMAIC 185	product quality 172	

DISCUSSION QUESTIONS

1. Pick a product (good or service) that you are interested in consuming sometime in the near future (for example, a textbook, apartment rental, cell phone, etc.). Analyze the offerings of two competing firms. How do the products compare on various dimensions of quality? From these differences, what can you infer about each company's strategy and the customers that they seem to be targeting?

2. Employee empowerment is an essential element of quality management, especially in services. From your own experience, cite instances where a service provider empowered its employee to go the extra mile to delight you. Then indicate an instance where the opposite happened.

3. You have been appointed head of quality control for your organization (either a firm you have worked for or your college). During the first month, you interview disciples

of Deming, Juran, and Crosby. Each seems to be equally affable and competent. Which consultant would you hire for your organization? Why?

4. It has been said that quality management is really a "people" system, more than a technical system. If this is true, what conditions must first be in place for a firm to be successful with quality management? What are the possible repercussions for the firm if the employees aren't committed to the quality management program?

PROBLEMS

1. Given the following cost information for Company XYZ, calculate:
   a. Total appraisal cost
   b. Total prevention cost
   c. Total cost of internal failures
   d. Total cost of external failures
   e. Total cost of quality

Cost item	Total for the Year
Quality assurance	$450,000
Equipment maintenance	$205,000
Product redesign	$310,000
Product warranty and repair	$550,000
Product testing and inspection	$372,000
Training	$250,000
Process improvement/Kaizen	$120,000
Material scrap	$230,000
Rework labor	$426,000
Incoming materials inspection	$323,000
Customer support (after sale)	$150,000
Travel to suppliers/process certification	$ 75,000
Travel to customers/problem solving	$ 80,000

2. Rachel loves to bake cookies, but she has an old oven that has trouble maintaining a constant temperature. If the acceptable temperature range for making the cookies is 350 plus or minus 5 degrees, what is the allowable standard deviation in the temperature of her oven in order to achieve a Six Sigma level of quality?

3. Six Sigma quality (3.4 defects per million units produced) is probably a bit much to ask of Rachel's old oven (see problem 2).
   a. What would the standard deviation in the temperature of her oven need to be if she settled for a "Three Sigma" level of quality?
   b. If her oven exactly meets a "Three Sigma" quality level, what percentage of the time would her oven be operating at a temperature outside the acceptable range? (*Hint:* See Table 6-5.)

4. Suppose that the Dallas School District wants to achieve Six Sigma quality levels of performance in delivering students to school. It has established a 20-minute window as an acceptable range within which buses carrying students should arrive at school.
   a. What is the maximum allowable standard deviation of arrival times required in order to achieve this standard of quality?
   b. If the school district achieves this standard, about how many times out of a million deliveries will a bus deliver students either too early or too late?

CASE

Aqua-Fun

Roberta Brown sat at her desk and looked through the preliminary slide deck she had prepared. This presentation had to be good. In two weeks she would be giving the presentation to the top management team of Aqua-Fun. The goal: To secure their commitment to a new program aimed at improving quality. Improvements were to come through a new (to Aqua-Fun) corporatewide program to implement Six Sigma. Involvement in this program was the principal reason that Roberta had been hired by Eric Tremble, the vice-president of operations/supply chain management at Aqua-Fun, some six months earlier.

Demand for Aqua-Fun's products had grown from an emerging interest in home swimming pools over the past few decades. During that time, the founders of Aqua-Fun recognized that there was a need for good quality, fun water toys and swimming pool accessories. Since then, Aqua-Fun had grown to its current state of $195 million in annual sales, employing some 650 employees. The secret to its growth: A fair price, reliable products, and the ability to design and introduce interesting and fun new toys and accessories quickly. However, in the last two years, there was evidence that Aqua-Fun's reputation was suffering. Sales growth had slowed, and, as some of the accessories (such as pool automatic cleaners) became more sophisticated, warranty claims had grown dramatically. Top management's best estimate of the costs of dealing with poor quality in the field was about $6.7 million. However, Eric Tremble was convinced that Aqua-Fun's managers did not fully comprehend the total costs associated with managing quality and quality failures.

Before joining Aqua-Fun, Roberta Brown had worked for two years in a firm that had successfully improved quality, reduced costs, and increased revenues by implementing a companywide Six Sigma program. Roberta had been part of the Six Sigma planning and deployment team; she had gone through Green and Black Belt training; and she had successfully carried out three high visibility Six Sigma projects. Now, she was being asked to introduce a similar approach at Aqua-Fun. For both Aqua-Fun and Roberta, the time seemed right for Six Sigma.

The Presentation

Critical to this presentation was Roberta's COQ analysis (shown in the table following). She worried that the analysis was missing important cost categories. She was also unsure regarding which costs should be included. Items with question marks "????" in the COQ were items that she either did not have data for or was unsure about including. For example, she wasn't sure how the marketing managers would feel about including marketing research as a category in the COQ, though she knew that this was a large expense for the company, well above $10 million per year. Other missing categories could be quite substantial as well. Besides, Roberta still felt that there might be even more "hidden" costs of quality not captured in the analysis.

As Roberta reviewed the presentation, she noted points that she wanted to make and questions she still needed to answer:

- Aqua-Fun had tended to underestimate the true costs of quality. For example, the external failure cost estimate of $6.7 million neglected lost sales and damaged customer goodwill that might occur from poor quality products.

- The initial costs of training for a Six Sigma program (between $20,000 and $30,000 per Green Belt and $40,000–$50,000 per Black Belt) were high. In typical Six Sigma implementations, companies trained 2 to 5 percent of employees as Black Belts and they trained 50 to 100 percent of employees as Green Belts.

- There were significant benefits to be gained by such investments. Other firms had achieved 10 to 20 percent reductions in the COQ each year for the first few years of the Six Sigma program.

- To be successful, this program had to be corporatewide. It had to involve everyone from top managers to the people working on the floor. It had to involve not only operations, purchasing, logistics, and supply chain areas but also finance, personnel, training, marketing, engineering, and accounting.

Questions

1. Review the COQ Analysis. Should marketing research and other similar cost categories be included? What other cost categories should be included? Where should Roberta go to get estimates for these other costs? Who else might need to be involved?

2. If Aqua-Fun implements Six Sigma, what costs might be expected to go up, at least in the short term? What costs should be expected to go down? Can this program be financially justified? How?

3. Thinking about the core values of quality management, what factors should Roberta encourage the management team to consider as they design a Six Sigma implementation?

	Estimated Annual Cost ($)	Total Category Cost ($)
I. Prevention costs		9,507,000
A. Marketing/customer/user		
1. Marketing research	????	
2. Customer/user perception surveys/clinics	????	
B. Product/service/design development		
1. Design quality progress reviews	1,300,000	
2. Design support activities	900,000	
3. Design qualification and test	3,600,000	
C. Purchasing		
1. Supplier reviews, ratings, and certifications	564,000	
2. Purchase order tech data reviews	260,000	
3. Supplier quality planning	????	
D. Operations (manufacturing or service)		
1. Operations process validation (planning and equipment design)	750,000	
2. Operations support quality planning	25,000	
3. Operator quality education	95,000	
4. Operator SPC/process control	623,000	
E. Quality administration		
1. Administrative salaries and expenses	1,330,000	
2. Quality program planning and reporting	????	
3. Quality education	25,000	
4. Quality improvement projects	20,000	
5. Quality audits	15,000	
6. Other prevention costs	????	
II. Appraisal costs		8,612,000
A. Purchasing appraisal costs		
1. Receiving or incoming inspections and tests	2,260,000	
2. Measurement equipment (annualized cost)	856,000	
3. Qualification of supplier product	????	
4. Source inspection and control programs	????	
B. Operations (manufacturing or service) appraisal costs		
1. Planned operations inspections, tests, audits	3,950,000	
2. Inspection and test materials	225,000	
3. Process control measurements	325,000	
4. Laboratory support	145,000	
5. Outside endorsements and certifications	????	
C. External appraisal costs		
1. Field performance evaluation	-	
2. Special product evaluations	75,000	
3. Evaluation of field stock and spare parts	776,000	
D. Review of tests and inspection data	????	
E. Miscellaneous quality evaluations	????	

	Estimated Annual Cost ($)	Total Category Cost ($)
III. Internal failure costs		12,639,000
A. Product/service design failure costs (internal)		
1. Design corrective action	1,230,000	
2. Rework due to design changes	560,000	
3. Scrap due to design changes	3,650,000	
B. Purchasing failure costs		
1. Purchased material reject disposition and rework costs	1,330,000	
2. Purchased material replacement costs	230,000	
3. Supplier corrective action	????	
4. Uncontrolled material losses	????	
C. Operations (product or service) failure costs		
1. Material review and corrective action costs	356,000	
2. Operations rework and repair costs	1,700,000	
3. Re-inspection/retest costs	23,000	
4. Extra operations	????	
5. Scrap costs (operations)	3,560,000	
6. Downgraded end product or service	????	
7. Internal failure labor losses	????	
D. Other internal failure costs	????	
IV. External failure		6,695,000
A. Complaint investigation/customer or user service	845,000	
B. Returned goods	1,200,000	
C. Recall costs	650,000	
D. Warranty claims	3,250,000	
E. Liability costs	750,000	
F. Customer/user goodwill/lost sales	????	
G. Other external failure costs	????	
	Total COQ	$ 37,453,000

CASE

A Comment on Management Attitude

I visited my old pal Dinsmore recently. He had called to let me know that he had taken over as general manager of the Flagship hotel about six months ago, and he thought that I might be interested in seeing a real hotel from the inside. He also indicated that I might learn something about the hotel business.

When I drove up to the front door, a steady rain kept me inside the car for 10 to 15 minutes. During that time,

I noticed that the doorman was peering at me from inside the lobby. Sensing that the rain was not going to quit, I made a dash for the doors and pushed my way in, dripping on the carpet in the process. The doorman told me that I could only leave the car there for about 10 minutes because it was a no-parking zone, but that the hotel garage in the next block would be glad to store it for me. He offered to lend me his umbrella in order to unload the trunk.

Accepting his offer, I retrieved my suitcase and clothes bag and dropped both at the front desk. Announcing myself as Mr. Dinsmore's guest didn't seem to make much of an impression on the clerk, who was chatting with the cashier. She seemed a little irritated at my interference.

There was no reservation for me, but they said they could fix me up since I had said the general manager had invited me. After only three rings of the "front" bell, the bellhop came to lead me to my room, which, as it turned out, wasn't made up. He commented that it was only 3 o'clock and the room would probably be fixed up by the time I returned from my business. I tipped him, dropped my bags, and remembered the car.

It wasn't necessary to worry because the police had just towed the vehicle away. The doorman said that he had waved to the tow truck but they hadn't been able to see him for the rain. He assured me that I could pick up the car in the morning with no problem. A cab could take me to the police lot, and the fine was only $25 plus the towing charge. The garage charged $6. He noted that it was interesting how they could move a car like that without having the key. He said they would make good thieves.

I found Dinsmore's office on the third floor. One of the elevators wasn't working so I took the brisk walk up the stairs. His secretary nodded and suggested that I move some magazines off that bench and sit down as "Elmer" would be with me as soon as he got off the telephone. She went back to her book.

After a few minutes, she seemed to notice my presence again and offered me some coffee from the percolator in the corner of the reception room. (She didn't like the hotel coffee, and neither, apparently, did Elmer.) I accepted with thanks, telling her I was still damp, having not been able to shower and change because the room was not prepared. She said I really shouldn't expect much else because, although checkout time was noon, they didn't like to push their guests out on rainy days like this. I said I thought that was very considerate of them.

I asked about my automobile, and she repeated the information I already had about the $25 fine and towing charges. Happens all the time, she indicated. The police have no class.

Dinsmore emerged from his office and greeted me effusively. Now, he told me, I was going to see how a hotel should be run. He took me into his office, cleared some reports off a chair, and offered me a cigar. After remarking on my trip, and how fortunate it was of him to catch me in an off moment, he asked me how I liked the place so far.

I told him about the car, the doorman, the room clerk, the room, the bellhop, and the elevator. He told me how to get the car back and dismissed the other incidents as growing pains.

Then, lowering his voice, he asked me if I would mind checking out the restaurant for him. He would pay, naturally. But he wasn't sure if the restaurant manager was really operating the place right. She didn't seem to get along with the other department heads and barely spoke to Elmer. Something funny is going on, he thought. Also, the hotel occupancy had been dropping steadily. He was sure that this had something to do with the food.

Then, straightening his tie, rolling down his sleeves, and putting on his favorite old hunting jacket, he took me on a tour of the hotel. He emphasized that I had only seen the front side of hotels in my travels. He was going to show me the real guts.

In the maid's room, nine or ten women were involved in a discussion with the housekeeper about their assignments. Those of the lower floors had to wait until the vacuum cleaners were available from the upper floors, so naturally everyone wanted to work on the upper floors. Dinsmore suggested that they might vacuum every other day; then they could share the machines on a rotating basis. The maids thought that this was a great idea, although the housekeeper didn't seem too pleased.

Dinsmore remarked to me about the lack of some people's decision-making ability. He sighed that he had to make more and more decisions each day because his staff seemed reluctant to take the initiative.

We toured all the floors. I mentioned the number of room service trays that seemed to be standing in the hall. Dinsmore said that this was a normal part of the hotel scene. The guests didn't mind because it reminded them that room service was available.

The cigar and newspaper stand looked like it belonged in the subway. The old man behind the counter offered some stale alternatives to the cigars I requested. He was very pleasant about it. Only a few magazines could be seen. "Guests don't go in for magazines anymore," Dinsmore told me. With a nudge, he reminded me that I didn't understand the hotel business.

The restaurant seemed to belong to a different world. It was packed. The maitre d' rushed over, bowed, seated us at a window, and took our drink orders. An atmosphere of quiet efficiency seemed to blanket the room. Two drinks appeared before us while attractive menus were deftly placed to our left. Elmer didn't seem happy. The restaurant, he told me, was a concession left over from the previous owners. He was trying to buy out the leases so he could turn it into a real moneymaker. At present, it made only about 10 percent net. I mentioned that most hotels lose money on their restaurants. He countered by showing me how many people were there even on that rainy day. He insisted that raising the prices while cutting back on the help was bound to increase the take.

The next morning, I retrieved my car, placed it firmly in the hotel garage, and returned for a farewell meeting with Dinsmore. He asked my opinion concerning his stewardship. He commented on the failing standards of today's workers, noted that he had ever-increasing difficulty in getting people who wanted to do quality work, and bemoaned the fact that the big grand hotels like his were losing out to the motels.

Questions

1. How would you rate Dinsmore's hotel? What evidence would you provide to support your position?

2. What are some of the most interesting examples of quality found in the case? How does Dinsmore view these examples? How would you, as the customer, view these same instances?

3. What do you think of Dinsmore's handling of the dispute involving the vacuums?

4. What would you recommend to Dinsmore about the manager of the restaurant?

5. If you were hired as a consultant by the owners of this hotel, what would you do? Why?

SELECTED
READINGS & INTERNET SITES

Antony, J. "Six Sigma for Service Processes." *Business Process Management Journal* 12, no. 2 (2006), pp. 234–48.

Breen, M.; B. Jud; and P. E. Pareja. *An Introduction to ISO 9000.* Dearborn, MI: Society of Manufacturing Engineers, Reference Publication Division, 1993.

Breyfogle III, F. W.; J. M. Cupello; and B. Meadows. *Managing Six Sigma: A Practical Guide to Understanding, Assessing, and Implementing the Strategy That Yields Bottom-Line Success.* New York: John Wiley & Sons, Inc., 2001.

Crosby, P. B. *Quality Is Free.* New York: McGraw-Hill, 1979.

Deming, W. E. *Out of Crisis.* Cambridge, MA: MIT Center for Advanced Engineering Study, 1986.

Furterer, S., and A. K. Elshennawy, "Implementation of TQM and Lean Six Sigma Tools in Local Government: A Framework and a Case Study." *Total Quality Management & Business Excellence* 16, no. 10 (December 2005), p. 1179.

Garvin, D. A. *Managing Quality.* New York: Free Press, 1988.

Goetsch, D. L., and S. B. Davis. *Quality Management,* 5th ed. Englewood Cliffs, NJ: Prentice Hall, 2005.

Hoyle, D. *ISO 9000 Quality Systems Handbook,* 5th ed. New York: Butterworth-Heinemann, 2005.

Imai, M. *Kaizen: The Key to Japan's Competitive Success.* New York: Random House, 1986.

Juran, J. M., and F. M. Gryna, Jr. *Quality Planning and Analysis.* New York: McGraw-Hill, 1980.

Kotter, J. P. "Leading Change: Why Transformation Efforts Fail." *Harvard Business Review* 85, no. 1 (January 2007), p. 96.

Pyzdek, T. *The Six Sigma Handbook: A Complete Guide for Greenbelts, Blackbelts, and Managers at All Levels,* 2nd ed. New York: McGraw-Hill, 2003.

Stevenson, W. J., and A. E. Mergen. "Teaching Six Sigma Concepts in a Business School Curriculum." *Total Quality Management & Business Excellence* 17, no. 6 (July 2006), pp. 751–56.

Swink, M., and B. Jacobs, "Six Sigma Adoption: Operating Performance Impacts and Contextual Drivers of Success," *Journal of Operations Management* 30, no. 6 (2012), pp. 437-53.

Yeung, A. C. L. "Strategic Supply Management, Quality Initiatives, and Organizational Performance." *Journal of Operations Management* 26, no. 4 (2008), pp. 490–502.

American Society for Quality
www.asq.org

ISO—Organization for Standardization
www.iso.org

Macolm Baldrige National Quality Award information
www.nist.gov

6

Chapter Supplement: Quality Improvement Tools

LEARNING OBJECTIVES *After studying this supplement, you should be able to:*

LO6S-1 Apply quality management tools for problem solving.

LO6S-2 Identify the importance of data in quality management.

OVERVIEW

Quality management programs make managers and employees better problem solvers by giving them the tools and procedures required to measure and improve processes, identify potential problems, and describe these problems to others. These tools can help managers determine whether processes are "under control," that is, whether they are capable of producing outcomes within the specifications needed to make products acceptable to customers. In this supplement, we use an example to illustrate the applications of important quality management tools, highlighting the types of problems they are designed to solve. While this supplement focuses on quality issues, these tools are universal and applicable to almost any process setting.

STANDARD PROBLEM SOLVING APPROACH

Chapter 6 introduced two problem solving approaches: (1) the Six Sigma improvement process known as DMAIC (define, measure, analyze, improve, and control) and (2) the plan-do-check-act (PDCA) cycle. Both approaches are good at standardizing improvement processes and giving everyone in the organization a common language for describing problems and related improvement efforts. A standard problem solving process also ensures that all employees use systematic, data-driven methods. While problem solving processes may vary from company to company, most follow the same fundamental steps represented in the DMAIC process and the PDCA cycle. Most of the tools described in this supplement deal with the measure, analyze, improve, and control steps of the DMAIC, or alternatively, steps P, D, and C of the PDCA cycle.

LO6S-1 Apply quality management tools for problem solving.

LO6S-2 Identify the importance of data in quality management.

QUALITY IMPROVEMENT TOOLS

The major goal of quality improvement is to move from uncovering the *symptoms* of a problem to determining the underlying root *causes* of a problem in a structured and logical manner. In this process, quality management decisions should be based on data whenever possible. Data fall into one of two categories: variable data or attribute data. **Variable data** measure quantifiable conditions such as speed, length, weight, temperature, density, and so forth. **Attribute data** measure qualitative characteristics of a process output (pass/fail, go/no go, good/bad). All variable data can be transformed into attribute data. However, it is not possible to transform attribute data into variable data.

variable data Data that measure quantifiable or numerical conditions.

attribute data Data that measure qualitative dimensions or conditions.

Consider the following example. To ensure safety, amusement parks have minimum height requirements for riders of roller coasters. At the Cedar Point amusement park, guests must be at least 52 inches tall to ride the Top Thrill Dragster.® The park could measure and record the actual height of each guest, gathering variable data. Instead, only those guests whose height is in question are measured. Their height is compared with a standard set at 52 inches; each guest is either tall enough to ride or not. Thus, Cedar Point is measuring an *attribute,* as opposed to a *variable.*

The various quality tools are just that—tools. They are used to address a specific question and to help managers understand what is taking place in operational processes. Table 6S-1 gives a summary of the tools and their usages.

Pear Computers: Using Quality Tools to Improve Performance

Pear Computers is a small Midwestern manufacturer of personal computers and data collection devices specifically targeting usages in the medical and dental fields. Pear has been successful in serving the needs of this market and in fending off the forays of larger computer makers such as Dell, Lenovo, and HP by relying on a strategy that emphasizes constant innovation, flexible product configurations, on-time delivery, and extremely high levels of quality.

TABLE 6S-1   Quality Improvement Tools

Quality Tools	Typical Usage
Histogram	To uncover underlying patterns (range and frequency) in data variability.
Cause-and-effect analysis	To uncover possible contributors to an observed problem; to facilitate group brainstorming.
Check sheets	To identify the frequency and location of problem causes.
Pareto analysis	To identify the most critical (relatively frequent) causes of problems.
Scatter diagrams	To determine if two variables are related to each other (whether the two variables move together in some predictable manner).
Process flow analysis	To graphically display and analyze the steps in a process.
Process capability analysis	To predict the conformance quality of a product by comparing its specification range to the range of its process variability.
Process control charts	To monitor process outputs and determine whether a process is operating according to normally expected limits.
Taguchi method/design of experiments	To evaluate and understand the effects of different factors on process outputs.

Recently, however, quality has slipped. Given where Pear Computers are used (often, literally life-and-death situations), this issue has become a major management concern. Increased final inspections have revealed that an unacceptably high number of computers are leaving final assembly DOA (dead on arrival—not working properly). Some computers have refused to boot up; others begin the start-up procedure only to stop and restart continuously without finishing the boot-up. Still others have started up and then become frozen at the start-up screen. Bob Feller, the operations manager in charge of the assembly line, has been charged with the task of eliminating these problems and ensuring that Pear delivers a computer that its customers can rely on.

Histograms

histogram A graphical representation of the distribution of values.

Variance exists in every activity or process. A **histogram** graphically displays a distribution of the values of the data of one variable to show the extent and type of variance. To create a histogram, one needs at least 30 observations, but more are better. Also, the analyst must determine the number of ranges or categories for grouping the data. The number of ranges is typically between 5 and 20, increasing with the number of observations.

Figure 6S-1 shows examples of histograms (each number identifies the frequency of occurrence of a given outcome). Histograms help problem solvers recognize and understand three critical traits of distributions:

- *Center:* The theoretical or desired mean (μ) should fall at the center of the distribution. Any gap between the observed mean and μ may indicate bias—a consistent tendency to exceed or fall short of a target.
- *Width:* The range (the difference between the highest and lowest values) is shown graphically by a histogram. The width indicates the unpredictability of the process (i.e., the wider the distribution, the less predictable it is).
- *Shape:* The overall shape of a distribution can indicate the degree of variability in outcomes and the types of factors that may be influencing the overall distribution.

Examine the five different distributions shown in Figure 6S-1. Most students are familiar with the first, normal, bell-shaped distribution. However, the other four distributions

FIGURE 6S-1   Common Histogram Shapes

Histrogram Distribution	Implications	
Bell-shaped	This is the typical or normal distribution that we expect to see when dealing with variable data. It is centered and symmetrical about the mean. This can be viewed as the baseline to which the subsequent histograms are compared.	
Double or twin-peaked	Often indicates that two normal distributions have been combined (signifying that we may have more than one process at work).	
Plateau	Often the result of combining multiple data sets, where the data sets themselves are moving.	
Comb	Typically occurs if there are errors in the process, faulty measurement, error in data collection, rounding errors, or poor grouping of data into categories.	
Skewed	A symmetrical pattern of data, typically indicating that there is some limit that is restraining the process on one side of the distribution. Skewed can either be positively skewed (with the tail extending to the right as shown here) or negatively skewed (with the tail extending to the left).	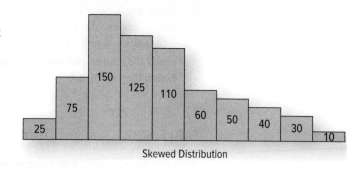

contain important information that can be used to uncover the potential underlying problems and to improve the performance of the system.

Histograms can provide a great deal of useful information. In the case of Pear Computers, Bob Feller may decide to collect initial time-to-failure data. When the computer goes through initial burn-in (test), he will look to see the frequency with which failures occur throughout the test. If the failure times are normally distributed, or skewed left or right, this information will give him an idea of the timing and stage where most failures occur. However, if Bob sees distributions that are either double-peaked or exhibiting a plateau, then this will indicate that multiple factors may be affecting performance.

Cause-and-Effect Diagrams

cause-and-effect diagrams (CEDs)
Diagrams that show the causes
of certain outcomes. Also known
as *fishbone diagrams* or *Ishikawa
charts*.

The **cause-and-effect diagram (CED)** examines complex interrelationships, identifies a problem's root causes (which are often hidden), and links them to the symptoms (which are often very visible). The CED is also known as a *fishbone diagram* (because a completed diagram looks like a fish skeleton), or an *Ishikawa chart,* in honor of Dr. Kaoru Ishikawa, who first developed this tool. In practice, CEDs offer users several important advantages. First, they are useful as brainstorming tools. They are best developed by a group of people who represent a variety of perspectives. Second, they discourage the presence of *management myopia*—"I know the root cause; don't confuse me with data." That is, CEDs help managers to see all of the potential causes, rather than limiting their attention to only a few. Third, they help to uncover the logic chain that leads from the root causes to the effects, thus showing how the various factors interact with each other to cause the observed problems.

The process of building a CED diagram consists of the following steps:

1. *Identify the problem to examine.* State the symptom or the effect (outcome) that must be explained in the form of a variance statement (e.g., reject rates are too high). Placed on the extreme right of the diagram, an arrow is next drawn from left to right. This arrow denotes the root effect—the link between the effect and the root causes.

2. *Identify the major categories of causes.* Identify the major categories of potential causes that could contribute to the effect. Represent them as main branches off the problem arrow, indicating the name of each category at the end of its branch. These main branches gather potential causes into categories and begin to structure the cause and effect relationships. The categories often reflect universal issues such as manpower (i.e., labor), materials, machines, and measurement. Firms often introduce additional categories that are appropriate to the situations and problems being studied. Table 6S-2 lists some commonly used categories.

3. *Identify more specific causes.* On each main branch, place smaller branches to represent detailed causes that could contribute to the primary categories of causes. For each detailed cause, ever-smaller branches represent still more specific and detailed causes. Brainstorming methods are used to identify major categories of causes and the more detailed causes.

4. *Circle likely causes.* After the diagram has been developed to show all potential causes, review all of the causes and circle the most likely ones. Further analysis and data collection can then focus on those causes.

5. *Verify the causes.* After identifying the most likely causes, use the other tools to ensure they really are the root cause of the problem.

TABLE 6S-2   Commonly Used Categories of Causes

Minimum Set	6 Ms (used in manufacturing)	7 Ps (used in service industry)	5 Ss (used in service industry)
People	Machine (technology)	Product/Service	Surroundings
Machine/Equipment	Method (process)	Price	Supplies
Methods/Processes	Material	Place	Systems
Material	Manpower/Mindpower	Promotion	Skills
	Measurement (inspection)	People/Personnel	Safety
	Mother Nature (environment)	Process	
		Physical Evidence	

To understand how a CED can be developed, let's return to Bob Feller and Pear Computers.

Bob still faces the problem of how to reduce the high failure rate of the new generation of Pear computers. An initial study has determined that CPUs are being damaged during assembly. To uncover causes of the damage, Bob has assembled a group consisting of a process engineer, a maintenance technician, a line employee, and an inspector. From the resulting group brainstorming session, Bob has been able to construct the CED found in Figure 6S-2.

In developing this diagram, Bob and the team have discussed each category to drill down into root causes. For example, Bob asked, "Why does the CPU chip lead to the CPU being damaged during assembly?" He received multiple answers from different participants. These are shown in Figure 6S-2 as arrows coming out of the CPU category arrow (e.g., received defective, pins not aligned). Bob then went through each one of these explanations asking why, until each logic chain answered at least five levels of why. This is illustrated in Figure 6S-2, where the main problem is the first why. The CPU chip category is the second why. The pins not aligned is the third why. Poor design is the fourth why. And, in answer to his question, "Why does poor design lead to pins not being aligned?" Bob is told the fifth why, that "the specifications are not precise." Consequently, Bob is able to understand the line of logic that leads from imprecise specifications to the problem of CPUs being damaged during assembly. With the insights generated from the CED, Bob is now able to collect data to determine if the insights gained from the CED are correct; he is also able to formulate, introduce, and evaluate the effectiveness of a corrective action program aimed at correcting the potential problems uncovered by the CED.

Check Sheets

A check sheet is a simple tool used to collect, organize, and display data to reveal patterns. An attribute check sheet consists of categories such as problem types, problem categories, or time. The categories may come from a cause-and-effect analysis. These categories typically represent factors that are seen as playing an important role in explaining what is happening. The goal of the analyst in collecting these data by category is to determine if there is a tendency for the data to be systematically associated with certain categories.

check sheet A tool for collecting, organizing, and displaying data with the goal of revealing underlying patterns.

FIGURE 6S-2
Cause-and-Effect Diagram for Pear's CPU Damage Problem

FIGURE 6S-3

Example of Attribute
Check Sheet

Reason for Reject	Number Rejected
Item damaged	✓✓✓✓✓✓✓✓✓✓✓
Wrong case shipped	✓✓✓✓✓✓✓
Part does not work	✓✓✓✓
Component(s) missing from part	✓✓✓✓✓✓✓✓✓✓✓✓✓✓✓✓✓✓✓✓✓✓✓✓
Not properly marked (no bar code on inside of case)	✓✓✓ ✓✓✓✓✓✓✓
Scratches found on case	✓✓✓✓✓✓✓✓✓✓✓
Other (factors not noted above)	✓✓✓✓

Figure 6S-3 shows a check sheet developed by Bob Feller to explore the reasons for rejecting component shipments received from a supplier (in this case, he is tracking problems with computer cases supplied by a vendor). Every time Pear rejects a shipment, it is examined to determine the reason for the rejection (as is done in Figure 6S-3). The most frequent reason for rejecting a shipment is that it is not marked properly. With this information, Pear could work with the supplier to determine why this problem is occurring. More detail can be used in the check sheet classification scheme. For example, time of day could be added, if relevant. Extra columns could be added to represent time of day and data collected to see if the time of day had any impact on rejects.

Pareto Analysis

Pareto analysis A technique for separating the critical few causes of problems from the trivial many.

Pareto analysis sets priorities for action based on the assumption that roughly 80 percent of problems typically result from 20 percent of the possible causes. Thus, not all possible causes of problems are equally important. Pareto analysis identifies the most critical (most frequent) causes of problems so that improvement efforts can be focused where the investment of time, effort, and money will yield the largest return.

Pareto analysis consists of a four-step procedure:

1. *Identify categories about which to collect information.* For example, specify categories that describe possible causes or types of defects. Such categories could come from a cause-and-effect analysis.
2. *Gather the data and calculate the frequency of observations in each category for an appropriate time period.* A check sheet could be used to guide data collection.
3. *Sort the categories in descending order based on their percentages.*
4. *Present the data graphically and identify the vital few categories that account for most of the variation.*

Pareto Analysis at Pear Computers

While working on the problems discussed previously, Bob Feller has become aware of problems involving the new Pear 6000 model. Performance analysis of the Pear 6000 has indicated that performance has not been up to the levels expected. Furthermore, tests have indicated that many of the computers are endlessly cycling during start-up. After talking with assembly workers, Bob Feller, the operations manager in charge of the assembly line, has identified the possible causes of these problems and gathered information about the frequency of problems. Over a four-week test period, 15,000 computers have been assembled. Table 6S-3 shows the defects that have been identified.

Figure 6S-4 charts the data constructed using Pareto analysis. The chart shows that the last two causes together account for about 47 percent of all defects. This chart suggests that Bob should begin his improvement efforts in these two areas. Just by eliminating these two problem types, he could reduce defects from 1,084 per 15,000 assemblies to 578.

TABLE 6S-3   Frequency of Problems Occurring in Pear Computer Assemblies

Problem Type	Number of Occurrences	Percent	Rank
Chips inserted incorrectly	43	3.97	8
CPU chip/memory chips popping out during burn-in	117	10.79	4
Traces cut on motherboard (during assembly)	78	7.20	6
Loose power connections	150	13.84	3
Connections not made on motherboard	34	3.14	9
Dust getting into critical areas of the computer	90	8.30	5
Wrong components put on computer	51	4.71	7
Motherboard incorrectly seated	15	1.38	10
Motherboard damaged during installation	245	22.60	2
CPU damaged during assembly	261	24.08	1
	1,084	100.00	

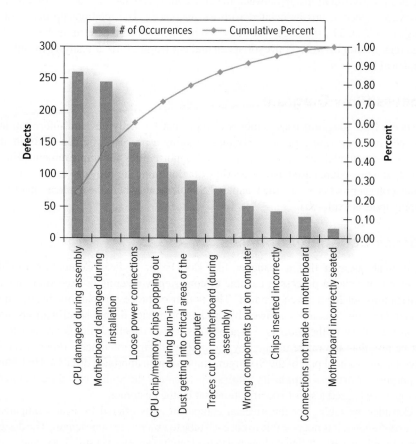

FIGURE 6S-4   Pareto Analysis for Pear Computers

Scatter Diagram

A **scatter diagram** graphically illustrates data points that indicate the relationship between a pair of variables, such as how the number of defects per batch relates to changes in the speed of the production line, or how production time per unit relates to hours of training. This information can help to confirm or deny hypothetical causes of observed effects.

scatter diagram A graphic illustration of the relationship between two variables.

FIGURE 6S-5 Scatter
Diagram for Conveyor
Speed and Cut Length

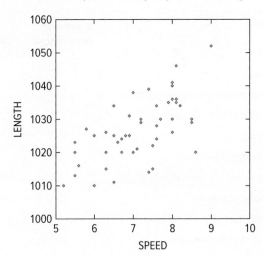

Scatterplot for Conveyor Speed vs. Cut Length

Pear Computers offers a medical equipment cart. This cart requires piping (which is cut internally) for the frame. Figure 6S-5 shows a scatter diagram that compares the speed of a conveyor line and the lengths of cut metal tubing. The diagram weakly suggests there is a positive relationship between the conveyor speed and the cut length; an increase in conveyor speed seems associated with longer pieces. The relationship does not seem strong, as indicated by the large space covered by the points. To determine the significance of the relationship between conveyor speed and cut length, further analysis would include a statistical test.

Process Flow Diagram

process flow diagram A graphic
technique for mapping activities
and their interrelationships in an
operating process.

A **process flow diagram** uses symbols to represent the activities and interrelationships contained in an operating process. By diagramming a process, you can study its details and uncover potential causes of variance and opportunities for improvement. The basic symbols and procedures used in process flow diagramming are fully discussed in Chapter 3 (which looks at processes) and the Chapter 3 Supplement (where the application of process mapping tools is explored).

Process Capability Analysis: C_p and C_{pk}

One critical question that a manager like Bob Feller at Pear Computers would like answered is whether a process is capable of consistently meeting or exceeding the design specifications set for a given product. The notion of process capability brings together two elements: the tolerances allowed by product or service design specifications, and the natural variability in the process. For a process to be "capable," limits on its variability must be less than the range defined by the product design tolerances. Process capability analysis is an essential part of the Six Sigma improvement approach discussed in Chapter 6.

process capability analysis A
tool for assessing the ability of
a process to consistently meet
or exceed a product's design
specifications.

The purpose of **process capability analysis** is to assess the ability of a process to consistently meet or exceed a set of specifications set by the customer.

Consider the tubing for the medical equipment carts offered by Pear Computers. As Figure 6S-5 shows, it is not possible to cut each tube to *exactly* the same length. The design tolerances for tubing parts designate how much the lengths can vary yet still fit together properly in the cart assembly. Suppose the design specification for a tube length is 1030 millimeters ± 10 millimeters. This would allow tubes to be usable if they ranged from 1020 millimeters to 1040 millimeters. This range is referred to as the *specification width* (*S*). The specification width may be based on product functionality requirements (e.g., cereal boxes cannot be closed if there is too much cereal in them), or it might be based on economic considerations (e.g., customers don't want to pay for boxes of cereal with too little cereal in them).

Processes have natural variation. When cutting a metal tube, machine vibration, cutting tool wear, worker experience, and metal characteristics can cause variations in the length. *Process width (P)* denotes the actual range of outcomes generated by the production process itself. If the cutting process can maintain length from 1025 millimeters to 1035 millimeters, it is *capable* since $P \leq S$. Alternatively, if much of the process output is longer or shorter than the specification allows, then it is not capable. If the process is not capable, then either the process variability must be reduced through improvements, or the product design tolerances must be widened (if allowable) in order to avoid an unacceptable number of defective outcomes.

Mathematically, process capability is represented by the capability index, C_p (and its associated measure, C_{pk}). The C_p is essentially the ratio of the specification width to the process width. It is calculated as follows:

$$C_p = \frac{\text{Specification width}}{\text{Process width}} = \frac{S}{P}$$

where:

S = Upper specification limit − Lower specification limit

$P = 6\sigma$

σ = Standard deviation of process output

P is expressed as a function of σ because most process output distributions are open-ended; that is, there is some probability, albeit small, that any output value could be produced. By convention, managers in the past have chosen to set $P = 6\sigma$ because six standard deviations define a range that covers about 99.7 percent of the output for processes that vary according to a normal distribution. Thus, a C_p value less than 1 would indicate that more than 0.3 percent of produced units will not meet design specifications.

To illustrate the application of C_p, consider Figure 6S-6. Returning to Bob Feller and his problems at Pear Computers, we find him considering a proposal regarding different quality improvement options for the metal tube cutting process. Recall that the tube has a design specification of 1030 ± 10 millimeters, so the specification width, *S,* equals 20 millimeters. Figure 6S-6 shows the existing tube cutting process in distribution A. The resulting C_p value of 0.67 indicates an incapable process (product would meet specifications only about 95.5 percent of the time). Distribution B, representing some incremental improvements in the process, shows that the process would be barely capable, with a C_p value of 1.0. Any slight disruption or movement of the process distribution would send it outside acceptable limits. Finally, distribution C, representing the anticipated results of a comprehensive process redesign, is capable because a C_p value of 1.67 indicates that it can deal with many unplanned but short-term variations in *P.*

In selecting between the three options, Bob would need to weigh the costs of making the proposed process improvements against the costs associated with having defective parts. If the costs of defective parts are low, or they can be corrected quickly, then he may decide that the second proposal (resulting in distribution B) is good enough. However, if the costs of defective parts are high, or if it is difficult to quickly repair the defects, then he may opt for the higher performance option offered by distribution C.

C_{pk}: Improving on the C_p Statistic

The C_p value effectively measures process capability *only* when a process is centered; that is, when the center of its output distribution is the same as the center of the product specification range. This is not the case for the distribution found in Figure 6S-7. In this figure, the process width and specification width are the same as in distribution C from Figure 6S-6, so both distributions have the same C_p value. However, while distribution C showed a highly capable process, the distribution in Figure 6S-7 is not capable. It is clear that many of the units of output from this distribution will have values that are outside the specification range. To deal with noncentered process distributions, we must use an adjusted version of the C_p metric known as the C_{pk}.

C_p A measure of process capability that compares the specification width with the process width—not adjusted for lack of process centering.

C_{pk} A measure of process capability that compares the specification width with the process width—adjusted for lack of centering.

FIGURE 6S-6 Sample Distributions and their Associated C_p Measures

Distribution A identifies a process that is *incapable* of meeting the customer specifications. Distribution B identifies a process that is *just capable*. Distribution C identifies a process that is *capable*.

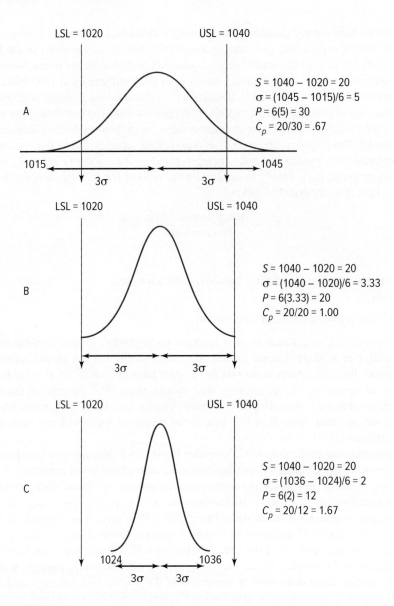

LSL = 1020   USL = 1040

A

$S = 1040 - 1020 = 20$
$\sigma = (1045 - 1015)/6 = 5$
$P = 6(5) = 30$
$C_p = 20/30 = .67$

1015 ←——— 3σ ———→ ←——— 3σ ———→ 1045

LSL = 1020   USL = 1040

B

$S = 1040 - 1020 = 20$
$\sigma = (1040 - 1020)/6 = 3.33$
$P = 6(3.33) = 20$
$C_p = 20/20 = 1.00$

3σ   3σ

LSL = 1020   USL = 1040

C

$S = 1040 - 1020 = 20$
$\sigma = (1036 - 1024)/6 = 2$
$P = 6(2) = 12$
$C_p = 20/12 = 1.67$

1024 ←— 3σ —→ ←— 3σ —→ 1036

FIGURE 6S-7 Deceptive C_p Value: The Problem of Lack of Centering

LSL = 1020   D = 1030   USL = 1040

$S = 20$
$\sigma = 2$
$P = 6(2) = 12$
$C_p = 20/12 = 1.67$

1016   1028

←— 3σ — $\overline{X} = 1022$ — 3σ —→

Mathematically, the C_p and C_{pk} can be written as follows:

(6s.1)
$$C_p = S/P = (USL - LSL)/6\sigma$$

(6s.2)
$$K = \frac{|D - \overline{X}|}{S/2}$$

(6s.3)
$$C_{pk} = (1 - K) * C_p$$

where:

USL = Upper specification limit
LSL = Lower specification limit
  D = Center of the product specification range = (USL + LSL)/2
  $\overline{X}$ = The average of the process output distribution
  K = Adjustment for differences between the specification center and the process mean

The C_{pk} and C_p are almost the same, except for the correction term, $(1 - K)$. The calculation of K involves a new parameter, D, which is the design center of the specification width S. D is the target value for performance data, while $\overline{X}$ is the process average. When D equals $\overline{X}$ then C_{pk} is identical to C_p.

There is another way of thinking about these two measures. C_p deals with the extent to which the process is *consistent*, while C_{pk} looks at the extent to which the process is *centered*. Consider the following example: Suppose you enjoy playing basketball and you want to become better at making shots. The hoop is 18 inches in diameter, while the basketball is 9.39 inches in diameter. If you become so good that your shots land within 5 inches of where you aim (that is, they land within a 10-inch range), then you will have become quite consistent—this is what is measured by C_p. However, as you practice you might find that, on average, your shots are mostly landing on the left side of the rim—they are not centered. That is what is measured by C_{pk}. Thus, you may have the consistency to make most of your shots, but if your aim is off center, you will still miss a lot of baskets. To prevent defects, you need to develop a process that is both consistent and centered.

Returning to the process for Pear Computers shown in Figure 6S-7, given that the process mean $\overline{X} = 1022$, we calculate the C_{pk} value as follows:

$$C_p = 1.67$$

$$D = (1020 + 1040)/2 = 1030$$

$$K = abs(1030 - 1022)/(20/2) = 0.8$$

$$C_{pk} = (1-0.8)\,(1.67) = 0.33$$

Since this value of C_{pk} is less than 1, it indicates an unreliable process that cannot reliably meet design specifications. Table 6S-4 shows the number of defective parts per million produced at different levels of C_{pk}.

TABLE 6S-4 C_{pk}, PPM, and Process Management

C_{pk}	PPM Defective	Process Implications
0.50	133,610	Process is incapable; 100% inspection may be needed.
1.00	2,700	
1.33	64	Process capable, normal sampling would be typical.
1.50	7	
2.00	0.00198	For values of 2 or more, no inspection may be needed; process is very stable.

Alternative Method for Computing C_{pk}

The C_{pk} formula presented in the preceding section emphasizes the need to adjust C_p for the difference between the process mean and the center of the product specification limits. C_p and C_{pk} can also be calculated using the following formula:

$$C_p = (USL - LSL)/6\sigma$$

$$(6s.4) \qquad C_{pk} = \min\left[(USL - \overline{X}) / 3 * \sigma, (\overline{X} - LSL) / 3 * \sigma\right]$$

The alternative calculations for C_{pk} are frequently found in discussions of Six Sigma. Either is acceptable.

Process Control Charts

Once a process is determined to be capable, it should be monitored over time to ensure that it remains stable. Sometimes things can change such that the range of process output changes, or the mean (i.e., centering of the process), shifts. Process control charts are tools used to monitor process output to detect such changes. The terms *statistical process control (SPC)* and *process control charts* are often used synonymously.

A control chart plots values for samples of process output collected over time. The plotted outputs are compared to a set of limits for the upper and lower boundaries of the process width (see Figure 6S-8), as defined by a confidence interval (usually 99 percent or 3σ). Any output sample value that lies between the upper and lower limits is within the expected normal random variation of the process. However, points that fall outside these limits are not likely to have occurred by chance, suggesting that the process may have changed. Thus, process control charts identify when a process has deviated from its normal operation (i.e., when it is "out of control"). Such a change prompts the process operator to stop, investigate, and correct the process. For example, over time a saw blade may wear, causing a change in the distribution of process output. A process control chart would indicate when a blade needs to be replaced. In services, one might use a control chart to track the order completion times for services (say, a drive-through window at McDonald's).

Process control charts are similar to process capability studies (C_p and C_{pk}) in that both tools evaluate the variability of processes. However, there are some important differences between these two tools. Process control charts are used to regularly monitor the output of a process to ensure that output lies within the *expected variation limits of the process.* Process control compares summary statistics (e.g., mean and range) for samples of output against predetermined process limits. Process capability studies, on the other hand, evaluate the extent to which process output lies within *design specification limits.* Process capability studies look at the variation in a large population of output, rather than

process control charts A statistical tool used to monitor a process output to detect significant changes.

FIGURE 6S-8 Process Control Limits

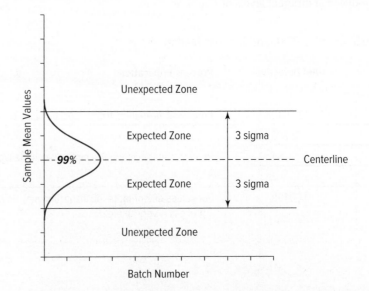

TABLE 6S-5   Types of Control Charts and Data Covered[1]

Type of Data	Control Chart Used	Types of Data
Variables—Continuous/Nondiscrete	$\bar{X} - R$	Measurement (inches, mm), volume, product weight, power consumed
Attributes—Discrete	np	Number of defects
Attributes	p (probability of defect)	Fraction defective
Attributes	U	Number of pin holes in pieces of plated sheet, differing in area (area/volume is not fixed)
Attributes	C	Number of pin holes in a specified area (area is fixed)

the variation of sample means and ranges. It is important to understand that the use of process control charts only ensures that the process is operating normally; it does not ensure that product output meets design specifications. Evaluating consistency with design specifications is the purpose of a process capability study.

There are five common types of control charts, listed in Table 6S-5. Each type of chart is used with a particular type of data. In the following sections, we will explain the $\bar{x} - R$ control chart, which deals with variable data, and the p control chart, which deals with attribute data. These are the most commonly used control charts.

Constructing an $\bar{x} - R$ Chart

This control chart is really the combination of two charts. The first is the $\bar{x}$ chart, which compares an output sample mean $\bar{x}$ against the upper and lower control limits to determine whether a process has shifted to the point that it is no longer "in control." The R chart plots the value of the range for each output sample and compares this range to a control interval to determine whether the width of the process distribution is in control. Since the $\bar{x}$ chart plots only average values, we also need to use the R chart to evaluate the gap between the largest and smallest observations in each sample. The following section illustrates the procedure for constructing and using $\bar{x} - R$ charts.

$\bar{x} - R$ chart A technique used to monitor the mean and range values for samples of variable data describing a process output.

Constructing and Using $\bar{x} - R$ Charts for Pear Computers

Bob Feller of Pear Computers wants to track hard disk seek times to make sure that the process of building the disks is under control. To make this assessment, he builds an $\bar{x} - R$ chart using the following steps:

1. *Collect data to calculate control limits.* To calculate control limits for both charts, data samples should come from a process known to be under control (not experiencing problems). An adequate amount of data (about 100 observations is typically considered adequate) is needed. Table 6S-6 shows data from 20 samples of 5 observations each. The sample size, n, should balance the cost of sampling against the added confidence that comes from larger samples. In this case the sample size is $n = 5$.
2. *For each sample, calculate the sample mean.* For each sample, calculate the sample mean using the following formula:

(6s.5)
$$\bar{x} = \frac{\sum_{i=1}^{n} xi}{n}$$

For the first sample from Table 6S-6, the first sample mean is 12.3. Repeating this calculation for each sample gives the 20 sample means.

[1]Kaoru Ishikawa, *Guide to Quality Control,* Second Revised Edition (Tokyo: Asian Production Organization, 1982). Reprinted with permission.

TABLE 6S-6 Hard Disk Seek Times (milliseconds)

Nominal Mean Seek Time = 12 Msec Sample #	1	2	3	4	5	$\bar{X}$	R
1	12.2	12.3	12.4	11.8	12.7	12.3	0.9
2	12.3	12.1	11.8	12.2	12.3	12.1	0.5
3	12.4	12.7	12.3	12.5	12.3	12.4	0.4
4	12.5	12.3	12.3	12.1	12.1	12.3	0.4
5	12.1	12.4	11.9	12.0	12.3	12.1	0.5
6	12.6	11.8	12.2	11.9	11.9	12.1	0.8
7	11.8	12.1	12.5	12.8	12.5	12.3	1.0
8	12.5	12.8	12.0	12.5	11.9	12.3	0.9
9	12.1	12.3	12.0	11.9	12.1	12.1	0.4
10	11.2	12.3	11.8	11.7	11.9	11.8	1.1
11	11.7	12.2	12.2	11.7	12.1	12.0	0.5
12	12.4	12.2	12.1	12.1	12.1	12.2	0.3
13	11.7	12.1	11.9	11.8	11.9	11.9	0.4
14	11.8	12.2	12.2	12.1	12.2	12.1	0.4
15	11.9	12.3	11.8	11.9	12.1	12.0	0.5
16	12.3	12.4	13.0	12.3	12.2	12.4	0.8
17	11.9	12.6	12.6	12.9	12.1	12.4	0.9
18	11.9	12.0	12.7	12.7	11.9	12.2	0.8
19	11.4	11.6	12.4	11.9	11.8	11.8	1.0
20	11.6	11.8	12.4	12.3	11.2	11.9	1.2

3. *For each sample, find the range, R.* The range measures the difference between the largest and smallest values. For the first sample in Table 6S-6, R equals 12.7 minus 11.8 = 0.9.

4. *Calculate the overall "grand" mean, $\bar{\bar{x}}$.* Summing the sample means, $\bar{x}$, and dividing by the total number of samples gives the mean for the entire data set. From the data in Table 6S-6, the sample means sum to 242.7, so the overall mean equals 12.14 (242.7 / 20). This number defines the centerline for the control chart. We expect future sample mean values to vary normally around this centerline.

5. *Calculate the mean range ($\bar{R}$).* The R chart needs a centerline as well. To define this line, sum the R values from all of the samples and divide by the number of samples to arrive at the mean R, or $\bar{R}$. The range values for the data samples in Table 6S-6 sum to 13.7, so $\bar{R}$ is 0.69 (13.7/20). We expect future sample range values to vary normally around this centerline. Besides defining the centerline for the R chart, $\bar{R}$ also helps to estimate the upper and lower control limits, since the range gives a proxy measure of the standard deviation for samples ($\sigma/\sqrt{n}$).

6. *Compute control limits and construct the charts.* To calculate the values of the control limits, enter values for A_2, D_3, and D_4 found in Table 6S-7 into the equations below:

Equations for the $\bar{x}$ and R control charts:

$\bar{x}$ chart:

(6s.6) $$\text{Central line} = \bar{\bar{x}}$$

(6s.7) $$\text{Lower control line} = \bar{\bar{x}} - A_2\bar{R}$$

(6s.8) $$\text{Upper control line} = \bar{\bar{x}} + A_2\bar{R}$$

TABLE 6S-7   Values for Setting Control Limit Lines

n = Number in Each Sample	$A_2 = \bar{x}$ Limits for 99.7% (3 sigma)	$D_4 = R$ Upper Limit	$D_3 = R$ Lower Limit
2	1.88	3.27	0
3	1.02	2.58	0
4	0.73	2.28	0
5	0.58	2.12	0
6	0.48	2.00	0
7	0.42	1.92	0.08
8	0.37	1.86	0.14
9	0.34	1.82	0.18
10	0.31	1.78	0.22
11	0.29	1.74	0.26
12	0.27	1.72	0.28
13	0.25	1.69	0.31
14	0.24	1.67	0.33
15	0.22	1.65	0.35
16	0.21	1.64	0.36
17	0.20	1.62	0.38
18	0.19	1.60	0.39
19	0.19	1.61	0.40
20	0.18	1.59	0.41

R control chart:

(6s.9) $$\text{Central line} = \bar{R}$$

(6s.10) $$\text{Lower control limit (LCL)} = D_3\bar{R}$$

(6s.11) $$\text{Upper control limit (UCL)} = D_4\bar{R}$$

Table 6S-8 gives the control chart parameters for the data in Table 6S-6. The control charts are shown in Figure 6S-9. By convention, the centerline appears as a solid line and the control limits appear as broken or dashed lines.

7. *Plot new $\bar{x}$ and R values on the control charts.* With the centerline and control limits established, the control charts are ready to be used.

TABLE 6S-8   Control Limits Calculated for the Example Control Chart

Data Points	$\bar{X}$ Chart	R Chart
Central Line	12.14 ms	0.69
Lower Control Limit (LCL)	$12.14 - 0.577*0.69 = 11.74$	0
Upper Control Limit (UCL)	$12.14 + 0.577*0.69 = 12.54$	$2.115*0.69 = 1.459$

FIGURE 6S-9 $\bar{X}$ and R Chart for the Example Data

After installing the new control charts on the hard disk production line, Bob Feller recorded the 12 sample means and ranges in Table 6S-9. When they were plotted (Figure 6S-9), Bob noticed that the sample mean for batch 10 was outside of the upper control limit. In practice, this would have triggered an immediate reaction—production would have been stopped with the goal of identifying the reasons for the problem. In flagging

TABLE 6S-9   Sample Means and Ranges for Hard Disk Drives

Sample	Sample Mean $\bar{X}$	Sample Range (R)
1	11.82	0.30
2	11.90	0.92
3	12.10	0.86
4	11.95	1.23
5	12.32	1.40
6	12.20	1.30
7	12.50	0.56
8	11.86	0.89
9	12.30	1.10
10	12.60	1.32
11	12.49	1.01
12	12.30	0.42

the out-of-bounds value for sample 10, Bob also realized something important: This value was a symptom; it indicated that something was wrong, but it did not tell Bob *what* was wrong. For Bob to uncover the underlying root causes, he and the team responsible for the hard disk production line would have to make use of tools such as the cause-and-effect diagram (previously discussed) in order to uncover possible root causes.

p Attribute Control Chart

$\bar{x} - R$ charts analyze samples of data for continuous variables. In some cases, the observed data are attributes. Such cases occur when we are dealing with pass/fail, live/die, or good/bad outcomes. In these cases, managers are usually interested in determining if the proportion of nonconforming product is stable and if the process generating such products is under control. To answer these questions, we use a *p* **attribute control chart**.

Consider the data presented in Table 6S-10. Bob Feller has been informed that the research team at Pear Computers has introduced the Mercury HD 6900, a new video graphics board for its top end computers. Since this product is new, Bob decides to construct a *p* attribute control chart. He is interested in whether the process can produce fewer than 5 percent defects, a minimum standard considered acceptable at Pear.

p attribute control chart A technique used to assess if the proportion of nonconforming product is stable. Applied to attribute data.

TABLE 6S-10   Reject Rate Analysis for Mercury HD 6900

Batch	Sample Size	Defective	Fraction Defective
1	100	5	.05
2	100	6	.08
3	100	2	.02
4	100	4	.04
5	100	6	.06
6	100	2	.02
7	100	3	.03
8	100	7	.07
9	100	1	.01
10	100	3	.03
11	100	2	.02
12	100	4	.04
13	100	4	.04
14	100	1	.01
15	100	1	.01
16	100	3	.03
17	100	2	.02
18	100	4	.04
19	100	5	.05
20	100	2	.02
Totals	2000	67	Average .0335

To carry out this analysis, Bob uses the following procedure:

1. *Collect and organize the data under normal operating conditions:* Table 6S-10 shows the data that were collected when the production line was running normally and presumably under control. Note that we are using constant sample sizes.

2. *Compute control limits and construct the chart:* To calculate the $\bar{p}$ and control lines, we use the following equations:

(6s.12) $\bar{p} = (\text{Number of Defects/Total Parts Inspected})$

(6s.13) $\text{Upper control line} = \text{UCL} = \bar{p} + 3\sqrt{\bar{p}(1-\bar{p})/n}$

(6s.14) $\text{Lower control line} = \text{LCL} = \bar{p} - 3\sqrt{\bar{p}(1-\bar{p})/n}$

where n = sample size. If the sample size varies from batch to batch, then an average sample size can be used.

Note that here, the 3 is the control limit. In this example, we have essentially specified the mean ($(\bar{p})$ +/−3σ). The value of 3 can be changed to increase or decrease this interval.

For the Mercury HD 6900 data:

$$\bar{p} = 67/2000 = 0.0335$$

$$\text{UCL} = 0.0335 + 3\sqrt{0.0335\,(1-0.0335)/100} = 0.0335 + 0.0540 = 0.0875$$

$$\text{LCL} = 0.0335 - 3\sqrt{0.0335\,(1-0.0335)/100} = 0.0335 - 0.0540 = \sim 0$$
$$\text{(we cannot have a negative LCL)}$$

3. *Create the control chart and begin monitoring results:* The parameters computed in the preceding step create a p chart with which Bob can monitor and control future production batches.

Table 6S-11 shows data for 20 samples that Bob drew from production after creating the control chart, and Figure 6S-10 plots the number of defects from each sample. The chart shows that the process is under control (i.e., no samples are outside the control limits). However, the defects seem to exhibit *cycling.* That is, there seems to be a pattern of the defects going up and down in a consistent pattern. This is not the kind of random behavior that one would expect from a process. Bob should initiate an effort to uncover root factors contributing to this outcome (applying a technique such as cause-and-effect diagrams). Cycling indicates that something systematic (rather than random) is affecting the underlying processes.

Interpreting Control Charts

A process is out of control whenever the sample means or range values appear outside the control lines. This signals managers or workers to stop the process to identify and correct the underlying problems that caused a change in the process. Control charts may also

FIGURE 6S-10 *Np* Control Chart for the Mercury HD 6900, Sample Evaluation

TABLE 6S-11   Sample Data Collected

Sample Number	Sample Size	Number Defective
1	100	3
2	100	3
3	100	4
4	100	5
5	100	6
6	100	7
7	100	8
8	100	7
9	100	6
10	100	4
11	100	3
12	100	2
13	100	2
14	100	1
15	100	2
16	100	2
17	100	3
18	100	4
19	100	5
20	100	6

indicate a need for intervention in the process in four conditions: trends, runs, hugging, and periodicity.

Trends. A control chart indicates a trend when successive points seem to fall along a line moving either upward or downward. A trend in control chart data indicates some continuing change in the process. This signal may warrant intervention before the trend line crosses control limits.

Runs. Truly random variations should not form any pattern in the distribution of data around the central lines. A run of points above the central line followed by a run of points below indicate systematic changes in the process that require attention.

Hugging. Hugging occurs when various points appear so closely grouped around the central line that they seem to show no variation. Hugging usually indicates some external intervention in the process to limit or eliminate variation (thus masking the problems). This intervention might be the action of some employee who wants the process to look good. With hugging you cannot judge whether the process is really operating under control or if some outside force is taking unusual measures to produce acceptable results.

Periodicity. If the plotted points show the same pattern of change over equal intervals, it is called *periodicity*. It looks much like a uniform roller coaster of the same size ups and downs around the centerline. This process should be watched closely as something is causing a defined uniform drift to both sides of the centerline.

Taguchi Methods/Design of Experiments

One of the first quality researchers to recognize the importance of linking product design to process improvement was Professor Genichi Taguchi, director of the Japanese Academy of Quality and four-time recipient of the Deming Prize. He recognized that managers could eliminate the need for mass inspection by building quality into both the products and the processes at the design stage.

Taguchi methods Statistical methods for improving the design of a product and the processes used to produce it.

Taguchi developed a straightforward, well-integrated system (now called the Taguchi methods) for improving the design of both a product and the process used to produce it. The objective of this system is to identify easily controllable factors and their settings to minimize variation in product features while keeping the mean values (or "response") of these features on target. Taguchi developed a methodology for designing experiments than can help managers identify the optimal settings of product specifications and process controls. One result of identifying these settings is that a product can be made robust with respect to changes in its operating and environmental conditions. Ultimately, this results in more stable, "process capable" designs. In other words, by focusing on both the product and the process and using well-developed designs, managers can develop products and processes that are properly centered and have performance distributions with reduced spread.[2]

Other Quality Control Tools

This supplement has provided only a brief introduction to the wide range of quality control tools that are available to operations managers. In addition to the tools discussed, there are other tools that you might want to explore either in other courses or by reading about them. Other important tools include:

1. Acceptance sampling.
2. Operating characteristics curves.
3. Taguchi loss functions.
4. CTQ tree (critical to quality—a tool used to decompose broad customer requirements into more easily quantified requirements).
5. Quality storyboards (a visual method for displaying a quality control story that helps the personnel go from plan and problem definition to actions).

---

[2]For more information on this system, see N. Logothetis, *Managing for Total Quality* (Englewood Cliffs, NJ: Prentice Hall, 1992), Chapters 11–14.

SUPPLEMENT SUMMARY

1. Effective quality management is data-driven. Data can be quantitative variable data, such as length and width, or it can be attribute data (e.g., good/bad). The appropriate data analysis tool depends upon the type of data.
2. Tools such as the histogram, check sheet, and Pareto analysis are graphical techniques that help to identify and prioritize problems.
3. Cause-and-effect diagrams and scatter diagrams are used to explore relationships and understand underlying causes of problems.
4. Process capability indicates if a process is able to meet the customer's quality requirements. Process control is used to monitor whether a process has changed. Taguchi's system for the design of experiments can be used to identify the settings of process factors that make a process capable.

SOLVED
PROBLEMS

1. Given the information presented in Figure 6S-11, calculate the process capability.

Solution:

$C_p = S/P = (20 - 10)/(16 - 10) = 10/6 = 1.667$
$K = abs\ [D - \bar{X}] / (S/2) = abs\ [15 - 13] / 5 = 0.40$
$C_{pk} = (1 - K)\ C_p = (0.4)/1.667 = 1.00$

2. You have been given the following data for a production process that is responsible for filling bags of flour.

Production specifications: $10.00 \pm .20$ pounds
Process standard deviation (σ):   0.05 pounds
Process distribution centered at: 10.10 pounds
Specification width (S): $10.20 - 9.80 = .40$
Process width (P):   we need 99% or 3σ on each side or $10.10 - .15 = 9.55$
                                     $10.10 + .15 = 10.25$
                                     $10.25 - 9.55 = .30$

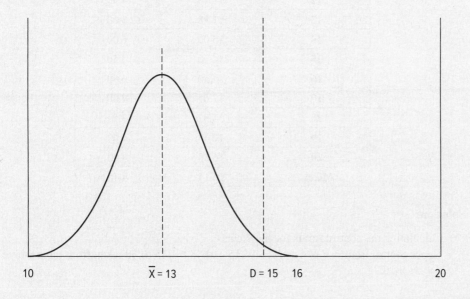

FIGURE 6S-11
Calculating C_{pk}

10          $\bar{X} = 13$ D = 15   16   20

With these data, you have been asked by management to determine the answers to two questions:

- Is the process capable?
- If it is not, then what has to be done to bring the process back in control (i.e., make it capable again)?

Solution:

$C_p = S/P = .40/.30 = 1.333$

Based on the C_p value alone, the process is capable . . . but barely.

$K = |D - \overline{X}| / (S / 2) = |10.00 - 10.10| / (.40/2) = .10 / .20 = .5$

$C_{pk} = (1 - K) * C_p = .5 * 1.333 = .667$

This indicates that the process is not capable. The first step for management is to recenter the production process. That is, the center of the production process must be shifted from 10.10 to 10.00. This action, while improving things, is not enough. The next is to reduce the variance of the process. The two actions, when combined, should result in a process that is now capable.

3. You have been given the following data taken from 20 samples, where each sample consists of five observations. You have been asked to calculate the limits for the $\overline{x} - R$ charts.

Sample Number	Sample Mean ($\overline{x}$)	Range (R)
1	12.25	4.50
2	12.75	5.00
3	10.63	0.50
4	15.88	1.00
5	12.00	4.00
6	14.75	4.00
7	13.25	3.00
8	13.48	8.00
9	15.50	3.00
10	15.25	7.00
11	15.75	5.00
12	13.13	4.50
13	11.88	3.00
14	15.00	6.00
15	14.30	4.50
16	14.50	6.00
17	17.65	9.00
18	14.88	3.50
19	12.63	4.00
20	16.88	4.00
Means	14.15	4.45

Solution:

Calculating the control limits for the $\overline{x}$ chart:

Upper control limit $= \overline{x} + A_2 * \overline{R} = 14.15 + 0.58 * 4.45$ (0.58 taken from table where $n = 5$) $= 16.73$

Lower control $= \bar{x} + A_2 * \bar{R} = 14.15 - 0.58 * 4.45 = 11.57$

Note: As long as $\bar{x}$ remains between 11.57 and 16.73, these data are under control. Calculating the control limits for R charts:

Upper control $= D_4 * \bar{R}$ (where D_4 taken from table) $= 2.11 * 4.45 = 9.39$

Lower control $= D_4 * \bar{R} = 0 * 4.45 = 0.0$

Note: As long as R remains between 0 and 9.39, then the sample is under control.

4. Dick Ross, the plant manager for ABC Housing Tiles, was concerned about the on-time delivery performance of one of his departments. This department manufactures bathroom tiles specifically for large "big box" home improvement stores (such as Home Depot, Menards, Lowe's, and Rona [Canada]). The buyers from these various customers were sending strong signals that they expected consistent on-time delivery (with future pressure to be on improving the level of on-time delivery).

Solution:

To help assess whether the department's on-time delivery was consistent, Dick collected two years' worth of information for calculating the parameters of the p control chart. The data are summarized as follows:

Month	Period	Sample	On-Time	p
January	1	250	230	0.921
February	2	250	229	0.916
March	3	250	229	0.918
April	4	250	228	0.915
May	5	250	228	0.912
June	6	250	230	0.923
July	7	250	226	0.905
August	8	250	223	0.892
September	9	250	228	0.913
October	10	250	226	0.905
November	11	250	227	0.908
December	12	250	228	0.912
January	13	250	228	0.912
February	14	250	233	0.932
March	15	250	230	0.921
April	16	250	227	0.911
May	17	250	229	0.918
June	18	250	224	0.896
July	19	250	226	0.905
August	20	250	230	0.923
September	21	250	227	0.910
October	22	250	227	0.908
November	23	250	229	0.916
December	24	250	228	0.914
Averages		250	227.92	0.913

Using this information, he calculated the overall $\bar{p} = 0.913$

He also calculated the UCL and LCL:

$$\text{LCL} = 0.913 - 3 \times \sqrt{\frac{0.913(1 - .913)}{250}} = 0.913 - 0.054 = 0.859$$

$$\text{UCL} = 0.913 + 3 \times \sqrt{\frac{0.913(1 - .913)}{250}} = 0.913 + 0.054 = 0.967$$

He also did a quick plot to see if these 24 months were really stable (they are; you can do it yourself to check). With these control parameters, he next took the on-time delivery data for the current 12 months (see the following table):

Month	Period	Sample	On-Time	p
January	25	250	224	0.896
February	26	250	229	0.916
March	27	250	235	0.940
April	28	250	220	0.880
May	29	250	221	0.884
June	30	250	234	0.936
July	31	250	223	0.982
August	32	250	230	0.920
September	33	250	231	0.924
October	34	250	233	0.932
November	35	250	233	0.932
December	36	250	235	0.940

These data are plotted on the following control chart:

In reviewing these data, Dick noted that the process was under control. However, beginning in August there was an upward trend. Such a trend is problematic as it indicates that a systematic change is taking place. Dick took note of this so he could talk with the area supervisor. These data told Dick that his process delivers on time about 92 percent of the time. However, the data did not tell him how late the late orders were. This would require further analysis.

5. You are responsible for the production of *Always Bright* bicycle flashers (the lights that we put on our bicycles to ensure that drivers see us). Recently, top management has noted that customers have been complaining about the quality of these products. Consequently, you decide to collect some data so that you can better understand the problem. You collect production data and rejects over a one-week period

(see following table). A "✓" indicates a defect. You have decided to organize the data by type of defect and by time of day (you have a feeling that some of the problems might be worse at certain times of the day).

Orders	7 a.m. – 9 a.m.	9 a.m. – 11 a.m.	11 a.m. – 1 p.m.	1 p.m. – 3 p.m.	3 p.m. – 5 p.m.	Sum
Insufficient plating	✓✓✓✓✓✓✓		✓		✓✓✓✓✓	15
Inability to meet heat specs	✓✓✓✓✓✓	✓✓✓✓✓✓✓✓✓✓	✓✓✓✓✓✓✓✓✓	✓✓✓✓✓✓✓✓✓	✓✓✓✓✓✓✓✓	42
Scratched lens	✓✓✓✓✓✓✓✓✓	✓✓	✓✓✓✓	✓✓✓	✓✓✓✓✓✓✓✓✓✓	28
Failed leak test	✓✓	✓✓	✓	✓✓✓	✓✓	12
Glue on lens			✓✓✓	✓✓✓	✓	7
Cracked body	✓	✓✓		✓✓		5
	27	16	18	20	28	109

Solution:

1. Carry out a Pareto analysis on the types of defects irrespective of time of day.

   Here, we would first organize the data in terms of number of occurrences going from most frequent to least frequent.

Defect Type	Number	Percentage	Cumulative Percentage
Inability to meet heat specs	42	38.53	38.53
Scratched lens	28	25.69	64.22
Insufficient plating	15	13.72	77.98
Failed leak test	12	11.01	88.99
Glue on lens	7	6.42	95.41
Cracked body	5	4.59	100.00

   What this analysis tells us is that were we to focus on the first three items, we would account for about 78 percent of all defects. This is where we should start. This can be graphically summarized as a histogram:

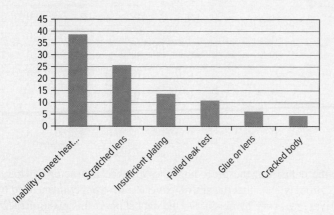

2. Does the time of the day have any impact?

   Yes, for insufficient plating and scratched lenses (both are more likely to occur before 9 a.m. or after 3 p.m.) and glue on lens (which is most likely to occur from 11 a.m. to 3 p.m.). These observations might be good candidates for CEDs.

PROBLEMS

1. The time students entered the classroom of OM 390, Introductory Operations Management, was recorded by the professor in the table below for five class meetings. Create and analyze a histogram of these data. Please note that a negative time means that the student arrived after the start of class.

Minutes Arrival Before Class (class starts at time 0)	Class 1	Class 2	Class 3	Class 4	Class 5
15	3	4	6	1	4
14	0	0	2	1	3
13	1	2	0	3	1
12	1	0	0	1	0
11	1	1	2	1	0
10	2	0	0	1	1
9	4	2	0	2	0
8	0	1	4	3	0
7	1	5	1	0	3
6	1	1	2	1	2
5	5	6	2	4	5
4	6	1	7	4	6
3	0	0	3	2	0
2	3	2	0	5	0
1	2	2	0	0	4
0	1	2	0	0	1
−1	0	0	0	0	1
−2	0	0	0	0	0
−3	0	0	0	1	0
−4	0	0	0	0	0
−5	0	1	0	0	0
−6	0	0	0	0	0
−7	0	0	0	0	0
−8	0	0	1	0	0
−9	0	0	0	1	0
−10	0	0	0	0	0

2. Using the data from the preceding question, the instructor in charge of these five classes strongly feels that the arrival patterns are strongly influenced by the class (i.e., the arrival rates vary by class). Do the data support this position? (*Hint*: Look at the histograms for each class separately.)

3. Using the data from question 1, you have been asked to develop an overall cause-and-effect chart explaining why students arrived so early.

4. The injection-molded caps of disposable ballpoint pens must meet tight specifications to fit snugly on the pen. One specification that is tracked is the cap's weight, which

should be 0.2 grams. A sample of 100 pens is taken each day. Make a histogram of the data for one day's production, given the data in the table below.

Weights of Molded Caps in Grams									
0.225	**0.243**	**0.239**	**0.231**	**0.228**	**0.215**	**0.161**	**0.161**	**0.207**	**0.177**
0.190	0.186	0.203	0.230	0.228	0.180	0.230	0.194	0.243	0.177
0.210	0.210	0.185	0.225	0.204	0.152	0.245	0.231	0.152	0.150
0.161	0.171	0.208	0.208	0.170	0.204	0.250	0.178	0.205	0.236
0.159	0.229	0.173	0.228	0.184	0.223	0.240	0.193	0.170	0.241
0.161	0.193	0.165	0.154	0.192	0.214	0.189	0.208	0.227	0.169
0.163	0.196	0.181	0.197	0.248	0.238	0.205	0.207	0.244	0.208
0.200	0.207	0.225	0.162	0.229	0.151	0.224	0.169	0.220	0.182
0.214	0.233	0.194	0.181	0.208	0.249	0.220	0.197	0.204	0.247
0.216	0.160	0.210	0.222	0.157	0.174	0.173	0.240	0.203	0.247

5. The specification for the weight of a box of cereal is 16.2 oz $\pm$ .1 oz. The actual mean and standard deviation from a sample of 200 boxes is 16.1 oz. and 0.05 oz., respectively. What are the C_p and C_{pk}?

6. A professor who teaches the Introduction to Management course has noticed that 20 percent of the students in her sections receive a grade lower than 2.0 on a 4.0 scale. This is the first management course that any of these students have taken. The text for the course is a standard survey text, which is used at many other colleges and universities. All of the students in the class are first semester junior, business students. The students work in teams to manage a simulated factory. As part of this they must use a computer spreadsheet to do simple income statements, balance sheets, and cash flow problems. Prepare a cause-and-effect diagram (CED) to analyze the problem: "Why do students in this class receive low grades?" For the main branches of the CED, use the following titles: student, books, faculty, and equipment.

7. Create a check sheet to organize the data in problem 1 above.

8. Create a check sheet to analyze the data in problem 2 above.

9. In an apparel factory, every time a sewing machine breaks, the symptom is recorded. In the past 30 days, all of the sewing machine breakdowns were recorded in the table below. Create a check sheet to organize and analyze these data.

Day	Machine Number	Reason for Breakdown	Day	Machine Number	Reason for Breakdown
	1	217 Dull knife		2	201 Dull knife
	1	145 Skip stitch		2	172 Breaking needles
	1	193 Stuck pedal		2	195 Stuck pedal
	1	187 Skip stitch		3	187 Skip stitch
	1	234 Breaking needles		3	234 Breaking needles
	2	165 Air pressure low		3	165 Air pressure low
	2	192 Breaking needles		3	192 Breaking needles
	2	217 Thread breaks		3	151 Skip stitch
	2	217 Skip stitch		4	187 Skip stitch
	2	165 Skip stitch		4	234 Breaking needles
	2	181 Breaking needles		5	195 Stuck pedal

Day	Machine Number	Reason for Breakdown
	5	187 Skip stitch
	6	165 Air pressure low
	6	192 Breaking needles
	6	165 Other
	6	192 Breaking needles
	6	217 Thread breaks
	6	217 Skip stitch
	7	165 Skip stitch
	7	195 Stuck pedal
	7	187 Skip stitch
	7	234 Breaking needles
	7	165 Air pressure low
	8	192 Other

Day	Machine Number	Reason for Breakdown
	8	234 Breaking needles
	8	165 Air pressure low
	9	192 Breaking needles
	9	217 Thread breaks
	9	151 Other
	9	187 Skip stitch
	9	234 Breaking needles
	9	151 Breaking needles
	10	234 Skip stitch
	10	165 Air pressure low
	10	192 Breaking needles
	10	187 Skip stitch
	10	131 Other

10. The quality inspectors at Windows Inc. visually inspect each sheet of 4 ft × 8 ft glass when it is through with the annealing process. They record all of the defects onto a form. The defects that have been found this week are given in the table below. Use these data to create a location check sheet.

Corner	Body	Defect
Left upper		chipped corner
	center	indentation
Left upper		chipped corner
Right lower		scratch
	left of center	bump
Left upper		chipped corner
Left upper		chipped corner
Left lower		scratch

Corner	Body	Defect
	center	scratch
Left upper		chipped corner
Right upper	chipped corner	
Right lower		scratch
	right of center	indentation
Left upper		chipped corner
Left lower		scratch
Left upper		crack

11. Use the data in problem 9 to create a Pareto diagram.

12. Use the data in problem 10 to create a Pareto diagram.

13. For the following check sheet, assume that o indicates a surface scratch, x a blowhole, D a defective finish, * improper shape, and ? others. How would you go about analyzing the following check sheet?

	Worker	Mon AM	Mon PM	Tue AM	Tue PM	Wed AM	Wed PM	Thur AM	Thur PM	Fri AM	Fri PM
March 1	1	oox*	ox	oxx	oooxxxo	ooooxxxo	ooxx	oooo	oxx	Oo	oDxx
March 2	2	oxx*	oooxx*	oooooxx	oooxx	oooooxx*	ooooox*	ooooxx	ooox**	Ooxx*	ooooo

For this problem, analyze the data using Pareto analysis. Is stratification (studying each class separately) appropriate for this type of a problem? How would you stratify the data? That is, identify those variables that you think have an important effect on the observed results.

14. Construct an $\bar{x} - R$ chart for the following data set.

Sub Group No.	6:00	10:00	14:00	18:00	22:00	$\bar{x}$	R
1	14.0	12.6	13.2	13.1	12.1	13.00	1.9
2	13.2	13.3	12.7	13.4	12.1	12.94	1.3
3	13.5	12.8	13.0	12.8	12.4	12.90	1.1
4	13.9	12.4	13.3	13.1	13.2	13.18	1.5
5	13.0	13.0	12.1	12.2	13.3	2.72	1.2
6	13.7	12.0	12.5	12.4	12.4	12.60	1.7
7	13.9	12.1	12.7	13.4	13.0	13.02	1.8
8	13.4	13.6	13.0	12.4	13.5	13.18	1.2
9	14.4	12.4	12.2	12.4	12.5	12.78	2.2
10	13.3	12.4	12.6	12.9	12.8	12.80	0.9
11	13.3	12.8	13.0	13.0	13.1	13.04	0.5
12	13.6	12.5	13.3	13.5	12.8	13.14	1.1
13	13.4	13.3	12.0	13.0	13.1	12.96	1.4
14	13.9	13.1	13.5	12.6	12.8	13.18	1.3
15	14.2	12.7	12.9	12.9	12.5	13.04	1.7
16	13.6	12.6	12.4	12.5	12.2	12.66	1.4
17	14.0	13.2	12.4	13.0	13.0	13.12	1.6
18	13.1	12.9	13.5	12.3	12.8	12.92	1.2
19	14.6	13.7	13.4	12.2	12.5	13.28	2.4
20	13.9	13.0	13.0	13.2	12.6	13.14	1.3
21	13.3	12.7	12.6	12.8	12.7	12.82	0.7
22	13.9	12.4	12.7	12.4	12.8	12.84	1.5
23	13.2	12.3	12.6	13.1	12.7	12.78	0.9
24	13.2	12.8	12.8	12.3	12.6	12.74	0.9
25	13.3	12.8	12.0	12.3	12.2	12.72	1.1
					Σ of $\bar{X} - R$	323.50	33.8
					Grand Mean $(\overline{\overline{X}})$	12.94	1.35

15. You are responsible for managing a process that manufactures electronic capacitors. This process has experienced an unacceptable level of rejects. Consequently, you have asked the people responsible for the manufacturing process for these products to collect data regarding defects and the reasons for these defects. This information has been collected in the following table (assume that the data are representative).

Observation	Reject Cause	Observation	Reject Cause	Observation	Reject Cause
1	Corrosion	2	Oxide defect	3	Contamination
4	Oxide defect	5	Oxide defect	6	Misc.
7	Oxide defect	8	Contamination	9	Metallization
10	Oxide defect	11	Contamination	12	Contamination
13	Oxide defect	14	Contamination	15	Contamination
16	Contamination	17	Corrosion	18	Silicon defect
19	Misc.	20	Contamination	21	Contamination
22	Contamination	23	Contamination	24	Contamination

Observation	Reject Cause	Observation	Reject Cause	Observation	Reject Cause
25	Misc.	26	Doping	27	Oxide defect
28	Oxide defect	29	Metallization	30	Contamination
31	Contamination	32	Oxide defect	33	Contamination

What conclusions can you draw from these data? What techniques would you use? How would you manage the data?

16. As a result of a Six Sigma exercise, the process described in the preceding question has been modified. Data have been collected again and summarized in the following table. To what extent have the improvements introduced by the process modification been successful in improving the process?

Failure Cause	Number Observed
Doping	0
Corrosion	2
Metallization	4
Misc.	2
Oxide defect	1
Contamination	8
Silicon defect	2

17. Big Turkey Burger Farms (BTBF) produces a large turkey burger that is world famous. This burger is known not only for its quality, but also its size and consistency. BTBF produces a turkey burger that on average is 12 ounces (with a standard deviation of 0.10 ounces). Currently, BTBF has been approached by two major restaurant chains: Monarch Burgers and Audrey's.

1. Monarch wants a turkey burger that is between 11.77 and 12.23 ounces.
   i. For this customer, calculate the C_p.
   ii. Calculate the C_{pk} value.
   iii. How well would BTBF's products meet the demands of Monarch Burgers?

2. Audrey's, in contrast, wants a turkey burger that is 11.95 ounces on average with a tolerance of 0.30 ounces.
   i. For this customer, calculate the C_p.
   ii. Calculate the C_{pk} value.
   iii. How well would BTBF's products meet the demands of Audrey's?

3. If BTBF had a choice of restaurant chains to serve (it can only pick one), which one should it select? Why?

18. In an article in *Quality Engineering,* a research article presented individual measurement data on sand compactibility, as follows:

46	43	41	42	40	44	40	41	40	42
41	41	43	43	40	38	45	42	41	43
42	43	39	44	44	45	43	42	41	46
41	39	40	40	42	44	42	40	43	

For these data, the author reported that the lower and upper specifications for sand compactibility are 38 and 46, respectively. Use this information to calculate the C_p and C_{pk} values.

19. Calculate the C_p and C_{pk} for a process characterized by the following data:
    Production specifications: 1.00 ± 0.08 cm
    Process standard deviation: 0.005 cm
    Process distribution centered at 0.95 cm.

20. Suppose that you collect data for 15 samples of 30 units each and find that, on average, 2.5 percent of the products are defective. What are the UCL and LCL for this process?

21. Peerless Windows is a major manufacturer and installer of windows into new homes. Currently, management has found that it has experienced a large number of customer claims (about 15% of all orders placed) against Peerless. These customers, often builders, are claiming that they are receiving shipments of windows that are built to the wrong specifications. Correcting these errors has cost Peerless a great deal in terms of time, resources, and disrupted schedules. To determine if the order entry process is at fault, management has collected orders from the last two years. For each month, 100 orders were withdrawn and reviewed. The results are summarized in the table below. Experience with this product has resulted in the mean defect rate being 7.5 with the LCL being 0 and the UCL being 15. As an analyst, you have been asked to review the order entry process with the goal of assessing whether this process is causing the problems.

Month	Number of Orders Reviewed	Number of Orders with Errors
1	100	11
2	100	10
3	100	6
4	100	14
5	100	8
6	100	10
7	100	9
8	100	12
9	100	2
10	100	14
11	100	18
12	100	7
13	100	12
14	100	12
15	100	14
16	100	13
17	100	11
18	100	10
19	100	8
20	100	6
21	100	19
22	100	17
23	100	25
24	100	24

22. You are concerned about the quality of parts that you are receiving from your supplier. Consequently, you decide to take 25 batches of samples (where each sample consists of 50 units) and conduct a 100% inspection on these samples. The results are summarized below.

Batch number	Defectives	Sample size ($n = 50$)
1	5	50
2	6	50
3	5	50
4	6	50
5	3	50
6	3	50
7	6	50
8	5	50
9	3	50
10	5	50
11	5	50
12	7	50
13	8	50
14	10	50
15	10	50
16	6	50
17	5	50
18	4	50
19	5	50
20	5	50
21	6	50
22	5	50
23	6	50
24	3	50
25	4	50
Totals	136	1250

This forms the basis for your further analysis. Next, you collect information about 20 recent orders that you have received from your supplier in the last month. By the way, it is important to note that your supplier is aware that your firm is concerned about the quality of its parts. These are summarized below:

Sample Data – June		
Sample Number	**Sample Size**	**Number of Defects**
1	50	3
2	50	2
3	50	3
4	50	4
5	50	1
6	50	2
7	50	4
8	50	3
9	50	1
10	50	1

Sample Data – June		
Sample Number	**Sample Size**	**Number of Defects**
11	50	2
12	50	2
13	50	3
14	50	1
15	50	3
16	50	3
17	50	4
18	50	5
19	50	5
20	50	5

a. Given the information in this problem, calculate the $\bar{p}$, UCL, and LCL from the baseline data. Use these parameters to construct a p attribute control chart.

b. Plot the data from the June samples on the p chart derived in (a). What issues, if any, does this analysis reveal? What management actions would you recommend and why?

c. You receive a telephone call from your supplier informing you that it (the supplier) has significantly changed the production process for your orders at its facility. How would this affect the previous analysis (p control chart)?

23. A store is concerned with the number of late shipments that it generates each day. Consequently, it decided to track the number of late shipments for the last seven days. The data are summarized in the list below:

Day	Number Late	p
1	10	0.20
2	5	0.10
3	8	0.16
4	12	0.24
5	9	0.18
6	11	0.22
7	12	0.24
	$\bar{p}$	0.19

24. Calculate the LCL and UCL for these data. Using the control chart developed in the previous question, plot the following data received from the store for a 10-day period. What insights for management do you have based on your analysis?

Day	Number Late	p
31	8	0.16
32	11	0.22
33	10	0.20
34	11	0.22
35	12	0.24
36	11	0.22

Day	Number Late	p
37	13	0.26
38	12	0.24
39	13	0.26
40	14	0.28

25. Management is concerned about the operation of its 123XYZ work center. From past studies, it knows that $\bar{x}$ is 12.14, the LCL is 11.74, and the UCL is 12.54. The following data were collected for a 20-day period (where each observation is the mean for the processing times for that day):

Day	Sample Mean
1	12.10
2	12.20
3	12.15
4	12.17
5	12.21
6	12.15
7	12.18
8	12.22
9	12.16
10	12.13
11	12.18
12	12.17
13	12.11
14	12.13
15	12.14
16	12.16
17	12.17
18	12.13
19	12.14
20	12.16

a. Plot and analyze the data using the control chart developed from the parameters provided.
b. What can you say about the process? Is it under control? Is there anything that bothers you about the process?

CASE

The Tragedy of R.M.S. Titanic

On the evening of Sunday, April 14, 1912, R.M.S. Titanic, while on her maiden voyage, struck an iceberg about two days from New York City. Within three hours, she was gone (Monday, April 15, 1912). On this voyage, there were 2,201 passengers and crew members, of which 711 survived. Initially, it was thought that the survivors came primarily from the first class compartments (with some from the second class). After all, the passengers in first class had paid the most to travel on the Titanic's maiden voyage (in some cases paying in excess of $100,000 in today's dollars). These people were closest to the lifeboats. They represented some of the most important people in 1912 society—John Jacob Astor IV and his wife Madeleine Force Astor, industrialist Benjamin Guggenheim, Macy's owner Isidor Straus and his wife Ida, Denver millionaire Margaret "Molly" Brown (who became known later on as the "Unsinkable Molly Brown"), Sir Cosmo Duff Gordon and his wife Lucy, and silent film actress Dorothy Gibson. In contrast, the third class was located the furthest away from the lifeboats. Also, as a result of the U.S. immigration requirements, the gates that would have given the third class passengers access to the lifeboats were locked when Titanic left Southampton.

You have been asked to study the passenger list for Titanic and to determine if the premises stated in the previous paragraph really did occur. Specifically, consider the following:

1. Using the Excel Spreadsheet, Titanic.xlsx on the text website (www.mhhe.com/swink3e), analyze the data to determine what type of passenger would be most likely to survive and least likely to survive.

2. Read about the Titanic and develop a CED to explain why so many people died on this ship. To help you in doing this assignment, you may want to read the note entitled, "RMS Titanic—Did you know??")

RMS Titanic—Did you know??

On April 14, 1912, RMS Titanic, while on her maiden voyage, struck an iceberg and sank. Up until this point, this was the single, most tragic maritime disaster in modern times (by the way, this loss has since been eclipsed–see if you can uncover the single, most tragic maritime disaster and why it occurred). To many, this event was unthinkable. After all, RMS Titanic was "unsinkable." This was not an idle claim, but the result of several modern innovations built into the Titanic, namely:

- *Double-hulled construction* – RMS Titanic was the first ship to use a double-hulled construction–with one hull constructed within another. The promise of this form of construction was that it made the Titanic less susceptible to sinking due to a punctured hull. Any puncture would have to go through two hulls–not one.

- *Electronic bulkheads* – The bulkheads, critical to locking compartments and keeping out water–were designed to be initiated electronically. The promise of this approach–speed and assuredness of closure.

- *The largest number of lifeboats on any ship* – The RMS Titanic carried lifeboats (both rigid and collapsible) for 1,168 passengers. This number was far in excess of the number mandated by the Maritime Commission.

- *Ability to stay afloat if up to five of her compartments were breached* – Based on past disasters, the designers were aware that a ship such as RMS Titanic might experience severe problems if multiple compartments were to be breached. Consequently, the Titanic was designed to float even if up to five compartments were to be breached. This was the most of any ship at the time.

- *The latest in Marconi wireless technology* for sending and receiving wireless messages.

Yet, late on April 14, 1912, at 11:40 p.m., RMS Titanic struck an iceberg. By 2:20 a.m., April 15, 1912, RMS Titanic had broken apart and was gone. People wanted to know why. The following are some (but not all) of the factors contributing to this disaster and its high loss of life:

- *Coal strike.* The departure of the RMS Titanic was delayed by some two weeks due to a British coal strike. The Titanic was delayed while sufficient coal stocks were accumulated for its maiden voyage. This had two major impacts. First, the delay put Titanic's crossing at a time when the ice floes in the mid-Atlantic were known to be worse. Second, since the ship was late, it increased the pressure for a quick voyage across the Atlantic.

- *A lost key in Queenstown.* When Titanic departed from Queenstown Ireland, on its way to New York, the crew was unable to access the binoculars needed for scouting or seeing icebergs in the distance. The reason: The key to the cabinet holding the binoculars had been left behind in Queenstown.

- *Weather conditions.* The night of April 14, 1912, was unusual in that it was perfectly still and calm–there were no waves on the ocean. Consequently, waves and wave splashes (one way that many crew located in the crow's nest could identify icebergs in the distance) were totally absent.

- *Moonless night.* Not only was the night calm, but it was also completely dark, thus further reducing the ability of the crew to spot icebergs in the distance.

- *The Blue Riband Award.* This was an award given to the ship that could record the fastest crossing of the Atlantic. Titanic was the most elegant of ships ever built but it was not the fastest (the Lusitania, which was built with Royal Navy funds, was inherently faster). However, Captain Smith, the commander of the Titanic, wanted to win this award. Consequently, he was pushing for a quick voyage.

- *Maiden voyage.* This was the first crossing for the Titanic, which meant that the crew had not worked with each other and they were still getting familiar with the ship.

- *No lifeboat drill.* Because of a late departure from Cherbourg (and an almost-collision with another ship) and another late departure from Queenstown, it was decided that there had been enough confusion for one day and the lifeboat drill was never carried out.

Consequently, many passengers did not know what to do if there was a problem. For example, they did not know where to go for their boats, where to find their lifeboat jackets, and how to get to the lifeboats. This last issue was a major one given the size of the Titanic.

- *Location of the lifeboats.* Most of the lifeboats were located amidships, on top of the ship. This, ironically, was where the first class passengers were located. However, most of the passengers were third class or steerage. These passengers were located either at the bow or stern.

- *The wireless system.* Critical to the safety of the Titanic was its wireless system. However, the wireless system was owned by the Marconi Company and manned by Marconi employees. These employees were paid on the number of messages that they sent. On April 12, Titanic was approaching New York and consequently many of its passengers wanted to send messages telling their friends and relatives that they were coming; the wireless office was simply overwhelmed with wireless volume.

- *Shut up.* The SS California had just traversed the same ice field that Titanic was about to enter. She (ships are always called *she*) found the ice field to be very dangerous. To cross it, the California had to move during the day at reduced speeds. In the evening, when the California found out that Titanic was entering the ice field, the radio operator repeatedly sent messages warning the Titanic of the potential danger ahead. The radio operators, because of the volume of work, found these messages irritating because they interrupted their ability to send out messages. One of the Titanic operators was so irritated that he sent a message to the California telling the operator to "shut up." The California operator, upon receiving this message, shut down his set (thus preventing him from receiving any other messages from Titanic until morning) and went to bed.

- *State of the water.* During early and mid-April, temperatures in the mid-Atlantic are very cold. Water temperature at night, for example, is about 40 degrees Fahrenheit (or less). At such temperatures, any person in the water for 15 to 30 minutes is likely to die from cardiac arrest and hypothermia.

- *Time delay.* From the time that the Titanic struck the iceberg until its passengers were being asked to move to their lifeboats, about an hour elapsed. Since the Titanic took less than three hours to sink, this was a critical loss of time.

- *Passenger reactions.* In many cases, the passengers could not understand the urgency. First of all, they were being asked to leave their warm rooms and to go outside where the night time temperatures were very cold. Second, many could not believe that there was a problem with the Titanic–after all, she was "unsinkable." Third, many of the crew, in asking the passengers to go to their lifeboat stations, did not convey the magnitude of the problem.

(Consider the following: Ismay from White Star, who was on the ship, and Edward Smith, the captain, both knew that the Titanic was doomed from the reports since six compartments were affected. This was one more than the five maximum that Titanic was designed to handle).

- *Immigration and naturalization practices.* Most of the passengers on the Titanic were traveling in third class; these passengers were coming to America to start a new life. In contrast, the passengers in first and second class were visiting. American Immigration practice was to secure (by lock) all access to third class. This was done to prevent any illegal immigration. However, when the Titanic struck the iceberg, the gates to third class remained locked.

- *Gates to third class compartments.* The crew did not open the gates to the third class compartments. When the Titanic struck the iceberg, the crew immediately went and manned their stations at the lifeboats; no one was formally tasked with the assignment of securing the key to third class and opening the gates.

- *The attitudes of the people.* Many of the people, especially those in third class, were used to being told what to do on the ship. When the Titanic struck the iceberg, many of these people (often families with young children) waited in their rooms for instructions.

- *The lack of lifeboats.* Simply put, the Titanic had too few lifeboats for its passengers and crew.

- *Lack of loading instructions.* Every officer in charge of a lifeboat had his own procedure and approach for loading and launching lifeboats. Some, like First Officer Charles Lightoller, only allowed women and children; others allowed men as long as they were from a reputable yachting club (not rowing club, but sailing large boats) and still others took the attitude of "first-come-first-served." In addition, some lifeboats were launched partially full while others were loaded to capacity.

- *Picking up survivors in the water.* Some lifeboats refused to pick up survivors because of fears of tipping over while others actively picked up survivors. Margaret (Molly) Brown of Denver was shocked when she learned that the person in charge of her boat refused to pick up any survivors even though the boat had the capacity to carry more passengers. Consequently, she convinced the other passengers of the need to save those in the water. They did so by threatening the boat captain with harm if he did not comply. That is why Molly Brown became known as the Unsinkable Molly Brown.

- *Rewards.* The Titanic carried a larger number than normal crew list. This was due in part to the practice of Harland and Wolfe of Belfast (the ship builders) to reward the good construction workers with berths on the Titanic for the maiden voyage (where they would be responsible for repairing any problems encountered). Nearly all of these people died when the Titanic went down.

CASE

The Bully Boy Bagging Line

Things were not going well at Bully Boy Products (BBP). BBP was a regional producer of organic fertilizer, potting soil, growing loam, and various gardening products for the discriminating gardener. It had been founded in 1976 when two agriculture students had decided that something had to be done to provide better supplies for gardeners. As one of the founders said, "Living better chemically may be great for chemicals but it has no place when it comes to gardening supplies."

Since its founding, BBP had grown by always remembering its core competencies—quality, variety, and innovative organic groups. As a result of this growth, the managers of BBP decided in 2011 to expand its production facilities, including installation of a new automated bagging line. This system was designed to provide quick product changeovers, something critical to BBP given its wide and ever-changing product line. The bagging system was brought online at the start of 2012. After four weeks of debugging, the system was thought to be ready for full-scale production. Yet, as soon as it started up, problems became evident. These problems took a variety of forms: bagging seams were poorly made at the top; some bags were overfilled, while other bags were underfilled; and some bags experienced various forms of rips (the most common form of defect). Whenever a bagging problem occurred, the standard operating procedure was to stop, clear the problem, write up the issue, and then restart production. Top management had decided that the situation in the bagging line was no longer acceptable—something had to be done. To that end, they asked Lisa Vickery to determine whether the bagging problems were random or systematic in nature.

Lisa reviewed the production on the firm's large-bag packaging line. There seemed to be much more variation in quality than she would normally expect. After calling for a summary of the data from production control, she received the BullyBoyBag.xlsx data (www.mhhe.com/swink3e) collected over the last 16 workweeks.

1. What do these data tell you?
2. Which tools did you use to determine what is happening? (*Hint*: Consider looking at the impact of staffing and day of the week.)
3. What management actions are appropriate? What would you recommend to Lisa Vickery?

SELECTED READINGS & INTERNET SITES

AT&T. *Statistical Quality Control Handbook,* 11th ed. Charlotte, NC: Delmar Publishing, 1985.

Deming, W. E. *Out of Crisis.* Cambridge, MA: MIT Center for Advanced Engineering Study, 1986.

Garvin, D. A. *Managing Quality.* New York: Free Press, 1988.

Gitlow, H.; S. Gitlow; A. Oppenheim; and R. Oppenheim. *Tools and Methods for the Improvement of Quality.* Homewood, IL: Irwin, 1989.

Ishikawa, K. *Guide to Quality Control.* White Plains, NY: Quality Resources, 1982.

Ishikawa, K. *What Is Total Quality Control? The Japanese Way.* Englewood Cliffs, NJ: Prentice Hall, 1985.

Juran, J. M., and F. M. Gryna, Jr. *Quality Planning and Analysis.* New York: McGraw-Hill, 1980.

Nelson, L. S. "Technical Aids." *Journal of Quality Technology* 16, no. 4 (October 1984), pp. 238–39.

American Society for Quality (ASQ)
www.asq.org

Six Sigma
www.isixsigma.com

7

Managing Inventories

LEARNING OBJECTIVES *After studying this chapter, you should be able to:*

LO7-1 Define the different types and roles of inventory in the supply chain.

LO7-2 Explain the financial impact of inventory on firm performance.

LO7-3 Explain and compute asset productivity and customer service–related measures of inventory performance.

LO7-4 Calculate inventory policy parameters to minimize total acquisition cost in continuous review, periodic review, and single period models.

LO7-5 Determine the cost of a company's service level policy.

LO7-6 Explain the advantages and disadvantages of different inventory location strategies.

LO7-7 Describe practical techniques for inventory planning and management.

Inventory Improvements at PolyOne Corp.

PolyOne Corp. is a global provider of specialized polymer materials, services, and solutions (such as metallic-look vinyl used in home appliances, the soft-touch plastic on the handle of your razor, and medical-grade polymers for tubing). A few years ago, it appeared that the company might have to file for bankruptcy. Instead, the company recently generated $218 million of free cash flow and reduced its net debt by $223 million. During this time its stock share price has risen 580 percent. How did the company increase cash flow in such a short time, and during one of the worst economic recessions in history? Largely through supply chain management improvements in two areas: better manufacturing efficiencies and much improved inventory management practices.

Inventory management improvements began when top managers formed a global inventory management team. The team's goal was to reduce inventory levels across businesses and regions while maintaining on-time delivery performance to customers. Major changes included consolidating operations into a smaller number of facilities, identifying and focusing on the highest total cost items, working with key suppliers on delivery reliability, and adjusting inventory reorder points. In one year, inventory management actions reduced inventory levels by $152 million—freeing up much needed cash while nearly doubling inventory turns.

As the PolyOne story suggests, inventory management is critical to a firm's financial success. In recent years firms have been very focused on reducing inventories, both within their organizations and across their supply chains. From a supply chain perspective, it does little good for one firm to reduce its inventory if the change requires another firm in the supply chain to increase its inventory holdings. Understanding the management of inventory is critical to virtually all aspects of operations management.

TYPES AND ROLES OF INVENTORY

In general, **inventory** is a supply of items held by a firm to meet demand. The demand may come from an external customer, or it may come from internal operations, such as the need for parts on an assembly line to complete production or for paper to produce copies of a report. It is useful, however, to think more specifically about different types of inventory that a firm might hold.

Types of Inventory

In a manufacturing firm, considerable quantities of inventory may be held to support the manufacturing process itself. **Raw materials and component parts** are items that are bought from suppliers to use in the production of a product. Once these items enter the production process, they become classified as **work in process inventory**. Finally, when the manufacturing is completed and products are ready for sale to a customer they become **finished goods inventory**. Retailers and wholesalers also hold finished goods inventory; in fact, their fundamental purpose is to have finished goods available for customer purchase.

There are other types of inventory that are held by all types of organizations. These items are generally referred to as **MRO inventory** or maintenance, repair, and operating supplies. MRO items include everything from office supplies and forms, to toilet paper and cleaning supplies, to tools and parts needed to repair machines. The need to manage MRO inventories makes the subject of inventory just as critical to service organizations as it is to manufacturing. Consider, for example, the vast quantity of paper used at your college to make copies of syllabi or exams in the courses you take. Also think of the supplies (such as food, water, blankets, and blood) held by the American Red Cross to support its ability to respond to disasters such as hurricanes or earthquakes.

Any given item may be classified as several different types of inventory, depending on who has it and for what purpose. For example, when copy paper comes off the production line at Mead Corporation, it becomes finished goods at Mead. When sold to your university, the same copy paper becomes part of your university's MRO inventory.

Some executives have gone so far as to suggest that holding any inventory at all is bad for an organization. Such a suggestion ignores the important roles that inventory plays in the supply chain. But it does emphasize the critical desire to minimize investments in inventory, as long as an organization can effectively meet its objectives.

The Roles of Inventory

There are several reasons that holding inventory is not necessarily bad. In fact, inventory has several important roles in a supply chain.

Balancing Supply and Demand

Holding inventory allows an organization to intermittently produce batches of products, instead of having to produce at exactly the same time and rate as demand. Inventory is used to satisfy demand for a product during the periods when it is not being produced. This may be needed when a firm produces several products using the same equipment and has to switch between producing the items from time to time. Producing or shipping inventories in batches enables firms to take advantages of economies of scale. In addition, inventory allows a firm to deal efficiently with seasonality of either supply or demand, as is the case with many agricultural products. For example, a potato farmer harvests potatoes only once each year and stores those potatoes in inventory, taking them out of storage when orders are received from customers. Inventories used for these purposes are known as cycle stocks and seasonal stocks.

Buffering Uncertainty in Demand or Supply

Managers rarely know with absolute certainty the amount of future demand for a product. Nor do they know for sure how long it will take to replenish inventory when more is needed. Consequently, companies frequently hold extra inventory to meet unexpected demand or delays in replenishment. Best Buy, for example, never knows how many units of a particular television model will be sold on a given day. There is also some uncertainty concerning exactly how long it will take to be resupplied with an item after an order is placed with the supplier. Therefore, Best Buy may carry more inventory than it actually expects to sell in any specific time period. Just about all organizations hold extra inventory of at least some products to guard against these potential uncertainties in demand or supply. This extra inventory is referred to as buffer (or safety) stock. Much of the attention in inventory management in recent years has focused specifically on reducing the quantity of safety stock needed.

Enabling Economies of Buying

For several reasons, supply managers may buy more inventory than they immediately need. Often, suppliers offer price discounts to encourage customers to purchase larger quantities at one time. Likewise, buying in large quantity may result in economies associated with transporting larger quantities at one time. Also related to the economics of buying are speculative holdings of inventory when supply managers buy ahead of need because they believe that prices may increase in the future or that there may be supply disruptions or shortages.

Enabling Geographic Specialization

Supply locations and demand locations are rarely the same. For example, Kimberly-Clark makes paper towels in only a small number of production facilities, but those paper towels are demanded virtually everywhere. It would be infeasible to locate production facilities in every demand location. Instead, the company holds inventory in distribution centers near major customer demand zones located around the world. Inventory frequently must be stored in such centers to quickly meet the demand of customers in different locales. Inventory that is being transported from one place to another (such as from a warehouse to a retail store) is known as transit inventory.

THE FINANCIAL IMPACT OF INVENTORY

Although most businesses recognize that inventory has many important roles, the primary reason that some executives think inventory is "bad" is that inventory has a significant financial impact on an organization. From the standpoint of financial accounting, inventory represents both an asset on the balance sheet and a cost that impacts the profitability of any firm.

Balance Sheet Considerations

Just as a manufacturing plant, a warehouse, or a retail store represents money invested in assets, so too does inventory. In fact, for many firms, and particularly for wholesalers and retailers, inventory represents a very significant portion (30 percent or more) of the company's total assets. Naturally, the funds for this investment must come from either the owners of the firm or through some sort of debt. Because most owners/stockholders prefer to keep their investment and their debt as low as possible, they prefer to keep inventories low. Additionally, a reduction in inventory frees up cash that can then be invested in other assets, used to reduce debt, or returned to shareholders.

Costs Related to Inventory

product cost The amount paid to suppliers for products that are purchased.

There are a number of costs and expenses a company incurs due to the fact that it holds inventory. First there is **product cost**. Product cost is simply the amount paid to suppliers for the products that are purchased.

Carrying Cost

carrying (or holding) cost Several expenses that are incurred due to the fact that inventory is held.

A very significant cost related to inventory is **carrying (or holding) cost**. Carrying cost actually encompasses a number of different expenses, which include the following:

- Opportunity cost, including the cost of capital.
- Cost of owning and maintaining storage space.
- Taxes.
- Insurance.
- Costs of obsolescence, loss, and disposal.
- Costs of materials handling, tracking, and management.

sustainability

Many companies drastically underestimate the opportunity costs associated with inventory and consider only the cost of capital in that category. In fact, there are other opportunity costs associated with inventory that are not immediately obvious. Holding large amounts of inventory frequently obscures other problems in an organization, such as inefficient receiving processes or inefficient production processes. In effect, the inventory leads to a failure to identify potential improvements in the company, such as the implementation of lean and just-in-time initiatives (as discussed in Chapter 8). Excess inventories also have societal costs. Disposal of unused inventories can contribute to air pollution, increased landfills, and hazardous wastes.

Most companies state carrying cost as a percentage of the value of the inventory that is held. It is not unusual for a company to value its annual carrying cost as high as 25 to 30 percent of product value. Consider the following example:

EXAMPLE 7-1

If a firm holds, on average, $100 million of inventory and its carrying cost percentage is 25 percent, it incurs $25 million annually in carrying cost. Reducing that inventory to $80 million would result in annual carrying cost of $20 million, a savings of $5 million, which basically drops straight to the bottom line as increased profit.

Carrying cost is also frequently translated into a monetary amount per unit of a product per unit of time. For example, suppose Whirlpool Corporation determines that its inventory carrying cost is 30 percent of product value annually. A particular refrigerator that Whirlpool makes and holds as finished goods has a value (cost) of $1,000. Whirlpool may then consider that its annual inventory carrying cost on one unit of the refrigerator is $300 ($1,000 × .30) or $25 per month ($300/12).

Order and Setup Cost

order cost The expenses incurred in placing and receiving orders from suppliers.

Order cost is a transaction cost associated with replenishing inventories. It includes the expenses incurred in placing and receiving orders from suppliers: order preparation, order transmittal, order receiving, and accounts payable processing.

setup cost Administrative expenses and the expenses of rearranging a work center to produce an item.

Conceptually, **setup cost** is similar to, but slightly different from, order cost. The difference lies in the fact that inventory is produced internally. In addition to administrative expenses, setup cost also includes the expenses of changing over or rearranging a work center to get it ready to produce an item. For example, Hershey may produce several different types of candy utilizing the same production equipment. After producing

Hershey production line making candy.
© Richard T Norwitz/Corbis

a batch of chocolate bars containing nuts, the equipment must be completely cleaned and sanitized and prepared for production of a different type of candy. The costs related to the time and tasks required to set up for production of a different item can be quite substantial.

Both order costs and setup costs are typically considered to be "fixed," irrespective of the size of the order or production batch. However, total annual order/setup cost varies with the number of orders (or setups) performed each year. If, for example, order cost is $100 per order, placing 10 orders per year results in $1,000 annual order cost. Five orders per year results in $500 annual order cost. Similarly, the cost of a setup may be fixed, but annual setup costs vary according to the number of times inventory is replenished.

Stockout Cost

Stockout (or shortage) cost is incurred when a company does not have inventory available to meet demand. A company may never know the actual amount of stockout cost for a product, because it does not know the actual amount of demand. In self-service retailing, for example, a consumer who can't locate an item may simply leave the store or buy a substitute item. Thus, one of the potential stockout costs is the cost of a lost sale (e.g., lost profit). In addition, the consumer who leaves the store may be so dissatisfied that she never returns to the store, and so the company loses future sales (and profits) as well. In cases where stockouts are known to exist, a company can incur significant back ordering and expediting costs. Stockouts also cause disruptions of materials flows in the supply chain. For example, if a production plant runs out of a component part needed to produce finished goods, the resulting cost of having to shut down the production line could run into the thousands or even hundreds of thousands of dollars.

stockout (or shortage) cost Cost incurred when inventory is not available to meet demand.

activity

student

Using your library's electronic databases or a Web browser, find three articles that describe specific companies and their efforts to reduce inventory. Summarize the different reasons given for the desire to reduce inventory.

MEASURES OF INVENTORY PERFORMANCE

There is a saying in business, "If you don't measure it, you can't manage it." Thus, measuring inventory performance is critical to provide information for effective management and control of inventory levels. There are two basic categories of inventory performance metrics. One category addresses issues of asset productivity, typically measured by *inventory turnover* and *days of supply.* The other addresses effectiveness in terms of meeting demand requirements, referred to as *service level.*

Asset Productivity: Inventory Turnover and Days of Supply

LO7-3 Explain and compute asset productivity and customer service–related measures of inventory performance.

Given the financial implications of inventory, companies are extremely concerned with the amount of inventory they hold. Two common measures of inventory asset productivity are inventory turnover and days of supply.

Inventory Turnover

inventory turnover The ratio between average inventory and the level of sales.

Inventory turnover measures the ratio between the average amount of inventory the company holds and its level of sales. There are, in fact, three different ways to measure inventory turnover, shown in the following three equations:

(7.1a)   Inventory turnover = Cost of goods sold/Average inventory @ cost

(7.1b)   Inventory turnover = Net sales/Average inventory @ selling price

(7.1c)   Inventory turnover = Unit sales/Average inventory in units

Equation (7.1a), in cost values, is by far the most common method and is used almost universally. Equation (7.1b), on the other hand, tends to be used primarily by retailers who use an accounting methodology known as the retail method of inventory valuation. Finally, equation (7.1c) may be a more accurate measure in situations where both the cost of an item and its selling price vary significantly during a year, such as gasoline.

EXAMPLE 7-2

As an example of calculating inventory turnover, suppose a firm has an annual cost of goods sold of $500 million and its average inventory level during the year is $80 million at cost. Then,

Inventory turnover = Cost of goods sold/Average inventory level = $500/80
= 6.25 turns

This can also be expressed as turning its inventory every 58.4 days (365 days in a year divided by the turnover rate of 6.25 times).

Table 7-1 provides data concerning inventory levels, turnover rates, and inventory carrying cost at 10 well-known business firms. While the data assume an inventory carrying cost of 20 percent for all 10 companies, the table illustrates the importance of inventory to all types of companies. In reality, the carrying cost differs among companies due to differences in capital cost and other expenses. Even service organizations such as Hyatt Hotels and Starwood, both well-known hotel and resort companies, carry significant inventories and can benefit from improved inventory management.

Companies that achieve high turnover rates enjoy several advantages, including:

• Increased sales volume due to having rapid flow of new or fresh items.
• Less risk of obsolescence or need to mark down or discount prices.
• Decreased expenses related to holding inventory.
• Lower asset investment and increased asset productivity.

TABLE 7-1   Example Inventory Levels, Turnover Rates, and Carrying Cost
(Fiscal Year 2011, $ figures in millions)

Company	Cost of Goods	Beginning Inventory	Ending Inventory	Average Inventory	Inventory Carrying Cost*	Inventory Turnover
Boeing	$55,867.00	$24,317.00	$32,240.00	$28,278.50	$5,665.70	1.98
Deere	22,034.40	3,063.00	4,371.00	3,717.00	743.40	5.93
Ford	113,345.00	5,917.00	5,901.00	5,909.00	1,181.80	19.18
Hewlett-Packard	97,529.00	6,466.00	7,490.00	6,978.00	1,395.60	13.98
Kellogg	7,750.00	1,056.00	1,132.00	1,094.00	218.80	7.08
Procter & Gamble	40,768.00	7,379.00	6,384.00	6,881.50	1,376.30	5.92
Target	48,306.00	7,596.00	7,918.00	7,757.00	1,551.40	6.23
Wal-Mart	335,127.00	36,318.00	40,714.00	38,516.00	7,703.20	8.70
Hyatt Hotels	2,957.00	100.00	87.00	93.50	18.70	31.63
Starwood	4,994.00	802.00	812.00	807.00	161.40	6.19

*Inventory Carrying Cost calculation assumes a 20% annual rate for all calculations.

However, there is a danger of having an inventory turn rate that is *too* high. These possible dangers include:

- Possible lowered sales volume due to running out of needed items (see the discussion of stockouts).
- Increased cost of goods sold due to inability to produce or purchase in quantity.
- Increased purchasing, ordering, and receiving time, effort, and cost.

Firms may differ in their inventory performance because of different circumstances in their supply and demand chains or because they have different strategies. Food retailers, for example, in general have higher turnover rates than appliance retailers due to the fast-moving nature of their products. Within the food retailing industry, however, turnover ratios differ between firms based on their financial strategy, their marketing strategy related to meeting customer demand, and their operational effectiveness.

Days of Supply

Inventory turnover is often considered a backward-looking measure because it looks at the company's performance in managing inventory during a previous time period, such as the previous year. Another common way that companies think about their inventory investment is in terms of days of supply, which is considered a forward-looking measure. **Days of supply** (also called *days of sales* or *days of inventory*) is the number of days of business operations that can be supported with the inventory on hand, given that no more inventory is bought or produced.

days of supply The number of days of business operations that can be supported with the inventory on hand.

Days of supply is most meaningful when it is expressed in terms of future expected demand, or daily rate of usage. The daily sales or usage rate may come from forecasts or may be computed from the most recent actual sales/usage experience. For example, inventory of finished automobiles is frequently stated as the number of days of consumer demand that could be satisfied from the existing inventory, based on the most recent daily sales rates. The general expression for computing days of supply is:

(7.2)   Days of supply = Current inventory/Expected rate of daily demand

EXAMPLE 7-3

Suppose there are currently 2,000,000 finished automobiles sitting in dealer or manufacturing facility lots. If expected sales of automobiles are 25,000 units per day, then days of supply = 80 days (2,000,000/25,000).

Of course, the calculated 80 days of supply for automobiles in Example 7-3 presumes that the existing inventory consists of automobiles that consumers actually want to buy. If consumers want to buy hybrid electric cars and the existing inventory consists primarily of cars with V-8 gasoline engines, the 80 days of supply would be extremely misleading. In inventory management, it is frequently more meaningful to measure performance for specific items rather than for overall inventory holdings.

The preceding calculation for days of supply can also be calculated in terms of costs or selling prices, rather than units.

activity

student

Choose three companies that are competitors in an industry of interest to you. Find their most recent annual reports and compute and compare their inventory turnover ratios. Explain the financial and marketing implications of the differences in inventory turnover rates for each of the three companies.

Service Level

service level A measure of how well the objective of meeting customer demand is met.

Since inventory exists in order to meet demand, companies need **service level** metrics to track how well this objective is accomplished. There are several different ways to measure service level. Many of these will be discussed more specifically in Chapter 9, "Customer Service Management." At this point, it is sufficient to think of service level in terms of a **stockout**, the situation that exists when there is demand for an item and no inventory is available. When companies experience stockouts of raw materials or component parts, production processes must be halted, with considerable potential cost implications. Stockouts of finished goods result in lost sales and potential customer dissatisfaction. Stockouts of MRO items may also have significant consequences. Consider, for example, what would happen if your university had no copy paper so your professor couldn't give you an exam on the scheduled date!

stockout An event that occurs when no inventory is available.

It is common to measure stockouts in terms of the number or percentage of inventory items for which there is no inventory on hand at the time of demand. For example, studies of retail stores across many industries consistently find that stockouts average about 8 percent of the items a store commonly offers for sale, at all times. Even more surprising is that for items that are specifically being advertised and promoted by a store, stockouts average about 16 percent![1] In another study, catalog retailers were found to have stockout levels that averaged more than 15 percent.[2]

activity

student

The next time you go shopping, prepare a list of the exact items you want to buy (brand, size, etc.). Visit a store that normally carries these items. Keep a record of how many of the items on your list are out of stock. Does your experience match the data cited above concerning retailer stockouts?

---

[1]Tom Gruen and Daniel Corsten, "Improve Out-of-Stock Methods at the Shelf," *Chain Store Age* (July 2006), p. 35.
[2]John C. Taylor and Stanley E. Fawcett, "Catalog Retailer In-Stock Performance: An Assessment of Customer Service Levels," *Journal of Business Logistics* 25, no. 2 (2004), pp. 119–35.

INVENTORY MANAGEMENT SYSTEMS

In this section we explain how to use inventory cost and service level parameters to determine how much inventory is required to support an operational process. The ultimate objective of any inventory management system is to minimize all inventory costs while meeting the organization's targeted service (product availability) objectives.

We first must distinguish between two different types of inventory management systems. **Independent demand inventory systems** are used when the demand for an item is beyond the control of the organization. This is typically the case for customer demands of end-items and repair parts. **Dependent demand inventory systems** are used when the demand for an item is derived from the demand for some other item.

To understand the distinction, think of a John Deere assembly plant. The demand for tractors and other agricultural equipment is somewhat unpredictable and outside the manufacturer's control, despite its best efforts to accurately forecast how many new pieces of equipment will be wanted by its customers. It is also extremely difficult to forecast how many tractors may break down while in use and therefore need to be repaired. Thus, managing inventory of finished goods and repair parts is best accomplished with independent demand systems. However, when John Deere has established a production schedule for tractors (typically based on a forecast), then it knows how many of each component it will need to fulfill that schedule. The inventory of these components is managed with dependent demand systems. Chapter 14 discusses dependent demand inventory systems. Here, we explain independent demand inventory planning.

The major independent demand inventory systems can be broken into two types: the **continuous review model**, where inventory is constantly monitored to decide when a replenishment order needs to be placed, and the **periodic review model**, where the management system reviews and orders inventory at some regular interval.

independent demand inventory systems Inventory management systems used when the demand for an item is beyond the control of the organization.

dependent demand inventory systems Management systems used when the demand for an item is derived from the demand for some other item.

continuous review model Inventory is constantly monitored to decide when a replenishment order needs to be placed.

periodic review model Management system built around checking and ordering inventory at some regular interval.

THE CONTINUOUS REVIEW MODEL

LO7-4 Calculate inventory policy parameters to minimize total acquisition cost in continuous review, periodic review, and single period models.

Two basic questions must be answered in planning inventories. First, how much should be ordered when an order is placed? For example, a John Deere dealer has to decide how many tractors to order from Deere to have them available for its customers. Second, when should an order be placed? The Deere dealer also has to decide in advance exactly when or at what level of remaining inventory it needs to order more tractors to replenish its inventory. Again, the objective is to minimize inventory-related costs.

To answer these questions we must first have a demand forecast. Chapter 12 explains how to develop demand forecasts. With a forecast of demand in hand, inventory planning then depends on whether a company has the capability to continuously monitor its inventory levels or whether it relies on a periodic review of its inventory. Because most (but not all) major organizations today maintain a computerized perpetual record of inventory on hand, we will first look at the continuous review model and how this system answers the "how much" and "when" questions.

The Case of No Variability

It is easiest to understand the basics of inventory management by first making a very naive and unrealistic assumption. In this first case we will assume that both the demand for an item and the supplier's lead time to replenish it are constant and known, with no variation. Later we will make adjustments to deal with variability.

In the example that follows, assume that you own a retail store that sells computer games. One particular game is Trexoid, a very popular fantasy game for which you pay your supplier $20.00 per copy, regardless of how many copies you buy. Each day you sell exactly 10 copies of Trexoid and the store is open 300 days per year; thus, annual demand is forecasted at 3,000 copies. In addition, you have done a detailed analysis of your costs and have determined that it costs $50.00 each time an order is placed. You also have determined that your inventory carrying cost is 20 percent of the item purchase cost annually. Suppose, finally, that when you place an order, it always takes exactly nine days for your supplier to get the shipment to you. How should you determine how much to order and when to order in a way that minimizes the total annual inventory cost?

How Much to Order: Economic Order Quantity

total acquisition cost (TAC) The sum of all relevant inventory costs incurred each year.

The quantity you order will impact your **total acquisition cost (TAC)**, the sum of all relevant inventory costs incurred each year. In this case the cost to purchase or produce the product is the same regardless of the quantity you order, so product cost isn't relevant to the decision. Stockout cost isn't relevant either because we have assumed no variability in the system. Because we know with certainty both the demand and the lead time, there should never be any stockouts. TAC in this case is simply the sum of your annual inventory carrying cost and annual ordering cost. Example 7-4 shows the impact of ordering 500 units each time.

EXAMPLE 7-4 CALCULATING TOTAL ACQUISITION COST

Suppose that you arbitrarily decide to order 500 copies of Trexoid every time you place an order. This order quantity requires that you place six orders during the year to acquire the needed 3,000 units.

(7.3)
$$N = D/Q$$
$$= 3,000/500 = 6$$

where

N = number of orders placed each year
D = annual demand
Q = order quantity

saw-tooth diagram An illustration of the pattern of ordering and inventory levels.

Figure 7-1 below illustrates the pattern of your ordering and inventory levels and is referred to as a **saw-tooth diagram**. Notice that the average inventory you will hold is 250 units. When no safety stock is held, the average inventory held across the year is one-half of the order quantity, or

(7.4)
$$\bar{I} = Q/2$$

where

$\bar{I}$ = inventory

We can now determine the TAC of your decision by determining the sum of the annual order cost and annual inventory carrying cost. The annual order cost is the number of orders per year (6) times the order cost ($50.00), or $300. The annual inventory carrying cost is the average inventory in units (250) times the unit value ($20.00) times the inventory carrying cost percentage (20%), or $1,000. Thus, the TAC of your inventory management policy is $1,300.

(7.5)
$$\begin{aligned} TAC &= \text{Annual ordering cost} + \text{Annual carrying cost} \\ &= C_o\,(D/Q) + UC_i\,Q/2 \\ &= \$50\,(3{,}000/500) + \$20\,(20\%)\,500/2 \\ &= \$1{,}300 \end{aligned}$$

where

C_o = order cost
U = unit cost
C_i = inventory carrying cost percentage per year

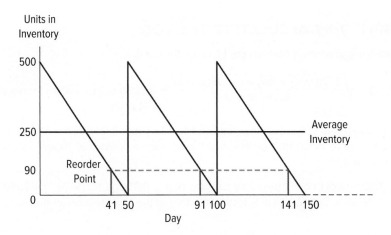

FIGURE 7-1
Trexoid Inventory
Saw-Tooth Diagram:
Order Quantity 500

What happens to TAC if you decide on a different policy? After all, ordering 500 was purely an arbitrary decision. Example 7-5 illustrates another policy.

EXAMPLE 7-5

Suppose you decide to order 200 units each time. This pattern, illustrated in Figure 7-2, results in placing 15 orders per year and an average inventory of 100 units. Annual order cost will be $750 (15 orders times $50 order cost). Annual inventory carrying cost will be $400 (100 units average inventory times $20 times 20%). Thus, the TAC of this policy is $1,150.

Ordering 200 units each time instead of 500 units each time saves you an expected $150 each year. How can you find the lowest cost ordering policy? Should you test every possible order quantity to determine the lowest TAC? Fortunately, that is not necessary. A formula exists that will solve the problem. This formula determines the order quantity that will yield the lowest TAC when the relevant costs are only annual inventory carrying cost and annual ordering cost. This order quantity is commonly known as the **economic order quantity (EOQ)**:

(7.6)
$$EOQ = \sqrt{\frac{2DC_o}{UC_i}}$$

economic order quantity (EOQ) The order quantity that minimizes the sum of annual inventory carrying cost and annual ordering cost.

You may have noticed in Example 7-6 that annual order cost and annual inventory cost using the EOQ are almost identical ($550 vs. $548). In fact, except for rounding, the two costs are equal. Essentially, the EOQ formula trades off the annual ordering cost and the annual inventory carrying cost and finds the quantity that yields the lowest combination.

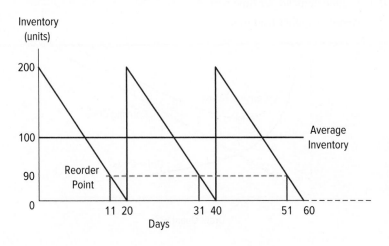

FIGURE 7-2
Trexoid Inventory
Saw-Tooth Diagram:
Order Quantity 200

EXAMPLE 7-6 CALCULATING THE EOQ

Using the preceding formula, the EOQ for Trexoid is

$$EOQ = \sqrt{\frac{2 \times 3{,}000 \text{ } units/year \times \$50/order}{\$20/unit \times .2}} = 273.86 \text{ units, or when rounded, } 274 \text{ units}$$

Given this order quantity, you will need to place 3,000/274 = 10.948 orders each year, rounded to 11 orders, and the average inventory of Trexoid will be 137 units. Thus,

TAC = Order cost + Inventory carrying cost = 11($50) + 137($20)(.2) = $550 + $548 = $1,098, which is less than either of the two previous alternatives.

This is the order quantity at which annual inventory ordering cost and annual inventory carrying cost are exactly equal to each other. Figure 7-3 depicts the relationship between the two costs and the total cost.

It is important to think about the EOQ and TAC discussion as more than simple calculations. Think about the variables in the EOQ formula and the impact of changes in those variables. For example, what happens to order quantity if demand increases? Because demand is in the numerator of the formula, the order quantity (and average inventory) goes up. What about a change in ordering cost? If ordering cost goes down, for example, order quantity and average inventory also decrease. Inventory carrying cost has a major impact; if it increases, EOQ goes down. These relationships will be further explored later in the chapter when we discuss managerial approaches to managing and reducing inventory.

When to Order: The Reorder Point

Now that we know how much to order, the second decision is to decide when to place an order. In the continuous review model, the answer to "when" is actually an inventory amount. That is, at what amount of remaining inventory should a replenishment order be placed? The amount is known as the **reorder point (ROP)**. The reorder point is a level of inventory that triggers the need to order more. The ROP is easy to calculate when no variability or safety stock is involved. We know exactly how long it will take to receive the order from the supplier. Also, we know exactly how many we will sell each day while waiting for that order to arrive. This leads us to the simple formula:

reorder point (ROP) The minimum level of inventory that triggers the need to order more.

(7.7) $$ROP = (\bar{d}) \, \bar{t}$$

where:

$\quad$ ROP = reorder point
$\quad \bar{d}$ = average demand per time period
$\quad \bar{t}$ = average supplier lead time

FIGURE 7-3
EOQ Cost Trade-Offs

EXAMPLE 7-7 CALCULATING THE ROP

Because it will take 9 days to be resupplied and you sell 10 copies of Trexoid per day, you will need to initiate an order with your supplier when you have 90 copies remaining on hand. That way the new shipment will arrive just as you sell the last copy you have in stock. Refer back to Figures 7-1 and 7-2. Notice that this reorder point is indicated in both figures.

EOQ Extensions

There are several assumptions underlying the EOQ formulation that often do not hold true in practice. Primary among these are the following:

- No quantity discounts—Product cost (production cost and transportation cost) is constant regardless of quantity ordered.
- No lot size restrictions—It is possible to order a lot size equal to the EOQ (i.e., there are no minimum or maximum order size requirements and capital is unlimited).
- No partial deliveries—The product is produced and delivered in a single batch (i.e., the entire replenishment order of inventory becomes available all at the same time).
- No variability—Product demand and replenishment lead time are known and constant.
- No product interactions—The ordering of one product is not tied to the ordering of some other product.

Because these assumptions are rarely met in real life, the EOQ formulation often needs to be modified. In the following sections we discuss modifications that can be made to accommodate the first four issues above. The issue of product interactions is quite complex and beyond the scope of this text.

Quantity Discounts

Quantity discounts are prevalent in the business world, so we will first explore how to extend the EOQ methodology when a supplier offers a discounted price for ordering larger quantities each time. The logic used for examining transportation discounts is similar and will therefore not be covered.

In general, the following steps must be taken to determine the order quantity when quantity discounts are available:

Step 1. Identify the price breaks offered by the supplier.

Step 2. Calculate the EOQ at each price break, starting with the lowest price possible.

Step 3. Evaluate the feasibility of each EOQ value. If the calculated EOQ for a given price is large enough to qualify for that specific price, then the calculated EOQ is feasible. If the EOQ calculated using the lowest price category is feasible, then it is the lowest TAC_{QD} order quantity. If it is not feasible (as in Example 7-8 below, where the EOQ for the $19 price is 281 units, but 1,000 units are required to qualify for that price), then go to Step 4.

Step 4. Calculate the TAC_{QD} for each feasible EOQ and for the minimum quantity required to attain each price break. TAC_{QD} includes the product cost itself, because the unit cost now varies as a function of the order quantity.

Step 5. Pick the order quantity that has the lowest TAC.

Example 7-8 shows how quantity discounts would affect the order amount for Trexoid. As you can see from the example, sometimes it is worthwhile to order more than the EOQ in order to take advantage of price breaks for larger quantities.

Lot Size Restrictions

How could the quantity discount approach be used to deal with the situation where products must be ordered in a particular batch size? For example, suppose that Trexoid must be purchased from the vendor in packs of 50 units each. In the case of the quantity discount (Example 7-8), this would pose no problem because 1,000 units is a multiple of 50. We would simply order 20 cases of the product. If there were no quantity discount, however,

EXAMPLE 7-8 CALCULATING EOQ WITH QUANTITY DISCOUNTS

Suppose your Trexoid video game supplier offers to sell the game to you for $19 per unit if you purchase 1,000 units or more each time you buy. Does this price discount justify paying the inventory costs associated with a larger order size?

To answer this question, we first determine the total annual cost of the existing policy. Because there is a price differential being offered by the supplier, the *annual product cost* must now be included in the TAC, which we now designate as TAC_{QD}. The TAC_{QD} for the existing policy ($Q = 274$) is

$$TAC_{QD} = \text{Annual ordering cost} + \text{Annual carrying cost} + \text{Annual product cost}$$

(7.8)
$$= C_O \, (D/Q) + UC_i \, Q/2 + UD$$

where:

U = unit cost
D = annual demand
For $U = \$20$:
Annual order cost = 3,000 units per year/274 units per order × $50 per order = $547
Annual inventory carrying cost = 274 units per order/2 × $20/unit × .2 = $548
Annual product cost = 3,000 units per year × $20/unit = $60,000

Therefore, the relevant TAC_{QD} of the current policy is $61,095.

As mentioned earlier, the annual order cost and annual inventory carrying cost are not exactly equal because we are using the rounded-up order quantity of 274 units, whereas the quantity that balances the two costs exactly is 273.86 units.

The next step is to determine the EOQ at the $19 price:

$$EOQ = \sqrt{\frac{2 \times 3,000 \, units/year \times \$50/order}{\$20/unit \times .2}} = 280.98 \text{ rounded to 281 units}$$

However, in order to receive the $19 price, you must order 1,000 units. Thus, in this case, the EOQ of 281 units is not feasible because the price for 281 units is $20. If the calculated EOQ at the discount price were higher than the quantity required (1,000 units in this case) we would continue the TAC_{QD} analysis using that EOQ. Because the calculated EOQ is not feasible, we need to determine the TAC_{QD} at the smallest order size necessary to get the discount price; that is, an order size of 1,000 units. At $Q = 1,000$, we can easily determine that the average inventory will be 500 units and the annual number of orders will be three.

Annual product cost = 3,000 units per year × $19 per unit = $57,000
Annual inventory carrying cost = 500 units × $19 per unit × .2 = $1,900
Annual order cost = 3 orders per year × $50 per order = $150
TAC = $59,050

Thus, it is more economical to take advantage of the quantity discount offered by the supplier of Trexoid. Even though ordering 1,000 units is actually a larger order than the calculated EOQ, it does result in the lowest TAC_{QD}. The annual savings of doing so are $61,095 − $59,050 = $2,045.

then from Example 7-6 we know that the EOQ of 274 would minimize costs. Unfortunately, we could not purchase exactly 274 units; we would need to purchase either 250 or 300. The simple solution is to calculate the TAC at an order size of both 250 and 300 and pick the order quantity that yields the lowest TAC.

activity

Think about several instances where you have bought a larger quantity of an item than you normally buy. What factors influenced you to do so? Explain how those factors relate to the discussion of EOQ and TAC.

Partial Order Deliveries—Production Order Quantity

Our previous EOQ models have assumed that inventory replenishments are produced and delivered in a single batch, and that an entire order is received and immediately available for use. In some situations, a replenishment order might be delivered in multiple shipments that occur as the product is produced. For example, a vendor may ship some product to us a little at a time, rather than making us wait until the entire batch is produced before the vendor ships anything. In this case, the first units in a replenishment order can be sold as the later units in the order are still being produced. In a production environment, units can be made available for sale immediately, one by one, as they are produced.

The EOQ modification used to deal with this situation is known as the **production order quantity**, the most economic quantity to order when inventory units become available at the rate of production and are sold as they are being produced. The basic concepts underlying the EOQ model can be applied to this situation. The difference is that replenishment inventory arrives or becomes available at the rate at which products are produced (or delivered) while inventory is simultaneously being depleted at the rate of demand. Example 7-9 illustrates this situation.

You can see from this example that calculating the optimal order quantity in a production environment is very similar to calculating the optimal order quantity in a purchasing environment. The difference occurs because of the $(1 - d/p)$ multiplier on the carrying cost. This is necessary in the production environment to adjust for the fact that inventory is being depleted at the same time that it is being produced.

production order quantity The most economic quantity to order when units become available at the rate at which they are produced.

activity

Verify for yourself the difference between the Q_p quantity and the EOQ. You can do that by using the standard EOQ formula and assuming that all items produced arrive simultaneously.

Enter Variability and Uncertainty

Life as an operations executive would be easy if it existed as we have described thus far, that is, in a world where both demand and supplier lead time were constant and known. Unfortunately, these factors are both variable and at least somewhat unpredictable (despite the best efforts of forecasting). The way that we accommodate this uncertainty is to hold safety stock. The question that now must be answered is, how much safety stock should be held?

To determine safety stock, two steps are required. First, the standard deviation of demand during the replenishment lead time must be calculated. Second, the company's policy on the desired service level must be determined. Let's start by examining the demand during the replenishment lead time.

Determining the Standard Deviation of Demand During Lead Time

Instead of the demand for Trexoid being 10 units per day, let's assume we have done a statistical analysis of past demand patterns and found that average demand is 10 units, but it ranges from as few as 4 units to as many as 16 units, with a standard deviation of 1.5 units per day. A similar analysis of supplier lead times for replenishment reveals an average lead

EXAMPLE 7-9 CALCULATING THE EOQ WITH PARTIAL DELIVERIES, AKA: THE PRODUCTION ORDER QUANTITY

Consider the manufacturer of the Trexoid video games you have been ordering for your store. The manufacturer expects annual demand from all retailers to be 500,000 units of Trexoid games. It receives orders from retailers for, on average, 2,000 units per day (250 days per year). To change from production of another game to production of Trexoid requires a setup cost of $2,000. Once production of Trexoid units begins, it can produce 5,000 units per day. The cost to produce a unit of Trexoid is $10. Finally, the manufacturer has determined that its inventory carrying cost is 25 percent annually. The fundamental question to answer is how many units of Trexoid should be ordered in each production run? It is also useful to know the length of the production run in days.

Solving this problem requires a slight modification to the basic EOQ model discussed previously, using the following data:

Q_p = production order quantity (the same concept as EOQ)
D = annual demand = 500,000 units
d = daily rate of customer demand = 2,000 units
p = daily rate of production = 5,000 units
C_o = setup cost (the same concept as ordering cost in EOQ) = $2,000
U = unit cost = $10
C_i = annual inventory carrying cost percentage = 25%

The formula for determining production order quantity is:

(7.9)
$$Q_p = \sqrt{\frac{2DC_o}{C_iU\left\{1-\frac{d}{p}\right\}}}$$

Substituting in the formula,

$$Q_p = \sqrt{\frac{2(500,000)(\$2,000)}{.25(\$10)\left\{1-\frac{2,000}{5,000}\right\}}}$$

Q_p = 36,514.84 = (rounded to) 36,515 units

Because the most economic size of a production run is 36,515 units and the production rate is 5,000 units per day, the length of a production run is simply 36,515/5,000 = 7.3 days.

time of 9 days but a range from 3 days to 18 days with a standard deviation of 2.5 days. Thus, it is possible that while waiting for replenishment after you have placed an order, demand could range from as little as 12 units (lowest daily demand of 4 units × shortest lead time of 3 days) to as much as 288 units (highest possible demand of 16 units per day × longest lead time of 18 days). The amount of demand that occurs while you are awaiting receipt of your order is known as **demand during lead time**. Of course, demand during lead time has a statistical distribution with its own standard deviation. The formula for determining the standard deviation of demand during lead time is

demand during lead time The amount of demand that occurs while awaiting receipt of an inventory replenishment order.

(7.10)
$$\sigma_{ddlt} = \sqrt{\bar{l}\sigma_d^2 + \bar{d}^2\sigma_l^2}$$

where

σ_{ddlt} = standard deviation of demand during lead time
$\bar{l}$ = average lead time
σ_d = standard deviation of demand

$\bar{d}$ = average demand

σ_t = standard deviation of lead time

EXAMPLE 7-10

Substituting our given information about Trexoid demand and lead time into the equation 7.10, we find

$$\sigma_{ddlt} = \sqrt{9 \ days \ (1.5 \ units)^2 + 10^2 \ units \ (2.5 \ days)^2} = 25.40 \ units$$

Thus, the combination of variance in demand and lead time yield a standard deviation of demand during lead time of 25.40 units.

The calculation of the standard deviation of demand during lead time is critical to determining the amount of safety stock that is to be carried. The next step is to determine a policy for customer service level.

Determining a Service Level Policy

A **service level policy** specifies the amount of risk of incurring a stockout that a firm is willing to incur. Ideally, this policy should weigh inventory carrying costs against stockout costs. However, because stockout costs are so hard to quantify, determining a service level

LO7-5 Determine the cost of a company's service level policy.

service level policy Specification of the amount of risk of incurring a stockout that a firm is willing to incur.

EXAMPLE 7-11

From our previous discussion, we know that, on average, demand by customers for Trexoid while waiting for replenishment from the supplier will be 90 units (the reorder point determined earlier). We now know that the standard deviation of demand during this lead time is 25.4 units. Suppose you have decided that you are only willing to have a 5 percent chance of being out of stock. Thus, your desired service level is 95 percent (100 minus the probability of a stockout while waiting for replenishment). Once you have made that decision, you can determine the required quantity of safety stock by

(7.11)
$$SS = z\,\sigma_{ddlt}$$

where:

    SS = safety stock

      z = number of standard deviations (σ_{ddlt}) required for the desired service level

    σ_{ddlt} = standard deviation of demand during lead time

The value of z can be determined from a table of cumulative probabilities of the normal distribution (we are assuming that demand follows a normal distribution, although that is not always an appropriate assumption). Table 7-2 displays some of the most commonly used standard deviations and probabilities in inventory management. A more complete table of the cumulative probability distribution of the normal distribution is included in Appendix A.

Table 7-2 indicates that, if you are willing to incur a 5 percent stockout probability, you must carry 1.65 standard deviations of safety stock because a 5 percent stockout probability is the same as a 95 percent probability of being in stock. Therefore, you must carry 42 units (1.65 standard deviations × 25.4 units) as safety stock.

How much does this decision cost you? You will, after all, incur inventory carrying cost on these units. Remember that we determined it was most economical to order Trexoid at a price of $19.

Safety stock inventory carrying cost   = $19 × 42 units × 20% Carrying cost

                           = $159.60 per year

(continued)

(continued)

TABLE 7-2 Standard Deviations and Probabilities

Z = Number of Deviations Required	Probability of Being in Stock	Probability of Stockout
1	84.13%	15.77%
1.04	85	15
1.28	90	10
1.65	95	5
1.96	97.5	2.5
2.0	97.72	2.28
2.33	99	1
3.0	99.86	0.14

policy is usually a matter of managerial judgment, not a quantitative analysis. While there are analytical methods that can help managers make more informed decisions, essentially, the decision depends upon the company's willingness to take a chance of being out of stock of an item while waiting for it to be replenished. As managers' tolerance for being out of stock decreases, service level targets will be raised and the required safety stock will increase.

Table 7-3 displays the inventory carrying cost incurred for Trexoid across a range of different service level policies. Notice that the difference in inventory carrying cost is increasing at an increasing rate. To go from a stockout probability of 15 percent to a probability of 10 percent costs an incremental \$26.60 (\$125.40 − \$98.80). From a stockout probability of 10 percent to a 5 percent probability costs another \$34.20 (\$159.60 − \$125.40). But look at the cost differential to move from the stockout probability of 5 percent to 1 percent—this will cost an additional \$64.60 (\$224.20 − \$159.60).

The general relationship between required inventory and increasing service level is depicted in Figure 7-4. As it shows, as companies attempt to offer higher levels of in-stock performance to their customers, inventory carrying costs become increasingly burdensome. The burden may not seem so large when you think about the inventory of a single item such as Trexoid, but consider that your store may carry hundreds of different

TABLE 7-3 Cost Related to Trexoid Service Levels

Std. Deviations of Safety Stock	Probability of in Stock	Probability of Stockout	Safety Stock Required	Safety Stock Inventory Carrying Cost
1	84.13%	15.77%	25	\$ 95.0
1.04	85	15	26	98.8
1.28	90	10	33	125.4
1.65	95	5	42	159.6
1.96	97.5	2.5	50	190.0
2.0	97.72	2.28	51	193.8
2.33	99	1	59	224.2
3.0	99.86	0.14	76	288.8

computer games. Could you afford the extra expense of a 99 percent in-stock policy on all of them? Ultimately, the decision about how much safety stock to carry requires a balancing between these costs and management's best estimate of the cost and lost goodwill that will occur with those customers whose demand for an item cannot be filled at the time they want to make a purchase.

Revisiting ROP and Average Inventory

Two revisions to earlier statements are required when uncertainty and unpredictability exist. The addition of safety stock to a firm's inventory increases both the reorder point and the average inventory held by the firm in the following ways:

(7.12) $$\text{ROP} = (\bar{d} \times \bar{t}) + SS$$

(7.13)   and average inventory $= Q/2 + SS$

where:

$\bar{d}$ = average daily demand

$\bar{t}$ = average lead time

SS = safety stock

EXAMPLE 7-12

For Trexoid, assuming you chose a 95 percent service level, the ROP now becomes (10 units × 9 days) + 42, or 132 units. When on-hand inventory plus any units that may already have been ordered reaches 132 units, an order should be placed.

What we earlier called average inventory (the order quantity/2) is actually known as **cycle stock**. Calculating average inventory requires adding safety stock to cycle stock. Thus, for Trexoid, the average inventory will be 500 units of cycle stock + 42 units of safety stock, or a total of 542 units.

cycle stock The portion of average inventory determined as order quantity divided by two.

THE PERIODIC REVIEW MODEL

LO7-4 Calculate inventory policy parameters to minimize total acquisition cost in continuous review, periodic review, and single period models.

While most large organizations use computerized inventory information systems, not all companies do. These companies usually rely on a periodic review model. Even when a company has the technology to use a continuous review, they may still choose a periodic review system because they want to place orders for multiple products at the same time. Remember that the continuous review system provides constant knowledge of the inventory status of an item, and an order of a fixed quantity is placed when the ROP is reached. In contrast, in the periodic review system an **order interval** is established. An order interval is a fixed time period that passes between each inventory review. The quantity ordered in each review varies, depending upon how much inventory is on hand at the time the review is done.

Let's evaluate the same scenario of ordering Trexoid from a supplier, this time using a periodic review system. For simplicity, assume that daily demand is still an average of 10 units with a standard deviation of demand of 1.5 units, and lead time is constant at 9 days. The only difference is that now you have no system for continuous inventory status information. Suppose that, given the high importance you place on this item, you decide to check inventory status every 30 days. At that time, after you have determined the quantity on hand, you will place an order to replenish the inventory. How will you determine the amount to order?

First, understand that this system has a built-in **uncertainty period**, a period of time in which you are uncertain about how much inventory is on hand. This time is determined by the order interval as well as the supplier's lead time. Expressed as an equation,

$$(7.14) \qquad UP = OI + \bar{t}$$

where:

UP = uncertainty period

OI = order interval

$\bar{t}$ = lead time

The uncertainty period spans the time period between today, when we perform a review and place an order, and some future date, when the next order we place is expected to arrive. This is the period over which we are at risk of a stockout. Order quantity in the periodic review system is determined by the amount of inventory we expect to use or sell during the uncertainty period, plus safety stock, minus the amount of inventory we currently have on hand, as shown in the following equation:

$$(7.15) \qquad Q = \bar{d}\left(UP\right) + z\sigma_{ddup} - A$$

where:

Q = order quantity

$\bar{d}$ = average daily demand

UP = uncertainty period

z = standard deviations of safety stock desired

σ_{ddup} = standard deviation demand during the uncertainty period

A = amount of inventory on hand when the count is conducted

EXAMPLE 7-13

Given the data for Trexoid,

UP = 30 days + 9 days = 39 days

Average demand during this time period will be 390 units (39 days × 10 units per day), but there will actually be a distribution of possible demands with a standard deviation. To determine a safety stock level, we have to determine the standard deviation of demand during the uncertainty period through the formula

$$(7.16) \qquad \sigma_{ddup} = \sqrt{(UP)\ \sigma_d^2}$$

Because the standard deviation of daily demand was determined to be 1.5 units, the standard deviation of demand during the uncertainty period is then

$$\sigma_{ddup} = \sqrt{(39)\left(1.5^2\right)} = 9.37$$

EXAMPLE 7-14

Suppose you have counted your inventory at the order review time and determine you have 105 units of Trexoid on hand. You now have to determine the order quantity. Assume that you desire to maintain the 95 percent service level. Your order quantity will be

$$Q = 10 \text{ units per day (39 days)} + 1.65 \text{ (9.37 units)} - 105 \text{ units}$$
$$Q = 390 + 16 - 105 = 301 \text{ units}$$

The periodic order system does not require investment in a computerized inventory information system and the maintenance that such systems generally require. However, it does require costs associated with monitoring and counting physical inventory on hand. The more frequently counts are conducted, the higher the associated costs. On the other hand, less frequent counts require higher levels of safety stock to maintain a given service level. Here, you can begin to see that trade-offs among inventory monitoring costs, ordering costs, and safety stock carrying costs can be complex.

SINGLE PERIOD INVENTORY MODEL

In many situations, managers must determine the order size for a one-time purchase, such as a retailer deciding the number of swimsuits to purchase to sell for the summer season. In these situations, there is no need or opportunity to issue a replenishment order. This situation requires a **single period inventory model**, because inventory is ordered and used only one time, and it may have little value after the period is over. The situation is frequently referred to as the *newsvendor problem,* named for the situation in which a newspaper vendor must determine an amount of papers to stock before actual demand is known. If the vendor doesn't buy enough papers to satisfy demand, a stockout cost will occur (C_{so}). The stockout cost includes lost profit due to lost sales and, possibly, lost future sales and lost customer goodwill. On the other hand, if the vendor stocks more newspapers than are demanded, there is a cost of being overstocked (C_{os}). The cost of being overstocked is the cost of the product itself, plus any costs associated with disposing of the extra product, less any salvage value of the excess.

There are several variations of the single period model. The method we describe requires estimates of an expected demand and a standard deviation. There are methods of analysis to use when this is not the case. However, if you understand the basic analytical approach shown in Example 7-15, you can easily understand the other methods as well.

single period inventory model Model used to determine the order size for a one-time purchase.

EXAMPLE 7-15

Suppose you open a kiosk at the mall every October to sell Halloween costumes. The most popular costume historically has been a skeleton costume. You can buy the costume for $10 and sell it for $30. Any costumes not sold have to be disposed of because the design changes each year and customers will not purchase a previous year's costume. Disposal and salvage costs are minimal and can be considered zero. Thus,

(7.17) C_{so} = Unit selling price − Unit cost = $30 − $10 = $20
C_{os} = Unit cost + Disposal cost − Salvage value
(7.18)   = $10 + 0 − 0 = $10

The next step is to determine the **target service level (TSL)**. The target service level is the probability of meeting all demand for an item. We want the TSL to be

© Mark Lennihan/AP Images

target service level (TSL) The probability of meeting all demand for an item.

(continued)

(continued)

set such that the expected cost of being out of stock of costumes is equal to the expected cost of having more costumes than needed. Mathematically,

(7.19) $(1 - TSL)(C_{so}) = TSL(C_{os})$

where

TSL = target service level
C_{so} = cost of a unit stockout
C_{os} = cost of being overstocked by one unit

Solving the above equation we find that

$$TSL = \frac{C_{so}}{C_{so} + C_{os}}$$

Substituting data for your Halloween kiosk,

$$TSL = \frac{\$20}{\$20 + \$10} = \frac{\$20}{\$30} = .667$$

This TSL will provide a 66.7 percent chance of meeting all of the demand for skeleton costumes. Suppose that in the past, sales of skeleton costumes have averaged 200 units per year with a standard deviation of 15 units. How many costumes should be ordered this year given the TSL? By looking at the table of the cumulative normal distribution in Appendix A, we see that this target probability equates to .43 standard deviations. Thus, the target order quantity should be

(7.20)   Order quantity = Expected demand + *SS*
Q = 200 constumes + .43(15 costumes)
= 200 + 6.45 = 206.45, rounded to 206

IMPACT OF LOCATION ON INVENTORY

LO7-6 Explain the advantages and disadvantages of different inventory location strategies.

In addition to determining *how much* inventory to order and *when* to order it, many companies must also determine *where* to stock inventories of different items. Many companies have several manufacturing plants, distribution centers, or other facilities that maintain inventories of the same items. Generally, firms hold stocks closer to customers so that they can satisfy demands more quickly. While each location may use the models described previously to plan its inventory of an item, the sum of the inventory held across all of the locations is of concern as well. It is this **total system inventory** that represents the company's asset investment that must be financed and for which carrying cost will be incurred.

total system inventory The sum of the inventory held across all of the locations in a company.

Suppose a company is currently serving all of the demand in the United States for its product from a single location in Michigan. It has applied the principles discussed previously and, as a result, has decided to hold 1,000 units of safety stock. What would happen if the company decided to open a second warehouse in California? Each warehouse will serve half of the company's total demand. However, as a result of adding this location, the variation in demand that each location will face individually is greater than the variation in demand that was faced by serving the entire country from a single location. This occurs because from a single location, some of the variations in demand that exist across different markets are essentially offset by one another. Increasing the number of locations means that this offsetting does not occur. Thus, while the two locations will each carry safety stock that is less than required by a single location, the total safety stock carried by the firm will have to be increased to provide the same protection against stockouts. The impact of the change in the number of locations can be estimated by using the following formula, known as the **square root rule**:

square root rule A method of estimating the impact of changing the number of locations on the quantity of inventory held.

(7.21) $$SS_n = \frac{N_n}{N_e} \times SS_e$$

where:

SS_n = system safety stock for the new number of locations
N_n = total number of new locations
N_e = number of existing locations
SS_e = system safety stock for the number of existing locations

It is important to note that the square root rule gives only a rough approximation of the impacts of inventory location strategies. It is based on the assumption that demands in different locations are independent (not correlated) and that inventories are not shared across stocking locations. In fact, if demands are correlated, then the square root rule might under-estimate the impact of consolidating stocks and overestimate the impact of increasing the number of stocking locations.

EXAMPLE 7-16

Because of opening a second warehouse, the company needs a total safety stock of

$$SS_n = \frac{\sqrt{2}}{\sqrt{1}} \times 1{,}000 \text{ units} = 1.41 \times 1{,}000 \text{ units} = 1{,}410 \text{ units}$$

Thus, the impact of adding the additional facility is an overall increase in total system inventory of 410 units. As additional locations may be added by the firm, the total system inventory will continue to increase, but at a decreasing rate, as shown in Figure 7-5.

FIGURE 7-5
Inventory Related to Number of Locations

MANAGING INVENTORY

LO7-7 Describe practical techniques for inventory planning and management.

Planning and management of inventory levels is both an art and a science. The inventory models presented provide the foundation for order quantities and timing. In practice, however, there are numerous other issues related to efforts to effectively reduce, track, and manage inventory levels. To reduce inventory it is useful to think about the causes of cycle stocks, safety stocks, and so on, and the variables that drive the different types.

Managing Cycle Stocks

The primary driver of cycle stock is the order quantity. One way to reduce total average inventory is to reduce the order quantity. Recall that the EOQ is a function of annual demand, order (or setup) cost, inventory carrying cost, and product price. If order costs can be reduced, order quantity declines, with a resulting decline in cycle stock. Order costs may be reduced through such techniques as online ordering, reducing receiving costs, and automated payment of invoices. Setup costs in production can be similarly reduced through automation and process improvements. All other things remaining the same, lowering order costs will lower the order quantity that provides the lowest total acquisition cost. For example, the original problem involving purchasing Trexoid from the manufacturer assumed an order cost of $50. If that order cost could somehow be reduced to only $1, the EOQ would be reduced to 39 units, resulting in average cycle stock of 19.5 units, as compared to the EOQ of 274 units and average cycle stock of 137 units in the original problem. This change moves the inventory management system toward a more lean operation, as described in Chapter 8.

Additionally, working more closely with suppliers to discourage quantity discounts (which typically result in larger order quantities) and instead offer the lowest possible price per unit regardless of order quantity would result in smaller order quantities. Companies that develop more JIT/lean processes may make longer-term commitments to suppliers in return for an agreement to deliver smaller quantities at the lowest price per unit.

relationships

Managing Safety Stocks

Much of the attention in reducing total inventory is focused on safety stock. Recall that the reason that safety stock is required is that there is uncertainty (due to variability) in both demand and lead time. If you can reduce this uncertainty, then you reduce the need for safety stock. Better forecasting models can be developed to reduce demand unpredictability. Companies also use such techniques as marketing promotions and pricing incentives to reduce demand variability. These topics are covered in detail in Chapter 12, "Demand Planning." It is also critical to focus on lead times in attempting to reduce inventory. Average lead time impacts the amount of safety stock, as does the standard deviation of lead time. Both of these may be reduced by some combination of buying from a supplier that is located more closely to the company, using a more reliable method of transportation, and/or using a faster method of transportation.

A frequently used approach in managing safety stock is **ABC analysis**. This analysis requires that every item in inventory be ranked according to some criterion of importance. The purpose of ranking items is to focus on the most important items, as opposed to the less important ones. For finished goods, items can be classified according to their annual sales volume or annual item profit. Raw materials, component parts, and MRO items can be classified according to their cost, their annual usage in the organization, or the difficulty of acquiring the items.

ABC analysis The ranking of all items of inventory according to importance.

Once a ranking of items is accomplished, you will generally see the effect of **Pareto's law**: a small percentage of the items account for a large percentage of the sales (or profit, or items that are either important or difficult to obtain). It is then common to classify the inventory items by assigning them an alphabetic code. For example, a small percentage of items (frequently 10 to 20 percent) that account for a large percentage of sales (often 70–80 percent) may be classified as A items; moderate volume items as B items; and the low volume items as C items. Frequently, the B and C items are about 30 percent and 50 percent of the total number of items, respectively. It should be noted that these percentages are offered as guidelines only, and that some firms actually use four or five classes rather than three.

Pareto's law The rule that a small percentage of items account for a large percentage of sales, profit, or importance to a company.

Figure 7-6 provides an example of ABC analysis. In this figure, A items account for about 70 percent of sales but are only 20 percent of the items carried; B items provide 20 percent of sales (30 percent of the items); and C items provide only 10 percent of sales from the 50 percent of items they represent.

The general procedure for a quantitative ABC analysis is:

- Determine annual usage/sales for each item (units and/or value).
- Determine the percentage of the total usage/sales by item.
- Rank the items from highest to lowest percentage.
- Classify the items into ABC categories.

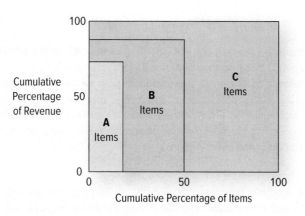

FIGURE 7-6
ABC Classification of
Inventory

EXAMPLE 7-17

Table 7-4 provides an example of how an ABC analysis might be conducted for finished goods inventory. In the table, 20 products have been ranked according to annual sales volume and percentage of total sales. Four of the 20 items (20 percent) in this example are classified as A, as they (in total) account for 80 percent of the

TABLE 7-4   Example ABC Analysis for Finished Goods

Product ID	Annual Sales (in 000s)	% of Total Sales	Cumulative % of Total Sales	Class
12345	$90,000	30.0%	30.0%	A
23456	70,000	23.3	53.3	A
34567	50,000	16.7	70.0	A
45678	28,000	9.3	79.3	A
56789	18,000	6.0	85.3	B
67890	10,000	3.3	88.6	B
09876	8,000	2.7	91.3	B
98765	6,000	2.0	93.3	B
87654	4,000	1.3	94.6	B
76543	2,000	0.7	95.3	C
65432	2,000	0.7	96.0	C
54321	2,000	0.7	96.7	C
43210	2,000	0.7	97.4	C
43258	1,500	0.5	97.9	C
46598	1,500	0.5	98.4	C
57589	1,500	0.5	98.9	C
24367	1,000	0.3	99.2	C
89566	1,000	0.3	99.5	C
76888	1,000	0.3	99.8	C
21345	500	0.2	100	C
Total	$300,000	100		

(continued)

(continued)

sales; 5 of the items (25 percent) are classified as B; and 11 of the items (55 percent) are classified as C because their combined sales volume is only slightly more than 5 percent of total sales. However, these quantitatively determined classifications may be modified by managerial judgment factors. For example, suppose item #76543 in the table is absolutely essential to the company's most important customers. Even though it represents only 0.7 percent of annual sales, managers may determine that it should be treated as an A item.

Without ABC analysis, companies frequently fall into a trap of assuming that all inventory items are of equal importance. Therefore, they establish the same safety stock policy for every item. ABC analysis can be used to establish different policies for different items. For example, A items usually have higher safety stock levels than B items. For C items, little or even no safety stock may be maintained. The result is a much smaller likelihood of stockouts on the most important items, yet the total amount of inventory in the company is less than would be required if all items had large safety stocks. This approach ensures that money (investment in safety stocks) is put to the best use.

Operations policies for cycle stocks and other inventories may also be based on ABC analysis. More purchasing effort may be warranted for A items than B or C items. Additionally, as we discuss later in this chapter, more time and effort may be devoted to monitoring inventory levels of A items as compared to other inventory items.

Managing Locations

The discussion of location impact on inventory levels also has important managerial implications for inventory management. Many firms have made an effort to reduce the number of warehouses and distribution centers in their logistics networks. The driving force behind this effort is the substantial reduction in inventory that this consolidation of facilities allows.

Chain retailers such as Walmart and Target utilize distribution centers to replenish the inventory of individual stores. In effect, the distribution centers reduce, rather than increase, the total amount of inventory that is actually held by the companies. While this may seem counter-intuitive at first, consider the alternative for the chains. The alternative is to treat each store location as a totally independent location, ordering inventory from far-distant suppliers, likely with very long and variable lead times. The result would be extremely large inventories required at each store location to service consumers. By utilizing distribution centers, many stores can draw on the stocks held at the local center and receive very rapid and consistent lead times, reducing the amount of inventory held at each location.

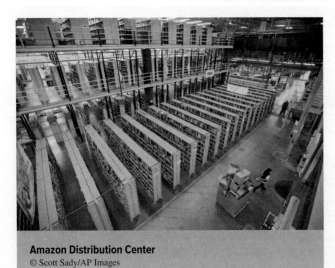

Amazon Distribution Center
© Scott Sady/AP Images

Similarly, consider the differences between Amazon and Barnes & Noble in the book industry. From a small number of distribution centers, Amazon can offer tens of thousands of different book titles with a relatively small inventory of each, as compared to the total inventory of a specific book title accumulated across all of the hundreds of Barnes & Noble store locations.

Another approach used in some situations is to share inventory among different locations within a firm. For example, dealers of Caterpillar equipment sometimes share repair parts and supplies among themselves. Thus, each dealer can reduce its inventory, knowing that there may be another dealer located close by who can provide a part if needed. This type of system can work particularly well when locations share information about what items are in stock.

Inventory Information Systems and Accuracy

Managing inventory requires an information system that provides accurate data concerning, among other things, quantities of inventory on-hand and expected arrivals of replenishment items. Any system is only as good as the data that it contains, and inventory systems are no different. Inaccurate inventory records create uncertainty, which usually requires firms to hold additional safety stocks.

Inventory record accuracy is affected by a number of things. As items are received or produced, they must be logged into the system correctly and in a timely fashion. Technologies such as bar codes and electronic identification tags can help in this effort. Point-of-sale scanning systems help with accuracy and up-to-date information as well.

Despite everyone's best efforts, records can and do become inaccurate. Human error or accidents can never be totally eliminated. Sometimes someone forgets to log in receipts of products or makes an error in the entry. Consider, for example, a clerk at the checkout in a retail store. A customer arrives at the checkout with 10 three-liter bottles of Coca-Cola products. Some are Diet Coke, some are regular Coke, and perhaps some are Sprite. To save time, the clerk takes one bottle and scans it very rapidly 10 times. The clerk may think this is acceptable because all three items are the same price. However, the clerk may not realize (or even care) that the store inventory records are now incorrect.

Inventory audits are important to ensure that entry and count errors are identified and corrected. A common audit approach is **cycle counting**, where each item in inventory is physically counted on a routine schedule. An easy way to set these audit cycles is to use the ABC classification discussed earlier. For example, A item inventories might be checked every week, B items checked every month, and C items checked every quarter. These checks are then spread out over the audit cycle so that a little is checked each day.

> **cycle counting** A process where each item in inventory is physically counted on a routine schedule.

The Get Real box below describes how American Apparel has used a new technology, RFID tags, to aid in more rapid replenishment of inventory, introduce efficiency in the process of physically tracking the on-hand inventory, and obtain greater accuracy in inventory records.

GET REAL

American Apparel Introduces RFID

At American Apparel, radio frequency identification (RFID) tags were recently deployed for item-level replenishment. This company's experience illustrates how RFID can be both cost-justified and rolled out with relative ease and expediency.

The company's business model calls for each store to maintain at least one piece of every size, color, and style on the sales floor at all times—which translates to roughly 40,000 pieces representing 12,000 to 13,000 unique items. The item-level RFID system demonstrated 99.9 percent accuracy on inventory replenishment throughout the store. Prior to RFID, this aggressive replenishment goal had sales associates running in circles and spending excessive hours manually counting and managing inventory. The pilot project showed American Apparel not only that RFID could work, but that employees could be significantly more productive because of the technology.

"We were seeing a huge savings in labor," noted an executive at American Apparel. "Before the pilot, we were doing inventory twice weekly and it required four to six employees working up to six hours. Now we can maintain inventory accuracy on the floor and do inventory just once a week. Two employees walking around the store with handheld RFID readers can scan everything in the entire store in under two hours."

© Scott Olson/Getty Images

Source: Adapted from Connie Robbins Gentry, "RFID Speeds Replenishment," *Chain Store Age* **84, no. 6 (June 2008), pp. 54–55.**

Implementing Inventory Models

A final issue to understand regarding inventory models is that no one model is likely to be used exclusively in an organization. Because most companies stock many different inventory items that differ in importance and value, a mix of different models is usually required. The most critical products may be managed with the continuous review model. This model lowers safety stock requirements but may also be the most expensive to implement due to the cost of information technology and system administration.

Many items may be managed using the basic concepts of the continuous review model but without the need for high-level technology. For example, in a **two-bin system**,

two-bin system Inventory of an item is stored in two different locations.

inventory of an item is stored in two different locations. Workers withdraw items as needed from one location until that location (or bin) is empty. When it is empty, workers immediately know that it is time to issue an order for more. This information is immediately given to purchasing, frequently by removing a form attached to the bin. While awaiting arrival of the order, inventory is taken from the second bin. The normal level of inventory in the second bin is determined as the ROP. When the order arrives from the supplier, the first bin is refilled and any remaining is put in the second bin. This system is frequently used in practice to manage inventory of low-value but necessary items, such as office supplies, and high-volume parts, such as bolts, screws, and similar pieces.

MANAGING INVENTORY ACROSS THE SUPPLY CHAIN

Thus far, we have focused on fundamentals for inventory management within a single firm. However, a firm must also consider how its actions and decisions may impact inventory of other firms in the supply chain.

Inventory Value in the Supply Chain

As discussed earlier, an item that is considered a finished product for one firm may well be a raw material or component part for a downstream supply chain member. The further downstream an item is in the supply chain, the more expensive it is to stock that item. As an item moves in the supply chain, value is constantly being added to it. For example, an automobile seat delivered by a seat manufacturer to a car assembly plant has value added of transportation. Once installed, the seat gains the added value of the labor and effort required to install it. Further, once it is installed, it becomes a part of a much more valuable product, the finished automobile. In fact, the finished automobile has a value that is much greater than the sum of its individual parts. A clear understanding of how inventory items gain value as they progress through the supply chain helps managers identify the best stages at which to hold inventories.

The Bullwhip Effect

bullwhip effect A small disturbance generated by a customer produces successively larger disturbances at each upstream stage in the supply chain.

The **bullwhip effect** occurs when a small disturbance in the flow of orders generated by a customer produces successively larger disturbances at each upstream stage in the supply chain. Bullwhip effects are of great concern. They incite excessive expediting (moving certain orders ahead of others), increased levels of inventory, uneven levels of capacity utilization (where plants go from being idle to working overtime), and, ultimately, increased costs.

To understand how a bullwhip effect is created, consider a hypothetical supply chain for a consumer product such as baby food. In this hypothetical chain, consumers buy baby food from a retailer, who, in turn, buys from a distributor. The distributor buys from the manufacturer. Under normal circumstances, the amount of baby food purchased by consumers ought to be fairly stable and predictable. It is easy to determine the number of babies who are at the appropriate age for consumption of baby food and the amount typically consumed per baby, per day, and so on.

Now, suppose that a large retailer decides to run an advertising promotion. In order to stock up for anticipated increases in sales, the retailer temporarily boosts orders to the distributor, as indicated in Figure 7-7 by an increase in order size in weeks 3 and 4. How should the distributor react? If it knows nothing about the retailer's promotional plan, the increased orders from the retailer come as a surprise. The distributor might worry that it won't be able to fill future orders of this magnitude.

A natural response would be for the distributor to place even larger orders with the manufacturer. After all, as far as the distributor knows, the retailer might place even larger orders in the future. This phenomenon is replicated upstream, until finally the orders that the manufacturer places on its suppliers are quite large indeed. Once the retailer's promotion campaign is over, it returns to placing normal smaller orders. How might the distributor react? By now it has lots of excess inventory sitting around. As a result it will probably decide to reduce future orders drastically. And so this opposite effect cascades up the supply chain.

What are the root causes of this bullwhip effect? Without information, suppliers are likely to overreact to changes in order sizes from their customers, regardless of whether they are larger or smaller than expected. Also, differences in ordering policies (batch sizes and order timing) at different stages of the supply chain can create unevenness in the flows. The ultimate outcome is continual fluctuations of excesses and shortages of inventory in the supply chain. In order to reduce these effects, operations managers have developed several approaches for more integrated supply chain inventory management.

Integrated Supply Chain Inventory Management

Every day, supply chain operations managers uncover new ways of improving performance by more thoroughly integrating decision making and execution. Two initiatives to accomplish this are vendor-managed inventory and collaborative planning, forecasting, and replenishment.

In the past, it was standard practice for operations managers to own and manage all the inventories on their property. More recently, an increasing number of firms have implemented **vendor-managed inventory (VMI)** arrangements. As the name suggests, the vendor (supplier) is responsible for managing the inventory located at a customer's facility. The vendor stocks the inventory, controls its flow in and out of the facility, and places replenishment orders. Often the vendor owns the inventory until the customer uses it, and a vendor representative often is located at the site where the inventory is stocked.

vendor-managed inventory (VMI) The vendor is responsible for managing the inventory located at a customer's facility.

This approach offers several important advantages to both the customer and the vendor. The customer saves the costs associated with managing inventories, including the labor costs usually incurred by both the materials and purchasing managers. The customer also receives more responsive service from the vendor because the on-site vendor

FIGURE 7-7

The Bullwhip Effect: An Example

representative works directly with production schedulers and other production personnel, thereby gaining a better understanding of the customer's schedule and quality needs.

The vendor gains better insights into the customer's operations and, surprisingly, often does a better job of scheduling inventory replenishment orders than the customer does. By controlling the order schedule, the vendor can also accommodate the needs of its own internal operations. For example, the vendor has the liberty to batch orders to reduce costly production setups. In addition, the production personnel at the vendor site receive higher quality and more timely information because the person generating the information has the vendor's interests at heart. The Get Real box about Stryker Instruments provides an example of vendor-managed inventory.

VMI approaches often blur the boundaries between the vendor's and customer's operations management systems. If secrecy is a high priority, this lack of separation sometimes poses a threat to the customer or vendor. Successful VMI arrangements require a fairly long-term commitment from both parties. Consequently, most VMI partnerships are usually reserved for only a few, important vendor relationships.

collaborative planning, forecasting, and replenishment (CPFR) A method by which supply chain partners periodically share forecasts, demand plans, and resource plans in order to reduce uncertainty and risk in meeting customer demand.

Another well-known supply chain initiative is known as **collaborative planning, forecasting, and replenishment (CPFR)**. Using this approach, partner firms periodically share information and forecasts in order to jointly develop their production, distribution, and replenishment plans. Chapter 12 discusses the CPFR process in more detail.

We are not finished with our coverage of the subject of inventory in this book. As you will see, most of the remaining chapters reference inventory in some way.

GET REAL

Vendor-Managed Inventory at Stryker Instruments

Staying in stock of the component parts for medical products such as this gurney was a major problem for Stryker Instruments. Much of the problem was solved through a vendor-managed inventory system.

© Brand X Pictures/Stockbyte/Getty Images

Stryker Instruments, a manufacturer of hospital equipment and instruments, had a classic inventory problem: It wasn't able to share real-time information with its key suppliers. Although its inventory levels were too high, the company was hesitant to lower them for fear of stockouts.

Using an inventory management solution from TradeBeam, Inc., Stryker instituted a new four-step process with its suppliers:

1. Stryker sets monthly inventory targets for each part number. Suppliers are responsible for keeping inventory within the target inventory range.

2. The inventory management system gives suppliers real-time visibility into Stryker's on-hand inventory levels, forecasts, current and future production schedules, and order commitments. More than 90 percent of Stryker's direct materials supply is now managed through the vendor replenishment process.

3. Using these data, the system helps suppliers determine how and when to ship materials to Stryker to ensure that inventory remains within target levels.

4. Suppliers enter into the TradeBeam inventory management solution promises for future ship dates with projected quantities, and they also provide advance shipment notice (ASN) information for products shipped.

As a result, Stryker has seen a 30 percent reduction in direct materials inventory for its manufacturing facilities in Michigan and Ireland. It also has seen a 30 to 40 percent reduction in finished goods inventory sent to Stryker distribution centers in the U.K. and Japan.

Source: Adapted from David Blanchard, "Stryker's 4-Step Inventory Reduction Process," *IndustryWeek* 256, no. 4 (April 2007), p. 48.

CHAPTER SUMMARY

This chapter has discussed fundamental aspects of inventory and inventory management in supply chain and operations management.

1. Inventory can be held as finished goods, raw materials and component parts, MRO (maintenance, repair, and operating supplies), or transit inventory.

2. The key roles of inventory are to balance supply and demand, buffer against variability and uncertainty, and assure that the economics of buying are maintained.

3. Inventory represents a financial investment by an organization as an asset. The costs related to inventory management include product cost, inventory carrying cost, ordering cost, and stockout cost.

4. Inventory policy involves determining how much of an item to order and when to place an order for replenishment.

5. Continuous review systems are used when the firm is able to continuously monitor inventory status.

6. The service level provided to customers depends on the level of safety stock held. The cost of different levels of safety stock can be quantified and then evaluated in relation to the potential impact of stockouts on customers.

7. Periodic review systems are used when companies do not have real time information on inventory levels, and must, instead, rely on physically counting inventory levels on a predetermined schedule.

8. When inventory is held in many locations, total inventory increases because of location impact on demand and lead time uncertainty.

9. While the mathematical models explained in the chapter can be used to establish the critical inventory parameters, in a practical sense managers attempt to reduce inventory requirements by changing and managing the variables (demand and its variation; lead time and its variation) that are components of those models.

10. To properly manage inventory, each item must have a unique identification and accurate inventory records must be maintained. Several different numbering systems have been developed for item identification. Record accuracy requires careful entry of information and typically can be supplemented with a program of cycle counting.

11. The bullwhip effect occurs when a small change in demand at the end-customer level of a supply chain results in increasingly large changes in the upstream supply chain.

12. Vendor-managed inventory is one approach taken in some supply chains to reduce the bullwhip effect and to reduce overall inventory levels in a supply chain.

KEY TERMS

ABC analysis   260

buffer (or safety) stock   239

bullwhip effect   264

carrying (or holding) cost   240

collaborative planning, forecasting,

and replenishment (CPFR)   266

continuous review model   245

cycle counting   263

cycle stock   239

days of supply   243

demand during lead time   252

dependent demand inventory systems   245

economic order quantity (EOQ)   247

DISCUSSION QUESTIONS

1. Why do some executives believe that inventory is "bad"? Explain why this thinking is incorrect.

2. Explain the different types of costs related to inventory planning.

3. Explain the trade-offs involved in the economic order quantity. How do these change when quantity discounts are considered?

4. Why does total system inventory increase as a company increases its number of stocking locations?

5. Early in the chapter it was stated that planning inventory levels is both an art and a science. Explain in your own words why this is true.

6. A firm is presently using the basic EOQ model and is considering switching to the production order quantity model (i.e., receiving gradual deliveries over time). If all the cost and demand parameters stay the same, what changes should the firm expect?

7. Suppose you have been given the task of reducing inventory in your company, without negatively impacting customer service. What actions might you be able to take to accomplish this task?

8. What steps do you think companies can take to improve the accuracy of their inventory information systems?

9. Why should one company in a supply chain consider total supply chain inventory as well as its own inventory levels?

PROBLEMS

1. Jiffy Print Shop, located close to a major university, does an enormous amount of printing of documents, papers, course packs, and dissertations for students and faculty. The shop uses an average of 20 cases of copy paper each day during the 320 days per year that it is open. Each case of paper costs $40.00. It conducts a count of its paper inventory at the end of every quarter of the year. Jiffy began the year with 1,200 cases of paper and at the end of each of the next four quarters had 800 cases, 1,050 cases, 950 cases, and 1,100 cases, respectively. Jiffy management has determined that its inventory carrying cost is 25 percent annually. What is Jiffy's average inventory for the year, inventory turnover rate, and annual inventory carrying cost for paper? Assuming that Jiffy expects demand for the next year to remain at an average of 20 cases per day, how long can Jiffy satisfy demand given its ending inventory (end of the fourth quarter) of 1,100 cases?

Solution:

Annual demand for paper is 20 cases/day (320 days) = 6,400 cases
Each case cost $40.00, therefore cost of goods = 6,400 cases * $40.00 = $256,000

Average inventory = (1,200 + 800 + 1,050 + 950 + 1,100) / 5 = 1,020 cases
Average inventory cost value = 1,020 cases * $40.00 per case = $40,800

Inventory turnover in this problem can be computed either in units or in dollars of cost:
Inventory turnover (units) = 6,400 cases used / 1,020 cases average inventory = 6.27 times
Inventory turnover (cost) = $256,000 cost of goods / $40,800 average inventory = 6.27 times

Annual inventory carrying cost = $40,800 average inventory * .25 = $10,200

Days of supply of inventory for the next year = 1,100 cases / 20 cases per day = 55 days

2. Johnson Widgets Inc. is examining its inventory of maintenance supplies in its warehouse. It wants to conduct an ABC analysis of these supplies. It maintains inventory of 10 parts and the history of part usage is contained in the following table.

Item #	Item Cost	Annual Usage	Annual Value
G-507	$ .45	50,000	$ 22,500
G-680	.80	600	480
K-100	1.70	2,000	3,400
K-300	2.20	250	550
K-303	.90	8,000	7,200
K-601	.50	4,000	2,000
N-005	8.50	80	680
N-035	4.00	24,000	96,000
P-440	1.20	900	1,080
Z-212	.02	100,000	2,000
Total			$135,890

What would you recommend to Johnson Widgets?

Solution:

In the table below, the percentage of total annual value for each item has been calculated (shown for the first item) and items have been ranked by this percentage value.

Item #	Annual Value	% of Annual Value	Cumulative % of Usage Value
N-035	$ 96,000	(96,000/135,890) = 70.65%	70.65%
G-507	22,500	16.56	87.21
K-303	7,200	5.30	92.51
K-100	3,400	2.50	95.01
K-601	2,000	1.47	96.48
Z-212	2,000	1.47	97.95
P-440	1,080	0.79	98.74
N-005	680	0.50	99.24
K-300	550	0.40	99.64
G-680	480	0.36	100
TOTAL	$135,890		

As for specific recommendations, some judgment is required. It seems clear that item # N-035 should be classified as an A item. Beyond that, it could be argued that item G-507 may be an A or B item, while the remainder would most likely be classified as Cs. However, even these classifications based on the quantitative analysis may be modified by managerial factors. For example, notice that item Z-212 is a very low-cost item and annual value is only 1.47 percent of the total. However, since it has the highest usage quantity of 100,000 units, it may be very important to overall operations at Johnson Widgets and therefore classified as an A or B item, thus maintaining higher safety stocks and/ or receiving more managerial attention than some of the other items. The quantitative analysis is a very useful first step in ABC classification, but it must be tempered with other factors.

3. Foods Galore is a major distributor to restaurants and other institutional food users.

   a. Foods Galore buys cereal from a manufacturer for $20.00 per case. Annual demand for cereal is 200,000 cases, and the company believes that the demand is constant at 800 cases per day for each of the 250 days per year that it is open for business. Average lead time from the supplier for replenishment orders is eight days, and the company believes that it is also constant. The purchasing agent at Foods Galore believes that annual inventory carrying cost is 10 percent and that it costs $40.00 to prepare, send, and receive an order. How many cases of cereal should Foods Galore order each time it places an order? What will be the average inventory? What will be the inventory turnover rate?

Solution:

The economic order quantity for cereal is

$$\sqrt{\frac{2 \times 200,000 \times \$40}{\$20 \times .10}} = 2,828.5 \text{ or } 2,829 \text{ cases}$$

Average inventory will be

$$2,829/2 = 1,414.5 \text{ cases}$$

Inventory turnover will be

$$200,000/1,414.5 = 141.4 \text{ times per year}$$

   b. Foods Galore conducts an in-depth analysis of its inventory management practices and discovers several flaws in its previous approach. First, it finds that by ordering 10,000 or more cases each time, it can obtain a price of $18.00 per case from the supplier. What order quantity should Foods Galore place? Why?

Solution:

The economic order quantity for the $18.00 price is

$$\sqrt{\frac{2 \times 200,000 \times \$40}{\$18 \times .1}} = 2,981.4 \text{ or } 2,981 \text{ cases}$$

However, Foods Galore is required to order 10,000 cases in order to receive the $18.00 price. Therefore, the total acquisition cost of ordering 10,000 cases must be compared to the total acquisition cost of ordering 2,829 cases at a time.

The TAC_{QD} of ordering 2,829 cases is:

Annual product cost = $200,000 \times \$20 = \$4,000,000.00$
Annual inventory carrying cost = $1,414.5 \times \$20 \times .1 = \$2,829.00$
Annual ordering cost = $(200,000/2,829) \times \$40 = \$2,827.85$
Total cost = $\$4,005,656.85$

(*Note:* Annual inventory carrying cost and annual ordering cost are not equal in this case due to rounding.)

The TAC_{QD} of ordering 10,000 cases is:

Annual product cost = $200,000 \times \$18 = \$3,600,000.00$
Annual inventory carrying cost = $5,000 \times \$18 \times .1 = \$9,000.00$
Annual ordering cost = $(200,000/10,000) \times \$40 = \$800.00$
Total cost = $\$3,609,800.00$

Foods Galore should order 10,000 cases of cereal each time because it will save a total of $395,856.85 per year by doing so.

    c.   In its analysis, Foods Galore determined that demand and lead time are not constant. In fact, demand has a standard deviation of 60 cases per day and lead time has a standard deviation of 1.5 days. Foods Galore management wants to evaluate two service level policies. One policy would incur a 5 percent risk of stockout while waiting for replenishment, and the other policy would incur only a 1 percent risk of stockout. What would be the cost of carrying the safety stocks for each of the two policies?

Solution:

The standard deviation of demand during lead time for cereal is:

$$\sqrt{8 \, days \, (60 \, cases)^2 + (800 \, cases)^2 \, (1.5 \, days)^2} = 1,211.94, \text{ or } 1,212 \text{ cases}$$

A 5 percent risk of stockout is equal to a 95 percent probability of being in stock, which will require 1.65 standard deviations of safety stock, or $1.65(1,212) = 2,000$ cases (rounded). Because the $18 price was determined to provide the lowest total acquisition cost, the cost of carrying the safety stock for this service level is $(2,000 \text{ cases} \times \$18 \times .1) = \$3,600.00$.

A 1 percent risk of stockout is equal to a 99 percent probability of being in stock, which will require 2.33 standard deviations of safety stock, or $2.33(1,212) = 2,824$ cases (rounded). The cost of this safety stock policy is $(2,824 \text{ cases} \times \$18 \times .1) = \$5,083.20$.

    4.   Thomas Toys Ltd. uses a periodic review inventory management system. One important item for the company is building blocks, which sell, on average, five sets per day. However, the standard deviation of demand is two sets per day. The company checks the status of inventory for building blocks every 21 days. When blocks are reordered from the supplier, it takes 14 days to be replenished. Thomas has just checked its inventory and found that it currently has 160 sets in stock. The company desires to maintain a 97.5 percent service level. How many sets of building blocks should Thomas Toys order?

Solution:

For building block sets, the uncertainty period is 21 days (the review period) plus 14 days (the lead time), or 35 days.

The standard deviation of demand during the uncertainty period is

$$\sqrt{2^2}(35) = 11.8 \text{ sets}$$

The order quantity for building blocks is

(5 sets per day)(35 days) + 1.96 (11.8 sets) − 160 sets = 175 + 24 − 160 = 39 sets

5. Johnson Plastics makes and sells, among many other things, specialty plastic display cases for retail stores. Johnson's expected demand for the display cases is 1,000 units, and average daily demand is 4 units. The production process is most efficient when 16 units per day are produced at a cost of $100 per unit. Setup cost is $50. Inventory carrying cost at Johnson is determined to be 10 percent annually. What is the best production order quantity, and how many days is a required production run?

Solution:

The production order quantity is

$$Q_p = \sqrt{\frac{2(1,000)\$50}{.10(\$100)\left(1 - \frac{4}{16}\right)}} = 115.47 \text{ units or (rounded up) 116 units}$$

Producing 116 units in a production run at a rate of 16 per day requires 116/16 = 7.22 days.

6. Concert Productions is planning an appearance of the top band Iggy Wiggy. It plans to buy custom-designed t-shirts to sell at the stadium where the concert will take place. The t-shirt will sell for $25.00 and the cost per shirt is $8.00. Previous experience at Concert Productions suggests that after the concert is over, t-shirts can still be sold, but the selling price will be only $5.00 per shirt. Based on analysis of previous similar concerts, the company estimates sales of the t-shirt will be 6,000 units. However, the analysis also shows that the standard deviation in similar situations is 800 units. How many Iggy Wiggy t-shirts should the company order?

Solution:

The cost for a stockout (C_{SO}) of a t-shirt = Unit selling price − Unit cost = $25 − $8 = $17
The cost of overstock (C_{OS}) of a t-shirt is = Unit cost + Disposal cost − Salvage value
$$= \$8 + 0 - \$5 = \$3$$
Target service level = $C_{SO}/(C_{SO} + C_{OS})$
Therefore, the target services level (TSL) for the t-shirts = $17/($17 + $3) = 0.85

This TSL will provide an 85% probability of meeting all demand for the Iggy Wiggy t-shirts. From the table of cumulative probability in Appendix A, we see that this target probability is closest to 1.04 standard deviations. Therefore, the target order quantity for t-shirts is:

Order quantity = Expected demand + Safety stock = 6,000 T-shirts + 1.04(800 T-shirts)
$$= 6,832 \text{ T-shirts}$$

PROBLEMS

1. Akers Inc. maintains average inventory of $1,000,000 (at cost). Last year, Akers' sales volume was $10,000,000 and cost of goods sold was $7,000,000. Akers has determined that its inventory carrying cost is 15 percent annually.
   a. What was the inventory turnover rate?
   b. How much was the inventory carrying cost for the year?
2. The following table contains data about the inventory for five items at Jones Corporation. Complete the missing items in the table.

Item #	Beginning Unit Inventory	Ending Unit Inventory	Average Unit Inventory	Annual Unit Sales	Inventory Turnover
1	150,000	120,000		400,000	
2	40,000	60,000		80,000	
3	85,000	97,000		190,000	
4	200,000	170,000		350,000	
5	50,000	60,000		165,000	
Total					

3. Suppose Jones Corporation in the above problem determined that its annual inventory carrying cost = 18 percent. The item unit cost was as follows:

   Item 1 = $25.00

   Item 2 = $60.00

   Item 3 = $5.00

   Item 4 = $10.00

   Item 5 = $1.00

   Compute the dollar values for the information in the above table and determine the annual inventory carrying cost for each item and the total annual inventory carrying cost.

4. Again, using the data for Jones Corporation in problems 2 and 3, suppose Jones believes that in the upcoming year, the rate of sales expected for each of the five items is as follows:

   Item 1 = 4,000 units per day

   Item 2 = 2,000 units per day

   Item 3 = 15,000 units per day

   Item 4 = 7,000 units per day

   Item 5 = 2,000 units per day

   Compute the days of supply for each item.

5. Complete an ABC analysis of the five items that Jones Corporation carries in inventory.

6. Suppose management of Foods Galore (in solved problem 3) found that it had drastically underestimated its annual inventory carrying cost. Rather than the 10 percent carrying cost assumed in the solved problem, carrying cost is actually 25 percent. Rework all parts of the solved problem assuming the 25 percent carrying cost.

7. Suppose Thomas Toys Ltd. (in solved problem 4) decides to reduce the review period from 21 days to 10 days. Rework the problem assuming everything else remains the same.

8. Suppose Johnson Plastics (in solved problem 5) reduces setup cost to $20. Rework the problem.

9. Ergonomics Inc. sells ergonomically designed office chairs. The company has the following information:

   Average demand = 20 units per day

   Average lead time = 30 days

   Item unit cost = $50 for orders of less than 200 units

   Item unit cost = $48 for orders of 200 units or more

   Ordering cost = $25

   Inventory carrying cost = 25%

   The business year is 250 days

   The basic question: How many chairs should the firm order each time? Assume there is no uncertainty at all about the demand or the lead time. There are many associated questions, such as what will the firm's average inventory be under each alternative? What will be the breakdown of costs for each alternative?

10. A sporting goods company has a distribution center that maintains inventory of fishing rods. The fishing rods have the following demand, lead time, and cost characteristics:

Average demand = 100 units per day, with a standard deviation of 12 units

Average lead time = 12 days with a standard deviation of 2 days

250 days per year in the business year

Unit cost = $25

Desired service level = 95%

Ordering cost = $50

Inventory carrying cost = 20%

The basic question: How many fishing rods should the distribution center carry to provide the desired service level? There are, of course, many other specific questions, such as what is the EOQ? What is the average cycle stock?

11. A company experiences annual demand of 1,000 units for an item that it purchases. The rate of demand per day is very stable, with very little variation from day to day. The item costs $50 when purchased in quantities less than 100 and $48 for 100 items or more. Ordering costs are $40 and the carrying cost is 25 percent. How much should the company buy each time an order is placed?

12. Meyer Stores carries a specialty line of flavored syrups. On average, Meyer sells 30 bottles per week of its popular raspberry syrup. Meyer's cost is $8 per bottle. Meyer has determined its order cost to be $50 and inventory carrying cost is 20 percent. Meyer is open for business 52 weeks per year.

    a. What is the EOQ for raspberry syrup?
    b. If Meyer orders the EOQ quantity each time, what will be the inventory turnover rate for raspberry syrup?

13. Talbot Industries is evaluating its service level policy for a product that is considered critical to customers. Demand for the item averages 100 units per day and the lead time from the supplier of the item averages 6 days. An analysis of demand and lead time patterns has shown that the standard deviation of demand during lead time is 110 units. The existing service level policy allows for a stockout probability of 10 percent during the replenishment cycle. Marketing managers claim that the item is so critical that the firm should carry three standard deviations of safety stock. If the item cost is $60 and Talbot's inventory carrying cost is 20 percent, what is the incremental inventory carrying cost of following the suggestion of the marketing managers?

14. Johnson Corporation has the following information about a product that it carries in stock:

Average demand = 40 units per day

Average lead time = 15 days

Item unit cost = $55 for orders of less than 400 units

Item unit cost = $50 for orders of 400 units or more

Ordering cost = $30

Inventory carrying cost = 20%

The business year is 300 days

Standard deviation of demand = 2.5 units

Standard deviation of lead time = 1.5 days

Desired service level = 97.5%

    a. What is the annual total acquisition cost of ordering at the $55 price?
    b. What is the annual total acquisition cost of ordering at the $50 price?
    c. What level of safety stock should Johnson maintain for the item?
    d. If Johnson chooses the ordering policy that results in the lowest total annual acquisition cost and maintains the safety stock level for 97.5 percent service, what will Johnson's average inventory be for this item?
    e. Given your answer in d, what will the annual inventory turnover rate be for this item?
    f. What will the reorder point be for the item?

15. Michigan State Figurine Inc. (MSF) sells crystal figurines to Spartan fans. MSF buys the figurines from a manufacturer for $10 per unit. It sends orders electronically to the manufacturer, costing $20 per order, and it experiences an average lead time of eight days for each order to arrive from the manufacturer. Its inventory carrying cost is 20 percent. The average daily demand for the figurines is two units per day. MSF is open for business 250 days a year. Answer the following questions:

    a. How many units should the firm order each time? Assume there is no uncertainty at all about the demand or the lead time.

    b. How many orders will it place in a year?

    c. What is the average inventory?

    d. What is the annual ordering cost?

    e. What is the annual inventory carrying cost?

16. Suppose the supplier problem 15 decides to offer a volume discount. It now will sell the crystal figurines at $8 per unit for orders of 250 units or more. Answer items (a) through (e) based on this revised set of data.

17. Freeport Corporation finds that average demand for surfboards is 10 units per day, with a standard deviation of 3 units. Lead time from the supplier averages 12 days, with a standard deviation of 2 days. The item costs $50 and the inventory carrying cost is 30 percent.

    a. Suppose management decides to offer a 95 percent service level; that is, it is willing to experience a stockout probability of 5 percent during the order cycle. How much safety stock should be carried?

    b. How much is the annual inventory carrying cost of the safety stock because of this decision?

    c. You decide that you want this company to give better service to its customers. You decide that a 99 percent service level is appropriate. How much safety stock must be carried to offer this service level?

    d. What is the *additional* inventory carrying cost that will be incurred on this item because of your decision to increase the service level?

    e. What will the reorder point be for the company *if your decision is implemented?*

18. Suppose you are a corporate buyer. One of your suppliers delivers a particular part in 12 days on average, with a standard deviation of 3. The daily usage averages 20 units per day with a standard deviation of 4. What is the standard deviation of demand during lead time? If you use a continuous review policy, how much safety stock would you want on hand to ensure at least 90 percent availability of the part while waiting for replenishment?

19. Korner Hardware manager Emerson Jones is interested in determining how many nativity scenes to order for the 10-day holiday season. Past experience indicates that demand for these nativity scenes averages eight per day during this 10-day period, with a standard deviation of two per day. Demand is approximately normal. Emerson purchases the nativity scenes for $15 per unit and sells them for $30 each during the season. After Christmas, they are marked down as sale items for $10 each. How many should Emerson order for the coming holiday season?

20. You have a one-time chance to purchase an item for $5. The item can be sold to customers for $30. After one day, the item has no salvage value because it becomes rotten at the end of the day. It will then cost you $15 per item to properly dispose of any unsold items. You think you can sell 1,000 units in one day, but you also know that the standard deviation of demand for the item is 50 units. How many units should you order?

21. Jasper's Grocery places an order for Monster every three weeks. Once the order is placed, delivery to the store typically occurs in one week. Average demand is 100 cases per week and the standard deviation of demand is 20 cases per week. The store policy is to stock an amount of inventory that allows for an average stockout condition of 10 percent while waiting for replenishment. It is time to place an order, and there are 420 cases on hand. How many units should be ordered?

22. Dreyfus Company has a policy of counting on-hand inventory of one of its products every 45 days. When a replenishment order for the product is placed with the supplier,

lead time is 8 days. Demand for the product averages 6 units per day with a standard deviation of 1.5 units. It has just been determined that the company currently has 42 units on hand. How many units should the company order if it strives to maintain a 99 percent service level on this item?

23. You manage inventory for your company and use a continuous review inventory system to control reordering items for stock. Your company is open for business 300 days per year. One of your most important items experiences demand of 20 units per day, normally distributed with a standard deviation of 3 units per day. You experience a lead time on orders from your supplier of six days with a standard deviation of two days. If you order 1,000 units or less, you pay the supplier $5.00 per unit. Orders of 1,000 or more can be bought at a unit price of $4.75. Your ordering cost is $50. Your inventory carrying cost is 20 percent. You have established a service level policy of 97.5 percent on this item.
    a. What is your optimal order quantity?
    b. What is your reorder point?
    c. How much safety stock do you carry?
    d. What is your average inventory?

24. Suppose in problem 23, you were able to reduce your order cost to $10. What is the impact of this change on the other variables?

25. After you reduce your order cost, as described in problem 24, the supplier in problem 23 changes its pricing policy to a standard $4.75 per unit, regardless of the order quantity. What is the impact of this policy change on the other variables?

26. You are the buyer for your university bookstore. One of the textbooks has a cost to you of $100 and you sell it to students for $140. Any copies of the book that you order and do not sell to students can be returned to the publisher for an average $80 credit. (Sometimes you can get full credit, but sometimes a new edition is published so you get no credit.) In one particular course, demand has averaged 400 books each semester, with a standard deviation of 40. What is your target service level? What is your target order quantity for the course?

27. Continuing with problem 26, one of the textbooks in your bookstore costs $100 and sells for $200. In this case, however, you cannot salvage any value from copies that do not sell because a new edition is published every semester. Demand for this text averages 80 copies each semester, with a standard deviation of 10 copies. How many copies should you order each semester?

28. Charles Cycles produces bicycles and tricycles. The setup cost when switching production from one to the other is $1,000. On average, retail customers order 150 tricycles per day (consider a 250-day year). The daily production rate for tricycles is 600 units. Unit cost of a tricycle is $60 and the company has determined inventory carrying cost to be 15 percent. What should the production order quantity be?

29. Bryson Carpet Mills produces a variety of different carpets. Changing from production of one carpet to another involves a setup cost of $1,000. One particular carpet costs $5 per yard to produce. Annual demand for this style is 120,000 yards. Bryson Carpet Mills produces carpet 300 days per year. The production process is most efficient when 4,000 yards per day are produced. Inventory carrying cost is estimated at 20 percent annually. What should be the production order quantity?

30. In problem 29, suppose Bryson Carpet Mills develops a production process that is most efficient when 6,000 yards per day are produced at a cost of $4.50 per yard. Everything else remains the same. How does this affect the calculation in problem 29?

31. After implementing the change described in problem 30, Bryson Carpet Mills now finds that it can reduce its setup cost to $500. Does this further change the calculations of production order quantity? How?

32. Steve Carter is CFO of a small temporary labor supplier. Steve is setting up an account to hold cash that the company needs to pay its monthly bills. Cash needs average $10,000 each month with a standard deviation of daily demand of $50. Steve estimates the company's opportunity cost of capital (the cost to hold cash for a year) at about

30 percent. Adding more cash by taking it from operating funds or short term loans takes one day and costs $50 to process required transactions.

a. How often should Steve add money to the cash account?

b. How much should he add to the account each time?

c. How much extra cash should Steve hold on hand to provide at least a 95 percent chance that the company will never run out of cash?

d. How much cash should be left in the account when Steve orders more cash?

e. How much cash will the company hold on average?

33. Suppose that Steve in problem 32 does not want to have to continuously monitor the company's cash account. He instead would like to do a monthly audit (every 30 days) and then order the appropriate amount of cash each time. If the June monthly audit shows $500 cash on hand, how much cash should Steve order in this review period? How much more safety stock is required to support the periodic review policy? Why is more needed?

34. Hartley Incorporated buys plastic resin by the ton and then packages and distributes it in smaller amounts to industrial users. The resin typically costs $50 per ton, and Hartley uses 80,000 tons each year. Placing an order for more resin costs $500 in allocated labor cost for purchasing personnel. Holding costs for the resin are estimated at 1 percent of the product value each month. Hartely operates 365 days a year.

a. How much resin should Hartley order each time?

b. What will be the average inventory and annual holding cost?

c. Suppose that instead of having each replenishment order delivered all in one shipment, Hartley asks its resin supplier to deliver each order in equally sized shipments, one shipment per day, with each shipment big enough to cover two days' worth of demand. How will this affect Hartley's order quantity, average inventory, and annual holding costs? (*Hint:* Realize in this second scenario that Hartley's inventory level will never reach Q.)

35. Rachel is making t-shirts that she hopes to sell at the upcoming "War on War" concert. The t-shirts cost $6 each to produce, and she will price them at $20 each. She expects that she can donate any unsold t-shirts to a local charity for a tax write-off of $2 each. Based on her experience at past concerts, Rachel expects to sell 1,000 t-shirts, with a standard deviation of 100 t-shirts.

a. How many t-shirts should Rachel make?

b. What is the probability that she will run out of shirts to sell?

36. Suppose that in problem 35, Rachel can spend $1,000 to buy a well-placed booth at the concert. Doing so would raise the expected sales of t-shirts from 1,000 to 1,200 and lower the standard deviation of demand from 100 to 50.

a. Should she decide to pursue this option, how many t-shirts should Rachel make?

b. Should Rachel spend the money for the better placed booth? (You may not know exactly how to answer this question, but at least write down what you would need to know in order to compute an answer.)

CASE

Inventory at Champion Electric

Champion Electric, a regional supplier of electrical and electronic components, keeps thousands of SKUs (stock keeping units) of various products on hand for its customers. A new operations manager, Barb Patterson, has just been hired to replace Bob, who resigned because of customer complaints and management pressure to keep inventories in check.

Gil, a longtime warehouse manager reporting to Barb, has been filling her in on past performance. Gil tells Barb, "Bob was a good manager who always did what the bosses wanted him to do. He just couldn't do everything. Management was upset with Bob about customer service, the number of people we have working in this area, and more recently, with the overall level of inventory.

"Barb, I think you need to put some pressure on marketing to stop adding products, and while you're at it, we should get rid of many of the items that sell so infrequently that you have to dust the box off to read the label. We always have the higher volume, more profitable items in stock—we keep lots of safety stock so we never run out.

"We are always getting hammered because of customer complaints, and yet our records show that we have a fill rate of 99.9 percent. With over 30,000 SKUs, you can't get much better than that. None of our competition has that kind of service. At the same time, every other order has a request for some piddly item that we don't have in stock. Sometimes our system even shows we should have stock but we don't. When we don't have an item, we have to reorder it or expedite it or do something extraordinary to make sure the customer gets the product—and many times it's late. That takes people and time. It drives us crazy. We shouldn't sell all of these things. You just can't keep enough inventory."

Gil continues, "But adding product every day just makes it worse. Marketing always makes the case that it is our strategy to supply customers a 'full line' of supplies—that means we have to add a product if there is demand for it. Customers often decide they want a new and improved version of what we are stocking and we almost always try to get them what they need."

Barb questions, "How do we add these items—what's the process?"

Gil considers her question and responds, "Sales makes an estimate of what they think they can sell and then we place an order. We try to determine the best 'economical' volume to buy of that item when we place the order. The problem is that even though customers say they want these new items, many times these things are never ordered after the first time. Would you believe that we have some 20 percent of our inventory classified as dead—it hasn't moved in over three months."

Later that day in President Campos's office, Barb gets some more information on her new mandate. "I have continued to invest money in inventory but there is a limit to how much we can afford. Customers are still complaining. I know that our inventories are higher than our competitors—I have backed that idea so that we could get a higher customer service rating than our competitors. But I'm not sure our service is any better; and, I know our inventory is higher. You have to get this thing under control."

Questions

1. Why, in your opinion, is senior management so concerned about the "high" inventory levels at Champion Electric?

2. What steps would you suggest that Barb take in addressing the concerns of President Campos?

CASE

Tasty Treats

Tasty Treats is a distributor of candy and snack products serving customers in a six state region of the midwestern United States. Bill Jones, chief operations officer, has been concerned about inventory levels and inventory performance at Tasty Treats for quite some time. In speaking with Jim Busfield, chief executive officer of Tasty Treats, Bill voiced some of his concerns: "Jim, we carry over 5,000 different items in inventory. I have a feeling that we just don't have a good handle on the proper approach to managing this part of our operations. We don't have any real analysis that tells us how much we should carry of each item. We just use simple rules of thumb to determine how much we should order from our suppliers. For example, we sell an average of 100 cases of Chocolate Chewies every day. When we order Chocolate Chewies from our supplier, it usually takes about 10 days for us to get the order. So, we order 1,000 cases of Chocolate Chewies every 10 days. I also try to keep an extra 200 cases on hand just in case something unexpected happens. Sometimes we run out of stock anyway and sometimes I look and see an enormous number of cases of Chocolate Chewies on hand. The same basic approach is used for every item we sell. There's got to be a better way."

Jim briefly thought over Bill's concerns before he replied. "I think you're right, Bill. As you know, my background is in finance, not operations, but I can tell you that we have a lot of money tied up in inventory and we spend a lot of money not just in buying it but in maintaining it, too. We pay insurance, taxes, and a lot of other costs just because of the amount of inventory. If we manage it better, we may be able to free up a lot of capital, too. There has to be a more sophisticated approach than what we are doing. I tell you what let's do. We have a summer intern who is majoring in supply chain management at State University. Let's turn her loose on this project."

Jim and Bill called the intern, Rachel Atkins, into the office and explained the situation to her. She happily accepted the assignment. She explained to Bill and Jim that she would need to gather a lot of information from them in order to complete the assignment. They agreed that she could have access to any data she needed and that they would tell other managers at Tasty Treats to cooperate with her in the project.

First, Rachel conducted a detailed analysis of demand for the past two years. For each of the 300 days per year that Tasty Treats ships to customers, she found that Bill was correct in saying that demand averaged 100 cases per day. However, in fact, the demand pattern had a standard deviation of 8 cases per day. She also looked at the supplier's performance and found that the 10-day lead time was a good average, but it also varied and had a standard deviation of 2 days.

From the supplier of Chocolate Chewies, Rachel learned that Tasty Treats paid $25.00 per case for Chocolate Chewies. The supplier's sales representative then remarked, "I've always wondered why Tasty Treats orders 1,000 cases every time. They've never asked about any of our discounts. If they order 3,000 cases, our selling price drops to $24.50. That's a 2 percent discount."

Rachel had several discussions with Jim and Bill. After explaining to them what "order costs" and "inventory carrying costs" consist of, they provided her with their estimates of each. Jim suggested that she should use 15 percent as the annual inventory carrying cost. Bill determined that a good estimate of order cost would be $100 per order.

As her final step in gathering information, Rachel talked with Jim, Bill, and the sales staff about the importance of customer service. She explained about service levels and stockouts and their importance in inventory management. The sales staff was insistent that a 99 percent service level policy was needed. Jim and Bill were a little hesitant to accept that and suggested instead that Rachel consider a 95 percent service level. Rachel commented, "I'll do both and we can see what the difference is." Jim said, "That'll be great, Rachel. I'm scheduling a meeting of all senior managers for next Tuesday to hear your report. I'm looking forward to it."

Questions

What recommendations should Rachel make in her presentation to Tasty Treats's senior management?

SELECTED READINGS & INTERNET SITES

Bhattacharya, A.; B. Sarkar; and S. K. Mukherjee. "Distance-Based Consensus Method for ABC Analysis." *International Journal of Production Research* 45, no. 15 (2007), pp. 3405–20.

Boute, R. N.; S. M. Disney; M. R. Lambrecht; and B. Van Houdt. "A Win-Win Solution for the Bullwhip Problem." *Production Planning and Control* 19, no. 7 (October 2008), pp. 702–11.

Gruen, T., and D. Corsten. "Improve Out-of-Stock Methods at the Shelf." *Chain Store Age,* July 2006, p. 35.

Hung, K-T, and S. Ryu. "Changing Risk Preferences in Supply Chain Inventory Decisions." *Production Planning and Control* 19, no. 8 (December 2008), pp. 770–80.

Kator, C. "Inventory Costs Rise Dramatically." *Modern Materials Handling* 62, no. 7 (July 2007), pp. 9–10.

Taylor, J. C., and S. E. Fawcett. "Catalog Retailer In-Stock Performance: An Assessment of Customer Service Levels." *Journal of Business Logistics* 25, no. 2 (2004), pp. 119–35.

Trunick, P. A. "Get Down to Detail on Inventory." *Logistics Today,* September 2007, pp. 16–18.

Vollman, T. E.; W. L. Berry; D. C. Whybark; and F. R. Jacobs. *Manufacturing Planning and Control Systems for Supply Chain Management.* 5th ed. New York: McGraw-Hill, 2004.

Wang, C. X. "Random Yield and Uncertain Demand in Decentralised Supply Chains under the Traditional and VMI Arrangements." *International Journal of Production Research* 47, no. 7 (2009), pp. 1955–68.

Zipkin, P. H. *Foundations of Inventory Management.* New York: McGraw-Hill/Irwin, 2000.

Inventory Operations Consulting
www.inventoryops.com/articles.htm

Supply Chain Brain
www.supplychainbrain.com/content/index.php

8

Lean Systems

LEARNING OBJECTIVES *After studying this chapter, you should be able to:*

LO8-1 Explain how the lean system approach improves value for internal operations and across the supply chain.

LO8-2 Describe the cultural changes, tools, and techniques needed to implement a lean approach.

LO8-3 Recognize the strengths and limitations of lean systems.

LO8-4 Apply the concept of lean systems to product design.

© David Joel/Stone/Getty Images

Imagine managing the operating room (OR) staff of a 250-bed community, not-for-profit medical center. How do you get more surgeries done per day without spending more money? In studying the problem directly through the use of **gemba kaizen**, in which managers and employees are obligated to see the problems and issues in person rather than relying on reports, a process improvement team discovered that capacity was being wasted through excessively long setups. It simply took too much time to change over operating rooms between surgical cases in the 11-OR-suite inpatient surgery department. Every minute saved in operating room changeover time could be used for more surgery or for ensuring better patient quality. Adding capacity in this way would help the staff improve both patient care and physician satisfaction.

To reduce changeover time, the team applied various lean tools such as process mapping, SMED (single minute exchange of dies—a process for setup reduction), and work standardization. The staff worked to streamline processes by identifying and moving work steps that had been internal to the changeover and making these steps external (i.e., identifying steps that could be done simultaneously with other activities). Visual indicators such as color coding were used to clarify the process and to standardize the OR changeover process. These and other changes were achieved through a four-day Kaizen Event. The impact: a 60 percent reduction of operating room changeover time. As a result, patient care has improved; nurses are more satisfied; and doctors feel that they have more time to focus on patient care rather than facility issues.

_____

[1]http://leanhealthcareperformance.com/leancasestudies.html

The focus of this chapter is *lean*—a systematic approach that has been developed to help managers identify and reduce/eliminate waste and variance in the processes under their control. To many, lean is something that a manufacturer of cars and farm equipment would apply; it is not something that a hospital or restaurant owner would consider using. Yet, as can be seen from the medical center's experience in the opening story, the lean approach to managing operations across the supply chain is broad-based and it has been successfully applied in a wide variety of product and service operational settings. In addition to traditional high-volume production settings and hospitals, lean systems have been applied to the production of unique, short-run collector dolls (Madame Alexander Dolls), high-end designer luggage (Louis Vuitton), jet airplanes (Boeing), and in services (Jefferson Pilot Insurance Company, now known as Lincoln Financial Group) (see Figure 8-1). Starbucks (a leading maker and retailer of specialty coffees) uses lean principles and practices to enable its baristas (coffee preparers) to speed up drink preparation, while maintaining product quality. The principles, tools, and procedures that make up the lean management system are highly versatile.

In sectors such as automobiles and electronics across the world, the lean system approach has become the dominant way that operations managers view their businesses. Because lean offers such a powerful way to eliminate wastes and variance in operational processes, it is important for all business professionals to understand its underlying principles and tools. This chapter focuses on what *lean* means and how it can be applied in various settings.

global

just-in-time (JIT) An older name for lean systems.

Toyota Production System (TPS) Another term for lean systems; refers to the specific lean system implemented at Toyota.

LEAN SYSTEMS DEFINED

Managers have used a variety of terms to describe lean systems, including lean production, just-in-time (JIT) manufacturing, stockless production, zero inventories, and the Toyota Production System (TPS). Currently, *lean systems* has become the term most commonly

FIGURE 8-1 Firms That Have Successfully Implemented Lean Systems

LO8-1 Explain how the lean system approach improves value for internal operations and across the supply chain.

Madame Alexander Dolls®
© Steven Chernin/Getty Images

Louis Vuitton luggage
© Koichi Kamoshida/Getty Images

Boeing
© Roslan Rahman/AFP/Getty Images

Lincoln Financial Group
© Joseph Kaczmarek/AP Images

used to describe the increasingly broad application of lean principles across manufacturing and service supply chain settings. While formal definitions of lean vary, this book uses the following definition:

> The **lean systems approach** is a *philosophy* of operations management that emphasizes the minimization of the amount of all the resources (including time) used in the various activities of the enterprise.[2]

lean systems approach A philosophy that emphasizes the minimization of the amount of all resources used in the various activities of the enterprise.

Just as a lean athlete has mostly muscle and little fat, operational processes can be described as being lean when they are very efficient and have few wasted resources. The elimination of *waste* is actually the defining objective of lean. More importantly, lean is also a philosophy—that is, a way of thinking and a way of viewing business activities and their associated resources. As a philosophy, lean offers managers guidelines that must be adapted to fit the firm's situation—the needs of its critical customers, the specific form of product value delivered, and the operations setting in which lean is deployed. Consequently, practices that work well in one setting may not work as effectively in another.

Origins of Lean Systems and Just-in-Time Production

Though elements of lean systems thinking have been around since the dawn of industrialization, credit is given to Taiichi Ohno of Toyota for organizing these elements into what eventually became the Toyota Production System.[3] Beginning in 1937, Ohno discovered that American laborers were nine times as productive as Japanese laborers. He borrowed important concepts of lean systems thinking from two distinct American institutions: Henry Ford's mass production system and the supermarket. The merging of these elements into what eventually became *lean* occurred during the 1950s when a delegation from Toyota led by Ohno visited the Ford plant at River Rouge (see Figure 8-2), then considered the most advanced car manufacturing system in the world.

At Ford, Ohno studied practices such as setup reduction, work standardization, focused factories, ongoing employee training, supply chain integration, and variance control and reduction. He also noted the presence of large amounts of inventory and rework. While he was greatly impressed with the operations at Ford, it was in the American supermarket that Ohno found his vision of the ideal operating system:

> We made a connection between supermarkets and the just-in-time system. . . .
>
> A supermarket is where a customer can get (1) what is needed, (2) at the time needed, (3) in the amount needed. From the supermarket, we got the idea of viewing

global

© Associated Press

FIGURE 8-2 Ford's River Rouge Plant: Once a Symbol of American Mass Production, 1942

[2]*APICS Dictionary,* 9th edition, 1998.
[3]Yasuhiro Monden, *Toyota Production System* (Norcross, GA: Industrial Engineering and Management Press, 1983), p. v.

the earlier processes in the production line as a kind of store. The later process (the customer) goes to the earlier process (the supermarket) to acquire the required parts (the commodities) at the time and in the quantity needed. The earlier process immediately produces the quantity just taken (restocking the shelves). We hoped that this would help us approach our just-in-time goal, and . . . we actually applied the system to our machine shop at the main plant.[4]

From this vision, the idea of just-in-time manufacturing was born. Initially, many North American managers felt that Toyota's approach could not succeed in the United States. However, the publication of a three-year study of worldwide automobile manufacturing[5] ended the debate about whether lean systems created real, lasting benefits. Table 8-1 shows that in the 1980s, Japanese-owned automotive plants following lean were as much as 30 percent more productive than U.S.–owned plants using traditional methods—quite a turnaround from the situation in the 1930s. Furthermore, the Japanese plants delivered cars with fewer defects using facilities that required less floor space and lower inventories. The data showed that the Japanese lean effect was significant, whether the plant was located in Japan or in the United States.

TABLE 8-1 Performance Characteristics for Lean Systems

	Japanese in Japan*	Japanese in North America	Americans in North America	All Europe
Performance				
Productivity (hours/vehicle)	100	126.19	149.40	215.48
Quality (assembly defects/100 vehicles)	100	108.33	137.17	161.67
Layout				
Space (sq. ft. / vehicle / yr.)	100	159.65	136.84	136.84
Size of repair areas (as % of assembly space)	100	119.51	314.63	351.22
Inventories (days for 8 sample parts)	100	800.00	1450.00	1000.00
Workforce				
% of workforce in teams	100	102.89	24.96	0.87
Job rotation (0 = none; 4 = freq.)	100	90.00	30.00	63.33
Suggestions/ Employee	100	2.27	0.65	0.65
# of job classes	100	73.11	563.87	124.37
Training of new production workers (hours)	100	97.29	12.20	45.57
Absenteeism	100	96.00	234.00	242.00
Automation				
Welding (% of direct steps)	100	98.61	88.40	88.86
Painting (% of direct steps)	100	74.54	61.54	69.96
Assembly (% of direct steps)	100	64.71	70.59	182.35

Source: James P. Womack, Daniel T. Jones, and Daniel Roos, *The Machine That Changed the World* (New York: Rawson Associates, 1990), p. 92.

*For these data, the Japanese plants represent the benchmark–they are set at 100. The numbers reflect the percentage that the other three systems performed at relative to the Japanese. For example, for productivity, we can see that the Japanese plants in North America need 26.19 percent more hours per car.

---

[4]William H. Davidow and Michael S. Malone, *The Virtual Corporation* (New York: Harper Business, 1992), pp. 119–20.

[5]J. P. Womack, D. T. Jones, and D. Roos, *The Machine That Changed the World* (New York: Rawson Associates, 1990).

Strategic Benefit of Lean Systems

The foregoing automotive comparison highlights the productivity and operational gains created by a lean approach. More importantly, lean can produce strategic benefits. As illustrated in Figure 8-3, by becoming lean a firm can significantly lower its break-even production quantity; that is, it can lower the minimum amount of output the firm needs to sell in order to make profit. Lean does this in two ways: by increasing the contribution margin (the difference between price and the firm's direct costs) and by reducing fixed overhead costs.

By eliminating wastes of all sorts in the system, the lean approach lowers variable production costs associated with labor, materials, and energy, thus raising the unit profitability of products. Since lean also emphasizes building exactly the products customers need, exactly when they need them, the contribution margin may also increase if the firm is able to charge higher prices. Lean also attacks waste associated with the fixed costs of facilities, equipment, capital, and support labor such as management, engineering, and so on. Together, improvements in the use of resources that affect both fixed and variable costs drive the production break-even point downward, enhancing the firm's flexibility. The firm can afford to produce smaller quantities, allowing niche marketing, and it can change outputs more quickly in response to changes in customer demand.

Lean Systems Objectives, Culture, and Guiding Principles

The objectives and principles of lean systems thinking are well established. They are to produce:

1. Only the products (goods and services) that customers want,
2. Only as quickly as customers want them,
3. With only features that customers want, and no others,
4. With perfect quality,
5. In the minimum possible lead times,
6. With no waste of labor, materials, or equipment, and
7. Using methods that reinforce the occupational development of workers.

FIGURE 8-3   Changes in Cost Structure under Lean Systems

Note that the first three objectives emphasize producing exactly what customers want just-in-time; that is, building products at the same rate that customers demand them. If operations managers can *synchronize* their production with demand (i.e., building at the same rate as customers demand the products), they can eliminate many sorts of waste (which are discussed later). Objectives 4–6 emphasize the quality, timeliness, and cost elements associated with creating value for customers. For the first three objectives to be met, operational processes and their personnel must embrace objectives 4 through 6 (since these objectives describe the desired traits of the products and the associated processes). The last objective reflects lean's greater emphasis on employees as the primary agents for improving operations. For operations to become flexible and responsive, employees closest to the underlying causes of waste and variance must become active problem solvers.

As stated earlier, a lean systems approach is not just a set of techniques; rather, it is a management philosophy that emphasizes the creation of value with the minimization of waste. To achieve the objectives identified above, lean is guided by important shared cultural beliefs and values, a common language, and five important principles:[6]

Principle 1. Precisely specify value for each specific product.

Principle 2. Identify the value stream for each product.

Principle 3. Make value flow without interruptions.

Principle 4. Let the customer pull value from the producer.

Principle 5. Pursue perfection.

Principle 1, "Precisely specify value for each specific product," maintains that the final consumer ultimately determines the value of a product or service. Consequently, the firm must engage in a dialogue with the consumers of its products and services to determine which outcomes, features, functions, and capabilities are most valuable. This dialogue provides the basis for continual improvement since it allows everyone to understand what attributes are valued and what attributes are "wasteful." As Henry Ford once noted, any action that does not generate value must ultimately be regarded as waste.

Principle 2, "Identify the value stream for each product," suggests that a firm must clearly understand and link together all of the activities involved in product development, order processing, production, and delivery. A strong value is placed on viewing and organizing these activities as processes within an overall system. Operations analysts often map out these processes in order to identify value-adding and non–value-adding steps. This type of analysis identifies different types of *muda* (the Japanese word for waste) in the process.

Waste is viewed as a symptom of problems elsewhere. Wastes of all kinds can usually be categorized into one of **seven basic types of waste** (see Table 8-2).[7]

seven basic types of waste
A classification of wastes into one of seven basic categories.

To reduce waste, workers must quantify its impact, uncover its underlying root causes, and then attack its root causes. For example, if inventory is too high, study the problem, uncover the root cause, and then attack it. As we can see from Table 8-2, high inventory (which is a symptom of overproduction) can be caused by several possible factors. If the root cause is long process setups, then the appropriate response is to attack setup time and cost. As workers begin to eliminate waste from internal value streams, they typically become aware of waste throughout the supply chain as well.

activity

student

See how many different wastes you can identify on your next visit to a doctor's office, hair salon, hotel, or restaurant.

Principle 3, "Make value flow without interruptions," means that the movements of materials and information in value streams should be swift and even. Sometimes operations managers use the saying, "Once in motion, always in motion" to characterize the ideal state of a

---

[6]J. P. Womack and D. T. Jones, *Lean Thinking* (New York: Simon and Schuster, 1996).

[7]These seven basic types of waste are foundational. Some managers have expanded the categories to include areas such as "underutilization of the problem-solving capabilities of employees."

TABLE 8-2   Seven Basic Types of Waste

Waste	Symptoms	Root Causes	
Overproduction (processing more units than needed)	• Extra inventory • Excessive floor space utilized • Unbalanced material flow • Complex information management • Disposal charges • Extra waste handling and treatment • High utility costs	• Product complexity • Misuse of automation • Long process setups • Unlevel scheduling • Overengineered equipment / capability • Lack of reuse and recycling • Poor market forecast	**waste of overproduction** Processing more units than are necessary.
Waiting (resources wasted waiting for work)	• Underutilization of resources • Reduced productivity • Increase in investment • Idle equipment • Large waiting / storage rooms • Equipment running, not producing • Unnecessary testing	• Unbalanced workload • Unplanned maintenance • Long process setup times • Misuse of automation • Unlevel scheduling • Ineffective layout • Too much specialization	**waste of waiting** Resources wasted waiting for work.
Transportation (units being unnecessarily moved)	• Extra handling equipment • Large storage areas • Overstaffing • Damaged product • Extra paperwork and hand-offs • Excessive energy consumption	• Mislocated materials • Unlevel scheduling • Unfavorable facility layout • Poor organization / housekeeping • Unbalanced processes	**transportation (move) waste** An activity that moves an input from one place to another without changing any of its other characteristics.
Processing (excessive or unnecessary operations)	• Extra equipment • Longer lead time • Reduced productivity • Extra material movement • Sorting, testing, inspection • Inappropriate use of resources • Excess energy consumption • Processing by-products	• Product changes without process changes • Just-in-case logic • Lack of communication • Redundant approvals and inspections • Undefined customer requirements • Stop-gap measures that become routine • Lack of reuse / recycling	**processing waste** Excessive or unnecessary operations.
Inventory (units waiting to be processed or delivered)	• Complex tracking systems • Extra storage and handling • Extra rework / hidden problems • Paperwork / documents • Stagnated information flow • High disposal costs • In-process packaging	• Just-in-case logic • Incapable processes (poor quality) • Unbalanced workload • Unreliable supplier shipments • Inadequate measurement and reward system	**inventory** A supply of items held by a firm to meet demand.
Motion (unnecessary or excessive resource activity)	• Reduced productivity • Large reach / walk distances • Excess handling • Reduced quality • People / machines waiting	• Poor ergonomics / layout • Machine / process design • Nonstandardized work methods • Poor organization / housekeeping	**waste of motion** Unnecessary or excessive resource activity.
Product defects (waste due to unnecessary scrap, rework, or correction)	• Rework, repairs, and scrap • Customer returns • Loss of customer confidence • Missed shipments / deliveries • Hazardous waste generation • High disposal costs	• Lack of process control and error-proofing • Deficient planned maintenance • Poor product design • Customer needs not understood • Improper handling • Inadequate training	**waste from product defects** Waste due to unnecessary scrap, rework, or correction.

"Picturing" Waste and Value: A Process Mapping Story

Process mapping (discussed in the Chapter 3 Supplement) is an invaluable tool for identifying waste. At one company, managers had every employee take pictures of every activity they performed. The pictures were used to create a pictorial flowchart. The chart surprised both the managers and the employees because the process involved over 1,100 steps. As the employees developed ways to eliminate each wasteful activity, they removed the photograph of that activity from the process flow collage and pinned it to a picture of a trashcan on another bulletin board. In this way the process improvement team was able to visually chart its progress as well as recognize those workers who had eliminated non–value-adding activities.

lean system. The key indicator that this state is attained is very little inventory. Inventory is often sitting still; therefore, it represents an interruption to material flows. Even worse, inventory often hides or covers other types of waste. This effect of inventory is illustrated in Figure 8-4, where the "rocks" below the surface represent problems and wastes. Too much inventory allows production to continue in spite of these problems, and consequently they are never addressed.

Excess inventory in a system often removes the urgency needed to identify and address problems created by root causes such as poor quality, long process setups, and unreliable machines. Inventory is sometimes used to protect the operation just in case these kinds of problems occur. Though this use of inventory may be unintentional, it nevertheless makes flow-interrupting problems difficult to find and solve. Process managers are likely to use inventory to satisfy shortages caused by problems and to worry about addressing the root causes of the problems later when they have time (which, in many situations, is never).

Inventory serves as a measure of the health of an operating system (just like a thermometer measures a patient's temperature). The more inventory needed for the system to work, the less healthy the system is. While using some inventory as a buffer against uncertainty makes sense in some cases, it can be overdone. In a service setting, excess capacity and increased lead times are often the buffers that hide problems. Inefficiencies in the system are hidden by having too many people and by allowing lengthy lead times.

Principle 4, "Let the customer pull value from the producer," is the source of the term, **pull system**. In a pull system, activities in operating processes are initiated by actual customer demands, not by schedules that are based on forecasts. In doing so, the process produces only what customers want, when they want it, and where they want it. The pull system approach is discussed later in this chapter in the section, "Kanban (Pull) Scheduling."

Principle 5, "Pursue perfection," suggests that continuous improvement is always possible. As long as workers are implementing the first four principles, they will always uncover more opportunities to improve processes and eliminate waste. A part of the lean

pull system Activities in the operating processes are initiated by actual customer demands, and not by forecasted demands.

FIGURE 8-4 Inventory Hides Operating Problems

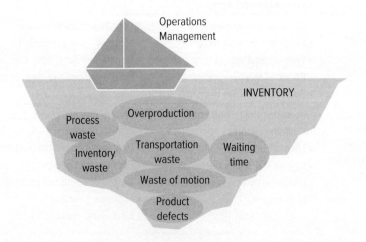

systems philosophy is the belief that everyone in the organization, from top managers to frontline workers, must be engaged in this ongoing effort to seek perfection.

Underlying the successful implementation of these five principles is the need for a **lean system culture**. The lean system culture places a high value on respect for people in the system. Employees must be empowered—given the training, tools, and authority to make continuous process improvements. Recall that the last major objective of lean systems is to produce "using methods that reinforce the occupational development of workers."

In the lean systems philosophy, employees are viewed as critical resources for success, for several reasons:

- *Acceptance:* Lean requires that everyone from top to bottom must buy into the goals and approaches underlying lean. Veteran employees must be willing to teach new employees the basics of lean through both words and actions.

- *Source of flexibility:* At the heart of lean is an emphasis on building the flexibility to respond directly to customers' demands (pull system). This type of flexibility depends on employees who are multiskilled and cross-trained, workers who can move quickly to fill constantly changing demand requirements.

- *Working in teams:* Lean places a high value on teamwork. Problems are best solved when representatives from different functional areas, suppliers, and customers work together in a team environment. Employees must be able and willing to work in teams.

- *Power in their hands:* More commonly referred to as **employee empowerment**, the responsibility for improving product quality and flow lies with the frontline workers who are the most familiar with the processes that must be improved. These employees have the power to stop work, for example, should they see instances of problems emerging in the system. Managers and engineers must be willing to trust and work with frontline workers in a partnership.

The lean system culture is based on certain shared values and beliefs. Of these beliefs, the following are the most important:

- *Manage with data.* Problems and solutions are identified, solved, and evaluated with data (quantitative, objective information). Data analysis replaces opinions, and the focus is placed on process performance rather than personal feelings.

- *Waste is a symptom.* Inventory and other visible forms of waste are never attacked directly. Rather, they are seen as the results of problems elsewhere.

- *Goals are to be met.* Managers must set realistic, achievable goals. The expectation is that everyone will meet their goals. It is management's role to find out how to help everyone meet their goals.

- *Standardization is fundamental to performance improvement.* Standardization highlights variation and abnormalities. It simplifies problem solving. Under lean, the motto is, "Without Standardization, There Is No Opportunity for Improvement."

- *Process orientation.* If you don't like the outcomes (the level of quality, the cost, the lead time), then you change the process. Lean involves attaining superior behavior by identifying the critical processes and changing them.

These values are inculcated into each person who works in a lean system. They become part of the belief structures that guide how everyone operates. It is important for managers to allow workers the time and social interactions needed to foster a lean culture.

IMPLEMENTING LEAN SYSTEMS: TOOLS AND TECHNIQUES

Along with a common culture and language, lean encourages a common view of work processes and improvement techniques. Table 8-3 classifies lean tools and techniques according to their areas of primary operational impact. Some of the tools work together synergistically. For example, a 5-S program is usually an essential prerequisite to a setup

lean system culture The culture that is present in lean systems and that places a high value on respect for people in the system.

employee empowerment Putting the responsibility for attacking waste with the employees directly involved in the processes.

LO8-2 Describe the cultural changes, tools, and techniques needed to implement a lean approach.

TABLE 8-3 Lean Systems Tools and Techniques

Area of Primary Impact		
Development of Facilities and Resources	**Operational Scheduling and Control**	**Continuous Process Improvement**
Total productive maintenance	TAKT time flow balancing	Quality at the source
Group technology	Kanban (pull) scheduling	Kaizen Events
Focused factories	Mixed model scheduling	Process analysis / Value stream mapping
	Setup reduction	Poka-yoke (fail-safing / mistake-proofing)
	Statistical process control	5-S program
	Visual control	Simplification / Standardization

reduction effort. Also note that there is a high degree of overlap between these tools and the procedures discussed in the quality improvement tools and techniques supplement to Chapter 6. Quality management programs and lean systems work well together.

Total Productive Maintenance (TPM)

total productive maintenance (TPM) The processes and systems that work to identify and prevent all possible equipment breakdown.

Equipment breakdowns create variance and costs within operational processes, not to mention user frustration (think about the frustration that an out-of-order sign can cause). Equipment failures, setups, processing speed losses, and quality defects often all can be traced to a lack of preventive maintenance. Total productive maintenance (TPM) works to identify and prevent all potential causes of breakdowns to achieve an ambitious goal of zero unplanned downtime. Typical TPM programs emphasize shop floor organization, disciplined adherence to operating procedures, rigorous equipment design and upkeep, and a focus on preventing problems rather than fixing them. In addition to manufacturing equipment, TPM can be applied to computer networks and automated service kiosks.

Group Technology—Cellular Manufacturing

group technology (GT) An approach to work layout and scheduling that gathers in one location all of the equipment and work skills necessary to complete production of a family of similar products.

In contrast to a functional layout (which puts the same types of equipment together in departments), or a product layout (which assigns workers to highly specialized, individual machines and tasks), group technology (GT) gathers in one location all of the equipment and work skills necessary for complete production of a family of similar products. Part families are created based on similarities in design features or in processing requirements. For each family, operations managers organize a work cell that lays out the equipment and facilities in the optimum sequence needed to build the items of the product family.

Focused Factories

focused factory Organizing operations systems by grouping together similar customers and then designing and implementing product systems to serve these specific customers.

The focused factory applies the same logic of group technology at the plant level. This approach reduces customer-induced variance by grouping together similar customers and then designing and implementing production systems (factories) to serve these specific customers (and no one else). The underlying logic is that a factory focused on a few specific tasks will outperform a factory that attempts to serve many disparate demands. A factory can be *market-focused,* supplying a range of products to customers with similar or complementary demand patterns and value propositions, or it can be *product-focused,* producing products that have similar technological processing requirements. Frequently, a "factory-within-a-factory" approach is used where two separate factories are housed

GET REAL

Applying the Focused Factory Idea to an Insurance Firm

Jefferson Pilot Insurance Company (a part of the Lincoln Financial Group) applied lean concepts to its application processing operations. Early on, managers noticed that differences in requirements created a high degree of variance in application processing times. One major difference in applications was that some required time-consuming attending physician statements, while others did not. The improvement team decided to create two processing lines, or "factories," one for each type of application. In this way, two steady moving streams of work were created. Fast-moving applications would no longer sit behind slow-moving applications waiting for physician statements. By making this change, along with other lean improvements, the company reduced application-processing time by 70–80 percent and overall labor costs by 26 percent.

within one overall building structure. Jefferson Pilot Insurance Company (as described in the nearby box) provides a good example of this approach in a service organization.

TAKT Time Flow Balancing

TAKT time flow balancing is a lean systems scheduling approach aimed at synchronizing the output rate with the rate of customer demand. *Takt* is a German word that means pace or rhythm of operations. Consider this example. Suppose that each week an insurance company has 33 hours of operating time to process an average of 100 applications submitted. This means that the company should adjust its capacity to process applications at a TAKT time rate of about three applications per hour, or one application every 20 minutes. In order to achieve this output, the company needs to balance its processing line and ensure that the bottleneck (slowest) operation in the overall process can work at least at this rate. Chapter 5 shows calculations for this type of line balancing.

> **TAKT time flow balancing** A scheduling approach aimed at synchronizing the output rate with the rate of customer demand.

Kanban (Pull) Scheduling

In keeping with the principle of letting customers pull value from the producer, the lean approach uses a scheduling system that can immediately and clearly communicate the demands of the customer to the delivery system. A **kanban (pull) scheduling** system does this. *Kanban* is the Japanese term for a signal. Kanbans are most often a system of control cards that govern material movements through a process. However, empty bins, colored golf balls, lights, or other types of items also have been used as kanban signals.

> **kanban (pull) scheduling** A scheduling system that builds output in response to actual customer demand.

A common approach uses two basic types of kanbans: *production kanbans* and *withdrawal kanbans* (also known as *conveyance kanbans*). A production kanban authorizes a worker to replenish an empty bin, specifying the type of parts and the number to build. When an empty bin arrives at a workstation with a production kanban attached, it is a signal to build a new batch of items to fill the bin. A withdrawal kanban authorizes someone to withdraw a standard amount of specific parts from a container. If a worker processing the job runs out of a part, the withdrawal kanban that accompanied the job gives that person the authority to take an empty bin to a replenishment area and to exchange it for a full bin.

These two kinds of kanbans control interactions between workstations such that no product is produced or withdrawn before it is needed at the downstream consuming work center. In a "push" system, by contrast, movements are controlled by a schedule that is based on forecasted demand and fixed operating times. Often, forecasted demands do not materialize and supposedly fixed operating times vary. Kanban scheduling provides the ability for the system to react to these uncertainties, as opposed to forcing movements according to a prearranged schedule. Further, the kanban system links work centers together in a way that eliminates the need for paperwork, complex computer technology, and order tracking. This aspect of the kanban system can be seen in the Get Real box "Using Kanbans to Schedule a Steel Mill."

Using Kanbans to Schedule a Steel Mill

The picture below shows a kanban system in use. Each cradle can store a steel coil; the cradles are organized by operation; the coils are organized in order of processing. Management can control the number of coils produced and stored by taping off the unneeded cradles. As we can see in this picture, a number of cradles are taped off. This tells everyone that we can produce steel coils until we reach the taped off cradles. At that point, we have to stop. Production is initiated as inventory is pulled, exposing open cradles; once these open cradles are filled, production stops. In this plant, the introduction of lean has resulted in a 50 percent reduction in lead times, improved on-time delivery, and a $5,000,000 per month improvement in profitability.

Source: www.handsongroup.com/articles-kanban.php3. The HANDS ON Group, 2009.

© The Hands-On Group, Inc. www.handsongroup.com.

Kanban (pull) scheduling can be effectively viewed as a complement to materials and requirements planning (MRP) systems (as discussed in Chapter 14). MRP tells the system what to produce and when the end items are needed; kanban determines the exact order and flow with which production is to be carried out.

Kanban pull scheduling can be contrasted with push scheduling, where a product is sent to the next stage of production or delivery irrespective of whether or not an actual demand for the product exists. Such deliveries are determined in advance by a schedule based on a forecast of demand or simply by the fact that the preceding operation has completed the item and wants to send it on. With push scheduling, line imbalances or bottlenecks become hidden because production still takes place even though there is no demand for it. With pull scheduling, process problems become immediately visible (and urgent) because activities stop and wait until more demand initiates production. This difference is one of the factors that makes pull scheduling so attractive to many managers (especially when lean is used).

push scheduling A system in which activities are initiated and products are moved according to a schedule, irrespective of whether or not the customer demands it.

Level, Mixed-Model Scheduling

An important goal in lean systems is to schedule work so that flows are smooth and predictable. Level, mixed-model scheduling, also known as heijunka, is the practice of leveling production of different product models over a period of time, with the goal of reducing batch sizes and lead times. It consists of two linked steps: load leveling and mixed-model scheduling. *Load leveling* is essentially a calculation of the average rate of production needed for each item based on the overall TAKT time. Then, one uses *mixed-model scheduling* to decide how to distribute the production of different products over the workday.

level, mixed-model scheduling The practice of leveling quantities of different product models produced over a period of time, with the goal of reducing batch sizes and lead times.

heijunka A form of level, mixed-model scheduling.

The level, mixed-model scheduling approach apportions batches of each product to be produced evenly throughout the day. For example, in a plant that produces four products, small production runs of product A, B, C, and D (ideally one unit in each run) are sequenced again and again throughout the day. The number of occurrences of each product in the schedule is proportional to its relative demand.

Level, mixed-model scheduling promotes the lean systems goal of simple flows through relatively simple methods. The technique offers a way to achieve swift, even response to market demand, simpler coordination of supply because consumption is at a constant rate, more consistent production learning, and minimal inventories.

Setup Reduction

In order for level, mixed-model schedules to be efficient, changeovers required to switch from one product to the next must be minimized. In general, setup reduction lowers changeover times and costs and makes it possible to produce outputs in smaller batch sizes more efficiently. Chapter 7, shows this relationship mathematically.

Setup reduction efforts usually involve process mapping and analysis to identify steps that can be eliminated, executed faster, or done in parallel. Think about the ways that a pit crew works together to execute extremely fast tire changes and refueling for race cars. Operations managers in factories and service centers similarly make use of careful planning, process analysis, good housekeeping, specialized training, tooling and technologies, and teamwork to make setups faster.

The most commonly used approach for setup reduction is that of single minute exchange of dies (SMED). This is a systematic three-stage procedure for reducing long setups:

- *Stage 1: Separate internal and external setups.* An *internal setup* includes any setup procedure that occurs while the equipment sits idle. In contrast, an *external setup* is any setup activity that workers complete while the equipment operates.
- *Stage 2: Convert internal setups to external setups.* Again, this is done by examining the flow process chart and developing a new process.
- *Stage 3: Streamline all activities in a setup.* This stage tries to eliminate any activities performed to make adjustments, calibrations, elaborate positioning, unnecessary tightening, or trial runs.

> **setup reduction** The processes used to reduce setup and changeover times with the goal of making output of smaller batches more efficient.

> **single minute exchange of dies (SMED)** A systematic three-stage procedure for reducing long setups.

Statistical Process Control

Statistical process control (SPC) makes use of various statistical tools for analyzing the capabilities of a given process and for monitoring its performance. The essential goal of SPC is to put controls in place that help ensure the quality of production and give quick notice when unusual events occur that might lead to product or service defects. SPC tools are discussed in greater detail in the Chapter 6 Supplement, "Quality Improvement Tools."

> **statistical process control (SPC)** The use of various statistical tools to analyze the capabilities of a given process and monitor its performance, with the goal of flagging potential problems before they occur.

> **visual control** Making current performance and potential problems immediately visually apparent.

> **quality at the source** The practice of eliminating defects at their root cause origination points.

Visual Control

Visual control is like SPC in that its goal is to immediately make the status of an operation visible and continuously updated for all interested parties. Bulletin boards, SPC charts, large electronic displays, and lighting systems are some of the means used to make real-time performance metrics available to large numbers of people. The nearby Get Real box that provides an example of an andon board illustrates one form of visual control. Visual control reduces waste by reducing reaction time and maintaining a sense of urgency.

Mobile technologies are creating new opportunities for visual control. With devices like the iPad or the Android-based tablet, firms are introducing new ways of interacting with operations data. Previously, a worker might have had to look at fixed computer screens or process boards in different locations to see what was taking place. Now, common procedures can be stored (with accompanying videos) and real-time status reports can be obtained on wireless, handheld devices. With such devices, workers need fewer resources and less lead time to identify, diagnose, and solve problems. Mobile access to information is changing the shop floor, transportation, and operations all across the supply chain.

© Joshua Hodge Photography/Getty Images

Quality at the Source

Quality at the source (often abbreviated as Q@S) is an emphasis on eliminating defects at their origination points. Ensuring quality at the source

GET REAL

Example of Visual Control in Action: Andon Board

Lines 1 and 3 indicate machines; lines 2 and 4 indicate what is taking place. For example, from this figure, we can see that machines 1C, 8, 9, 14, and 17 are experiencing problems, with quality control (QC) being the issue at 1C, 9, and 17. From this andon board, the entire operations system and its status is immediately evident to the manager.

Source: www.pcmsigns.com/andon2.htm.

Source graphic: www.salescaster.com.

reduces the potential for quality problems downstream, because the quality of the outputs of later stages of production depends substantially on the quality of their inputs. Three techniques are often associated with quality at the source: jidoka, stop-and-fix (or line-stop) systems, and andons (trouble lights).

Jidoka

jidoka A focus on developing technological features of equipment and processes that automatically detect and flag problems.

Japanese for *autonomation,* jidoka represents a focus on developing technological features of equipment and processes that automatically detect and flag problems while the systems run. For example, a limit switch on a machine might monitor the contents of a feeding bin and either light a signal or sound a tone when the bin becomes nearly empty, alerting the operator to refill it.

Stop-and-Fix (Line-Stop) Systems

stop-and-fix (or line-stop) system The practice by which an operator should stop the process and immediately fix problems, rather than allowing it to continue making poor-quality output.

A stop-and-fix (or line-stop) system works on the simple premise that an operator should stop the process and immediately fix any significant problem that arises, rather than allowing it to continue making poor-quality output. Besides guarding against low quality, such a system brings focused attention to the source of the problem because its failure has shut down the process in a highly visible and immediate way, perhaps disrupting other operations that depend on the problem activity.

Andons (Trouble Lights)

andons (trouble lights) The use of visual indicator systems such as flashing lights to help management assess current performance and quickly identify the location of current problems.

Programs to enhance quality at the source may rely on visual signals to identify the exact locations of problems in the system. Lean systems often combine these andons (trouble lights) with jidoka and stop-and-fix systems to make problems highly visible, allowing workers to develop visual control of a process. We can see an example of an andon system in the Get Real box.

Kaizen Event A short-term (i.e., lasting one week or less) approach to enhancing efficiency that focuses on improving an existing process or an activity within a process.

Kaizen Events

A Kaizen Event is a short-term project (usually one to four days) aimed at improving an existing process. In that time period, cross-functional team members document a process,

Using an Andon Board to Spot a Problem

This andon board is used to help management assess the performance of a five-line plant. This board gives management a lot of useful information. It tells management what the output target is, what each line is doing, and if any line(s) is experiencing problems. From this board, we can see that lines 2 and 4 are under control, lines 1 and 5 are running slow (indicated by the yellow), and line 3 has stopped. Because line 3 has stopped, this is where management should focus its attention.

Source: www.london-electronics.com/andon-displays.php.

assess different options for performance, and develop and document the implemented process changes. This highly focused effort emphasizes fast action improvements, verifiable measures of improvement, and disciplined documentation of the ideas to be used in future improvement efforts.

Critical to the success of the Kaizen Event is gemba kaizen, briefly mentioned at the beginning of this chapter. The term *gemba* (meaning "actual place") emphasizes the notion that managers and employees are obligated to see the problems and issues in person, rather than relying on reports. They must travel to where the problems are taking place. This may sound expensive, but a lean systems belief is that these expenses will pay off in terms of faster and higher-quality problem solving. More information about Kaizen Events is found in Chapter 3, "Managing Processes and Capacity."

> gemba kaizen Managers and employees are obligated to see the problems and issues in person rather than relying on reports.

Process Analysis/Value Stream Mapping

Process analysis/value stream mapping is a graphic mapping technique (as discussed in Chapter 3 and the Chapter 3 Supplement) that helps managers understand the material and information flows as a product makes its way through the process. Value stream mapping also considers factors such as capacity, quality, and variability. One of the major metrics/outputs of a value stream mapping exercise is to identify the percentage of the total lead time that is value-adding.

Value stream mapping generates two different process maps. The first is the "current state" map, which describes the value stream as it currently exists. Figure 8-5 presents an example of such a map. The second is the "future state" map. This map lays out the revised process designed to increase the percentage value metric by identifying and eliminating any non–value-adding steps in the process.

> process analysis/value stream mapping A graphical technique that helps managers understand material and information flows as a product makes its way through the process.

Poka-Yoke

To produce perfect quality the first time and every time, managers and workers must develop processes and systems that make performing tasks correctly every time easy and inevitable. The Japanese term poka-yoke (also known as *fail-safing* or *mistake-proofing*) indicates an emphasis on redesigning processes in such a way as to make mistakes either impossible or immediately apparent to the worker. For example, before giving medicines or blood, a nurse checks bar codes on the item and on the patient's bracelet to ensure that the patient is receiving the right treatment.

> poka-yoke (foolproofing) An emphasis on redesigning processes in such a way as to make mistakes either impossible or immediately apparent to the worker.

FIGURE 8-5 Value Stream Mapping: An Example of a Current State Map

[Figure 8-5: Value stream mapping current state map diagram showing flow from Michigan Steel Co. through Production Control, MRP, Weekly Schedule, and processes STAMPING (200 T), S. WELD #1, S. WELD #2, ASSEMBLY #1, ASSEMBLY #2, SHIPPING to State Street Assembly]

- Michigan Steel Co.
- 6-week Forecast
- PRODUCTION CONTROL
- Weekly Fax
- MRP
- 500-ft. coils
- 90/60/30 day Forecasts
- State Street Assembly
- Daily Order
- 18,400 pcs./mo.
  - −12,000 "L"
  - −6,400 "R"
  - Tray = 20 pieces
  - 2 Shifts
- Weekly Schedule
- Daily Ship Schedule
- Tues. + Thurs.
- 1x Daily

STAMPING 200 T	S. WELD #1	S. WELD #2	ASSEMBLY #1	ASSEMBLY #2	SHIPPING Staging
1	1	1	1	1	

- Coils 5 days
- 4600 L / 2400 R
- 1100 L / 600 R
- 1600 L / 850 R
- 1200 L / 640 R
- 2700 L / 1440 R

STAMPING	S. WELD #1	S. WELD #2	ASSEMBLY #1	ASSEMBLY #2
C/T = 1 second	C/T = 39 seconds	C/T = 46 seconds	C/T = 62 seconds	C/T = 40 seconds
C/O = 1 hour	C/O = 10 minutes	C/O = 10 minutes	C/O = Ø	C/O = Ø
Uptime = 85%	Uptime = 100%	Uptime = 80%	Uptime = 100%	Uptime = 100%
27,600 sec. avail.	2 Shifts	2 Shifts	2 Shifts	2 shifts
EPE = 2 weeks	27,600 sec. avail.	27,600 sec. avail.	27,600 sec. avail.	27,600 sec. avail.

- 5 days — 1 second
- 7.6 days — 39 seconds
- 1.8 days — 46 seconds
- 2.7 days — 62 seconds
- 2 days — 40 seconds
- 4.5 days

Production Lead Time = 23.6 days
Processing Time = 188 sec.

sustainability

5-S Program

Effective housekeeping is an important discipline in lean systems. It prevents wastes of waiting and inventory by reducing the chances of lost tools, equipment breakdowns, and damaged goods. One popular housekeeping program is known as the **5-S program**. The term *5-S* refers to the first letters of the five Japanese words that describe the five major activities. Table 8-4 shows the Japanese words along with their English counterparts and

5-S program A systematic program for effective housekeeping in operational processes.

TABLE 8-4 Major Activities of the 5-S Program (and Its Variants)

5-S Elements (Japanese)	5-S Elements (English)	The 5-C Campaign	Intent
Seiri	Sort	Clear out	Red tag suspected unnecessary items. After a monitoring period, throw out unnecessary items.
Seiton	Straighten	Configure	Put everything in an orderly fashion so that it can be located—"a place for everything and everything in its place." This is frequently done using "footprinting," which creates a painted outline for each item.
Seiso	Scrub	Clean and check	Clean everything and eliminate the sources of dirt.
Seiketsu	Systematize	Conform	Make cleaning and checking routine. Set the standard, train and maintain.
Shitsuke	Standardize	Custom and practice	Standardize the previous four steps into one process and continuously improve it. Use visual control through performance boards, checklists, and graphs.

a *5-C* equivalent program that is used in some companies. Some managers have added a sixth S to the list of 5-S activities—Safety. Safety has always been an important part of social responsibility for operations managers.

Simplification/Standardization

In lean systems, simplification and standardization are means used to reduce lead time and process variances of all sorts. *Simplification* focuses on eliminating non–value-added activities in a process. *Standardization* is aimed at clarifying and documenting the steps in a process so that they are executed exactly the same way every time by every worker.

simplification and standardization An emphasis on eliminating non–value-adding process steps and executing process steps in exactly the same way each time by every worker.

LEAN SYSTEMS: RANGE OF APPLICATION

Table 8-5 describes the level of adoption and application of the lean approach in a number of different business environments. Lean has been applied in many manufacturing companies across many industrial settings. It has become the dominant manufacturing paradigm around the world. Service companies have also adopted a *lean services* approach, especially for services that involve the repeated processing of similar jobs, such as logistics services, airlines, banks, insurance firms, call centers, software development, hospitals, and law offices. Tools such as 5-S, visual control, pull systems, and poka-yoke (mistake-proofing) have been successfully applied in service environments.

Applying Lean Systems within the Firm

The application of lean systems needs to move beyond the shop floor in order to produce maximum benefits. In the most successful firms, all functions have adopted lean principles. The lean approach requires tight coordination of marketing, sales, and operations to increase communication and decrease order processing lead times. Some firms have achieved this coordination by creating integrated product teams responsible for marketing, sales, design, production, and distribution. Importantly, marketing managers must reassess promotional programs and sales incentives that can create large swings (high variance) in demand, as these shifts are inconsistent with the lean approach.

Human resources practices for recruitment and selection, training, and performance evaluation and compensation must reflect the goals of lean. Though the lean approach tends to empower workers, not all potential workers desire to work in a lean environment. Recruitment and selection must strive to hire engaged, self-motivated employees who have a strong interest in solving problems through process innovation. Employees must also be able to work effectively with others in teams. In addition, the design of training programs needs to be driven by lean objectives.

relationships

TABLE 8-5   The Extent of Lean Systems Applications

Operational Setting	Level of Lean Systems Application
In manufacturing	Heavy adoption
In services	Growing adoption
Within firms	Heavy adoption and application
Across supply chains	Growing application
In execution activities	Mature application
In design activities	Early application
In stable business environments	Optimal application
In moderately dynamic business environments	Application with some buffers
In turbulent business environments	Very limited application

Applying Lean Systems Across the Supply Chain

LO8-3 Recognize the strengths and limitations of lean systems.

Managers have also extended lean concepts to supply chain management. However, applications of the lean approach across the supply chain have experienced a mix of benefits and problems. In stable environments, lean can enhance the performance of the supply chain by reducing lead times (thus making the supply chain more responsive to customer demands), improving quality, reducing cost, and improving customer service. Many companies have deployed lean techniques jointly with their suppliers and customers, including Toyota, John Deere, Honda, Harley-Davidson Motorcycles, Nissan, Dell, Apple, Hewlett-Packard, Nike, SYSCO (food products), Cisco (IT), Gap/Limited (clothing), Walmart, and Boeing.

Lean supply chains strive to eliminate the need for inventory, lead time, and capacity buffers. This is best achieved if suppliers and customers work together as partners in streamlining the system. Visibility plays an important role. Partners must work together to develop an environment where suppliers can "see" into their customers' operations, and vice versa. This visibility enables the partners to better understand each other's needs and capabilities, so they can be more responsive with higher quality. Finally, lean supply chains require close coordination of processes and tight integration of the transportation system to ensure the constant flow of materials and information between supply chain partners. Applying lean principles to supply chain relationships leads to the following prescriptions:

global

- Buy to achieve the lowest total cost (as compared to the lowest unit price).
- Keep distances between partners short (in the case of Toyota, this has been restated as "buy in the country where manufacturing is performed").
- Minimize the number of suppliers.
- When a problem occurs, treat the problem as a symptom and focus on what in the supply chain processes could have contributed to the emergence of that problem.
- Work with your suppliers and not against them; the firm is only as strong as the weakest supplier.

The lean supply chain produces benefits, yet it can also open up risks. Since lean supply chains are more tightly linked and have reduced buffers (in the form of excess capacity, inventory, and lead time), a problem that takes place anywhere in the supply chain can quickly and negatively affect the entire supply chain. A strike at a supplier's plant could starve the rest of the supply chain; a hurricane that destroys roads and rails can prevent shipments; a lightning storm can disrupt communications, preventing a critical order from being scheduled. Being lean can make a company more susceptible to these types of events. Additional examples are presented in Table 8-6. When protection from buffers is reduced to the lowest levels, the resulting supply chain becomes fragile; that is, when a breakdown occurs, then the supply chain stops performing. This concept is also discussed in Chapter 10, "Sourcing and Supply Management."

Applying Lean Systems to Product Innovation

LO8-4 Apply the concept of lean systems to product design.

Lean concepts can also be applied to product and process engineering and innovation. Choices made in product and process design have huge effects on the potential to achieve lean objectives. Engineers must ensure that product designs exploit any possible commonalities in processing methods or components, as these commonalities reduce the need for setups.

lean design The application of lean principles and tools to the task of designing products.

Lean design applies lean principles and tools to the task of designing products. Lean design has three major goals:

- Design products that exactly meet customers' needs (i.e., to generate real value).
- Design products that support corporate strategic objectives and that meaningfully differentiate the firm and its products from those offered by the competition.
- Design products that reduce/minimize the opportunities for waste.

Just as lean thinking seeks to reduce waste in operations, lean design seeks to reduce opportunities for product design waste. Table 8-7 lists some of the types of waste that can be reduced in lean design.

TABLE 8-6   Types of Events Causing Problems for Lean Supply Chains

Category of Event	Examples	Real World
Operational/Technological	Forecast errors Capacity constraints IT disruptions	Nike—A glitch in planning software in 2000 caused a shortage of Air Jordans. Boeing 787, 2008—A new lean process allowed very little time for startup issues and other problems.
Social	Labor strikes Sabotage	A strike at West Coast ports in 2002 starved many manufacturing plants and retail stores.
Natural/Hazard	Fire, flood, monsoon, earthquake	Japan—On March 12, 2011, an earthquake and tsunami severely impacted production and supply (especially in the computer industry). Thailand—In March/April 2011, severe flooding delayed deliveries to companies such as Nikon, Sony, and Seagate.
Economy/Competition	Interest rate fluctuations Bankruptcy of supply partners	In 2008, logistics firms encountered problems due to increasing fuel prices.
Legal/Political	Lawsuits, wars, border customs, regulations	Mattel Toys and lead paint in toys—In November 2007, lead was found in the paint used on Fischer-Price, Barbie, Polly Pockets, Batman, and Cars toys; too little time was allowed to respond to problems.

TABLE 8-7   Reducing the Opportunity for Product Design Waste

Seven Wastes in Product Design	What Does It Mean?
Complexity	Many different processes; high quantity required to deliver the product's value both on the factory floor and in the customer's use.
Precision	Product design requires precision at the outer limits of our ability to produce the product or the customer's ability to use it.
Variability	Product specifications make it difficult to control processes on the factory floor, within our supply base, or in the customer's domain.
Sensitivity	Product design results in a situation where the resulting product can be easily flawed or damaged during factory operations (either internally or within the supply base) or in the customer's domain.
Immaturity	The use of the solution found within the product design has not been previously validated for a specific application (we are not sure whether the solution offered by the product design is either valid or valued by the customer).
Danger	The use of the product design may unintentionally expose users or the environment to potentially dangerous impacts.
High skill	The product design requires processes or components that demand high degrees of training and experience (either within our internal factory or within our suppliers' operations).

Product innovation can be radical or incremental. Radical innovations sometimes make existing business models and products obsolete. For example, innovations such as the ballpoint pen, compact discs, jet engines, digital photography, and antibiotics all made their predecessors obsolete. Lean design approaches are most compatible with incremental innovation.

To be successful, radical innovation depends on unfettered idea generation with lots of exploration and testing. Employees are encouraged to generate as many new ideas as possible using new and different approaches and processes (something that runs counter to the strong emphasis on standardization found in lean systems). Furthermore, radical innovation demands the presence of slack—excess and unused resources. Slack is needed to free up time for outside-the-box idea generation, for debugging, to absorb the impact of innovation failures (not every idea works), and for pursuing unexpected opportunities. The radical innovation approach can be seen as "wasteful" from a lean perspective, because a primary goal of lean is to reduce slack.

Recognizing that a lean environment may not be consistent with the needs and demands of radical innovation raises an important fact of operations management. Not every system, such as lean systems and total quality management systems, works well in all settings. The task facing every operations manager is to identify the demands that must be satisfied and pick the system that works best in that setting.

CHAPTER SUMMARY

Lean systems and techniques have now become integral to operations and supply chain management in many industries. In this chapter, we have examined many of the concepts, management tools, and developments associated with these systems. The following are some of the major issues raised in this chapter:

1. Lean systems is a corporatewide approach that works to continuously identify, control, and eliminate all sources of waste both within the firm and across the supply chain. This requires that variance at all levels of the firm be eliminated.

2. The lean approach has seven major objectives: produce only what customers want, at the rate that customers want it, with only the features that customers want, with perfect quality, with minimum lead times, without wasting resources, and with methods that support people's development.

3. Workers implementing lean systems use many tools to reduce variance and waste. These tools work together synergistically and are highly consistent with quality improvement tools.

4. In order to be most successful, firms should expand lean thinking and the lean culture across functions within the firm and with partners across the supply chain.

5. The lean approach is not universally applicable. It is less successful in turbulent business environments, and it is not conducive to radical innovation.

1. While Taiichi Ohno was impressed by certain aspects of the Ford Production System, he was bothered by other aspects. These included: large, special-purpose equipment; a focused, specialized workforce; and an ever-driving emphasis on cost efficiency. Why are these aspects inconsistent with lean?

2. Figure 8-4 illustrates the analogy of a boat hitting rocks as the water level falls. Why is water a good analogy for inventory? Is the sequence in which rocks are encountered a good way to prioritize inventory reduction activities? How might this prioritization scheme differ from one used in an accounting department?

3. Why is achievement of the following goals critical to the success of lean systems?
   a. Setup time and cost reduction.
   b. A relatively stable shop load.
   c. Employee empowerment.
   d. Statistical quality control.

   Give an example of how each area contributes to the success of a lean system.

4. You work in the marketing department of a firm that sells mountain bicycles and related gear. Its manufacturing division has decided to wholeheartedly adopt the lean systems philosophy. Will this affect your ability to delight your customers? Make a list of the potential pluses and minuses of this lean systems decision.

5. Discuss how lean systems might apply to a fast-food hamburger stand. How will it have to be modified to deal with daily demand variation?

6. Using the discussion of lean design, consider the design of an iPod competitor. Give examples of each of the following design wastes:

   - Complexity
   - Precision
   - Immaturity
   - Danger
   - High skill

7. What would happen if you tried to introduce a new strategy based on radical innovation into an organization in which the lean culture has been wholeheartedly adopted?

8. How would a restaurant use the 5-S program? How would an operating room use this program?

9. Why should you *not* include setup times when calculating the TAKT times?

10. What is the relationship between bottlenecks and TAKT time?

11. One lean systems' consultant has stated that, "Without standardization, there can be no improvement." Explain the reasoning behind this statement.

12. Can lean systems enhance a worker's quality of life? Discuss the pros and cons from an employee's point of view.

13. Where would you most successfully apply lean systems principles, during the introductory or growth stages of the product life cycle?

14. Can a supply chain ever be *too* lean? What would happen to the supply chain if an unexpected disruption/interruption were to occur? How might you as a supply chain manager reduce the effects of such an unexpected disruption, while staying consistent with the lean approach?

15. Imagine that your customer base is located in North America and your suppliers are located in China. Is it possible to implement lean supply chain management under such conditions? What are the challenges now facing the firm?

CASE

Good Guy Hospital Supply

Good Guy Hospital Supply (GGHS) was founded in the 1960s to serve the hospital and nursing home industry. Since then, its sales have grown an average of 26 percent per year, through both geographical expansion and increased existing-market penetration. Key to GGHS's success is service. It prides itself that it is able to fill 99.4 percent of all requests within 24 hours, and many requests actually are delivered more quickly. Recently, GGHS's quality service coordinator developed a plan to improve service levels. The new system uses a just-in-time approach to the medical supply needs of GGHS's clients. GGHS's clients had been using personal computers in their hospital medical supply stockrooms to place GGHS orders. While these clients could still purchase from other supply houses, the GGHS order entry system made it much easier for the clerical staff to place an order with GGHS. The new JIT plan, however, eliminates supplies going through GGHS's clients' medical supply stockrooms. Now the medical facility's staff and GGHS will determine the type and desired level of supplies at each stocking point. GGHS plans to place supplies at each of these stocking points; and a GGHS sales representative will tour the medical facility, identify items that have been used, and immediately restock them using inventory in the sales representative's van. Using bar coded stock and a mobile sales register, GGHS will give the hospital a detailed invoice for the items consumed each day. These reports will be designed to support each facility's medical cost control system.

GGHS's quality service coordinator argues that the increased distribution costs of this proposed system will be offset by increased product and service pricing and by the increased share of each hospital's business and that GGHS will become the vendor of choice for all items covered by its system. She argues that the hospitals will find this system attractive because it will greatly reduce their costs for stocking, ordering, and distributing medical supplies within the medical facility.

1. Is Good Guy's plan an appropriate application of JIT? Why, or why not?

2. Identify each of the stakeholders in this situation. What will each give up and get if the proposed system is accepted by GGHS's clients?

CASE

Purchasing at Midwestern State University

Jane Polski, the newly hired director of university purchasing, took one final look at the report from her purchasing manager, removed her glasses, and rubbed the bridge of her nose. Surely, she thought, things could not be that bad. According to the report, which she had commissioned, the centralized ordering process at Midwestern State University was simply "out of control." Various academic departments that placed orders through the purchasing system had complained that orders were often lost. Furthermore, the amount of time that it took for an order to be filled was difficult to predict. For example, the chemistry department had placed an order for two identical mass spectrometers, separated by three weeks. The first one took two weeks to arrive; seven months later the second order was still unfilled. Orders were often incorrectly entered. When this occurred, if the ordering department did not want to accept the incorrect order and if the item could not be returned (something that often happened because the items ordered were unique), the purchasing department was obligated to assume responsibility for the ordering error. A separate budget category had been set up for this problem (last year, it accounted for over 10 percent of total costs). Once a year, the purchasing department sold off all the misordered items—often at a significant loss. Finally, university personnel complained that, when they called the purchasing department to identify the status of an order, no one seemed to know how to locate it.

This was bad, and Jane knew that she had to do something—that was one reason that she was hired—to significantly improve operations within the purchasing department. Midwestern University had grown tremendously in the number of programs it offered. It had been decided some 40 years ago to centralize purchasing activities in one department (previously, each unit managed its own purchases). The reason for this decision was to reduce costs and improve operating and acquisition efficiencies. The current department was staffed by some 40 buyers, planners, and clerks. Most of these people had little or no prior professional purchasing experience. Furthermore, many had little more than a high school education. Most of them saw their jobs as consisting mainly of simply placing orders. With the growth in technology and the rapid changes taking place in academic research, placing orders efficiently was becoming more difficult. Systems that had worked before were not working well now.

Jane had commissioned a series of purchasing team meetings aimed at identifying areas of possible improvement. As she reviewed the report, she noted the following issues uncovered by the team:

- The department had more than 6,000 different forms. Many of the forms were developed by individual buyers for their own uses.

- The forms were difficult to complete since critical terms were often undefined and were thus interpreted in different ways.

- The department lacked a standard approach to processing orders. Workers often felt that they had many "exceptional" items to purchase that required special processing. These exceptions were not well documented.

- Except for notification of when the orders were filled, there was little contact with the customers once the request for an order was submitted.

- Department performance was evaluated in terms of utilization and cost—the percentage of the staff time devoted to receiving and processing orders.

- Every buyer processed orders differently. For example, one buyer tended to place all orders on the last day of the week, while another worked on each order to completion as soon as it arrived.

- Orders were typically worked on in the order received without any consideration of urgency or importance.

There were other issues, but Jane knew that she had enough to start devising a plan for change. The question was, where to start?

Jane is considering the application of lean services in this department. To help her, she needs the following questions addressed:

1. What should the desired outcome (objective) for this department be? How does the purchasing department create value?

2. Purchasing personnel feel that since Midwestern State University is a public, rather than private, institution, they really do not deal with customers. What is your assessment of this view? Why?

3. What measures should be used to evaluate the performance of this department?

4. Evaluate the suitability of lean services in this department.

5. What lean tools and procedures would you suggest Jane introduce into this department? Why?

CASE

Western Telephone Manufacturing

It was a tough year for Western Telephone Manufacturing (WTM) of Canton, Michigan. Until this year, WTM had been the darling of Wall Street. This company had become one of the first to wholly embrace the concepts of Six Sigma and Total Quality Management. Management had invested significantly in Six Sigma. Every employee had been trained in the tools and application of Six Sigma; an internal consulting group (Operational Services, or the OS Group, as it was referred to internally) was established to support these efforts. Furthermore, management had decided to complement its Six Sigma efforts with the implementation of lean principles and practices.

As a result, WTM had transformed itself completely over a 15-year period. Prior to the "journey" (how people at WTM referred to the process of implementing Six Sigma and Lean), quality was poor (field reports indicated that between 10 to 12 percent of all telephones produced failed in the field on initial usage by the customer, as compared to 2 to 4 percent failure rates for the competition); lead times were long (about 20 percent longer than the competition); and costs were high (a WTM telephone cost about 12 percent more than the competition). Eventually, WTM became the leader in cost control, quality (with failure rates running less than 1 percent per million), and lead times. At the heart of this quality storm was the Messiah of Six Sigma, Ted Hendrix, who also happened to be WTM's CEO.

To understand WTM's, success, all that was needed was a simple visit to any one of its manufacturing operations. Everywhere you would see posters encouraging employees to do a better job:

- Without standardization, there is no opportunity for improvement.
- First time, every time, right—that is the goal.
- You are at the heart of Quality.
- Our customers want products that work; not products that fail.
- Attack slack.
- Attack waste in every form that it appears.
- Perfect Quality—not simply a goal but what the customer expects.

Consistent with this emphasis, Ted had instituted a program that measured and monitored cost savings closely and regularly. To be promoted at WTM, it was widely recognized that you had to participate in the various programs, and you had to show that you could identify and implement projects that reflected the Six Sigma goals and that generated verifiable and significant cost savings ($25,000 over a one-year period for a Green Belt and $100,000 over a one-year period for a Black Belt). All management candidates for promotion had to generate at least 10 quarters of above average performance (i.e., actual costs were less than standard costs by a minimum of 10 percent).

Ted Hendrix was known for the quirky things he did to ensure that everyone at WTM knew the importance of Six Sigma and Lean. It was not unusual for Ted to show up in a plant where he would recognize an employee for efforts "above and beyond the call of duty." Such employees were designated as "Six Sigma Samurai." They also received a free one-week vacation for themselves and their families to anywhere in the United States, a check for $1,000 (for spending money), and a Japanese samurai sword (a Katana). Their pictures would be taken and posted in the Six Sigma Hall of Fame at corporate headquarters. Finally, and most importantly, they could expect to be on the fast track for promotion.

Until two years ago, this approach appeared to be working: WTM stock prices were above the industry average;

many business magazines had printed feature articles about WTM; cases on WTM and its journey with Six Sigma had been written and published by prestigious business schools. Then, technological innovation hit WTM. Wireless systems, Skype, cellular systems, and cloud computing were causing companies like WTM to rethink the role played by their systems—a role that was continuously changing as new technology emerged.

After hiring a major consulting company to carry out a project focusing on the future of the telephone receiver and then receiving its report, Ted Hendrix had decided that for WTM to survive into the next 20 years, the emphasis on quality had to be replaced by an emphasis on product and technological innovation and responsiveness. Innovation, Ted had decided, was the new mantra for WTM.

Consequently, Ted went around to the various plants to discuss the need for innovation. He spent time with plant management and with the employees discussing why cost and quality were no longer enough and why innovation was so important. With the support of the board of directors and his top management team, Ted made a number of highly visible changes at WTM:

- Extensive training in product innovation was carried out.
- Employees were exposed to presentations from such well-known innovation companies as GE Transport, Procter & Gamble, 3M, Apple, and Netflix.
- A new program of grants aimed at encouraging investment in innovation (and known as the WTM Innovation Grant, or WIG) was introduced.
- A new Research and Development Center was introduced at Michigan State University. This center was to work with certain faculty in North America with the goal of introducing truly new and radical innovations in telephone technology.
- Changes were made in the performance measurement scheme. Specifically, a new metric, percentage of revenue generated from products less than three years old, was introduced.

Finally, Ted tried to ensure that everyone understood the new mantra at WTM. It was no longer "Lean and Mean" but rather "Fast and New." After calling numerous consultants to review the changes made, Ted felt that WTM was now poised to become the innovator in this business.

Reality, however, has not fulfilled management expectations. Specifically, the personnel, who have always felt comfortable with Six Sigma and Lean, were distressed by the new emphasis on innovation. New, innovative products were experiencing in-field failure rates around

5 percent—well in excess of the current failure rates of less than 0.0001 percent. When WTM delayed the launch of these products so that it could drive out the root causes of the failure, it was often beaten to the market by competitors. Consequently, WTM had to be satisfied with accepting lower prices (even though its development costs were just as high as those of the competition). Employees felt comfortable with the predictability of Lean and Six Sigma; they were frustrated by the lack of predictability of innovation. Telephones that everyone at WTM thought were going to be winners often turned up being losers. Finished goods inventory went up; costs were also beginning to creep up. When a winner did occur, WTM often found itself unable to respond fast enough to the increase in demand.

In frustration, the workers at one plant went on strike. Their grievance was that management was now preventing them from doing their jobs with this new emphasis on innovation. Corporatewide grumbling with this new shift in strategy was also heard; many argued that there were still numerous opportunities for Six Sigma and Lean to do their magic; the emphasis on innovation, consequently, was seen as being premature.

As Ted Hendrix surveyed the state of WTM, he was not assured by what he saw. He saw a company experiencing real difficulties in bringing new technology to the market. What really frustrated Ted was that he knew that WTM was making great strides in developing just the technology demanded by the marketplace—only to have the advantage offered by this new technology lost once the product was released for production.

The challenge facing WTM and Ted Hendrix was to make WTM as successful with innovation as it once was with quality and cost control. Given recent changes in the firm's stock price, it appeared that Wall Street was betting against WTM.

Questions

1. Describe the culture developed at WTM as a result of the movement to Six Sigma and Lean.

2. What type of culture is most appropriate for the successful introduction of a strategy based on innovation?

3. To what extent is the current culture consistent with the requirements of an innovation strategy? Why?

4. Given expected failure rates of 5 percent in really new products, how should a firm like WTM respond? Why is this response so different from what was observed?

5. What recommendations would you make to Ted Hendrix?

SELECTED READINGS

Bhote, K. R. *Strategic Supply Management: A Blue Print for Revitalizing the Manufacturer-Supplier Partnership*. New York: American Management Association, 1989.

Bicheno, J., and M. Holweg. *The Lean Toolbox*. 4th ed. Buckingham, UK: PICSIE Books, 2009.

Dennis, P. *Lean Production Simplified*. New York: Productivity Press, 2002.

Ford, H. *Today and Tomorrow*. Cambridge, MA: Productivity Press, 1989.

Goldratt, E. M., and J. Cox. *The Goal: A Process of Ongoing Improvement*. Great Barrington, MA: North River Press, 2004.

Grieco, P. L.; M. W. Gozzo; and J. W. Claunch. *Just-in-Time Purchasing: In Pursuit of Excellence*. Plantsville, CT: PT Publications, 1988.

Huthwaite, B. *The Lean Design Solution*. Mackinac Island, MI: Institute for Lean Design, 2004.

Imai, M. *Gemba Kaizen*. New York: McGraw-Hill, 1997.

Imai, M. *Kaizen: The Key to Japan's Competitive Success*. New York: Random House, 1986.

Little, J. D. C. "A Proof for the Queuing Formula: $L = \lambda W$," *Operations Research* 9 (1961), pp. 383–87.

Melnyk, S. A., and L. Fredendall. *Lean Systems Tools and Procedures*. Burr Ridge, IL: Primis On-Line Custom Publishing, 2006.

Monden, Y. *Toyota Production System*. Norcross, GA: Industrial Engineering and Management Press, 1983.

Nakajima, S. *TPM: Introduction to TPM, Total Productive Maintenance*. Cambridge, MA: Productivity Press, 1988.

Shingo, S. *A Revolution in Manufacturing: The SMED System*. Cambridge, MA: Productivity Press, 1985.

Sugimori, Y. K.; F. C. Kusunoki; and S. Uchikawa. "Toyota Production System and Kanban System—Materialization of Just-in-Time and Respect-for-Human System." *International Journal of Production Research* 15, no. 6 (1977), pp. 553–64.

Suzaki, K. *The New Manufacturing Challenge: Techniques for Continuous Improvement*. New York: Free Press, 1987.

Womack, J. P., and D. T. Jones. *Lean Thinking: Banish Waste and Create Wealth in Your Corporation*. New York: Simon and Schuster, 1996.

Womack, J. P.; D. T. Jones; and D. Roos. *The Machine That Changed the World*. New York: Rawson Associates, 1990.

INTEGRATING RELATIONSHIPS ACROSS THE SUPPLY CHAIN

		relationships	sustainability	global
9	Customer Service Management	X		
10	Sourcing and Supply Management	X	X	X
11	Logistics Management	X	X	X

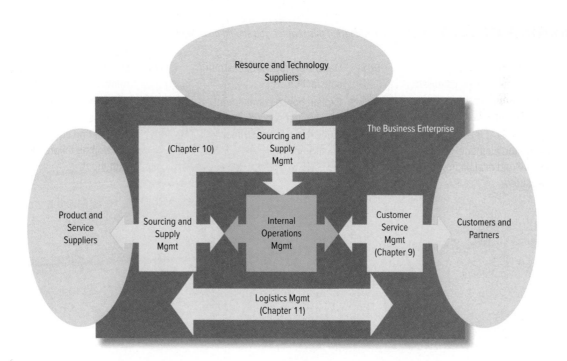

How do operations managers make the most of their relationships with other functions and organizations? Operations management activities take place both inside and outside organizations. Each of the chapters in Part 3 describes how to manage flows of information, materials, and associated organizational relationships to reach their greatest potentials. **Chapter 9** defines customer service and explains how operations and order fulfillment activities relate to meeting customer needs. **Chapter 10** similarly describes the importance of identifying, selecting, assessing, and managing suppliers who provide key inputs to the organization. **Chapter 11** shows how logistical decisions create the physical and informational networks that tie these supply chain partners together. Collectively, these three chapters explain how operational relationships in the supply chain can be improved for the benefit of all partners.

9 Customer Service Management

LEARNING OBJECTIVES *After studying this chapter, you should be able to:*

LO9-1 Describe how operations management helps establish and fulfill different levels of organizational commitment to customers.

LO9-2 Define the elements of basic service and explain how they are measured.

LO9-3 Describe a model of customer satisfaction.

LO9-4 Explain how a commitment to customer success is the highest level of customer management.

LO9-5 Describe the technological and relational aspects of customer relationship management.

LO9-6 Describe a strategy for segmenting customers and for developing tailored relationships with them.

© Jason E. Miczek/AP Images for Macy's

Macy's is betting that its recent investments will help it survive in a retail world dominated by Amazon. Macy's (http://www1.macys.com/) plans to protect its position as the leading apparel retailer in the United States by investing in "omnichannel" marketing. This strategy includes the following initiatives:

- My Macy's – This initiative targets marketing efforts on specific groups, including Latinos, small-footprint stores, and millennial shoppers in particular (Macy's has launched over 24 millennial brands).

- Omnichannel shopping – This includes investments in improving the Macy's website and mobile apps, with the goal of making shopping easier and faster. In addition, Macy's has adopted numerous digital technologies that track and leverage a 360-degree view of customer shopping behaviors, while enabling collaboration on merchandising strategies across all channels.

- Omnichannel fulfillment – This is the ability to fulfill online orders from inventory at fulfillment centers and/or from stores. The goal is to enable ordering by phone, online, or in-store and then provide delivery according to customer choices, including store pick-up or fast delivery (even same day delivery).

- Magic Selling – This initiative includes training and coaching of sales associates so that they can better manage customer engagements and selling. One component of this strategy is to teach its associates to think "omnichannel" – selling customers goods that may not be in the store and embracing customers who are making returns.

This omnichannel strategy enables customers to buy from Macy's anywhere and from any digital retail platform, pick up products or have them delivered, and return them by mail or in stores. As a result, buying from Macy's is easier over the entire buying process (from search to purchase to return).

LO9-1 Describe how operations management helps establish and fulfill different levels of organizational commitment to customers.

customer service management The design and execution of the processes that provide customers with products and services they desire.

relationships

In Chapters 1 and 2, we argued that customers are the focal point in design and management of operations across the supply chain. To prosper in today's dynamic and demanding economy, every company needs to excel in attracting customers and keeping them. Due to many factors, this task has never been more challenging. Recent advances in technology (e.g., smartphones) and growing numbers of global competitors are shaping the attitudes and expectations of customers either directly or indirectly.

For operations and supply chain management personnel, this means that the "wall" separating operations activities from marketing activities is breaking down. As can be seen from the Macy's example, many aspects of operations management are now becoming highly visible to customers. For example, order fulfillment is now a point of differentiation that customers care about. In addition to being able to place orders easily, customers expect products to be delivered quickly and easily, and they want companies to shape their various fulfillment processes to fit customer needs (and not the other way around). Operations managers are responsible for the design and execution of these processes, under the broad responsibility of **customer service management**. This requires an intense focus on understanding customers' desires and requirements and translating this understanding into specific operational capabilities and processes. These efforts include the design of sales and order fulfillment processes. However, they extend far beyond order fulfillment to collaboration, information gathering, and customer relationship management.

As the concept of supply chain management has evolved over the past two decades, so too has thinking about the nature of customer relationships. The use of the term *relationship* implies at least two participants, in this case a customer and a supplier. Just as suppliers must manage relationships with their customers, customers also have programs in place for managing relations with their suppliers. This chapter discusses general aspects of relationship management, as well as the specifics of how suppliers manage customer relationships. Chapter 10 discusses customers' efforts in managing relationships with their suppliers.

Figure 9-1 depicts a hierarchy of organizational commitment to customer service. Historically, operations managers tended to concentrate on providing excellent basic service. Today, excellent service is considered to be the foundation of customer service management. In addition, operations managers now think more holistically, in terms of customer satisfaction and success. Customer satisfaction requires a higher-level commitment than basic service in that it explicitly addresses expectations customers have regarding the organization's performance. A commitment to customer success focuses on leveraging the organization's operations capabilities to help customers meet their critical objectives.

In the following pages we will describe each of these approaches and their implications for operations management. Keep in mind throughout this discussion that customer management is customer-specific. That is, not all customers need or want the same thing from a supplier. Thus, a supplier's operational capabilities must have the flexibility to meet

FIGURE 9-1 Hierarchy of Commitment to Customers

Customer Success
Assist customers in meeting their objectives

Customer Satisfaction
Meet or exceed customer expectations

Basic Service
Product availability
Lead time performance
Service reliability

the requirements of different customers. In fact, research has shown that customer-specific knowledge is vital in developing operational supply chain strategies.[1]

BASIC SERVICE

Most operations managers agree that service is important, yet they often find it difficult to explain exactly what "customer service" means. While common expressions include "easy to do business with" and "responsive to customers," it is more meaningful to think of service as providing six basic "rights" to customers:

LO9-2 Define the elements of basic service and explain how they are measured.

- The *right* amount
- The *right* product
- The *right* place
- The *right* time
- The *right* condition
- The *right* information

Traditionally, it has been common to think of a company's **basic service** program in terms of product availability, lead-time performance, and service reliability.

basic service A supplier's ability to provide product availability, lead-time performance, and service reliability.

Product Availability

Product availability is the capacity to have inventory present when and where it is desired by a customer. To make products consistently available, managers have to make good decisions concerning safety stock and service level policies (as discussed in Chapter 7). From the standpoint of providing basic service, product availability is usually measured in terms of stockouts and fill rates.

product availability The capacity to have inventory present when and where it is desired by a customer.

Recall from Chapter 7 that a *stockout* refers to the situation when a firm has depleted inventory of an item that is supposed to be in stock. For example, a study was cited that revealed that at any point in time during a week, the average supermarket is out of stock of approximately 8 percent of the items that are supposed to be on its shelves. It is important to note, however, that a stockout does not necessarily result in failure to fulfill customer demand. A stockout only leads to a service failure when a customer actually attempts to order the product. Nevertheless, the aggregation of stockouts across products and over time is an indicator of how well a firm is positioned to provide basic service commitments. While this measure does not consider that some products may be more critical than others, it provides a good starting point for assessing product availability.

Store shelves empty of stock.
© Jae C Hong/AP Images

The most common way to report levels of product availability is in terms of fill rates. A **fill rate** measures the impact of stockouts over time or over multiple orders from customers. There are many ways that fill rates can be estimated; the most common measures include *unit fill rate, line fill rate,* and *order fill rate.*

fill rate A measure of the impact of stockouts over time or over multiple orders from customers.

The **unit fill rate** is the percentage of the total quantity of units ordered by customers that are actually delivered. It is calculated using the following equation:

(9.1a)   Unit fill rate = Total units delivered / Total units ordered

unit fill rate The percentage of total quantity of units ordered by customers that are actually delivered.

The **line fill rate** is a more stringent measure of fill rate performance. It measures service performance as the percentage of purchase order lines that are filled in total.

line fill rate A measure of service performance as the percentage of purchase order lines that are filled in total.

---

[1]Alice H. W. Yeung, Victor H. Y. Lo, Andy C. L. Yeung, and T. C. Edwin Cheng, "Specific Customer Knowledge and Operational Performance in Apparel Manufacturing," *International Journal of Production Economics* 114, no. 2 (August 1, 2008), p. 520.

Thus, even if most of the units of a specific item can be provided, the inability to provide all of them is considered to be a failure. Line fill rate is calculated using the following equation:

(9.1b) Line fill rate = Number of order lines delivered complete / Total order lines

Finally, order fill rate (orders shipped complete) is the most stringent measure of a firm's performance relative to product availability; it measures the percentage of orders that are shipped complete with all items ordered by a customer. An order that is missing only one unit of one item on a purchase order is considered to be incomplete. Order fill rate is measured as follows:

(9.1c) Order fill rate = Total complete orders delivered / Total orders

In practice, there are many variations to these fill rate measures that operations managers use to assess service. Fill rate performance can be used to differentiate the level of service offered on different products, keeping in mind that different customers may have different requirements. For example, if a customer needs 20 parts to repair a machine and receives only 19 of them, the failure to deliver a complete order means that the machine cannot be repaired. In situations where some of the items are not critical to a customer, receiving 19 of the 20 may be acceptable. The customer may be willing to accept a back order or reorder the product at a later time.

EXAMPLE 9-1

Table 9-1 presents a summary of customer order information that a company might collect to examine its fill rate performance.

Unit fill rate = Total units delivered/Total units ordered
= 19,500/20,000 = 97.5%

Line fill rate = Number of order lines delivered complete/Total order lines
= 4,800/5,000 = 96%

Order fill rate = Total complete orders delivered/Total orders
= 910/1,000 = 91%

TABLE 9-1 Summary Order Data

Orders Received	Total Units Ordered	Total Order Lines	Total Units Delivered	Total Complete Order Lines Delivered	Total Complete Orders Delivered
1,000	20,000	5,000	19,500	4,800	910

Lead-Time Performance

Operations managers use the term lead time to describe the amount of time that passes between the beginning and ending of a set of activities. Value tends to be enhanced when lead time and lead-time variability are reduced. Of critical importance to customers is the order-to-delivery (OTD) lead time, which is the time that passes from the instant the customer places an order until the instant that the customer receives the product. Many different time-consuming activities may constitute OTD lead time, including:

1. *Product design lead time* is the time interval needed to conceptualize, design, and test a new product.
2. *Order lead time* is the time required to place an order for a product plus the time to schedule the order so that operations can begin working on it.

3. *Procurement lead time* is the time associated with obtaining (through purchases) the inputs required for processing the order.

4. *Production lead time* begins at the moment the production or service system begins working on an order. It ends when the completed order is transferred to the distribution system for delivery.

5. *Delivery lead time* measures the time consumed by the distribution system, including warehousing and transportation. It ends the moment that product reaches the customer.

For some businesses, only certain lead-time elements apply. Customers who get a haircut, for example, only experience order and production lead time. On the other hand, customers who purchase highly customized goods will probably experience all five elements of lead time. From the customer's point of view, the elements of lead time that comprise the OTD lead time depend on the market orientation of the product. As discussed in Chapter 5, any product has one of four market orientations:

- Engineer to order (ETO)
- Make to order (MTO)
- Assemble to order (ATO)
- Make to stock (MTS)

These four categories describe how a firm processes customer orders as well as who (the supplier or the customer) bears the cost of lead time. Figure 9-2 illustrates differences in lead time according to market orientation.

Lead time is often an important source of value for customers. With ETO products there is a strong incentive to reduce lead times, because shorter total OTD lead times are often very attractive to customers. For example, an airline buying new aircraft from Boeing historically has experienced total lead time measured in years, or at least many months. Reducing this total lead time to a matter of a few months would be a very attractive offering for most airlines.

While a reduction in lead time may be desirable, lead-time reliability is generally more important to customers. The reason that reliability is particularly important can best be understood by thinking of our discussion of safety stocks in Chapter 7. Variation in OTD lead time is a major reason that customers must plan for safety stocks. If suppliers can be counted on to always deliver with the same lead-time performance, customers can significantly reduce the amount of safety stock they keep on hand. The same principle applies for service products. If a customer can depend on a service provider to be on time, then the customer can reduce any resources that would be needed for workarounds or contingency plans.

FIGURE 9-2   Market Orientation and Order-to-Delivery Lead Time

LO9-2 Define the elements of basic service and explain how they are measured.

service reliability A firm's ability to perform all order-related activities error-free. It also encompasses a firm's ability to provide customers with critical information regarding inventory and order status.

Service Reliability

Service reliability involves many specific attributes of customer order fulfillment. Overall, it refers to a firm's ability to perform all order-related activities error-free. It also encompasses a firm's ability to provide customers with critical information regarding inventory and order status. Attributes of reliability mean that orders arrive damage-free; invoices are correct and error-free; shipments are made to the correct locations; and the exact amount of product ordered is included in the shipment. While all aspects of reliability are difficult to enumerate, the point is that customers demand that suppliers handle details routinely and correctly.

Increasingly, customers indicate that advance notification of problems such as incomplete orders is more critical than the complete order itself. Customers hate surprises! More often than not, customers can adjust to an incomplete or late delivery if they have advance notification. While this is particularly true in business-to-business relationships, it is equally important in dealing with consumers. Imagine the situation where a consumer takes time off work to stay at home, expecting a new appliance to be delivered and installed. If the appliance does not arrive, the consumer has not only been inconvenienced, but he has also possibly lost a day's wages.

The Perfect Order

The ultimate goal in providing basic service is to do everything right and to do it right the first time. In the past, most operations managers used several independent measures to evaluate service performance. If each of these separate measures was acceptable relative to some standard, then overall service performance was considered acceptable.

Recently, however, operations executives across the supply chain have begun to focus attention on zero-defect performance across all elements in the OTD cycle. They have realized that, even if performance meets a standard on each independent measure, a substantial number of customers may have some type of order-related failure.

perfect order The notion that an order should be delivered without failure in any attribute.

The notion of the perfect order is that an order should be delivered without failure in any attribute. In other words, total order cycle performance must be executed with zero defects. This means that availability and operational performance must be perfectly executed and that all support activities must be completed exactly as promised to the customer. Typical perfect order failures include shipping the wrong products or the wrong quantities, late delivery, missing or incorrect information, damaged items, and incorrect documentation. While it may not be possible to commit to zero defects as a basic service strategy offered across the board to all customers, such high-level performance may be an option on a selective basis.

EXAMPLE 9-2

Suppose a company determines that its service performance on four attributes of service is:

97 percent of orders are shipped complete (as the customer originally requested).
97 percent of orders are delivered on time (at the customer's requested date and time).
97 percent of orders are delivered damage-free.
97 percent of orders have correct documentation (including invoicing).

The probability that any order will be *perfect* with respect to these four attributes is approximately 88.5 percent ($.97 \times .97 \times .97 \times .97$). This means that 11.5 percent of all orders will have some kind of problem, even though performance on any given metric appears to be good.

Limitations of Basic Service

Implementing a policy involves specifying the level of basic service commitment to customers in terms of availability, lead-time performance, and reliability. The fun-

activity

Using any Web browser or your library's electronic databases, enter the term *perfect order.* Look for articles that discuss the perfect order measure. Find and summarize an article that discusses specific companies and their ability to provide perfect orders to their customers.

damental question is, "How much basic service should the operational system provide?" Managers usually answer this by considering order winners, qualifiers, and losers as discussed in Chapter 2. They attempt to provide high performance levels on those service attributes they perceive as the order winners, and performance that is at least as good as their competitors' for order qualifiers and order losers. In many industries, minimum and average service performance levels are generally well known by both suppliers and customers. Operations and supply chain executives frequently speak of basic service commitments in terms of "doing as well as the competition" or "beating our major competitors' performance." For example, in the consumer packaged goods industries, it is common to hear major manufacturers and retailers talk in terms of 97–98 percent item fill rates and order-to-delivery lead times of three to five days. Suppliers who are unable to perform within these service parameters suffer significant competitive disadvantages.

A company's competitive strategy guides this decision. A firm that competes primarily on low price most likely will commit to lower levels of service due to the high costs of a high-level commitment. Firms desiring to differentiate themselves based on service are willing to spend more to do so. Yet even firms with a high level of basic service commitment generally do not seek to provide zero-defect service for all customers, because associated cost and resource requirements are too high. Instead, they seek to accommodate customers as well as or better than competitors.

It is important to realize that just because a firm outperforms its competitors on service, this does not necessarily mean that its customers are *satisfied.* For example, how many of us are truly satisfied with the performance of airlines, even the better ones? Customer satisfaction must be assessed from the customer's viewpoint, using measures that are external to the firm. The traditional approach to establishing a basic service platform is critical, but greater competitive advantage comes by ensuring that customers are, in fact, satisfied.

CUSTOMER SATISFACTION

In building a customer satisfaction program, the first question that must be answered is, "What does it mean to say that a customer is satisfied?" The simplest and most widely accepted method of defining customer satisfaction is meeting or exceeding customer expectations. If a customer perceives that a supplier's performance meets or exceeds her expectations, the customer is satisfied. Conversely, if perceived performance is less than what the customer expected, the customer is dissatisfied. A number of companies have adopted this framework for customer satisfaction, and an often-heard phrase within many organizations is: "We strive to meet or exceed our customers' expectations."

customer satisfaction
Meeting or exceeding customer expectations.

While this framework for customer satisfaction is relatively straightforward, its implications for building customer relationships are not. To build upon this platform it is necessary to answer certain questions: What do customers expect? How do they form these expectations? Why do many companies fail to satisfy customers? If a company satisfies its customers, is that sufficient? The following sections provide some answers to these critical questions.

Customer Expectations

When customers transact business with a supplier, they have numerous expectations concerning the supplier's performance. Many of these expectations revolve around the supplier's basic service platform, including availability, lead time, and service reliability performance, and they may have formal monitoring programs in place addressing each of these dimensions. However, research on service expectations and service quality has identified a larger set of categories of customer expectations, each of which has implications for supply chain operations management.[2] Customers usually have expectations regarding each of the following:

- *Reliability:* Suppliers will perform all activities as promised, including dimensions of basic service as well as special requests.
- *Responsiveness:* Suppliers will provide prompt service that goes beyond mere delivery to include issues related to quick handling of inquiries and resolution of problems.
- *Access:* Suppliers will provide easy contact for order placement, obtaining information regarding inventory, order status, and so on.
- *Communication:* Suppliers will proactively keep customers informed, rather than waiting for customer inquiries concerning order status, particularly if problems with delivery or availability arise.
- *Credibility:* Suppliers' communications will be believable and honest.
- *Security:* Suppliers will work to limit customers' feelings of risk or of doubt in doing business with them. This includes risks associated with resources customers commit based on orders placed, as well as risks associated with their need for confidentiality.
- *Courtesy:* Suppliers will be polite, friendly, and respectful. This can be a challenge considering that customers may have contact with numerous individuals in the organization (sales representatives, inventory managers, other operations executives, customer service personnel, truck drivers, etc.). Failure by one individual may destroy the best efforts of all the others.
- *Competence:* Suppliers will be competent in their execution of every interaction.
- *Tangibles:* Suppliers will maintain a level of physical appearance of facilities, equipment, and personnel. Consider, for example, the shock if a UPS delivery driver was not dressed in the well-known brown uniform.
- *Knowing the customer:* While suppliers may think in terms of groups of customers and market segments, customers think of themselves as individuals. Each customer expects a supplier to understand and adapt to his or her specific requirements.

In a business-to-business setting, customer expectations are particularly complex because a customer is a business organization made up of numerous functions and individuals. Different personnel in a customer organization may prioritize the criteria of performance differently, or they may have different levels of expectation for the criteria. For example, some personnel may be most concerned with responsiveness and rapid handling of an inquiry regarding order status, while others may be more concerned with order completeness or meeting a delivery appointment. Meeting customer expectations requires an understanding of how expectations are formed and the reasons many companies fail to meet those expectations. It is also important to recognize that customers' expectations are always changing. For example, consider how the growth of Amazon has influenced consumers of retail and other products.

The "Amazon Effect": Changing What Customers Expect

Amazon has become a modern retail juggernaut. Founded in 1998, with headquarters in Seattle, Washington, by 2015 Amazon surpassed Walmart as the most valuable retailer in the United States by market capitalization.[3] Amazon has grown from being simply an online

[2]This discussion and Figure 9-3 are based on: A. Parasuraman, V. Zeithaml, and L. L. Berry, *A Conceptual Model of Service Quality and Its Implications for Future Research,* Report No. 84–106 (Cambridge, MA: Marketing Science Institute, 1984).

[3]Jodi Kantor & David Streitfeld "Inside Amazon: Wrestling Big Ideas in a Bruising Workplace." *The New York Times.* August 15, 2015. http://www.nytimes.com/2015/08/16/technology/inside-amazon-wrestling-big-ideas-in-a-bruising-workplace.html

bookstore to a one-stop omnichannel retailer. It offers a wide range of products including DVDs, CDs, video downloads/streaming, software, electronics, apparel, furniture, food, tools, toys, and jewelry. It now has retail presence in the United States, Canada, the United Kingdom, Ireland, France, Germany, Italy, Spain, the Netherlands, Australia, Brazil, Japan, China, India, and Mexico. Amazon also has expanded successfully into cloud computing and storage. More importantly, it has changed how customers shop and what customers expect, known as the "Amazon Effect."

These changes are most evident in the following areas:

Amazon Effect The impact exerted on both customers and competitors by Amazon, due to its on-going emphasis of developing and continuously refining (and quickly implementing) new ways of connecting customers with solutions.

- **24/7 customer service:** Amazon always has customer service available by various means—online chats, telephone, or e-mail. In addition, Amazon service is known for being very accommodating.

- **Easy-to-place orders:** Amazon has developed a unique reputation with its customers is the ease with which orders can be placed. Once you set up your account, establish the method of payment, and allow one-click shopping, then all that you have to do is click on the "place order" button and your order is placed. There is no re-entry of credit card information or address—that has all been taken care of. If you place orders using an iPhone, then you can use the finger print scanner to validate the order and its placement.

- **Continuous flow of information about the order:** Once the order has been placed, then Amazon continuously communicates with the customer regarding the status of the order (it has shipped, it will arrive by such a date). There is continuous visibility regarding the order.

- **A relentless focus on improving customer service:** Amazon realizes that its customers want (and are willing to pay for) products that are fairly priced but quickly delivered. Consequently, Amazon is always searching for and experimenting with new ways of placing orders and reducing delivery lead times when the customer needs the product *now.* For example, Amazon has recently introduced Amazon Echo— a product that allows the customer to restock previously purchased Prime-eligible products by simply ordering them by voice. Amazon has experimented with drone delivery, one-hour delivery of food and other products in large cities, and the use of bicycle messengers and UBER carriers for product delivery.

- **An informed buying process:** When you buy from Amazon, you are provided customer reviews and alternative/complementary products. You are also given the option of buying from non-Amazon sources. The result is a reduction in buyer-regret—the feeling that you could have gotten a better deal elsewhere.

- **A trusted source:** Ultimately, with Amazon, you get a good price, although maybe not the best. Perhaps more important, Amazon has become a well-known, trusted source that will honor its sales commitments.

- **Reliable deliveries:** If you are an Amazon Prime[4] customer, then your orders will be delivered in two days—free. If you want next day delivery, it is extra. The result is one of the most predictable delivery systems in the retail market. This trait has also helped to set customer expectations for delivery—no more than four (4) business days from the time that you place the order.

Amazon's "Echo" device
© Mark Lennihan/AP Images

---

[4]Amazon Prime is a membership service offered to Amazon customers. In exchange for a yearly membership fee, customers are offered free two-day shipping and discounted one-day shipping rates. Furthermore, Amazon Prime gives its members access to unlimited, ad-free streaming of over one million songs, as well as free access to many movies and television shows.

- **Easiest return process in the retail market:** Finally, Amazon has made it easy to return products. Simply go online, click on the order placed, and then indicate the item that you wish to return. After recording the reason for the return, Amazon sends you a preprinted, prepaid UPS label. More importantly, your money (less shipping) is credited back to your account when the package has been scanned as received by the UPS pickup service.

These various attributes have shaped not only how customers view their interactions with Amazon but also their interactions with other companies. For example, at the Supply Chain Outlook Summit conference held in Chicago from November 2–3, 2015, one of the participants—a manufacturer of automation equipment—observed that his customers were now demanding that he provide the same things that Amazon was offering: full information, reliable deliveries, and 24/7 service. Likewise, as we noted at the beginning of this chapter, Macy's omnichannel approach is a strategy directly influenced by its desire to counter the Amazon effect. The Amazon effect is real and it is changing what customers expect of the firm's operations management/supply chain management system.

Customer Satisfaction Model

LO9-3 Describe a model of customer satisfaction.

Figure 9-3 provides a framework for understanding the process by which customers form their expectations of supplier performance. It also suggests that there frequently exists a number of gaps that a supplier must overcome as it seeks to satisfy its customers.

Customers' expectations regarding priorities and performance are influenced by several factors. The first is their defined requirements. These requirements come from a customer's specific strategies and performance goals. Interestingly, however, customer expectations are frequently not the same as their stated requirements or needs. Previous supplier performance also influences their expectations. A supplier which consistently delivers on time will most likely be expected to deliver on time in the future. Similarly, a supplier with a poor record of performance will be expected to perform poorly in the future. Also, a customer's experience with one supplier may influence his expectations of other suppliers. For example, when Federal Express began delivering small packages on a next-day basis, many customers began to expect the same performance from other suppliers.

Word-of-mouth also shapes expectations. Customers frequently tell each other about their experiences with specific suppliers. At trade and professional association meetings, the subject of suppliers' performance capabilities is a common topic of discussion among companies. For consumer products, consumers get word-of-mouth inputs from acquaintances, product comparison publications, online user blogs, and so on, which influences their expectations.

Perhaps the most important factor influencing customer expectations is the communication coming from the supplier itself. Promises and commitments made by sales personnel or customer service representatives, statements contained in marketing and promotional messages, and even the printed policies and procedures of an organization serve to influence customers' expectations. Suppliers can, to a major extent, proactively manage customer expectations through their communications. Unfortunately, companies often set themselves up for failure by overpromising in an attempt to influence customer expectations.

Figure 9-3 also provides a framework for understanding what an organization must do to deliver customer satisfaction. The failure of firms to satisfy their customers can often be traced to one or more of the gaps identified in the framework.

- *Gap 1: Knowledge Gap.* The first and the most fundamental gap that may exist is the gap between customers' real expectations and managers' perceptions of those expectations. The knowledge gap reflects management's lack of knowledge or understanding of customers. Reasons for this lack of understanding often include a lack of marketing research or a lack of intimacy with important customers.

knowledge gap The gap between customers' real expectations and managers' perceptions of those expectations.

- *Gap 2: Standards Gap.* Even if a supplier fully understands a customer's expectations it still might fail to establish appropriate standards of performance.

A Model of Customer Satisfaction

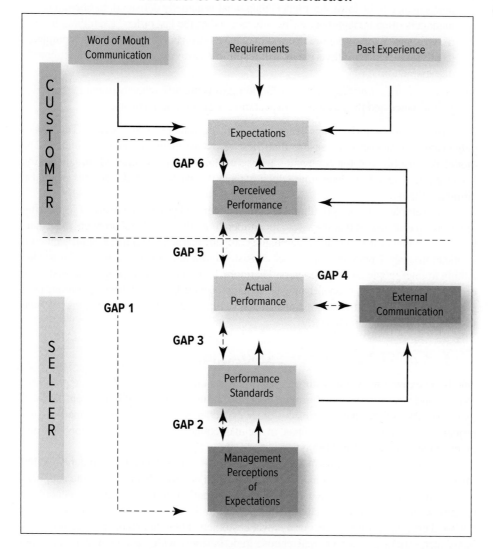

FIGURE 9-3 A Model of Customer Satisfaction

The **standards gap** exists when internal performance standards do not adequately or accurately reflect the organization's understanding of customer expectations. Sometimes it is difficult to translate customer expectations (for example, "I want courteous service") into specific operational standards. This gap also occurs when operations managers develop their service platform based on what they feel they can deliver or what their competitors deliver, rather than based on their understanding of what customers expect.

- *Gap 3: Performance Gap.* The **performance gap** is the difference between the operational standard and actual performance. If the standard is a fill rate of 98 percent and the firm actually performs at 97 percent, a performance gap exists. It should be pointed out that many firms focus on eliminating the performance gap in their efforts to improve satisfaction. It may be, however, that the dissatisfaction exists due to a poor understanding of customer expectations in the first place (the knowledge gap).

- *Gap 4: Communications Gap.* The **communications gap** is the difference between a company's actual performance and what a company communicates about its performance. The role of communications in customer satisfaction cannot be overemphasized (this is especially important when the product is an intangible service). As discussed previously, overcommitment, or promising higher levels of performance than can actually be provided, is a major cause of customer dissatisfaction.

standards gap The gap that exists when internal performance standards do not adequately or accurately reflect customer expectations.

performance gap The difference between standard and actual performance.

communications gap The difference between a company's actual performance and what a company communicates about its performance.

perception gap The gap that exists when customers perceive performance to be different than what is actually provided.

- *Gap 5: Perception Gap.* The **perception gap** exists when customers perceive performance to be lower (or higher) than what is actually delivered. In operations, managers often lament that "we're only as good as the last order." Even though performance over a long time period may have been very good, a late or incomplete or otherwise subpar delivery may still result in a customer's expression of extreme dissatisfaction.

satisfaction gap The difference between perceived performance and the customer's expectation regarding performance.

- *Gap 6: Satisfaction Gap.* The **satisfaction gap** is the difference between perceived performance and the customer's expectation regarding performance.

Any of the first five gaps leads to gap 6, customer dissatisfaction. The key to delivering satisfaction is to ensure that these gaps are identified and eliminated. This model is a useful tool for companies whose customers have expressed dissatisfaction. It can guide research to determine which gaps exist and to prescribe actions needed to eliminate them.

For example, a major agricultural chemical company learned that many of its distributors were so dissatisfied that they were recommending other suppliers' products to farmers. Using the model to structure its research, the company learned that it had a significant communications gap. Operations personnel consistently underestimated delivery times when talking to salespeople and to customers. Therefore, both internal salespeople and customers expected delivery much sooner than what actually occurred. As a solution, operations managers trained personnel to better estimate delivery times. Over the next 12 months customer satisfaction improved dramatically.

Limitations of Customer Satisfaction

Due to its explicit focus on customers, an emphasis on customer satisfaction represents a step beyond a basic service platform in an organization's efforts to build relationships with its customers. A firm that satisfies customer expectations better than its competitors will probably gain a competitive advantage in the marketplace. Nevertheless, an emphasis only on customer satisfaction has limitations, too.

The first limitation is that many executives make a fundamental (yet understandable) mistake in assuming that customers who are satisfied are also "happy" with the suppliers' performance. That may or may not be the actual situation. Remember that satisfaction is the customer's perception of actual performance in relation to performance expectations. Satisfied customers are not necessarily loyal customers. Even though their expectations are being met, satisfied customers may choose to do business with a competitor because they expect a competitor to perform at a higher level, or at least as well as the organization in question. Research has frequently shown that many customers who report being satisfied are still likely to do business with competitors.

activity

student

Think of a time that you were dissatisfied with a service provider. Which of your expectations were not met? How did you form these expectations? Which gap do you believe resulted in your dissatisfaction?

Another limitation to a focus on customer satisfaction is that firms frequently forget that satisfaction is an individual customer phenomenon. The "standards gap" frequently exists in an organization because standards are established based on the presumption that all customers have the same expectations. There is a tendency to aggregate expectations across customers and to neglect their differences. What satisfies one customer may not satisfy other, much less all, customers. When a single standard is used, some customers' expectations are exceeded while others are underserved.

Despite these limitations, a customer satisfaction platform does represent a forward step in a firm's efforts to manage relationships with its customers. Firms that primarily focus on industry and competitor standards of basic service performance are much less likely to find that their customers are very satisfied or highly satisfied with their performance. Simply stated, the only way to know if customers are really satisfied is to ask them.

CUSTOMER SUCCESS

There is yet another step that can be taken in the attempt to gain competitive advantage through customer service management. A firm's ability to grow and expand market share depends on its ability to attract and hold the industry's most successful customers. Thus, a supplier should develop its performance capabilities to enhance the success of those customers. A focus on customer success shifts the emphasis from customers' expectations to customers' "real" requirements. Recall that customer requirements, while helping form expectations, are not the same as expectations. Requirements are frequently downgraded into expectations due to perceptions of previous performance, word-of-mouth, or communications from the firm itself. This explains why simply meeting expectations may not result in "happy" customers. For example, a customer may be satisfied with an average 98 percent fill rate. However, for the customer to be successful in executing its strategy, a 100 percent fill rate on certain key products may be necessary.

LO9-4 Explain how a commitment to customer success is the highest level of customer management.

customer success Helping customers to meet their real business requirements.

Achieving Customer Success

A customer success program involves a thorough understanding of individual customer requirements and a commitment to focus on long-term business relationships that have high potential for growth and profitability. Such commitment most likely cannot be made to all potential customers. A supplier must work intensively with a customer to understand the customer's requirements, internal processes, competitive environment, and what it takes for the customer to be successful in its own competitive arena. Further, the supplier organization must understand how it can utilize its own capabilities to enhance customer performance.

This level of understanding requires a supplier to consider how its customers deal with *their customers.* Ideally, the supplier develops a comprehensive understanding of the competition and strategy for each level of customers within its supply chain. In then can develop programs that ensure that its immediate customers are successful in meeting the requirements of customers further down the supply chain.

For example, in the electronics industry, one supplier of component parts adopted the slogan, "We take pride in helping customers compete." This statement implies that the supplier attempts to do more than provide basic service and meet customer expectations. This supplier attempts to understand the real requirements of its customers so it can develop products and operational capabilities that help its customers succeed in their own competitive environments. Managers disseminated their slogan throughout the company, from the reception area to the manufacturing plants. A senior executive of the company summarized the benefits of this customer orientation in stating, "If they are more successful due to our ability to provide them with better products, more timely delivery, lower total costs, or whatever, then they will gain market share and grow. Of course, when they grow, we grow!"[5]

The Get Real box concerning Procter & Gamble's new service approach provides a clear example of focusing on the requirements of individual business customers. P&G's commitment demonstrates its desire to help key retail customers by meeting the requirements critical for their success.

relationships

---

[5]This example and quote have been adapted from Stanley E. Fawcett and M. Bixby Cooper, "Customer Service, Satisfaction, and Success," *Innovations in Competitive Manufacturing,* Paul M. Swamidass (ed.) (Norwell, MA: Kluwer Academic Publishers, 2000), p. 43.

GET REAL

Procter & Gamble's New Service Program

Procter & Gamble (P&G) recently established a new service measurement approach: Service as Measured by Customer (SAMBC). With SAMBC, P&G now measures its customer service in terms of how well it performs against the individual metrics of each customer included in the new program. SAMBC is defined as: *The percent of customers for which P&G is meeting or exceeding all customer-unique expectations.*

SAMBC is built on the reality that different customers have different requirements and levels of importance for certain dimensions of performance. Even universally embraced metrics such as fill rate and on-time delivery are calculated differently by various retailers, and there is a wide variety of expectations. For example, some customers want 98 percent on-time delivery, while others are satisfied with 94 percent.

SAMBC obviously requires a very collaborative approach with customers, as they may find it difficult to immediately define the metrics and levels of performance that they require. In its discussions with retailers, P&G many times found that retailers define metrics differently than P&G does. Also important, once customer-specific metrics are defined, they must be applied backward through the supply chain, all the way to individual manufacturing

sites. Plant managers need to be aware of how they are performing, not just at an aggregate level, but at a customer-specific level, for each of perhaps dozens of key customers. Applying this approach has a major impact on supply chain performance management, as well as on supply chain planning and execution.

Adapted from: Dan Gilmore, *Supply Chain Digest*, November 3, 2011, http://www.scdigest.com/.

© Al Behrman/AP Images

To achieve customer success, a supplier may need to reinvent the way a product is produced, distributed, or sold. It often requires suppliers and customers to collaborate in ways that create new relationships, processes, and other avenues for success. For example, the Get Real box regarding Tesco shows how a major retail company understood the unique needs of a segment of its customers in South Korea and developed a totally new approach to online retailing to make the entire shopping experience more convenient for those consumers. Companies that are adopting a customer success focus have also been leaders in implementing customer relationship management programs (discussed next) as a tool for accomplishing customer success.

Table 9-2 presents a selected set of companies (10 of the 25 total) ranked by *BusinessWeek* magazine as outstanding in aspects of customer service management, as described in this chapter. It also includes some of their actions in recent years. Notice that these actions start with improving basic service, with some oriented toward satisfaction and others focused on customer success.

relationships

Customer Relationship Management

customer relationship management (CRM) A software and information technology–based approach used to collect and analyze customer data from numerous sources for the purpose of developing strategically appropriate relationships with customers.

Customer relationship management (CRM) is a relatively new term in supply chain management; it does not yet have a standard definition across different businesses. For many, CRM is equated with computer software and information technology that is used to manage and analyze data from numerous sources within an organization (sales calls, call centers, actual purchases, etc.) in order to gain greater insight into customers' buying behaviors. To others, CRM includes not only technology, but also all forms of information and communication that help suppliers develop better relationships with customers.

GET REAL

Tesco's Virtual Store

To compete against Korean supermarket retailer E-Mart's dominant retail store presence, Tesco Homeplus (its local Korean brand) took the bold move of not trying to match E-Mart's number of physical store locations. As the number-two grocery retailer in the Korean market, Tesco's research showed that Koreans are among the most hard-working people in the world, and grocery shopping is a dreaded task for many of them. Based on the research, Homeplus developed the concept of a virtual store in a space where masses of people were already located (subways) at a time when they had nothing else to do (waiting for the next train) and using an ordering mechanism that most consumers carry with them at all times (smartphones).

The implementation was simple but incredibly effective. Photos of the Homeplus grocery shelves are blown up into huge wall-sized posters that cover the subway walls, with all of the typical products consumers look for when grocery shopping. Each product has a price and QR code attached; each shopper simply snaps a picture with his/her mobile camera to arrange for home delivery. The idea allows busy commuters to scan their groceries on their way to work in the morning and, as long as their order is placed before 1:00 p.m., their items will be delivered home that same evening. This creates even greater speed and convenience for the whole shopping

experience. All of this occurs without a single Tesco staff member needed on site.

In the first three months, Homeplus online sales increased 130 percent. Homeplus became number one in the Korean online market and a very close second in the offline market. The concept has been so popular that Tesco is expanding it to other markets, including its home country, the United Kingdom.

A shopper using the Homeplus virtual display.

© Paul Brown/Rex Features/AP Images

The objective of customer relationship management is to develop a customer-centered organization that utilizes every opportunity to delight customers, foster their loyalty, and build long-term, mutually beneficial relationships. CRM involves the science of first gathering and analyzing data that describe individual customer needs and purchasing habits and, second, developing the operational capability to meet those individual needs more completely. In this way, CRM systems can ensure rapid response to customer requirements, achieving the goal of better serving customers at lower cost and in less lead time. The Get Real box concerning Amazon describes how CRM technology can be used to benefit both a company and its customers.

CRM is not only based on technology. It involves developing personal and organizational relationships as well. For example, it is becoming increasingly common for suppliers to have their own personnel maintain an office very near, or even inside, the facilities of key customers. In this way, the supplier gains critical knowledge of the customer's needs and plans and can anticipate the customer's actions with a high degree of certainty.

Companies may include numerous other activities in a CRM approach, including the actions described in Table 9-2. Many companies also establish customer councils to provide customers with an opportunity to provide feedback on proposed products and plans. A full discussion of CRM technology and processes is beyond the scope of this text. In fact there are entire textbooks devoted to the topic. Our purpose here is to establish that customer–supplier relationships can involve many layers of cross-functional interaction. However, it is usually not desirable (or possible) for all relationships to involve

LO9-5 Describe the technological and relational aspects of customer relationship management.

TABLE 9-2   Examples of Actions for Customer Service Management

Company/Industry	Actions
Amazon.com (Online/Catalog Retail)	Some 30 percent of sales come from outside retailers who sell goods on Amazon. Amazon rolled out new services for these retailers, including aid in setting up shop or managing order fulfillment.
Lexus (Auto)	Lexus awards cash to dealers—as much as $50,000 to dealers with the best new service ideas.
The Ritz-Carlton (Hotel)	To lure corporate event planners worried about spending on high-end meetings, Ritz will donate 10 percent of meeting fees to charity.
Publix Super Market (Supermarket)	To ensure consumers always find what they come looking for, Publix adopted "automated replenishment" for fresh items. Scanners indicate when inventory levels are low and software automatically orders replenishment.
Hewlett-Packard (Consumer Electronics)	In 2008, HP opened eight new customer service centers and gave experienced agents access to Instant Care, a tool that allows tech support reps to remotely control a customer's desktop.
Key Bank (Banking)	Key Bank unveiled new online tools that give entrepreneurs many of the cash management services long reserved for large companies.
Cadillac (Auto)	Despite General Motors' cash crunch, Cadillac has not scaled back on guaranteeing loaner cars to customers while their cars are in the shop.
Amica (Insurance)	Investing in new technology to speed claims processing, Amica also invests heavily in staff, which has a turnover rate of less than 7 percent.
JetBlue Airways (Airlines)	JetBlue created the industry's first Customer Bill of Rights, which includes compensation for problems caused by the carrier, and introduced free e-mail and instant messaging on some flights.
Charles Schwab (Brokerage)	A new direct-dial feature lets clients call back a Schwab rep directly rather than navigate the automated system a second time.

Source: Adapted from "Customer Service Champs," *BusinessWeek,* March 2, 2009, pp. 32–33. See the article for the entire list and ranking of 25 companies.

GET REAL

Amazon's Automated CRM Technology

Amazon.com has been one of the leaders in automating CRM functionality to gather information and communicate with customers. For example, Amazon customers frequently receive e-mail messages from Amazon informing them of new books written by authors of books that they previously purchased. In addition, every time repeat customers log on to Amazon.com, they get tips on other products they might like based on their previous purchases. Also, when a customer selects a particular title from Amazon's website, the customer is informed of book titles that other customers have ordered in conjunction with the title selected.

All of these actions certainly benefit Amazon by increasing sales revenue. However, most customers also appreciate this ability on the part of Amazon, as it adds significantly to their reading enjoyment. This service provided by Amazon is made possible by its online interface and its massive data storage and computational capabilities. By recording customers' searches and selections, Amazon is able to develop customer profiles that give a clear picture of each customer's interests and purchasing habits.

© Ron Wurzer/AP Images

the intensity of a customer success commitment. In the next section we discuss different types of relationships that suppliers and customers might develop.

CUSTOMER MANAGEMENT AND RELATIONSHIP STRATEGY

A basic principle of supply chain management is that companies must segment customers based on their needs and adapt supply chain operations to serve those segments. In many instances a segment may consist of only one customer. For example, Procter & Gamble has a highly publicized relationship with Walmart that includes many specialized operational characteristics. Many P&G employees live and work in Bentonville, Arkansas, the headquarters of Walmart. P&G is extensively involved in managing inventories for Walmart, determining when Walmart distribution centers should be replenished with P&G products. In addition they have collaborated on numerous initiatives to reduce cost across the two organizations.

Earlier, we noted that moving beyond basic service and satisfaction and committing to the level of customer success is extremely time-consuming and resource-intensive. The P&G Get Real box in previous section demonstrates that the company collaborates with customers other than Walmart, but certainly not with every customer, and none to the extent that it does with Walmart. Clearly, no company can implement such an approach with every potential customer. In fact, many customers may not desire such relationships with all (or any) suppliers. From a strategic point of view, then, a company must determine which level of commitment and relationship is appropriate for each customer segment.

One approach for determining levels of commitment makes use of Pareto's law, which we introduced in Chapter 7. Just as some products are more critical than others, so too are some customers more critical. It is not uncommon for a company to find that the vast majority of its revenue comes from a small percentage of its customers. The same is true for a company's profit. Finally, it is also often true that the customers who account for a large portion of revenue are not necessarily the most profitable customers with whom to do business. The combination of these facts leads to the diagram presented in Figure 9-4.

Procter & Gamble has a customer success relationship with Walmart.

© Danny Johnston/AP Images

FIGURE 9-4 Selection of Appropriate Customer Relationships

Typically, only a small number of customers are both high revenue generators and also highly profitable. These customers are naturally the most deserving of a customer success relationship, as depicted in the upper right-hand corner of Figure 9-4. On the other hand, suppliers should carefully question whether they should continue serving customers that provide both low revenue and low profit (the lower left-hand corner of Figure 9-4). In many instances there may be good reasons to continue. For example, they may be new customers or they may be small but rapidly growing companies. In some instances it may simply be a wiser decision to stop doing business with them.

Customers who occupy the other two areas of Figure 9-4 are candidates for a level of commitment that emphasizes a high degree of basic service or satisfaction. The choice between service and satisfaction often depends on the supplier's potential to influence the customer to increase the quantity it buys or its potential to serve the customer more efficiently, thereby raising profitability. Recall that in the opening vignette for the chapter, Macy's found that many customers desired much shorter lead times, and some desired the ability to significantly modify orders. Supplier ability to provide these types of operational modifications can significantly influence customer buying preferences.

Customers can be segmented and analyzed in many different ways that are suggestive of strategic actions. The important point to remember is that commitment at the level of customer success should be reserved for a few customers; for others an emphasis on basic service or satisfaction is appropriate. Like all other operational activities, managing customer relationships consumes scarce resources. Therefore, it is important to spend these resources in ways that provide the greatest returns with the lowest risks.

student activity

The text references the close relationship between P&G and Walmart. Conduct a literature search on the Web to learn more about P&G's relationships with major retail customers. Next, see what else you can learn about Walmart's relationships with suppliers other than P&G.

CHAPTER SUMMARY

In this chapter we have explored the evolution of customer management in supply chain operations. Over the past two decades the focus has shifted from provision of basic service to customer satisfaction and customer success. The major issues discussed in the chapter are:

1. Traditionally, it has been common to think of a company's basic service program in terms of product availability, lead-time performance, and service reliability.

2. Of critical importance to customers of an organization is the order-to-delivery lead time (OTD), which is the lead time that passes from the instant the customer recognizes the need for a product until the instant that product is received. The components of OTD differ depending upon a product's market orientation.

3. Customer satisfaction is achieved when customers perceive that a company's performance meets or exceeds the customers' expectations.

4. A customer success program focuses on a customer's strategic objectives and involves a thorough understanding of individual customer requirements.

5. Customer relationship management involves the science of first gathering and analyzing data that describe individual customer needs and purchasing habits and, second, building systems that enable the organization to meet those individual needs more completely.

6. There are several different types of relationships and levels of commitment that may exist between suppliers and customers. Excellent companies tailor their customer relationships and associated operational capabilities to maximize revenue and profit, while minimizing risk.

7. Customer expectations and demands have been greatly influenced by the various actions and initiatives introduced by Amazon, creating the "Amazon effect."

KEY TERMS

Amazon effect   317

basic service   311

communications gap   319

customer relationship management (CRM)   322

customer satisfaction   315

customer service management   310

customer success   321

fill rate   311

knowledge gap   318

lead time   312

line fill rate   311

order fill rate (orders shipped complete)   312

order-to-delivery (OTD) lead time   312

perception gap   320

perfect order   314

performance gap   319

product availability   311

satisfaction gap   320

service reliability   314

standards gap   319

unit fill rate   311

DISCUSSION QUESTIONS

1. Explain the critical differences between basic service, customer satisfaction, and customer success.

2. Consider some of your recent shopping experiences and discuss instances in which a store was out of stock of items you were planning to purchase. What did you do as a result of the stockout?

3. Consider products you consume. Identify purchases you have made from firms with the following market orientations:
   a. Make to stock
   b. Make to order
   c. Assemble to order
   d. Engineer to order

   In each case, describe the components and your estimate of order-to-delivery lead time that you as the customer experienced.

4. Which market orientation would you consider for a standard product that has low, infrequent demand? What are the trade-offs you would consider in making this decision?

5. How can a company use the gap model of customer satisfaction to improve its operations management processes?

6. Why don't companies attempt to offer a commitment at the level of customer success with all of their customers?

7. What aspects of operations management can contribute to customer success?

8. The chapter offers one approach to customer management and relationship strategy based on sales volume and profitability. Can you think of other criteria that might be used to determine the most appropriate form of relationship?

9. One of the observations made in this chapter focuses on the relentless series of changes continuously being introduced by Amazon. How would these changes affect your firm and decision making within the firm, as it pertains to the customer?

10. In this chapter, we began with a discussion of Macy's and its omnichannel strategy. What are the possible implications of this strategy for the relationships between (a) marketing and operations/supply chain management? (b) operations/supply chain and the key customer?

11. You are a manager for a firm that sells computer and technological equipment through its stores and various online sites. You recently found out that Amazon is releasing a new line of products (through its AmazonBasics line) that are in direct competition with your firm's products. What customer-focused actions would you consider introducing to counter Amazon (and why)?

SOLVED PROBLEM

The accompanying table presents order fulfillment data for a company. Compute the unit, line, and order fill rates.

Orders Received	Total Units Ordered	Total Order Lines	Total Units Delivered	Total Complete Order Lines Delivered	Total Complete Orders Delivered
8,000	40,000	20,000	37,500	18,250	7,150

Solution:

Unit fill rate = 37,500/40,000 = 93.75%

Line fill rate = 18,250/20,000 = 91.25%

Order fill rate = 7,150/8,000 = 89.375%

PROBLEMS

1. Aldo Inc. was reviewing its quarterly performance in providing service to customers. An analysis of order and shipping data was prepared and is shown in the table below. How well did Aldo perform in unit, line, and order fill rate?

Orders Received	Total Units Ordered	Total Order Lines	Total Units Delivered	Total Complete Order Lines Delivered	Total Complete Orders Delivered
450	15,000	3,000	14,250	2,700	360

2. The following quarter, Aldo's senior executive (see problem 1) was interested in knowing whether performance had improved. The following table presents order and shipping data collected for the next quarter. How would you answer the senior executive?

Orders Received	Total Units Ordered	Total Order Lines	Total Units Delivered	Total Complete Order Lines Delivered	Total Complete Orders Delivered
500	18,000	3,200	17,200	2,950	425

3. Suppose a firm, in discussions with customers, learns that customers identify eight factors that they evaluate for every order they receive from suppliers. The firm then finds that its performance is 95 percent on six of these factors and 92 percent on the other two factors. What is the firm's probable perfect-order performance?

4. In problem 3, suppose the firm's performance on two of the 95-percent factors falls to 90 percent. What impact does this have on the firm's perfect-order performance?

5. ABBA Inc. collected the following data concerning orders and shipments during the most recent year:

Orders Received	Total Units Ordered	Total Order Lines	Total Units Delivered	Total Complete Order Lines Delivered	Total Complete Orders Delivered
25,000	5,000,000	150,000	4,800,000	146,500	24,150

How well did ABBA perform in providing product to its customers?

6. In addition to the information concerning product availability in problem 5, ABBA collected the following data concerning service performance:

Late delivery—6 percent

Damage—1 percent

Incorrect documentation—4 percent

Assuming these are the critical attributes for perfect orders, how well did ABBA perform?

7. Jones Company found the following results when analyzing its delivery performance:

Total Orders	Total Units Ordered	Total Order Lines	Total Units Delivered	Order Lines Delivered Complete	Complete Orders Delivered
1,245	22,350	5,830	18,750	4,824	898

How would you assess Jones Company's performance in product availability?

8. Jones Company (see problem 7) also found the following information about delivery to customers. Late deliveries were made for 8 percent of the orders. Early arrivals, which are unacceptable to customers, occurred for 2 percent of the orders. The company also experienced a 1.5 percent damage rate during delivery. It also had incorrect information on 3 percent of the invoices billed to customers. Based on this information, what was the approximate perfect-order performance at Jones Company?

CASE

Tiler Industries

Harry Chamberlain, vice president of Tiler Industries, closed the phone call by saying, "Well thanks, Jim. We appreciate the call even though it was bad news. We're sorry we didn't get the contract for the SRW installation from Phoenix, but we understand. And, we'll do better next time." Most of the executive committee members heard the news as they filed in for the division's weekly status meeting. In the few minutes before the meeting started, Harry started to organize his thoughts, concerns, and ideas as to where to go from here with the loss of a major sale to a long-standing customer.

As the meeting convened, he said, "Well, as most of you have just heard we didn't get the contract for this year's SRW installation at Phoenix Engineering. That would have been a $12 million project plus ongoing service and parts business. That call was from Jim Gray, their head of purchasing. He said our price was okay. But their new cross-functional commodity team was unanimous on many benefits, some tangible and some intangible, and supply chain approaches that were provided in the proposal from Eastern Star Electronics. We took a bad hit on this one. The real harm is the long-term impact by Eastern Star with a customer who has been very loyal to us over the years."

Tiler Industries is a manufacturer of industrial tools and machinery with headquarters in Wisconsin. It also has operations in Europe and South America and makes nine specialty lines of equipment. The SRW equipment line is used by customers for precision shaping, forming, and assembly of fluid dynamics components that are subsequently sold to original equipment manufacturers of such items as diesel engines, electrical generation equipment, jet engines, turbines, and marine motors. It involves precise measuring, cutting, and forming processes. Tiler has traditionally been number two in the industry, behind Acton Tools, the dominant price leader. Acton and Tiler have led the industry for many years.

The Executive Committee Meeting

"We lost the job to Eastern Star, and it wasn't on price. Eastern Star came at us from out of nowhere and we were caught without warning," Harry said.

Bill Mathews, sales and marketing head, spoke up: "Eastern Star is starting to become a major player now. We just came back from the Milan Machine Tool Show last week, and they were there in a big way. That's the third time I've seen their displays at major trade shows this year. Each time they have new and innovative features in their equipment. It makes ours look weak in comparison. Our products show only minor modifications and small efficiency changes, but theirs have technical leaps. They have a new laser module component that looks quite good. None of the U.S. firms are close to that technology. And you can't beat Eastern Star's output quality."

Sally Morgan, finance director, said, "Our quality is good. In fact, it's great. All of our benchmark warranty and survey studies against Acton Tools show we are comparable or better. And they are still the industry leader."

Harry asked Phil Chung, director of research, "OK, just what makes this latest equipment from Eastern Star better than our SRW?"

Phil replied, "Well, this is the first trade show the company ever sent me to. And it was a real eye-opener for me. As Bill Mathews said, Eastern Star has a real state-of-the-art line. At first look, it does just what our machine does. And it doesn't really perform any better in comparison to the SRW or Acton's units. But the real advantage is that Eastern also sells a module that a company like Phoenix can attach to components that go onto the OEM's generator, turbine, or motor. A technician can then come along with a diagnostic reader and determine if those units are performing properly. If there is a problem, fine-tuning adjustments can be made. This just isn't possible with our SRW line."

He continued, "They also spend a lot of time talking about the supply chain. They look a lot at the end users of turbines and diesel engines. And, they talk to their customers about issues like lead times and delivery. Eastern can promise a customer like Phoenix that they'll be able to install a big system similar to our SRW in two months. We couldn't possibly do that since it would take us almost that long just to get the components we need to start making the SRW. The best we could do would probably be in the neighborhood of four months."

Bill Mathews said, "Phil's right. We don't really know much about Phoenix's customers. What's happening with cars, boat engines, and power generation equipment? One time a couple of years ago I went with Phoenix's people to visit Ford and Cummins Engine. I thought that was a big deal."

Harry brought the conversation back into focus. "Seems like we're playing by the old rules of the ballgame, and this is an entirely different one. Eastern pretty well blindsided us while we were happy trying to make sure we were at least as good as Acton. This is a good lesson for us. We need an across-the-board approach to figure out what to do. Maybe we ought to get some people here from Phoenix to talk over these issues. It might not hurt to get someone from Detroit Diesel or a power generation company. What do you think about getting some people from a couple of our key suppliers to meet with us? What we end up doing may change this company, more than just our products and marketing. There are some issues that may fundamentally change how we do business."

As the meeting ended, Harry's thoughts returned to Jim Gray's comment about the tangible and intangible benefits. He wondered what all of this would mean for the organization, structure, planning, and operations of the company. He had an uneasy feeling that some fundamental changes were in order.

Questions

1. What do you think are the intangible benefits Eastern Star provides to customers? What is the role of operations management in providing these benefits?

2. What changes in organization and/or planning would help Tiler respond to the challenges raised by Eastern Star?

Source: Adapted from a case prepared by Joseph L. Cavinato, Department of Business Logistics, The Pennsylvania State University.

CASE

Johnson Snacks

Murray Griffin, manager of distribution for Johnson Snacks, was faced with a difficult task. Harold L. Carter, the new CEO, had circulated a letter from Johnson Snacks' only mass merchandise customer, Discount 2 You, complaining of poor operating performance. Among the problems cited by Discount 2 You were: (1) frequent stockouts, (2) poor basic service responsiveness, and (3) high prices for Johnson Snacks' products. The letter suggested that if Johnson Snacks were to remain a supplier to Discount 2 You, it would need to eliminate stockouts by: (1) providing direct store delivery four times per week (instead of three), (2) installing an automated order inquiry system to increase basic service responsiveness ($300,000 investment), and (3) decreasing product prices by 5 percent. While the previous CEO would most certainly have begun implementing the suggested changes, Harold Carter was different. He requested that Murray prepare a detailed analysis of profitability by customer segment. This was something that Murray had never previously attempted, and it was needed first thing in the morning.

Johnson Snacks is a small manufacturer of salty snacks in the southeastern United States. The company was founded in 1922 and following an unsuccessful attempt at national expansion has remained primarily a local operation. The company currently manufactures and distributes several varieties of potato chips to three different types of retail accounts: grocery, drug, and mass merchandise. The largest percentage of business is concentrated in the grocery segment, with 250 retail customer locations accounting for 2,100,000 annual unit sales and more than 74 percent of annual revenue. The drug segment comprises 140 customer locations which account for 365,000 annual unit sales and more than 14 percent of annual revenue. In the mass merchandise segment, Johnson Snacks has one customer with six locations that account for 400,000 annual unit sales and almost 12 percent of annual revenue. All distribution is store-direct, with delivery drivers handling returns of outdated product and all shelf placement and merchandising.

Recently, the company has actively sought growth in the mass merchandise segment because of the perceived profit potential. However, while the company is acutely aware of overall business profitability, it has never conducted an analysis on a customer segment basis.

Murray began by gathering data about the service to the customers. All deliveries were store-direct with two deliveries per week to grocery stores, one delivery per week to drugstores, and three deliveries per week to mass merchandiser stores. The cost of delivery to each store was dependent on the type of vehicle used. Standard route trucks were used for drugstores and grocery stores, while extended vehicles were used to accommodate the volume at mass merchandisers. Johnson's selling prices for each unit were different for grocery ($1.70), drug ($1.90), and mass merchandise ($1.40) customers. Murray was also aware that Discount 2 You required Johnson Snacks to cover the suggested retail price (generally about $3.00 per unit regardless of channel) with a sticker bearing its reduced price at the store. Murray knew that many costs could be directly related to the specific type of customer. There were, of course, other costs that Johnson incurred but could not be related to a specific customer segment. Murray's analysis of the costs and expenses revealed the following:

Costs and expenses directly associated with:

Grocery stores:	$3,230,000
Drugstores:	$ 652,000
Discount 2 You:	$ 542,000

As Murray sat in his office compiling this information to complete the analysis of profitability, he received several unsolicited offers for assistance. Bill Smith, manager of marketing, urged him not to bother with the analysis, saying:

Discount 2 You is clearly our single most important customer. Look at the sales per store. We should immediately implement the suggested changes.

Steve Brown, director of manufacturing, disagreed. He felt the additional manufacturing cost required to meet Discount 2 You requirements was too high:

We should let Discount 2 You know what we really think about their special requirements. Stickers, of all things! What business do they think we are in?

The sales force had a different opinion. Jake Williams, sales manager, felt the grocery segment was most important:

Just look at that volume! How could they be anything but our best customers?

Questions

1. Using the framework in Figure 9-4, how would you categorize each of the three customer segments?

2. How should Johnson Snacks respond to the letter from Discount 2 You?

Anderson, D. L.; F. F. Britt; and D. J. Favre. "The Best of Supply Chain Management Review: The Seven Principles of Supply Chain Management." *Supply Chain Management Review* 11, no. 3 (April 2007), p. 57.

Bensaou, M. "Portfolios of Buyer–Supplier Relationships." *Sloan Management Review,* Summer 1999, pp. 35–44.

Chauhan, S. S., and J. M. Proth. "Analysis of a Supply Chain Partnership with Revenue Sharing." *International Journal of Production Economics* 97, no. 1 (July 2005), p. 44.

Fawcett, S. E., and M. B. Cooper. "Customer Service, Satisfaction, and Success." In *Innovations in Competitive Manufacturing,* ed. P. M. Swamidass. Norwell, MA: Kluwer Academic Publishers, 2000, pp. 35–44.

Fawcett, S. E.; J. A. Ogden; G. M. Magnan; and M. B. Cooper. "Organizational Commitment and Governance for Supply Chain Success." *International Journal of Physical Distribution & Logistics Management* 36, no. 1 (2006), p. 22.

Hart, C. W. "Beating the Market with Customer Satisfaction." *Harvard Business Review,* March 2007, p. 30.

Parsons, A. L. "What Determines Buyer–Seller Relationship Quality? An Investigation from the Buyer's Perspective." *Journal of Supply Chain Management* 38, no. 2 (Spring 2002), pp. 4–12.

Stading, G., and N. Alta. "Delineating the 'Ease of Doing Business' Construct within the Supplier–Customer Interface." *Journal of Supply Chain Management* 43, no. 2 (Spring 2007), p. 29.

Customer Relationship Management Association
www.crmassociation.org

Supply Chain Brain
www.supplychainbrain.com/content/home/

10 Sourcing and Supply Management

LEARNING OBJECTIVES

After studying this chapter, you should be able to:

LO10-1 Define supply management and understand its impact on a firm's performance.

LO10-2 Define and describe each of the six supply management goals.

LO10-3 Analyze costs and make insourcing/outsourcing decisions.

LO10-4 Explain the steps in a strategic sourcing process.

LO10-5 Describe the components in a sourcing strategy.

LO10-6 Assess and select suppliers.

LO10-7 Understand ways to manage ongoing supplier relationships.

© Stephen Brashear/AP Images

Sourcing and supply management are essential for the success of Chipotle Mexican Grill®. With over 1,700 company-owned restaurants, Chipotle® is one of the most successful "fast casual" restaurant chains. Burritos, tacos, and salads are assembled to order using high quality, fresh, and often, locally sourced ingredients. The menu concept—"a few things, thousands of ways"—keeps the number of ingredients small, simplifying sourcing and inventory management. Chipotle® builds close relationships with its suppliers, reducing its exposure to price increases and ensuring the highest quality ingredients are available for its customers.

Sustainability is a key driver in the company's strategic goal of serving "Food with Integrity®." Beans are sourced from organic farms and, when in season, vegetables are sourced from within 350 miles of its restaurants. The chain also plans to eliminate all genetically modified organisms (GMOs) from its ingredients. In addition to its focus on the environment, Chipotle is committed to the ethical treatment of animals for its dairy and meat products.

However, its sourcing strategy also exposes the company to supply chain risk. Sourcing from specialized suppliers means the company may have higher costs and the potential for a supply disruption. In fact, in 2015, Chipotle® stopped serving pork carnitas in about one-third of its locations because an audit of its supplier showed that the pigs were not being raised in a manner that met its ethical treatment standards. Within six months, Chipotle's sourcing team found a qualified pork supplier in the UK that met its ethical standards, at the expense of its local sourcing goals.[1]

Suppliers provide a wide range of resources to companies. As shown by Chipotle, sourcing and supply management are essential for success. This chapter discusses the role that supply management plays in the operations of a firm and its supply chain. We examine how managers decide what to purchase and what to make internally, whom to purchase from, how to get the best value, how to mitigate risk, and how to manage suppliers after the contract is signed.

---

[1]Source: Adapted from Chipotle Mexican Grill 2014 Annual Report and http://chipotle.com/carnitas

SUPPLY MANAGEMENT'S IMPACT ON FIRM AND SUPPLY CHAIN PERFORMANCE

supply management The identification, acquisition, positioning, and management of resources and capabilities that a firm needs to attain its strategic objectives.

sourcing The identification, evaluation, selection, and management of suppliers.

LO10-1 Define supply management and understand its impact on a firm's performance.

Supply management is the identification, acquisition, positioning, and management of resources and capabilities that a firm needs to attain its strategic objectives. Organizations buy raw materials, parts, and components that go into the products they make. They also buy indirect materials that support operations such as office supplies, capital equipment, and a wide range of different services. **Sourcing**, which is the identification, evaluation, selection, and management of suppliers, is an important part of supply management.

Supply management is critical to an organization's success. In many industries, purchased goods and services account for a large percentage of a product's cost. For example, 75–80 percent of the cost of a car made by Honda of America comes from purchased parts and components. The parts costs for Apple's iPhone 6S® are over 50 times larger than the costs to assemble it. The phone itself is assembled by suppliers rather than Apple. Thus, for Honda and Apple, the cost, quality, delivery, and degree of innovation of their products depend heavily upon suppliers.

Corporate purchases go beyond raw materials, parts, and equipment. As firms focus on their core competencies, suppliers take on noncore business functions such as accounting, information systems, maintenance, inventory management, office support services, human resources management, and engineering design. Further, companies turn to suppliers for integrated solutions that combine both goods and services. For example, Diebold Corporation. whose products include ATM machines, vaults, and automation technologies for banks, positions itself as providing integrated solutions that improve the customer banking experience, reduce security risk, and improve efficiency.

Supply Management Goals

LO10-2 Define and describe each of the six supply management goals.

Effective supply management enables a firm to meet its strategic objectives and improve performance. Its goals are to:

- Ensure timely availability of resources.
- Identify, assess, and mitigate supply chain risk.
- Reduce total costs.
- Enhance quality.
- Access technology and innovation.
- Foster sustainability.

Ensure Timely Availability of Resources

Ensuring that the right purchases are available at the right time to support new product launches, operations, and shipments is an important supply management goal. Late supplier deliveries or poor supplier quality can halt operations, causing deliveries to customers to be late. Think about the problems that would occur if the right materials were not available for a surgery or if the security team for a concert failed to show up. In the automotive industry, stopping an assembly line costs thousands of dollars per minute in idle time. Deliveries that are too early also cause problems, as they increase inventory costs, waste resources, and reduce flexibility for the buyer. Identifying and managing supply chain risks can help to ensure that deliveries are on time.

Identify, Assess, and Mitigate Supply Chain Risk

supply chain risk The probability of an unplanned event that negatively affects a firm's ability to serve its customers.

Supply managers gather information and carefully evaluate supply markets and suppliers' capabilities to assess **supply chain risk**, the probability of an unplanned event in acquisition, delivery, and use that negatively affects a firm's ability to serve its customers. Supply chain risks include delivery disruptions, thefts of intellectual property, price increases, product safety problems, tampering with products or information, or harm to a firm's reputation. Sources of supply chain risk are often upstream in the supply chain, beyond a firm's first tier suppliers.

Operations and supply chain practices can increase exposure to supply chain risk. Lean manufacturing, just-in-time deliveries, reliance on a single supplier for each component, and global sourcing increase supply chain risks. Factors contributing to risk include:

- Supplier technical, operations, or quality problems.
- Supplier financial problems.
- Labor disputes.
- Major increases or decreases in demand.
- Lack of transparency in the supply chain.
- Inadequate physical, information, and intellectual property security.
- Disasters such as fires, earthquakes, hurricanes, and floods.
- Political instability.
- Changes in government regulations.
- Concentration of suppliers within the same geographical region.

Firms use supply chain risk management (SCRM) practices to identify, assess, and reduce risk exposure and to speed recovery if a disruption occurs. Risks are assessed based on their probability of occurrence and their impact on the firm. For high likelihood/high impact risks, firms invest to increase **supply chain resilience**, which is the capability to resist and recover from supply chain disruptions. See the nearby Get Real box to see how Flextronics is using software to gather real-time data to increase resilience in its supply chain. Other ways to increase supply chain resilience include:

supply chain resilience The capability of a supply chain to minimize the impact of a disruption and to recover after a disruption.

- Holding higher inventory levels of critical materials to allow more time to react if a disruption occurs.
- Using more than one supplier for critical purchases so that there is a "back-up" just in case.
- Working closely with suppliers to improve their capabilities.
- Requiring suppliers to have geographically dispersed operations.

global

GET REAL

Real-time Data Increases Supply Chain Resilience

Flextronics, a supply chain solutions supplier to major corporations such as Ford and Apple, uses real-time data to monitor its supply chain risk. Using cloud-based software provided by Elementum, a Flextronics spin-off company, employees monitor their supplier chains for potentially disruptive events. If a disaster happens in any part of the world, the software shows which suppliers may be affected and the current inventory on hand. The software also allows video chatting and video footage of Flextronics production facilities. Supply chain managers can quickly assess the potential for disruption and implement continuity plans if needed.

Source: http://www.wsj.com/articles/flextronics-will-manage-global-supply-chain-with-new-real-time-software-1436311241

© Elementum

Reduce Total Costs

The true cost of using a product can be much greater than its purchase price. Think about purchasing a used car. The car that is the lowest price may need more repairs, be less reliable, have lower fuel economy, and may not last as long. Similarly, selecting a supplier based solely on purchase price can be a bad business decision. The supplier with the lowest price may not have the capabilities to meet the buyer's quality or delivery requirements, ultimately resulting in delays and higher costs.

total cost of ownership (TCO) All of the costs incurred before, during, and after a purchase.

The **total cost of ownership (TCO)** considers all the costs incurred before, during, and after the purchase of a good or service. These include sourcing costs, purchase price, transportation, handling, inspection, quality, rework, maintenance, and disposal, as shown in Table 10-1. Returning to the used car example, think about the costs that happen before, during, and after your purchase. Your costs increase as you take more time and drive to various locations to look at cars, hire a mechanic to inspect potential cars, and make repairs after the purchase.

Consider the total costs of ownership associated with global sourcing. For example, for a firm located in the United States, sourcing in Vietnam will have a lower purchase price in comparison to a U.S. supplier. However, purchasing from a low-cost country such as Vietnam can increase costs and problems such as:

global

- Long lead times.
- Higher transportation costs.
- Higher inventory costs because of higher safety stock and in-transit inventory.
- Lack of flexibility to make changes in quantity or specifications because of the inventory in the long transportation pipeline.
- Costs of travel and communication.
- Complexity, delays, and costs from customs clearance, duties, and border security.
- Potential quality problems because of differing standards and difficulty in monitoring.
- Cost of poor quality because the entire transportation pipeline from the supplier could be filled with poor-quality materials.

Supply managers have to consider all of the relevant costs when making purchases. Although some costs such as purchase price and transportation costs are easy to evaluate, other costs such as defects in finished goods, warranties, safety recalls, replacements, repairs, lost sales, liability, and customer satisfaction are difficult to accurately estimate in advance.

TABLE 10-1   Total Cost of Ownership

When the Costs Occur	Type of Costs
Before the transaction	Time spent and costs of searching for, visiting, evaluating, and certifying suppliers.
During the transaction	Purchase price and costs of ordering, transporting, expediting, receiving, inspecting, and following up.
After the transaction	Costs of inventory, supply risk, production downtime, defects in finished goods, warranties, safety recalls, replacements, repairs, lost sales, liability, and damaged reputation.

Source: Adapted from L. Ellram, "Total Cost of Ownership," *International Journal of Physical Distribution and Logistics Management* 25, no. 8/9 (1995), pp. 4–24.

Enhance Quality

A product's quality depends in large part upon the quality of all of its inputs. For example, if you have a question about your credit card, the service provided by the customer service representative, an employee of a supplier, impacts your impression of the credit card company. Similarly, the failure of low-cost parts, such as thermostats, can cause engines to overheat, increasing warranty costs and impacting a car manufacturer's reputation. For many of the world's largest automakers, a supplier quality problem caused an important safety feature, air bags, to turn deadly (see the nearby Get Real box).

A supplier's quality is an order qualifier with a specified level of quality required to do business with the buyer. If a supplier's quality is poor, buyers will often look for a new supplier. Most large corporations require that their suppliers have extensive quality management systems such as ISO 9000 and statistical process control, as discussed in Chapter 6. Many companies expect suppliers to demonstrate continuous improvement in quality and use continuous improvement as a key performance indicator.

Access Technology and Innovation

Firms look to suppliers as sources of innovation and new technology to aid the design of new products and the improvement of existing ones. Very few firms have all the necessary expertise to develop needed innovations on their own. For example, Procter & Gamble acquires innovative ideas from suppliers using a process called "Connect + Develop." Key ingredients for its Olay® Regenerist line of skin creams were developed by a French supplier. Suppliers often provide essential technical knowledge and expertise by being directly involved in early product development activities.

Foster Sustainability

sustainability

Supply managers play important roles in fostering sustainability, which simultaneously addresses how decisions made within the firm and throughout the supply chain affect people, the planet, and company profits. Firms develop policies and procedures designed to

---

GET REAL

Air Bag Supplier Responsible for Largest Recall in U.S. History

In 2015, Takata air bag inflators caused the largest automotive recall ever in the United States. Eleven automakers, including Honda, Toyota, General Motors, Ford, Fiat Chrysler, and BMW, purchased the faulty air bags. Quality problems with air bag inflators designed and produced by Takata have been blamed for at least eight deaths and numerous injuries. Takata and the automakers are investigating the root cause of the quality problems.

The external costs of quality have been enormous for Takata and the automakers. To begin with, they must compensate the victims and their families and will most likely face years of lawsuits. Further, they must replace inflators in almost 34 million vehicles. In addition, the automakers have had to scramble to find alternative suppliers with the capacity to meet their requirements for new vehicle production. Because of the size of the recall, customers faced long waits to have their cars repaired; in the meantime, these customers were concerned about safety while driving their vehicles.

FO4305OZ02

© Caspar Benson/fStop Images/Getty Images

sustainability The ability or capacity of the system (the firm and its supply chain) to maintain or sustain itself by improving its performance in terms of how it manage pollution (planet), people, and changes in the business model (profit).

improve sustainability. Sustainability has become increasingly important in recent years due to customer expectations, growing government regulations, and social pressures.

Sustainability typically addresses the following goals:

Goals	Supply Management Example
Support and provide value to the community	Provide jobs in the supplier's community
Increase social diversity	Use minority, women, and veteran-owned suppliers
Encourage environmental responsibility	Require environmental compliance from suppliers
Display ethical behavior	Engage in fair contract negotiations
Practice and promote financial responsibility	Accurately report financial dealings with suppliers
Respect human rights	Use suppliers who conform to child labor laws
Ensure a safe working environment	Use suppliers who conform to safety standards

activity

student

Review the most recent list of the 100 Best Corporate Citizens as ranked by *Corporate Responsibility Officer* (**www.thecro.com**). Select a company from the list, visit its website, and search for "supplier code of conduct." If you were a supplier, how would this code affect the way you do business? Why?

Sustainability can improve financial performance, lower total costs, increase quality, instill customer loyalty, and enhance a firm's reputation. Most large corporations have a code of conduct that communicates expectations for sustainability in their own organizations and across the supply chain. The nearby Get Real box shows how Caribou Coffee is working to improve sustainability. Coffee production in many parts of the world can occur in conditions that are very poor for workers and detrimental to the environment. Caribou Coffee is committed to sustainable sourcing and works with suppliers to ensure that coffee beans are grown using sustainable farming practices.[2]

GET REAL

Sourcing Increases Sustainability for Caribou Coffee

Sourcing plays a key role in implementing Caribou Coffee's corporate sustainability strategy, "Do Good." In fact, 100 percent of the coffee purchased by Caribou Coffee is certified by the Rainforest Alliance to be grown in conditions that ensure the basic human rights of the farm workers, such as fair wages and reasonable living conditions. Farming methods also protect wildlife and the environment.

The pursuit of the Rainforest Alliance certification is a way for farmers to aim for a premium price for their coffees, "green up" their practices, gain some production efficiencies, and feel a great sense of pride and accomplishment once certification is achieved.

Caribou Coffee's sourcing team did not stop its sustainability efforts at coffee. The team collaborated with suppliers to reduce the materials used in its cups and coffee sleeves, reducing waste and costs. It is also working with suppliers to use recycled materials and/or compostable materials.

© Tim Boyle/Getty Images

---

[2]http://www.cariboucoffee.com/page/1/responsible-coffee-sourcing.jsp.

MAKING AN INSOURCING/OUTSOURCING DECISION

After supply management goals are agreed upon, you must determine which resources and activities should be provided by the firm (**insourcing**) and which should be provided by its suppliers (**outsourcing**). On a personal level, deciding whether to make dinner at home or get take-out is an example of an insourcing (cook) or outsourcing (take-out) decision. Strategically, organizations must focus on their current or future core competencies. Noncore activities are candidates for outsourcing to suppliers whose expertise and capabilities are a better fit with the activities. For example, universities often outsource dining and food service operations to suppliers whose core competency is in managing these operations.

Advances in information technology and globalization have enabled many processes such as manufacturing, customer care, logistics, supply management, information services, engineering, and human resource management to be outsourced. A **make or buy decision** considers insourcing or outsourcing the production of parts and components. The same type of analysis can be done when deciding whether to perform a service using internal resources or to buy it from a supplier. When outsourcing to a different country, the term *offshoring* is sometimes used.

Outsourcing offers several advantages and disadvantages, as shown in Table 10-2.

Outsourcing may give suppliers critical expertise and access to intellectual property. This is especially a concern when sourcing in low-cost countries. Suppliers then compete against the buyer or may transfer knowledge to other customers. Without having to invest in R&D and product development, suppliers can sell products at a lower price. Trying to stop theft of intellectual property using the legal system can be slow and costly, and the outcome is uncertain. To avoid having suppliers become competitors, some companies, such as Honda and Toyota, spend three months or more assessing and working on-site with their potential suppliers. Other firms outsource only mature technology, protecting their competitive advantages.

Because of its complexity, insourcing/outsourcing analysis should be done by a cross-functional team. The team must consider quantitative and qualitative issues. The steps in making an insourcing/outsourcing decision are shown in Figure 10-1.

Step 1. Assess Fit with the Firm's Core Competencies. Evaluate the product's or process's relationship to the firm's current or future core competencies. Compare the savings from outsourcing to the risk of losing core competencies or intellectual property. To reduce risk, firms usually insource processes in their areas of core competencies, even if outsourcing is a lower cost alternative.

LO10-3 Analyze costs and make insourcing/outsourcing decisions.

insourcing Acquiring inputs from operational processes provided within the firm.

outsourcing Acquiring inputs from operational processes provided by suppliers.

make or buy decision The choice between making a product internally or purchasing it from a supplier.

global

TABLE 10-2   Outsourcing Advantages and Disadvantages

Internal Factors	
Outsourcing Advantages	**Outsourcing Disadvantages**
Capital is not needed for equipment and facilities	Can be difficult to communicate what is needed to suppliers, especially for services
Easier to add or remove capacity if demand changes	Supplier may have quality or delivery problems Supplier may increase costs
Lower costs because suppliers gain economies of scale and suppliers often pay lower wages	Must have sourcing and supply management capabilities
Increased flexibility to change technology or suppliers	May be difficult to integrate information and materials flows with supplier
Better access to supply market information	Loss of intellectual property

FIGURE 10-1
Insourcing/Outsourcing
Decision Process

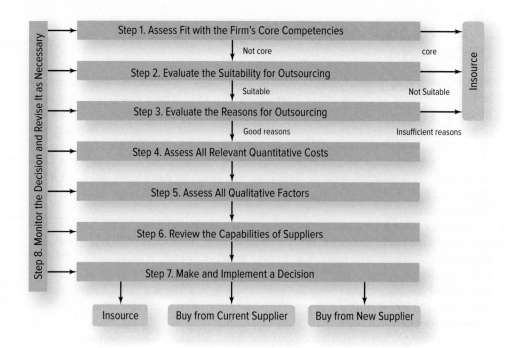

Step 2. Evaluate the Suitability for Outsourcing. Certain characteristics favor outsourcing. Mature products with standard processes and requirements are often outsourced. Known technology means that there are many capable suppliers and the intellectual property risk is low.

Step 3. Evaluate the Reasons for Outsourcing. If the product or process seems appropriate for outsourcing, compare the benefits of outsourcing to those of insourcing. For example, outsourcing might free up internal resources to produce other, more profitable products. However, costs will not be lower if freed-up resources sit idle.

Step 4. Assess All Relevant Quantitative Costs. If previous steps indicate that outsourcing makes sense, compare the costs to make the product internally against the total cost of purchasing it. Classify costs as either fixed or variable:

fixed costs per contract Costs incurred at the start of production or the beginning of a new contract.

fixed costs per order Costs incurred each time an order is placed, regardless of the size of the order.

variable costs Costs that change in proportion to the quantity of units produced or service delivered.

- **Fixed costs per contract**. These are the one-time costs incurred by the buying firm at the start of the contract or when beginning to make a product. For example, the firm may have to acquire tools in order to produce the product in-house or it may have to pay reorganization costs to purchase the product.
- **Fixed costs per order**. The firm will incur costs each time it places a new order. For example, it will incur costs to inspect and refurbish tools for individual production runs.
- **Variable costs**. These are costs associated with each unit produced, including labor, materials, asset depreciation, energy, or the purchase price.

Step 5. Assess All Qualitative Factors. It is not always possible to quantify all factors affecting the insourcing/outsourcing decision. Numerous qualitative factors are often important, including:

- Loss of control by releasing work to a supplier.
- Risk of dealing with a supplier.
- Importance assigned to a supplier's location and the convenience of site visits.
- Quality of the supplier's management team.
- Compatibility of organizational cultures and values.
- Supplier's willingness to remain flexible and accommodate changes.
- Supplier's labor–management climate.
- Supplier's warranty, repair, and support systems.
- Proprietary information and degree of secrecy required.

Step 6. Review the Capabilities of Suppliers. After assessing the costs and qualitative factors of insourcing and outsourcing, determine whether to use current or new suppliers. This requires a review of the technical, financial, manufacturing, and quality-related capabilities of suppliers as described later in this chapter.

Step 7. Make and Implement a Decision. After extensive study, make a decision based on the available information. If you decide to outsource, select a supplier and document the anticipated benefits of outsourcing. If you decide to insource, document the reasons for this decision. Then, negotiate the terms of the purchase contract or acquire assets to initiate internal production.

Step 8. Monitor the Decision and Revise It as Necessary. Insourcing/outsourcing analysis does not end with the start of production or a purchase. Compare the actual results of the decision against estimates and identify potential problems. This information may indicate a need for corrective action, such as terminating or renegotiating the contract.

EXAMINING THE STRATEGIC SOURCING PROCESS

If the decision is to outsource, suppliers must be identified, evaluated, selected, and managed. The processes that are used to identify, evaluate, and award business to suppliers must be linked with an organization's strategic objectives. A typical strategic sourcing process is shown in Figure 10-2. The remainder of this chapter will discuss each step of the strategic sourcing process.

Analyze Spend and Supply Markets

The first step of the strategic sourcing process is to understand what your firm is buying. Often different people within a firm purchase the same or similar products from different suppliers at different prices. **Spend analysis** is a process used to understand what purchases are being made, at what price, and from which specific suppliers. A spend analysis at Boeing found that it was buying 200 different types of safety glasses when two or three different types would suffice. Based on a spend analysis, specifications can be standardized so purchases can be consolidated with fewer suppliers, reducing administrative costs, inventory costs, and often leading to lower prices. Spend analysis reports are typically available through e-procurement systems.

When doing a spend analysis you should consider all purchases, even those that traditionally have not been made by supply managers. For example, purchases made in human resources management (worker benefits programs), marketing and sales (advertising), information technology (hardware and software), and other functional areas should be included in spend analysis.

A market analysis gathers data on the market's structure, including the number of suppliers, the number of buyers, and the nature of competition. This analysis provides information to assess the level of supply chain risk and to help develop an appropriate sourcing strategy, in coordination with other functions. Future price increases or decreases can be forecast using market analysis data.

student activity

Many universities are outsoucing services that were traditionally insourced. Make a list of the major services that your university offers. Which are opportunities for outsourcing and which should be insourced? Why?

LO10-4 Explain the steps in a strategic sourcing process.

spend analysis A process that identifies what purchases are being made in an organization.

FIGURE 10-2 Typical Strategic Sourcing Process

Source: Adapted from L. Smeltzer, J. Manship, and C. Rossetti, "An Analysis of the Integration of Strategic Sourcing and Negotiation Planning," *The Journal of Supply Chain Management* 39, no. 4 (2003), p. 18.

LO10-5 Describe the components in a sourcing strategy.

purchase requisition A document that communicates needs between the user and supply management.

Develop a Sourcing Strategy

When managers reevaluate sourcing practices as the result of a spend analysis, or when something new needs to be purchased, they develop a sourcing strategy. To communicate details such as what, when, and how many to the supply management department, people use an internal company document referred to as a **purchase requisition**. The requisition should be clear, correct, and complete because this is used to develop the criteria used to select suppliers. Otherwise, purchases may not meet the users' needs. For example, the requisition for a cell phone cover would include a blueprint showing dimensions, acceptable tolerances, acceptable materials, and color.

A sourcing strategy is developed using information from the spend analysis and the market analysis. A classic framework developed by Kraljic in 1983 is still relevant today. The framework categorizes sourcing strategies based on supply risk and the value of the total amount spent by the firm and recommends a sourcing strategy (see Figure 10-3).

Sourcing approaches and tactics vary by category:

- *Strategic purchases* represent a high spend level and are high risk. Typically these purchases are unique and core to the firm's performance. Tactics—Use one or two suppliers and build partnerships with them to foster collaboration and innovation.
- *Bottleneck purchases* are high risk and low spend and typically are not core to the firm's performance, but lack of availability can cause delays. Tactics—Use at least two suppliers to assure supply, develop new suppliers, and explore using different materials.
- *Leverage purchases* are low risk but represent a high level of spend. They typically involve standard goods or services where many possible suppliers are available. Tactics—Standardize purchases across the company, use competition to select suppliers, and consolidate purchases with one or a few suppliers to get discounts.
- *Noncritical items* typically are a low percentage of overall spend and have little impact on performance. Tactics—Use vendor-managed inventory (discussed in Chapter 7) and allow users to make their own purchases using online catalogs or corporate credit cards (called *purchasing cards*) to lower the transaction costs of purchasing.

The sourcing strategy determines which suppliers to use for which purchases. The strategy must support the corporate strategy as well as the other functional strategies within the firm. A sourcing strategy must consider:

- Number of suppliers to use.
- Capabilities and location of suppliers.
- Type of relationship and contract length.

FIGURE 10-3
Sourcing Strategies

Source: P. Kraljic, "Purchasing Must Become Supply Management," *Harvard Business Review* 61, no. 5 (1983), p. 112.

	Low — Level of Supply Risk — High
Leverage (High Value of Spend to Firm)	**Strategic**
Standardize purchases	Build collaborative partnerships
Use competition to select suppliers	Single or dual source
Consolidate purchases	Have executive champions in both companies
Noncritical	**Bottleneck**
Increase efficiencies	Use multiple sources
Electronic catalogs	Find substitute materials
Purchasing cards	Develop new suppliers
Vendor managed inventory (Low Value of Spend to Firm)	

Number of Suppliers

How many suppliers should a firm use? Making this decision is called supply base optimization. Using too few suppliers increases supply chain risk and reduces competition. Lack of competition means that prices may be higher, and sources of innovation are limited. Using too many suppliers increases complexity and administrative costs and makes communication and control difficult.

supply base optimization The determination of the number of suppliers to use.

To reduce suppliers you can standardize purchases and buy families of similar items from a single supplier. Another approach is to use a modular design. Rather than purchasing many individual parts from many different suppliers, you can purchase a module from a single supplier. For example, automobile dashboard modules assembled by first-tier suppliers integrate electronics such as the speedometer and fuel gauge and plastic parts. The first-tier suppliers purchase these parts from second-tier suppliers, reducing the number of direct suppliers for the automobile assembler.

When considering a single type of purchase, you can choose either single or multiple sourcing. Single sourcing is the deliberate choice to use a single supplier for a specific purchase. Multiple sourcing involves purchasing a specific material or service from more than one supplier. Multiple sourcing may be too costly if there are high start-up costs, as is the case when specialized tooling must be purchased. Further, with multiple sourcing, suppliers may be unwilling to share information and ideas for fear these will be shared with their competitors.

Some purchases should be single sourced and others should be multiple sourced (Figure 10-3). In bottleneck situations, multiple sourcing decreases supply risk because backup suppliers are available. For strategic purchases, using single sourcing increases cooperation, and for leverage purchases single sourcing leads to quantity discounts and more consistency. Firms with multiple product lines, such as car manufacturers, can get the benefits of both approaches by single sourcing for each model but using different suppliers for different models.

Capabilities and Location

An important part of a sourcing strategy is determining the capabilities and the location of suppliers. Because of advances in transportation and communications it is possible to source from almost anywhere in the world. Consider the following questions when deciding upon a supplier location.

- How important is it to use a close, local supplier? Close proximity makes it easy to communicate, collaborate, and keep delivery costs low. Quality, safety, and sustainability are other reasons that firms choose to source locally. For example, as we saw in the opening vignette, Chipotle Mexican Grill locally sources as part of its commitment to high quality and sustainability. Purchasing locally helps the local economy and creates goodwill in the community.

sustainability

- Is it important to source nationally/regionally? Countries sometimes have laws requiring a company to source in the same country in which it sells products, especially for large purchases such as airplane and construction projects. Other firms use suppliers within regions because of lower transportation costs, quicker response, and lower trade barriers because of agreements such as the North American Free Trade Agreement (NAFTA).

- Should the supplier have a global presence? This can be important so that the supplier can expand into the same regions as the firm. Many global companies, such as Ford, work with global first-tier suppliers.

global

- Is low cost the primary objective? If so, sourcing from suppliers in emerging economies can be considered. During the last 20 years, the trend has been to outsource operations to emerging economies. In the 1990s China was a key offshoring destination but as wage rates increased, companies began sourcing from other Asian countries such as Cambodia, Vietnam, and Bangladesh. Products are manufactured in China increasingly to serve its growing middle class.

Sourcing location analysis must consider the total cost of ownership, not just purchase price. Increasing supply chain risks, higher transportation costs, the need to respond faster to customers, and new manufacturing technologies have some companies *reshoring* (moving operations back to the United States) or *nearshoring* to Central America, the Caribbean, and Mexico. For example, as discussed in the nearby Get Real box, K'Nex has moved toy production back to the United States.

Type of Supplier Relationship and Contract Length

relationships

adversarial relationships Relationships characterized by distrust and limited communications.

arm's-length relationships Relationships limited to simple purchasing transactions.

What types of relationships should a firm have with its suppliers? Buyers and suppliers interact in different ways, depending on the circumstances. Sometimes, they simply receive and fill orders. Other times they work closely together and seamlessly integrate many activities from initial product or process design through routine deliveries of standing orders. The relationship's design should fit with the situation. Four types of relationships categorize the degree of interaction, information sharing, and collaboration between buyers and suppliers, as shown in Figure 10-4.

At one end of the spectrum, adversarial relationships represent the traditional way that buyers and suppliers have approached each other. These relationships are typified by distrust, limited communications, and short-term business transactions. Adversarial relationships can be serious obstacles to effective supply chain management. Arm's-length relationships tend to be limited to simple purchasing transactions, but they lack the high levels of distrust and antagonism often associated with adversarial relationships. For some supplier relationships, an arm's-length relationship is sufficient.

In adversarial and arm's-length relationships, buyers attempt to minimize dependency through multiple sourcing. Suppliers also try to minimize dependency on any one buyer, to minimize the buyer's power in negotiations. Price is the focus in adversarial or arm's-length relationships. Suppliers try to obtain the highest possible price while buyers try to squeeze the supplier's profit margin to a minimum. Buyers and suppliers do not share information about cost, the market, competition, or their strategies. They view information as a resource to be used to gain power over the other party. Lack of trust, loyalty, and

GET REAL

K'Nex® Reshoring Toy Production

As child, many of you may have played with K'Nex®, the snaptogether plastic building set toys in which you can create planes, robots, and roller-coasters. Like most toys, K'Nex's products were primarily made by suppliers in China. In the last few years, K'Nex has been reshoring much of its production back to the United States. Greater control over material quality and toy safety were key factors driving the reshoring decision, but increasing wages in China also were a factor.

After reshoring, K'Nex has realized a savings of over 20 percent, primarily because of lower inventory and transportation costs. By producing products closer to its retail customers, the company can make and deliver the toys that are in hot demand faster. This capability is especially critical given the seasonal nature of toy sales. In moving production back to the United States, K'Nex has made some design changes to make production more economical and has automated its packaging process using robotics.

© John L. White/KRT/Newscom

Adapted from: http://www.wsj.com/articles/SB10001424127 8873232937045783340 62190251402.

FIGURE 10-4 Spectrum of Supplier Relationships

Transaction-Oriented ←→ Collaborative

Adversarial Relationship	*Arm's-length Relationship*	*Acceptance of Mutual Goals*	*Full Partnership*

Maintain independence
Focus on price
Short-term focus
Hoard information
Buyer-sales relations
Focus on self-interest

Recognize mutual dependence
Focus on total cost
Long-term focus
Share information
Cross-functional relations
Share risk/reward

commitment typically limit these relationships to the short term. Price competition and high stress levels make for high turnover in adversarial and arm's-length relationships.

Acceptance of mutual goals represents a major step toward collaboration, but it lacks the commitment of resources associated with full partnership. Also called strategic alliances, **full partnerships** have close working relations, trust, mutual respect, and highly integrated operations. Full partners acknowledge their interdependencies and work together to reduce total costs so both parties benefit. Partners frequently exchange schedules, information and specifications for new product designs, and cost data, along with other information. Many buyers allow suppliers direct access to their information systems, and vice versa. By working together, partners expect to create better solutions than they could create alone. In Brazil, Ford Motor Co.'s Camaçari assembly plant is an excellent example of buyer–supplier partnerships (see the Get Real box below).

It takes a long time to build true partnerships; thus, long-term contracts are common. Partnerships foster long-term loyalty and mutual respect, ultimately leading to many of the advantages of vertical integration. Partners must trust each other. Trust is elusive, but it tends to grow when both the supplier and buyer benefit. Further, a partnership requires close, open, informal interactions and frequent contact among members of several different functions in the respective firms (sales, engineering, operations, and so on). In many cases, this contact extends beyond the professional level and includes social interactions.

The Japanese keiretsu system used by Toyota and Honda provides an example of partner relationships. Toyota and Honda have long-term relationships with their suppliers and work closely with them to improve the entire supply chain. Honda and Toyota spend an extensive amount of time understanding their suppliers' operations and organizations.

acceptance of mutual goals A collaborative relationship that lacks the commitment of a full partnership.

full partnerships Relationships that have close working relations, trust, mutual respect, and highly integrated operations.

global

GET REAL

Supplier Partnerships at Ford Brazil

Rural Brazil has turned out to be a success story for the Ford Motor Co. Ten years ago Ford was struggling in Brazil, but its amazing turnaround is due in part to a state-of-the-art assembly plant with a twist. At Ford's Camaçari assembly plant, more than two dozen suppliers work side-by-side with Ford employees inside the complex. For example, Visteon Corp. workers connect the wiring in a dashboard module for a Ford EcoSport while Lear Corp. employees in the manufacturing cell next to them build seats for the same vehicle.

By working together, both Ford and its suppliers benefit. Inventories are minimized as subassemblies flow directly into the main Ford assembly line at the precise point and time they are needed. Suppliers have more flexibility and better understand

Ford's needs. When quality problems occur they are fixed quickly through collaboration with Ford and supplier engineers.

© Bill Waugh/AP Images

They supervise suppliers and provide constant feedback. In addition, they improve suppliers' technical capabilities and work together to improve processes. Honda and Toyota encourage suppliers to collaborate with each other through supplier study groups.

Ultimately, the type of relationships developed with a given supplier should be consistent with the category it fits, as shown in Figure 10-3. Most firms reserve partnerships for only the most critical suppliers who provide strategically important purchases. Arm's-length relationships are appropriate for bottleneck or noncritical items. However, a commitment to purchase more over a period of time reduces transaction costs, confirms supply availability, and reduces price uncertainty. For leverage purchases, annual contracts are often used. For strategic purchases, longer-term contracts lasting through the product's life are the norm.

Identify Potential Suppliers

Once you have a sourcing strategy, the next step is to identify potential suppliers. There are many ways to do this. A starting point is to consider the firm's current suppliers or those used in the past. Using current suppliers saves time, reduces sourcing costs, and is consistent with supply base optimization. To reduce the time and effort needed to find qualified suppliers, supply managers develop preferred supplier lists that are used when a new supplier is needed. Sources of information about potential new suppliers include the Internet, catalogs, trade directories, trade journals, and networking through trade associations.

Assess and Select Suppliers

LO10-6 Assess and select suppliers.

As you know from experience, you need to spend much more time evaluating suppliers for some purchases than for others. For example, when buying detergent, typically you make a quick decision based on the lowest price or a brand name that you trust. However, when buying a new car, you will spend much more time researching the car's performance, options, reliability, warranty, cost for service, and financing packages, and you will most likely visit several dealers to take test drives before making your purchase.

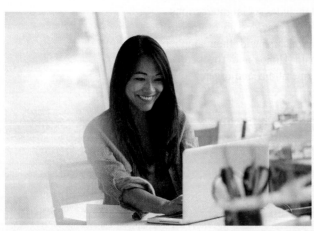

© Tim Robbins/Mint Images/Getty Images

Similarly, the evaluation and supplier selection processes differ for corporate purchases. How suppliers are assessed and selected depends upon the level of spend, the nature of the purchase, and the type of relationship desired. Purchases that account for a large amount of spend, are strategically important, are from a new supplier, or need a full partnership require an extensive formal evaluation. To understand all aspects of the supplier's capabilities and organization, cross-functional teams typically do these evaluations. For smaller spend levels and noncritical purchases, the supply manager typically makes the selection decision.

Most organizations use e-procurement systems to automate the entire procurement process, including developing requirements, communicating with suppliers, obtaining quotes from suppliers, issuing purchase orders, obtaining supplier's invoices, and making payments. Within the e-procurement system, employees within the firm can communicate the requirements of what they need to buy using a purchase requisition.

request for proposal (RFP) or request for quotation (RFQ) Documents sent to suppliers to request bids. These must describe the purchase requirements as specifically as possible.

After the requirements are determined, the supply manager develops a **request for proposal (RFP)** or a **request for quotation (RFQ)** in the e-procurement system. These documents describe the purchase requirements as clearly as possible in terms of technical specifications, quality, quantity, delivery requirements, packaging, shipping, and any other characteristics. When purchasing services, a statement of work (SOW) also is used to explain specific activities, performance measures, and timelines. The RFP, RFQ, and SOW must be correct, because they communicate the requirements to suppliers so they can develop quotations.

If the supplier wishes to do business with the firm, a salesperson submits a quotation that is then evaluated by the supply manager and a cross-functional team, if it is a major purchase. Each quotation is carefully evaluated compared to the requirements. For major strategic purchases, if the supplier is new to the firm, the sourcing team may visit the supplier to gather first-hand information about the supplier's capabilities, such as:

- Operations processes and systems.
- Quality processes and systems.
- Labor skills, training, and morale.
- Technological capabilities.
- Supply management processes.
- Logistics systems.
- Financial stability.
- Management capabilities and attitudes.

When potential suppliers have different strengths and weaknesses, direct comparisons of quotations and capabilities can be difficult. Tools for analyzing and comparing suppliers' capabilities range from simple methods such as categorical ratings and weighted-point models, to more comprehensive approaches such as the analytic hierarchy process (AHP) (see Chan, "Interactive Selection Model" in the Selected Readings at the end of the chapter for more details) and mathematical programming models.

A **weighted-point model** links the supplier's performance rating to the firm's competitive priorities. Working with members from key functions, each performance category is weighted so the total sum of the weights equals 100 percent. The weights should reflect the company's priorities for the purchase. As business needs change, the weights are adjusted to reflect new priorities.

weighted-point model Establishes performance categories that are weighted according to importance.

After assigning weights, the data gathered in the assessment is used to rate each supplier on each category using scales of 1 to 3 or 1 to 5, with the higher score indicating better performance. The rating for each category is then multiplied by the weight to get its score, as

activity

Assume that you will be selecting a new apartment. Develop a weighted-point model to assist in your decision-making process.

shown in Table 10-3. Based on this model, Supplier B would be selected because its score is the highest. Although this method results in a numerical score, it is important to note that both the ratings and the weights are based on managerial judgment and therefore subjective. In practice, judgment, and not just the total score, should be used to determine which suppliers to select. The weighted-point model also is used for ongoing supplier evaluations in supplier scorecards.

TABLE 10-3 Weighted-Point Model for Supplier Selection*

Category	Weight	Supplier A		Supplier B		Supplier C	
		Rating	Score	Rating	Score	Rating	Score
Quality systems	40%	3	1.2	5	2.0	3	1.2
Delivery capability	40%	2	0.8	3	1.2	4	1.6
Price	20%	5	1.0	3	0.6	2	0.4
Weighted score	100%		3.0		3.8		3.2

*All scores on a five-point scale with 1 = poor, 5 = excellent.

Online Competitive Bidding and Reverse Auctions

competitive bidding A selection process in which suppliers submit bids to win the buyer's business.

After you have assessed suppliers, online competitive bidding, online reverse auctions, or negotiation are used to select the supplier or suppliers to receive the contract. **Competitive bidding** is used when price is the most important factor, the specifications are known and clear, the spend level is large enough, and there are a number of equally qualified suppliers who are willing to compete. Mature, standard products are often sourced using competitive bidding because price is often the only difference among suppliers. Competitive bidding is often required for purchases by local, state, and the federal governments. Competitive bidding is used when relationships are adversarial or arm's-length.

online reverse auctions Competitive bidding systems that allow suppliers to submit multiple bids within a fixed time.

Online reverse auctions allow suppliers to competitively bid for a buyer's business in real time. During a fixed time period, suppliers submit multiple bids and typically can see the bid prices submitted by other suppliers, creating competition. It is important that all suppliers included in the auction are qualified. The auction process is similar to e-Bay, but instead of an auction to sell an item—driving prices higher—reverse online auctions use bidding to drive prices lower. Procter & Gamble reportedly identified over $290 million in potential savings through online reverse auctions.

Negotiation

negotiation A bargaining process involving a buyer and seller seeking to reach mutual agreement.

If one supplier is preferred or is the only one qualified, *negotiation* establishes the price and other details and terms of the contract. **Negotiation** is an exploratory bargaining process (planning, reviewing, analyzing, compromising) involving a buyer and seller seeking to reach mutual agreement on all aspects of a contract—including price, service, specifications, technical and quality requirements, contract length, delivery frequency, shipping, and payment terms.

Normally, negotiation is the preferred method of supplier selection for strategic purchases that require full partnerships. Unlike the situation for competitive bidding and online reverse auctions, negotiation is a better choice when:

- A high degree of uncertainty in the requirements exists or the requirements may change because of a long lead time.
- Different combinations of requirements may be acceptable.
- Early supplier involvement in product development is required.
- A complex start-up or customized equipment is needed.

activity

student

Find an example of a negotiation in a TV show or movie. Was the negotiation successful? Why, or why not? What went well in the negotiation and what would you change if you were handling this negotiation?

Unlike the typical Hollywood depiction of negotiation, ideally, both the buyer and the supplier should be able to meet their objectives. During the face-to-face meeting, problem solving creates solutions where both the buyer and the supplier benefit. The information sharing and give and take that occurs can build close, cooperative relationships. The outcome of a successful negotiation should be a contract and a good working relationship between the buyer and the supplier.

A successful negotiation starts well in advance of the actual face-to-face meeting. Planning is the most important stage in negotiation. For major negotiations, the supply manager facilitates a cross-functional team whose role is to gather and analyze information. During planning, a negotiation range is set for all of the important aspects of the negotiation, including price. The range must have a minimum, target, and maximum level, with room to move. The overlap of the buyer's and the supplier's ranges is where the give-and-take occurs. For example, if you are buying a used car, your target might be $10,000, and you would be willing to pay up to $12,000, but you suspect that the seller will not go below $9,000. Then, your negotiation range is $9,000 to $12,000. The seller's range is actually $10,000 to $13,000, so the actual area for negotiation is the overlap of $10,000 to $12,000. The price that you eventually agree upon will be in this range.

It is important to note that price is rarely the most important factor in negotiation. Negotiation should include all factors that are important to the buyer and supplier, such as quality, delivery, contract length, performance measurement, technical support, continuous improvement, and contract terms and conditions.

Manage Ongoing Supplier Relationships

The signing of a contract and a handshake is just the beginning of a buyer–supplier relationship. Buyers and suppliers must develop processes to share information and coordinate their activities. Buyers must monitor supplier performance and ensure that suppliers improve if necessary. Many firms take a holistic approach called *supplier relationship management.* Each of these aspects of managing the ongoing relationship is discussed in this section.

LO10-7 Understand ways to manage ongoing supplier relationships.

Information Sharing and Coordination with Suppliers

To signal to the supplier that goods or services are needed, the supplier managers use the e-procurement system to issue a *purchase order (PO).* A purchase order (PO) is a legally binding document prepared by a buyer to describe all terms and conditions of a purchase. The buyer and supplier share business documents needed for the purchase transaction, including purchase orders, invoices, and shipping notices, in electronic formats based on agreed upon standards. The payment process requires matching of the PO, the supplier's invoice, and the receiving documents that show what was actually sent.

Buyers and suppliers must carefully coordinate forecasting, planning, and scheduling so products arrive exactly when needed. For example, when an oil refinery undergoes a shutdown for routine maintenance, the work of over 1,000 different equipment and service suppliers must be coordinated. Sharing sensitive information such as forecasts and customer demand underscores the importance of trust among supply chain members. Better information reduces the need for inventory within a supply chain. Chapter 12 explains collaborative planning, forecasting, and replenishment (CPFR), in which supply chain members collaborate to meet customer demand while reducing supply chain inventory and costs.

Firms integrate information systems with key suppliers. For example, many share planning and scheduling information using materials requirements planning (MRP—see Chapter 14). Buyers have supplier portals on their websites so suppliers can access the buyer's scheduling information. Current scheduling information helps suppliers set priorities and do a better job of operations planning. Representatives of the buyer and the suppliers can share reactions to the schedules and discuss the impact of changes. These discussions educate each party about the other's capabilities, helping both to plan for the future. They allow the supplier and the buyer to cooperatively adjust production schedules to optimize throughput, ultimately reduce costs and lead time, and enhance quality.

© fatihhoca/Getty Images

As described in Chapter 7, some firms, especially big-box retailers and grocery stores, use vendor-managed inventory (VMI) in which the supplier manages its customer's inventory. Walmart was a leader in adopting VMI, and many other retail firms now use this approach. The supplier regularly reviews the customer's inventory and restocks as needed. With VMI, suppliers understand what their customers are actually using and thus can plan their own operations more effectively, reducing excess inventory and waste in the supply chain.

sustainability

supplier scorecard Used to report a supplier's performance on key performance indicators (KPI).

Supplier Performance Monitoring and Improvement

For ongoing supplier relationships, it is important to set formal goals for suppliers and to measure performance against these goals on a regular basis. Supply managers identify the key performance indicators (KPI) in terms of quality, delivery, cost reduction, service, or other performance attributes that are important for their firms. Suppliers receive regular feedback, typically monthly or quarterly, in a **supplier scorecard**. For example, Philips, an electronics company, rates its suppliers on five main performance areas: delivery, quality, cost, responsiveness/support, and innovation. Large companies post scorecards on their websites in supplier portals that can be accessed by suppliers using a secure login.

Supplier scorecards are used in several ways. Some firms categorize suppliers based on an overall score. For example, Federal Mogul, a first-tier automotive supplier, categorizes suppliers as preferred, acceptable, and developmental. Firms give preferred suppliers the opportunity to participate in product development and to win new business. Acceptable suppliers must develop a plan for improving their performance to the preferred level. Developmental suppliers must improve performance, or they are targeted to be replaced. Rather than replacing suppliers, companies such as Honda and Toyota work with suppliers to help them improve their performance and capabilities (for example, by implementing lean practices). Once they have received the business, buyers expect their suppliers to continually improve, especially by reducing costs.

A firm's best suppliers can become certified. The type of certification varies with the industry and firm needs. **Supplier certification** is an assessment that verifies that the supplier operates, maintains, improves, and documents effective procedures related to the buyer's requirements. Quality certification reduces the need for incoming quality inspections. When suppliers are certified, buyers do not have to do incoming inspection, a process called "dock to stock."

supplier certification An assessment that verifies effective procedures related to the buyer's requirements.

Some firms develop their own processes to certify suppliers. For example, suppliers who consistently demonstrate excellence in quality, reliability, delivery, cycle time, and productivity and who provide evidence of an effective quality management system become certified. Typically, a formal audit, including a site visit, is done as part of the certification process. To reduce certification costs and to provide objectivity, some companies rely upon certifications done by external organizations such as ISO certifications in quality (ISO 9000) and environment (ISO 14000). Chapter 6 describes ISO 9000 quality certifications.

Supplier Relationship Management (SRM)

supplier relationship management (SRM) A comprehensive system, facilitated by software, that works on managing the firm's interactions with its supply base.

Supplier relationship management (SRM) tries to do for supplier management what CRM (Chapter 9) does with customers. That is, SRM is a comprehensive system, facilitated by software, that manages the firm's interactions with its supply base. The goal of SRM is to streamline the processes and interactions that exist between the firm and its various suppliers so they are more efficient and transparent. SRM helps the firm identify critical suppliers and to improve how the firm works with those suppliers on such activities as reducing costs, introducing new products, creating cash (through inventory reduction and payment term management—i.e., how the firm pays its suppliers), mitigating supply and regulatory risks, and ensuring a secure supply of scarce materials. SRM deals with all stages of the supply management process (identifying suppliers, working with suppliers, placing orders, and postorder contract activities, which include inventory management and warranty recoveries). SRM is widely used and can be found in media and entertainment, automotive, pharmaceutical and medical products, and health care industries.

CHAPTER SUMMARY

1. Effective supply management contributes to an organization's performance by ensuring availability and timely delivery; identifying, assessing and mitigating supply chain risk; reducing total costs; enhancing quality; accessing technology; increasing innovation; and fostering sustainability.

2. The strategic decision to insource or outsource goods or services is based on a thorough analysis that considers both cost and qualitative factors.

3. Strategic sourcing is a process used to identify, evaluate, and award business to suppliers that meet a firm's strategic objectives.

4. A sourcing strategy is a plan for the number of suppliers, their capabilities and locations, and the types of buyer-supplier relationships.

5. Suppliers are selected using online competitive bidding, online reverse auctions, or negotiations. A weighted-point model can be used to compare suppliers with different capabilities and offerings.

6. Managing the ongoing relationship with suppliers involves developing processes for information sharing and coordination and measuring supplier performance. Supplier relationship management is a systematic approach to managing all supply management processes.

KEY TERMS

acceptance of mutual goals   347
adversarial relationships   346
arm's-length relationships   346
competitive bidding   350
fixed costs per contract   342
fixed costs per order   342
full partnerships   347
insourcing   341
make or buy decision   341
negotiation   350

online reverse auctions   350
outsourcing   341
purchase requisition   344
request for proposal (RFP)   348
request for quotation (RFQ)   348
sourcing   336
spend analysis   343
supplier certification   352
supplier relationship management (SRM)   352

supplier scorecard   352
supply base optimization   345
supply chain resilience   337
supply chain risk   336
supply management   336
sustainability   340
total cost of ownership (TCO)   338
variable costs   342
weighted-point model   349

1. Can you think of an organization that has benefited by extending sustainability to its supply chain? What about one whose supply chain practices have hurt its reputation?

2. Consider the purchase of a new mobile phone. How would you determine the total cost of ownership? What are the costs that you might incur before the purchase, during the purchase, and after the purchase?

3. How would you do a spend analysis if you were the supply manager for a large state university? What are likely to be the most important spend categories (excluding dining services and residence life)?

4. The top management team at your company is considering outsourcing the supply management function. Do you support this idea? Why, or why not?

5. Many universities have outsourced dining services. Do you think this is a good idea? Why or why not?

6. Marriott and Hilton corporations have hotels around the world. What type of purchases should be local, national/regional, or global? Why?

7. For an organization with which you are familiar, provide an example of each of the four categories of purchases shown in Figure 10-3. What sourcing strategy would you use for each? Why?

8. Why don't companies seek full partnerships with all of their suppliers?

9. When evaluating a supplier's financial stability, what are some key indicators to consider? Why?

10. What are the costs and challenges involved with switching suppliers?

1. Insourcing/Outsourcing Decision Process

A major corporation that develops and manufactures lawn care products such as fertilizer, herbicide, and seed is evaluating whether it should insource or outsource the landscaping and lawn care of its corporate headquarters located outside of Augusta, Georgia. Currently, the landscaping is outsourced, and the supplier's performance has been excellent. In the Augusta area, there are a number of landscaping companies that have the capabilities to do this job.

To maintain the corporate headquarters grounds, approximately 5,000 hours per year are needed. The annual fixed costs to insource are estimated to be $10,000 per year and the variable costs are $14/hour. Bids from 10 qualified landscaping companies range from a low of $78,000 to a high of $90,000 for a one-year contract. The current supplier's bid is $81,000/year.

Apply the insourcing/outsourcing decision process in Figure 10-1 to make a recommendation.

Solution:

Developing and producing lawn care products are core competencies of the company. However, *doing* landscaping and lawn care is not. There are many capable suppliers available, the process is standard, technology is known, and risk is low, suggesting that landscaping and lawn care are suitable for outsourcing. By outsourcing, the company can focus its internal resources on its core business rather than lawn maintenance.

The cost to insource is $80,000. Suppliers are able to provide this service at the same or a lower price.

$$\text{Total Cost} = [(\text{Variable Costs} \times \text{Volume}) + \text{Fixed Costs}]$$
$$= [(\$14/\text{hour} \times 5{,}000 \text{ hours/year}) + \$10{,}000]$$
$$= \$80{,}000/\text{year}$$

The current supplier's performance has been excellent. Based on the lack of fit with the company's core competencies, the good suitability for outsourcing, the cost analysis, and the current supplier's excellent performance, outsourcing is recommended. Further, it makes sense to continue to use the current supplier. Although other suppliers quoted a lower price, the cost of switching to a new, unproven supplier is likely to consume the small $3,000 cost savings.

2. **Weighted-Point Model for Supplier Evaluation**

Dazzling Lighting Inc. in Cincinnati, Ohio, is evaluating suppliers for its new line of lighting products to be sold to home builders. Three potential suppliers have been identified and evaluated by a cross-functional team. Using the data gathered from a supplier survey and site visits, the team applied a weighted-point model to be used in the supplier selection decision.

Overview of Suppliers

Supplier Name	EZ Lite	North-South Trading	Zhenjiang Lighting
Annual Sales	$200 million	$350 million	$100 million
Location	Fremont, Ohio	Matamoros, Mexico	Zhenjiang, China
Defective Parts per Million (ppm)	75	130	120
Transportation Time	1 day	5 days	45 days
On-time Delivery	99%	92%	86%
Purchase Price	$4.50/unit	$3.00/unit	$2.15/unit

Supplier Evaluation Scores*

Category	Weight	EZ Lite		North-South Trading		Zhenjiang Lighting	
		Rating	Score	Rating	Score	Rating	Score
Quality Performance and Systems	40%	4	1.6	3	1.2	3	1.2
Management Capabilities and Attitudes	30%	4	1.2	3	0.9	3	0.9
Delivery Performance	20%	5	1.0	4	0.8	2	0.4
Purchase Price	10%	1	0.1	4	0.4	5	0.5
Total Weighted Score			**3.9**		**3.3**		**3.0**

*All scores on a five-point scale with 1 = poor, 5 = excellent.

Solution:

EZ Lite received the highest overall weighted score. However, the final decision of which supplier to use should be based on judgment.

PROBLEMS

1. The supply manager at a dishwasher manufacturer is assessing whether the company should purchase the pump from a supplier or assemble the pump in-house. Forecasts suggest that 15,000 pumps are needed per year. The annual fixed costs to assemble the pumps are $120,000 per year. The variable costs per unit to assemble the pump are $25/unit. The pumps can be purchased for $30/unit. Does the cost analysis support insourcing or outsourcing pump assembly?

2. An online retailer must decide if it should insource or outsource its website maintenance. The company estimates that 4,000 hours per year will be needed to maintain its website. To insource maintenance requires $25,000 in fixed costs per year and $27/hour in variable costs. Quotes from suppliers show that website maintenance can be outsourced for $35 per hour. Does the cost analysis support insourcing or outsourcing website maintenance?

3. A furniture manufacturer is assessing whether it should make or buy the wooden frames for upholstered dining room chairs. The forecast is for 100,000 chairs to be produced per year. The fixed costs per year to make the frames are $150,000 and the variable costs are $5/frame. The supplier's bid is $8/frame. Does the cost analysis support insourcing or outsourcing the chair frames?

4. A construction equipment manufacturer is considering outsourcing the assembly of dashboard components. Strategically the company is focusing on design and final equipment assembly. The company expects to make 75,000 units next year. The total variable cost to assemble the dashboard component is $270/unit, including both direct labor and direct materials. The fixed costs associated with the assembly process are $500,000 per year. A supplier has quoted a delivered price of $280/unit for up to 80,000 units per year. What are the total costs to insource and to buy the assembly from the supplier? Considering cost and strategic factors, should dashboard assembly be insourced or outsourced to the supplier? Why?

5. WatchNU is a company that designs and manufacturers drones for military use. The supply manager is getting ready to renegotiate the contract with the security service provider that it uses for its offices and manufacturing plant. Three suppliers responded to the RFP for security services for the next three years. The current security services provider, SecureIT, quoted $990,000 per year. Two suppliers that have not been used by WatchNU in the past quoted $890,000 and $965,000, respectively.

   The supply manager is also analyzing the costs associated with insourcing security services rather than using a supplier as a way to reduce costs and provide greater control over security. The salary and benefits package for a full-time security services manager is estimated to be $100,000. Other fixed costs are estimated to be $30,000/year. Three security guards are needed 24 hours/day, 365 days per year. The salary and benefits for the security guards is $30/hour.

   What are the costs to insource the security services? Do you recommend insourcing or outsourcing the security services? Why?

6. The Big Apple Pizza Company, a manufacturer and distributor of frozen food products, is introducing a new frozen Chicago-style pizza. The new sauce for this pizza is a unique, special recipe and it resulted in very positive taste test ratings in market research studies. The supply manager is trying to decide if the company should make or buy this sauce. The current forecast is for 120,000 total gallons of the sauce to be used over the estimated three-year life of the product. In the first year 30,000 gallons are forecast, with 45,000 gallons each in years two and three.

   Currently, Big Apple purchases all of the sauce used in its products, ready-made, from a single source, Top Tomato. The supplier's production plant is located 320 miles from Big Apple's production plant, and weekly truckload deliveries are currently used. The company buys approximately 600,000 gallons of sauce per year from Top Tomato. The sauce supplier has provided high-quality, low-cost standard pizza sauces to Big Apple and other pizza makers for over five years. The current sauce supplier has quoted a delivered price of $2.85/gallon for the sauce if a three-year contract is used. Conformance to quality standards for Top Tomato's sauce has been 99 percent and on-time delivery has been 95 percent.

Big Apple's manufacturing manager has stated that a facility and sauce-making equipment are needed at an investment of $60,000 because the company does not make any sauces. The manufacturing manager stated that he had been considering laying off several workers because of lower demand for frozen pot pies, so he was in favor of making the sauce. The following direct costs have been estimated for making the sauce. Typically, overhead costs for Big Apple's production facility are allocated to products at a rate of 200 percent of direct labor.

Apply the eight steps for the insourcing/outsourcing decision. Should Big Apple Pizza make or buy the sauce? Why?

| Direct labor | $0.25/gallon |
| Direct materials | $2.00/gallon |

7. Your company has used competitive bidding to select a supplier for janitorial services. Three suppliers returned acceptable bids within the allotted time frame. Based on these ratings from the supplier assessment, which supplier appears to be the best? Why? How would the final selection decision be made?

Category	Weight	Supplier A	Supplier B	Supplier C
		Rating	Rating	Rating
Quality Systems	40%	3	3	4
Financial Stability	25%	2	3	1
Management Experience	20%	2	3	3
Price	15%	4	4	5

Note: All scores are based on a five-point scale, with 1 = poor and 5 = excellent.

8. As the buyer for the city of Perrysburg, you are evaluating a supplier for garbage cans to be used in the city's parks. Three suppliers returned acceptable bids within the allotted time frame. Based on these ratings from the supplier assessment, which supplier appears to be the best? Why? How would the final selection decision be made?

Category	Weight	Supplier A	Supplier B	Supplier C
		Rating	Rating	Rating
Design	10%	4	3	2
Delivery	30%	2	3	5
Warranty	20%	5	1	2
Price	40%	3	5	4

Note: All scores are based on a five-point scale, with 1 = poor and 5 = excellent.

9. Simply Chocolate, a retailer selling gourmet candy, has decided to expand its market by adding online sales. The supply and marketing managers must select a company to develop a website. Based on an initial screening, the team has narrowed the list to four potential suppliers. Based on these ratings, which supplier appears to be the best? Why? How would the final selection decision be made?

Company	Weight	WebTex	CoolWeb	Dazzling Designs	Major Marketing
		Rating*	Rating*	Rating*	Rating*
Number of Sites Developed	45%	3	1	4	5
Technical Expertise	30%	3	3	5	4
Responsiveness	15%	4	5	3	1
Price	10%	4	5	3	1

*All scores on a five-point scale with 1 = poor, 5 = excellent.

10. The senior buyer at How Does Your Garden Grow Inc. needs to select a supplier for plastic patio chairs for a one-year contract. The chairs will be shipped to the company's distribution center in Toledo, Ohio. Three potential suppliers have been identified and data have been gathered. Develop a weighted-point model. Based on this model, which supplier should be selected? What other factors should be considered?

Company	ABC Molding	Perfection Plastics	I-Products
Annual Sales	$ 9 million	$ 80 million	$ 30 million
Plant Location	Erie, PA	Oakland, CA	St. Louis, MO
Purchase Price per Unit	$9.50	$11.39	$11.25
Quality (defective parts per million)	300 ppm	60 ppm	160 ppm
Delivery (% on time)	99.5%	90%	94%
Transportation Time	1 day	5 days	2 days

Supplier Assessment Scores

		ABC Molding		Perfection Plastics		I-Products	
Category	Weight	Rating*	Score	Rating*	Score	Rating*	Score
Quality Performance and Systems	50%	2		5		3	
Management Capabilities and Attitudes	10%	3		5		3	
Delivery Performance	20%	5		1		3	
Purchase Price	20%	5		2		2	

*All scores on a five-point scale with 1 = poor, 5 = excellent.

CASE

Strategic Sourcing at Best Banks

Karen Williams, the new director of supply management at Best Banks, was excited to be working at her new job. After gaining over 10 years of experience in various supply management positions at a first-tier automotive supplier, she was looking forward to being in a new industry.

Best Banks is a medium-sized bank with assets of over $1 billion. It is a community-focused financial services company with 35 branches in northwest and central Ohio. Providing competent and friendly service to its customers is critical while keeping the costs of banking affordable. Bank employees are encouraged to remember their customers and call each by name.

Historically, each branch manager did purchasing. However, within the last five years, the bank created a centralized supply management department that is responsible for the bank's major purchases. For instance, this group handled the sourcing when the bank upgraded its information system to make online banking easier for its customers.

Based on her experience in the automotive industry, Karen knew strategic sourcing could be a way to increase the value of supply management at Best Banks. As a first step she conducted a spend analysis. After information systems (30 percent), the two top spend categories for the bank were temporary personnel (15 percent) and print advertising and promotional materials (8 percent).

Karen decided to explore each of these categories in more detail. She found that each of the branch locations selected and made its own decision for which temporary agency to use. In fact, over 20 different temporary personnel agencies were being used. The marketing department at the bank's headquarters made all of the sourcing decisions for advertising spend, and Karen was surprised to learn that the supply management department was not involved.

Questions

1. Using the framework in Figure 10-3, how would you categorize information technology, temporary personnel, and advertising as spend categories for the bank? Why?

2. What recommendations do you have with respect to sourcing temporary personnel? Why? What challenges should Karen expect to encounter?

3. Should the supply management department be involved in the purchasing of print advertising and promotional materials? Why, or why not? What should supply management's role be?

CASE

Trail Frames Chassis: Insourcing/Outsourcing Decision

Trail Frames Chassis (TFC) of Elkhart, Indiana, is a major manufacturer of chassis for the motor home and van markets. Two unemployed truck-manufacturing engineers founded TFC in 1976. Since then, the company has grown into one of the largest suppliers of chassis. In the past, TFC has produced only a pusher type of chassis, one that is powered by a diesel engine located in the rear. This design offers many advantages (e.g., no tunnel for the transmission, reduced engine noise, better handling). However, these chassis tend to be expensive, and they are used in motor homes that are very expensive ($150,000 and up). Recently, TFC entered into an agreement with Gulf Stream to produce low-end pusher-type chassis for motor homes priced under $100,000. These new designs offer some of the features of the higher-end pushers, but at a lower cost.

Today's market for motor homes and vans is increasingly made up of people in their late 40s to 60s. These older customers want a motor home that rides like a car, and they are willing to pay for innovations such as ABS (anti-lock breaking systems), assisted steering, and computer-balanced suspension. TFC is the technological leader in this market. TFC sells to large manufacturers such as Winnebago, Airstream, and Gulf Stream. In general, these companies order small quantities (5 to 10 in a batch), and many of the units in a batch are customized to a specific customer's requirements.

Achieving continued success in the motor home and van markets is difficult because of the rate of change taking place. TFC has become successful because of its ability to develop new product designs in a timely fashion. This ability stems from TFC's extensive experience with motor home users and TFC's knowledge of new technological advances. It is generally recognized that no one in the industry can match TFC's design and marketing knowledge base. Until recently, TFC could design and build a chassis in less than 30 days. However, the lead times have been growing. As a result of limited capital, TFC has found itself unable to keep up with demand. Management has identified the design department as the major bottleneck. While pondering this problem, the management team was approached by Computer-Images, a design house located in Grand Rapids, Michigan. Computer-Images has made an attractive offer to take over the design responsibilities for the low end of TFC's product line. Furthermore, Computer-Images has offered to work with TFC as a virtual corporation—one in which specifications would be generated by TFC and sent electronically to Computer-Images. The new drawings would then be designed and electronic copies sent back to TFC. Outsourcing the low-end work to Computer-Images would free up TFC's staff to focus on meeting the demand for medium- to high-end chassis.

Based on the information provided in Table 10-4, complete the insourcing/outsourcing analysis. Prepare a report for the company president with the findings and your recommendation. Only one option can be recommended.

TABLE 10-4 Information for the Analysis

	Computer-Image Proposal	TFC Make Option
Contract Period	3 years (with option to cancel after first year with 45 days warning)	Not applicable
Cost per Design	$225 per chassis	$490 per chassis (arrived at by summing direct labor computers and including corporate overhead)
Number of Chassis per Year	1,000 minimum to 2,500 maximum (1,250 expected)	2,000 chassis maximum (assuming stable growth in other chassis lines)
	TFC must commit to 1,250 designs per year	
Setup Costs (one-time cost)	$300,000 (computer systems, training, establishing computer linkages)	$200,000 (to expand design capacity)
Lead Times (sending specifications to receipt of new design)	< 2 working days	5 to 10 working days
Quality	All designs to be tested via computer simulation and certified feasible	Feasibility of designs based on expertise of designers
Time until Delivery of Design 1	3 months	Immediately
Other Terms and Conditions	Understood that Computer-Images would be free to work with any other chassis builder	To significantly expand design capacity would require a period of between 6 and 8 months
	All designs generated by Computer-Images would remain the property of Computer-Images	
	Computer-Images insists on a training period of 6 months in which the designers of TFC would teach Computer-Images designers about the critical design tasks encountered in the motor home market	

SELECTED
READINGS & INTERNET SITES

Arruñada, B., and X. Vázquez. "When Your Contract Manufacturer Becomes Your Competitor." *Harvard Business Review* 84, no. 9 (2006), pp. 135–44.

Cavinato, J. L. "Supply Management Defined," Jan. 2010, **https://www.instituteforsupplymanagement.org/content.cfm?ItemNumber=5558**.

Chan, F. "Interactive Selection Model for the Supplier Selection Process: An Analytical Hierarchy Process Approach." *International Journal of Production Research* 41, no. 15 (2003), pp. 3549–79.

Eisenstein, P. "Takata Air Bag Recall Shrinks, but Investigation Widens, NBC News, Sept. 5, 2015, **http://www.nbcnews.com/business/autos/takata-air-bag-recall-shrinks-investigation-widens-n422071**, accessed Oct. 13, 2015.

Ellram, L. "Total Cost of Ownership." *International Journal of Physical Distribution and Logistics Management* 25, no. 8/9 (1995), pp. 4–24.

Engardio, P. "The Future of Outsourcing: How It's Transforming Whole Industries and Changing the Way We Work." *BusinessWeek,* January 30, 2006.

"GM Gently Squeezes Its Suppliers as Collaboration in Cost-Cutting Is Encouraged," *Crain's Detroit Business,* Feb. 17, 2010, **http://www.crainsdetroit. com/article/20140217/NEWS/140219887/gm-gently-squeezes-its-suppliers-as-collaboration-in-cost-cutting**.

Hagerty, J. A. "Toy Maker Comes Home to the U.S.A." *The Wall Street Journal,* March 11, 2013, **.http://www. wsj.com/articles/SB1000142412788732329370457833406 2190251402** accessed Oct. 13, 2015.

Handfield, R., and S. Straight. "What Sourcing Channel Is Right for You?" *Supply Chain Management Review* 7, no. 4 (2003), pp. 62–69.

Hoffman, B. G. "Ford's Test Bed: Brazil's Cama-çari Plant Is Model for the Future." *The Detroit News,* August 22, 2007, **www.detroitnews.com/apps/pbcs.dll/ article?AID=/20070822/AUTO01/708220407/1148.**

Holmes, S. "Cleaning Up Boeing." *BusinessWeek,* March 13, 2006, p. 68.

King, R. "Flextronics Will Manage Global Supply Chain with New Real-Time Software." *The Wall Street Journal,* July 7, 2015, **http://www.wsj.com/articles/ flextronics-will-manage-global-supply-chain-with-new-real-time-software-1436311241**, accessed Oct. 13, 2015.

Kraljic, P. "Purchasing Must Become Supply Management." *Harvard Business Review* 61, no. 5. (1983), pp. 109–17.

Liker, J., and T. Choi. "Building Deep Supplier Relationships." *Harvard Business Review* 82, no. 12 (2004), pp. 104–13.

Melynk, S.; D. Closs; S. Griffis; C. Zobel; and J. Macdonald. "Understanding Supply Chain Resilience." *Supply Chain Management Review* 18 (2014), pp. 34-41.

Petersen, K. J.; R. B. Handfield; and G. L. Ragatz. "Supplier Integration into New Product Development: Coordinating, Product, Process, and Supply Chain Design." *Journal of Operations Management* 23, no. 3/4 (April 2005), pp. 371–88.

"Rejoice! Chipotle Finally Has a New Carnitas Supplier." **http://money.cnn.com/2015/07/10/news/chipotle-carnitas-source/**, accessed Oct. 12, 2015.

Roberts, J. "Responsible Business—Good Business." *Inside Supply Management,* May 2004, pp. 5–7.

Sandholm, T.; D. Levine; M. Concordia; P. Martyn; R. Hughes; J. Jacobs; and D. Begg. "Changing the Game in Strategic Sourcing at Procter & Gamble: Expressive Competition Enabled by Optimization." *Interfaces* 36, no. 1 (January–February 2006), pp. 55–68.

Smeltzer, L.; J. Manship; and C. Rossetti. "An Analysis of the Integration of Strategic Sourcing and Negotiation Planning." *The Journal of Supply Chain Management* 39, no. 4 (2003), p. 18.

Smock, D. "Strategic Sourcing: It's Now Deeply Rooted in U.S. Buying." *Purchasing Metals Edition* 133, no. 14 (2004), p. 20.

Spector, M. "Takata Executive Says Air Bag Death Toll Could Rise." *The Wall Street Journal,* June 23, 2015, **http://www.wsj.com/articles/takata-executive-says-air-bag-death-toll-could-rise-1435079352**.

"Upgraded Components in iPhone 6S Plus Costs Apple an Extra $16 per Device," Sept. 29, 2015, **http://press.ihs. com/press-release/technology/upgraded-components-iphone-6s-plus-costs-apple-extra-16-device**, accessed Oct. 12, 2015.

"Wal-Mart Unveils 'Packaging Scorecard' to Suppliers," **http://walmartstores.com/FactsNews/NewsRoom/6039. aspx**.

Zsidisin, G., and L. Ellram. "An Agency Theory Investigation of Supply Risk Management." *Journal of Supply Chain Management* 39, no. 3 (2003), pp. 15–27.

Chipotle Mexican Grill 2014 Annual Report **http://ir.chipotle.com/phoenix. zhtml?c=194775&p=irol-reportsAnnual**

Diebold Corporation **http://www.diebold.com/solves**

Elementum **http://www.elementum.com/**

Federal-Mogul Corporation **www.federal-mogul.com**

Flextronics **www.flextronics.com**

Institute for Supply Management **https://www.instituteforsupplymanagement.org/**

Philips **www.philips.com**

Procter & Gamble **www.pgconnectdevelop.com**

Walmart **www.walmart.com**

11

Logistics Management

LEARNING OBJECTIVES

After studying this chapter, you should be able to:

LO11-1 Explain logistics and the major decisions made by logistics managers.

LO11-2 Estimate cost savings from consolidation.

LO11-3 Choose efficient transportation modes and carriers.

LO11-4 Make decisions regarding warehouses, distribution centers, and facility networks.

LO11-5 Explain the importance of packaging and materials handling.

LO11-6 Locate facilities using the center-of-gravity model.

LO11-7 Describe the benefits of integrated service providers.

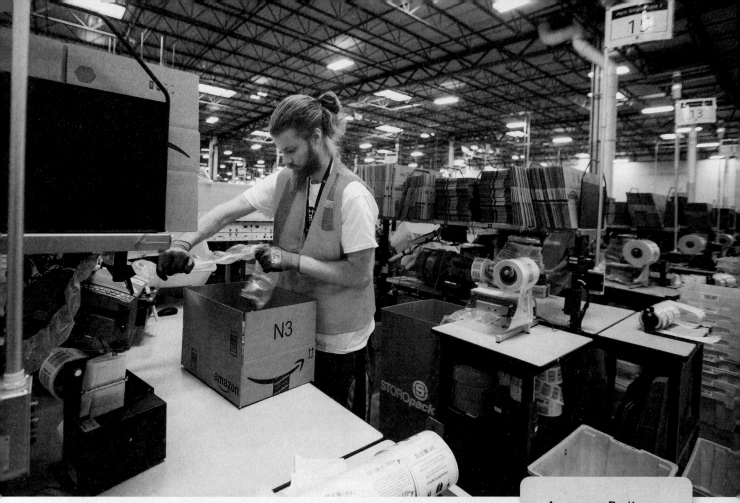

Amazon Delivers Innovation

Amazon, which started in 1994 as an online bookstore, has transformed itself into one of the most innovative logistics and technology companies on the planet. Its vast logistics network includes over 170 fulfillment and sortation centers worldwide and it continues to add centers at a fast pace every year. Each new large fulfillment center incorporates state-of-the-art technology, including thousands of robots helping to fill customer orders quickly and correctly.

To meet its goal of being the most "customer-centric" company on earth, Amazon is focusing on reducing delivery time and effectively delivering products the "last mile" direct to customers' homes. For example, Amazon Fresh, available in select cities, enables customers to order groceries, meals, and other items for same-day delivery. But for Amazon, one-day delivery is not fast enough. In support of its rapidly expanding one-hour delivery service, Prime Now, Amazon is opening small fulfillment centers in key urban locations to keep inventory close to customers. Amazon is leading this emerging trend of "micrologistics."

Think one-hour is too slow? Managers at Amazon's Prime Air do. They are working toward 30-minute delivery of small packages within 10 miles of a distribution center using unmanned aerial vehicles (drones). Although there are technical and regulatory challenges to overcome, if Prime Air is successful, delivery by drone one day may be as commonplace as delivery by truck.

Humans are still at the core of some of Amazon's fast delivery strategies. Amazon is experimenting with an Uber-like app that would pay ordinary people to deliver its packages. As its logistics capabilities evolve, Amazon may no longer rely upon third-party shipping companies such as UPS and FedEx for many of its deliveries.

From the beginning of civilization it has been necessary to move, store, and handle products. Today, as a result of globalization, technological advances, and rising customer expectations, logistics is critical to competitive success, as demonstrated in the opening vignette about Amazon. This chapter explains the strategic role of logistics in the supply chain, and it describes the basic operating principles that you can use to make logistics decisions.

THE ROLE OF LOGISTICS IN SUPPLY CHAIN MANAGEMENT

LO11-1 Explain logistics and the major decisions made by logistics managers.

logistics management
Management of the movement and storage of materials at lowest cost while still meeting customers' requirements.

relationships

The Council of Supply Chain Management Professionals (CSCMP) defines logistics management as "that part of supply chain management that plans, implements, and controls the efficient, effective forward and reverse flow and storage of goods, services, and related information between the point of origin and the point of consumption in order to meet customers' requirements"[1]. In short, it is concerned with moving and storing materials at lowest cost while still meeting customer requirements. As shown by Amazon, strong logistics capabilities can lead to a competitive advantage.

Figure 11-1 illustrates the primary activities involved in accomplishing logistics management objectives: (1) inventory management; (2) order management; (3) transportation management; (4) warehousing; (5) packaging and materials handling; and (6) network design. By its very nature, logistics is an integrating activity. Logistics managers work closely with suppliers and supply managers to ensure that the inbound flow of materials meets the firm's requirements for its own operations. Logistics managers also have responsibility for flows of information, products, and materials internally, among a firm's different facilities. Finally, logistics managers work with marketing and sales personnel, as well as with customers, to ensure that customer requirements are satisfied. Integrating these activities accomplishes the dual objectives of providing service to customers and efficiently managing costs.

Logistics Service Benefits

Logistics plays a critical role in fulfilling the customer service benefits of availability, lead-time performance, and service reliability. Logistics managers are responsible for ensuring that customers receive the right products at the right time. They determine how much inventory should be held and where it should be held in the supply chain. They also determine how to ship products to customers, which is a critical aspect of overall lead-time

FIGURE 11-1 The Activities of Integrated Logistics Management

[1]See the organization's Web site at: www.cscmp.org.

performance. Many aspects of service reliability are also the responsibility of logistics. Delivery must include all items ordered by the customer (no shortages or overages) and be made on-time, to the right location, without damaging the product. Ultimately, logistics has primary responsibility for the execution of perfect orders. Because of its importance, research studies show that logistical service is critical to industrial buyers' selection of suppliers.

Logistics Cost Minimization

Logistics activities can be costly. In many firms the total cost of logistics is as much as 25–30 percent of each dollar of sales revenue. While these costs may be less significant in other firms, another way to think about the importance of logistics cost is to consider the facts: In 2014, the total cost of U.S. logistics was $1.4 trillion, or approximately 8.3 percent of the U.S. gross domestic product (GDP), according to the 2015 CSCMP State of Logistics Report.

The challenging aspect of managing logistics is that providing ever-higher service levels typically increases cost. Logistics managers make two types of trade-offs as they strive to minimize total logistics cost: cost-to-service trade-offs and cost-to-cost trade-offs.

1. The **cost-to-service trade-off** means that as service levels increase, typically so do costs. For example, to avoid stockouts, more inventory is needed, increasing carrying costs. Shorter lead-times can be accomplished by using faster, more expensive transportation—for example, air versus truck. Thus, you must first determine what level of service performance customers require and then determine how to provide that service most cost efficiently.

   > **cost-to-service trade-off** As service levels increase, typically so do costs.

2. A **cost-to-cost trade-off** occurs when increasing the cost of one logistics activity reduces the cost of another activity. For example, having many warehouses in different locations increases operating costs. However, because warehouses are closer to customers, transportation costs are lower. As the number of warehouses gets very large, transportation costs begins to rise again. (The rationale for this relationship will be explained later in this chapter.) There are many other such cost-to-cost trade-offs.

   > **cost-to-cost trade-off** Increasing the cost of one logistics activity reduces the cost of another.

From a systems perspective, the objective of logistics management is to minimize the total of all logistics costs, not just one element. Ultimately, companies should make their strategic decisions based on **total landed cost**, which is the sum of all product- and logistics-related costs. Consider how a total landed cost comparison would affect the decision of where to locate manufacturing plants. Many companies have "offshore" manufacturing (that is, they have located manufacturing plants in global locations far from customers). These are the companies most at risk when crude oil prices fluctuate wildly, labor costs rise in developing countries, and the U.S. dollar declines in value compared to other currencies. Does this mean that plants should always be located closer to customers? Not necessarily. It is important to use a manufacturing strategy that minimizes a product's total landed cost. The relevant costs in such a decision include:

global

> **total landed cost** The sum of all product- and logistics-related costs.

- Costs within each country of manufacture: raw materials, storage, labor, quality, overhead, obsolescence, packaging, risk of supply chain disruption, and exchange rates.
- Costs in transit from country of manufacture to country of sale: fuel, insurance, port charges, handling, security, banking, charges for delays in loading or unloading, duties, handling agency charges, and in-transit inventory.
- Costs within the country of sale: local handling, transportation, taxes, safety stock, productivity implications, maintenance, and environmental impact.

It is also important to include costs related to lead times and lead-time variability. These can differ significantly depending on shipping distance. All of the relevant costs are summed to compare the total landed cost of manufacturing a product domestically and the total landed cost of manufacturing a product offshore (while taking exchange rates into account). Logistics managers use a similar total landed cost approach to evaluate all sorts of operational decisions affecting supply chain design and execution.

Inventory Management

Managing inventory is a fundamental concern of all managers involved in supply chain operations, but it is especially important to logistics managers. The details of inventory management were discussed in Chapter 7, and it is important to understand that inventory is linked to all logistics management decisions.

Critical inventory decisions include deciding how much inventory of each material item to hold, where in the supply chain to hold each item, in what form (raw material, work in process, finished goods), and how often to replenish each item. A popular mantra in business today is, "information replaces inventory." Logistics managers seek ways to provide more accurate and timely information, thus reducing the need to hold inventory as a buffer against uncertain product demand, supply, or lead times.

The amount and location of inventories in a supply chain are strongly influenced by logistics decisions. For example, the level of inventory is influenced by the mode of transportation. Slower transportation modes (such as rail versus truck) increase in-transit inventory and cost. The location and number of warehouses in the system also affect inventory levels. All other things being equal, total inventory is lower with just a few large warehouses than with many smaller geographically disbursed warehouses. Inventory is lower when firms offer lower levels of customer service; for example, longer delivery times or less choice of products.

Logistics managers continually weigh the costs and benefits of holding different quantities of inventories at different locations in the supply chain. They also influence management policies, procedures, and technological investments needed to improve inventory management.

Order Processing

Order processing systems should be designed to ensure accuracy, efficiency, and speed. Specific customer requirements flow into a firm as customers' orders. Many orders are placed by customers electronically online or via mobile apps and flow directly into a company's information system. Websites and apps should be designed to be easy to use and help prevent errors. For example, Amazon's ordering system reminds customers what they have ordered in the past and allows them to pay with "one-click." Companies can reduce costs and delays by reducing the number of orders that are entered manually, such as those taken over the phone. Domino's encourages customers to create a online "pizza profile" and offers discounts for online orders.

TRANSPORTATION MANAGEMENT

Transportation is perhaps the most visible aspect of logistics and has taken on even more importance as companies have increased their global reach, both selling and sourcing products across the world. The increased distances and more complex geographical span lead to long lead times, the potential for delays and disruptions, security issues, and increased exposure to other supply chain risks.

Government's Role in Transportation

Because transportation is so vital to the overall economy, governments typically play a major role. All governments realize that a stable and efficient transportation system is vital to economic development. In some situations, governments own and provide transportation services. In others, governments regulate private industry, which provides transportation services. Governmental concern regarding transportation addresses both economic regulation and safety regulation.

Economic Regulation

Economic regulation is designed to ensure that transportation services are available to everyone at reasonable cost. Governments may actively control the entry, rates, and services provided by transportation carriers. In the early history of the United States, significant federal legislation and many governmental agencies existed to control who could form a transportation company, where they could operate, what services they could provide, and what rates they could charge. As a result, logistics managers had few choices and little influence on pricing and costs. While the vast majority of these regulations no longer exist in the United States at the federal level (having been repealed in the 1980s), some individual states still maintain such control.

Economic deregulation at the federal level has benefited logistics managers. New companies have entered the industry as transportation carriers. Logistics managers now can develop and negotiate new arrangements, terms, and conditions with the transportation carrier of their choice. Deregulation also has created opportunities for innovation and companies have created new logistical solutions aimed at reducing costs, improving customer service, and increasing efficiency.

economic regulation Government controls of the entry, rates, and services provided by transportation carriers.

Safety Regulation

While the economic regulation of transportation has lessened in the United States in recent years, **safety (and social) regulation** has increased significantly. This form of regulation is designed to ensure that transportation carriers conduct their activities in a safe and responsible manner. There is tremendous concern, for example, about the movement of hazardous goods, the number of hours that a truck driver can work without rest, and the traffic congestion caused by transportation vehicles. Other regulations addressing environmental concerns already exist or are being considered. A full description of the regulations regarding these issues is beyond the scope of this text, but numerous regulations exist and more can be expected in the future.

Since 2001, another issue of concern has been the security of the transportation system. The concerns range from the potential to contaminate products (especially food) while they are in transport to the potential use of a transportation vehicle as a weapon of destruction. Because countries around the world have very different levels of security, the U.S. Customers & Border Protection introduced an anti-terror partnership process (C-TPAT) to increase cross-border security while reducing costs and delays for low-risk shipments.

safety (and social) regulation Regulation designed to ensure that transportation carriers conduct their activities in a safe and responsible manner.

sustainability

Transportation Economics

There are two fundamental economic principles underlying the efficiency and the cost of transportation movements: transportation *economy of scale* and *economy of distance*. **Economy of scale** is described by the fact that the cost per unit of weight decreases as the size of the shipment increases. Thus, it is less costly per pound to move 10,000 pounds of product a given distance than it is to move 5,000 pounds that same distance. This is because the fixed costs associated with transportation (equipment and expenses at the origination and destination points) are spread over a larger weight (or quantity of items). Although the total cost of the larger shipment is higher, the cost per pound is less. This principle helps to explain the recent growth in new mega-container ships. For example, the MSC Oscar is so big that in 2015, there were no U.S. ports where it could enter. Figure 11-2(A) graphically illustrates economy of scale.

The second principle, **economy of distance**, refers to the principle that the cost per unit of distance decreases as the distance moved increases. The rationale for this relationship is essentially the same as for the economy of scale. Longer distances traveled allow the fixed costs to be spread over a larger number of miles. Economy of distance is illustrated in Figure 11-2(B).

LO11-2 Estimate cost savings from consolidation.

economy of scale The cost per unit of weight decreases as the size of the shipment increases.

economy of distance The cost per unit of distance decreases as the distance moved increases.

Consolidation

Given these economic principles, logistics managers often use consolidation strategies to improve transportation efficiency. **Consolidation** is the practice of combining small orders

consolidation Combining small orders or shipments into one larger shipment to take advantage of transportation economies.

FIGURE 11-2
Economies of Scale and
Distance

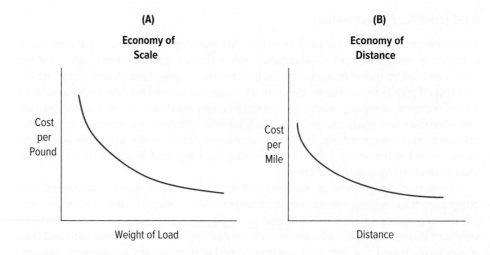

or shipments into one larger shipment to take advantage of economies of scale or distance.
There are three basic consolidation strategies:

market area consolidation
Combining several small shipments from one shipper that are going to the same market area into one shipment.

1. **Market area consolidation** is achieved by combining several small shipments from one shipper that are going to the same market area into one shipment. Suppose, for example, that Kellogg's has several orders from different customers located in Alabama. Rather than put each order on a separate transportation vehicle, Kellogg's combines shipments into a single load to be moved to the destination point.

pooled delivery consolidation
Combines small shipments from *different shippers* that are going to the same market area.

2. **Pooled delivery consolidation** is similar to market area consolidation, except that it combines small shipments from *different shippers* that are going to the same market area. Generally, pooled delivery consolidation is handled by independent transportation companies such as UPS or FedEx (and many other transportation carriers). These firms merge the freight from numerous shippers into large shipments headed for the same market area. By doing so, each shipper can achieve some economy that would not be possible if the individual shipments were separately delivered.

scheduled delivery consolidation
Establishing specific times when deliveries to customers will be made.

3. **Scheduled delivery consolidation** refers to establishing specific times when deliveries will be made to customers. Customers then adjust their pattern of ordering to fit the schedule. For example, rather than delivering to a customer or a market area every day, which might result in daily small quantity orders, shipments to that customer or market might be scheduled for delivery only on Thursday. The result is larger quantity orders and less frequent shipment. While the economic advantage of this practice is easily understood, it is only possible to accomplish within the constraints of customers' requirements for delivery. It is quite possible that customers may decide to use a different supplier who does not limit their ordering practices. This represents one of the cost-to service trade-offs that logistics decision makers face.

The cost reduction from consolidation comes from the transportation economies discussed previously. Example 11-1 demonstrates how these economies might work to justify consolidation. The cost savings represented by consolidation strategies are clearly quite considerable.

Transportation Modes

LO11-3 Choose efficient transportation modes and carriers

A **transportation mode** is simply a form or method of transporting items. There are five basic transportation modes: rail, truck, water, air, and pipeline. Transportation managers decide which mode of transportation to use for each order that must be delivered. To decide which mode to use you need to consider the service characteristics and the cost of each mode. The five dimensions of service characteristics are:

transportation mode A form or method of transporting items.

- *Speed:* the elapsed time required to move from the point of origin to destination.
- *Availability:* the ability to service any possible location.

EXAMPLE 11-1

Spartan Company, located in Atlanta, has orders from three customers located in Lansing, Michigan. The weight of each individual shipment is 12,000 pounds. The transportation carrier quotes a freight rate of $15.75 per hundredweight (or cwt.) for individual direct shipments between the two cities, as is the normal practice in the transportation industry. Alternatively, the carrier's rate for a shipment that weighs more than 30,000 pounds is $10.50 per cwt. However, if the orders are combined into one shipment, the carrier will charge $300 for each stop it is required to make. Should Spartan consolidate the orders into one shipment?

SOLUTION

The total cost of one individual shipment is:

$15.75 × (12,000 pounds / 100 pounds) = $15.75 × 120 hundredweight = $1,890

Therefore, three separate shipments will total $1,890 × 3 = $5,670. A consolidated shipment of 36,000 pounds will cost:

$10.50 × (36,000 pounds / 100 pounds) = $10.50 × 360 hundredweight = $3,780

Adding three stop-off charges of $300 each to the cost of the consolidated shipment brings the total cost of the consolidation to $4,680, providing a cost savings of $990 in the transportation bill.

- *Dependability:* the variance in the expected delivery times.
- *Capability:* the ability to handle any type of product and/or size of load.
- *Frequency:* the number of scheduled movements that can be arranged by a shipper.

The modes also differ significantly in their cost characteristics and, therefore, the rates they charge to shippers. Because of the differences in capabilities and costs, you should choose the mode of transportation that best meets the needs of each order. Table 11-1 compares the operating characteristics of the five transportation modes.

Truck

Given the combination of service characteristics, it is no wonder that trucks are used for about 70 percent of the freight shipped in the United States. Virtually all consumer goods

TABLE 11-1   Characteristics of Transportation Modes

Operating Characteristics*	Truck	Rail	Water	Pipeline	Air
Speed	2	3	4	5	1
Availability	1	2	4	5	3
Dependability	2	3	4	1	5
Capability	3	2	1	5	4
Frequency	2	4	5	1	3
Cost to shippers**	2	3	4	5	1
Typical uses	Medium and light manufacturing; Wholesale and retail distribution	Heavy bulk commodities	Bulk commodities; cement; agricultural products	Petroleum; natural gas; slurry	Small shipments; emergency shipments

*1 = best, 5 = worst.
**1 = highest, 5 = lowest.

move at least partially, if not entirely, via truck. Trucks (also referred to as motor carriers) have been a major mode of transportation since the 1910s (unlike rail, which has been present since the 1800s).

The extensive use of trucks in the United States is due to several factors. The vast system of highways and roads, which has been financed largely at public expense (both state and federal), is the most influential factor. This is in contrast to rail, which has been largely financed by corporations obtaining the right-of-way and paying for construction and maintenance. Thus, trucks have relatively low fixed costs (because the government builds and maintains the roads) and relatively high variable costs (due to high labor content). Availability is also key. Trucks can offer door-to-door service anywhere.

Similar to many other industries, technology is changing the trucking industry. Additional vehicle features such as braking assistance and roll-over prevention are increasing safety. Cellular and satellite technology enable drivers to be monitored in real-time, improving efficiency and safety. The nature of competition is changing as well, as discussed in the nearby Get Real box regarding mobile apps.

The trucking industry is categorized into three distinct segments:

truckload (TL) Truckload carriers generally carry only full trailers of freight (i.e., with shipments in excess of 15,000 pounds).

1. **Truckload (TL)** carriers generally carry only full trailers of freight (i.e., with shipments in excess of 15,000 pounds). Since the loads are full, there is no need for consolidation. Trucks can be routed directly from the shipper to the consignee. In the United States, this segment consists of many relatively small carriers who are cost competitive, although several large firms compete in this segment as well, such as Schneider National and J. B. Hunt Transportation Services.

less-than-truckload (LTL) Less-than-truckload carriers usually move loads of less than 15,000 pounds.

2. **Less-than-truckload (LTL)** carriers usually move loads of less than 15,000 pounds. Unlike the TL carriers, the LTL carriers experience relatively higher fixed costs because of the need to stop at a terminal for load consolidation. The cost of the terminals is part of the fixed costs. Also, LTL carriers typically pay higher marketing costs because they want to generate full loads. Because of these factors, the LTL segment is dominated by a few large carriers that you may often see on the highways (carriers such as FedEx Freight, YRC National, Con-Way Freight, and ABF Freight).

specialty carriers Specialty carriers include package haulers such as FedEx and United Parcel Service (UPS).

3. **Specialty carriers** include package haulers such as FedEx and United Parcel Service (UPS).

GET REAL

Mobile Apps Are Transforming the Trucking Industry

In the trucking industry, third-party logistics providers (3PLs) often play key brokering roles in matching supply and demand. These brokers connect shippers (customers who need to have products shipped) to drivers with trucks looking for business. However, the over $700 billion U.S. trucking industry may be in for a radical change as "uberization" takes hold. A number of tech start-up companies such as Trucker Path (https://truckerpath.com/) and Convoy (https://convoy.com/) have developed apps to directly connect drivers and customers for shipping a single package or a truckload without using a broker.

In larger metropolitan areas, shipping apps are likely to reduce the time to find a truck from hours to minutes. With the apps, customers know exactly where their shipments are at any point, any time. Drivers benefit, too. Greater efficiency should lead to more profit. However, it is yet to be seen how many drivers and customers will embrace the new technology.

© Trucker Path, Inc.

Rail

In the United States, rail is the second most commonly used transportation mode after truck. Historically, rail has been best suited to moving large shipments over long distances. Rail has high fixed costs, due to the costs of expensive equipment (e.g., railroad engines, railcars), rights-of-way (railroads must build and maintain their own tracks), switching yards, and terminals. In contrast, variable costs are relatively low. For example, a good deal of energy is expended in starting and stopping a train. Once a train is moving, relatively little energy is needed to keep it moving. Advances in diesel and electrical technology (used by the locomotives) have further reduced the variable costs.

Rail is well suited to the movement of bulky, low cost commodities such as oil, grain, and chemicals. However, rail transportation is relatively slow. And, because trains move according to fixed and rigid schedules, shipping flexibility is low.

Still, rail is currently experiencing a renaissance in the United States. Almost any product can be transported by rail. Therefore, rail is used by many companies that need to move large quantities of product economically. Railroads have significantly improved operations in recent years, making rail a more attractive choice for shippers. In addition, railroad companies have formed alliances with carriers from other modes of transportation. The result has been an increase in the total amount of freight moving by rail.

Water

Of the five transportation modes, water is the oldest. In North America, this mode consists of two segments: domestic and deep-water transport. Domestic transport consists of the Great Lakes, all canals, and all navigable rivers. Deep-water transport consists of the oceans surrounding the United States.

© Slow Images/Getty Images

The major advantage of water transportation is its ability to move extremely large shipments economically. One tow barge, for example, can carry the equivalent of over 800 truckloads of freight. The major disadvantages of water are speed and availability. Ships and barges are relatively slow, and water transport simply doesn't serve that many locations. In addition, to load freight on a ship requires first getting the freight to a dock or loading area, usually by truck or rail. At the destination port, products must then be unloaded and transported by truck or rail to the final destination. In general, water transport is an attractive way to move large tonnage at very low cost when speed is not critical.

global

Deep-water transport is essential for global business. The invention of the shipping container over 50 years ago dramatically improved deep-water transport. To take advantage of economies of scale, the size of newly produced container ships has been growing dramatically. The largest container ships have the capacity to hold 19,000 shipping containers, each of which are 20 feet long. Further, shipping routes are changing due to factors such the Panama Canal expansion and new Arctic shipping routes that are emerging because of global climate change. For example, from July through November, use of the Arctic route can reduce the transit time for ships traveling from China to Europe by at least 12 days.

Pipeline

Pipelines are appropriate for moving products that exist in a gaseous, liquid, or slurry form. Slurry is created when a solid product is suspended in a liquid. For example, crushing coal and then mixing it with water makes coal slurry. At the end of the pipeline, the slurry is taken out, the water is evaporated, and the product is made ready for use. Pipelines are used to move natural gas, oil, gasoline, chemicals, and even orange juice (in Florida).

Pipeline transportation offers users several advantages. First, it operates 24 hours a day, seven days a week, 52 weeks a year. It never stops, except for maintenance or cleaning. Second, pipeline transportation is typically not affected by the weather. A dense fog or ice storm that would immobilize airplanes, trucks, and trains has no impact on product flows within a pipe. Of the five modes, transportation by pipeline has the highest fixed costs and the lowest variable costs. The fixed costs are associated with getting rights-of-way combined with the construction and maintenance of pipelines, the control stations, and the pumping capabilities. The very low variable costs are due to the lack of labor required to move product within the pipe. However, logistics managers are required to plan and schedule pipeline flows, a job that can be very challenging.

Air

Air transport is both the newest and the least utilized mode. The major advantage of air is clearly speed. Against this advantage (which is important under certain conditions), air offers some significant disadvantages. It is relatively limited in the sizes, shapes, amounts, and types of freight that it can carry. It may seem strange that air is rated worst on dependability. The reason for this is that, although the speed is extremely fast (a matter of hours), air transport is subject to frequent delays due to weather or maintenance issues. A delay of several hours on a six-hour shipment represents a significant difference from the expected delivery time.

Another major disadvantage is the relatively high cost of air for shipping products. In general, air is most appropriate for very high value, low-bulk items or those that are extremely perishable. Air is basically used when speed is critical. Air transport is frequently used for moving Christmas presents, high fashion items, medical supplies and items (e.g., hearts for transplants), fresh flowers, and fresh fish. It is also frequently used for products such as repair parts when the need for rapid delivery outweighs the high cost.

activity

student

Search the Internet to find out which transport mode produces the least damage to products. Which one is the safest to operate? Which one consumes the least amount of energy? Which one is least subject to disruptions from events such as labor strikes or natural disasters?

Intermodal Transportation

Intermodal transportation combines two or more modes to take advantage of the economies and service characteristics of each. The most common form of intermodal transportation is commonly referred to as *piggyback service* and integrates truck and rail transportation. Piggyback service is more technically called either *trailer on flatcar (TOFC)* or *container on flatcar (COFC)*. In this arrangement, a trailer or a container is placed on a rail flatcar for the long distance movement between cities (say Chicago to Los Angeles). At the destination city, a truck picks up the trailer or container to complete the delivery. This arrangement allows for the service availability of truck combined with the cost efficiency of rail.

The popularity of piggyback service has led to the development of many other intermodal formats. In fact, any two or more modes might be combined into an intermodal arrangement. The nearby Get Real box concerning Tuesday Morning provides an interesting example of the advantages of intermodal transportation.

intermodal transportation
A combination of two or more transportation modes to take advantage of the economies and service characteristics of each.

Carrier Types

Not only are there different transportation modes to choose from, you also have several types of carriers (transportation service providers) to choose from, especially in truck transportation. Many logistics managers make use of more than one type of carrier, depending on the specific situation they face. There are three classes of carriers:

common carriers Transportation companies that provide service to the public.

1. **Common carriers** are transportation companies that provide service to the public. Common carriers publish their rates, although negotiation between shippers and common carriers regarding specific charges results in many discounts off the published rate schedules.

contract carriers Carriers that have specific contracts with a limited number of shippers.

2. **Contract carriers**, as the name implies, have specific contracts with a limited number of shippers. Many of the trucks you see on the highways may bear the

GET REAL

Tuesday Morning Shifts Modes

Tuesday Morning is a Dallas-based retailer specializing in upscale closeout merchandise with 769 stores across the United States. Since Tuesday Morning's stores function on an event basis, a challenge is getting store merchandise from its origin through distribution channels and into stores by a specified date and time for its more than 20 specialty sales events per year.

Tuesday Morning started looking for ways to save money while meeting its tight deadlines—and what the team came up with was a solution ahead of its time. They decided to use intermodal transport out of the West Coast ports (where merchandise arrives

© Marmaduke St. John/Alamy Stock Photo

from Asia) to a single, national distribution center (DC) just outside of Dallas.

"We started to take a hard look at intermodal for our inbound needs," says Cheryl Bailey, Tuesday Morning's logistics manager for transportation. "We found that it gave us many options."

Tuesday Morning's outbound distribution to its network of stores is unique among national retailers in that it has chosen to cover the nation with its one DC in Farmers Branch. One of its primary carriers was Averitt, which provides both TL and LTL services. And while Averitt understood that sometimes the deadlines for this link of the supply chain were tight, it felt intermodal services could meet the majority of time demands while earning major savings.

Given the cost savings, Tuesday Morning now looks at intermodal service as a viable transportation option in all lanes that exceed 500 miles. And Averitt, one of its main transportation partners, says it's fine with that. "Tuesday Morning is an excellent customer," says Averitt's Mark Richards, Director of Truckload Sales, "Intermodal is a piece of that, and it's going to grow a lot with them. In fact, I don't want to call them a customer or client—it's a true partnership. We share a lot of knowledge and we share a lot of ideas."

Source: Adapted from John D. Schulz, "Tuesday Morning Shifts Modes," *Logistics Management* **(February 2012), pp. 24–27.**

name of a well-known manufacturer, but in fact they are owned and operated by a contract carrier.

3. **Private carriers** are companies that own and operate transportation equipment to transport their own products. There has been a shift away from private carriers to common or contract carriers because, for manufacturers and distributors, transportation is not their core competency. Nevertheless there are still firms, such as Walmart and Steelcase, who operate their own truck fleets in addition to using the services of other types of carriers in some situations.

private carriers Companies that own and operate transportation equipment to transport their own products.

Transportation Service Selection

Selecting a mode of transportation, or a particular carrier within a mode, is not a trivial problem. The decision involves several factors: the cost related to transportation itself; the cost of inventory while in transit; and the service requirements related to speed, availability, and so on. However, to illustrate the basic cost-to-cost trade-offs in the decision, we will assume that the service dimensions are negligible. When managers are faced with this decision, they usually seek to balance the inventory costs of products in-transit against the costs of moving these products. Faster delivery means less in-transit inventory, yet faster modes are usually more expensive. Other things being equal, managers typically pick the mode that offers the lowest total cost. Example 11-2 illustrates the calculation of the lowest total cost in making this decision.

EXAMPLE 11-2

Consider the choice faced by a manufacturer of high-end wristwatches (such as Omega or Rolex) that must ship an assortment of 30 watches valued at $500 each from its manufacturing warehouse to a distributor located 1,000 miles away. The manufacturer is paid for the watches upon receipt at the distributor, so the manufacturer owns the in-transit inventory. Assume that the two most favorable transportation options include parcel 8-day ground service or air express 2-day air service. The basic question is: Does the inventory cost savings from faster shipping justify the additional cost of air versus ground shipping? Given the cost information shown below, the total cost for each transportation option would be calculated as follows:

Shipping weight = 10 pounds   Total Product value = $15,000

Parcel ground cost = $50.00   Air express cost = $90.00

Inventory holding cost rate = 20% of product value per year

(11.1)   Total cost = In-transit inventory holding cost + Carrier cost

In-transit inventory holding cost = # of days in-transit/365 × Shipment

(11.2)   value × Annual inventory carrying cost percentage

Total cost for ground = [(8 days/365) × $15,000 × .2] + $50.00

= $65.75 + $50.00 = $115.75

Total cost for air = [(2 days/365) × $15,000 × .2] + $90.00

= $16.64 + $90.00 = $106.44

In this case, the inventory savings of a faster mode of transportation outweighs the additional carrier cost, so the transportation manager should use the air express service option.

The primary cost variables driving the transportation service decision are the value and weight of the items being shipped. Product value drives inventory costs, and product weight drives transportation costs. If the weight of the shipment is much greater, the transportation cost is much higher. Thus, in Example 11-2, if the same decision is made at a less-expensive watch manufacturer, ground might easily be the lowest cost choice. Because of this relationship between total transportation cost, product value, and weight, a shipping load's **value density** is usually a key determinant of the transportation mode used to move it. Value density is simply the ratio of a product's value to its weight. All other things being equal, faster, more expensive transportation is usually justified for more value-dense items. Sometimes the ratio of a product's value to its volume (i.e., the cubic space it fills) is also important. The final decision depends on whether weight or volume is the driving factor affecting freight charges.

value density The ratio of a product's value to its weight.

The analysis in Example 11-2 is based purely on inventory and carrier cost considerations. In many situations, of course, other factors would come into play. It may be that the customer is simply unwilling to wait eight days to receive shipment. Also, differences in delivery reliability, the potential for damage or loss, packaging requirements, or other factors might ultimately drive the transportation decision.

Increasingly, managers are considering environmental sustainability issues related to transportation decisions, including energy consumption and greenhouse gas emissions (GHG). For each of the transportation modes, Table 11-2 shows estimates of GHG per ton of freight transported per kilometer. Rail, pipeline, and water are relatively low in GHG emissions because these modes carry large quantities at relatively slow speeds. Trucking,

sustainability

TABLE 11-2   Freight Transportation Mode Greenhouse Gas Emissions

Mode	Grams/Ton-km
Air	1,000–1,800
Light duty delivery truck	350–450
Long-haul truck	80–150
Rail	20–70
Bulk vessel/barge	10–60
Container vessel	10–30

particularly light duty local delivery, generates higher GHG, and air transport produces extremely high levels of GHG.

There are many ways to reduce the environmental impact of freight transportation. Advances in technology such as alternative fuels and better fuel efficiency are obvious steps. For example, using compressed natural gas as a fuel in trucks instead of diesel fuel reduces GHG emissions. You can also choose lower-impact modes such as rail or water as long as service commitments to customers can still be met.

WAREHOUSE MANAGEMENT

LO11-4 Make decisions regarding warehouses, distribution centers, and facility networks.

Historically, a warehouse was simply a place to store inventory. While storage is an important function, warehouses today are often used for other activities, including creating final product configurations and assortments for customers. In fact, ideally, storage is minimized as inventory moves continuously throughout the supply chain. Of course, some storage is typically justified on the basis of cost or service requirements, but to emphasize the difference between the storage activity and the strategic role of warehouses, many people today use the term distribution center rather than *warehouse*.

distribution center Term used to describe the strategic role of warehouses in storage and in creating assortments that meet customer requirements.

Primary Functions of Warehousing

Like all other areas of logistics management, warehousing tends to center on cost and customer service improvements. In terms of customer service, warehouses located near customers enable quicker product fulfillment than remote manufacturing plants or stocking locations. As described in the opening vignette, Amazon is using this strategy for faster delivery. In addition, having a warehouse visibly located in a given customer market frequently leads customers to believe that they will be better supported.

Warehouses are often the most cost-effective means to provide an assortment of products to geographically dispersed customers because of the transportation economies associated with consolidation. In addition, warehouses are increasingly being used as transshipment points, or sortation centers. At a transshipment point, products are received, sorted, sequenced, and selected into loads consistent with the customer's needs. Transshipment warehouses are most evident in grocery and retail businesses. The activities that follow describe some of the primary functions provided by warehouses.

transshipment point A facility where products are received, sorted, sequenced, and selected into loads consistent with the customer's needs.

Stockpiling

Stockpiling is the storage of inventory in warehouses to protect against seasonality either in supply or demand. For example, ketchup can only be produced during the times of the year when tomatoes are harvested, yet there is year-round demand for this product. Demand seasonality is evidenced in products such as lawn furniture, snow blowers, and toys.

stockpiling The storage of inventories in warehouses to protect against seasonality either in supply or demand.

Production Support

Today, manufacturers often require suppliers to locate warehouses near their major manufacturing plants. A production support warehouse is dedicated to storing parts and

production support warehouse A warehouse dedicated to storing parts and components needed to support a plant's operations.

components needed to support a plant's operations. The cost of stopping a production line due to a lack of needed material can be very high (hundreds of thousands of dollars each day). Thus, it is sometimes worthwhile to dedicate a supporting warehouse, especially if supplier lead times would otherwise be very long, for example, with global sourcing, or if the usage of material is quite variable.

Break-Bulk, Warehouse Consolidation, and Cross-Docking

When suppliers use market area consolidation strategies to reduce transportation costs, they send large shipments to a warehouse in a local market area. That warehouse then conducts break-bulk, splitting the shipment into individual orders and arranging for local delivery to customers. Break-bulk is illustrated in Figure 11-3(A).

Warehouse consolidation occurs when a warehouse receives shipments from a number of sources and combines those shipments into one larger shipment going to a single location. This allows the customer to receive an assortment of products in a single shipment, thus reducing the time and effort required for the customer. It also takes advantage of transportation economies by combining small shipments into a single large shipment. Figure 11-3(B) illustrates the warehouse consolidation activity.

Cross-docking combines break-bulk and consolidation activities. In cross-docking, large shipments from many sources are scheduled to arrive at the facility's receiving docks simultaneously. Meanwhile, several vehicles are positioned at the shipping docks, each bound for a different destination. As the incoming shipments are unloaded, they are broken into the quantities needed at each customer location and loaded into the appropriate

break-bulk Splitting a large shipment into individual orders and arranging for local delivery to customers.

warehouse consolidation Combining shipments from a number of sources into one larger shipment going to a single location.

cross-docking Combines break-bulk and warehouse consolidation activities.

FIGURE 11-3
Break-Bulk, Consolidation, and Cross-Docking Warehouse Operations

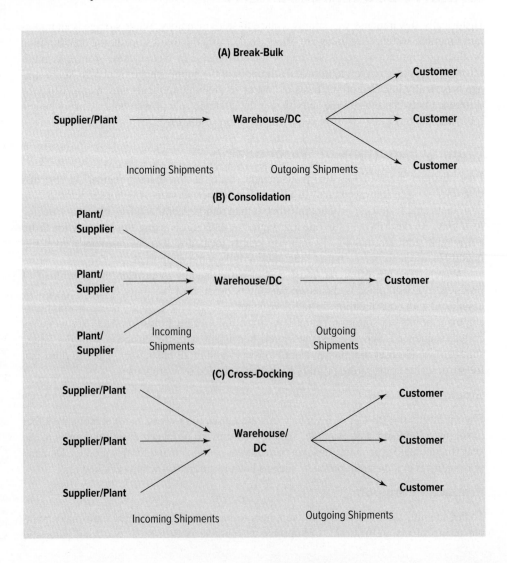

outbound vehicles. Generally, customers have specified exactly how much of each product is required at each location and suppliers have presorted their shipments into these quantities. This approach simplifies the unloading and reloading process. Once the trucks have the loads of mixed products completed, they depart for their final destinations. Cross-docking provides tremendous efficiency in transportation, avoids the need for product storage, and provides a sizable service benefit to customers by providing one shipment containing their requirements for many different products. Many retailers, especially grocery and mass merchants, use cross-dock facilities extensively to replenish their stores. Figure 11-3(C) illustrates how cross-docking works.

Sometimes cross-docking is not practical because it requires precise scheduling of shipments from suppliers or trucks destined for customers. Even in these instances, however, warehouses provide important benefits by mixing or creating assortments. While this function is similar to cross-docking, the difference lies in the fact that incoming shipments do not have to be scheduled as precisely. They may be put into storage until all of the needed products are available.

A U-Shaped Cross-Dock. Trailers with inbound shipments are staged at the outside walls of the cross-dock facility, while trailers bound for customer destinations are staged on the inside of the U-shaped facility. Inside the building, workers unload the inbound trailers and quickly fill the outbound equipment with an assortment of products.

Courtesy of John J. Bartholdi, III and warehouse-science.com

Reverse Logistics Support

As products become more complex and as consumers become more environmentally conscious, the number of products that are returned and reclaimed is growing dramatically. The growth of leasing and online purchasing has also contributed to this growth (some online sellers process returns equaling as much as 50 percent of their sales). With many online retailers offering free shipping on returns, the need for reverse logistics is expected to increase.

To cope with this increasing need, warehouses are being used as collection points for reverse logistics; that is, the logistics needed to send products or packaging materials back to disassembly, reclamation, or disposal sites. Sometimes this activity involves the handling of hazardous materials or requires special handling of damaged or defective products. Frequently, returned products can be remanufactured or updated for resale. For example, many electronics manufacturers disassemble and/or remanufacture used equipment, which can then be sold at a discounted price. In fact, the retailer GameStop has made reverse logistics a key part of its business strategy, as described in the nearby Get Real box.

sustainability

GET REAL

GameStop Depends upon Reverse Logistics

With about 25 percent of its revenues coming from refurbished, pre-owned video gaming systems, mobile phones, tablets, and video games, reverse logistics plays an important role for GameStop. Games and equipment are cleaned, repaired, and restored to their original operating conditions in company-owned refurbishment operations centers. GameStop has 10 such centers located around the world, including one outside of Dallas, Texas, with over 1,000 employees. In addition, through reverse logistics at GameStop, over 13 million pounds of waste each year are kept out of landfills.

Source: Adapted from 2014 GameStop Annual Report.

© Paul Moseley/MCT/Newscom

The Defense Logistics Agency is another organization that is extensively involved in transferring or selling used equipment among the various military services and to other governmental agencies. Increasingly, firms are recognizing that reverse logistics offers opportunities for reducing costs, increasing profits, and differentiating the company from its competition.

Value-Added Services

value-added services Any work that creates greater value for customers.

The demand for highly customized service has transformed modern distribution warehouses into facilities that specialize in performing value-added services. A value-added service is any work that creates greater value for customers. These services may change the physical features or configuration of products so they are presented to customers in a unique or customized manner. For example, companies frequently postpone final product configuration by completing packaging, labeling, and even light manufacturing in a warehouse facility. A well-known application of this occurs in food processing. Many food processors sell canned vegetables to different customers who want their own labels to be placed on the cans. Vegetables can be processed and canned in "brights" (cans without labels) at the processing plants. Once a specific customer order is received, the warehouse completes labeling and packaging. Other examples range from packaging pharmaceuticals to customizing appliances to installing software on electronics.

Warehouse Operations

Once the roles of a warehouse have been determined, the next step is to design and manage the operations. It is useful to think of this as an exercise in process design. In the case of a warehouse, the primary process activities involved are:

- *Receiving and unloading:* Inbound shipments must be received and unloaded from the transportation vehicles. Part of this activity may also involve checking the shipment for the correct quantities and for potential damage to products.
- *In-storage handling:* Once unloaded, the goods must be moved to the desired destination within the facility, which may be an actual storage location or, in the case of a cross-dock facility, a shipping area.
- *Storage:* Products are held, even if for only a few minutes, in a storage area.
- *Order picking:* The products are removed from storage and assembled into appropriate quantities and assortments to fill customer orders.
- *Staging:* The assembled orders are moved to an area in the warehouse in readiness for loading into a transportation vehicle bound for customer locations.
- *Shipping:* Shipping involves verifying that the assembled orders are correct, as well as the actual loading of the transportation vehicles.

Designing and operating a warehouse is no different in concept than designing and managing any other process. Capacity must be determined, activities and flows must be managed, and potential bottlenecks and delays must be identified.

Companies have three options in choosing warehouse facilities: private warehouses, public warehouses, or contract warehouses. A private warehouse is owned and operated by the firm that owns the products. A private warehouse offers more control over the products, opportunities to integrate the warehouse operations with the other activities within the logistics system, and flexibility in operating policies and procedures. However, ownership requires that financial resources be committed to fixed physical assets.

A public warehouse is a firm that offers warehouse services to the public for a fee based on the amount of space used and the number of shipments into or out of the facility. Using public warehouses may be especially appropriate for a firm whose needs for warehouse capacity vary substantially throughout the year; for example, firms moving products into critical markets only at certain times of the year are most likely to use public warehouses. Agricultural chemical companies make extensive use of public warehouses, storing herbicides and pesticides in markets only for the growing seasons.

Contract warehouse companies offer to build, own, and operate warehouse facilities for the benefit of clients who do not want to undertake those responsibilities themselves. In addition, contract warehouse operators typically offer expanded services in such areas as transportation, inventory control, order processing, customer service, and returns processing.

MATERIALS HANDLING AND PACKAGING

LO11-5 Explain the importance of packaging and materials handling.

At its core, logistics management is very much about materials handling. Both transportation and warehousing managers must plan the best ways to load, offload, move, sort, and select products. They also work closely with packaging engineers to design or select packaging materials that facilitate materials handling. Packaging and materials handling decisions affect value in many ways. First, materials handling costs can be substantial, and improved labor and equipment productivity can significantly improve profits. Second, materials handling is usually the number one cause of product damage and loss in logistics. Poor handling practices and improperly packaged items lead to scratched, dented, and broken products that no one wants to buy. Usually, the less a material is handled, the better.

Packaging protects the product while it is in the logistics system. Beyond this basic function, however, packaging can facilitate ease of handling in a number of ways. First, packaging schemes are often devised to create one large container out of several smaller units. For example, individual soft drinks are frequently packaged in six-packs. The six-packs may be grouped together into cases of four six-packs. Cases are then grouped together into one unit of many cases. This process, called containerization or unitization, greatly reduces overall handling cost.

containerization or unitization Creating one large container out of several smaller units.

automated storage and retrieval systems (AS/RS) Computer-controlled systems that use robots to automatically select, find, retrieve, and convey product items from storage bins to loading docks.

Packages also contain information about the products they contain (useful when sorting products and processing orders). Today, many new packaging and labeling approaches are improving the speed and ease with which products can be identified, selected, and routed. For example, many warehouses today use automated storage and retrieval systems (AS/RS). These computer-controlled systems use robots to automatically select, find, retrieve, and convey product items from storage bins to loading docks. For these systems to work reliably, products need to be packaged in generic, unitized containers. Furthermore, labels need to be designed so that automated scanners are able to easily scan packaging information. The advantages of systems such as AS/RS include reduced labor requirements, reduced picking errors, more densely packed storage bays, and greater facility utilization (because racks can be built several stories high, much higher than human workers could safely operate).

Packaging and materials handling is a rapidly changing field in logistics management. There are numerous opportunities to improve logistics efficiency through advanced technologies such as AS/RS, new data communication technologies, and computerized control. In addition, supply chain managers are integrating operations across corporate boundaries by standardizing packaging designs, instruction formats, and data protocols.

Radio frequency identification (RFID), discussed in Chapter 7, is another technology that has rapidly gained acceptance in packaging and materials handling. RFID places a coded electronic chip in or on a package that emits a signal identifying its contents as it moves through facilities or is conveyed on transportation equipment. For example, when you buy a new shirt at a clothing retailer, the security tag is a type of RFID.

An AS/RS system. The photograph shows an aisle in a warehouse with an automated picking capability. The robot moves on a rail to the appropriate location and then automatically pulls products from their storage location.

© Craig Cozart/Getty Images

www-lib.icu.ac.jp/ASRS/index-e.htm

GET REAL

General Dynamics Develops AS/RS for the Navy

General Dynamics Armament and Technical Products, a business unit of General Dynamics, was awarded a $4.8 million contract to develop a land-based demonstrator of technology for the automated storage and retrieval system, an automatic warehouse system designed to be used aboard ships. The automated storage and retrieval system (AS/RS) will accept a palletized load from a fork truck, automatically identify the load through radio frequency identification (RFID), verify load size and weight, and then securely stow the load within the hold of a ship. This next-generation, low-maintenance storage and retrieval technology will allow the automatic inventory and total visibility of all material within the hold, greatly improving shipboard efficiency and reducing the need for dedicated manpower. The AS/RS design will be adaptable to a wide variety of ships and hold configurations.

Source: Adapted from "General Dynamics Awarded $5 Million to Develop Automated Storage and Retrieval System for U.S. Navy," *PR Newswire*, June 20, 2005.

Walmart and other major retailers are requiring that their major suppliers place RFID tags on their cases to facilitate processing in distribution centers and reduce handling expense. The U.S. Department of Defense uses RFID to list the contents of containers so that they can be tracked as they are loaded on transportation equipment or moved through facilities. The Get Real box on General Dynamics provides an interesting and rather unique application of both AS/RS systems and RFID.

sustainability

Finally, many firms are reexamining their approaches to packaging to improve environmental sustainability. For example, companies have reduced the plastic used to make beverage bottles. Using less packaging reduces costs and improves sustainability, but the quality and integrity of the product through the entire supply chain also must be ensured. Since 2011, Nike engineers have been working toward the goal of reducing the weight of its shoe boxes by 10 percent—a goal that has yet to be reached due to product damage. Many companies use recycled materials in packaging as a way to reduce costs and increase sustainability. Nike has been making its shoe boxes from 100 percent recycled materials for over 20 years.

NETWORK DESIGN

Perhaps no other set of decisions impacts supply chain operations more than network design. Network design determines the number and location of facilities. It also establishes the linkages among facilities through which information and material transportation flows occur in the network. For example, network designers decide which customers will be served by which facilities and which facilities will share inventories. These network decisions clearly impact a firm's cost and ability to service customers.

Numerous factors influence location decisions. Some of the most important of these are:

- Labor (availability and cost)
- Proximity of suppliers
- Proximity of customers
- Construction costs
- Land costs
- Taxes
- Regulations
- Incentive packages
- Transportation infrastructure
- Quality of life for employees
- Supply chain risk

Within each of these factors there are many specific items to evaluate. For example, regulations may be federal, state, and local. Building a facility at a specific place can require approval from each level of government. Even if a proposed facility meets all federal and state regulations, local officials could refuse to grant permission due to local zoning regulations.

Given the importance of location, sophisticated computer software is used to aid in decision making. In-depth discussion of those models is beyond the scope of this text, but we will briefly review a few fundamental location principles. First we examine issues related to choice of a location. Then we address issues related to determining the number of facilities needed.

Facility Location

There are several quantitative approaches that can help in facility location decisions. The center-of-gravity method provides an example of the distribution-related considerations involved in location. The center-of-gravity method attempts to find the lowest-cost location for a facility based on demand and distance.

The first step in the center-of-gravity method is to position the demand locations on a map with X and Y coordinates. Figure 11-4 shows a plot for three locations (A, B, and C), which represent markets to be served. The coordinate system's scale and origin do not matter as long as the relative distances between the locations are correct. The next step is to determine the amount of demand at each location. Demand can be measured in a number of ways. Often it is estimated as a function of the population at each location. Other factors, such as historical weight of products shipped, number of shipments, or sales dollars are also used as measures of demand.

The center of gravity is then determined by solving for the X and Y coordinates as follows:

(11.3a) $$\text{X coordinate of center of gravity} = \text{X}^* = \frac{\sum_i D_i X_i}{\sum_i D_i}$$

(11.3b) $$\text{Y coordinate of center of gravity} = \text{Y}^* = \frac{\sum_i D_i Y_i}{\sum_i D_i}$$

where:

D_i = Demand at location i

X_i = X coordinate of location i

Y_i = Y coordinate of location i

The center-of-gravity method involves certain assumptions. One of the most critical of these is the assumption of straight-line distances between all locations. In reality, roads or other transportation infrastructure are not straight lines. Another assumption is that amount of demand is a good proxy measure of transportation cost, which is not always true.

LO11-6 Locate facilities using the center-of-gravity model.

center-of-gravity method Attempts to find the lowest-cost location for a facility based on demand and distance.

FIGURE 11-4
Coordinate Locations of Markets and Their Center of Gravity

EXAMPLE 11-3

Suppose, given the locations plotted in Figure 11-4, we determine the following information:

Location	X Coordinate	Y Coordinate	Weight Shipped
A	20	90	200,000 lbs.
B	95	75	100,000 lbs.
C	60	30	500,000 lbs.

Solving for the center-of-gravity coordinates results in:

$$X^* = \frac{20(200,000) + 95(100,000) + 60(500,000)}{200,000 + 100,000 + 500,000} = \frac{43,500,000}{800,000} = 54.375$$

$$Y^* = \frac{90(200,000) + 75(100,000) + 30(500,000)}{200,000 + 100,000 + 500,000} = \frac{40,500,000}{800,000} = 50.625$$

The calculated center-of-gravity coordinates are plotted and represented by the "⊕" in Figure 11-4.

In addition, there are no qualitative factors included in the determination of location using the center-of-gravity method. For example, there is no consideration of environmental regulations or other costs associated with a given location.

Despite these assumptions and limitations, the center-of-gravity method does give a reasonable first approximation of where a facility might be located. This methodology, with considerable enhancement, forms the core of several of the more sophisticated computerized location models.

Number of Facilities

The basic principles driving the number of facilities in the network can be looked at from the perspective of transportation consolidation, the impact of facilities on inventory requirements, and customer service considerations. All of these directly impact the number of facilities and their location in a network.

Transportation Cost

Earlier in the chapter we demonstrated the financial savings possible from transportation consolidation. Frequently, this consolidation is achieved by positioning facilities in local markets to receive large inbound shipments from remote locations; the shipments are then distributed locally. The local facilities could be storage warehouses, break-bulk terminals, or cross-dock facilities. As long as the cost of operating the facility and the cost of local market delivery are less than the cost of making direct, small quantity shipments from the remote location, a facility can be justified on a total cost basis.

A company serving a large geographic area would find it advantageous to add local facilities as long as this relationship holds true. As a general rule, total cost will initially decline as the number of facilities increases. However, a point will be reached where the total cost is minimized and then increases as the number of facilities goes up. This point is reached because continual expansion of the number of facilities not only increases total facility costs, it also eventually results in each facility beginning to receive smaller inbound shipments, resulting in the loss of the consolidation benefit. Thus, inbound transportation costs also begin to increase. As an illustration of this point, consider the maximum number of potential network locations that would exist if a firm were to put a facility at each customer location. In this case, there is no consolidation and therefore the inbound transportation cost is the same as direct shipments to customers, with the added costs of all of the facilities in the network. Figure 11-5 illustrates this general relationship between transportation cost and the number of warehouse facilities.

Inventory Cost

Recall that in Chapter 7, we discussed basic fundamentals of inventory management. A critical point to remember from that discussion is that if you expand your network from one warehouse to two warehouses, you don't just divide your inventory in half and split it between the two locations. The reason that this will not work is that each facility must maintain its own safety stock. In fact, the total amount of inventory a company must hold increases as the number of warehouse locations increases.

Total Network Cost

Total network cost can be derived by combining the cost curves for transportation and inventory and adding the fact that facility costs also increase as the number of facilities increases. The result is depicted in Figure 11-6. Note in the figure that the "ideal" number of locations does not occur where inventory or facility costs are the lowest, which would be one facility. Neither does it occur where transportation cost is minimized, as that would require high inventory and facility costs.

Logistics Postponement

At the beginning of this chapter, we said that logisticians are concerned with both cost and service. The number of facility locations has a significant impact on the service provided to customers, particularly with respect to delivery speed. When customers require short lead times, the company must have a larger number of warehouses. For example, Grainger Distribution, a distributor of maintenance, repair, and operating supplies, has a network of over 400 warehouses throughout the United States, driven primarily by the fact that many customers have emergency needs for repair parts for major equipment. While maintaining such an extensive network is certainly not the lowest-cost alternative, it is profitable for Grainger because customers are willing to pay higher prices to receive delivery within a few hours.

FIGURE 11-5
Transportation Cost Related to Number of Warehouse Locations

FIGURE 11-6
Total Network Cost

logistics postponement Strategy that involves stocking products in a single or only a few locations rather than spreading inventory across a large number of warehouses.

In contrast to Grainger's approach, the strategy of logistics postponement is to stock in a single or only a few locations rather than spread inventory out across a large number of warehouses. Logistics postponement is practiced by many firms, particularly those that manufacture high–value density products. In this situation, it would be very expensive to position inventory in a large number of locations in anticipation of a customer order arising in any given area. It may be substantially less expensive, for example, to maintain one central location of inventory and then to use a premium mode of transportation such as FedEx or UPS Air to deliver directly to customers. The savings in warehousing and inventory costs could make it more economical, even though the transportation cost may be high. Of course, logistics postponement is only feasible if the transportation mode chosen can still meet customer requirements regarding delivery speed.

Imagine all of the cost trade-offs and customer service issues that you would have to consider when making structural changes such as logistics postponement. Such decisions should not be made from a short-term point of view. Network designers must consider changes in customers (e.g., the opening of a new market), changes in technology, changes in supply and demand, changes in competitive actions, changes in products (e.g., new or modified products), and changes in costs. Modifications to the logistics network often require substantial investments in information systems, land, facilities, training, and transportation infrastructure. Consequently, logistics network design is an area of strategic concern that often constrains many other operating decisions. The Get Real box about Kimberly-Clark illustrates the complexity of these decisions.

GET REAL

Kimberly-Clark Redesigns the Network

Kimberly-Clark, the maker of Kleenex facial tissue, Huggies diapers, Scott paper towels, and many other health and hygiene brands, is based in Irving, Texas. Kimberly-Clark began to address facility network questions when it started a project to update its supply chain. The primary goal was "customer-centric, to improve customer service," said Mark Jamison, vice president of customer service at Kimberly-Clark North America. According to Jamison, "the second goal was to fashion a lower-cost network."

The company examined its network, which comprised 70 mill and plant distribution centers. "Each manufacturing location had multiple warehouses, and many were not located near major markets. So the intent was to streamline the distribution network," he said.

Kimberly-Clark has reduced those 70 facilities to nine regional megacenters that are located close to its key retail customers and markets. The change enables the company to reach 90 percent of the North American population within eight hours. The nine regional distribution centers are located in Chicago; Scranton, Pennsylvania; Atlanta; Graniteville, South Carolina; Dallas; Redlands, California; Kansas City, Missouri; Conway, Arkansas; and Seattle.

"As we have seen the cost of oil increase and its significant impact on distribution expenses, the decision to consolidate and streamline the network has become a real positive," Jamison said. "Our inventory is no longer scattered among many manufacturing and distribution centers."

Kimberly-Clark figures that in its first year the network restructuring saved 473,000 gallons of fuel and decreased the number of miles driven from distribution centers to customer locations by 2.8 million. Another initiative that Kimberly-Clark recently began will move some 22 co-packaging facilities into the regional distribution centers. Under the current system, the company has to move its product from the manufacturing and distribution plant to the co-packer and then ship it back to the distribution center for shipment. "This will eliminate moving the same product twice, and it eliminates the costs of shipping to the co-packer and the additional material-handling costs," Jamison said.

© Ron Heflin/AP Images

Source: B. DiBenedetto, *The Journal of Commerce Online*, June 17, 2008.

INTEGRATED SERVICE PROVIDERS

More and more, firms are foregoing the costs of owning private transportation and warehousing in favor of purchasing logistical services from specialists. For example, in the transportation industry there are thousands of carriers who specialize in product movement between geographic locations. Over the years, a comprehensive network of common and contract carriers has emerged. In addition, a large number of service companies have traditionally provided public or contract warehouse services.

In recent years there has been a radical shift from single function to multifunctional specialists. Today, **integrated service providers (ISPs)** provide a range of logistics services. For example, United Parcel Service (UPS) stocks Nike shoes and warm-up suits at a Louisville warehouse and processes orders hourly. All related communication and administration activities are handled by a UPS call center, and UPS provides delivery to retail customers. Thus, Nike has effectively outsourced basic logistics services to UPS. The common name used throughout the industry to describe ISPs is **third-party logistics service providers (3PLs)**.

The continuing globalization of business has put tremendous pressure on logistics executives. Lead times are considerably longer and more subject to variation. It is more difficult to determine shipment status and anticipate arrival times. In addition, there is a substantial increase in the volume and type of documentation required to deal with international logistics, much of which is country-specific. As a result, few companies have the resources and capabilities to deal with these issues internally. Integrated service providers provide a potential solution to these problems for many organizations.

LO11-7 Describe the benefits of integrated service providers.

integrated service providers (ISPs) Companies that provide a range of logistics services.

third-party logistics service providers (3PLs) A common term used in the industry to describe integrated service providers (ISPs).

global

CHAPTER SUMMARY

This chapter describes the role of logistics in supply chain operations. We explored the following issues:

1. Logistics management provides for the flow and storage of information and products between: (1) the firm and its suppliers (inbound logistics); (2) the firm and its customers (outbound logistics); and (3) the various plants, divisions, and units of the firm (internal logistics).

2. The objective of logistics management is to provide customers with their required service benefits at the lowest total logistics cost.

3. A complete logistics management system comprises six major decision areas: (1) facility network design, (2) information and inventory management, (3) order management, (4) transportation management, (5) warehousing management, (6) and packaging and materials handling management.

4. Economies of scale and distance offer opportunities to lower cost through consolidation in transportation management. The transportation modes each have significant advantages and disadvantages, which makes the choice of transportation service a complex decision.

5. Warehouses perform several functions over and above storage. They also provide benefits through consolidation, break-bulk, cross-docking, and assortment activities.

6. Network design and facility location are extremely complex decisions involving a number of considerations. Quantitative techniques such as center-of-gravity can be used to approximate ideal locations. Determining the proper number of locations involves many cost trade-offs as well as a clear understanding of customers' service requirements. Integrated service providers are increasingly being utilized by companies due to their expertise in accomplishing logistics activities.

automated storage and retrieval systems (AS/RS)   379

break-bulk   376

center-of-gravity method   381

common carriers   372

consolidation   367

containerization or unitization   379

contract carriers   372

cost-to-cost trade-off   365

cost-to-service trade-off   365

cross-docking   376

distribution center   375

economic regulation   367

economy of distance   367

economy of scale   367

integrated service providers (ISPs)   385

intermodal transportation   372

less-than-truckload (LTL)   370

logistics management   364

logistics postponement   384

market area consolidation   368

pooled delivery consolidation   368

private carriers   373

production support warehouse   375

safety (and social) regulation   367

scheduled delivery consolidation   368

specialty carriers   370

stockpiling   375

third-party logistics service providers (3PLs)   385

total landed cost   365

transportation mode   368

transshipment point   375

truckload (TL)   370

value-added services   378

value density   374

warehouse consolidation   376

1. What are the two types of trade-offs that are of concern to logistics managers? Provide examples of each type of trade-off, beyond those given in the text.

2. Why has the importance of logistics management been growing over the past few decades?

3. What is the role of government in transportation? Do you believe economic deregulation is positive or negative for the overall economy?

4. What is transportation consolidation? How do consolidation strategies take advantage of the basic economic characteristics of transportation?

5. Which mode of transportation would you use for the following products? Why?
   a. Steel.
   b. Oil from Alaska.
   c. Roses from Texas bound for New York.
   d. Cancelled checks moving from Hartford to Chicago.
   e. A contract that must be signed within 24 hours.

6. Why do you think so many firms are concerned about logistics issues when they move into new markets such as China and Russia?

7. Why is the use of warehouses for cross-docking and for transshipment much more attractive to retail and grocery firms, compared to their more traditional use as storage points?

8. What are the critical trade-offs involved in logistics postponement?

9. Based on the information contained within this chapter, what are the critical linkages between the logistics management system and other functions such as production and purchasing?

10. Think about the increasing importance of environmental sustainability and the likelihood that regulations designed to protect the environment will become increasingly strict. What do you think the impact of these changes will be on logistics management?

PROBLEMS

1. Jones Nurseries has received orders from four different customers located in Alabama. Each order has a shipment weight of 6,000 pounds. In discussions with transportation carriers, the best rate Jones received was $28 per hundredweight for a 6,000-pound shipment. However, one carrier quoted a transportation cost of $20 per hundredweight for a consolidated shipment, with an additional charge of $200 for each stop on the delivery. Should Jones choose the consolidated shipment alternative?

Solution:

The cost of four individual shipments is:
$4 \times (6,000$ pounds$/100) \times \$28 = \$6,720$
The cost of a consolidated shipment is:
$(24,000$ pounds$)$ x $(\$20/$hundredweight$) + (4$ stops$)$ x $(\$200$ per stop$) = \$5,600$
Jones Nurseries should choose the consolidated shipment, which saves $1,120 in transportation expense.

2. Bill's Glass needs to ship an order of five chandeliers to a builder about 1,000 miles away. The chandeliers cost about $5,000 each, and Bill will be paid upon delivery. Bill plans to ship the order by truck at a cost of $250. The delivery will take five days. Bill uses a 20 percent annual inventory carrying charge with an operating schedule of 360 days per year. What will be the approximate total shipping and transit inventory cost of the shipment?

Solution:

The cost of carrying the inventory while it is in transit is:
$(5$ days$/365)$ x $(5$ chandeliers$)$ x $(\$5,000/$chandelier$)$ x $.2 = \$68.49$

Since the transportation cost is $250, the total cost is $318.49.

3. Johnson's Department Store has decided to build a warehouse to serve its store locations. It has one large store in each of the following cities: Sparta, Troy, and Athens. The map coordinates of these cities and the weight of shipments per month to each is shown in the following table:

City	X Coordinate	Y Coordinate	Weight/Month
Sparta	25	50	100 tons
Troy	75	10	200 tons
Athens	90	80	50 tons

Calculate the X and Y coordinates of the center-of-gravity for Johnson's Department Store.

Solution:

$$X^* = \frac{25(100) + 75(200) + 90(50)}{100 + 200 + 50} = \frac{22,000}{350} = 62.86$$

$$Y^* = \frac{50(100) + 10(200) + 80(50)}{100 + 200 + 50} = \frac{11,000}{350} = 31.43$$

PROBLEMS

1. Richard's Sporting Goods needs to fill an online order for a gross (144) of hockey sticks. The manager is considering shipping the order by truck to the customer in Wisconsin, at a carrier charge of $75. The delivery will take five days and the order is paid on delivery (Richard's doesn't get paid until the sticks are received). The hockey sticks are valued at $50 for each stick and Richard's uses a 25 percent annual inventory carrying charge.

   a. What will be the total shipping and transit inventory cost of the shipment?
   b. If the shipment could be delivered in only two days at a cost of $100, should the manager do it? How much money would be saved or lost?

2. The following table provides shipping rates for packages using UPS next-day air or ground service options. The rates vary according to both the weight of the package and the distance of the shipment (larger numbered zones are farther away). Note that the zone number also indicates the number of days required to deliver a package using ground service. For example, it would take three days and cost $7.40 to send a 10-pound package to zone 3 using ground service.

   a. Suppose you have a package weighing 15 pounds that needs to be shipped to zone 5. The value of the material is $10,000 and the annual inventory holding rate is 40 percent of the product value. Which transportation mode (air or ground) minimizes the total shipping and transit inventory cost?
   b. How high would the inventory holding rate have to be in order to justify next-day air service?

Table of Shipping Rates							
Next-Day Service Weight (in pounds)	Domestic Zones Transit Time (in Days)						
	1	2	3	4	5	6	7
1	$ 16.25	$ 19.25	$ 22.75	$ 24.75	$ 27.00	$ 28.25	$ 29.00
2	$ 17.25	$ 20.75	$ 25.50	$ 27.75	$ 30.25	$ 31.25	$ 32.00
3	$ 19.00	$ 21.75	$ 28.25	$ 30.50	$ 33.50	$ 34.75	$ 35.50
4	$ 20.00	$ 22.75	$ 31.00	$ 33.50	$ 36.50	$ 37.75	$ 38.50
5	$ 21.25	$ 24.25	$ 33.50	$ 36.25	$ 39.50	$ 40.75	$ 41.75
6	$ 22.00	$ 25.25	$ 36.00	$ 39.00	$ 42.75	$ 44.00	$ 45.00
7	$ 22.75	$ 27.00	$ 38.50	$ 42.00	$ 46.00	$ 47.00	$ 48.25
8	$ 23.75	$ 28.25	$ 41.00	$ 44.75	$ 49.25	$ 50.25	$ 51.25
9	$ 24.50	$ 29.75	$ 43.75	$ 47.50	$ 52.50	$ 53.75	$ 54.50
10	$ 25.25	$ 31.00	$ 46.25	$ 50.25	$ 55.25	$ 56.75	$ 57.75
11	$ 26.25	$ 32.50	$ 48.75	$ 52.75	$ 58.00	$ 60.00	$ 60.75
12	$ 27.00	$ 33.50	$ 51.25	$ 55.50	$ 60.75	$ 63.00	$ 63.75
13	$ 27.75	$ 34.75	$ 53.75	$ 58.00	$ 63.25	$ 65.75	$ 66.50
14	$ 28.50	$ 36.00	$ 55.75	$ 60.50	$ 65.75	$ 68.50	$ 69.25
15	$ 29.50	$ 37.50	$ 58.00	$ 63.00	$ 68.25	$ 70.75	$ 72.00

Ground Service Weight (in pounds)	Domestic Zones Transit Time (in Days)						
	1	2	3	4	5	6	7
1	$ 4.75	$ 4.90	$ 5.25	$ 5.35	$ 5.65	$ 5.70	$ 5.85
2	$ 4.85	$ 5.15	$ 5.65	$ 5.80	$ 6.25	$ 6.40	$ 6.80
3	$ 5.00	$ 5.40	$ 6.00	$ 6.25	$ 6.70	$ 6.90	$ 7.55
4	$ 5.15	$ 5.60	$ 6.30	$ 6.60	$ 7.10	$ 7.30	$ 8.05
5	$ 5.40	$ 5.80	$ 6.60	$ 6.95	$ 7.40	$ 7.75	$ 8.55
6	$ 5.55	$ 6.00	$ 6.75	$ 7.20	$ 7.65	$ 8.05	$ 8.85
7	$ 5.75	$ 6.15	$ 6.90	$ 7.45	$ 7.95	$ 8.35	$ 9.25
8	$ 6.00	$ 6.35	$ 7.10	$ 7.60	$ 8.25	$ 8.75	$ 9.90
9	$ 6.20	$ 6.55	$ 7.25	$ 7.80	$ 8.45	$ 9.25	$ 10.55
10	$ 6.40	$ 6.70	$ 7.40	$ 8.00	$ 8.80	$ 9.90	$ 11.25
11	$ 6.60	$ 6.90	$ 7.55	$ 8.25	$ 9.20	$ 10.60	$ 12.05
12	$ 6.80	$ 7.10	$ 7.70	$ 8.45	$ 9.60	$ 11.35	$ 12.95
13	$ 7.00	$ 7.35	$ 7.85	$ 8.65	$ 10.05	$ 12.05	$ 13.80
14	$ 7.15	$ 7.55	$ 8.00	$ 8.85	$ 10.60	$ 12.75	$ 14.65
15	$ 7.35	$ 7.80	$ 8.15	$ 9.05	$ 11.15	$ 13.45	$ 15.55

3. Use the table in problem 2 to answer the following question. A transportation manager must ship orders of materials weighing three pounds each to destinations in each of the seven zones listed in the table. The daily inventory holding rate is $7.50 per day for all orders. The manager has decided to use next-day air service for all shipments. Would you agree that this is the right course of action? Why, or why not?

4. Using the table in problem 2, determine whether or not economies of scale (weight) and economies of distance exist. (*Hint:* Assume that distance from each zone to the next farthest zone is approximately constant across all zones.)

5. You are shipping 200 diamonds to a customer located 2,000 miles away. The average value of the diamonds is $1,500. You can ship via air for $500 and the diamonds will arrive in two days or you can ship via a specialty ground carrier for $200 and the diamonds will arrive in six days. You figure your inventory carrying cost is 25 percent. Your customer will immediately transfer funds to your bank account on receipt of the shipment. What is your total cost if you use the ground carrier? The air carrier? What other considerations are involved besides the cost?

6. Suppose Jones Company has orders from three customers located in the same market area. One order has a total weight of 4,000 pounds, the second weighs 8,000 pounds, and the third weighs 14,000 pounds. The transportation carrier quotes a freight rate of $20.00 per hundredweight (or cwt.) for direct shipment to the customer for shipments weighing 1,000 to 4,999 pounds; $18.00 per cwt. for orders weighing 5,000 to 9,999 pounds; and $16.00 for shipments weighing between 10,000 and 15,000 pounds. Alternatively, the carrier's rate for shipments weighing more than 20,000 pounds is $13.50 per cwt. However, if the orders are combined into one shipment, the carrier will charge $200 for each stop it is required to make. Should Jones consolidate the three shipments?

7. Suppose you have three shipments to make. One shipment has a weight of 3,000 pounds, the second weighs 7,000 pounds, and the third weighs 14,000 pounds. The transportation rates are: $18/cwt. for shipments of 1,000–5,000 pounds; $16/cwt. for 5,000–10,000 pounds; and $14/cwt. for shipments over 10,000 pounds. For consolidated shipments, there is a charge of $200.00 per stop. How much will you save if you choose to consolidate the shipments rather than ship each individually?

8. A trucking company publishes the following rates:

Shipment Weight	Cost per 100 Pounds
Less than 500 lbs.	$20.00
500–999 lbs.	$18.00
1,000–4,999 lbs.	$15.50
5,000–9,999 lbs.	$14.00
10,000 lbs. or more	$13.00

Suppose you have 10 shipments to make, each of which weighs 800 pounds. The carrier offers to consolidate them into one shipment of 8,000 pounds but will charge an additional $300 (total) to do so. Should you agree to this offer?

9. Using the rates in problem 8, suppose you have eight shipments of 900 pounds each that the carrier will consolidate into one shipment, for an additional charge of $200 (total). Should you agree to this?

10. Dansville Cabinets is considering a new warehouse to serve its major markets. Find the center of gravity using the following information:

Market	X Coordinate	Y Coordinate	Demand
North	45	80	200 truckloads
East	85	45	100 truckloads
South	45	10	500 truckloads
West	10	45	50 truckloads

11. Creative Crafts needs to determine where to locate a new warehouse to serve its retail stores in Ohio. Find the center of gravity location using the following information.

Retail Location	X Coordinate	Y Coordinate	Shipments/Year
A	10	18	395
B	25	5	385
C	35	45	290
D	50	10	210
E	55	35	435

12. A manufacturing company wants to locate its new plant to facilitate shipping from its suppliers. Using the information below, determine the location using the center of gravity.

Supplier Location	X Coordinate	Y Coordinate	Shipments/Year
1	8	68	1,000
2	26	5	200
3	43	55	1,700
4	64	21	350
5	79	73	1,500

13. Determine the center of gravity location for a company that wants to serve customers located in Chicago, Detroit, Indianapolis, and Cincinnati. To do this, you can find the X and Y coordinates by looking at the longitude and latitude for each city. Estimate demand for each city by simply looking up the population of each.

14. Atlas Corporation is considering a distribution center which will serve three primary market areas: Dallas, Texas; Atlanta, Georgia; and, St. Louis, Missouri. Atlas has determined that the latitude, longitude, and populations of the three metropolitan areas are:

Metropolitan Area	Approx. Latitude	Approx. Longitude	Approx. Population
Atlanta	33.75	−84.39	5.4 million
Dallas	32.80	−96.77	6.5 million
St. Louis	38.62	−90.20	2.8 million

Using the center-of-gravity method, determine the latitude and longitude of the best location for the distribution center. Use Google Maps or some other resource to plot the location. Then suggest other factors to consider in determining a location for the distribution center.

CASE

Spartan Plastics

Elise Lovejoy, the new logistics coordinator at Spartan Plastics, was looking at the stack of papers and the two computer screens in front of her. It was Friday afternoon—the Friday before the long weekend—and she still had not come to a resolution. She knew that first thing Tuesday morning she would have a meeting with Bob Barley, CEO and major owner of Spartan Plastics. The issue that they would be discussing: how to get the increasing shipping costs under control. With the forecasts for the upcoming year looking promising, shipping volumes were expected to increase by 10 to 25 percent. Consequently, the shipping costs had to be addressed because, simply put, they were too high.

Spartan Plastics—Background Information

Spartan Plastics was a medium-sized producer of high-quality, highly engineered plastic components. These components were typically found on the interior of most trucks and cars. They tended to come in variety of colors and finishes—everything from small door panels to panels that looked like wood. Typically, their critical major customers consisted of the Big Three (General Motors, Ford, and Chrysler) and were located in the Detroit-Toledo-Lansing area. During the last year, Spartan Plastics had shipped approximately 10,000 pounds of components per day to each assembly plant served.

Located in St. Louis, Missouri (where the company was known for its aggressive policy of recruiting minorities for its workforce and for its progressive supplier diversification program), Spartan Plastics employed 450 people: 200 direct assembly line employees, 150 engineers, and 100 others.

Originally begun in 1976, the company had grown quickly. However, management's primary focus was on engineering and product design. Management's mantra was simple and known to everyone: High-quality components, designed right, built right, sold at a fair price, and delivered on-time.

The Shipping Problem

Logistics and shipping, as a result, were traditionally not a high priority at Spartan Plastics. Until recently, shipping was seen as simply being a clerical task. Consequently, this responsibility was assigned to a shipping clerk who simply called a local shipping company. Unsurprisingly, shipping costs tended to be high.

In the past, Spartan Plastics had used an LTL carrier from its plant to each of the assembly plants. The carrier charged Spartan Plastics $0.05 per hundredweight per mile. What this policy meant was that to ship one day's worth of components to the Lansing plant, for example, it would cost Spartan Plastics $2,435 (over $600,000 per year).

With its customers becoming more cost sensitive, top management agreed that something had to be done. The first step was to increase the "professionalism" of the logistics and shipping department. One of the first actions triggered by this step was the hiring of Elise Lovejoy. Elise had previously worked as a manager in a shipping department of a local St. Louis company that was widely respected for its expertise in this area. Upon arriving at Spartan Plastics, Elise undertook an assessment. After three weeks, she agreed with top management—the shipping costs were simply too high; there were no controls on them.

Consequently, she approached several Midwestern logistics/shipping companies and asked them to submit proposals in response to her RFQ (request for quotes). After an initial screening review, she identified two proposals that seemed to be highly attractive.

Consolidated Shipping LLC (CS): The first proposal recommended a consolidated delivery approach. That is, CS would consolidate the three shipments into one 30,000-pound truckload. The carrier would then use a "milk-run" approach in which the truck would stop first at the Lansing assembly plant, then continue on to Detroit, and finish in Toledo. The carrier's charge for the milk-run approach would be based on distance only with a charge of $6.00 per truck mile, plus a stop-off charge of $250/stop, including the final stop in Toledo.

Amalgamated Integrated Services (AIS): The second proposal came from AIS, which could provide both transportation and cross-docking capability. AIS proposed to handle deliveries to the various automotive plants by consolidating the shipments into a full truckload in St. Louis. This full truckload would then travel from St. Louis to Ypsilanti, Michigan, where the shipment would then be broken down into cross-docked shipments for delivery to the appropriate assembly plants (again handled by AIS). AIS established a cost of $6.00 per mile to the cross-dock facility and then a flat cost per delivery to each assembly plant from Ypsilanti of $500.

To help in evaluating these two proposals, Elise put together a mileage table for all of the relevant origin/destination points. She also knew that she would have to consider the cost implications of the alternatives. Yet, she felt that there were some potential qualitative and service considerations present as well.

Origin	Destination	Distance
St. Louis, MO	Lansing, MI	487 miles
St. Louis, MO	Detroit, MI	552 miles
St. Louis, MO	Toledo, OH	499 miles
Lansing, MI	Detroit, MI	88 miles
Detroit, MI	Toledo, OH	65 miles
St. Louis, MO	Ypsilanti, MI	521 miles

As Elise proceeded to turn off her computer and to put the various notes and calculations into her briefcase, she knew that on Tuesday, she would have to be ready with a comprehensive, well-reasoned analysis and set of recommendations.

Questions

1. What are the cost implications of each delivery option?

2. What are the qualitative and service characteristics of each delivery option?

3. Based on your analysis, what would you recommend to Bob Barley?

CASE

Lear Corporation

Lear Corporation, headquartered in Southfield, Michigan, is one of the world's 10 largest independent automotive suppliers and the leading player in the $45 billion global auto interiors market. This market consists of such items as seating systems, interior carpets, safety restraining systems, and interior paneling. By most measures of performance, Lear is a very successful company. It has experienced a compound annual growth rate of 33 percent over a 13-year period.

One of the most successful plants within the Lear system is the Romulus I plant. This facility, located about 250 yards from the on- and off-ramps of I-275 (a major highway located in the Detroit area), was initially built to serve a GM plant that has now been shut down. The plant today provides seat assemblies for the Chrysler Warren Plant, which is located some 38 miles away. The Chrysler Warren Plant assembles the Dodge Ram and Dakota trucks.

All seats are assembled at Lear on a just-in-time basis. Lear has a five-hour window between the time that Lear's Romulus plant receives notice of the specific types of seats that it must deliver and the time that the seats are needed at Chrysler Warren. Thus, Lear must assemble, test, sequence (i.e., arrange them on the trucks so that the seats can be withdrawn in the exact order that they are needed), and deliver the seats within five hours. This plant has met these demands in a number of ways. First, the entire production line has been rethought. Operations have been extensively analyzed and simplified (thus reducing the need for highly skilled employees). All employees are cross-trained. The plant also is electronically linked to the Warren plant. The Romulus plant receives information about type of vehicles and their seating options as the trucks move through framing. This information ensures that the right types of seats are made in the right order. The material for seats comes off trailers parked near the assembly lines. These trailers bring material up from suppliers located in Mexico. All material is bundled (one bundle per seat) and sequenced by a daily schedule so that the material can be brought in as needed. When the seats are finished, they are temporarily stored on-site. This storage is used to consolidate loads and to ensure that the loads are correctly sequenced (i.e., the first seats needed are loaded last, the last seats are loaded first). When a load is completed, it is shipped by truck to the Warren plant.

How successful is the Romulus plant? In recent years the plant has turned its inventory in excess of 200 times each year.

Questions

1. What elements define value for the customers of the Romulus plant?
2. What is the role of logistics and logistics considerations in the success of the Romulus plant? In your answer, focus on such issues as information processing, warehousing, mode of transportation, and network design.

SELECTED READINGS & INTERNET SITES

Bowersox, D. J.; D. J. Closs; M. B. Cooper; and J. C. Bowersox. *Supply Chain Logistics Management,* 4th edition. New York: McGraw-Hill, 2013.

Bowman, R. "Is New Truck-Monitoring Technology for Safety or for Spying on Drivers? *Forbes/Logistics & Transportation,* Feb. 11, 2014, http://www.forbes.com/sites/robertbowman/2014/02/11/is-new-truck-monitoring-technology-for-safety-or-spying-on-drivers/.

Closs, David J.; Cheri Speier; and Nathan Meacham. "Sustainability to Support End-to-End Value Chains: The Role of Supply Chain Management." *Journal of the Academy of Marketing Science* 39, no. 1 (2011), pp. 101–16.

Closs, David, et al. "A Framework for Protecting Your Supply Chain." *Supply Chain Management Review* (March–April 2008).

Golicic, Susan; Courtney Boerstler; and Lisa Ellram. "Greening the Transportation in Your Supply Chain." *MIT Sloan Management Review* 51, no. 2 (2010), pp. 47–55.

Kim, E. "The Latest Data Shows Where Amazon Might Be Headed Next—and It Should Terrify UPS and FedEx." *Business Insider,* Oct. 19, 2015, http://www.businessinsider.com/amazon-logistics-facilities-update-2015-10.

Lynch, C. F. *Logistics Outsourcing: A Management Guide,* 2nd edition. Memphis: CFL Publishing, 2004.

Nicas, J. and L. Stevens. "Startups Accelerate Efforts to Reinvent the Trucking Industry," *The Wall Street Journal,* Oct. 27, 2015, http://www.wsj.com/articles/startups-accelerate-efforts-to-reinvent-trucking-industry-1445918403?alg=y.

Paris, C. and Chiu, J. "Chinese Shipping Group Cosco Planning Regular Trans-Arctic Sailing," *The Wall Street Journal,* Oct. 29, 2015, http://www.wsj.com/articles/chinese-shipper-cosco-to-schedule-regular-trans-arctic-sailings-1446133485.

Parkinson, J. "On Board the World's Biggest Ship," *BBC News Magazine,* March 11, 2015, http://www.bbc.com/news/magazine-21432226.

Peterson, E. and Klimczuk-Massion, S. "Uncertainty on the High Seas," *CSCMP Supply Chain Quarterly,* Quarter 2, 2015, http://www.supplychainquarterly.com/topics/Global/20150622-uncertainty-on-the-high-seas/.

Schulz, John D. "Trucking Game Changing Movement." *Supply Chain Management Review* (May–June 2010), pp. 56–66.

Stock, J.; T. Speh; and H. Shear. "Many Happy (Product) Returns." *Harvard Business Review* 80, no. 7 (2002), p. 16.

"To Fulfill Increasing Customer Demands, Go Small," *CSCMP's Supply Chain Quarterly,* July 22, 2015, http://www.supplychainquarterly.com/news/20150722-to-fulfill-increasing-customer-demands-go-small/.

Amazon
www.amazon.com

Convoy Trucking
www.convoy.com

Council of Supply Chain Management Professionals
www.cscmp.org

Dominos Pizza
www.dominos.com

GameStop
www.gamestop.com

Logistics Management
www.logisticsmgmt.com

Nike
www.nike.com

Supply Chain Brain
www.supplychainbrain.com

Supply Chain Digest
www.scdigest.com

Trucker Path
www.truckerpath.com

PLANNING FOR INTEGRATED OPERATIONS ACROSS THE SUPPLY CHAIN

 relationships sustainability   global

		relationships	sustainability	global
12	Demand Planning: Forecasting and Demand Management	X		X
13	Sales and Operations Planning	X	X	X
14	Materials and Resource Requirements Planning	X		X

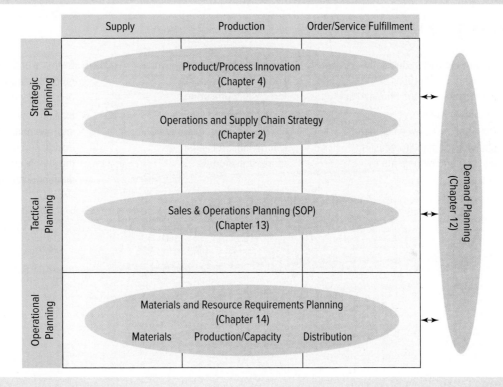

ow do operations managers make sure that they have the right products at the right place at the right time? Surely you have heard the adage, "If you fail to plan, you plan to fail." Part 4, *Planning for Integrated Operations Across the Supply Chain,* explains how operations managers develop resource plans and put them in place. As the figure above indicates, planning typically takes place at three levels: strategic (long term) planning, tactical (medium term) planning, and operational (short term) planning. At each level the primary goal is to ensure that capacity (the amount and types of resources available) is enough to satisfy demand. While this may sound simple, many planning processes at different levels must be coordinated, creating a hierarchy of decisions as shown in the figure above.

Because strategic planning decisions were covered in Part 2, this part of the book addresses tactical and operational planning. **Chapter 12** explains processes used to forecast and manage (influence) customer demand. This topic comes first because demand planning is the starting point for all the other types of planning. **Chapter 13** describes tactical planning, used to identify customer demands for aggregate product families and establish the inventory and capacity plans needed to satisfy those overall demands. **Chapter 14** discusses planning processes for the short term, addressing the most detailed levels of inventory and resources. These chapters will introduce you to several collaborative planning processes, such as collaborative planning, forecasting, and replenishment (CPFR) and sales and operations planning (S&OP). These types of processes help ensure that all the needed inputs from customers, suppliers, and internal operational functions are integrated to create effective and efficient plans for all supply chain partners.

12

Demand Planning: Forecasting and Demand Management

LEARNING OBJECTIVES *After studying this chapter, you should be able to:*

LO12-1 Explain the role of demand planning in operations management, in the firm, and in the supply chain.

LO12-2 Differentiate between demand planning, demand forecasting, and demand management activities.

LO12-3 Describe various qualitative and quantitative demand forecasting procedures.

LO12-4 Develop forecasts using moving average, exponential smoothing, and linear regression models.

LO12-5 Evaluate and select forecasting models using various measures of accuracy and bias.

LO12-6 Explain how certain improvements to both product design and operations across the supply chain can make demand planning easier.

© Kiichiro Sato/AP Images

The Longaberger Company (www.longaberger. com) is known primarily for its high-quality baskets—still handmade, just like when the company was born in 1918. In recent years Longaberger has experienced phenomenal growth; quite a feat considering the challenges of competing in the home decorating industry. Demand planning in general, and sales forecasting in particular, are usually quite tough for a fast-growing company with a complex set of continually changing product lines. Since these are "fashion" items subject to changing trends and customer tastes, it is often difficult to judge which products will be fast sellers and which will be slow. Moreover, keeping track of pricing changes and promotional programs can be a complex planning task.

Forecasting processes at Longaberger must consider many different factors, including the growth strategy of the company, seasonal and holiday demand patterns, and both regular and irregular promotional events. The forecasting approach used at Longaberger addresses these factors by integrating three sources of information: historical sales trends and seasonal patterns; economic data quantifying market, sales, and environmental conditions; and the qualitative judgmental expertise of managers.

For Longaberger, the key to forecasting success has not been to simply pick the "right" statistical analysis method, but rather to develop an integrated system of techniques to help managers accurately plan for future demand. Forecasts generated by the system drive all kinds of production, procurement, and capacity management plans. Ultimately, the accuracy and insights provided by the demand planning system have been instrumental in helping the Longaberger Company give customers the products they want, when they want them.

LO12-1 Explain the role of demand planning in operations management, in the firm, and in the supply chain.

DEMAND PLANNING: AN OVERVIEW

Almost all operational planning activities start with some estimate of what customers' demands will be. In order to develop demand estimates, every company has to forecast both the quantity and timing of demands, and many companies can also influence or "manage" customers' demand patterns through product pricing and through other means. These two activities, demand forecasting and demand management, are collectively known as *demand planning*.

demand planning The combined process of forecasting and managing customer demands to create a planned pattern of demand that meets the firm's operational and financial goals.

demand forecasting A decision process in which managers predict demand patterns.

demand management A proactive approach in which managers attempt to influence the pattern of demand.

Demand planning is the combined process of forecasting and managing customer demands to create a planned pattern of demand that meets the firm's operational and financial goals. **Demand forecasting** is a decision process in which managers predict demand patterns, whereas **demand management** is a proactive approach in which managers attempt to influence patterns of demand. Usually, demand management involves the use of pricing and promotional activities.

By doing a good job of demand planning, operations managers can more effectively plan for the amount of productive capacity and other resources their business will need, both in the short term and in the long term. Demand planning also helps operations managers know what customers they should serve and at what levels of service. Demand planning is especially difficult when products have highly varying and uncertain demand patterns. Precisely because it is so difficult, companies like Longaberger have built competitive advantages as a result of their superior abilities.

The Role That Demand Planning Plays in Operations Management

Demand planning drives almost all other activities in operations management. For many tangible products, making products to order is not an option. The lead time required is longer than customers are willing to wait. For example, you probably would not be willing to wait for a company to build a toaster oven from scratch for you. Consequently, managers have to anticipate demand and plan what materials and resources they will need well in advance of actual orders. In order to make these production plans, managers need to make good predictions of the quantities of products that will be demanded at a given time and place. Accurate planning information has many benefits, and there are severe costs to being wrong. The costs of making forecasts that are too high include money lost in holding inventory that is never sold, lost capacity that is spent making products that no one wants to buy, lost wages spent paying workers who are not needed, and so on. These costs are borne by firms throughout the supply chain, but they are also passed on to customers in the form of higher prices. Similarly, costs of making forecasts that are too low include lost sales and lower product availability for customers.

LO12-2 Differentiate between demand planning, demand forecasting, and demand management activities.

Planning Activities

Figure 12-1 illustrates how demand forecasting and demand management activities relate to one another and to other operational planning activities. Forecasting activities integrate information gathered from the market, from internal operations, and from the larger business environment to make predictions about future demand. This information includes past demand, past forecasts and their associated errors, business and economic metrics, and the judgments of experts. In addition, the forecasting system uses demand management plans that specify the firm's pricing strategies and promotional plans. By combining all of these factors, the forecasting system creates new forecasts of future demand. The demand management system in turn uses these forecasts as inputs for future demand management planning. In addition, the forecasts and demand management plans are passed on to materials and capacity planning and scheduling systems. These systems are used to manage resources and operating processes.

FIGURE 12-1 Elements of Demand Planning

Table 12-1 describes the types of demand planning that support various levels of operational planning across the supply chain.[1] In this chapter we will explore different

TABLE 12-1 Demand Planning for Different Time Horizons

Time Horizon/Type of Planning	Demand Planning Units	Uses of Forecasts and Demand Management Plans	Types of Decisions Involved
Long term/strategic: 1–5 years Discussed in Chapters 2 and 4	Total dollar or unit sales for a business unit across the sales network	–Supply chain network design –Technology investments –Capacity planning (investments or divestments)	–Find new sources of supply –Build or sell a plant –Contract for transportation services –Open or close new service location
Intermediate term/tactical: 6–18 months Discussed in Chapter 13	Total dollar or unit sales for a product family in a region	–Sales and operational planning –Product portfolio planning	–Aggregate production plans –Employee hiring and firing –Planned overtime work –Subcontracting –New product launches
Short term/operational materials and resources: 1–12 weeks Discussed in Chapter 14	Dollar or unit sales for a given item or service at a given location	–Inventory planning –Purchasing plans –Labor scheduling	–Daily production schedule –Daily work schedule –Purchase orders

---

[1]We will discuss different levels of operational planning in more detail in Chapter 13, "Sales and Operations Planning."

methods for demand forecasting and demand management. In addition, we describe sources of uncertainty in demand planning and what can be done to reduce them.

DEMAND FORECASTING

In this section, we discuss the objectives and techniques of demand forecasting. It is important to think of forecasting as a process, rather than simply as a technique or a model. The process should be sophisticated enough to achieve acceptable levels of forecast accuracy, but simple enough so that steps involved can be understood by the users. It is also important to continually improve the forecasting process to improve its accuracy, user-friendliness, and flexibility. The process almost always involves people at some level who may lack sophisticated knowledge of statistics and forecasting techniques. Consequently, forecasters must ensure that users of forecasts understand and accept the underlying logic of the system. Then users will have the confidence and knowledge to use forecasting processes intelligently.

Components of Demand

Most forecasting techniques seek to uncover predictors of and patterns in demand and to extrapolate them to the future. Figure 12-2 shows common demand patterns. These patterns suggest that some systematic forces are influencing the data. The forecaster's objective is to uncover and describe the processes generating these time series patterns. A demand pattern is typically made up of different component drivers of demand that work together.

stable pattern A consistent horizontal stream of demands.

A **stable pattern** is a consistent horizontal stream of demands. Mature consumer products, for example shampoo or milk, often exhibit this type of pattern.

seasonality and cycles Regular demand patterns of repeating highs and lows.

Seasonality and cycles are regular patterns of repeating highs and lows. Seasonality may be daily, weekly, monthly, or even longer. For example, restaurants experience seasonal patterns during the day with peaks for breakfast, lunch, and dinner. Banks typically experience a monthly seasonal pattern with peaks coinciding with company pay periods. Economic, political, demographic, and technological factors influence these patterns.

trend The general sloping tendency of demand, either upward or downward, in a linear or nonlinear fashion.

A **trend** identifies the general sloping tendency of demand, either upward or downward, in a linear or nonlinear fashion. New products in the growth phase of the life cycle typically exhibit an upward, nonlinear trend.

shift or step change A one-time change in demand, usually due to some external influence on demand.

A **shift or step change** in demand is a one-time change, usually due to some external influence on demand such as a major product promotional campaign, or a sudden economic shock.

autocorrelation The correlation of current demand values with past demand values.

Autocorrelation describes the relationship of current demand with past demand. If values of demand at any given time are highly correlated with demand values from the recent past, then we say that the demand is highly *autocorrelated*.

forecast error The difference between a forecast and the actual demand.

Forecast error is simply the "unexplained" component of demand that seems to be random in nature. If the straight line in each panel of Figure 12-2 represents the forecast and the curved line represents the actual demand, then the differences between these lines are the forecast errors.

A good forecasting process acquires and analyzes information inputs in ways that address all of the relevant components of demand, while not overreacting to random changes in demand. If successful in this way, then the forecasting process will produce smaller errors.

FIGURE 12-2   Patterns in Demand

Stable, no trend | Seasonal, cycle | Trend, probably linear | Step change

Designing a Forecasting Process

A forecasting process attempts to understand the various components of demand so that it can convert data inputs into reliable predictions of future events. As Figure 12-3 illustrates, the forecasting process often combines statistical data with judgments from knowledgeable sources. The sources of data and judgment may include information systems and experts both inside and outside the company. For example, suppliers and product distributors often can provide excellent information regarding overall market and sales trends.

The primary goal in designing a forecasting process is to generate forecasts that are usable, timely, and accurate. The following five steps can help managers achieve this goal.

1. *Identify the users and decision-making processes that the forecast will support.* The forecasting process needs to be designed with the following users' characteristics and needs in mind:

    Time horizon. The forecasting process should suit the period of time over which the user's current actions will affect future business performance. Most important is the lead time required to implement decisions influenced by the forecast. For example, if a production system requires an eight-week lead time, then a product demand forecast should cover a period of at least eight weeks.

    Level of detail. Forecasts can be generated for an individual product, for an entire product family, or even for an entire business or industry. Similarly, forecasted demand could be for a location, a country, a region, or worldwide. Levels of detail and time horizon characteristics are usually related (as shown in Table 12-1). It is important for forecasters to understand the levels of product and geographic detail that are needed by users of the forecasts.

    Accuracy versus cost. Greater forecast accuracy often requires greater effort and greater forecast system sophistication. It is important to weigh the costs created by forecast errors against the costs of achieving greater accuracy.

    Fit with existing business processes. In order for it to be useful, the forecasting process must be integrated into other business processes. For example, as much as possible the data for forecasts should come from collection processes that already exist. Also, the logic used to generate forecasts must be easily understood by the users. People are not likely to trust forecasting approaches that they don't understand.

2. *Identify likely sources of the best data inputs.* Today's information-rich environment typically provides numerous sources of information, including all kinds of experts, corporate records (past sales, promotion programs), transactional data, data from the Internet, the government (for information on the state of the economy), suppliers, and sellers of sales and customer databases. It is important to identify the potential drivers of demand and then find the data that best represent those drivers.

FIGURE 12-3   The Forecasting Process

For example, consumer confidence and feelings of personal wealth are drivers of purchases of luxury items (such as diamonds). Governments usually report disposable income and consumer confidence data, which can be used as leading indicators of luxury purchases.

3. *Select forecasting techniques that will most effectively transform data into timely, accurate forecasts over the appropriate planning horizon.* In short-term planning for stable demand environments, forecasters can usually create suitable forecasts using only simple statistical models based on historical demand. More volatile and longer term planning situations usually require multiple inputs including judgments, historical data, and leading indicator data. In this case, forecasting approaches also need to be more flexible or adaptive. Forecasters have access to many simple-to-use software programs that automate most of the tedious calculations and data management aspects of collecting and combining inputs from various sources. Some programs enable the user to quickly evaluate many different forecasting models in order to select the best forecast according to user-input criteria.

4. *Document and apply the proposed technique to the data gathered for the appropriate business process.* The entire set of assumptions and steps included in the forecasting process should be well understood by all people involved. This enables the users to identify those conditions under which the forecasts are most and least applicable.

5. *Monitor the performance of the forecasting process for continuous improvement.* Forecasters should carefully track and study the accuracy of the forecasts and work with users to refine the forecasting process. Periodic reviews of the basic assumptions that underlie the forecasts help to keep the process on target for future forecasts.

In the following sections we briefly discuss some broad categories of forecasting techniques: judgment-based techniques that gather and use subjective inputs, statistical model-based techniques that use quantitative data, and techniques for assessing forecast error and providing feedback to the forecasting system.

Judgment-Based Forecasting

LO12-3 Describe various qualitative and quantitative demand forecasting procedures.

Judgment-based forecasts are built upon the estimates and opinions of people, most often experts who have related sales or operational experience. Judgment techniques seek to incorporate factors of demand that are difficult to capture in statistical models. This approach is useful when there is a lack of quantitative historical information; for example, when a new product is about to be launched. It is also useful when information about the past may not support good decisions for the future (underlying demand-generating processes have changed). For example, historical sales patterns could not forecast the drop in demand for trucks and SUVs when gasoline prices rose dramatically in 2008. The following judgment-based forecasting techniques are among the most common approaches.

Grassroots Forecasting

grassroots forecasting A technique that seeks inputs from people who are in close contact with customers and products.

Grassroots forecasting is a technique that seeks inputs from people who are in close contact with customers and products. A marketing study, for example, might ask sales representatives for their sales estimates and comments on current market conditions in their respective sales areas. The nearby Get Real box shows how Texas Instruments and Sport Obermeyer use grassroots forecasting. A major limitation of this technique is that "experts" may unconsciously base their forecasts on their most recent experiences, rather than their entire set of experiences. They also may adjust their forecasts because of other motivations. For example, a sales representative who is rewarded for exceeding sales goals is likely to understate future sales forecasts.

Executive Judgment

executive judgment Forecasting techniques that use input from high-level, experienced managers.

While grassroots approaches are most useful for developing short-term forecasts for individual products, high level managers using their executive judgment are usually better equipped to make judgments regarding long-term sales or business patterns. High-level business managers have experience and access to sources of information upon which to base their judgments.

GET REAL

Two Examples of Grassroots Forecasting

Companies in two vastly different industries provide innovative approaches for gathering forecasts from employees on the operations front lines.

Managers at Texas Instruments developed an artificial "stock" market to solve the problem of extracting forecasts from sales representatives. The company issues securities to sales reps that represent different levels of product sales. Then, the sales reps can trade the securities so that they "invest" in securities representing their best guess of what actual product sales will be. At the end of the sales period, the value of the securities depends on the actual product sales. For example, if you sell pocket calculators and you expect next year's sales to be 800,000 units, you would try to buy securities denominated "800,000." You would want to unload any securities you have that are denominated "700,000" or "950,000" or other values, because you don't expect them to pay off. In this artificial market, if the "800,000" security ends up trading at the highest price, then forecasting managers use that number as the firm's best estimate of next year's calculator volume.

Sport Obermeyer, a designer and producer of ski apparel, uses an innovative grassroots approach to develop forecasts of sales for the items it offers each new season. The company invites retail store managers and sales associates from around the country to come "shop" at a simulated store located at headquarters containing all the new items. Each sales associate rates the desirability of each item using a seven-point scale. The ratings are then tabulated, and the items are ranked based on the average ratings.

Managers then create sales forecasts by allocating the total sales estimate for a given category of items to the individual items in that category using a graduated scale based on past sales. For example, managers know from experience that the top 10 most highly rated items in a category will account for a certain percentage of sales, the next 10 will account for a lower percentage of sales, and so on.

By using such innovative approaches, companies like Texas Instruments and Sport Obermeyer are able to gather unbiased judgments from the employees who interact with customers directly.

© STR/AFP/Getty Images

Historical Analogy

The historical analogy approach to forecasting uses data and experience from similar products to forecast the demand for a new product. For example, when next generation electronics (TVs, computers, phones) are introduced, managers use sales patterns for previous generations along with other information to predict the life cycle stages for the new products. Economists use historical analogy extensively when forecasting business cycles and related developments.

historical analogy A forecasting technique that uses data and experience from similar products to forecast the demand for a new product.

Marketing Research

Marketing research bases forecasts on the purchasing patterns and attitudes of current or potential customers. Marketers have developed a wide range of tools for evaluating the purchasing patterns and attitudes of current or potential buyers of a product, including consumer surveys, interviews, and focus groups. A panel of knowledgeable people (often potential customers) can be convened to develop a forecast by engaging in an open dialogue over a relatively short period of time. Recently it has also become much easier to track customer buying patterns and preferences through click streams and sentiment data recorded in Internet searches and purchases.

marketing research A forecasting technique that bases forecasts on the purchasing patterns and attitudes of current or potential customers.

Delphi Method

The Delphi method develops forecasts by asking a panel of experts to individually respond to a series of questions. The forecaster compiles and analyzes the respondents' inputs and shares the data with the group. Once everyone has seen the collective responses, they are

Delphi method Forecasts developed by asking a panel of experts to individually and repeatedly respond to a series of questions.

given the chance to revise their responses or to ask new questions. This question-answer-feedback process is repeated until a consensus is achieved that reflects input from all of the experts while preventing any single individual from dominating the process.

Statistical Model–Based Forecasting

LO12-4 Develop forecasts using moving average, exponential smoothing, and linear regression models.

Statistical model–based forecasting techniques transform numerical data into forecasts using one of three methods:

1. Time series analyses, which extrapolate forecasts from past demand data.
2. Causal studies, which look for causal relationships between leading variables and forecasted variables.
3. Simulation models, which try to represent past phenomena in mathematical relationships and then evaluate data to project future outcomes.
4. Artificial intelligence, in which a "smart" computer program "learns" from a combination of causal and simulation analyses using a wide array of data.

Table 12-2 provides a comparison of the requirements needed to implement the different techniques.

Time Series Analysis Models

time series analysis models
Forecasting models that compute forecasts using historical data arranged in the order of occurrence.

Time series analysis models compute forecasts using historical data arranged in the order of occurrence. Forecasting models that are based only on a series of past demands assume that a demand pattern of the past will continue in the future. Thus, if some new event changes the underlying drivers of demand, then these models will not work well. Forecasts are generated by summing weighted values of past demands, and the weighting schemes

TABLE 12-2 Comparing Different Statistical Forecasting Methods

Forecasting Method	Amount of Historical Data	Data Pattern	Forecast Horizon	Preparation Time	Personnel Background
Time series: Moving average and exponential smoothing based methods	10 to 15 observations to set the parameters	Stable, trend, and seasonality	Short	Short	Little to moderate sophistication
Time series: Regression	10 to 20 observations; for seasonality at least 5 per season	Trend and seasonality	Short to medium	Short	Moderate sophistication
Causal modeling	10 observations per each independent variable	Complex patterns	Short, medium, or long	Long development time, short time for implementation	Considerable sophistication
Simulation models and focused forecasting	50 or more observations	Distributions of demand-creating processes must be approximated	Medium or long	Long	High sophistication
Artificial intelligence	100s or 1000s of observations	Complex patterns	Short, medium, or long	Long	High sophistication

range from very simple to very complex. The type of weighting used depends upon the demand pattern. For example, with a stable demand pattern, the simplest time series forecasting model is a **naïve model**, which simply assumes that tomorrow's demand will be the same as today's. For example, if on a given day a restaurant served 55 customers, managers might expect to serve 55 customers on the following day as well. While this simple approach is sometimes effective, it ignores the trend, seasonal, or other components of the historical time series, and it creates highly erratic forecasts if these components or random variations are present. For this reason, most time series models use multiple values of past demands. For example, a restaurant manager might want to use a weighted average of daily demand over a week as a better forecast of tomorrow's demand. The following sections discuss two simple time series models, *moving average* and *simple exponential smoothing,* that are used when demand patterns are stable.

naïve model A simple forecasting approach that assumes that recent history is a good predictor of the near future.

Moving Average Models

One way to create forecasts that reflect changes in demand while dampening or smoothing out erratic movements is to forecast future demand as a simple average of past demand values. This model is used when the demand pattern is relatively stable, without trend or seasonality. A **moving average** forecasting model computes a forecast as the average of demands over a number of immediate past periods (*n*), as shown in equation (12.1).

moving average A forecasting model that computes a forecast as the average of demands over a number of immediate past periods.

(12.1)
$$F_{t+1} = \frac{d_t + d_{t-1} + d_{t-2} + \ldots + d_{t-n}}{n}$$

where:

F_{t+1} = the forecast for the next period
d_t = the demand from the most recent period
n = the number of periods used to compute the moving average

To use the moving average forecasting model, the forecaster must decide upon the number of past periods (*n*) to use. Increasing the number of periods (*n*) reduces the impact of random or atypical demands in isolated time periods, but it also reduces the sensitivity of the moving average to actual shifts in demand. Figure 12-4 compares the forecasts that would be created over time using moving average models with different values of *n*. Note that a smaller value of *n* produces forecasts that are more sensitive to changes in demand, while larger values tend to smooth out demand changes.

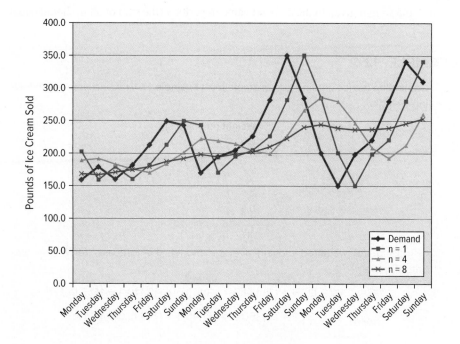

FIGURE 12-4
Comparing Moving Average Forecasting Models

EXAMPLE 12-1

Suppose the manager of an ice cream store is trying to forecast the pounds of ice cream that the store will sell based on what it has sold in the past four days. Recent actual sales numbers are:

Day	Sales (in pounds)
Sunday	137.1
Monday	123.6
Tuesday	134.9
Wednesday	160.0
Thursday	140.4

A four-day moving average forecast of Friday's demand would be computed as follows:

$$F_{\text{Friday}} = \frac{123.6 + 134.9 + 160.0 + 140.4}{4} = 139.7 \text{ lb.}$$

Suppose that the actual sales on Friday turn out to be 135.0 lb. Then, the forecast for Saturday would be:

$$F_{\text{Saturday}} = \frac{134.9 + 160.0 + 140.4 + 135.0}{4} = 142.5 \text{ lb.}$$

weighted moving average A forecasting model that assigns a different weight to each period's demand according to its importance.

An adjustment to the moving average model that is sometimes used for stable demand patterns is a **weighted moving average** model. This model assigns a different weight to each period's demand according to its importance, for example, giving more recent periods more importance than earlier periods. Typically, more weight is given to more recent demand, because this is thought to capture market effects that are more relevant to the current demand situation.

The equation for a weighted moving average model is:

(12.2) $\qquad F_{t+1} = a_t d_t + a_{t-1} d_{t-1} + a_{t-2} d_{t-2} + \ldots + a_{t-n} d_{t-n}$

where:

a_t = the weight given to the demand value in period t (the sum of all a_t should equal 1)

EXAMPLE 12-2

Continuing the ice cream store example from Example 12-1, let's assume the following weights:

Day	Weight (in pounds)
4 days ago	0.1
3 days ago	0.2
2 days ago	0.2
Yesterday	0.5
Total	1.0

Using the weighted moving average model, the forecasts for Friday and Saturday are

$$F_{\text{Friday}} = (.1)\,123.6 + (.2)\,134.9 + (.2)160.0 + (.5)\,140.4 = 141.5 \text{ lb.}$$

$$F_{\text{Saturday}} = (.1)\,134.9 + (.2)\,160.0 + (.2)140.4 + (.5)\,135.0 = 141.1 \text{ lb.}$$

Notice that Saturday's forecast is lower than Friday's forecast, yet in Example 12-1 Saturday's forecast was higher than Friday's forecast. This difference in results is because the weighted moving average puts more emphasis on recent demand, and demand has decreased in the last couple of days.

Exponential Smoothing

Another time series model used for stable demand patterns assigns weights to a moving average calculation in a systematic way; it is known as **exponential smoothing**. In this approach, an exponentially smaller weight is applied to each demand that occurred farther back in time. Each weight is a certain percentage smaller than the weight assigned to demand data for the previous period. The exponential smoothing model is shown in equation (12.3).

(12.3)
$$F_{t+1} = \alpha\, d_t + (1 - \alpha)\, F_t$$

exponential smoothing A moving average approach that applies exponentially decreasing weights to each demand that occurred farther back in time.

where α is a constant between 0 and 1, called the **smoothing coefficient**. The forecast for a given period is a linear combination of the most recent subsequent period's result, d_{t-1}, and the forecast for that period, F_{t-1}. For example, suppose that a manager uses a forecasting model with a smoothing coefficient to $\alpha = 0.1$. This model will create a new forecast by adding one-tenth of last period's demand plus nine-tenths of last period's forecast.

smoothing coefficient A parameter indicating the weight given to the most recent demand.

By rearranging the terms, equation (12.3) can be rewritten as:

(12.4)
$$F_{t+1} = F_t + \alpha\, (d_t - F_t)$$

In equation (12.4), the term $d_t - F_t$, is the *forecast error* (recall that we defined this earlier in the chapter). This new way of looking at the exponential smoothing model states that the new forecast is equal to the prior forecast, plus an adjustment to account for the forecast error from the last period. For example, if last period's forecast was too high, then the forecast error will be negative, and the new forecast will be adjusted downward. Later in this chapter, we show other ways that forecast errors can be monitored and used to improve the forecasting process.

EXAMPLE 12-3

Returning to our ice cream store example, let's say that actual sales for a given day totaled 115 pounds, while the forecast for that day was 110 pounds. With a smoothing constant of 0.10, the next day's forecast is:

$$F_{t+1} = 110 + (0.1)(115 - 110) = 110.5 \text{ lb.}$$

Note that the new forecast is slightly higher than the previous forecast, owing to the fact that our last forecast was 5 pounds too low. But the new forecast is only *slightly* higher. This is because we aren't putting much weight (only 0.1) on the most recent demand data. Using an $\alpha = 0.9$ would produce a forecast of 114.5, a value much closer to the recent actual demand. Thus, the higher the value of the smoothing coefficient, the greater the weight placed on the most recent actual demand value. Figure 12-5 shows the increasing sensitivity of forecasts when alpha is increased.

Moving forward one day, now let's say that actual sales for period $t + 1$ totaled 107 pounds. The forecast for the next day would be:

$$F_{t+2} = 110.5 + (0.1)(107 - 110.5) = 110.2 \text{ lb.}$$

(continued)

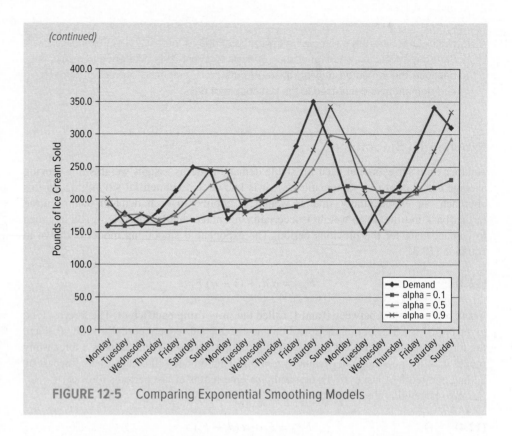

(continued)

FIGURE 12-5   Comparing Exponential Smoothing Models

By using the exponential smoothing equation again and again from one period to the next, each new forecast is implicitly built upon many past actual demands, each of which receives less and less weight as one goes back in time. This is because each past forecast (F_t in the equation) is itself a function of prior demands. In this way, the exponential smoothing approach is really just a sophisticated form of the weighted moving average model.

Figures 12-4 and 12-5 illustrate the fact that even the most sensitive simple exponential smoothing and moving average models are still only reactive; they do not *anticipate* the effects of a trend, or any seasonal or cyclical variations in demand. When such variations are present, the forecast will lag the actual demand time series. The forecaster can reduce the lag effect by increasing the value of α or reducing the n, but this also increases the risk of adding unwanted variability to forecasts as they overreact to random variations in demand. As a remedy to this problem, there are a number of enhancements that can be made to exponential smoothing models that make them more anticipative of trends and seasonal effects and more reactive to major shifts in demand patterns.

Estimating Trends

Exponential Smoothing with Trend Effects

Early users of the exponential smoothing model soon started to augment the simple model to accommodate trend and other components of demand in a more predictive way. The following equations show how to change each period's forecast to include an adjustment for a known trend:

(12.5)
$$FIT_{t+1} = F_{t+1} + T_{t+1}$$

(12.6)
$$F_{t+1} = FIT_t + \alpha(d_t - FIT_t)$$

(12.7)
$$T_{t+1} = T_t + \beta\,(F_{t+1} - FIT_t)$$

where:

FIT_t = the forecast including trend for period t

F_t = the "base" forecast for period t from the simple exponential smoothing model

T_t = the forecast of the trend component of demand for period t

α = the base smoothing coefficient

β = the trend smoothing coefficient

Equation (12.5) is simply the sum of the forecasts for the base and trend components of demand, respectively. Equations (12.6) and (12.7) are used together to compute the new smoothed forecasts for the base and trend components.

EXAMPLE 12-4

As an example of using the exponential smoothing model with trend effects, assume that the forecast for the last period is $FIT_t = 250$ units, and recent experience suggests a likely sales increase of 10 units each period. Actual sales for the last period reached 270 units. Assuming a smoothing coefficient of $\alpha = 0.20$ and a trend smoothing coefficient of $\beta = 0.10$, the forecast for the next period is given by

$$F_{t+1} = FIT_t + \alpha(d_t - FIT_t) = 250 + 0.20\,(270 - 250) = 254$$

$$T_{t+1} = T_t + \beta(F_{t+1} - FIT_t) = 10 + 0.10\,(254 - 250) = 10 + 0.4 = 10.4$$

$$FIT_{t+1} = F_{t+1} + T_{t+1} = 254 + 10.4 = 264.4$$

If the demand in period $t + 1$ turned out to be 260, then the forecast for period $t + 2$ would be

$$F_{t+2} = 264.4 + 0.20\,(260 - 264.4) = 263.52$$

$$T_{t+2} = 10.4 + 0.10\,(263.52 - 264.4) = 10.4 - 0.088 = 10.31$$

$$FIT_{t+2} = 263.52 + 10.31 = 273.8$$

Determining Trend Factors

The trend component of a time series normally results from some market force that causes a general rise or decline in values over time. In the United States, the number of people smoking cigarettes has declined each year for some time, as has the number of 1980 Ford LTD cars needing replacement front left fenders. The number of people over 65 has increased each year. Different causes have created these long-term trend effects.

A linear trend results when demand rises or falls at a constant rate, describing a straight line on a graph. Figure 12-6 shows graphs of exponential trends and the traditional sales growth trend for a new product. Of course, nothing dictates that any long-term trend must follow any of these familiar curves.

Exponential   Negative Exponential   Growth Curve

FIGURE 12-6 Common Nonlinear Trends

To estimate a trend, the forecaster should begin by graphing the data. Many times forecasters can make a good approximation of a trend by simply hand-drawing a line through the data. You will recall that the equation for a line is

(12.8)
$$d_t = a + b * t$$

where:

d_t = demand value for period t
t = number of periods from the origin
a = y-axis intercept of the line
b = slope of the line

Simple Linear Regression: Time Series

regression analysis A mathematical approach for fitting an equation to a set of data.

Regression analysis is the most commonly used method for estimating relationships between leading indicators and demand. Simple linear regression is a technique that finds "optimal" values for the parameters a and b shown in equation (12.8), that is, parameters that will most closely equate the independent variable, t, and the dependent variable, d_t, over a set of values. More specifically, simple linear regression computes values of a and b that minimize the expression

(12.9)
$$\sum_{t=1}^{t=n} (d_t - F_t)^2$$

where

d_t = actual demand value for period t
F_t = forecasted demand from the regression equation for period t

Recall that $d_t - F_t$ is the forecast error. Linear regression seeks to minimize the sum of the squared errors between the actual values of demand and the values of demand predicted by the straight line. For this reason, it is also known as least-squares regression. The linear regression formulas for values of a and b are:

(12.10)
$$b = \frac{\sum_{t=1}^{t=n} td_t - n\bar{t} * \bar{d}_t}{\sum_{t=1}^{t=n} t^2 - n\bar{t}^2}$$

(12.11)
$$a = \bar{d}_t - b\bar{t}$$

where

$\bar{t}$ = of all t values
$\bar{d}_t$ = of all d_t values
n = number of data points

Equations (12.10) and (12.11) use past demand values to compute the parameters a and b for the regression model. Most spreadsheet programs have functions that will automatically calculate regression parameters given a set of values for t and d_t.

EXAMPLE 12-5

Table 12-3 illustrates the calculations needed to specify a linear regression model using example data.

Using the linear regression formulae, the slope and the intercept are:

$$b = [17,785.1 - (16)(8.5)(127)] / [1,496 - (16)(8.5)^2] = 1.5 \text{ per period}$$

$$a = (127) - (1.5)(8.5) = 114.2$$

TABLE 12-3   Example Linear Regression Calculation

Period	Actual Demand		
t	d_t	$t * d_t$	t^2
1	117.8	117.8	1
2	117.1	234.2	4
3	123.7	371.1	9
4	117.1	468.4	16
5	118.3	591.5	25
6	129.2	775.2	36
7	121	847	49
8	127.9	1023.2	64
9	123	1107	81
10	129.8	1298	100
11	125.9	1384.9	121
12	129	1548	144
13	136.6	1775.8	169
14	130.8	1831.2	196
15	141.8	2127	225
16	142.8	2284.8	256
Total		**17785.1**	**1496**
Average	**8.5**	**127.0**	

The trend for the data given in our example is 1.5 units per period. The forecaster could use this trend value as the starting trend value in an exponential smoothing forecasting model. Alternatively, the forecaster might choose to use the regression model itself to make forecasts. Combining our parameter estimates, we get the following as the linear formula for the forecasted demand in each period:

$$F_t = a + bt = 114.2 + 1.5 * t$$

The forecasts for the next few periods are then

$$F_{17} = 114.2 + 1.5 * 17 = 139.8$$

$$F_{18} = 114.2 + 1.5 * 18 = 141.8$$

$$F_{19} = 114.2 + 1.5 * 19 = 142.8$$

Adjusting Forecasts for Seasonality

Seasonal variations in demand can be estimated by applying a seasonal index to adjust forecast values for each seasonal time period. Remember, a "season" can occur daily, weekly, monthly, or in larger periods. The seasonal index is computed by dividing each period's actual demand by an estimate of the average (or base) demand across all periods in a complete seasonal cycle; that is, the average demand that would be expected if no seasonality existed. For example, if there are four periods in a complete seasonal cycle, then one would compute the average demand across the four periods in the cycle. Alternatively, the average demand can be estimated using a time series regression model, because it creates estimates of average demand all across the time horizon. Using the regression

seasonal index An adjustment factor applied to forecasts to account for seasonal changes or cycles in demand.

approach to estimate average demand is better if there is a trend in the demand. In either case, it is usually wise to compute and compare seasonal indexes over several seasonal cycles to ensure that the indexes are stable.

EXAMPLE 12-6

Table 12-4 illustrates the procedure using data from the ice cream sales example. The actual daily sales for three weeks are divided by the forecasts from a simple regression model to obtain a seasonal index for each day. The regression model provides *deseasonalized* estimates of average demand; that is, estimates of demand that account for trend but remove seasonal influences. A daily seasonal index is estimated by averaging the values over all three weeks. For example, the seasonal index for Monday is the average across all three Mondays included in the data = (0.93 + 0.90 + 0.84)/3 = 0.89. As one might expect for ice cream sales, the indexes indicate that sales are above average (index > 1) on the weekends and below average (index < 1) on other days in the week.

Suppose that, instead of using the regression estimates as the base for calculating the seasonal indexes, we used the average demand in each week as the base. Using this approach, the seasonal indexes for week 1 would be:

Average demand for week 1 = (123.6 + 135.0 + 160.0 + 140.4 + 187.9 + 195.0 + 171.8)/7 = 159.10

Seasonal indexes using demands for week 1:

Monday SI = 123.6 / 159.1 = 0.78

Tuesday SI = 135.0 / 159.1 = 0.85

Wednesday SI = 160.0 / 159.1 = 1.01

Thursday SI = 140.4 / 159.1 = 0.88

Friday SI = 187.9 / 159.1 = 1.18

Saturday SI = 195.0 / 159.1 = 1.23

Sunday SI = 171.8 / 159.1 = 1.08

Performing the same calculations for weeks 2 and 3, we can fill out Table 12-5 .

TABLE 12-4   Calculating Seasonal Indexes Using Regression Estimates as the Base

		Actual Demand (a)	Average Demand Estimate (from regression) (b)	Seasonal Index SI = a/b	Three Week Average Indexes
Week 1	Monday	123.6	132.9	0.93	Average SI for Mondays = 0.89
	Tuesday	135.0	137.0	0.98	Average SI for Tuesdays = 0.90
	Wednesday	160.0	141.1	1.13	Average SI for Wednesdays = 0.93
	Thursday	140.4	145.2	0.97	Average SI for Thursdays = 0.90
	Friday	187.9	149.3	1.26	Average SI for Fridays = 1.16
	Saturday	195.0	153.4	1.27	Average SI for Saturdays = 1.17
	Sunday	171.8	157.5	1.09	Average SI for Sundays = 1.10
	Monday	145.9	161.5	0.90	
	Tuesday	130.0	165.6	0.78	
	Wednesday	145.0	169.7	0.85	

		Actual Demand (a)	Average Demand Estimate (from regression) (b)	Seasonal Index SI = a/b	Three Week Average Indexes
Week 2	Thursday	147.2	173.8	0.85	
	Friday	214.2	177.9	1.20	
	Saturday	190.0	182.0	1.04	
	Sunday	202.1	186.1	1.09	
	Monday	159.0	190.1	0.84	
	Tuesday	178.7	194.2	0.92	
	Wednesday	160.0	198.3	0.81	
Week 3	Thursday	181.5	202.4	0.90	
	Friday	212.8	206.5	1.03	
	Saturday	249.4	210.6	1.18	
	Sunday	242.9	214.7	1.13	

TABLE 12-5   Calculating Seasonal Indexes Using Average Demand per Cycle as the Base

		Actual Demand (a)	Average Demand for Week (b)	Seasonal Index SI = a/b	Three Week Average Indexes
	Monday	123.6		0.78	Average SI for Mondays = 0.82
Week 1	Tuesday	135.0		0.85	Average SI for Tuesdays = 0.84
	Wednesday	160.0		1.01	Average SI for Wednesdays = 0.89
Week 1	Thursday	140.4	159.1	0.88	Average SI for Thursdays = 0.89
	Friday	187.9		1.18	Average SI for Fridays = 1.18
	Saturday	195.0		1.23	Average SI for Saturdays = 1.21
	Sunday	171.8		1.08	Average SI for Sundays = 1.17
	Monday	145.9		0.87	
	Tuesday	130.0		0.77	
	Wednesday	145.0		0.86	
Week 2	Thursday	147.2	167.8	0.88	
	Friday	214.2		1.28	
	Saturday	190.0		1.13	
	Sunday	202.1		1.20	

(continued)

(continued)

		Actual Demand (a)	Average Demand for Week (b)	Seasonal Index SI = a/b	Three Week Average Indexes
	Monday	159.0		0.80	
	Tuesday	178.7		0.90	
	Wednesday	160.0		0.81	
Week 3	Thursday	181.5	197.8	0.92	
	Friday	212.8		1.08	
	Saturday	249.4		1.26	
	Sunday	242.9		1.23	

Note that the seasonal indexes in Tables 12-4 and 12-5 are not exactly the same, but they are fairly close. Using the average demand in each cycle as the base for calculating the seasonal index can be thought of as a looser approximation method than the regression approach. In practice, however, either approach can be effective.

The next step is to use the average seasonal indexes to adjust the future forecasts. For example, regression-based forecasts (the average demands) for the next two weeks (weeks 4 and 5) would be adjusted as shown in Table 12-6. Note that we could use a method other than regression for generating the base demand; it is up to the forecaster to decide what method best approximates trends or other demand patterns that exist before seasonal impacts.

TABLE 12-6 Seasonal Adjustments for Forecasts

		Forecasted Base Demand (from regression) (a)	Seasonal Index (b)	Adjusted Forecast a × b
	Monday	218.7	0.89	194.6
	Tuesday	222.8	0.90	200.5
	Wednesday	226.9	0.93	211.0
Week 4	Thursday	231.0	0.90	207.9
	Friday	235.1	1.16	272.7
	Saturday	239.2	1.17	279.9
	Sunday	243.3	1.10	267.6
	Monday	247.4	0.89	220.2
	Tuesday	251.4	0.90	226.3
	Wednesday	255.5	0.93	237.6
Week 5	Thursday	259.6	0.90	233.6
	Friday	263.7	1.16	305.9
	Saturday	267.8	1.17	313.3
	Sunday	271.9	1.10	299.1

Figure 12-7 shows the forecasts for weeks 3, 4, and 5 of the time series. Compare this to the forecasts shown in Figure 12-5. The seasonally adjusted forecasts clearly do a better job of matching seasonal shifts in the demand pattern. Note that the forecasts presented in Figure 12-5 lag the shifts by at least one period.

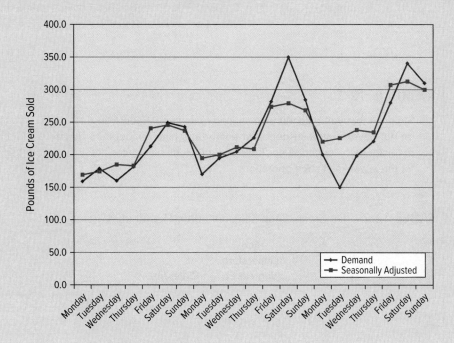

FIGURE 12-7
Seasonally Adjusted
Forecasts

Causal Models

Where time series models use only past demand values as indicators of future demand, causal models use other independent, observed data to predict demand. These models concentrate on external factors that are thought to *cause* demand. For example, the amount of household disposable income in an economy might be a good leading indicator of the sales of luxury items, such as sailboats.

As mentioned earlier, regression analysis is the most commonly used method for estimating relationships between leading indicators and demand. In fact, the technique can be extended to include multiple indicators in a multiple regression analysis. In this approach, a forecaster would gather past data describing demand and multiple independent indicators considered important as predictors of demand. The regression analysis computes the coefficients (indicator weights), forming an equation that best describes the past relationships between the predictors and the actual demand data. The resulting equation is then used to forecast future values of demand, based on observed values of the leading indicators. For example, we might see the following multiple regression equation used to forecast sailboats sales:

$$\text{Sales forecast} = B + b_d(D) + b_a(A) + b_f(F) + b_s(S)$$

where:

B = Base sales (computed y-intercept)
D = Disposable personal income
A = Advertising expenditures
F = Fuel prices
S = Sales from prior year

Each of the indicator weights (values of b) is computed by a regression method. Each value of b represents the incremental contribution of the corresponding leading indicator to the sales forecast.

Simple Linear Regression: Causal Modeling

Let's look at an example of causal modeling with one leading indicator using simple linear regresssion.

EXAMPLE 12-7

Suppose that you manage a small ice cream shop. People tend to buy ice cream on hot days, so you suspect that each day's high temperature might be a good predictor of ice cream sales. Table 12-7 provides daily sales and temperature data for three weeks of shop operations.

TABLE 12-7   Ice Cream Shop Sales and Daily High Temperatures

		High Temperature (degrees F)	Sales (lb.)		
		t	d_t	$t * d_t$	t^2
Week 1	Monday	70	123.6	8652.0	4900.0
	Tuesday	78	135.0	10530.5	6084.0
	Wednesday	75	160.0	12000.0	5625.0
	Thursday	60	140.4	8424.0	3600.0
	Friday	66	187.9	12401.4	4356.0
	Saturday	75	195.0	14625.0	5625.0
	Sunday	82	171.8	14087.6	6724.0
Week 2	Monday	75	145.9	10942.5	5625.0
	Tuesday	60	130.0	7800.0	3600.0
	Wednesday	63	145.0	9135.0	3969.0
	Thursday	64	147.2	9420.8	4096.0
	Friday	75	214.2	16065.0	5625.0
	Saturday	81	190.0	15390.0	6561.0
	Sunday	83	202.1	16774.3	6889.0
Week 3	Monday	78	159.0	12402.0	6084.0
	Tuesday	85	178.7	15189.5	7225.0
	Wednesday	85	160.0	13600.0	7225.0
	Thursday	82	181.5	14883.0	6724.0
	Friday	85	212.8	18088.0	7225.0
	Saturday	87	249.4	21697.8	7569.0
	Sunday	87	242.9	21132.3	7569.0
	Total			**283240.2**	**122900.0**
	Average	**76.0**	**174.9**		

Using the linear regression formulae with temperature as the leading indicator variable, the slope and the intercept are:

$$b = [283240.2 - (21)(76.0)(174.9)]/[122900 - (21)(76.0)^2] = 2.6 \text{ per degree F}$$

$$a = (174.9) - (2.6)(76.0) = -21.1$$

The trend results indicate that the ice cream shop should expect to sell an additional pound of ice cream each time the high temperature for a day rises by 2.6 degrees F. Suppose that the forecast is for a warming trend over the next three days with high temperatures of 82, 84, and 87 degrees, respectively. Using the causal regression model, the forecasted sales for the shop would be given as follows:

$$F_t = a + bt = -21.1 + 2.6*82 = 190.5 \text{ pounds}$$

$$F_t + 1 = a + bt = -21.1 + 2.6*84 = 195.6 \text{ pounds}$$

$$F_t + 2 = a + bt = -21.1 + 2.6*87 = 203.4 \text{ pounds}$$

Simulation Models

Simulation models are sophisticated mathematical programs that offer forecasters the ability to evaluate different business scenarios that might yield different demand outcomes. This evaluation helps forecasters to better understand how different variables and drivers of demand relate to one another.

A relatively simple simulation-based approach is known as **focused forecasting**. Focused forecasting combines common sense inputs from frontline personnel (such as sales managers) with a computer simulation process. The focused forecasting process asks managers to suggest rules of thumb that should be followed when developing forecasts. For example, one rule might be, "We will probably sell 10 percent more product this month than we did in the same month last year." These types of rules are embedded in a simulation model, and their usefulness is then tested by estimating how effective they collectively would have been in predicting demand data from the past. The forecaster then makes new forecasts using the combination of rules that would have provided the best forecasts for the past demands. Managers from different functional areas adjust the forecasts as they see fit. This approach has delivered better results than those provided by exponential smoothing or other time series–based models. However, the focused forecasting approach requires more preparation and user involvement.

simulation models Sophisticated mathematical programs that offer forecasters the ability to evaluate different business scenarios that might yield different demand outcomes.

focused forecasting A combination of common sense inputs from frontline personnel and a computer simulation process.

Artificial Intelligence

Artificial intelligence is a broad term that describes learning and decision making capability exhibited by machines or software. In the world of forecasting, artificial intelligence can be considered a next generation approach that combines time series analysis, causal modeling, simulation, and focused forecasting techniques. However, instead of requiring manager inputs (as focused forecasting does), learning algorithms that are embedded in forecasting software are able to develop rules and heuristics on their own. Artificial intelligence systems are linked to sources of data (e.g., the Internet, company sales, planning and transaction systems, and external data feeds) that they constantly scour for relevant information.

artificial intelligence Refers to learning and decision making capability that stems from software algorithms.

student activity

Interview one or two small business managers. Ask them to describe their demand forecasting processes.

By constantly analyzing correlations between massive amounts of diverse data and demand values, the software "learns" how to weight and adapt various inputs that represent drivers of demand. Artificial intelligence systems combine massive search capability, computational power, and learning algorithms to produce more accurate demand forecasts. The nearby Get Real box describes how Lennox Industries recently implemented such a system.

GET REAL

Lennox Uses Artificial Intelligence to Improve Its Demand Planning

Lennox Industries is a global producer and service provider for heating and air conditioning equipment. The company maintains over 250,000 SKU-locations throughout its growing global network. Lennox recently launched an initiative to improve its inventory and service levels while more than doubling the number of locations in its distribution and service network.

As an important component of the initiative, Lennox purchased the SO99+ forecasting system from ToolsGroup, a demand planning vendor. By integrating the SO99+ system with its enterprise resource planning (ERP) and other information systems, Lennox enabled the artificially intelligent system to automatically adjust demand predictions minute by minute as point of sale (POS) data are automatically loaded. Further, the platform can monitor social media and incorporate positive and negative product or brand mentions in order to augment demand forecasting. The system continuously updates its demand prediction algorithms by making corrections based on updates of data describing demand drivers and actual sales.

The company attributes the following improvements to its forecasting system implementation:

- Reduced inventory by 20 percent, despite a 250 percent increase in physical locations.
- Improved same-day delivery to 40 percent and increased orders that can be delivered the next morning from 35 percent to 98 percent.

- Reduced distribution costs as a percentage of sales by more than 15 percent.
- Improved service levels by 20 percent, with a 15 percent increase in fill rate.

Companies like Lennox are particularly good candidates for sophisticated forecasting systems. Lennox's customers demand high levels of service, and the company makes a wide range of products and replacement parts that have highly seasonal and unpredictable demands.

© lisafx/iStock/Getty Images

ASSESSING THE PERFORMANCE OF THE FORECASTING PROCESS

LO12-5 Evaluate and select forecasting models using various measures of accuracy and bias.

forecast accuracy The measurement of how closely the forecast aligns with the observations over time.

forecast bias The tendency of a forecasting technique to continually overpredict or underpredict demand. Also called *mean forecast error.*

The primary measure of forecasting performance is forecast error. As we noted earlier, forecast error is defined as the actual demand value minus the forecasted demand value for a given time period. Thus, a positive forecast error indicates an overly pessimistic forecast; a negative value indicates an overly optimistic forecast. Forecast errors can be examined to determine two primary aspects of forecast performance over time: *forecast accuracy* and *forecast bias*. Forecast accuracy measures how closely the forecast aligns with the observations over time. Every error, whether the forecast was too high or too low, reduces accuracy. Forecast bias, on the other hand, is simply the average error. Forecast bias indicates the tendency of a forecasting technique to continually overpredict or underpredict demand.

Forecast bias is the average forecast error over a number of periods:

$$(12.12) \qquad \text{Bias} = \text{Mean forecast error (MFE)} = \frac{\sum_{t=1}^{n}(d_t - F_t)}{n}$$

A positive forecast bias indicates that over time forecasts tend to be too low; a negative bias indicates that forecasts tend to be too high.

Forecast bias makes intuitive sense, and it is simple to calculate. However, it does not always allow easy comparisons across products when the average demands are different. Suppose that your company sells two different products, gadgets and widgets, at the rate of about 1,000 per month and 10 per month, respectively. Now suppose that the bias for each of the products over the past few months using both metrics is equal to 5. This means that, on average, the forecasts for each of these two products were below demand by about five units each month. Does this mean that both forecasting models are performing equally well? Certainly not! A bias of 5 units on 1,000 units of sales is outstanding performance, whereas a bias of 5 units on 10 units of sales is relatively poor performance.

For comparability's sake, forecasters often compute average error (bias) on a percentage basis. This metric is known as **mean percent error (MPE)** and is calculated as:

> **mean percent error (MPE)** Average error represented as a percentage of demand.

$$(12.13) \qquad \text{Mean percent error (MPE)} = \frac{\sum_{t=1}^{n}\frac{d_t - F_t}{d_t} * 100}{n}$$

Remember that both average forecast error and mean percent error are good indicators of bias, but they do not necessarily provide good indications of forecast *accuracy*. A measure of forecast accuracy seeks to indicate the overall errors, regardless of the direction of the errors. Forecasts that are too low or too high are both undesirable. The simplest measure of forecast accuracy is known as **mean absolute deviation (MAD)** (or the *mean absolute error*). This measure provides the average size of forecast errors, irrespective of their directions. It is computed as:

> **mean absolute deviation (MAD)** The average size of forecast errors, irrespective of their directions. Also called *mean absolute error.*

$$(12.14) \qquad \text{Mean absolute deviation (MAD)} = \frac{\sum_{t=1}^{n}|d_t - F_t|}{n}$$

EXAMPLE 12-8

Table 12-8 shows the calculation of bias or mean forecast error (MFE) and MAD for two different forecasting models. While the bias for model 2 is slightly higher than that of model 1, model 2 is preferred to model 1 because its MAD is far smaller (9.3 as compared to 50). A forecasting manager can use this approach to test many different model parameters and then select the model that yields the lowest errors.

TABLE 12-8 Computing Bias (MFE) and MAD

Period	Actual Demand	Forecast Model 1	Forecast Error	Absolute Error	Forecast Model 2	Forecast Error	Absolute Error
1	100	150	−50	50	104	−4	4
2	100	50	50	50	93	7	7
3	100	150	−50	50	88	12	12
4	100	50	50	50	102	−2	2

(continued)

	Period	Actual Demand	Forecast Model 1	Forecast Error	Absolute Error	Forecast Model 2	Forecast Error	Absolute Error
	5	100	150	−50	50	90	10	10
	6	100	50	50	50	107	−7	7
	7	100	150	−50	50	89	11	11
	8	100	50	50	50	83	17	17
	9	100	150	−50	50	110	−10	10
	10	100	50	50	50	113	−13	13
			Average	0	50		2.1	9.3
				MFE	MAD		MFE	MAD

(continued)

We should note that for normally distributed forecast errors, 1 MAD equals 0.80 standard deviations (or 1.25 MAD equals 1 standard deviation). We will return to this point later.

For purposes of comparability across products, forecasters sometimes adjust the MAD to create a related metric, the **mean absolute percentage error (MAPE)**. The MAPE indicates how large errors are relative to the actual demand quantities. Computationally, the MAPE is determined as follows:

(12.15) $$\text{Mean absolute percentage error (MAPE)} = \frac{\sum_{t=1}^{n} * \, 100 \frac{|d_t - F_t|}{d_t}}{n}$$

mean absolute percentage error (MAPE) The MAD represented as a percentage of demand.

Though intuitively appealing, measures like MAD and MAPE are sometimes inadequate as measures of forecast accuracy in that they do not recognize that forecasts that are really far off the mark may be more harmful to the user than forecasts that miss the actual demand by a small amount. To deal with this issue of sensitivity to the magnitude of the errors, researchers developed the **mean squared error (MSE)**.

mean squared error (MSE) A more sensitive measure of forecast errors that approximates the error variance.

(12.16) $$\text{Mean squared error (MSE)} = \frac{\sum_{t=1}^{n} (d_t - F_t)^2}{n - 1}$$

Because of the squared term, the MSE gives exponentially more weight to larger and larger errors. The MSE equation looks like the formula for the variance of the forecast errors. However, there are some important differences. The variance of errors would use the actual forecast errors and the mean of the forecast errors.

(12.17) $$\text{Forecast error variance} = \frac{\sum_{t=1}^{n} (e_t - \bar{e})^2}{n - 1}$$

where
  et = the forecast error for period t
  $\bar{e}$ = the mean forecast error

At the same time, the MSE usually does give a decent *approximation* of the variance of forecast errors. Thus, the square root of MSE provides a good approximation of the standard deviation. For this reason, forecasters often track the **root mean squared error (RMSE)**, or

root mean squared error (RMSE)
Gives an approximation of the forecast error standard deviation.

(12.18) $$\text{Root mean squared error (RMSE)} = \sqrt{\text{MSE}}$$

EXAMPLE 12-9

To compare the measures of forecast accuracy, let's apply them to the data presented in Table 12-9. Here, we calculate the MAD to be 6.7 and the RMSE to be 8.3. As was mentioned earlier, the MAD value is typically 80 percent of the value of the standard deviation of error. Dividing the MAD by 0.80 yields 8.4. Thus, both the adjusted MAD and RMSE provide good rough approximations to the actual standard deviation of forecast errors, which in this case is 8.2.

TABLE 12-9 Assessing Forecast Accuracy: A Comparison of MAD, RMSE, and Standard Deviation

Period	Actual	Forecast	Forecast Error (Actual− Forecast)	Absolute Error |Actual− Forecast|	Error Squared
1	345	340	5	5	25
2	328	341	−13	13	156
3	335	339	−4	4	18
4	330	339	−9	9	78
5	334	338	−4	4	16
6	340	338	2	2	6
7	338	338	0	0	0
8	328	338	−10	10	96
9	345	337	8	8	67
10	350	338	12	12	153
			8.2	6.7	8.3
			STD DEV	MAD	RMSE

Tracking Forecast Error Acceptability

Forecasters generally use forecasting metrics such as MAD and MSE to quickly and continuously evaluate forecasting models, sometimes for thousands of different products at a time. In this environment, metrics are often used to identify exceptional cases that require adjustments to model parameters. Managers need a simple test for determining when the forecast error is unacceptable. One way to test the forecast error is to develop a control chart in which forecast errors are plotted and compared to expected upper and lower control limits.[2] Such a control chart is illustrated in Figure 12-8. Several statistical tests can be done to determine with some level of confidence whether or not forecast errors are exhibiting new and unacceptable patterns.

---

[2]The logic and steps for building such a control chart are presented in the Chapter 3 Supplement.

FIGURE 12-8   Tracking
Signal Control Chart

tracking signal The ratio of a
running total of forecast error to
MAD that indicates when the pattern of forecast error is changing
significantly.

In lieu of these rather sophisticated tests, managers often opt for a simpler metric
known as the **tracking signal**. The tracking signal records the ratio of a running total
of forecast error to MAD. Mathematically, this signal is expressed as

(12.19)
$$\text{Tracking signal} = \frac{\sum_{t=1}^{n}(d_t - F_t)}{MAD_{t=1 \to n}}$$

The tracking signal is essentially a comparison of forecast bias (sum of errors, rather
than MFE) to forecast accuracy (MAD) over *n* periods. By tracking this metric over
successive periods of time, managers can observe whether undesirable trends or highly
biased errors are occurring. For example, managers might program a computer to compute
the tracking signal each month using the most recent six months of data. If the tracking
signal exceeds some control limit value, say +/−3, then the computer would send an alert
to the forecaster. Tracking signal control limits are typically set somewhere between +/−3
and +/−8. A smaller limit gives a more sensitive indicator and would probably be used for
high volume or high revenue items.

adaptive forecasting A technique
that automatically adjusts forecast
model parameters in accordance
with changes in the tracking signal.

Once a tracking signal control limit is exceeded, forecasters take action by changing
the forecasting approach or model parameters. In **adaptive forecasting**, the smoothing
coefficients in exponential smoothing models are automatically adjusted as a function of
the tracking signal (a larger tracking signal creates a larger smoothing coefficient). Such
automatic correction for unpredictable data can simplify the life of the manager, but when
a particular demand forecast routinely misstates actual results, it warrants some sort of
management intervention. For example, when the tracking signal frequently exceeds
control limits, this suggests that something in the underlying process that drives demand
has fundamentally changed and needs to be investigated. This investigation should include
some assessment of the real effects of poor forecasts on organization operations. For example, consistently low forecasts may suggest that the popularity of the product has grown.
Managers may also decide to raise the safety stock level to keep more inventory as a buffer
against the continuing uncertainty.

Past patterns of forecast errors can give managers hints about the processes that
generate both demand and errors. Such knowledge can help managers focus resources
to develop sales plans and eliminate the causes of undesirable errors. Hence, forecasters
should review the model and the parameters of a forecasting tool that fails to capture actual
demand accurately.

Situational Drivers of Forecast Accuracy

global

All forecasters want to develop accurate forecasts. However, some demand forecasting
situations create greater challenges than others. The following "rules" give an indication of
how situational characteristics tend to affect forecast accuracy:

Rule 1: Short-term forecasts are usually more accurate than long-term forecasts. It is
almost always easier to predict what will happen tomorrow than it is to predict what
will happen next week or next year (think about predicting the weather, for example).
As the time horizon for forecasting increases, more and more potentially unknown
factors can affect demand.

Rule 2: Forecasts of aggregated demand are usually more accurate than forecasts of demand at detailed levels. Aggregate forecasts benefit from a cancellation of errors that exist in item-level forecasts. For example, suppose you are tasked with forecasting demand for products A1 and A2. If your forecasts are unbiased, each forecast has a 50 percent chance of being either too high or too low. However, the chance that forecasts for both products are simultaneously too high (or simultaneously too low) is less than 50 percent (it is only 25 percent if the product demands are independent). Considering a larger number of products, there is a good chance that forecasts for some products will be too high and forecasts for other products will be too low. Thus, when the individual product forecasts are combined, the aggregate forecast is overall more accurate, because some of the negative errors are cancelled out by some of the positive errors. This same logic applies when you attempt to forecast aggregate demand directly (as opposed to summing up individual forecasts). The random forces that affect demand for individual products tend to be inconsistent across all products. The effects cancel one another. Thus, aggregate demand is more stable and predictable. This aggregation benefit also applies to geographic aggregation. For a single product, an overall global demand forecast is typically more accurate than forecasts of demand in any specific geographic region.

Rule 3: Forecasts developed using multiple information sources are usually more accurate than forecasts developed from a single source. Many different market forces may drive demand for a given good or service. It is difficult for any single source of information (historical demand data, executive judgments, sales force estimates, and so on) to comprehend all of these forces. In addition, any single source is potentially biased. Consequently, a forecast created by combining information from multiple different sources is likely to reflect a more complete and unbiased picture of actual demand patterns. It is unlikely that all sources will be "wrong" in the same direction.

DEMAND MANAGEMENT

Forecasting is essentially a reactive approach that considers fluctuations in demand to be mostly outside the firm's control. Rather than simply forecasting and reacting to changes in demand, however, business executives would prefer to influence the timing, pattern, and certainty of demand to whatever extent they can. They do this through demand management activities that adjust product characteristics including price, promotion, and availability. The purpose is to influence product demand to achieve sales objectives and to accommodate the supply chain resources and capacities that the firm has in place.

Demand management is especially important when customers' demands fluctuate in an unpredictable way. These fluctuations cause operational inefficiencies all across the supply chain, including:

1. Requiring extra resources to expand and contract capacity to meet varying demand.
2. Backlogging (delivering later than originally promised) certain orders to smooth out demand fluctuations.
3. Customer dissatisfaction with the system's inability to meet all demands.
4. Buffering the system through the use of safety stocks (excess inventories), safety lead time (lead times with a cushion), or safety capacity (excess resources).

To be effective, demand management requires coordination of many sources of demand information. Different people working throughout the organization and the supply chain may individually see only parts of the overall demand picture. Demand management planning often crosses organizational boundaries in the supply chain. It requires sales, marketing, supply management, and operations personnel, as well as suppliers and intermediate customers, to work together in planning strategies for developing and fulfilling orders. Sales and marketing personnel need to be aware of the costs and constraints of operations in order to make good pricing and product availability decisions. Furthermore,

relationships

operations managers must understand customer requirements regarding acceptable lead times, as well as priorities associated with different customer orders.[3]

Managers try to manage demand by using variants of three basic tactics:

1. *Influence the timing or quantity of demand through pricing changes, promotions, or sales incentives.* These moves are usually intended to increase demand during the low periods and to reduce or postpone demand during the peak periods. For example, automobile manufacturers sometimes offer promotional packages including zero percent financing or rebates to stimulate purchases. Many service operations such as hotels, airlines, and theaters use these approaches because their services cannot be inventoried.

2. *Manage the timing of order fulfillment.* In some situations, it is possible to negotiate with customers regarding when they will take delivery of their products. Information systems can be used to inform customers of the availability of certain products, including the expected delivery date. Different customers might be quoted different delivery dates depending on their importance to the business. In some services, customers are encouraged to choose when they will order, based on expected lead times. For example, amusement parks such as Disney World use this tactic when they place signs at points in a waiting line telling you how long you can expect to wait from that point.

3. *Substitute by encouraging customers to shift their orders from one product to another, or from one provider to another.* Suppose you are ordering a new computer, but the model with the features you desire is not readily available. You might be willing to take a near substitute, or perhaps an upgraded model, if you can get it immediately or at a lower price. Dell, a computer manufacturer, is famous for "selling what it has." Dell's information systems enable sales representatives to know exactly which products are immediately available, and marketing managers price products dynamically to move those items that are in stock.

Characteristics of the product, customers' lead-time expectations, and the operations environment all influence how the above tactics are employed in a demand management process. However, in every case the ultimate goal of demand management is to match demand and operational capacity in order to attain the business's competitive objectives.

IMPROVING THE CONSTRAINTS ON DEMAND PLANNING

LO12-6 Explain how certain improvements to both product design and operations across the supply chain can make demand planning easier.

Many business firms today are redesigning operations across their supply chains to facilitate more effective demand planning and order fulfillment. Improvement initiatives are aimed at changing information sharing systems, manufacturing and service processes, supply chain relationships, and even the product design itself, so that companies can reduce both the magnitude and the impact of forecast errors on their operations.

Improving Information Breadth, Accuracy, and Timeliness

The fashion-driven clothing industry vividly demonstrates the important role of information in demand planning. Predicting the sales of a new line of merchandise is difficult. Once the firm launches a product line, it needs quick information about the market's response to the new goods. Information systems that rapidly collect and distribute accurate sales information are important in the fashion industry and in many other industries as well. Quick sales data collection is important because current data are more relevant for forecasting future sales. Initial forecasts made at product launch can be hugely improved by incorporating

---

[3]Chapter 13, "Sales and Operations Planning," discusses in detail the coordination of demand management with operational constraints.

early sales data. In addition, rapid access to customer sales information, coupled with an operations system capable of rapid response, decreases a firm's reliance on forecasting, because the firm doesn't have to forecast as far into the future. The Get Real box describing Destination Maternity Corporation provides a good example of the impact of information accuracy and timeliness.

The Role of "Big Data" in Improving Information

The growth of available data in today's world is astounding. More information is created on the Internet each year than the total that existed five years previously. Similarly, data housed in corporate and social databases is growing exponentially. Each one of us creates more than 2–5 MB of data that is captured by our devices each day. And, consider this: There are more than three times as many interconnected devices as there are people on the planet!

These trends have given rise to the term big data, which refers to the voluminous amounts of information that are easily accessible through interconnected systems today. These data include highly structured forms (such as transaction data, location data, and descriptive data) as well as unstructured forms (such as e-mail and blog texts, social media, and Internet click streams). Devices are also creating and capturing massive amounts of sensor data (such as temperature, GPS, data from wearable technology, and RFID and bar-code data) and other types of data (for example, videos, digital images, and voice data).

> **big data** Large amounts of data made available through sensors and interconnected systems.

GET REAL

Destination Maternity Corporation

Destination Maternity Corporation (originally known as Mothers Work, Inc.) is a leading designer, manufacturer, and marketer of maternity fashion in the United States, with over 900 locations nationwide.

Since the time of its initial public offering in March 1993, Destination has increased its store base by over 1,300 percent and grown financially to more than 10 times its original size. A critical success factor has been the company's ability to gather extensive point-of-sale information at each store. Managers have developed an information system with the following capabilities:

- Capture all customer information and create a buying history.
- Run individual mailing lists by due date.
- Receive alerts about any operational errors that may have occurred the previous day.
- Review all orders on the way to their stores.
- Make customer-unique price tickets.
- Send and receive digital photos.
- Provide sales trend information.

The system also provides such features as custom profiles for each store, daily inventory replenishment, and daily updated selling information for each style. Complementing the information system are the company's fast-turn, in-house design and quick-response, material sourcing and replenishment processes:

- Real-time tracking of sales.
- Two-day replenishment of items from warehouses.
- Two- to three-week design cycle.
- Two-week manufacturing cycle.
- One- to four-month cycle for overseas sourcing.

These process times are far shorter than the typical cycles for average fashion merchandisers. By coupling current and accurate information with a very responsive supply chain, Destination has been able to avoid lost sales while maximizing in-store inventory turns and sales per square foot. Destination provides an excellent example of how improving the constraints that otherwise limit the effectiveness of the demand planning system can yield big operational and financial benefits.

© David Brabyn/Corbis

Source: Information taken from http://Motherswork.com/.

The availability of all these types of data provides a huge opportunity for making improvements in demand planning, as well as other planning and decision making in supply chain operations management. Imagine, for example, the improved demand forecasts that a consumer goods company could achieve if its planners had real-time access to consumer purchases, eating habits, entertainment choices, and the like. Such data exist and are being extensively analyzed by companies and their consulting partners. In industrial environments, data created by sensors, robots, and computers are being analyzed to better predict purchases of equipment and business-to-business services.

Overall, the growing availability of big data, along with systems that can analyze and interpret big data, offers the promise of more robust and accurate demand planning. Such systems make planning more effective because broader sets of data mean that more complete sets of demand influences can be captured, real-time sensors make data more current, and automated data capture makes data more accurate.

Reducing Lead Time

As we noted earlier in the chapter, it is a basic fact of forecasting that the longer the time period over which you have to forecast, the greater the forecast error. A forecast of demand for two years from now is far less accurate than a forecast of demand for next month. In most cases, the number of periods that managers have to forecast into the future is determined by the order-to-delivery (OTD) lead time provided by the supply chain, or the time required to source, make, and deliver the product. Thus, reducing lead time improves forecast accuracy, because shorter lead times require shorter-term forecasts.

Speeding up or eliminating process steps that are redundant, unnecessary, or poorly executed reduces lead time. Opportunities for improvement usually extend beyond the firm throughout the supply chain. The Get Real box about Calyx and Corolla gives an example of extreme lead-time reduction facilitated by the company's redesign of the supply chain. If lead times are reduced sufficiently, operations managers can move from a build-to-stock (build-to-forecast) process to a build-to-order process where little forecasting is required.

Redesigning the Product

For a firm offering a wide range of products, forecasting is especially challenging. Consider the problems faced by Hewlett-Packard when it comes to printers, which are consumed around the world in regions that have different power requirements and languages.

GET REAL

Calyx and Corolla Delivers Freshness by Redesigning the Supply Chain

Calyx and Corolla sells flowers from growers located around the world to customers located around the world. The company promotes itself as "the flower lover's flower company™" as it competes primarily through "freshness." Calyx and Corolla promises that its flowers will last 5 to 10 days longer than most others. How is it able to deliver on this promise? Most traditional florists must deal with a long supply chain. Growers grow the flowers. Distributors buy them and sell them to regional sellers, who in turn sell them to local florists. At each stage, the flowers are produced or purchased based on the party's forecast of demand.

A typical flower can last about 19 days, once it has been cut. The traditional supply chain consumes about 10 to 11 days of this time. The founders of Calyx and Corolla redesigned the supply chain to reduce lead time by working directly with the growers. Orders received from customers (in response to printed catalogs or the Internet) are placed by Calyx and Corolla directly with the growers, who then cut, package, and ship the flowers directly to the customer via FedEx. Consequently, flowers delivered this way spend three days or less in the supply chain. The benefit for the customer is that they arrive at their destination fresher, and they also last longer. The benefit for Calyx and Corolla is that it only needs to forecast demand for three to four days into the future in order to arrange for sufficient product and transportation capacities. Its competitors have to forecast demand for several weeks into the future.

As described in the nearby Get Real box, ultimately HP responded by developing *postponable products.* A **postponable product** is one that can be configured to its final form quickly and inexpensively once actual customer demand is known. In this operations system, only components, not finished goods, are stocked near sources of demand. The components are then assembled into finished product configurations once the actual demand materializes.

postponable product A product designed so that it can be configured to its final form quickly and inexpensively once actual customer demand is known.

The postponable product approach largely eliminates the need for large and complex forecasting systems, as only the demands for the relatively few individual components are forecasted, not the demands for the many different end-item configurations. The keys to this approach are redesign of the product and redistribution of production resources so that the products can be easily configured close to the source of demand. Electronics firms such as HP often use this approach. So do private-brand producers of grocery products (e.g., canned beans, corn, peas). The grocery producers stock unlabeled cans and then print the labels and make cartons for specific brands only after actual orders are received.

Collaborating and Sharing Information

The need for forecasting partially arises from a lack of information sharing across stages of the supply chain. Suppliers make assumptions about the actions of their customers, and vice versa. Many firms today use both formal and informal approaches to share planning information with their suppliers and customers, including forecasts of product demand and planned product promotions, as well as production plans and capacity limitations. The planning partners then make commitments to a collaboratively established overall sales and production plan, taking into account the demands and constraints of the various organizations involved. This approach reduces the risks associated with forecast errors; it reduces the inventories that supply chain players typically hold to guard against such risks; and it improves customer service levels by reducing lead times.

GET REAL

HP Improves the Constraints on Forecasting through Postponement

While the "guts" of a printer are basically the same regardless of where they are sold, instruction manuals, power supplies, and cables have to be made differently to accommodate differences in language and power grids in various countries. Initially, HP forecasted each country's demand for printers and then stocked all printer variants according to the forecasts. However, forecasts were never accurate enough to make this approach work— inventories were high, expediting was common, and customer service was low.

To solve this problem, HP decided to produce and stock only the generic printer bases, along with separate power supplies, cables, and instruction manuals, in regional warehouses around the world. The warehouses act as both storage locations and light assembly plants. Once an order is received for a printer in Germany, for example, the order is sent to the nearest regional warehouse. There, a generic printer base is withdrawn from stock and paired with the appropriate power supply, cable, and instruction manual. The entire system is then tested and packed in country-specific packaging.

Forecasts for printer bases and components are more accurate than forecasts for final product variants. At HP, this approach has

reduced total landed cost (manufacturing, shipping, and inventory) by 25 percent. In addition, HP has reduced total inventories by 50 percent while simultaneously increasing customer order fill rates significantly.

© Deepak G. Pawar/The India Today Group/Getty Images

"Smartek" chips stacked and ready for final assembly in HP printers in manufacturing plant.

collaborative planning, forecasting, and replenishment (CPFR)
A method by which supply chain partners periodically share forecasts, demand plans, and resource plans in order to reduce uncertainty and risk in meeting customer demand.

One systematic process for improving collaboration and information sharing in the supply chain is known as **collaborative planning, forecasting and replenishment (CPFR)**. The CPFR process requires buyers and sellers to collaboratively develop their demand plans and then to collaboratively adjust and execute those plans, with the goal of meeting customer demand with minimal inventories, lead times, and transaction costs.

To engage in CPFR, supply chain partners must first come to an understanding regarding their relationship and the roles they will play. Included in this mutual understanding are definitions of the accounts and operational processes involved and jointly developed business goals. Figure 12-9 illustrates one common version of the CPFR process, which typically consists of four collaborative activities:

- *Market planning.* The partners collaboratively discuss such issues as the introduction of new products, store openings/closings, changing inventory policies, and product promotions.
- *Demand and resource planning.* Customer demand and shipping requirements are forecasted.
- *Execution.* Orders are placed, delivered, received, and paid for. This includes preparation of shipments and recording of sales. Since logistics/distribution is critical, third-party logistics providers may be included in the CPFR effort.
- *Analysis.* Execution is monitored and key performance metrics are collected with the goal of identifying opportunities for future improvement.

FIGURE 12-9 The CPFR Approach

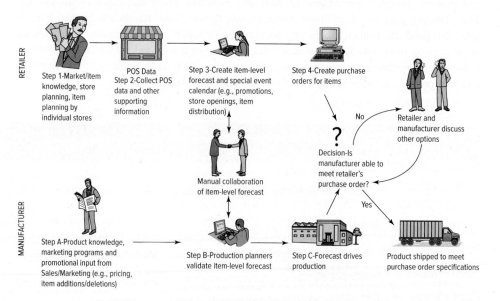

CHAPTER SUMMARY

Demand planning is a process that every firm must develop in order to deal with variability and uncertainty of product demand. This chapter discussed two fundamental elements of demand planning: demand forecasting and demand management. The following points and issues were raised:

1. The choice of a forecasting process depends on conditions in the operating environment, including the time horizon for management decisions, the level of detail that the user of the forecast needs to support decisions, the number of products for which the process must generate forecasts, the decision makers' emphasis on control or planning needs, the constancy of forecasted events, and the firm's current methods for developing forecasts.

2. Forecasting methods fall into two categories: judgment-based and statistical model–based methods. Judgment-based approaches gather inputs through grassroots methods, executive judgment, focused forecasting, historical analogy, market research, and the Delphi method. These techniques are appropriate in those situations where past data are either unavailable or no longer appropriate. They are also appropriate for forecasting technological innovations (another use of forecasting). Statistical model–based forecasting approaches try to extend the past by decomposing historical time series data and other causal factors into seasonal, trend, and other components to reveal the residual effects of unique, current forces on demand. Operations managers may develop naive forecasts or employ much more sophisticated methods.

3. Both accuracy and bias should be considered in the evaluation of forecasting errors. Mean forecast error (MFE) and mean percentage error (MPE) are good at measuring bias, while metrics such as mean absolute deviation (MAD), mean squared error (MSE), root mean squared error (RMSE), and mean absolute percentage error (MAPE) are used to monitor forecast accuracy. Managers often set up tracking signals for forecasting systems so that they can be notified when forecast errors become unusually large. This type of monitoring of forecasting performance leads to continuous updating and improvement of forecasting models.

4. Demand management involves varying the price, promotion, or availability of the product or service in order to increase, decrease, or shift the pattern of expected demand.

5. By improving supply chain constraints, operations managers can make the system more responsive to actual demand and less sensitive to forecast error. This can be done by improving information systems, reducing lead times (by changing the underlying processes and systems), redesigning the product to facilitate product postponement, and sharing information and collaborating with other supply chain partners.

6. Technology advances such as big data and artificial intelligence are improving demand planners' abilities to incorporate broader sets of considerations (and therefore less bias) into forecasts. These systems also provide more accurate and timely access to relevant information.

KEY TERMS

1. Think of four instances in your life when you confronted sellers' demand management practices. As a value-conscious customer, do you think that each of the four sellers served you well?

2. Your boss wants you to explain the term *exponential smoothing*. How do you reply?

3. Someone in your organization suspects a causal relationship between statistics on corrugated board shipments reported in *BusinessWeek* and your company's usage of corrugated board. How would you test this assertion? If you were to verify the relationship, how could you use it in your business?

4. In what way is an exponential smoothing model really a moving average model?

5. Your boss has less training than you have in business statistics. She asks you to explain the logic of the least squares regression method for determining a trend line. What will you tell her?

6. Your firm is considering reducing staff, and your forecasting department has been mentioned as a prime candidate for this treatment. Outline a brief memo to defend the value of your department's services to the firm. How could you quantify your claims?

7. Assume that you are the regional operations manager responsible for 27 Burger Queen restaurants. What types of demand forecast models do you think you would need for your short-term planning? What decisions would each forecast support? Identify the users of each forecast.

8. As the regional manager of 27 Burger Queens, you are thinking about expanding the number of outlets in your area. What types of forecasts would you want to create in order to support your decision?

9. What arguments would you use in order to justify tightening the limits used on a tracking signal control chart? What arguments would you use for loosening the limits?

10. Describe the likely effects of the following business trends on demand forecasting processes:

    a. Fast-to-market product design.
    b. Division of many markets into isolated niches.
    c. The Internet.
    d. More powerful and cheaper computers and forecasting software packages.

    How would you modify your firm's demand management or demand forecasting processes in response to these trends?

1. Vinod Malhotra is trying to decide how many wait staff he will need to support his restaurant operations for the next month. First he needs to identify a suitable forecasting model to estimate next month's demand. He is considering three alternative models:

   Model 1: Four-month moving average

   Model 2: Four-month weighted moving average with weights = .1, .2, .3, .4

   Model 3: Exponential smoothing with $\alpha = 0.7$

   Based on past performance, which model should Vinod use?

Solution:

To evaluate the three competing forecasting models, we need to compare the errors that would have been produced if they had been used in the past. The table below shows the forecasts created by each model using eight months of past demand.

Month	Actual Demand	Model 1 Forecast	Error	Abs Error	Model 2 Forecast	Error	Abs Error	Model 3 Forecast	Error	Abs Error
1	1940									
2	2250									
3	2301									
4	2630									
5	2264	2280.3	−16.3	16.3	2386.3	−122.3	122.3	2630.0	−366.0	366.
6	2736	2361.3	374.8	374.8	2379.8	356.2	356.2	2373.8	362.2	362.
7	2503	2482.8	20.3	20.3	2529.7	226.7	26.7	2627.3	−124.3	124.
8	2422	2533.3	−111.3	111.3	2537.8	−115.8	115.8	2540.3	−118.3	118

In order to complete the table, forecasts will be needed for each month. As an example, the calculations are shown below for forecasting demand for month 8:

Model 1: $F_8 = (2630 + 2264 + 2736 + 2503) / 4 = 2533.3$
Model 2: $F_8 = (0.1) 2630 + (0.2) 2264 + (0.3) 2736 + (0.4) 2503 = 2537.8$
Model 3: $F_8 = (0.7) 2503 + (1 − 0.7) 2627.3 = 2540.3$

Calculations of bias and MAD:

Model 1: Bias = $(−16.3 + 374.8 + 20.3 − 111.3) / 4 = 66.9$;
MAD = $(16.3 + 374.8 + 20.3 + 111.3) / 4 = 130.6$
Model 2: Bias = $(−122.3 + 356.2 − 26.7 − 115.8) / 4 = 22.9$;
MAD = $(122.3 + 356.2 + 26.7 + 115.8) / 4 = 155.3$
Model 3: Bias = $(−366.0 + 362.2 − 124.3 − 118.3) / 4 = −61.6$;
MAD = $(366.0 + 362.2 + 124.3 + 118.3) / 4 = 242.7$

Conclusion: Vinod would probably be advised to use model 2, the weighted moving average model, as it has provided the lowest amount of bias in the past. Though the MAD for this model is slightly worse than that for model 1, the bias is significantly better. Vinod might want to try some other model parameters to see if he can develop an even more accurate model.

2. Suppose that an electronics company has the monthly sales shown below. It wants to develop forecasts using a time series regression model and a trend enhanced exponential smoothing model using $\alpha = 0.30$ and $\partial = 0.40$, and then seasonally adjust these two models using the regression forecasts as the base for calculating the seasonal indexes. Finally, it wants to determine which forecasting model fits the data better and use this model to predict sales for the next six months.

Month	1	2	3	4	5	6	7	8	9	10	11	12
Sales ($1,000,000)	16	20	35	18	24	33	21	23	51	35	36	64

Solution:

The parameters for the regression model are calculated in Table 12-10.

TABLE 12-10   Regression Parameter Calculations

Month	Sales		
t	d_t	$t*d_t$	t^2
1	16	16	1
2	20	40	4
3	35	105	9
4	18	72	16
5	24	120	25
6	33	198	36
7	21	147	49
8	23	184	64
9	51	459	81
10	35	350	100
11	36	396	121
12	64	768	144
Total		2855	650
Average	6.5	31.3	

Using the linear regression formulae, the slope and the intercept are:

$$b = [2,855.1 - (12)(6.5)(31.3)]/[650 - (12)(6.5)^2] = 2.9 \text{ per period}$$
$$a = (31.3) - (2.9)(6.5) = 12.6$$

Regression-based estimates for each time period are calculated as:

Month 1 forecast = $12.6 + 2.9(1) = 15.5$
Month 2 forecast = $12.6 + 2.9(2) = 18.4$

Table 12-11 shows the regression forecast values for all 12 months.

The trend enhanced exponential smoothing model forecasts are calculated as follows. Since no starting values are provided, we choose the actual sales in month 1 as the initial base demand value and the slope from the regression model as the initial trend value. The forecasts are:

Month 1 forecast = $F_{t+1} + T_{t+1} = 16 + 2.9 = 18.9$
Month 2:

Base forecast = $FIT_t + \alpha(d_t - FIT_t) = 18.9 + 0.3(16 - 18.9) = 18.0$
Trend forecast = $T_t + \beta(F_{t+1} + FIT_t) = 2.9 + 0.4(18.0 - 18.9) = 2.5$
Month 2 forecast = $F_{t+1} + T_{t+1} = 18.0 + 2.5 = 20.5$

Table 12-11 shows the trend enhanced exponential smoothing forecast values for all 12 months.

To seasonally adjust these forecasts we need to first estimate the seasonal indexes. As shown in Table 12-11, this is done by simply dividing the sales in each month by the base sales provided by the regression forecast. By examining the indexes, it is clear that a quarterly demand pattern exists, with most sales occurring in the third month of each quarter. We average the seasonal indexes across the four quarters represented in the data, and then use these values to adjust the regression and trend enhanced forecasts, as shown in Table 12-11.

TABLE 12-11   Forecasts for the Solved Problem

Month	Sales (a)	Regression Forecasts (b)	Trend Enhanced ES Forecasts (c)	Seasonal Indexes = a / b	Average Seasonal Indexes (d)	Season Adjusted Regression Forecasts d × b	Season Adjusted Trend Enhanced ES Forecasts d × c
1	16	15.5	18.9	1.03	SI for first month = (1.03 + 0.75 + 0.64 + 0.85)/4 = 0.82	0.82(15.5) = 12.7	0.82(18.9) = 15.4
2	20	18.4	20.5	1.09		0.86(18.4) = 15.8	0.86(20.5) = 17.6
3	35	21.3	22.8	1.65	SI for second month = (1.09 + 0.89 + 0.65 + 0.81)/4 = 0.86	1.36(21.3) = 28.9	1.36(22.8) = 31.0
4	18	24.1	30.4	0.75		19.7	24.8
5	24	27.0	29.1	0.89		23.2	25.0
6	33	29.9	29.4	1.10	SI for third month = (1.65 + 1.10 + 1.32 + 1.36)/4 = 1.36	40.6	39.9
7	21	32.8	32.7	0.64		26.7	26.7
8	23	35.6	30.1	0.65		30.6	25.8
9	51	38.5	27.9	1.32		52.3	37.9
10	35	41.4	37.6	0.85		33.8	30.7
11	36	44.3	39.3	0.81		38.0	33.7
12	64	47.1	40.4	1.36		64.0	54.8

Now we can compare the forecasts provided by both seasonally adjusted models. Table 12-12 compares the bias, MAD, MAPE, and MSE for each of the forecast models.

TABLE 12-12   Comparison of Forecasting Errors

		Seasonally Adjusted Regression				Seasonally Adjusted Trend Enhanced ES			
Month	Sales	Forecast	Forecast Error	Absolute Error	% Absolute Error	Forecast	Forecast Error	Absolute Error	% Absolute Error
1	16	12.7	3.3	3.3	21%	15.4	0.6	0.6	4%
2	20	15.8	4.2	4.2	21%	17.6	2.4	2.4	12%
3	35	28.9	6.1	6.1	17%	31.0	4.0	4.0	11%
4	18	19.7	−1.7	1.7	9%	24.8	−6.8	6.8	38%
5	24	23.2	0.8	0.8	3%	25.0	−1.0	1.0	4%
6	33	40.6	−7.6	7.6	23%	39.9	−6.9	6.9	21%
7	21	26.7	−5.7	5.7	27%	26.7	−5.7	5.7	27%
8	23	30.6	−7.6	7.6	33%	25.8	−2.8	2.8	12%
9	51	52.3	−1.3	1.3	3%	37.9	13.1	13.1	26%
10	35	33.8	1.2	1.2	4%	30.7	4.3	4.3	12%
11	36	38.0	−2.0	2.0	6%	33.7	2.3	2.3	6%
12	64	64.0	0.0	0.0	0%	54.8	9.2	9.2	14%
	Average		Bias = − 0.9	MAD = 3.5	MAPE = 14%		Bias = 1.1	MAD = 4.9	MAPE = 16%

It is clear that the seasonally enhanced regression-based forecasting model outperforms the trend enhanced model, as it has better scores on all bias and accuracy metrics.

Using the seasonally enhanced regression model, the forecasts for the next six months would be

Month 13 forecast = [12.6 + 2.9(13)] (0.82) = 41.2

Month 14 forecast = [12.6 + 2.9(14)] (0.86) = 45.8

Month 15 forecast = [12.6 + 2.9(15)] (1.36) = 76.3

Month 16 forecast = [12.6 + 2.9(16)] (0.82) = 48.4

Month 17 forecast = [12.6 + 2.9(17)] (0.86) = 53.2

Month 18 forecast = [12.6 + 2.9(18)] (1.36) = 88.1

PROBLEMS

1. Assume you are forecasting with an exponential smoothing model using $\alpha = 0.6$. How much weight is placed on the most recent actual demand? How much weight is given to the demand one time period older than the most recent data? How much weight is given to data from two periods in the past?

2. Given the series of demand data below

Period	1	2	3	4	5	6	7	8	9	10
Demand	40	33	56	43	23	45	38	40	29	40

   a. Calculate the forecasts for periods 7 through 11 using moving average models with $n = 2$, $n = 4$, and $n = 6$.

   b. Calculate the bias and MAD for each set of forecasts. Which moving average model is best?

3. If last period's forecast was 27 and the demand was 30, what was the forecast error? What would be the forecast for the next period using an exponential smoothing model with $\alpha = .5$?

4. Use the Excel spreadsheet that accompanies this chapter to evaluate different forecasting models using the ice cream sales data. Try the following parameters for the moving average and simple exponential smoothing models: $n = 1, 4, 8$; $\alpha = 0.1, 0.5, 0.9$. Which parameters yield the best forecasting model for the periods under evaluation?

5. You have become concerned about the amount of copier paper used in your office after repeatedly running out of supplies. Your assistant keeps track of the number of reams (packages of 500 sheets) for 24 weeks:

Week	1	2	3	4	5	6	7	8	9	10	11	12
Reams of paper	232	263	271	248	235	261	207	243	237	293	243	260
Week	13	14	15	16	17	18	19	20	21	22	23	24
Reams of paper	253	270	230	253	238	272	222	243	289	238	262	234

   a. Compare the effectiveness of two-week, four-week, and six-week moving averages. Which should you use to forecast copier paper use during the next week?

   b. Compare the performance of the simple exponential smoothing model with smoothing constants of 0.01, 0.05, and 0.25. Assume a forecast for week 1 of 230 reams. Which constant worked best?

6. Assume that you are the production manager for Fast Current Kayaks of Washington State. One of the products that you make and sell is the "Fast Current" sea touring kayak paddle. You are responsible for ensuring that there is enough production capacity to meet demand (given the very high markup on the paddles).

Year	Quarter	Demand	Year	Quarter	Demand
Year 1	Q1	18	Year 5	Q1	42
	Q2	19		Q2	38
	Q3	18		Q3	59
	Q4	17		Q4	58
Year 2	Q1	19	Year 6	Q1	60
	Q2	21		Q2	61
	Q3	18		Q3	62
	Q4	19		Q4	62
Year 3	Q1	20	Year 7	Q1	64
	Q2	24		Q2	65
	Q3	28		Q3	66
	Q4	32		Q4	68
Year 4	Q1	30	Year 8	Q1	69
	Q2	31		Q2	68
	Q3	34		Q3	67
	Q4	40		Q4	68

a. Given the data shown above, beginning in quarter 1 of year 2, use a moving average based on four quarters to predict the demand in each quarter.
b. Using the same data, forecast demand using exponential smoothing. You are given an initial forecast for year 1, quarter 1, of 17. When generating your forecasts, assume that the smoothing coefficient is 0.10.
c. Which of the forecasting procedures performed the best? Why? (*Hint:* Plot the demand data to better understand what is going on.)

7. Using $\alpha = 0.5$ and the following data, compute exponential smoothing forecasts for periods 2 through 8.

Period	1	2	3	4	5	6	7
Forecast	10						
Actual demand	12	15	11	13	11	11	10

8. The owner of an online video rental service has recorded the following rentals each week:

Week	1	2	3	4	5	6	7	8
Rentals	1202	1503	1444	1254	1609	1499	1689	1555

a. Use a three-week moving average to forecast sales for each of the weeks 4 through 9.
b. Use a four-week moving average to forecast sales for each of the weeks 5 through 9.
c. Compare the forecasts created by these two methods using mean absolute deviation. Which forecasting method would you recommend?

9. A ski repair shop at a resort in Colorado sells replacement poles each season. The shop needs to develop a forecast of next season's sales so that it can place an order for poles with its supplier well in advance of the beginning of the season. Sales data for the past five years are shown below.

Year	1	2	3	4	5
Sales (units)	375	395	360	400	380

Develop and compare the forecasts given by the following models:
a. A five-year moving average model.
b. A weighted moving average model with weights of 0.1, 0.1, 0.2, 0.3, and 0.3 for years 1 through 5, respectively.
c. An exponential smoothing model with a year 1 forecast of 380 and $\alpha = 0.2$.

10. The following data show the number of laptop computers sold each month at a retail store:

Month	Unit Sales
January	200
February	230
March	225
April	240
May	210
June	180
July	160
August	310
September	320
October	270
November	250
December	300

a. Assuming the estimated trend from May to June was −4 and the forecast for June was 190, use trend-adjusted exponential smoothing with $\alpha = 0.3$ and $\beta = 0.2$ to forecast sales for each of the seven following months: July, August, September, October, November, December, and January.
b. Use regression for the data from January to June to create a forecast for each month from July to the following January.
c. Compare the two sets of forecasts generated in parts (a) and (b). Which forecast model produces a better MFE? Which produces a better MAD?

11. Use the data from problem 10 to solve the following:
a. Using the average demand for the year as the base, compute a seasonal index for each month.
b. Use regression to estimate the deseasonalized demand in each of the given months. Using these base values, compute a seasonal index for each month.
c. Are the seasonal indexes computed in parts (a) and (b) the same or different? Why?
d. Using the regression model and the seasonal indexes you computed in part (b), compute a seasonally adjusted forecast for January, February, March, April, and May of the next year.

12. Monthly usage data for pallets used in a distribution center are as follows:

Year	1	2	3	4
January	1484	1482	1792	1902
February	1394	1400	1586	1722
March	1552	1548	1770	1876

April	1796	1864	2110	2218
May	2060	2198	2408	2548
June	2214	2446	2652	2844
July	2330	2580	2606	2972
August	2432	2698	2872	3110
September	2416	2682	2946	3208
October	2262	2592	2906	3200
November	1942	2132	2340	2806
December	1566	1802	2046	2418

a. Calculate the monthly usage index for each month.
b. Use simple linear regression to forecast total usage of pallets for year 5.
c. Forecast the seasonally adjusted usage for pallets for each month in year 5.

13. Given the data shown below, use $\alpha = .2$ and $\beta = .4$ to create a trend enhanced smoothing based forecast for period 7. Assume that $FIT_1 = 22$ and $T_1 = 7.83$.

Period	1	2	3	4	5	6
Demand	19	33	37	49	52	60

14. Repeat problem 13 using $\alpha = .4$ and $\beta = .8$. Which model gives a better approximation of the demand pattern for periods 1 through 6?

15. Calculate the slope and intercept for the data in problem 13 using simple linear regression. You may want to use an Excel spreadsheet to check your answer.

16. Wamaco Corporation uses the same simple exponential smoothing forecasting model for all of its products. The model has yielded the following weekly forecasts:

Week	1	2	3	4	5	6
Product 1 forecast	12	10.6	10.9	12.4	13.5	12.5
Product 1 sales	10	11	13	14	12	10
Product 2 forecast	102	100.6	103	104.4	104.8	108.4
Product 2 sales	100	104	105	105	110	106

a. What value of α is Wamaco Corp. using in its forecasting model?
b. Calculate the forecast for period 7 for product 1 and product 2.
c. Using the first six periods of data, calculate the bias (MFE), MAD, MPE, and MAPE. Does the forecasting model provide approximately the same bias and accuracy for both products? What would you recommend?

17. Many supply managers use a monthly reported survey result known as the purchasing managers' index (PMI) as a leading indicator to forecast future sales for their businesses. Suppose that the PMI and your business sales data for the last 10 months are as follows:

Month	1	2	3	4	5	6	7	8	9	10
PMI	42.1	43.0	41.0	38.2	40.2	44.1	45.8	49.0	48.7	52.0
Sales (1000s)	121	123	125	120	118	118	122	127	135	136

a. Construct a causal regression model using PMI as the causal variable. How well does your model fit the data?
b. Suppose that the PMI is truly a *leading* indicator. That is, the PMI value in one period influences sales in the following period. Construct a new regression model using this information. Is the new model better or worse than the model you made for part (a)?
c. Pick the best model from parts (a) and (b), and create a forecast for sales given PMI = 47.3.

18. Assume that the following demands vary according to a four-period seasonal cycle:

Month	1	2	3	4	5	6	7	8
Demand	20	30	40	20	50	70	95	50

    a. Compute the seasonal indexes using the average demand in each cycle as the base.

    b. Compute the seasonal indexes using regression estimates as the base.

    c. How do the answers for parts (a) and (b) differ? How would you explain the difference?

19. Use the Excel spreadsheet that accompanies this supplement to evaluate different forecasting models using the ice cream sales data.

    a. Which model—time series regression, causal regression using temperature, or trend enhanced exponential smoothing--gives better forecast accuracy? Report all bias and accuracy metrics.

    b. What combination of parameters for the trend enhanced smoothing model gives the best results?

    c. Calculate seasonally adjusted forecasts, first using the average demand as the base, then using the time series regression forecasts as the base, then using the causal regression forecasts as the base. Which model is better? Why?

20. Given the data shown below, use $\alpha = .1$ and $\beta = .2$ to create a trend enhanced smoothing based forecast for period 6. Assume that $FIT_1 = 20$ and $T_1 = 3$.

Period	1	2	3	4	5
Demand	25	23	26	28	35

21. Re-solve problem 20 using a simple exponential smoothing model with $\alpha = .8$, and with a 2-period moving average model. Which model is best?

22. Using the data in the table below:

Period	1	2	3	4	5	6	7	8	9	10	11
Gasoline sales	100	150	130	150	180	200	120	130	140	180	200
Oil price	82	60	80	71	57	45	88	77	63	43	55

    a. Compute the forecast for period 12 using a causal regression model and assuming that oil price for period 12 is 65.

    b. Create a graph of the gasoline sales and oil price data and include a line representing the regression model. In which period is gasoline sales least well predicted by oil price? What is the amount of this error?

CASE

Rachel's Breakfast Café

Rachel Kirkpatrick thought to herself, "What a waste," as she threw away three bags full of unsold items and spoiled ingredients. "I have to get better at estimating how much food to order and prepare."

Rachel owned and operated a small café that specialized in fresh baked quiches, breakfast casseroles, and breads, as well as ready-made country style breakfasts. The café was open six days a week and closed on Sundays. Rachel had run her shop for over a year now, and business seemed to be taking off. While she had made a number of operating improvements related to the consistency and quality of her products, she still struggled between two extremes of the same problem. On some days Rachel did not have enough ingredients on hand to satisfy the day's customers. In this case, some of the people who expected to get one of her famous quiches were disappointed. Other days Rachel had far too much food on hand. On days like today, Rachel found herself throwing away food because she had vastly overestimated the number of customers she would have.

While it was difficult for Rachel to know exactly how many customers she served each day, she was able to accurately track the total dollar value of sales. It seemed to her that her business was growing, but she had not taken the time to see whether the increasing demand was a true trend or just her perception. Based on her assumption that business was growing, Rachel had been placing larger orders with her suppliers of milk, eggs, cheese, and other ingredients each week. Each day Rachel placed orders for supplies online at a nearby grocer's website, and he delivered each order five days later.

As Rachel considered how to improve her forecasts for needed items, she thought about possible factors that caused demand to be greater or smaller each day at her café. Fridays and Saturdays were usually busier than other days. Beyond the weekend effect, she noted that the weather had an impact. On rainy days people were less likely to go out for breakfast. Rachel wondered how she could use this information to improve her business.

Over the next four weeks Rachel collected the data shown in the following table. The "5 day forecast" column shows the probability of rain (percentage) for the area around Rachel's café, as predicted by the local weather service five days into the future. For example, the table shows a forecasted 10 percent probability of rain on the first Monday in the table; this was the forecast released by the weather service on the Wednesday five days earlier. Since it currently took Rachel five days to receive orders

for her supplies, she knew that she would need to have the weather forecast at least this far in advance in order for it to be of use to her. At the same time, she also knew that shorter term forecasts are usually more accurate. So, she also decided to track the "2 day forecast," that is, forecasts made two days in advance.

Day	Probability of Rain (%) 5 day forecast	Probability of Rain (%) 2 day forecast	Total Sales
Monday	10	40	5520
Tuesday	20	30	4320
Wednesday	30	10	4212
Thursday	50	40	4987
Friday	80	80	5545
Saturday	90	90	6023
Monday	60	30	4590
Tuesday	70	30	4733
Wednesday	90	30	4923
Thursday	100	50	4687
Friday	100	100	5988
Saturday	20	70	6132
Monday	10	10	5324
Tuesday	10	10	4526
Wednesday	10	10	5232
Thursday	50	50	5684
Friday	20	70	5911
Saturday	60	60	6328
Monday	20	20	4932
Tuesday	15	15	5235
Wednesday	20	50	5862
Thursday	20	20	4862
Friday	10	80	6100
Saturday	60	70	6255

Questions

1. Develop forecasts using regressions of sales on each of the series of rain forecasts, respectively. Calculate the MFE (bias), MAD, and MAPE for the two forecasting models. Which rain forecast seems to be better

at predicting Rachel's daily sales, the five-day forecast or the two-day forecast?

2. How can Rachel make use of the rain forecasts to improve her forecasts of total sales each day? What other changes to her business would she need to make in order to capitalize on this information?

3. How are order lead time and forecasting accuracy related to each other in this case?

4. Plot and visually inspect the sales data. What other suggestions would you give Rachel for improving her sales forecasts? What type of time series model would be appropriate? Why?

CASE

C&F Apparel, Inc.

Bill Smith, director of business planning for C&F Apparel, chewed on a pencil as he looked out the window of his fourth-story office. These bad forecasts are killing us, he thought. Forecast errors for the fall season's sales had ranged from 50 to 200 percent of demand. As a consequence, C&F had discounted its apparel heavily, with average markdowns of 30 percent. In addition, it had written off some 15 percent of inventory as obsolete.

C&F Apparel was a medium-sized designer and producer of sports apparel and active wear, including pants, shirts, sweaters, and some accessories. Though it did not own any retail stores, it sold through most of the larger retail outlets throughout North America. The clothes sold by C&F were considered by most consumers to be durable and reasonably priced. While its fashions were not cutting edge, C&F managed to keep up with trends and changing designs from season to season. Each selling season lasted about 15 weeks.

Developing good forecasts and maintaining product availability were constant challenges for C&F. To keep costs low, the company sourced most of its products from material and assembly plants located in the Pacific Rim countries, including China, Vietnam, and Thailand. The lead time to have new designs made and shipped from these countries was typically two to three months, so it was important for initial sales estimates to be as accurate as possible. Bill Smith and his marketing team took it upon themselves to develop forecasts each season. They used sales from the previous year's season, along with their judgments regarding upcoming changes in economic conditions and consumer tastes. While the aggregate sales forecasts

developed by Bill and his team were sometimes fairly accurate, forecasts for specific items were all over the map. Bill knew that their forecasting process was not as consistent from season to season as it could be, but he felt that flexibility was needed to cope with changing conditions.

Bill had recently heard about "fast fashion" apparel makers like Zara, a Spanish company that designs, produces, and sells expensive, top-of-the-line apparel. An article describing Zara's forecasting and fulfillment policies intrigued him. Zara had price markdowns that were much lower than industry averages, and its sales per square foot were 20–30 percent higher. The article attributed better performance to several factors. First, Zara was known for developing long-term purchase contracts, mostly with domestic suppliers. Its supply lead times were typically two to three weeks. Second, Zara used store manager inputs and sales information from its own retail stores to rapidly update its sales forecasts throughout each sales season. The company was known to invite store managers to corporate headquarters at the beginning of each season so that they could evaluate the new product lines. Finally, Zara had focused product teams responsible for developing the forecasting process for each product category.

Bill wondered if these approaches might work at C&F.

Questions

1. What are the advantages and disadvantages of Zara's methods?

2. Would these methods work at a company like C&F?

3. What advice would you give to Bill Smith?

Armstrong, J. S. (ed). *Principles of Forecasting: A Handbook for Researchers and Practitioners.* New York: Kluwer Academic Publishers, 2001.

Crosby, J. V. *Cycles, Trends, and Turning Points: Practical Marketing & Sales Forecasting Techniques.* Lincolnwood, IL: NTC Business Books, 2000.

Ghemawat, P., and J. N. Nueno. "ZARA: Fast Fashion." *Harvard Business Review,* April 1, 2003.

Gilliland, M. "Is Forecasting a Waste of Time?" *Supply Chain Management Review* 6, no. 4 (July/August 2002), pp. 16–23.

Kahn, K. B. "An Exploratory Investigation of New Product Forecasting Practices." *Journal of Product Innovation Management* 19, no. 2 (March 2002), pp. 133–43.

Makridakis, S., and S. C. Wheelwright. *Forecasting Methods for Management,* 5th ed. New York: John Wiley & Sons, 1989.

Robb, D. J., and E. A. Silver. "Using Composite Moving Averages to Forecast Sales." *Journal of the Operational Research Society* 53, no. 11 (November 2002), pp. 1281–85.

Woolsey, R. E. D., and H. F. Swanson. *Operations Research for Immediate Application: A Quick and Dirty Manual.* New York: Harper & Row, 1975.

Institute of Business Forecasting and Planning
www.ibf.org

13

Sales and Operations Planning

LEARNING OBJECTIVES *After studying this chapter, you should be able to:*

LO13-1 Describe the role and the process of sales and operations planning.

LO13-2 Define the contents of an aggregate plan.

LO13-3 Explain the relevant costs in developing an aggregate plan.

LO13-4 Contrast different types of aggregate production strategies.

LO13-5 Develop alternative aggregate production plans.

LO13-6 Explain the differences in aggregate planning in services versus manufacturing industries.

**Sunsweet
Growers Implements
Advanced S&OP**

In most supply chains, the key constraint lies either on the supply side or the demand side. But for dried-fruit producer Sunsweet Growers, both supply and demand are determined by factors beyond the company's control. The company's Yuba City plant operates throughout the year, but harvest takes place only during September and October. The fruit is dried and stored immediately after harvest and then processed and shipped throughout the year. Demand, however, is highly seasonal, with peak times occurring during the Christmas holiday period, resulting in costly overtime and difficulty in maintaining its 98 percent customer fill rate. The wide variety of products requires sophisticated scheduling and planning. For example, the fruit is packaged in clear bags, stand-up pouch bags, cartons, bulk cases, and cans. Containers range in size from one ounce to 50 pounds and are labeled in 20 languages, and there are 20 different sizes and grades of prunes to be processed and packaged.

Sunsweet recognized that sales and operations planning (S&OP) is key to running an optimized supply chain. Implementation of an S&OP process has provided all groups within the organization a better understanding of how to work together to reduce cost and improve order lead time. Sunsweet is now able to develop a more accurate forecast and has seen major improvements in delivery performance and cost management. The company has reduced the number of production lines, reduced changeovers, and reduced overtime from 30 to 10 percent.

By implementing a successful S&OP program, Sunsweet benefits from increased visibility into its supply chain and is better able to align all areas within the organization to make better business decisions. Participants in the process can now understand sales and marketing expectations and how they relate to realistic manufacturing scheduling and production. As a result, they can make better collaborative decisions on issues that affect the supply chain performance of the entire organization.[1]

---

[1]Adapted from H. Upton and H. Singh, "Balanced S&OP: Sunsweet Growers" Story," *Supply Chain Management Review* 11, no. 2 (2007), p. 51.

This chapter discusses a fundamental challenge that every organization faces: balancing supply with demand. It is often difficult to supply the exact quantity of products and services at the exact time customers demand them. Compounding the problem, in many organizations sales and marketing executives often do not discuss their plans with their counterparts in supply chain operations functions. Likewise, operations executives frequently do not tell sales and marketing personnel about supply constraints and capacity plans. The inevitable result is a mismatch between the organization's sales plan and its operations plan. For example, countless stories are told about companies who were not prepared for the amount of demand created by highly discounted promotions, resulting in product shortages and dissatisfied customers.

sales and operations planning (S&OP) A process to develop tactical plans by integrating customer-focused marketing plans for new and existing products with the operational management of the supply chain.

Sunsweet Growers found the solution to this problem in a process called sales and operations planning (S&OP). S&OP is a process to develop tactical plans by integrating customer-focused marketing plans for new and existing products with the operational management of the supply chain.

This chapter discusses S&OP by building on the inventory and demand planning principles discussed in Chapters 7 and 12. It describes the process of sales and operations planning and then focuses on procedures for developing an aggregate production plan. The chapter closes with a discussion of the application of these processes in service industries.

SALES AND OPERATIONS PLANNING

LO13-1 Describe the role and the process of sales and operations planning.

A formal sales and operations planning (S&OP) process is critical to success at the operational, corporate, and supply chain levels. For example, a recent study by the Aberdeen Group (Ball, 2013)[2] reported that greater than 60 percent of the best-in-class companies viewed a formal S&OP as a strategic priority and that best-in-class firms hold an 18 point advantage in forecast accuracy. The reason lies in what the S&OP process does.

The formal S&OP process gives companies a regular (e.g., monthly) opportunity for the S&OP teams to come together and to review the data, the current intelligence and information from the field, and to decide how the company should best respond. The formal S&OP process also gives the company the opportunity to challenge current execution plans and to either confirm or change the plan to meet the strategic and financial goals of the firm. Finally, it provides a forum where the members, drawn from groups such as accounting, operations, logistics, purchasing, marketing, engineering, finance, and top management, can discuss issues and arrive at critical decisions. It ensures that the planning process continuously generates realistic and credible commitments.

In the hierarchy of supply chain planning activities described at the beginning of Chapter 12, S&OP is considered to be intermediate-range planning; that is, it focuses on a time period ranging from 3 to 18 months. Typically, it is broken into time increments that are weekly, monthly, or quarterly, depending on the specific needs of a company. Planning occurs at the aggregated, product-family level, though it may include some detailed planning for critical items and special events such as new product launches. While the implementation of S&OP often varies from company to company, there are certain common features present in nearly all S&OP processes.

relationships

Figure 13-1 provides an overview of S&OP. Typically, sales and marketing executives bring to the S&OP meetings their ideal or unconstrained sales plans based on their analysis of existing customer orders, plus plans for new product introductions, promotions, expected competitive actions, and the like. Operations executives bring plans and knowledge concerning capacity constraints, inventory policies, suppliers' capabilities, materials availability, and transportation and storage capabilities. Financial managers bring budgets that define goals for managing inventories, cash flows, and other capital expenditures.

In S&OP, the parties involved try to resolve potential conflicts among the objectives of three primary functional groups: sales, operations, and finance. (See Tables 13-1 and 13-2.)

---

[2]B. Ball, *Sales and Operations Planning: A Global Comparison (S&OP): A Sure Path to Superior Performance,* (Aberdeen Group, September 28, 2012). http://blogs.aberdeen.com/supply-chain-management/sales-and-operations-planning-sop-a-sure-path-to-improvement/

FIGURE 13-1 Overview of Sales and Operations Planning

TABLE 13-1   Sales and Operations: Balancing Objectives

Sales	Operations
Aggregate forecasts	Detailed forecasts
Many product variations	Few product variations
Rapid response	Long production runs
High service	Stable production schedules
Maximize revenue	Maximize output; minimize costs

TABLE 13-2   Finance and Operations: Balancing Objectives

Finance	Operations
Maximize financial returns	Minimize costs
Reduce financial risk	Reduce variance
High returns on investment	Maintain up-time
Focus on customers with highest contribution margins	Focus on grouping orders together to enhance operational efficiency or to reduce setups

For example, sales personnel might want to offer many different variations of a product to attract more customers. However, operations and financial planners might prefer to limit product offerings in order to maximize production runs, avoid costly changeovers, and focus on the most profitable customers. In addition, the company may not have the capacity either internally or in the supply base to meet all of sales' objectives.

Similarly, finance and operations managers might disagree over scheduling decisions. Operations managers typically want to minimize costs and maximize equipment up-time and product quality, whereas finance managers typically focus more on working capital and profitability. How these competing concerns are resolved has major implications for how the firm positions itself competitively. S&OP forces the different functional managers to explicitly consider each other's concerns and to create a unified and balanced plan that fits with the firm's overall strategic objectives.

S&OP Benefits

Organizations that have effective S&OP processes have experienced both "hard" (quantifiable) and "soft" (qualitative) benefits. The hard benefits include:

- Improved forecast accuracy. Detailed discussions between executives representing all of the key functions results in a consensus forecast that is usually more accurate.
- Higher customer service with lower finished goods inventory levels, due to better forecasts and coordination of supply with demand.
- More stable supply rates, resulting in higher productivity (for purchasing, suppliers, and operations).
- Faster and more controlled new product introduction.

In addition, the soft benefits include:

- Enhanced teamwork at both the executive and operating levels.
- Better decisions with less effort and time.
- Better alignment of operational, marketing, and financial plans.
- Greater accountability for results.
- A window into the future to see potential problems soon enough to prevent them from becoming real problems.

The Get Real box concerning Heinz provides an example of the conflicting objectives that exist between functions and the benefits of developing an S&OP process.

relationships

The S&OP Process

While there is no specific set of steps that must be followed, Figure 13-2 summarizes a typical S&OP process. The S&OP team first reviews prior plans and results so that lessons learned

---

GET REAL

One-Number Forecasting at Heinz

Heinz North America (HNA) is well known for brands such as Heinz Ketchup, Pickles, Vinegar, and Relish, as well as sauces such as 57 Sauce, Home-Style Gravy, and Classico Pasta Sauces. HNA also has frozen brands, including Smart Ones Frozen Meals and Desserts, Boston Market Meals and Sides, Ore-Ida Potatoes, Bagel Bites, and TGIF Appetizers.

Until 2002, the responsibility for forecasting resided with marketing/brand management, which posed both benefits and challenges. In this approach, each brand manager led initiatives to grow his or her own business. However, challenges included the presence of different motives underlying different forecasts. Brand management teams tended to be optimistic in forecasting, while sales management was conservative because of sales quotas. Finance typically added more optimism to the forecast, while production planning often applied a bit of conservatism in its desire to maintain low inventories. The functional groups' estimates differed from each other because of their different assumptions and motivations. When shipments did not materialize as forecasted, everyone had their own explanation of why they missed the forecast.

Recently, Heinz began requiring the forecasting department to report to the vice president of supply chain, who was tasked in turn with the responsibility of providing the essential link between the front end (marketing/sales) and the back end (supply chain and operations), using the same forecast. Now, one forecast drives both the front-end business planning and the supply chain through constant communication and consensus meetings.

The one-number forecast has enabled the entire organization to plan based on the same assumptions, risks, and upsides. In addition, it has encouraged productive conversations around true planning for the first time. For instance, budgeting is now less confusing because the same volume forecast drives the plans of marketing, sales, production, inventory, transit/warehousing, manufacturing/co-packing, and, ultimately, financials. When spending increases or decreases, appropriate volume is either added or removed from the forecast. When large events at certain accounts shift in execution timing, the associated volume also is moved. When promotions change at the account level, deployment plans change accordingly.

With this approach, potential issues surrounding supplies/suppliers and capacity at factories and warehouses surface much earlier than before. Most importantly, everyone is held accountable for the inputs and assumptions that make up the final forecast.

Source: Adapted from S. Park, "One-Number Forecasting: Heinz's Experience and Learning," *The Journal of Business Forecasting* 27, no. 1 (2008), pp. 29–32.

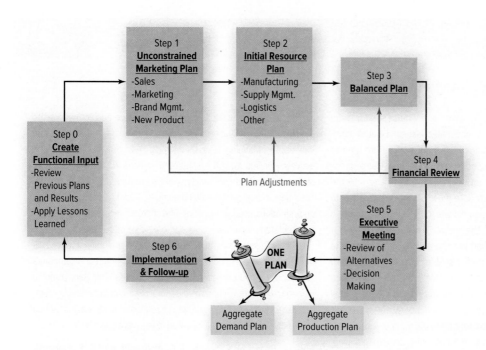

FIGURE 13-2
The S&OP Process

can be applied to the new planning period. The supply and demand functional reviews produce a consensus forecast that guides the initial functional plans. In reality, planning is usually an iterative process, where the S&OP team develops a consensus forecast and then each functional area develops its initial plans. The S&OP team then meets again (as indicated by the red lines in Figure 13-2), to work out problems or potential inconsistencies. For example, after being exposed to an initial aggregate production plan with its costs and constraints, the sales team may consider alternative sales strategies and tactics that impact the sales forecast and result in a more efficient production plan. Likewise, the operations team, once exposed to the sales plan, may be able to adjust the production plan to meet the sales objectives.

S&OP is a dynamic process, not a one-time event. It would be extremely rare for a company to establish an aggregate production plan at the beginning of a year and simply follow it blindly for the next six or twelve months. Most firms that have incorporated S&OP as a part of their overall management process hold monthly, or at least quarterly, review meetings. Operations personnel and marketing/sales personnel review performance to date and bring new information to the process. For example, two months into the year, sales and marketing personnel have some actual demand data, more information concerning future orders from customers, and possibly revised forecasts of sales for the remainder of the year. Likewise, based on events that occur, sales plans for new products or promotions may be revised.

Similarly, conditions in operations may change. Unexpected machine breakdowns, employee strikes, and other events can drastically change the aggregate production plan. Many companies incorporate **rolling planning horizons**, meaning that they replan each period (month or quarter), for a given number of periods into the future. This approach updates the S&OP sales plan and aggregate production plan as conditions change.

Working collaboratively with customers and suppliers is one of the main ingredients of a successful S&OP program. Bringing customers into the process through collaborative planning, forecasting, and replenishment (CPFR) initiatives (discussed in Chapter 12) provides much deeper insight into demand. Sharing aggregate production plans with key suppliers allows them to be better positioned to meet the requirements for materials, components, and supplies. Leveraging the capabilities and influence of customers and suppliers expands the scope of potential improvements for the organization and for the entire supply chain. The nearby Get Real box concerning Lowe's and Whirlpool describes how those firms have worked together to develop an integrated planning process that has resulted in better financial results for both companies.

rolling planning horizons Replan each period (month or quarter), for a given number of periods into the future.

relationships

GET REAL

Whirlpool and Lowe's Integrate Their Planning

Historically, interactions between Lowe's and Whirlpool addressed only immediate merchandising and sales issues. Limited communications between the two firms led to problems from time to time. For example, when Whirlpool introduced a new line of products, both Lowe's and Whirlpool wanted to get the line into the store quickly. When the launch date was set, the merchandising leader from Lowe's asked, "When did you know you were going to bring this line to the market?" The answer was, "We've known for months." Because Whirlpool had not shared this information, the two companies had to negotiate the split for tens of thousands of dollars of liquidation costs required for Lowe's to sell out its inventory of the existing line. A little trust and shared information would have saved both companies aggravation and money. Today, Lowe's and Whirlpool are working in an integrated planning process.

The effort began with a focus on collaborative demand planning. After developing a collaborative demand planning process, Lowe's and Whirlpool moved toward working more closely on supply planning. Lowe's' initial focus was on recognizing the capabilities and limitations

of Whirlpool's manufacturing divisions. Both companies worked to develop an understanding of each other's target inventory levels and new product planning. Next, their supply chain organizations became actively involved with the sales and merchandising organizations. Structured demand and supply reviews created a single set of forecasts and sales plans for both companies. They focused collaboration on promotions, product launches, and special-event planning, creating an integrated promotional calendar for each product category.

The two companies developed a shared planning process built around joint business objectives that emerged from each company's internal sales and operational planning process. This joint planning helped Lowe's and Whirlpool realize improvements in several key metrics. For example, unit sales growth increased over a three-year period by 12 percent, while overall inventory costs went down by 5 percent.

Source: Based on L. Smith, J. C. Andraski, and S. E. Fawcett, "Integrated Business Planning: A Roadmap to Linking S&OP and CPFR.," *The Journal of Business Forecasting* **29, no. 4 (2010), pp. 4, 7, 9–13.**

LO13-2 Define the contents of an aggregate plan.

aggregate production plan
Specifies the production rates, inventory, employment levels, backlogs, possible subcontracting, and other resources needed to meet the sales plan.

Ultimately, the output of the S&OP process is a balance of the demand plan and the **aggregate production plan**. The aggregate production plan specifies the production rates, inventory, employment levels, backlogs, possible subcontracting, and other resources needed to meet the demand plan. Aggregate planning is typically accomplished at the level of a product line or product family rather than the individual product or SKU, thus the term *aggregate*. Techniques and methods for modifying demand were discussed in detail in Chapter 12, "Demand Planning: Forecasting and Demand Management." The remainder of this chapter is devoted to techniques for modifying supply to meet demand through development of the aggregate production plan.

AGGREGATE PRODUCTION PLANNING

The overall goal of aggregate production planning (APP, also called *aggregate capacity planning*) is to set targets for inventory and various sources of capacity so that supply will match demand over the intermediate time frame in the most efficient way possible. The aggregate plan also takes into account other constraints formed by the company's strategy and the often conflicting wishes of each of the functional areas. Though it is called *production* planning, this type of planning is equally important in service businesses as well as in manufacturing. In either case, evaluating the merits of various plans requires the evaluation of a large number of cost trade-offs.

LO13-3 Explain the relevant costs in developing an aggregate plan.

Relevant Aggregate Planning Costs

To do aggregate planning, several different types of costs must be identified and quantified, including the following:

- *Inventory holding cost.* As discussed in Chapter 7, maintaining inventory involves a number of expenses related to the cost of capital invested in inventory, insurance, storage, obsolescence, and taxes.
- *Regular production cost.* The regular production cost includes the average labor cost to produce an aggregate unit and any benefits that are a part of the pay package.

- *Overtime cost.* In many instances, overtime may be scheduled for the labor force to gain additional output. Overtime costs are generally stated as some percentage of regular production cost.

- *Hiring cost.* This cost includes the cost of advertising for new workers, interviewing them, processing their applications, and then training them. In addition, new workers may not be as productive as veteran workers and this should be factored into the cost as well. In many instances, temporary workers may be hired for a short time period. Hiring and firing costs for temporary workers may be less than for permanent workers.

- *Firing/layoff cost.* When the workforce level is decreased, there are costs associated with either firing or laying off the workers. Separation costs can include unemployment compensation or lump sum separation payments. Some union contracts require that workers receive a portion of their normal pay for a period of time after they have been laid off.

- *Backorder/lost sales cost.* A firm may plan to either backorder a demand or lose the sales for that demand. In the backorder case, there will likely be an explicit penalty for late delivery, but there is also a good chance that there is a customer ill-will cost that is harder to quantify. In the case of lost sales, there is the direct loss of profit and the additional ill-will cost of not being able to meet demand.

- *Subcontracting cost.* A company may choose to subcontract (outsource) production to another firm for a period of time. Associated costs are generally stated on a per-unit basis. An additional cost is sometimes added above the contracted price because of the lack of control over quality and delivery, although this portion is difficult to estimate.

Some of these costs may be difficult to precisely measure, and estimates may be required. In some cases, where a cost is extremely difficult to determine, some firms choose to leave the costs out. They compare scenarios based on multiple criteria, making a judgment about the level of the removed factor as opposed to the cost impact of that factor. This is particularly true for the cost of backorders and possible lost sales.

In addition to these costs, there are other constraints on production plans. For example, company policy may limit the number of layoffs allowed in any one period. Subcontracting might be limited by corporate fiat due to the lack of control over quality. Limits on the level of working capital might limit the amount of inventory allowed. Companies often limit the degree to which backorders and lost sales can be included in a plan. The belief is that these can damage the company's image in the eyes of its customers. However, some companies might find meeting peak demand to be cost-prohibitive during very high demand periods, in which case backorders may be necessary.

Certain functional area requirements may create additional constraints in the production planning process. For example, marketing may want a minimum service level that can be expressed as a minimum inventory level for each period. This minimum inventory may be needed to provide protection against uncertain demands and to provide a proper mix of finished goods to meet customer demands. Similarly, human resource managers may limit the amount of overtime allowed, as the strain of working long hours may lead to safety and labor problems, lost productivity, or turnover. Thus, along with minimizing costs, aggregate planning must address other goals in a sustainable way.

sustainability

Aggregate Production Strategies

LO13-4 Contrast different types of aggregate production strategies.

Solving aggregate planning problems involves formulating alternative production strategies for meeting demand and determining the cost and feasibility of those alternatives. There are two "pure" strategies that form extreme alternatives of aggregate plans. In a **level production strategy**, the firm produces at a constant rate over the year, building inventory in periods of low demand and depleting the inventory in periods of high demand. In a **chase strategy**, the production rate is changed in each period to match the amount of expected demand. In reality, most firms typically use a mixed or hybrid strategy somewhere between these generic strategies, but these generic options are worth discussing to better understand the trade-offs involved in developing a good aggregate plan.

level production strategy The firm produces at a constant rate over the year.

chase strategy The production rate is changed in each period to match the amount of expected demand.

As mentioned earlier, aggregate planning is not limited to manufacturing firms. All organizations face a problem of matching supply (capacity) with demand. Consider the demand pattern of the hypothetical retailer illustrated in Figure 13-3. Retailers often attempt to manage demand to obtain somewhat more stable patterns; consider early bird specials and attempts to encourage early Christmas shopping, for example. However, at least some level of variation in demand is usually unavoidable. Retailers are therefore likely to adopt a plan that is closer to a chase strategy.

Level Production Strategy

A level production strategy is used when the costs of ramping production up and down are high and inventory costs are relatively low. If a firm's processes require highly skilled workers that are hard to find, it is more likely to use a level strategy. For example, a shop that employs highly skilled machinists is likely to avoid hiring and firing them, especially if they are hard to find or if they are protected by a strong union. Similarly, if the constraining resources are machines that cannot be easily scaled up or down (such as in a paper mill), the firm will likely pursue a level strategy.

The level production strategy provides a constant rate of output over the entire planning time period and requires no overtime, no changes in the workforce level, and no subcontracting. The disadvantage of this is that it can cause inventory levels to be quite high following low-demand seasons. It generally results in the highest investment in inventory, high inventory carrying cost, and risk of inventory obsolescence, and it requires storage space capacity. However, it requires the least overall investment in plant and equipment because an average production rate can be maintained throughout the year.

Chase Strategy

A chase strategy is generally used by firms that have either high per-unit inventory holding cost rates relative to their cost of changing the production rate or products that cannot be inventoried. They may use part-time seasonal workers who can be hired during peak-demand periods and laid off during low-demand seasons. Firms that require little in the way of labor skills or training, or those producing goods that are perishable or quickly become obsolete, are candidates for some form of a chase strategy.

Most service businesses use a chase strategy because they don't have the option of building inventory of their product. Retailers who have very high peak-demand periods, such as the Christmas season, make extensive use of temporary workers. Many firms in high-technology industries follow a chase strategy because product changes occur so rapidly that inventory held over any substantial amount of time can easily be rendered obsolete.

sustainability

A chase strategy can be executed by adjusting labor, subcontracting, or some mixture of the two. One approach is to hire and fire or lay off workers as needed. This, of course, involves the associated costs of hiring and terminating employees. It also might require higher investment in production plant/equipment, as enough capacity is needed to produce at the required rate in the highest-demand period. Consider the hypothetical retailer in Figure 13-3. Using a chase strategy, the retailer will need to have enough checkout lanes and equipment available to meet demand in the heaviest weeks, although much of

FIGURE 13-3 Retail Sales by Week

this equipment will be hardly used during the majority of the year. There are also ethical concerns involved in frequent changes to workforce size. In reality, most companies try to avoid continually hiring, firing, and laying off workers as much as possible given the impact of these practices on workers and their families and communities.

Managers can also use overtime to vary the production rate. Because workers generally earn premium wages for overtime work, the manufacturing cost per unit increases when this option is used. There is also a practical limit to the amount of overtime scheduled for employees. If too much overtime is used, worker burnout, safety risks, and/or quality problems can result.

A firm can use subcontracting to supplement output while maintaining a level workforce or production rate inside its own walls. Subcontractors are sometimes paid an amount that is higher than the per-unit cost of making the product internally. However, subcontracting allows firms to maintain less overhead and investment in fixed assets. There is some loss of control when subcontractors are used, with an increased possibility of problems related to product quality. One way firms manage this risk is by maintaining production of the high-value products or the components requiring the latest product or process technology and subcontracting the lower-value, more mature products or components.

Hybrid Strategies

Most firms implement a **mixed or hybrid strategy**. Such a strategy includes some elements of both level and chase strategies. For example, a company might use inventory to help smooth production during part of a season and then use workforce changes, including overtime and temporary workers, to supplement production during another part of the season. These mixed strategies tend to keep costs lower than pure strategies.

Regardless of the chosen strategy, aggregate production plans need to be revisited when circumstances change. The Get Real box concerning Canon describes how the unexpected downturn of the economy in 2008 affected that company's production plans.

mixed or hybrid strategy
A strategy that includes some elements of level production and some elements of chase production strategies.

global

GET REAL

Canon Struggles to Shrink Level of Digital Camera Inventory

The global economy's dizzying downturn brought an abrupt end to the digital camera boom. In the middle of the 2008 Christmas shopping season, digital camera makers cut prices deeply in a desperate effort to reduce their excess inventories. This was a dramatic reversal of fortunes for the industry. The global digital camera market expanded briskly for several years, with annual sales of about 126 million units in 2007, up 26 percent from the previous year. Digital camera makers had already manufactured products for the 2008 Christmas shopping season, based on projections that sales would continue growing at the same torrid pace as in the past several years. As a result, the industry found itself saddled with mountains of oversupply.

"The biggest waste for a manufacturer is inventory," said Canon Executive Vice President Toshizo Tanaka. His objective was to cut down on unnecessary spending as much as possible in the current tough environment." Even Canon's efficient and flexible supply chain management system failed to adjust production quickly enough to match the rapid collapse of final demand, allowing excessive output to build up.

Canon's sharp output reduction did not come without strain. Contract workers at the company's digital camera manufacturing unit in Oita Prefecture were laid off. Canon buys digital cameras from a contract manufacturer, which was forced to shed about 1,100 jobs when its order was slashed.

Source: Excerpted and adapted from "Canon Struggles to Shrink Level of Digital Camera Inventory," *Nikkei Weekly,* **Yoshiki Tanaka and Masamichi Hoshi, staff writers, January 5, 2009. © 2009 Nihon Keizai Shimbun, Inc. All rights reserved.**

© Kimimasa Myama/Bloomberg via Getty Images

CREATING AN AGGREGATE PRODUCTION PLAN

Suppose you have been given the responsibility of developing the six-month aggregate production plan at Sodas Galore, a manufacturer of soft drinks. Your company makes three types of soft drinks: regular, diet, and super-caffeinated. Fortunately, all three types are made using the same production process, and the costs related to switching between the three types are so minimal that they can be ignored. Thus, you can treat your problem as an aggregate planning exercise where the planning unit is cases of soft drinks, regardless of what types of drinks they are.

The S&OP team has developed a forecast of demand for the first six months of the year as shown in Table 13-3. The S&OP team has also provided you with the planning data shown in Table 13-4.

The material cost of a case of soda is the same regardless of whether it is produced in regular time or overtime. Also assume that Sodas Galore always plans to hold 5,000 cases of safety stock to meet unanticipated customer demand. Table 13-4 shows that at the beginning of January the only inventory on hand is safety stock.

Before comparing alternative aggregate production plans, it is necessary to convert some of the given data into common values for planning purposes. In this instance it is simplest to convert the labor costs into a cost per case. A worker earns $3,200 per month in regular wages (160 hours × $20.00/hour). This equates to a labor cost of $.80/case, since the monthly output per worker is 4,000 cases of soda ($3,200/4,000 cases). The overtime wage rate of $30.00 per hour is 1.5 times the regular wage rate; therefore a case of soda produced using overtime has a labor cost of $1.20 per case.

You have been asked to evaluate the cost of a level plan, a chase plan, and a hybrid plan in order to make a recommendation to the S&OP team.

TABLE 13-3   Monthly Demand at Sodas Galore

Month	Demand Forecast
January	24,000 cases
February	32,000 cases
March	32,000 cases
April	48,000 cases
May	60,000 cases
June	44,000 cases
Total Demand	240,000 cases
Average Monthly Demand	**40,000 cases**

TABLE 13-4   Sodas Galore Planning Data

Current workforce	8 workers
Average monthly output per worker	4,000 cases per month
Inventory holding cost	$.30 per case per month
Regular wage rate	$20.00 per hour
Regular production hours/month	160 hours
Overtime wage rate	$30.00 per hour
Hiring cost	$1,000 per worker
Subcontracting cost	$1.15 per case
Firing/layoff cost	$1,500 per worker
Beginning inventory	5,000 (all safety stock)

Level Production Plan

A level production plan (shown in equation 13.1) sets production at the average rate of demand, after adjusting for beginning inventory and desired ending inventory.

(13.1) $$P = (\Sigma D_i + EI - BI)/N$$

where

P = level production rate

D_i = demand in period i

EI = desired level of ending inventory

BI = beginning inventory

N = number of planning periods

Chase Plans

In a chase plan, the objective is to match production in each period to the demand in that period, thus avoiding the need to hold inventory. There are actually three options to accomplish this objective:

1. Produce all units internally by hiring workers in high-demand months and firing/laying off workers in low-demand months.

2. Produce internally the quantity required to meet demand in the lowest-demand month and use overtime production to meet demand in other months.

3. Produce internally the quantity required to meet demand in the lowest-demand month and use subcontracting to meet demand in other months.

student activity

Verify the ending inventory levels in Table 13-5 for the months after January.

EXAMPLE 13-1

The level production rate for the Sodas Galore plan is:

P = (24,000 + 32,000 + 32,000 + 48,000 + 60,000 + 44,000 + 5,000 − 5,000)/6
= 40,000 cases

In this case, the level production rate is equal to the average demand (40,000 cases) because the beginning and ending inventory levels are equal. In months when demand is less than average, the excess product produced will be stored in inventory. When demand is more than the monthly average, the inventory will be depleted to fill customer orders.

Next, you need to determine the number of workers needed to produce the required quantity each month. Because the average worker produces 4,000 cases in a month and the average demand is 40,000 cases, you will need a total of 10 production employees. Given that the current workforce is eight workers, you will need to hire two employees, resulting in hiring costs of $2,000.

Table 13-5 shows the impact of the level production plan on hiring and inventories. No firing, overtime, or subcontracting is required in the level plan.

Assuming that the inventory holding cost is incurred based on the number of cases of soda in inventory at the end of a month, the total inventory holding cost for the level production plan at Sodas Galore is 130,000 cases ($.30/case) = $39,000. The total production cost is 240,000 cases ($.80/case) = $192,000.

Total level plan cost = Regular production cost + Inventory cost
    + Hiring/firing cost
    = $192,000 + $39,000 + $2,000
    = $233,000

TABLE 13-5   Sodas Galore Level Production Plan

					Workers Required		
					Beginning inventory = 5,000; Beginning workers = 8		
Month	**Demand**	**Regular Production**	**Overtime or Subcontract Production**	**Ending Inventory***	**(4,000 cases/ worker)**	**Hire**	**Fire/ Lay Off**
Jan.	24,000	40,000	0	21,000	10	2	0
Feb.	32,000	40,000	0	29,000	10	0	0
March	32,000	40,000	0	37,000	10	0	0
April	48,000	40,000	0	29,000	10	0	0
May	60,000	40,000	0	9,000	10	0	0
June	44,000	40,000	0	5,000	10	0	0
Total	**240,000**	**240,000**	**0**	**130,000**		**2**	**0**

*Ending inventory in any month = Ending inventory in previous month + Current month production − Demand. For example, January ending inventory = 5,000 + 40,000 − 24,000 = 21,000.

EXAMPLE 13-2

Table 13-6 provides the data necessary to determine the total cost of option 1 at Sodas Galore, adjusting the size of the workforce to the amount of demand each month.

TABLE 13-6   Chase Plan: Adjust Workforce Size

					Workers Required		
					Beginning inventory = 5,000; Beginning workers = 8		
Month	**Demand**	**Regular Production**	**Overtime or Subcontract Production**	**Ending Inventory**	**(4,000 cases/ worker)**	**Hire**	**Fire/ Lay Off**
Jan.	24,000	24,000	0	5,000	6	0	2
Feb.	32,000	32,000	0	5,000	8	2	0
March	32,000	32,000	0	5,000	8	0	0
April	48,000	48,000	0	5,000	12	4	0
May	60,000	60,000	0	5,000	15	3	0
June	44,000	44,000	0	5,000	11	0	4
Total	**240,000**	**240,000**	**0**	**30,000**		**9**	**6**

The total cost of adjusting the workforce size to accomplish the chase plan is:

Total cost = Regular production cost + Inventory cost + Hiring/firing cost
= 240,000 cases ($.80) + 30,000 cases ($.30) + 9 hire ($1,000) +
6 fire/layoff ($1,500)
= $192,000 + $9,000 + $9,000 + $9,000
= $219,000

Notice that no inventory other than that required to meet current demand is created or used during the chase plan. The only carrying cost is due to the safety stock requirement.

To evaluate options 2 and 3 for the chase plan, we need to estimate the costs of maintaining a workforce large enough to meet the minimum monthly demand, supplementing output with either overtime or subcontracted labor in months when demand is greater than the minimum. These options are described in Example 13-3.

EXAMPLE 13-3

Table 13-7 below describes the options for supplementing capacity with either overtime or subcontract labor.

For this plan, it is assumed that the workforce is stable at six workers, which means that you must also include the cost of initially laying off or firing two workers (since the initial assumption was that eight workers are employed).

The total cost of a chase plan using overtime is:

Total cost = Regular production cost + cost + Inventory cost +
       Hiring/firing cost
       = 144,000 cases ($.80) + 96,000 cases ($1.20) + 30,000 cases ($.30)
       + 2 fire ($1,500)
       = $115,200 + $115,200 + $9,000 + $3,000 = $242,400

The total cost of a chase plan using a subcontractor to supplement regular production is:

Total cost = Regular production cost + Subcontract cost + Inventory cost +
       Hiring/firing cost
       = 144,000 cases ($.80) + 96,000 cases ($1.15) + 30,000 cases ($.30)
       + 2 fire ($1,500)
       = $115,200 + $110,400 + $9,000 + $3,000 = $237,600

TABLE 13-7   Chase Plan: Use Overtime or Subcontract Labor

Beginning inventory = 5,000; Beginning workers = 8

Month	Demand	Regular Production	Overtime or Subcontract Production	Ending Inventory	Workers Required (4,000 cases/ worker)	Hire	Fire/ Lay Off
Jan.	24,000	24,000	0	5,000	6	0	2
Feb.	32,000	24,000	8,000	5,000	6	0	0
March	32,000	24,000	8,000	5,000	6	0	0
April	48,000	24,000	24,000	5,000	6	0	0
May	60,000	24,000	36,000	5,000	6	0	0
June	44,000	24,000	20,000	5,000	6	0	0
Total	240,000	144,000	96,000	30,000		0	2

Hybrid Plans

Usually, the actual production plan combines some aspects of level production and building inventory with aspects of chase, or it varies the production rate during each period to match production and demand. In either case a company may face some of the constraints mentioned earlier or simply may have policies related to the use of personnel.

EXAMPLE 13-4

Suppose Sodas Galore has an established policy of maintaining a stable workforce. It is believed that constantly adjusting workforce size is not practical, and there is a desire to keep morale high among the permanent employees by allowing them the opportunity to earn some overtime pay. After much internal discussion, the company decides to maintain a permanent workforce of eight production workers. Therefore, in periods of relatively low demand, the company will allow inventory to build. In periods of higher demand, the inventory will be used to satisfy as much demand as possible and overtime or subcontract production will be used to satisfy remaining demand. The costs associated with this hybrid plan are presented in Table 13-8.

TABLE 13-8 Sodas Galore: A Hybrid Solution

Beginning inventory = 5,000; Beginning workers = 8

Month	Demand	Regular Production	Overtime or Subcontract Production	Ending Inventory	Workers Required (4,000 cases/ worker)	Hire	Fire/ Lay Off
Jan.	24,000	32,000	0	13,000	8	0	0
Feb.	32,000	32,000	0	13,000	8	0	0
March	32,000	32,000	0	13,000	8	0	0
April	48,000	32,000	8,000	5,000	8	0	0
May	60,000	32,000	28,000	5,000	8	0	0
June	44,000	32,000	12,000	5,000	8	0	0
Total	**240,000**	**192,000**	**48,000**	**54,000**		**0**	**0**

The total cost of this hybrid aggregate plan is:

Total cost = Regular production cost + Overtime cost + Inventory cost

= (192,000 cases)($.80/case) + (48,000 cases)($1.20/case) + 54,000 cases ($.30)

= $153,600 regular production + $57,600 overtime production + $16,200

= $227,400

Comparing Aggregate Production Plans

Table 13-9 compares the costs related to the five alternative aggregate plans for Sodas Galore. Given the various planning assumptions used in this exercise, the plan that results in the lowest total cost is the chase plan with monthly hiring and firing.

In evaluating these plans, we should consider the assumptions we have made. For example, we have assumed that newly hired workers are just as productive as experienced workers. For that matter, it was also assumed that workers are in fact available. Worker availability can be a serious issue for a firm that has a reputation of frequently hiring and then laying off employees. The overtime example assumes that the existing workforce is capable of working enough overtime hours to meet the total demand. There are often limitations to the amount of overtime that the workforce can handle. Moreover, workers may become less productive the longer they work. We also assumed that the operation has a make-to-stock (MTS) orientation. Since make-to-order (MTO) and assemble-to-order

TABLE 13-9 Comparison of Five Plans at Sodas Galore

Aggregate Plan	Reg. Prod. Cost	Overtime Cost	Subcontr. Cost	Inventory Cost	Hire Cost	Fire/Lay Off Cost	Total Cost
Level	$192,000	0	0	$39,000	$2,000		**$233,000**
Chase— Hire/Layoff	$192,000	0	0	$ 9000	$9,000	$9,000	**$219,000**
Chase— Overtime	$115,200	$115,200	0	$ 9000	0	$3,000	**$242,400**
Chase— Subcontract	$115,200	0	$110,400	$ 9000	0	$3,000	**$237,600**
Hybrid	$153,600	$ 57,600	0	$16,200	0	0	**$227,400**

(ATO) operations do not build finished goods inventory ahead of demand, they follow something closer to a chase strategy.

There are, of course, many other possible hybrid solutions to the Sodas Galore planning situation. It is likely that a hybrid solution exists that is less costly than the pure chase plan. Sometimes operations may employ more workers than are actually needed in low demand periods just to avoid other hidden costs or risks associated with hiring/firing, overtime, and/or subcontracting (such as labor strikes, quality problems, and so on). A manager could easily set up a spreadsheet on a personal computer in order to quickly evaluate many different scenarios. If used interactively, this methodology can be effective at generating a solution that all major functions can agree on. In addition, the interactive process allows managers to see the effect of the changes as they are made, which can uncover unrealistic cost assumptions and unworkable situations. This is especially important when all of the constraints haven't been identified up front. Dialogue between managers and eventual agreement on a good production plan could actually be better than an optimal plan that is forced on everyone.

Sophisticated modeling techniques such as linear programming, integer programming, and others can be applied to the aggregate production planning process. These techniques require precise specification of assumptions, constraints, costs, and objectives in a mathematical format. For those who are interested in the more sophisticated models, the supplement to this text demonstrates an optimal solution using linear programming and spreadsheet modeling.

AGGREGATE PLANNING FOR SERVICE INDUSTRIES

As mentioned earlier, S&OP and aggregate planning are just as critical in service industries as in manufacturing. In some ways such planning is even more critical because there is no ability to build inventory in anticipation of demand. When supply and demand do not match, the impact is almost always on human resources.

Yield Management

Because of the inability to inventory demand, service companies often make extensive use of the demand management tactics discussed in Chapter 12. Consider, for example, how airlines and hotels change prices almost constantly in an attempt to fill flights or rooms. These companies use a process called **yield management**, which adjusts prices as demand occurs (or does not occur) for a service (such as seats on a specific scheduled flight or hotel rooms for a specific night).

The purpose of yield management is to shape demand in a way that yields greater revenues or profits. For example, in Michigan, there is a wonderful vacation spot known as

yield management A process that adjusts prices as demand for a service occurs (or does not occur).

Mackinac Island, home of the Grand Hotel. As you might expect, demand for hotel rooms on the island is greatest during the summer. Consequently, room rates fall in September and remain low until the end of May. Airlines routinely practice yield management by adjusting prices and travel restrictions to maximize revenues on each flight. Their computer systems periodically compare the expected revenue of offering a seat on a flight at the normal fare against the expected revenue from offering it at a discount. As the date of the flight approaches, the airline increases the ticket's price.

Yield management can involve very sophisticated mathematical models that simulate customer behaviors under different scenarios. Complex computer programs have been developed in certain industries to continuously analyze demand versus available capacity and make the price adjustments. Effective yield management requires extensive analysis of past demand so that typical demand patterns and trends are clear. It also requires continuous tracking of actual demand for the service. The Get Real box on yield management in the hotel industry provides more insight into this practice.

GET REAL

Yield Management in the Hotel Industry

Hotels pose an interesting problem when it comes to maximizing revenue. Why? Because fundamentally, like any service, they are a perishable product. You cannot store an unused hotel room until it is needed; if you have an empty hotel room that is unused, then it loses value and revenue every day that it is unsold. So how you deal with this challenge?

In the past, the price was to offer discounts to encourage people to come to your hotel or to extend their stays. Yet, today, we realize that such approaches are often ineffective. They are not linked to the customer's preference; they treat every customer as being the same. How do we deal with this challenge? The answer is a new development—yield management.

Yield management (also called *revenue management*) provides a means to maximize revenue from a perishable, fixed product such as a hotel or an airline. Yield management is a variable pricing strategy that is based on understanding, anticipating, and influencing customer behavior to maximize revenue from such assets. It seeks to "sell" the product to the "right" customer at the right time for the right price.

In principle, yield management tactics are fairly straightforward. In practice, applying yield management is complex. It is also multi-disciplinary in that it blends elements of market, operations, supply chain, and financial management. Yield management recognizes that what is important to one customer is not necessarily important to another. It also recognizes that some activities cannot be eliminated or temporarily stopped—a pool cannot be shut down because only a handful of guests use it; front desks must be staffed around the clock because that is what most customers expect.

In the hotel industry, yield management seeks to offer those benefits that specific customers want in order to encourage them to book a room or extend the length of their stay. For example, costs associated with a hotel's breakfast buffet, including food preparation and waste disposal, will exist whether the hotel is fully or sparsely occupied on any given day. A "free breakfast" offering

© Jupiterimages/Getty Images

during slow periods can encourage more guests to stay at your hotel, improving overall revenue with only a marginal effect on food and beverage costs. Likewise, offering complimentary phone and Internet use to corporate users as part of the negotiated rate is another way of offering certain customer segments with access to assets that they value but that are essentially fixed costs for the hotel. Thus, hotels are now better able to target and lure in specific customers—and as a result, the customers and the hotel both win!

Source: Excerpted from S. Sampson, "Yield Management in 2009: How to Keep Your Hotel Up and Running in a Downturn," *Hospitality Trends,* **March 10, 2009. Copyright (c) 2009 Shannon Sampson. Reprinted with permission.**

An Example of a Service Aggregate Plan

LO13-6 Explain the differences in aggregate planning in services versus manufacturing industries.

Ultimately, most service businesses have to develop aggregate plans based on human resource requirements. The process is not greatly different from that already discussed, except that there is no inventory to be considered. Instead, demand for services is often stated in terms of the amount of service labor required rather than the amount of product required.

EXAMPLE 13-5

Suppose Nile Inc., an Internet retailer, needs to develop an aggregate plan for its warehouse operation. Demand in the warehouse is stated in terms of the number of labor hours required each quarter to pick, pack, and ship customers' orders. Because the business is seasonal, demand is expected to be as follows:

Quarter 1: 15,000 labor hours
Quarter 2: 12,000 labor hours
Quarter 3: 10,000 labor hours
Quarter 4: 18,000 labor hours

Full-time employees work 500 hours per quarter, and their total compensation (including benefits) is $10.00 per hour. A worker can work overtime, up to a maximum of 100 hours per quarter, for $15.00 per hour. If, however, a full-time employee is not busy for 500 hours, the employee is still paid for those hours.

Part-time workers can be hired as needed, as long as each works no more than 400 hours per quarter (there is no minimum requirement of hours for a part-time employee). Part-time workers earn $8.00 per hour. The company currently employs 20 workers. The hiring and firing cost for a part-time employee is $1,000 for each hire or fire.

In this case, a level plan would require maintaining a stable workforce, meaning that the number of full-time employees must be able to fulfill the maximum demand. The level plan is shown in Table 13-10. Because the maximum number of hours a full-time employee can work is 600 hours per quarter (regular 500 hours plus 100 overtime hours), the level number of workers required is 18,000 hours maximum/600 = 30 workers. Keep in mind that these 30 workers will have 15,000 hours of regular time pay each month regardless of the number of hours actually worked. A total of 10 workers must be hired immediately to meet the first quarter demand.

Cost of level plan = Regular pay + Overtime pay + Hiring cost
   = (60,000 hours) ($10.00/hour) + (3,000 hours) ($15.00/hour)
      + 10($1,000)
   = $655,000

TABLE 13-10   Level Plan for Nile Inc.

Quarter	Demand (hours)	Regular Hours Paid	Overtime Hours Paid	Number of Hires
1	15,000	15,000	0	10
2	12,000	15,000	0	0
3	10,000	15,000	0	0
4	18,000	15,000	3,000	0
Total		**60,000**	**3,000**	**10**

(continued)

(continued)

There are several possible variations on a chase plan for Nile Inc. We will evaluate a pure chase plan. In this instance, the permanent workforce will be large enough to only meet the minimum demand requirement of 10,000 hours, working the regular hours (500 hours). Thus, the permanent workforce is 20 workers. This results in a maximum of 2,000 hours of overtime available. The permanent workforce will always work the maximum possible before part-time workers are used. Finally, since you can't hire part of a person, when part-timers are hired, you must incur the full hiring cost even though the person may not work the maximum of 400 hours that part-timers are allowed to work. Table 13-11 shows the results of this plan.

Cost of plan = Regular pay + Overtime pay + Part-time pay + Hire/fire costs
= (40,000 hours)($10.00) + (6,000 hours)($15.00) + (9,000)($8.00)
+ (31 hire/fire)($1,000)
= $593,000

TABLE 13-11   Chase Plan for Nile Inc.

Quarter	Demand	Regular Hours Paid	Overtime Hours Paid	Part-Time Hours	Part-Time Workers Needed	Hire	Fire
1	15,000	10,000	2,000	3,000	7.5 = 8	8	0
2	12,000	10,000	2,000	0	0	0	8
3	10,000	10,000	0	0	0	0	0
4	18,000	10,000	2,000	6,000	15	15	0
Total		40,000	6,000	9,000		23	8

activity

Rework the Nile Inc. chase plan assuming that the permanent workforce is 17 workers. How does your answer differ from the chase plan illustrated in Table 13-11?

As in the planning for Sodas Galore, there are again many alternatives that might be considered for Nile Inc., depending upon assumptions concerning how the labor force might actually be utilized. For example, the chase plan would be different if Nile Inc. were to decide that the permanent workforce only needs to be large enough to meet minimum demand by working maximum hours (in this case, 600 total hours). Thus, the permanent workforce would consist of only 10,000 hours/600 = 16.67, or rounded up, 17 workers. All other aspects of the plan would be different from those shown.

CHAPTER SUMMARY

This chapter has dealt with the sales and operations planning process, with specific emphasis on aggregate production planning. The major issues discussed in the chapter were as follows:

1. All firms experience difficulty in balancing supply and demand.
2. Sales and operations planning is a cross-functional process that brings representatives from sales, marketing, manufacturing, purchasing, and logistics together to develop plans for most efficiently and effectively meeting expected customer demand.

3. The sales and operations planning process results in two plans: a sales plan, which attempts to influence demand to match supply, and an aggregate production plan (APP), which attempts to match supply to demand.

4. Sales and operations planning should be a dynamic process conducted frequently during the year to update plans as new information becomes available.

5. The relevant costs in aggregate production planning are inventory holding cost, regular production cost, overtime cost, temporary workforce cost, firing/layoff cost, backorder/lost sales cost, and subcontracting cost.

6. The three basic aggregate production strategies are level production, chase, and mixed strategies. The alternatives should be compared to determine which one provides the lowest total cost.

7. Service industries have aggregate planning approaches similar to manufacturing. The major difference is that there is no inventory to consider.

KEY TERMS

aggregate production plan   448

chase strategy   449

level production strategy   449

mixed or hybrid strategy   451

rolling planning horizons   447

sales and operations planning (S&OP)   444

yield management   457

DISCUSSION QUESTIONS

1. What is the value of the S&OP process to an organization? Why should it be a dynamic process rather than a one-time annual event?

2. Explain in your own words the typical differences in objectives for production managers and sales managers.

3. Do you think chase strategies might be more appropriate in some industries than in others? Give some examples and explain why.

4. What are the key cost advantages of a level production strategy over a chase strategy? What are the key cost advantages of a chase strategy over a level production strategy?

5. Suppose your firm is using a level production planning approach to manage seasonal demand. Your production manager is evaluated on lowest production cost but the logistics manager is evaluated on the amount of inventory the firm holds. Explain the issues.

6. Explain why the following is not necessarily a true statement: "If a company is chasing demand, then it is overinvesting in balance sheet assets because inventories will be high."

7. If most aggregate production planning problems include assumptions and ignore many needs of the company that are difficult to quantify, then what is the benefit of the process?

8. In most companies that are considered to be successful users of the S&OP process, the resulting plans and commitments are treated, essentially, as "quasi-contracts." That is, the agreement reached between the various parties cannot be unilaterally broken or changed by any party. To change the schedule requirements participation of all the parties. They must agree to the changes before they can be implemented. What are the implications of a position as it pertains to how the firm and its functional areas deal with changes?

PROBLEM

Neal Industries manufactures blue jeans for the teen market. The S&OP team has agreed upon a demand forecast for the following year, as shown below. Given the planning information, determine the cost of a level production plan and a plan to chase demand by adjusting the size of the workforce each month. The company begins with 1,000,000 jeans in safety stock and desires to maintain this level consistently (and end with this level).

Quarter	Demand
1	6,000,000
2	9,000,000
3	15,000,000
4	10,000,000

Current workforce	400 workers
Average output per worker	20,000 jeans per quarter
Inventory holding cost	$.10/pair per quarter
Regular wage rate	$16.00 per hour
Regular production hours	500 hours per quarter
Hiring cost	$300 per worker
Firing/layoff cost	$200 per worker
Beginning inventory	1,000,0000

Solution

The total demand for the year is 40,000,000 jeans. Therefore, the average demand per quarter is 10,000,000 jeans, and 10,000,000 jeans is the level production rate.

The average worker produces 20,000 jeans per quarter. Therefore the current workforce can produce 8,000,000 jeans per quarter. To produce 10,000,000 per quarter using a level production plan will require the addition of 100 workers (2,000,000 jeans/20,000 jeans per worker).

An average worker earns $8,000 per quarter (500 hours × $16.00 per hour) and produces 20,000 jeans. Therefore, the regular production (labor) cost is $0.40 per unit.

Beginning Workers = 400 Beginning Inventory = 1,000,000						
Quarter	Demand	Production	Ending Inventory	Workers Required	Hire	Fire
1	6,000,000	10,000,000	5,000,000	500	100	0
2	9,000,000	10,000,000	6,000,000	500	0	0
3	15,000,000	10,000,000	1,000,000	500	0	0
4	10,000,000	10,000,000	1,000,000	500	0	0
Total	40,000,000	40,000,000	13,000,000		100	0

The total cost of the level production plan for Neal Industries is $0.40/unit (40,000,000 jeans) + $0.10/unit (13,000,000 jeans) + 100 hires ($300) = $16,000,000 + $1,300,000 + $30,000 = $17,330,000.

A plan to chase demand has the following results:

Quarter	Demand	Production	Ending Inventory	Workers Required	Hire	Fire/ Lay Off
1	6,000,000	6,000,000	1,000,000	300		100
2	9,000,000	9,000,000	1,000,000	450	150	0
3	15,000,000	15,000,000	1,000,000	750	300	0
4	10,000,000	10,000,000	1,000,000	500		250
Total	40,000,000	40,000,000	4,000,000		450	350

The total cost of this plan is:

$0.40/unit (40,000,000 jeans) + $0.10/unit (4,000,000 jeans) + 450 hires ($300) + 350 fires (200) = $16,000,000 + $400,000 + $135,000 + $70,000 = $16,605,000

The level production plan costs $725,000 more than this chase plan.

PROBLEMS

1. For the Sodas Galore problem discussed in the chapter, assume that employees negotiate an increase in the regular production wage rate to $24.00 per hour and $36.00 per hour for overtime. Rework all aspects of the problem using the new wage rates.

2. Using the existing data in the solved problem (Neal Industries), assume that the overtime production wage rate is $24.00 per hour. Compute the cost of a chase plan using a stable workforce of 300 workers.

3. The Johnson Company manufactures expensive medical diagnostic equipment. It plans to meet all of its projected demand (given below for the next year by quarter). The firm plans to use a constant production rate of 300 units/quarter. Production costs are $20,000 per unit and holding costs are $2,000 per quarter per unit.

Quarter	1	2	3	4
Demand	200	300	400	300

   What is the cost of this production plan?

4. The current aggregate demand requirements for a firm are shown below for the next six months:

Month	May	June	July	Aug	Sept	Oct
Demand	120	100	100	100	130	150

   The firm always plans to meet all demand. The firm currently has 120 workers capable of producing 120 units in a month (1 unit/worker). The workforce can be increased (at a cost of $500 per worker) or decreased (at a cost of $1,000 per worker). Inventory holding cost is $100 per unit per month. The firm currently has 40 units of inventory on hand, and it would like to have 40 units available at the end of each month. Regular production cost is $3,000 per unit.

   a. What should the aggregate plan be if the inventory holding cost is to be minimized?
   b. What is the cost of this plan?

5. A firm must plan production for the next six months. Each unit costs $250 to produce and has an inventory holding cost of $10 per unit per month based on ending inventory levels. The cost to hire a worker is $100, and the cost to fire a worker is $200 per worker. Each worker produces 10 units per month. There are 20 persons on the payroll

at the beginning of the first month. The company currently has 100 units of inventory in stock, and it wants to hold these as safety stock.

Month	1	2	3	4	5	6
Demand	300	300	300	300	400	500

    a. From the information given above, what level production rate will meet demand for the next six months?

    b. Given the production rate determined in (a), what is the maximum end-of-period inventory experienced at some time during the six months? What is the cost of a level production plan?

    c. From the information given above, what is the total cost of a chase (hire and fire only) production plan?

6. JokersRWild makes playing cards in several different styles, but a "standard" deck of cards is used for planning purposes. The average worker at JokersRWild can make 10,000 decks of cards per month at a cost of $1.00 per deck during regular production and $1.30 during overtime. The company currently employs 25 workers. Experience shows that it costs $500 to hire a worker and $500 to fire a worker. Inventory carrying cost is $.25 per deck per month. Given the following demand estimate, develop a six-month production plan based on (a) level production, (b) chase using overtime (no workers will be fired and inventory increases if necessary), and (c) chase by changing workforce level. The beginning inventory is 50,000, and at least that amount is desired each month.

Month	January	February	March	April	May	June
Demand	200,000	150,000	200,000	400,000	550,000	250,000

7. Trexoid Inc. makes a popular video game console. Demand varies each month, with highest demand coming in the last quarter of the year. Regular production costs are $120 per unit and inventory carrying cost is $5 per unit per quarter. Overtime production cost is $150 per unit. Assume that the 10 current Trexoid employees can produce 50,000 units per quarter in regular production and can work enough overtime hours to produce the amount required if a chase plan is employed. On the other hand, hiring cost is $5,000 per employee and firing cost is $10,000 per employee. Trexoid currently has zero inventory on hand, and it would like to have zero inventories at the end of the year. Forecasted demand is as follows:

Quarter 1	30,000 units
Quarter 2	20,000 units
Quarter 3	70,000 units
Quarter 4	120,000 units

What would you suggest to Trexoid management?

8. Appliances Inc. is preparing an aggregate production plan for washers for the next four months. The company's expected monthly demand is given below in the chart. The company will have 500 washers in inventory at the beginning of the month and desires to maintain at least that number at the end of each month. Below are other critical data:

Production cost per unit = $300

Inventory carrying cost per month per unit = $50 (based on ending month inventory)

Hiring cost per worker = $1,000

Firing cost per worker = $2,000

Beginning number of workers = 10

Each worker can produce 100 units per month.

Level Plan

Month	Demand	Regular Production	Ending Inventory	Workers Required	Hire	Fire
1	4,000					
2	6,000					
3	3,000					
4	7,000					
Total	20,000					

Chase Plan

Month	Demand	Regular Production	Ending Inventory	Workers Required	Hire	Fire
1	4,000					
2	6,000					
3	3,000					
4	7,000					
Total	20,000					

Complete the tables and determine the cost of the two plans.

9. Togo makes riding lawn mowers and tractors. The company's expected quarterly demand is given below in the chart. The company will have 300 mowers in inventory at the beginning of the quarter and desires to maintain at least that number at the end of each quarter. Other critical data include:

Production cost per unit = $200
Inventory carrying cost per quarter per unit = $60 (based on ending quarter inventory)
Hiring cost per worker = $500
Firing cost per worker = $750
Beginning number of workers = 40

Each worker can produce 100 units per quarter.

Level Plan

Quarter	Demand	Regular Production	Ending Inventory	Workers Required	Hire	Fire
1	5,000					
2	9,000					
3	7,000					
4	9,000					
Total	30,000					

Chase Plan

Quarter	Demand	Regular Production	Ending Inventory	Workers Required	Hire	Fire
1	5,000					
2	9,000					
3	7,000					
4	9,000					
Total	30,000					

Complete the tables and calculate the cost of the two plans.

10. Jones Inc. is preparing an aggregate production plan for next year. The company expects demand to be 1,000 units in quarter 1; 2,000 units in quarter 2; 4,000 units in quarter 3; and 3,000 units in quarter 4. The company will have 100 units in inventory at the beginning of the year and desires to maintain at least that number at the end of each quarter as safety stock. Other information includes:

Regular production labor cost = $100 per unit
Overtime production cost per unit = $150
Inventory carrying cost = $25/unit/quarter based on quarter-ending inventory
Hiring cost = $2,000 per worker
Firing/layoff cost = $3,000 per worker
Beginning number of workers = 15
Each worker can produce 100 units per quarter.

   a. What is the total cost of a level plan?
   b. What is the total cost of a chase plan utilizing hiring and firing?
   c. Suppose Jones management is reluctant to constantly change the workforce by hiring and firing. The company decides to hire seven additional workers at the beginning of the year. The company will build inventory in low-demand months and use it in high-demand months. In addition, if necessary, overtime will be used to meet demand requirements if there is not sufficient inventory available. What is the total cost of this plan?

11. Dale's Dance Studio currently has three full-time instructors who are each paid $2,500 per month. A dance instructor can work a maximum of only 100 hours per month because instruction normally takes place at night. Instructors receive $2,500 even if they do not work 100 hours, however. Part-time instructors can be hired at a cost of $40 per hour. Dale's has forecasted that demand for the next six months will be as follows:

Month	1	2	3	4	5	6
Hours	380	280	450	420	520	390

   Should Dale hire more full-time instructors or rely on part-time instructors to meet demand?

12. Make-Believe-You is a company that produces "cosplay" costumes for those people who want to live like their favorite action heroes. Currently, out of its catalog of hundreds of costumes, Make-Believe-You has identified six costumes that are demanded on a regular basis (with the following traits) and that are made in the same system:

Model	# Hours	Price	% of Sales
Harley Quinn	4.2	285	32
Guardians of the Galaxy – Star Lord	4.9	345	21
Star War – Storm trooper	5.1	395	17
Lord of the Rings – Gandalf	5.2	425	14
Batman - Dark Knight	5.4	525	10
Iron Man – from Iron Man 3/Avengers	5.8	725	6

Make-Believe-You also has developed the following agreed-upon forecast for overall demand:

Month	Predicted Demand (aggregate units)
January	220
February	280
March	460
April	190
May	310
June	145
July	110
August	225

Management has decided that it would like to begin with 200 units at the end of December and end with 100 units on hand at the end of August.

a. Using these data, identify the monthly production levels using a chase strategy.

b. Using the data in your solution to the previous question, develop an aggregate plan using a constant workforce. (*Hint:* Convert the individual units into aggregate units using a summed weighted approach. For example, Iron Man contributes 5.8*.06 = 0.35 hours of demand for capacity, while Harley Quinn contributes 4.2*.32 = 1.34 hours of demand for capacity. Use the same approach for each item to determine the overall aggregate demand for capacity.)

c. Review your answers to the previous questions.

1. Under what conditions would you go with a chase strategy even though the costs might be lower with a level strategy?

2. What actions can you introduce to improve the quality of your aggregate planning?

CASE

Med-Chem Products: Hospital Division

The following case is based on one of the coauthor's experiences with an actual company and its management.

Fiona Richey knew that she had been given the opportunity of a lifetime. She had just been hired to be an internal troubleshooter and consultant by the Hospital Division of Med-Chem Products. This was quite a feat. After all, she had graduated about four years ago with an undergraduate degree in Operations Management and Logistics from a large midwestern university. During that time, she had developed a reputation for being a good team player, a creative thinker, and someone who got things done quickly (and correctly). That was one of the major reasons that Med-Chem had hired her. Originally, she had been working for a supplier to Med-Chem. About six months ago, she was approached by one of the managers of Med-Chem, with a very attractive job offer.

Even though she had been at Med-Chem for only four weeks, she had begun to get a feel for the division,

its products, its operating plans and procedures, and its problems. During this time, she had not been given any major projects. Rather, she was told to get to know people and to look around. As a result, she was ready and eager when Todd Hall, the division director, called her and gave her the first real assignment, and what an assignment. At this time, over coffee, Todd told Fiona that he had been concerned about the current planning system that was in place. He seemed to be finding out about problems after they occurred. The marketing and operations groups within the division always seemed to be making after-the-fact corrections to the plans that they each had generated. More important, no one in the division seemed to feel any responsibility for the plans. Whenever things went wrong, everyone took the position of blaming everyone else. What Todd wanted Fiona to do was twofold: he wanted her to review the current system and to prepare a critique of it. In addition, he wanted her to recommend changes. Fiona knew that she had to do well on this project.

The Hospital Division of Med-Chem

Med-Chem was a Fortune 100 drug and chemical manufacturer, headquartered in Germany and with divisions and plants located worldwide. The Hospital Division was a division of this company. In the United States, it was headquartered in Atlanta, Georgia. This division manufactured a line of pharmaceuticals and testing equipment for use in hospitals, emergency rooms, nursing homes, and so on. Within this division, there were two major groups: marketing and operations.

Marketing was responsible for three major activities: sales, distribution, and forecasting. Of these three, forecasting was considered to be the most important. The products offered by this division were essentially make-to-stock. As a result, it was important that the right amounts be in stock at any point in time. As the marketing people had told Fiona, forecasting was a nightmare task. First, Med-Chem had a very broad product line, consisting of some 5,000 items. In addition, not all of the products were equally important. The group had adopted the product model developed by the Boston Consulting Group when describing the products. According to this model, the various products could be assigned to one of four categories. The first category was that of a *star*. A star product was one that was seen as being important. A product could be important because of a high contribution margin, its unique position in the marketplace, or because it helped to enhance the reputation of the division (for being a leader in this product). These were products that management always wanted to ensure were delivered at or near 100 percent of actual demand. About 10 percent of the products fell into this category. Next came the *cash cows*. These products, about 35 percent of the current catalog, were highly stable, highly predictable in nature. They generated a very good revenue stream. Management never wanted to stock out of these items. The third group was comprised of the *question marks* (25 percent). In general, these were new products or ones that had not yet established their value in the marketplace. The final category, *dogs*, were products that were considered low performers. Typically, such product lines were old, were positioned in segments where the competition was severe, had very low contribution margins, or were not unique (i.e., there were a number of equally effective generic substitutes available). Many dogs were kept because marketing felt that they helped to round out Med-Chem's product offerings. For all four groups, marketing rarely informed operations of large orders by major customers or its attempts to stimulate ordering through special promotions or discounts. Marketing was allowed to change the forecasts at any point, up to and including the point at which the products were scheduled to be shipped.

Operations was responsible for building the products required by marketing. At present, operations personnel viewed this as a major problem because of marketing's constant modifications to the forecasts and the lack of any data concerning actual sales occurring in the marketplace. After talking with some of the plant managers, Fiona knew that their primary objective was to minimize the total production cost, including the cost of holding inventory. With the frequent production changes dictated by changes in the forecasts, operations personnel found themselves expediting orders and undertaking dramatic production changes. If left alone, Fiona knew that operations would schedule operations to reduce cost.

Med-Chem's Current Planning System

The current system at Med-Chem had been in place for as long as anyone could remember. This system did not differentiate between the performance of marketing and the performance of operations. Everyone agreed that all the information needed by management to reduce the problems existed but no one really knew how to proceed. As Todd told Fiona before she left, there had to be a better way of planning at Med-Chem.

Questions

1. Describe the current system in use as it applies to the operations personnel and marketing personnel. To what extent does this system help or hinder Med-Chem's ability to achieve its objectives? Why?

2. For marketing and operations, what are the critical activities that they must do well for Med-Chem to be successful in the marketplace?

3. What general recommendations would you make to Todd regarding the current situation?

CASE

Fitch and Hughes, P.C.

Fitch and Hughes, P.C., is a small law firm specializing in family law, wills, estates, and trusts. The firm, begun in 1980 by Jason Fitch and George Hughes, currently has three attorneys who are shareholders and three associate attorneys. The firm is managed by George Hughes since the retirement of his cofounder of the firm, Jason Fitch.

In early December, Hughes was thinking about the firm's workload for the first half of next year.

Given the current client load and projections for the next six months, Hughes estimated the number of billable hours for the firm is as follows:

Month	Hours
Jan.	1,100
Feb.	1,150
Mar.	1,450
Apr.	1,450
May	1,250
June	1,200

The three attorneys who are shareholders each receive a monthly salary of $10,500, while the associate attorneys are paid $7,000 each month. The three shareholders, of course, also receive additional compensation at the end of each year when the firm's profits are distributed to them based on their proportionate shareholdings.

Under normal circumstances, each of the six attorneys can bill a total of 175 hours per month. When any attorney bills more than 175 hours, he or she receives additional compensation of $80 per hour for associate attorneys or $120 per hour for the shareholders. The four shareholders (one of whom was Hughes) have agreed that no attorney can bill more than 225 hours per month. In the interest of

fairness, they also have decided that any "overtime" work required would be divided equally among all attorneys. This arrangement would allow each attorney the opportunity to increase income while preventing a few from benefiting excessively over the others.

While Jason Fitch does not really want to work any longer, he has agreed that he would be willing to help out in extreme situations at a rate of $150 per hour, as long as he is guaranteed a minimum of 30 hours during any single month. The firm could, of course, hire an additional associate attorney at the same salary as the current associates. If an additional attorney is hired, Hughes wants to do so by the beginning of the year so that the new attorney is familiarized with the firm as soon as possible. He is strongly opposed to letting any attorney go during the six-month period.

Questions

1. Determine the cost of a plan which uses only overtime and the services of Jason Fitch.

2. Suppose clients pay the same hourly rate regardless of which attorney bills the hours, and Hughes is interested in determining the lowest-cost plan for the firm. What should Hughes do, given the current policies of the firm?

3. What other considerations might influence the plan that Hughes develops?

SELECTED READINGS & INTERNET SITES

Ball, B. *Sales and Operations Planning: A Global Comparison.* (Aberdeen Group), January 2013 (**http://www.aberdeen.com/assets/report-preview/7854-RA-sales-operations-planning.pdf**).

Bower, P. "How the S&OP Process Creates Value in the Supply Chain." *The Journal of Business Forecasting* 25, no. 2 (Summer 2006), pp. 20–32.

Fisher, M. L.; J. H. Hammond; W. Obermeyer; and A. Raman. "Making Supply Meet Demand in an Uncertain World." *Harvard Business Review* 72, no. 3 (May–June 1994), pp. 83–93.

Lapide, L. "S&OP: The Linchpin Planning Process." *Supply Chain Management Review* 15, no. 6 (2011), pp. 4–5.

Muzumdar, M., and J. Fontanella. "The Secrets to S&OP Success." *Supply Chain Management Review* 10, no. 2 (April 2006), pp. 34–41.

Smith, L., J. C. Andraski, and S. E. Fawcett. "Integrated Business Planning: A Roadmap to Linking S&OP and CPFR." *The Journal of Business Forecasting* 29, no. 4 (2010), pp. 4, 7, 9–13.

Smith, M. "Sales and Operations Planning: Making BPM Work." *Business Performance Management Magazine,* March 2008, pp. 4–6, 8, 10.

Spiegel, R. "Tallying the Benefits of S&OP." *Supply Chain Management Review* 15, no. 3 (2011), pp. 54–56.

More case studies on sales and operations planning can be found at the following websites:

Supply Chain Brain
www.supplychainbrain.com

Supply Chain Management Review
www.scmr.com

14

Materials and Resource Requirements Planning

LEARNING OBJECTIVES

After studying this chapter, you should be able to:

LO14-1 Explain the materials requirements planning (MRP) process and when it should be used.

LO14-2 Conduct MRP planning for items at multiple levels in the bill of materials (BOM).

LO14-3 Explain how distribution requirements planning (DRP) is used.

LO14-4 Conduct capacity requirements planning (CRP) using an infinite loading approach.

LO14-5 Describe how materials requirements and resource planning functions work together within an enterprise resource planning (ERP) system.

LO14-6 Explain how advanced planning and scheduling (APS) systems improve the requirements and resource planning processes.

© Matthew Mead/AP Images

Do you want a home-cooked meal but just do not have the time to search through recipes and go grocery shopping? Blue Apron's co-founders, Matt Salzberg, Illia Papas, and Matt Wadiak, recognized this as a business opportunity. In 2012, they started a food-tech business that delivers recipes and premeasured seasonal ingredients directly to consumers in a refrigerated box. Consumers have everything they need to make meals such as "sumac-spiced steak and honeynut squash with pickled onion and apple-walnut salad." By 2015, Blue Apron was sourcing, assembling, and delivering five million meals a month to its subscription customers.

Requirements planning is an essential ingredient in Blue Apron's success. Meals are planned months in advance, considering the seasonal crops that will be available at the best price. Because Blue Apron sources ingredients directly from suppliers and small businesses, freshness and quality are high. Using software, operations planners predict demand based on the number of subscribers and historical data about how many will cancel an order in any week.

Planning is not easy given that the company's creative recipes are never used twice in a year. However, limiting all customers to a predetermined menu helps to simplify the planning process. Complexity has increased with the addition of wine with meals, and the company may offer customers more choices in the future. Based on production plans, meals are assembled in distribution centers in New Jersey, Texas, and California and shipped to customers all around the country, perhaps even to your front door.[1]

---

[1] Adapted from A. Konrad, "Blue Apron's Got Big Plans for Dinner—But So Do Its Hungry Rivals," *Forbes*, Oct. 14, 2015. http://www.forbes.com/sites/alexkonrad/2015/10/14/inside-blue-apron-and-the-meal-kit-rush/ and https://www.blueapron.com/

In a supply chain, managers make plans at many levels to ensure the right materials and resources are available to make and deliver the products that customers want at the right price. For example, Blue Apron relies upon its requirements planning process to make sure it has the right quantities of the right fresh ingredients to fill customer orders, while minimizing the inventory costs due to spoilage. Chapter 13 described the sales and operations planning process and explained how to develop aggregate production plans. This chapter explains how aggregate production plans are translated into operational level production and distribution plans for individual products. Specifically we discuss three requirements planning processes: materials requirements planning (MRP), distribution requirements planning (DRP), and capacity requirements planning (CRP).

- MRP calculates when and how much of raw materials, parts, and subassemblies are needed for production.
- DRP plans when and how to supply finished goods at the right time to the right places in the distribution system.
- CRP determines if sufficient resources (labor, equipment, space, suppliers) are available when needed for production.

These planning processes share information with customers and suppliers for their own planning processes. It can be difficult to coordinate planning across the supply chain. Consider a company such as Conair, which makes a wide variety of health and beauty products such as hair dryers. Many different retailers sell Conair's products, including Bed Bath & Beyond, Best Buy, Walmart, Kohl's, Amazon.com, and Conair's own online store. Conair combines information gathered from all its retailers and uses it to develop production plans. To assemble its products, Conair purchases parts and subassemblies from many different suppliers, which purchase from other companies that are their suppliers. All this complexity makes supply chain coordination and planning a very important and challenging process.

Planning processes differ for independent demand and for dependent demand. You will recall from Chapter 7 that **independent demand** is created by customers; it includes the demand for finished products (for example hair dryers) and replacement parts. **Dependent demand** is *dependent* on decisions made by internal operations managers and is usually derived from demand for other items. After managers decide how many finished products to make in a given period, they calculate the dependent demand quantities for materials and resources needed to make those products. The hair dryer's heating element and fan are examples of dependent demand items; their demand depends on the production schedule set for hair dryers. When used for dependent demand, inventory management approaches such as reorder point and periodic review (discussed in Chapter 7) can lead to high inventory costs and poor customer service. These approaches are more appropriate for independent demand items.

Consider the following example. When you order a large pepperoni pizza for delivery, this creates independent demand for the pizza shop. A pizza ordered by one customer is independent of an order placed by another. The shop's manager does not know exactly how many pepperoni pizzas will be ordered on any day, but she can develop and use a forecast to decide how many pizzas she will plan to produce. From this production plan, the manager calculates dependent demand for the dough, sauce, pepperoni, cheese, and a pizza box. She also can determine how many cooks, ovens, delivery drivers, and other resources will be required. In this way, dependent demand for materials and resources is calculated directly from actual orders and forecasts.

The following sections explore dependent demand operational planning processes. In a supply chain, the distribution requirements planning (DRP) process is downstream from the manufacturer, closer to the end consumer (see Figure 14-1), and can be an input into the materials requirements planning (MRP) process. However, to illustrate the planning logic that is similar in both MRP and DRP, we will start with a discussion of MRP and then describe DRP, followed by an explanation of capacity requirements planning (CRP).

independent demand Demand that is created by customers.

dependent demand Demand that depends upon decisions made by internal operations managers.

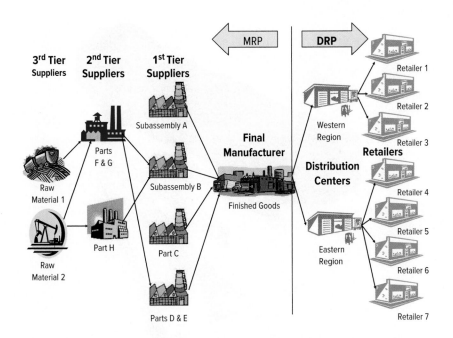

FIGURE 14-1 MRP and DRP in the Supply Chain

MATERIALS REQUIREMENTS PLANNING (MRP)

A primary function of materials requirements planning (MRP) is to match supply with demand, so the right quantities of raw materials, parts, and subassemblies are available when needed for production. It determines how much and when to produce using a time-phased schedule that is based on lead time. The time-phased schedule typically considers both actual orders and forecasts and is considered a *push* system. The MRP schedule pushes work from one workstation to the next without considering if the downstream station is ready for the work. Thus, MRP differs from kanban (pull) scheduling, described in Chapter 8. In kanban (pull) scheduling, production is triggered only when it is needed by the next workstation in the process. In practice, firms often use a combination of MRP for planning and kanban (pull) scheduling to trigger production on the shop floor.

MRP is used widely, especially in manufacturing; it is a standard function found in enterprise resource planning (ERP) software. According to one study, 80 percent of high-performing manufacturing plants have implemented MRP.[2] Operations that assemble complex, discrete products in batches are especially good candidates for MRP. For example, MRP works well for computers, appliances, furniture, and motor homes. Operations that make large volumes of less complex products, for example soft drinks or laundry detergent, or those that make-to-order unique products, can also use MRP, but the benefits may be less. Services such as hotels and hospitals also use MRP for planning, as described in the Get Real box in the next section.

The next section describes the detailed planning steps for MRP and discusses MRP inputs, the detailed calculation process, and MRP outputs in turn. As an example, we will use a BBQ grill gift set (see Figure 14-2) as a product to illustrate the MRP process. The gift set consists of a tote bag, a fork, a spatula, and tongs.

MRP INPUTS

Accurate input information is essential for MRP performance. Operations managers must coordinate activities closely within the organization and with other firms in the supply chain to ensure that forecasts, product information, inventory data, and lead-time estimates are current and correct. If the inputs are wrong, the outputs of MRP will be wrong.

materials requirements planning (MRP) A planning system used to ensure the right quantities of materials are available when needed.

LO14-1 Explain the materials requirements planning (MRP) process and when it should be used.

---

[2]D. Bartholomew, "9 Lives and Counting," *Industry Week,* May 2006, p. 44.

FIGURE 14-2 BBQ Grill
Gift Set

© Gastromedia/Alamy Stock Photo

As shown in Figure 14-3, MRP uses three key information inputs—the master production schedule (MPS), the bill of materials (BOM), and inventory records. Together, the information contained in the MPS, the BOM, and the inventory records files enables the MRP process to determine the quantity and timing of requirements for all components needed to make related products.

FIGURE 14-3 Overview of the Materials Requirements Planning (MRP) Process

GET REAL

MRP in Services

Although less widely used than in manufacturing, MRP also can be applied to services. Hotel chains use MRP for renovation planning. For example, if a hotel chain plans to renovate 1,000 rooms, a planner can calculate the number of dressers, beds, chairs, and mirrors needed and work with suppliers to understand how long it takes for each to be delivered and when they should be ordered. The goal is to have all of the right materials arrive at the right time so renovations can be completed on time.

To increase operating room efficiency, many hospitals purchase preassembled surgical kits from suppliers. These kits contain almost everything that a surgeon needs to complete a specific surgical procedure. Medical suppliers, who sell surgical kits to many different hospitals, use MRP to plan and assemble surgical kits for their customers. Surgical kits are a good candidate for MRP because of the complexity created by a high variety of different kits that are assembled from a wide variety of items.

© Dina2001RF/Alamy Stock Photo

Master Production Schedule (MPS)

The **master production schedule (MPS)** shows the quantities of end items to be completed in each time period (hour, day, week) into the future. The time period used for planning is called a **time bucket**. The MPS shows how many of each individual end item must be completed each period. The MPS is developed from the aggregate production plan and aggregate sales plan, which are the outputs from the sales and operations planning process (Chapter 13). For example, the aggregate production plan for Conair might show the total number of all hair dryers to be produced each month for the next year. The MPS would indicate how many hair dryers of each type must be completed each week for the next quarter. In making this plan, managers would consider forecasted demands, actual customer orders, orders generated through distribution requirements planning (DRP), demand for replacement parts, interplant transfers, lead times, and current inventory levels.

The entire time period covered by MPS is the **planning horizon** and must be at least as long as the longest lead-time path in the overall assembly of the product, called the **cumulative lead time**. This ensures that there is enough time to plan, order, receive materials, and make the end items. Global sourcing has increased the lead times for some items (think about purchasing furniture parts from Vietnam), requiring plans that extend even further into the future. The size of time buckets depends on the overall planning horizon and the dynamics of the market. Most companies plan in weekly buckets, though a company like Dell plans in terms of hours.[3]

An MPS for the BBQ grill gift set is shown in Figure 14-4. To develop the MPS, the first step is to calculate the projected end item on-hand inventory at the beginning of each time bucket. Projected on-hand inventory is the previous period's on-hand inventory minus *either* the actual customer orders *or* the forecast orders. The largest quantity of either the customer orders or the forecast is used. When the projected on-hand inventory in any time

master production schedule (MPS) The quantities of each finished product to be completed each period.

time bucket The individual time period for planning.

planning horizon The entire time period covered by the MPS.

cumulative lead time The longest lead-time path in the BOM.

global

---

[3]Research shows that using smaller time buckets improves performance. See Steele et al., "Comparisons between Drum-Buffer-Rope and Materials Requirements Planning: A Case Study," *International Journal of Production Research* 43, no. 15 (2005), pp. 3181–3208.

FIGURE 14-4   MPS for the BBQ Grill Gift Set

MPS Beginning inventory = 10	April					May		
	Week 1	Week 2	Week 3	Week 4	Week 5	Week 6	Week 7	Week 8
Forecast	35	20	25	40	50	40	30	30
Actual customer orders	40	30	30	25	25	20	10	0
Projected on-hand inventory	0	0	0	0	0	0	0	0
Available to promise	0	0	0	15	25	20	20	30
MPS	30	30	30	40	50	40	30	30

Part Name: BBQ grill gift set

period is negative, more end items are needed. Look at Figure 14-4. In week 1, the number of actual customer orders (40) exceeds the forecast of 35. So, the number of additional items needed is the beginning on-hand inventory of 10 minus the customer orders of 40; this equals negative 30. If we order 30 BBQ gift sets to be built in week 1, this will leave 0 projected on-hand inventory for week 2.

Some part of the production planned in the MPS may be committed to specific customers that have placed firm orders. The remaining planned production is **available to promise** to other customers as orders arise. The number of items that are available to promise are communicated to sales and marketing personnel so that they can arrange feasible delivery times and quantities for customers that wish to place new orders. For example, Figure 14-4 shows that in week 4, there are 15 units available to promise because only 25 of the 40 units in the MPS have been committed to actual customer orders.

The MPS does not consider whether the critical resources needed to complete the end items according to schedule are available during the planning horizon covered by the MPS. Recall that the aggregate production plan considers resources, but it does so using larger time buckets than the ones used in the MPS. Critical resources might include space, labor, equipment, suppliers, and even money. **Rough-cut capacity planning** estimates the availability of the critical resources needed by the MPS. If the resources are not available, then the MPS or the resource levels must change. For example, you could change the MPS by increasing the delivery time for some customers, acquiring critical resources, or diverting resources from other products. Some planning software systems calculate "capable to promise," which considers capacity when determining if new customer orders can be met.

available to promise The part of planned production that is not committed to a customer.

rough-cut capacity planning An estimation of the availability of the critical resources needed to support the MPS.

Bill of Materials (BOM)

The **bill of materials (BOM)** is a detailed description of an "end item" along with a list of all of its raw materials, parts, and subassemblies. The BOM is essentially a "recipe" for the product; it shows the number of each type of component that is required to make *one unit* of the end item. The BOM also shows the sequence of assembly. The BOM is created when a new product is developed. Product engineering managers are responsible for making updates to the BOM.

The BOM is shown as an indented list, a parts list (see Figure 14-5), or a product structure diagram, also called a *product structure tree* (see Figure 14-6). In our example, the BBQ grill gift set is the end item, shown as level 0 in the BOM. Each set consists of four "level 1" inputs: a tote bag, a fork, a spatula, and tongs. The dependent demand for the level 1 items is driven by the needs of the level 0 item. Similarly, the demand for the level 2 items is driven by the needs of the level 1 items, and so on. The BBQ grill gift set (level 0)

bill of materials (BOM) A detailed description of an "end item" and list of all of its raw materials, parts, and subassemblies.

LO14-2 Conduct MRP planning for items at multiple levels in the bill of materials (BOM).

Indented Bill of Materials	Parts List
Boxed BBQ grill gift set	Boxed BBQ grill gift set
* Tote bag (1)	Tote bag (1)
* Fork (1)	Fork (1)
** Metal fork (1)	Spatula (1)
*** Steel sheet (1)	Tongs (1)
** Handle A (1)	
*** Wood block (1)	Fork
** Rivet (2)	Metal fork (1)
** Leather tie	Handle A (1)
* Spatula (1)	Rivet (2)
** Metal spatula (1)	Leather tie
*** Steel sheet (1)	
** Handle A (1)	Spatula
*** Wood block (1)	Metal spatula (1)
** Rivet (2)	Handle A (1)
** Leather tie	Rivet (2)
* Tongs (1)	Leather tie
** Metal tong (1)	
*** Steel sheet (1)	Tongs
** Handle B (2)	Metal tong (1)
*** Wood block (2)	Handle B (2)
** Rivet (8)	Rivet (8)
	Metal fork
	Steel sheet (1)
	Handle A
	Wood block (1)
	Metal spatula
	Steel sheet (1)
	Metal tong
	Steel sheet (1)
	Handle B
	Wood block (2)

FIGURE 14-5 Indented Bill of Materials (BOM) and Parts List

can be thought of as the "parent" of the tote bag, fork, spatula, and tongs. These items are components, or "children," of the gift set.

The trends toward modular products and toward purchasing subassemblies from suppliers rather than making them in-house reduce the number of levels in a product's BOM, making it flatter. For example, the tote bag is purchased as a finished item from a supplier. For this reason, its children (raw materials,

activity

student

Select an item such as a chair or desk and develop a product structure BOM.

FIGURE 14-6 Product Structure Bill of Materials (BOM)

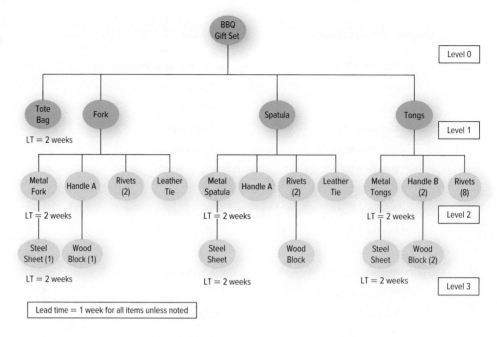

parts, and subassemblies) are not shown in the company's BOM. These raw materials, parts, and subassemblies are shown on the supplier's BOM for the tote bag.

Inventory Records

inventory status file A file that contains detailed inventory and procurement records.

Inventory records are contained in an **inventory status file**. Each inventory record includes:

- The item number.
- Description of the item.
- The lead time to order and receive the item from a supplier or to produce it internally.
- The preferred order quantity (lot size).
- Safety stock quantity.
- Other information such as cost or process descriptions.
- Quantity of on-hand inventory.
- Amount of inventory committed to a use.

scheduled receipts The quantity that has been ordered but not yet received.

- **Scheduled receipts** (the quantity that has been ordered but not yet received).

One of the key managerial decisions in MRP is the order quantity, or production lot size. Operations managers consider carrying costs, ordering costs, product costs, and stockout costs when deciding upon the appropriate lot-sizing strategy. For purchased items, suppliers typically set the lot sizes. Consider the choices at your local grocery store for purchasing milk—typically one gallon, one quart, or a single serving. Some of the typical lot-sizing strategies are:

lot-for-lot (L4L) An order for the exact amount needed.

- **Lot-for-lot (L4L).** An order is placed for exactly the amount that is needed in each period. L4L minimizes carrying costs, but maximizes setup or ordering costs.

fixed order quantity (FOQ) An order for the same amount each time.

- **Fixed order quantity (FOQ).** The same amount is ordered each time. For example, the economic order quantity (EOQ) (discussed in Chapter 7) might be used. A slight variation of FOQ is *multiples of FOQ,* where purchased items may be available only in a fixed order quantity, such as a carton of 10 items. In this case, if 14 items were needed, the order quantity would be two cartons of 10 (20 items) rather than 14.

periodic order quantity (POQ) An order for an amount that covers a fixed period of time.

- **Periodic order quantity (POQ).** An amount that covers the requirements for a fixed number of future periods is ordered. For example, enough is ordered to cover two periods' worth of net requirements each time an order is placed.

Use of fixed order quantities, multiple fixed order quantities, and periodic order quantities can create "lumpy" orders rather than a smooth continuous flow of materials. These lot-sizing rules can minimize ordering or setup costs for the firm. However, spikes in orders become accentuated and more dramatic as orders flow upstream in the supply chain to direct suppliers, and then to their suppliers, contributing to the bullwhip effect. When this effect occurs, inventory can fluctuate dramatically, going from excesses to stockouts. Coordination and information sharing among supply chain members help to reduce this effect and its associated costs.

relationships

MRP PROCESS

MRP calculations are done using computer software. However, managers need to know the mechanics in order to make good decisions using MRP outputs. Let's work through the MRP process using the BBQ grill gift set as an example. The planning process always starts with the level 0 items in the BOM and then continues down each successive level. The planning logic determines when items are needed and then works backward to determine when to place orders. As we go step-by-step through the process we will define the key items that are shown in an MRP record (see Figure 14-7).

Gross requirements refers to the total amount of an end item (finished good, subassembly, or part) that is required by *all* of its parents during each period. This must include end items that are used as replacement parts, interplant transfers, or service items. Start with the MPS for the BBQ grill gift set. The production schedule for the MPS creates the gross requirements in the MRP record for each week, as shown in Figure 14-8.

gross requirements The total amount of an end item that is required.

As discussed earlier, *scheduled receipts* are the total quantity of items from orders placed in the past and due to be delivered by the beginning of the period in which the quantity is shown. The scheduled receipts of 30 BBQ grill gift sets in week 1 (see Figure 14-9) were ordered one week ago. Note that the *order* is not shown on the current record form, just the *delivery*. The order placement was on last week's version of the record form, because the lead time for the gift sets is one week.

The next step in the process is to determine how many additional units, if any, are needed to meet the week's gross requirements. This calculation is called **requirements explosion**, and it determines the *net requirements* (see Figure 14-10). **Net requirements** are the minimum quantity required in the period based on gross requirements minus the sum of scheduled receipts and available inventory at the end of the last period (which is the inventory available at the start of the current period). When safety stock is needed, the net

requirements explosion The determination of how many additional units are needed.

net requirements The minimum amount needed in the period.

FIGURE 14-7   Example of an MRP Record

	Part Name:							
MRP Record **Lead time =** **On-hand inventory =** **Safety stock =** **Order quantity:**	**Week** **1**	**Week** **2**	**Week** **3**	**Week** **4**	**Week** **5**	**Week** **6**	**Week** **7**	**Week** **8**
Gross requirements								
Scheduled receipts								
Available inventory								
Net requirements								
Planned order receipts								
Planned order releases								

FIGURE 14-8 Gross Requirements for the BBQ Grill Gift Set

					Part Name: BBQ grill gift sets			
			April				**May**	
MPS **Beginning inventory = 10**	**Week** **1**	**Week** **2**	**Week** **3**	**Week** **4**	**Week** **5**	**Week** **6**	**Week** **7**	**Week** **8**
Forecast	35	20	25	40	50	40	30	30
Actual customer orders	40	30	30	25	25	20	10	0
Completed end items	(30)	30	30	40	50	40	30	30

					Part Name: BBQ grill gift sets			
MRP Record **Lead time = 1 week** **On-hand inventory = 0** **Safety stock = 0** **Order quantity: L4L**	**Week** **1**	**Week** **2**	**Week** **3**	**Week** **4**	**Week** **5**	**Week** **6**	**Week** **7**	**Week** **8**
Gross Requirements	(30)	30	30	40	50	40	30	30

FIGURE 14-9 Scheduled Receipts for the BBQ Grill Gift Set

					Part Name: BBQ grill gift sets			
MRP Record **Lead time = 1 week** **On-hand inventory = 0** **Safety stock = 0** **Order quantity: L4L**	**Week** **1**	**Week** **2**	**Week** **3**	**Week** **4**	**Week** **5**	**Week** **6**	**Week** **7**	**Week** **8**
Gross Requirements	30	30	30	40	50	40	30	30
Scheduled Receipts	(30)							

Ordered last week.

requirements are calculated based on the gross requirements plus safety stock minus the sum of scheduled receipts and available inventory at the end of the last period (the starting inventory of current period). Of course, if the total of available inventory plus scheduled receipts is greater than the gross requirements, then the net requirements is zero. Available inventory is the inventory quantity that is available *at the end* of a period (see equation 14.1).

(14.1) Available inventory = Available inventory at the start of the period + Scheduled receipts + Planned order receipts − Gross requirements

FIGURE 14-10   Net Requirements for the BBQ Grill Gift Set

MRP Record **Lead time = 1 week** **On-hand inventory = 0** **Safety stock = 0** **Order quantity: L4L**	**Week 1**	**Week 2**	**Week 3**	**Week 4**	**Week 5**	**Week 6**	**Week 7**	**Week 8**
Gross requirements	30	30	30	40	50	40	30	30
Scheduled receipts	30							
Available inventory								
Net requirements		30	30	40	50	40	30	30

The next step is to calculate the planned order receipts for each week. The quantity that is planned to arrive at the *beginning* of a period is the **planned order receipt**. These arrivals come from orders that are planned to be placed at the designated time in the future. In this example, because we use a L4L policy, the planned order receipts exactly equal the net requirements, as shown in Figure 14-11.

The last step is to determine *when* to place the order. A **planned order release** is the quantity of an item that is planned to be ordered in the period. Because of the rolling time horizon of MRP records, when an order is placed (released), it shifts from being a *planned* receipt to being a *scheduled* receipt. To determine the planned order release for each period, count backward from the planned order receipt using the lead time. In the example, the planned order releases are scheduled one week before the planned order receipts, as shown in Figure 14-12.

planned order receipt The amount that is planned to arrive at the beginning of a period.

planned order release The amount of an item that is planned to be ordered in a period.

FIGURE 14-11   Planned Order Receipts for the BBQ Grill Gift Set

MRP Record **Lead time = 1 week** **On-hand inventory = 0** **Safety stock = 0** **Order quantity: L4L**	**Week 1**	**Week 2**	**Week 3**	**Week 4**	**Week 5**	**Week 6**	**Week 7**	**Week 8**
Gross requirements	30	30	30	40	50	40	30	30
Scheduled receipts	30							
Available inventory								
Net requirements		30	30	40	50	40	30	30
Planned order receipts		30	30	40	50	40	30	30

FIGURE 14-12   Planned Order Releases for the BBQ Grill Gift Set

MRP Record Lead time = 1 week On-hand inventory = 0 Safety stock = 0 Order quantity: L4L	Week 1	Week 2	Week 3	Week 4	Week 5	Week 6	Week 7	Week 8
Gross requirements	30	30	30	40	50	40	30	30
Scheduled receipts	30							
Available inventory								
Net requirements		30	30	40	50	40	30	30
Planned order receipts		(30)	30	40	50	40	30	30
Planned order releases	(30)	30	40	50	40	30	30	

Part Name: BBQ grill gift set

After the planned order releases for the BBQ grill gift sets are known, the planning process continues through the BOM for each component, level by level. Look back at Figures 14-5 and 14-6, which show the BOM for the BBQ grill gift set. The next step would be to develop MRP records for the level 1 items: the tote bag, the fork, the spatula, and the tongs. Once the MRP records for the level 1 items are complete, then MRP records are developed for the level 2 items: the metal fork, the metal spatula, the metal tongs, handles A and B, the rivets, and the leather ties. Similarly, after the level 2 records are complete, MRP records for the level 3 items are calculated. This process, called an MRP "explosion," continues until the planning is complete for all levels of the BOM.

Let's walk through the calculation steps for the tote bag. Then we'll show the MRP records for the fork and spatula and develop the gross requirements for handle A, which has the fork and spatula as parents. Tote bags are purchased in cartons of 100 bags each from a supplier in China, and the lead time is two weeks with shipment by air. Because of the risk of delays, one carton (100 bags) is held as safety stock. If the available inventory drops below the safety stock level of 100, the MRP process calculates the net requirements needed to bring the inventory level back up to a minimum of 100.

First determine the tote bag's gross requirements by asking who its parents are. Because the tote bag is only used in the BBQ grill gift set and no replacement bags are purchased, the gross requirements come *only* from the planned order releases for the BBQ grill gift set. Note in Figure 14-13 that the numbers in the gross requirements line for tote bags are identical to the numbers in the planned order releases line for the BBQ grill gift set. If tote bags were used in multiple products, the planned order releases for *all* of its parents would be combined to determine its gross requirements.

Next, calculate the net requirements and associated orders. The scheduled receipt of 100 in week 1 covers the gross requirements for the first three weeks, so the first net requirement occurs in week 4. In week 4, the net requirement is 50 bags. Schedule a planned order release of 100 bags, which is the lowest order quantity possible. Because of the two-week lead time, the order must be released in week 2 so that it can be received in week 4. This same logic is used to complete the rest of the record, as shown in Figure 14-13.

Continue with the MRP records for the fork and spatula (see Figure 14-14). The gross requirements for each come from the planned order releases from the BBQ grill gift set. Let's develop the MRP record for one level 2 item: handle A, as shown in Figure 14-15.

FIGURE 14-13   MRP Requirements for Tote Bags

Part Name: BBQ grill gift set

MRP Record
Lead time = 1 week
On-hand inventory = 0
Safety stock = 0
Order quantity: L4L

	Week 1	Week 2	Week 3	Week 4	Week 5	Week 6	Week 7	Week 8
Gross requirements	30	30	30	40	50	40	30	30
Scheduled receipts	30							
Available inventory								
Net requirements		30	30	40	50	40	30	30
Planned order receipts		30	30	40	50	40	30	30
Planned order releases	(30)	30	40	50	40	30	30	

Part Name: Tote bag

MRP Record
Lead time = 2 weeks
On-hand inventory = 100
Safety stock = 100
Order quantity:
Multi = 100

	Week 1	Week 2	Week 3	Week 4	Week 5	Week 6	Week 7	Week 8
Gross requirements	(30)	30	40	50	40	30	30	
Scheduled receipts	100							
Available inventory 100	170	140	100	150	110	180	150	
Net requirements				50		20		
Planned order receipts				(100)		(100)		
Planned order releases		(100)		(100)				

The gross requirements for handle A come from the planned order releases from its parents (fork and spatula). The BOM (Figures 14-5 and 14-6) shows that one handle each is needed for the fork and the spatula. There are no other sources of demand for handle A. Notice that there is beginning on-hand inventory of 60 units. When needed, handle A is always produced in fixed order quantity (FOQ) lot sizes of 100.

To complete the entire materials requirements plan, MRP calculations would be done for all of the remaining level 2 items and then all of the level 3 items in the BOM. Some organizations use MRP for planning the higher level items in the BOM but use kanban (pull) systems to replenish the lower level items.

FIGURE 14-14   MRP Records for the Fork and the Spatula

Part Name: Fork

MRP Record Lead time = 1 week On-hand inventory = 0 Safety stock = 0 Order quantity: L4L	Week 1	Week 2	Week 3	Week 4	Week 5	Week 6	Week 7	Week 8
Gross requirements	30	30	40	50	40	30	30	
Scheduled receipts	30							
Available inventory								
Net requirements		30	40	50	40	30	30	
Planned order receipts		30	40	50	40	30	30	
Planned order releases	30	40	50	40	30	30		

Part Name: Spatula

MRP Record Lead time = 1 week On-hand inventory = 0 Safety stock = 0 Order quantity: L4L	Week 1	Week 2	Week 3	Week 4	Week 5	Week 6	Week 7	Week 8
Gross requirements	30	30	40	50	40	30	30	
Scheduled receipts	30							
Available inventory								
Net requirements		30	40	50	40	30	30	
Planned order receipts		30	40	50	40	30	30	
Planned order releases	30	40	50	40	30	30		

MRP OUTPUTS AND USE

MRP outputs include primary and secondary reports. The primary reports are schedules of the planned order releases that trigger purchases and the production of items in the proper time frame. Secondary reports provide cost, inventory, and schedule attainment information that helps managers judge how well the operation is performing. If a major difference between actual performance and the MRP plan occurs, then an exception report is generated.

Once set, numerous changes made to the MPS can cause **nervousness** throughout the system. Significant MPS changes can modify the timing and quantities of orders for raw

nervousness Inconsistencies in the plan caused by changes to the MPS.

FIGURE 14-15   MRP Record for Handle A

MRP Record **Lead time = 2 weeks** **On-hand = 60** **Safety stock = 0** **Order quantity: FOQ = 100**	**Week 1**	**Week 2**	**Week 3**	**Week 4**	**Week 5**	**Week 6**	**Week 7**	**Week 8**
Part Name: Handle A								
Gross requirements	(60)	80	100	80	60	60		
Scheduled receipts		100						
Available inventory 60	0	20	20	40	80	20		
Net requirements			80	60	20			
Planned order receipts			100	100	100			
Planned order releases	100	100	100					

60 = 30 forks + 30 spatulas

materials, parts, and subassemblies, making suppliers' planning very difficult. As a result, users may not trust the MRP plan.

MRP assumes that parts produced or received from suppliers are defect-free and delivered as scheduled. This is especially important if an L4L lot-sizing strategy is used. Thus, quality management is critical within the firm and by its suppliers. If quality and delivery performance are not perfect, then safety stock or increased lead times are required. These increase cost and decrease the effectiveness of the planning process.

DISTRIBUTION REQUIREMENTS PLANNING (DRP)

Distribution requirements planning (DRP) calculates the positioning and replenishment of *finished goods inventories* throughout the distribution network using logic similar to MRP. DRP is typically a module in enterprise resource planning (ERP) system software. Distribution networks can be very complex, with multiple levels of distribution centers and thousands of retailers (think about Conair, for example). Thus, planning and coordination across the supply chain can be difficult. The output of DRP is used for input into operations and logistics planning processes.

Similar to MRP, inventory replenishment decisions are based on a time-phased schedule considering forecasts and actual orders. The DRP process starts by combining forecasts and firm orders, ideally at each customer or the contact point as close as possible to the customer, such as the retailer or regional distribution center. Forecasts and actual orders at the customer or contact points are added to create the independent demand for the finished goods, and planned order receipts are determined for each of these locations for the planning horizon. Looking back at Figure 14-1, forecasts and actual orders create the planned order releases for the seven retailers. For Retailers 1, 2, and 3, these planned order releases are combined to form gross requirements for the Western Region distribution center, while those for Retailers 4, 5, 6, and 7 form the gross requirements for the Eastern Region distribution center.

distribution requirements planning (DRP) Determination of replenishment and positioning of finished goods in the distribution network.

LO14-3 Explain how distribution requirements planning (DRP) is used.

As with MRP, the planning horizon must extend far enough into the future so that replenishment orders can be scheduled in plenty of time to make the required shipments. For each future week at each customer location, the gross requirements estimate is compared with the amount of inventory projected to be on-hand at that location. If the projected inventory available is less than the estimated gross requirements, a replenishment order is planned for the net requirements.

The next step is to compare the schedule of gross requirements at each distribution center against its projected on-hand inventory for each week into the future. This comparison creates net requirements and planned orders, and these orders are consolidated to make gross requirements for the next upstream source of supply, while considering required lead times. The process continues to consolidate requirements and orders across all stages in the distribution network up to the production plant that makes the finished goods. The result is a week-by-week plan of demands placed on the plant that ultimately reflects the forecasted independent demands taking place at each of the customer locations. At this point, MPS and MRP processes take over.

UNDERSTANDING CAPACITY REQUIREMENTS PLANNING (CRP)

LO14-4 Conduct capacity requirements planning (CRP) using an infinite loading approach.

DRP and MRP focus on material feasibility—can we get the right amount of material at the right time? To meet customer needs, an operation also needs sufficient capacity of key resources. A load is the amount of work given to a worker, machine, work center, or facility during a specific period of time. To make sure a plan is feasible, the load is compared to the capacity, which is the output that can be done during a period of time.

Though rough-cut capacity planning suggests an MPS is feasible, after development of an MRP plan, a more detailed assessment of capacity is needed to ensure this is still the case. MRP does not compare the planned orders to the available capacity in the supply chain. Most MRP plans assume **infinite loading**; that is, they assume an infinite amount of capacity is available, which is not realistic. **Capacity requirements planning (CRP)** determines if all the work centers involved have the capacity to implement the MRP plan. The CRP process uses planned order releases and scheduled receipts to estimate work center loads. A **load profile** compares weekly load needs against a profile of actual capacity.

infinite loading The assumption that there is an infinite amount of capacity available.

capacity requirements planning (CRP) An estimate of the capacity needed at work centers.

load profile A comparison of production needs to actual capacity.

Figure 14-16 shows available capacity and a load profile for the spatula. The planned order releases are from the spatula's MRP record (Figure 14-14). The CRP table in Figure 14-16 estimates the number of production hours needed to make the spatulas, based on a machine rate of 30 minutes per spatula. The available machine capacity is 20 hours per week. The table and load graph show that the process will be overloaded in week 3, when the load of 25 hours exceeds the available capacity of 20 hours. The load exactly equals capacity in weeks 2 and 4. Underloading occurs in weeks 1, 5, and 6.

Having too much or too little capacity can be problematic. When underloading occurs, the extra capacity could be used to build anticipation inventory, but this increases costs. If underloading is an ongoing problem, the firm should find new business or develop new products to use the capacity or reduce the capacity. If there is not enough capacity to meet the production requirements, the use of overtime or outsourcing some operations are options, but costs increase. Alternatively, you can increase delivery lead times or create a backlog of orders, but this may reduce customer satisfaction and sales. If capacity is available earlier, goods can be made in advance and held in inventory until needed. Because of the differences between the load and available capacity for the spatula, managers must decide to change capacity or to change the MPS. One alternative would be to produce 10 of the units needed in week 3 in week 1, when capacity is available, and hold these units in inventory. A cross-functional team including operations, sales, marketing, finance, supply, and engineering should decide upon the best approach to manage capacity to meet the company's objectives.

FIGURE 14-16   Capacity Requirements for Spatulas

Processing Time = 30 minutes per unit	Part Name: Spatula							
	Week 1	Week 2	Week 3	Week 4	Week 5	Week 6	Week 7	Week 8
Planned order releases	30	40	50	40	30	30		
Processing load (hours)	15	20	25	20	15	15		
Available capacity (hours)	20	20	20	20	20	20		

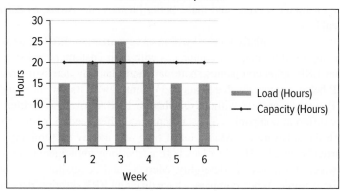

ADVANCES IN PLANNING SYSTEMS

The logic of requirements and resources planning has been around for a long time. The U.S. Army's ordering system used in World War II was essentially a manual MRP system. In the past few decades, however, the benefits of DRP, MRP, and CRP processes have become more fully realized because of the dramatic increase in computer power and the availability of low-cost MRP software. Today, the planning for very complex operations can be done using fairly low-cost requirements planning software systems.

Over the years, requirements planning systems have evolved. Initially, the focus of MRP was on manufacturing planning and scheduling. However, managers soon recognized that the output from MRP would be useful for planning in other functions such as accounting, purchasing, marketing, sales, finance, distribution, and engineering. MRP evolved into manufacturing *resource* planning, or MRP II, which considers a wider range of cross-functional issues. MRP II also has the capability to simulate the impacts of different plans. This was a precursor of the enterprise resource planning (ERP) systems that have been adopted by many firms. Recent advances in requirements and resources planning systems being implemented today include: (1) enterprise resource planning (ERP) systems, (2) advanced planning and scheduling (APS) systems, and (3) extended planning across the supply chain using demand-driven MRP. APICS—a professional organization for supply chain and operations managers—is an excellent source of information on the latest trends and directions in materials and resources planning across the supply chain.

Enterprise Resource Planning (ERP)

Rather than existing as independent, stand-alone systems, DRP, MRP, and CRP are usually embedded as integral parts of an **enterprise resource planning (ERP)** system. An ERP system consolidates all of the business planning systems and related data throughout a

enterprise resource planning (ERP) system Software that consolidates all of the business planning systems and data throughout an organization.

LO14-5 Describe how materials requirements and resource planning functions work together within an enterprise resource planning (ERP) system.

company, so the planning processes across all business functions can be integrated and consistently applied. The goal of ERP systems is to allow business processes to function seamlessly and in unison. Companies such as SAP and Oracle are the leading providers of ERP software and cloud-based applications.

A typical ERP includes the functionality of many requirements and resource planning systems, including sales, billing, accounting, finance, human resource management, and project management, along with the supply chain planning systems discussed in this chapter. Before ERP, these different planning functions were done using "legacy" software systems that were developed and used within each function, such as accounting, operations, and human resources, but were not linked or compatible with one another. As a result, data needed by other legacy systems (say, operations data were needed by accounting) had to be manually transformed via spreadsheets or databases, thus wasting time and creating errors. By allowing all business data to be in one ERP system, planning and coordination across business functions is easier, time is saved, and errors are reduced. All types of companies can gain benefits from an ERP system. An ERP system helped Red Door Spas reduce costs, improve customer service, and make better business decisions, as discussed in the nearby Get Real box.

Although they were initially focused within an organization, ERP systems and add-on software are being used to integrate companies with their customers and suppliers. In the same ways that ERP helps companies share data and planning across internal functions, expanded ERP helps a company share data and planning with its suppliers and customers. However, ERP systems are not without drawbacks. ERP software is written to meet the needs of many different companies. Thus, companies either need to modify their business processes to fit the software or spend a lot of time and money customizing the software to fit their particular needs. This involves high costs, long implementation times, highly complex software, and a lack of flexibility. Mergers and acquisitions can be especially challenging, for example. When companies have different ERP systems, data must be combined into a single system and processes must be standardized.

GET REAL

ERP Improves Performance at Elizabeth Arden Red Door Spas

ERP systems are not just for manufacturing. Elizabeth Arden Red Door Spas has 30 locations designed to provide the ultimate in pampering through salon and spa services. The management team was planning to add locations both within the United States and internationally. However, its human resource, finance, and logistics systems were not integrated, making decision making difficult. In 2006, to give its business performance a makeover, Red Door Spas replaced its legacy business systems with an ERP system by SAP. The system made it easier to track orders. Inventory at its salons and distribution center dropped, reducing costs. Employees could spend more time with customers and less time on administrative tasks. More importantly, the ERP system provided more consistent data that could be used for making better business decisions.

© ZUMA Press/Newscom

Advanced Planning and Scheduling (APS)

Conventional requirements planning systems were sequential and iterative in nature, and today many still are. In this chapter, we have described a process in which distribution requirements planning (DRP) output feeds the master production schedule (MPS), which feeds materials requirements planning (MRP), which feeds capacity requirements planning (CRP). Problems identified in the CRP process must be remedied by a revision to the MPS, and the process repeats itself until a feasible solution is found. This approach, which emerged in the past because of the lack of computer power and connectivity across legacy data systems, is fundamentally inefficient.

Imagine a planning process that simultaneously considers materials requirements along with resource capacity constraints. In this process a plan could be developed that optimizes all related costs, for example, inventory, labor, capital, and other costs. This level of joint optimization is the goal of **advanced planning and scheduling (APS) systems**, which are often included in ERP systems. APS systems use the same fundamental explosion logic of MRP. However, they integrate materials and capacity planning into one system. APS is possible because of vast improvements in computing power coupled with the development of sophisticated mathematical algorithms that help to solve very complex scheduling problems. The result is better plans that are generated much faster.

Requirements and resource planning systems have achieved a high level of acceptance because of the important advantages that they offer to a firm. As multiple firms work together to adopt and share compatible planning systems, the supply chain can experience significant benefits. Planning systems that are extended across supply chain partners provide greater visibility into the current status and into plans for the future. By anticipating supply and demand conditions into the future, APS systems help managers to identify and avoid problems and quickly evaluate alternatives. Supply chain partners can jointly plan their operations using what-if analyses. APS systems evaluate different scenarios of changes in customer demand and material delays. This analysis helps supply chain partners to identify options and create contingency plans.

Supply chain partners who work to coordinate and share planning systems typically see tremendous reductions in order fulfillment lead times, large improvements in information accuracy, reductions in inventory, and lower costs. Demand-driven MRP goes beyond a single organization to extend planning across the entire supply chain. Understanding leadtimes, variations in supply and demand, bottleneck operations, and flexibility across the entire supply chain leads to better decisions. For example, decisions about where inventory should be held within the supply chain can increase responsiveness while reducing costs.

LO14-6 Explain how advanced planning and scheduling (APS) systems improve the requirements and resource planning processes.

advance planning and scheduling (APS) systems Systems that integrate materials and capacity planning into one system.

CHAPTER SUMMARY

This chapter defined dependent demand and described materials and resource planning processes.

1. Dependent demand refers to the demand for raw materials, parts, and subassemblies needed to make end items.

2. Inputs to MRP include the master production schedule (MPS) for the end items, the bill of materials (BOM), which shows what components are needed, and inventory records.

3. The key steps in the MRP process include calculating the gross requirements, determining net requirements, establishing the timing for planned order receipts, and offsetting to determine planned order releases.

4. MRP outputs include primary reports used for operations planning and secondary reports used for performance measurement and process improvement.

5. Distribution requirements planning (DRP) uses the logic of MRP to determine the positioning and replenishment of finished goods inventories (independent demand) within a distribution network.

6. Plans developed by MRP may not be feasible unless there is adequate capacity available within the supply chain. With basic MRP, an additional step, capacity requirements planning (CRP), is used to determine if the plan developed by MRP is feasible.

7. Advances in computer technology are streamlining the planning process by combining materials and capacity planning into advanced planning and scheduling (APS) systems that are part of ERP systems.

KEY TERMS

DISCUSSION QUESTIONS

1. Why are spare parts and service parts considered to be independent demand, rather than dependent demand?

2. Why is collaboration within an organization and the supply chain important when using DRP and MRP?

3. The planning process involves a rolling time horizon. What does this mean to a planner?

4. What is the relationship between cumulative lead time and changes in the MPS? Why?

5. What types of companies are likely to benefit the most from using MRP? Why?

6. What problems can MRP create for suppliers as you go upstream in the supply chain? Why?

7. As an organization increases its level of outsourcing, what is the impact on its bill of materials? Why?

8. How do L4L, FOQ, and POQ ordering policies impact setup/ordering costs and inventory costs? Why?

9. What impact will a supplier's quality and delivery problems have on a company using MRP? Why?

10. In what ways are DRP and MRP similar and how are they different?

11. How have advances in computer technology changed the planning process? Why? What changes do you expect in the future?

SOLVED PROBLEMS

The Comfort Chair Company makes furniture that is used in waiting rooms for doctors' offices. Its most popular model is an upholstered chair that comes in two colors of fabric: blue and burgundy. The BOM, provided as a product structure diagram, is shown in Figure 14-17. All of the components are the same for the blue and burgundy chairs, with the exception of the fabric. Using this information, answer questions 1, 2, and 3.

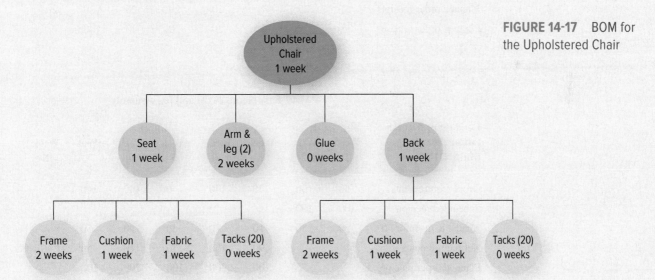

FIGURE 14-17 BOM for the Upholstered Chair

1. What is the cumulative lead time for the chair, and why is this important?

   Solution:

   The cumulative lead time is four weeks. The longest path is one week (upholstered chair) plus one week (seat or back) plus two weeks (frame). Thus, the planning horizon for the MPS must be at least four weeks to provide enough time to produce the chairs.

2. Given the MRP for the blue and the burgundy chairs, complete the MRP for the arm and leg assembly. Assume that the gross requirements for the arm and leg assembly depend only upon the blue and burgundy chairs.

Part Name: Blue upholstered chair								
Lead time: 1 week Order quantity: L4L	Week 1	Week 2	Week 3	Week 4	Week 5	Week 6	Week 7	Week 8
Gross requirements			50	50	50	50	50	50
Scheduled receipts								
Available inventory								
Net requirements			50	50	50	50	50	50
Planned order receipts			50	50	50	50	50	50
Planned order releases		50	50	50	50	50	50	

Part Name: Burgundy upholstered chair								
Lead time: 1 week Order quantity: L4L	Week 1	Week 2	Week 3	Week 4	Week 5	Week 6	Week 7	Week 8
Gross requirements		25		20	20	20	20	20
Scheduled receipts								
Available inventory								
Net requirements		25		20	20	20	20	20
Planned order receipts		25		20	20	20	20	20
Planned order releases	25		20	20	20	20	20	

Part Name: Arm and leg assembly								
Lead time: 2 weeks Order quantity: Multi = 100	Week 1	Week 2	Week 3	Week 4	Week 5	Week 6	Week 7	Week 8
Gross requirements	50	100	140	140	140	140	140	
Scheduled receipts	100	100						
Available inventory 0	50	50	10	70	30	90	50	
Net requirements			90	130	70	110	50	
Planned order receipts			100	200	100	200	100	
Planned order releases	100	200	100	200	100			

Solution:

The gross requirements for the arm and leg assembly come from both the blue and the burgundy chairs. Because each chair requires two arm and leg assemblies, planned order release quantities from the upholstered chairs must be doubled.

3. If it takes 45 minutes to assemble each upholstered chair, and there is one worker in the assembly department who works 40 hours per week, can the MPS for week 4 be met for both the blue and burgundy chairs? Why, or why not?

Solution:

The time required for each chair is 45 minutes/60 minutes = .75 hours. The requirements to complete 50 blue chairs and 20 burgundy chairs in week 4 is 70 chairs × .75 hours = 52.5 hours. This exceeds the available capacity with one worker.

4. The Organic Juice Co. produces a line of fresh, natural organic juices. Given the MPS and BOM for one type of juice, Passion Swirl, complete the MRP schedules for the components: orange juice, passion fruit juice, and mango juice. There are 128 fluid ounces per gallon.

MPS

Item	Week 1	Week 2	Week 3	Week 4	Week 5	Week 6	Week 7	Week 8
Passion Swirl Number of 16 oz. bottles	2,000	2,000	2,500	2,500	2,500	3,000	3,000	3,000

Item	Orange Juice	Passion Fruit Juice	Mango Juice
Lot size rule	Multiples FOQ = 120 gallons	Multiples FOQ = 50 gallons	Multiples FOQ = 50 gallons
Safety stock	50 gallons	10 gallon	10 gallons
Beginning inventory	80 gallons	10 gallons	40 gallons
Lead time	2 weeks	3 weeks	2 weeks

Solution:

MRP can be used to determine the schedule for continuous products, as is the case in this example. To determine the gross requirements, take the MPS quantity for a period and multiply it by the number of ounces that are in the product. In week 1, for example, 2,000 16-ounce bottles of Passion Swirl are needed. Because there are 10 ounces of orange juice in each bottle of Passion Swirl, the total number of bottles, 2,000, is multiplied by 10 ounces to get the gross requirements of 20,000 ounces. The order quantity for each of the juices is in gallons, so the total number of ounces required must be divided by the number of ounces in a gallon (128 ounces/gallon) to get the gross requirements in gallons as shown in the MRP records. Repeat for the remaining periods. Use a similar approach for passion fruit juice and mango juice.

After the gross requirements are determined, complete the MRP schedule using the same approach as for discrete products. In this example, for orange juice, 50 gallons of safety stock are required. This means that the inventory level should always be 50 or more gallons. Take a look at week 3 to see how the net requirements are calculated when safety stock is used. The gross requirements of 195.3 gallons plus the safety stock of 50 gallons make up the total requirements of 254.3 gallons in week 3. At the beginning of week 3 there are 127.4 gallons available in inventory. The net requirements in week 3 are 117.9 gallons (254.3 – 127.4 gallons).

MRP Record				**Material Name: Orange Juice**				
Lead time = 2 weeks **On-hand = 80 gallons** **Safety stock = 50 gallons** **Order quantity: Multiples** **FOQ = 120 gallons**	**Week 1**	**Week 2**	**Week 3**	**Week 4**	**Week 5**	**Week 6**	**Week 7**	**Week 8**
Gross requirements (gallons)	156.3	156.3	195.3	195.3	195.3	234.4	234.4	234.4
Scheduled receipts	240	120						
Available inventory 80 gallons	163.7	127.4	52.1	96.8	141.5	147.1	152.7	158.3
Net requirements			117.9	193.2	148.5	142.9	137.3	131.7
Planned order receipts			120	240	240	240	240	240
Planned order releases	120	240	240	2400	240	240		

MRP Record				**Material Name: Passion Fruit Juice**				
Lead time = 3 weeks **On-hand = 10 gallons** **Safety stock = 10 gallon** **Order quantity: Multiples** **FOQ = 50 gallons**	**Week 1**	**Week 2**	**Week 3**	**Week 4**	**Week 5**	**Week 6**	**Week 7**	**Week 8**
Gross requirements (gallons)	62.5	62.5	78.1	78.1	78.1	93.8	93.8	93.8
Scheduled receipts	100	50	100					
Available inventory 10 gallons	47.5	35	56.9	28.8	50.7	56.9	13.1	19.3
Net requirements				31.2	59.3	53.1	46.9	90.7
Planned order receipts				50	100	100	50	100
Planned order releases	50	100	100	50	100			

MRP Record									
Material Name: Mango Juice									
Lead time = 2 weeks On-hand = 40 gallons Safety stock = 10 gallons Order quantity: Multiples FOQ = 50 gallons	Week 1	Week 2	Week 3	Week 4	Week 5	Week 6	Week 7	Week 8	
Gross requirements (gallons)	31.3	31.3	39.1	39.1	39.1	46.9	46.9	46.9	
Scheduled receipts	50								
Available inventory 40 gallons	58.7	27.4	38.3	49.2	10.1	13.2	16.3	19.4	
Net requirements			21.7	10.8		46.8	43.7	40.6	
Planned order receipts			50	50		50	50	50	
Planned order releases	50	50		50	50	50			

PROBLEMS

1. Using the BOM shown below, how many of part E will be needed if 20 units of end item A are needed? How many of part C will be needed?

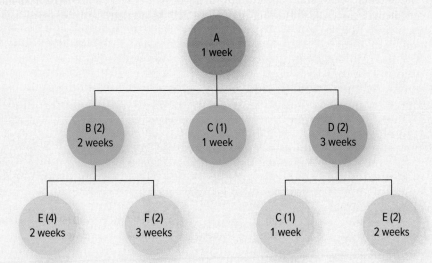

2. Based on the BOM in problem 1, what is the cumulative lead time for end item A? How will this information be used?

3. Develop an indented BOM for the product structure tree in problem 1.

4. Based on the BOM shown below, how many units of part F will be needed if 15 units of end item A are needed? If the company decided to purchase part D from suppliers, how would the BOM change? Assuming part D is purchased, how many units of part F are needed to make 15 units of end item A?

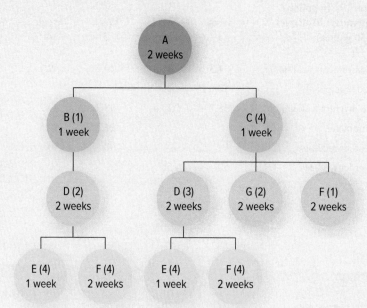

5. Based on the BOM in problem 4, what is the cumulative lead time for end item A?
6. Develop an indented BOM for the product structure tree shown in problem 4.
7. Based on the BOM shown below, how many of part D will be needed if 100 units of end item A are needed? How many of part F will be needed?

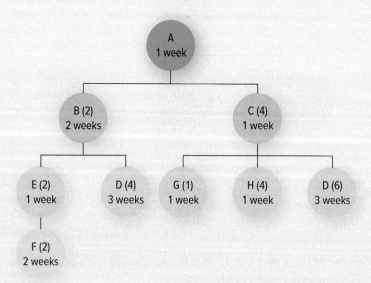

8. Using the information in problem 7, develop an indented BOM.
9. Based on the BOM shown below, how many of part J will be needed if 40 units of end item A are needed? Managers have decided to outsource part G. Revise the BOM for

end item A, assuming that item G is now purchased from a supplier. How many of part J will now be needed if 40 units of end item A are needed?

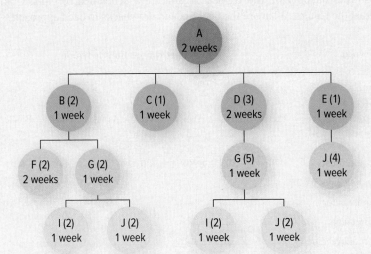

10. Draw a product structure tree for the baking pan using the BOM shown below. If there are plans to make 100 baking pans, how many handles are needed? How many bolt and nut sets are needed?

Baking Pan
* Pan (1)
** Pan shell (1)
** Handles (2)
** Bolt and nut set (4)
* Lid (1)
** Lid subassembly
***Glass (1)
***Steel rim (1)
** Handle (1)
** Bolt and nut set (2)

11. Draw a product structure tree for the patio planter using the BOM below. If there are plans to make eight patio planters, how many bolt and nut sets will be needed?

Patio Planter
* Planter box assembly
** Base assembly (1)
*** Base (1)
*** Rolling casters (4)
*** Bolt and nut set (4)
** Side assembly
*** Side panels (4)
*** Corner braces (8)
** Bolt and nut sets (4)
* Top (1)
* Bolt and nut sets (4)

12. Complete the MRP record for a bicycle frame using an L4L lot-sizing strategy. Considering the lead time, where should scheduled receipts be shown? Repeat using a fixed order quantity of 100 frames. Again, show scheduled receipts. Compare and contrast the results. What are the benefits and drawbacks to each approach?

MRP Record				Part Name: Bicycle frame				
Lead time = 2 weeks **On-hand = 0** **Safety stock = 0** **Order quantity: L4L**	Week 1	Week 2	Week 3	Week 4	Week 5	Week 6	Week 7	Week 8
Gross requirements	70	50	80	80	70	60	80	80
Scheduled receipts								
Available inventory								
Net requirements								
Planned order receipts								
Planned order releases								

MRP Record				Part Name: Bicycle frame				
Lead time = 2 weeks **On-hand = 0** **Safety stock = 0** **Order quantity:** **FOQ = 100**	Week 1	Week 2	Week 3	Week 4	Week 5	Week 6	Week 7	Week 8
Gross requirements	70	50	80	80	70	60	80	80
Scheduled receipts								
Available inventory								
Net requirements								
Planned order receipts								
Planned order releases								

13. Complete the MRP record for a bicycle seat.

MRP Record				Part Name: Seat				
Lead time = 1 week **On-hand = 40** **Safety stock = 20** **Order quantity** **FOQ = 100**	Week 1	Week 2	Week 3	Week 4	Week 5	Week 6	Week 7	Week 8
Gross requirements	70	50	80	80	70	60	80	80
Scheduled receipts								
Available inventory								
Net requirements								
Planned order receipts								
Planned order releases								

14. Based on the BOM and the MPS for end item A shown below, complete the MRP schedule for items A, C, D, and E.

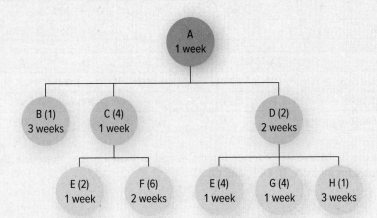

MPS

Item	1	2	3	4	5	6	7	8
A	60	20	50	120	100	50	80	40

Item	A	C	D	E
Lot size rule	L4L	L4L	L4L	Multiples FOQ = 500
Safety stock	0	0	0	100
Beginning inventory	0	0	0	300

15. Given the BOM and MPS for end items A and B shown below, complete the MRP schedules for items A, B, C, D, and E.

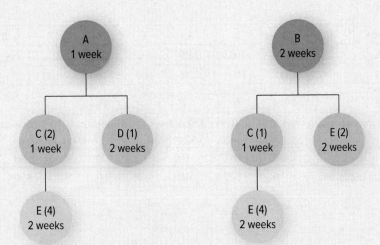

Item	1	2	3	4	5	6	7	8
A			200	200		200	200	
B				150			150	150

Item	A	B	C	D	E
Lot size rule	L4L	L4L	FOQ = 500	FOQ = 1,000	L4L
Safety stock	0	0	0	200	50
Beginning inventory	0	0	50	500	1,000

16. Given the BOM and MPS for end items A and B shown below, complete the MRP schedules for items A, B, C, F, and G.

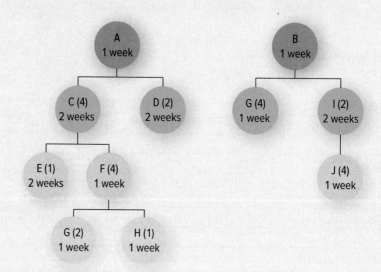

MPS

Item	1	2	3	4	5	6	7	8
A			200	250		300		
B		100	100	100	100	100	100	

Item	A	B	C	F	G
Lot size rule	L4L	L4L	Multiples FOQ = 500	Multiples FOQ = 1,000	Multiples FOQ = 1,000
Safety stock	0	0	100	500	500
Beginning inventory	0	0	400	500	800

17. The Natural Beauty Co. develops, makes, and markets a full line of hair care products that are sold through upscale salons. Natural Beauty Co. uses MRP for planning and scheduling. Given the MPS and BOM for Lemon Silk Shampoo shown below, complete the MRP schedules for the surfactant, the thickener, and the fragrance. Note that there are 128 fluid ounces in a gallon.

MPS

Item	Week 1	Week 2	Week 3	Week 4	Week 5	Week 6	Week 7	Week 8
Lemon Silk Number of 8 oz. bottles	500	500	600	1,000	800	700	800	1,000

Item	Surfactant	Thickener	Fragrance
Lot size rule	Multiples FOQ = 10 gallons	Multiples FOQ = 1 gallon	Multiples FOQ = 16 ounces
Safety stock	5 gallons	1 gallon	8 ounces
Beginning inventory	15.5 gallons	3 gallons	0

18. The computer keyboard assembly area has five employees who work 40 hours each week. Use this information to develop a load profile. What are your recommendations?

Part Name: Computer keyboard								
Processing time = 9 minutes	Week 1	Week 2	Week 3	Week 4	Week 5	Week 6	Week 7	Week 8
Planned order releases	1,000	1,200	900	1,300	1,400	1,000	800	1,100
Processing load (hours)								
Available capacity (hours)								

19. Calculate the processing load and develop the load profile for the computer assembly process. As the planner, what concerns do you have (if any)? What changes might you consider?

Part Name: Computer								
Processing time = 2 hours	Week 1	Week 2	Week 3	Week 4	Week 5	Week 6	Week 7	Week 8
Planned order releases	60	50	40	35	70	55	45	60
Processing load (hours)								
Available capacity (hours)	120	120	120	120	120	120	120	120

20. Calculate the processing load and available capacity and develop the load profile for the stereo speaker subassembly. Two employees work the assembly process for 40 hours each per week. As the planner, what concerns do you have and what changes would you make (if any)?

Part Name: Stereo speaker								
Processing time = 20 minutes	Week 1	Week 2	Week 3	Week 4	Week 5	Week 6	Week 7	Week 8
Planned order releases	210	180	220	260	200	180	230	190
Processing load (hours)								
Available capacity (hours)								

21. Calculate the processing load and available capacity and develop the load profile for a dishwasher. Eight employees work the assembly process for 40 hours per week each. As the planner, what concerns do you have and what changes would you make (if any)?

Part Name: Dishwasher								
Processing time = 30 minutes	Week 1	Week 2	Week 3	Week 4	Week 5	Week 6	Week 7	Week 8
Planned order releases	600	625	640	600	620	690	645	620
Processing load (hours)								
Available capacity (hours)								

22. Calculate the processing load and available capacity and develop a load profile for a baby stroller assembly process. The assembly process for baby strollers takes 18 minutes and the assembly line has 5 employees who work 8 hours per day. What concerns do you have (if any)?

	Baby Stroller				
Processing time = 18 minutes	Mon	Tue	Wed	Thurs	Fri
Planned order releases	116	144	148	110	156
Processing load (hours)					
Available capacity (hours)					

CASE

QP Industries—The Challenges of Integration

Adam Rodriguez, the vice president of supply chain management for QP Industries, sat in his office, contemplating what he had to tell the executive leadership team at tomorrow's meeting. During the last two years, lead times for transmitting orders between QP Industries' six strategic business units (SBUs) were getting longer and longer; meanwhile, the number of incorrect orders, inventory levels, and stockouts were dramatically increasing. Six weeks ago, the CEO of QP Industries, Ellen Higgins, had asked Adam to form a task force to identify the underlying problems and to develop a plan to solve them.

QP Industries—Corporate Background

QP Industries develops and makes gears and related engineered components, mostly used as replacement parts in heavy equipment. With sales of over $7 billion per year, QP serves the aerospace, automotive, recreational vehicle, medical, military, off-road, and power generation markets. QP is organized into six SBUs serving each of these markets.

Since its founding, QP Industries has grown by expanding on its core strengths—innovative designs, high-quality engineering, and a strict, almost fanatical adherence to quality standards and delivery schedules. The company prides itself on being the most responsive in the industry and offers "the 12-hour guarantee." For most of its product line, QP promises to pick (or produce, if necessary) and ship products within 12 hours of receiving customer orders.

Six years ago, QP's executive leadership team sought to grow sales by expanding beyond North America. They targeted Vietnam, India, Indonesia, Brazil, Argentina, China, and South Africa as desirable markets and rapidly expanded, primarily through acquisitions. During this time, QP Industries acquired over 30 different companies, many of which were leaders in their regional markets. With some 50,000 different stock keeping units (SKUs), there was a concern that the acquisitions caused unnecessary duplication of part numbers and SKUs. Subsequently, a corporate initiative identified and eliminated redundant or unnecessary SKUs (resulting in a 37 percent reduction in SKUs).

The 12-Hour Guarantee Problem

While expansion had given QP Industries 15 major distribution centers and a sales presence in 20 countries, increasingly QP was failing to meet its 12-hour guarantee.

The standard was to have 95 percent of orders meet the 12-hour guarantee. Two years ago, only 83 percent of orders were shipped within 12 hours. Last year this rate had fallen to 71 percent, and year-to-date performance suggests that the downward trend will continue.

To address this problem, Adam formed a task force consisting of the supply chain directors for each division. Over a very intensive six-week period, the task force visited customers (especially key accounts), distribution centers, and manufacturing facilities. The task force made several key conclusions.

- QP Industries was using at least 22 different MRP systems and four different DRP systems.

- Many of the acquired companies were still using legacy sales and billing systems, each with its own unique database.

- The different systems had difficulty in "talking" to each other. Often, communications were delayed and errors created as orders generated by one system were manually entered into the other system.

- Each group believed that it needed to maintain its own MRP/DRP system because its unique features were necessary.

- In many cases, the bills of materials were inaccurate because engineering changes introduced by the newly acquired companies had not been incorporated into the bills.

The Task Force's Recommendations

After consulting with some of the major MRP/ERP software providers (SAP, QAD, Oracle, and JDA), the task force recommended that the current systems be consolidated into one corporatewide ERP system and that all databases be consolidated into one database. In conjunction with this transition, core/critical processes were to be standardized and consolidated. It was estimated that this project would cost QP Industries around $25 million, but costs could run as high as $480 million (using 6.9 percent of total revenue as a proxy for the total cost of ownership). Implementation might take anywhere from 14 to 24 months. As Adam prepared for the meeting, he could not help wondering if these recommendations were sufficient and how they would be received by the executive team.

1. What are the benefits from implementing a single, companywide ERP system?

2. What challenges are likely to be encountered during implementation?

3. What additional recommendations would you make to Adam?

CASE

The Casual Furniture Company

The Casual Furniture Company (CFC) makes a variety of bookshelves for homes and businesses. The shelves come in various heights, widths, materials, and finishes. Effective requirements planning is essential for CFC's performance, and it uses MRP for planning.

The MPS and MRP records are shown for one of CFC's products, part number 4x3-01, a four-foot-high and three-foot-wide standard depth oak bookshelf. The BOM as a product structure diagram is shown in Figure 14-18.

CFC uses one-week time buckets and a planning horizon of eight weeks. The MPS for the 4x3-01 Bookshelf is shown in Figure 14-19.

The cabinets are built in the cabinet assembly department and the shelves, backs, sides, and ends are made in the cutting department. The component lot size, lead time, available inventory and safety stock are shown in Figure 14-20. Two associates work in the cutting department, making the available capacity 80 hours per week, without overtime. The processing time for each component in the cutting department is shown in Figure 14-21.

Questions

1. Develop the MRP for all of the components.

2. During week 1 of the plan, the bracket supplier notifies CFC that the order for 600 units will not arrive as planned. Instead, 300 will arrive this week and 300 will arrive next week, instead of all 600 arriving at

FIGURE 14-18

Bookshelf 4 × 3-01 BOM

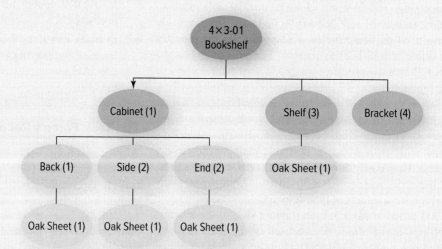

FIGURE 14-19

MPS Bookshelf 4 × 3-01

		Part Name: Bookshelf 4 × 3-01							
		Week 1	Week 2	Week 3	Week 4	Week 5	Week 6	Week 7	Week 8
MPS		70	70	80	90	60	80	80	70

FIGURE 14-20   Component Lot Size and Inventory Information

Item	Bookshelf 4 × 3-01	Cabinet	Back	Side	End	Shelf	Bracket	Oak Sheet
Lot size rule	L4L	L4L	L4L	L4L	L4L	FOQ = 500	FOQ = 600	FOQ = 1,000
Lead time	0	2 weeks	1 week	1 week	1 week	1 week	300	2 weeks
Available inventory	0	120	100	200	200	300	0	500
Safety stock	0	0	0	0	0	0	0	30

Component	Processing Time (minutes/part)
Back	10 minutes
Side	8 minutes
End	5 minutes
Shelf	7 minutes

FIGURE 14-21   Cutting Department Processing Time

the same time. Will this affect production and, if so, to what extent?

3. Now that the plan has been developed, is it feasible to consider the capacity of the cutting department? What recommendations do you have?

4. If you could change the lead times or lot-sizing policies used for any of the components, what changes would you make? Why?

APICS Dictionary, 14th ed. Chicago: APICS, 2013.

Bartholomew, D. "9 Lives and Counting." *Industry Week,* May 2006, p. 44.

Jacobs, F.; W. Berry; D. Whybark; and Vollmann, T. *Manufacturing Planning and Control for Supply Chain Management,* 6th ed. New York: McGraw-Hill, 2010.

Jonsson, P., and S. Mattsson. "Inventory Management Practices and Their Implications on Perceived Planning Performance." *International Journal of Production Economics* 46, no. 7 (2008), pp. 1787–1812.

Lee, H.; V. Padmanabhan; and S. Whang. "The Bullwhip Effect in Supply Chains." *Sloan Management Review* 38, no. 3 (1997), pp. 93–102.

Mabert, V. "The Early Road to Materials Requirements Planning." *Journal of Operations Management* 25, no. 2 (2007), pp. 346–56.

Ptak, C. and Smith, C. *Orlicky's Material Requirements Planning,* 3rd. ed. New York, McGraw-Hill, 2011.

Rettig, C. "The Trouble with Enterprise Software." *MIT Sloan Management Review* 49, no. 1 (2007), pp. 21–27.

Steele, D.; P. Philipoom; M. Malhotra; and T. Fry. "Comparisons between Drum-Buffer-Rope and Materials Requirements Planning: A Case Study." *International Journal of Production Research* 43, no. 15 (2005), pp. 3181–3208.

Taylor, D. A. "A Master Plan for Software Selection." *Supply Chain Management Review* 8, no.1 (2004), pp. 20–27.

Willcox, B. *Study Notes for Detailed Scheduling and Planning.* Chicago: APICS, 2004.

American Production and Inventory Control Society (APICS)
www.apics.org

Blue Apron
www.blueapron.com

5

MANAGING CHANGE IN SUPPLY CHAIN OPERATIONS

		relationships	sustainability	global
15	Project Management	X	X	X
15s	Project Management Supplement: Advanced Methods for Project Scheduling			
16	Sustainable Operations Management—Preparing for the Future	X	X	X

How do operations managers manage change and prepare for future challenges? Because social and economic conditions, government regulations, customer and supplier markets, and technologies are always changing, operations managers must continually plan, implement, and control changes to their operating processes. Part 5, *Managing Change in Supply Chain Operations,* explains how operations managers accomplish change in their organizations.

Chapter 15 and the accompanying supplement describe how projects serve as a means for managing change. A project is a one-time or infrequently occurring set of activities that creates outputs within prespecified time and cost schedules. **Chapter 15** describes the factors that make projects successful, and it lays out a series of steps that operations managers use to plan and control them.

Chapter 16 concludes this book by discussing the "sustainable perspective" as an approach for managing the important challenges that loom on the horizon for operations managers. The chapter describes how operations managers are seeking to develop successful outcomes for people and the planet, while maintaining profits in a rapidly changing world.

15

Project Management

LEARNING OBJECTIVES *After studying this chapter, you should be able to:*

LO15-1 Explain the difference between projects and other more routine operational processes.

LO15-2 Manage the social and technical factors that are critical for project success.

LO15-3 Choose the best type of project organizational structure for a given set of objectives.

LO15-4 Develop a comprehensive project plan, evaluating trade-offs, uncertainties, and risks.

LO15-5 Fashion criteria to guide project selection and management of a portfolio of projects.

© Jean-Pierre Clatot/AFP/Getty Images

Pixar Wins with Project Management

Pixar Animation Studios combines creative and technical artistry to create original stories in the medium of computer animation. Pixar has created some of the most successful and beloved animated films of all time, including: *Toy Story* (and its sequels), *A Bug's Life*, *Monsters Inc.* (and its sequel), *Finding Nemo*, *The Incredibles*, *Cars* (and its sequel), *Ratatouille*, *Wall-E*, *Up!*, *Brave*, and *Inside Out*. Its movies have won more than 18 Academy Awards® and have grossed billions of dollars at the worldwide box office.

What makes Pixar so successful? Project management certainly plays an important role. Pixar's approach for managing movie projects is quite different from the traditional Hollywood model. In the traditional approach, an ad hoc collection of actors, producers, and technicians come together around a film and then disband once it is finished. Highly talented people agree to terms, do their jobs, and then move on to their respective next projects. This model allows for flexibility, but it inspires minimum loyalty among project team members, and it requires a substantial period for team members to learn and accept their respective roles.

Turn that model on its head and you get the Pixar version: a tight-knit company of long-term collaborators who stick together, learn from one another, and strive to improve with every production. Project team members are professionals who have traded one-time contracts for long-term affiliations with Pixar. They contribute to multiple projects that take place over time, taking the lessons learned from one project and immediately applying them to the next. In addition, the company has created a work environment that keeps employees motivated.

Pixar also excels in the technical aspects of project management. It puts a high priority on project management skills in its new hires and offers courses on project management in its own Pixar University. The company is widely known as having the latest, most sophisticated project management software and movie production technologies.

By excelling in the management of both the social and technical aspects of project management, Pixar is able to put together enthusiastic project teams that are both creative and productive.

project A one-time or infrequently occurring set of activities that create outputs within prespecified time and cost schedules.

relationships

PROJECTS AND PROJECT MANAGEMENT

This chapter discusses a special form of operational process known as a project.[1] You will recall from Chapter 5 that a project is one of the five basic types of processes found in operations management.

A **project** is a one-time or infrequently occurring set of activities that creates outputs within prespecified time and cost schedules, while *project management* is the combination of planning, directing, and controlling resources (people, equipment, information, material) in a project to meet technical objectives within budget and schedule constraints.

Using these definitions, projects sound a lot like other operational processes discussed in this book, so why do we need a chapter dedicated to project management? There are several specific characteristics of projects that make them particularly challenging to manage:

- Every project is unique, having a planned beginning and end. Most business organizations are designed to efficiently manage repetitive, ongoing activities. Projects are not routine; they are used to manage change. Therefore, they require different management techniques.

- Most projects are multidisciplinary, involving many functional specialists who contribute to the overall project goals. The tasks that these specialists perform are interdependent, and because the project is a one-time set of activities, these interdependencies aren't always clearly understood. Imagine, for example, all of the complex relationships between tasks required to design an entirely new car using cutting-edge technologies.

- Projects are often staffed with people who are temporarily taken from functional groups (such as finance, operations, marketing, engineering, and supply management) that perform routine operations. Along with expertise, these people have their own functional points of view, and they may feel more loyalty to their functional homes than to the project.

- Projects often compete with routine operations or with other projects for resources and personnel. For this reason, projects often involve a good deal of conflict among project team members.

Because a project is usually a one-time event, it does not usually have the same degree of certainty or repeatability that routine operations do. So it is up to the project manager and her team to anticipate and plan ways to deal with all of the issues mentioned above. Although many operations management concepts may be applied to projects, there are special tools for planning, coordinating, and controlling project activities. This chapter describes these tools and discusses factors that drive project success.

student activity

Note from the following list that business projects can be long or short, big or small. Can you add to this list some types of projects in which you have participated? Think about the last event, class, party, or other "project" in which you participated. Write down the steps that were taken to plan for and execute the event.

Example projects:

Developing and launching a new product.

Merging two companies.

Constructing a new building.

Installing new equipment.

Planning and holding a company picnic.

Developing and launching a marketing campaign.

Holding an online auction or bidding event.

Starting up or closing a manufacturing plant.

---

[1]Portions of this chapter were adapted from K. A. Brown, "Project Management," in S. A. Melnyk and M. L. Swink (eds.), *Value Driven Operations Management: An Integrated Modular Approach* (New York: McGraw Hill/Irwin, 2002).

How Projects Succeed

A "successful" project meets the following objectives:

1. Completed within budget.
2. Completed on time.
3. Deliverables meet the expectations of customers, project team members, and other stakeholders.

Meeting "deliverables" objectives includes completion of the specific work outputs of the project, as well as achieving goals such as learning new lessons from the project, executing activities with minimal environmental impact, and other considerations.

As Figure 15-1 indicates, these outcomes usually conflict with one another. A general maxim in project management is, "faster, better, or cheaper; you can have two, but not three." This means that once a project has been planned and resources have been allocated, changes to the budget, schedule, and deliverables require trade-offs. For example, if management wants to reduce the project budget and speed up the schedule, then they must reduce either the quality or the scope of deliverables for the project. On the other hand, by changing the technologies used to execute the project, or by changing how project activities are defined, project managers can sometimes achieve improvements in all three areas.

In practice, there are many **technological factors** that make projects more or less successful. Think of technologies as including all "ways of doing things." Hard technologies, including equipment, facilities, computers, and communications systems, help project team members to execute tasks more quickly, more cheaply, and with better quality. In addition, soft technologies, including decision support and planning software, information systems, organizational structure, and measures and reward systems, can be very important contributors to success. Sometimes operations managers tend to focus on these technical factors. However, research has shown that **social factors** are often of equal or even greater importance to the success of projects. Social factors include the project team culture, norms of behavior, values, enthusiasm, experience,

LO15-2 Manage the social and technical factors that are critical for project success.

sustainability

activity

student

Think about all the activities involved in building a home. Can you identify a new technology that has enabled this type of project to be completed faster, better, and cheaper? On December 17, 2002, Shelby County Habitat for Humanity built a house in 3 hours, 26 minutes, and 34 seconds—breaking the previous record of 3 hours, 44 minutes, and 59 seconds. Go to an Internet search site and type "World's Fastest House." You will find a short video that shows the project through a time-lapse sequence. Imagine the project management work needed to set up and execute such an event!

technological factors Systems, equipment, and processes that define how project work is done.

social factors Project team culture, norms of behavior, values, enthusiasm, experience, authority, and influence of team members.

FIGURE 15-1 Three Primary Objectives in Project Management

In building thousands of homes, Habitat for Humanity has refined project management to a science.
© Associated Press

authority, and influence of team members. Project managers need to pay close attention to both the technical and the social aspects of their projects. The following list contains factors that are generally acknowledged to be important contributors to project success:

- A vision of project objectives that is clearly communicated and widely understood.
- A committed, talented, and well-connected project leader.
- Sufficient resources and top management support for the project.
- Disciplined procedures coupled with flexible project team members.
- Team members who have a "winning" spirit.

Stages in the Life of a Project

Figure 15-2 shows the stages in the life of a typical project, along with the level of resources typically required in each stage. Early project definition and planning activities may involve only a few people relative to the large number of personnel and other resources required in the execution of the project. However, the definition and planning stages are critical, because they define how the execution and completion stages will be done.

relationships

Though the project life profile shown in Figure 15-2 is "typical," not all projects follow this profile strictly. For example, new product development projects often have early testing and prototyping stages that precede the full-scale execution of the project. Many projects are characterized by numerous starts and stops. Sometimes projects are killed in early stages or even in the midst of execution. As business needs, technologies, and environmental conditions change, the definition, scope, and execution of projects change, too.

Because many of the project success factors discussed above are established in the early planning stages of a project, a project manager usually has the greatest influence on the success of the project in the planning stage. Once a project has been defined and planned, many of the potential outcomes of the project have been set. Once a project is under way, it is often difficult to make major changes. For this reason, most of this chapter focuses on project definition and planning activities.

FIGURE 15-2   Stages in a Project's Life

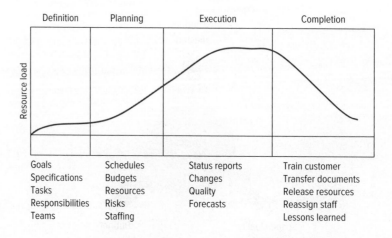

Definition	Planning	Execution	Completion
Goals	Schedules	Status reports	Train customer
Specifications	Budgets	Changes	Transfer documents
Tasks	Resources	Quality	Release resources
Responsibilities	Risks	Forecasts	Reassign staff
Teams	Staffing		Lessons learned

PROJECT DEFINITION

Project definition starts with the initial idea for the project. The definition is refined as the business case for the project is developed and evaluated and eventually selected and funded. In the early stages of project definition, it is very important to clarify who the project's clients or customers are and what they care most about. Too often, project personnel assume they know what the customer wants. Even when they do ask the customer, they may not dig deep enough to uncover unexpressed needs that are at the heart of a customer's requirements.

A useful approach is to define a project using a concise project objective statement that includes the following contents:

- *Scope and major deliverables*—desired results, milestones, documents, products.
- *Schedule*—start and end dates.
- *Resources required*—dollars, person-months, special needs (equipment, skills, etc.).

A good **project objective statement** contains all of these issues in specific, concise, clear, measurable terms. Consider the following example: "we will put a man on the moon and return him safely to earth by the end of the decade, at a cost of less than $10 billion."[2] Defining a project in this way has several advantages. First, stating things clearly and concisely creates a strong vision and challenge for the project team members. Second, it establishes a baseline for detailed activities needed to achieve this overall objective, as well as activities that should not be included. This list of activities should be reviewed with the customer to ensure that the expected deliverables can be achieved. For example, suppose your company is hired to produce a movie from a given screenplay within six months and at a cost of no more than $30 million. Does this include hiring of the actors? Promotion of the movie? In order to avoid surprises, your team must work with customers in determining all the deliverables associated with this objective statement.

> **project objective statement** The identification of project deliverables, schedule, and resources in specific, concise, clear, measurable terms.

Organizing the Project: Pure, Functional, and Matrix Projects

Most of the time, projects are planned and executed within an established organization. However, the project manager must organize the specific project team to maximize its potential for success. Projects typically fall along a spectrum of organizational forms, anchored by three specific types: functional project, pure project, and matrix project.

A **functional project** is housed and controlled within a single functional department during each project stage. Imagine, for example, a product development project in which the marketing function makes all of its promotional plans and inputs, then the engineering department creates all of the product designs, and then the operations department establishes all of the process plans needed to deliver the product. At each stage of the project, a different function controls the activities and the budget for the project. Once the activities by one function are completed, the project is handed off to the next function.

> **functional project** A project that is housed and controlled within a single functional department during each project stage.

A **pure (autonomous) project** is housed outside the normal functional departments in the business. The project team is made up of functional representatives that are fully dedicated to the project for the duration of the project's life. A pure project has a single project manager who is responsible for the budget, schedule, and all project activities. Consider, for example, a product development effort in which marketing, engineering, and operations personnel are all colocated and work together to simultaneously develop product promotional plans, product designs, and product process designs.

> **pure (autonomous) project** A project that is housed outside normal functional departments, with all stages managed by a single leader.

Efficiency is the primary advantage of a functional project approach because the project does not disrupt the existing organizational structure. A disadvantage is that project team members often have other job responsibilities, so the project may not receive top

[2]This is a paraphrase of a famous statement by John F. Kennedy in his 1960 inaugural address as president of the United States.

priority. This approach is appropriate for projects where the majority of work is in one specific function, little cross-functional integration is needed, and project leadership can be handled via the normal chain of command. The functional approach is mainly useful for incremental, fairly routine projects.

On the other hand, if various project activities requiring different functional expertise are interdependent, then a pure project can be much more effective. A pure project structure allows team members from each function to work together to solve problems faster and better. A major disadvantage to a pure project is its cost. Personnel dedicate 100 percent of their time to the project, though they may not always be needed at this level. Also, colocation and reorganization costs can be high. The pure project approach is best when:

- Speed is crucial.
- The project includes complex or uncertain tasks.
- Resource cost is not a tight constraint.
- Innovation is needed.
- Managers want to shield the project from organizational influences.
- A high degree of team commitment is needed.

matrix project A project in which a full-time project manager works together with functional managers to control budgets and to supervise functional workers who are loaned to the project from time to time.

The matrix project approach is probably the most commonly used organizational structure because it balances the advantages and disadvantages of the functional and pure project types. A matrix project utilizes people from different functional areas who are "loaned" to the project from time to time. A full-time project manager plans the project's tasks and schedules, while functional managers determine which people and technologies are used. This approach is appropriate when organizations cannot afford to tie up critical resources on a single project, and when efficient use of resources (cost) is important. From a team member's perspective, the matrix approach can be quite stressful. He or she must balance the requirements of working on several projects at once and working for several managers at the same time. Because of the conflicts that are inherent in the matrix project structure, the stature of the project manager within the organization is critical to the project's success. A "heavyweight" project manager gets the resources and priorities that the project needs by virtue of his ability to influence the functional managers who control the resources. Matrix projects with weak project managers are not likely to succeed. Table 15-1 lists the advantages and disadvantages of each of the project types.

Selecting a Project Manager

Project managers need to have both technical and social skills. Good project managers typically have many of the following traits:

- A leader, an enthusiastic influencer of people.
- A clear and sometimes forceful communicator.
- A good time-manager who is self-motivated.
- A high tolerance for ambiguity and stress.
- Politically astute and well-connected with the customer and with important people in the organization.
- Capable of understanding critical technical details of the project, including issues from different disciplines and functional areas.
- High ethical standards.

A project manager has to be both a generalist and a specialist. Good project managers can identify the most important schedule-, technical-, and resource-related details while not losing sight of the overall goals of the project and how they fit into the overall business strategy. They can speak the various "languages" of executives, technical personnel, and customers.

How does a person become an excellent project manager? Experience is the best teacher. However, because projects occur irregularly in many organizations, project

TABLE 15-1   Advantages and Disadvantages of Three Project Organizational Structures

Functional Project	Matrix Project	Pure Project
Advantages	*Advantages*	*Advantages*
• Functional manager controls both budget and activities	• Enhanced interfunctional communications	• The project manager has full authority over the project
• A team member can work on several projects	• Pinpointed responsibility	• Team members report to one boss
• The functional area is the team member's home after the project is completed	• Duplication of resources is minimized	• Shortened communication lines
• Technical expertise is maintained within the functional area (critical mass of specialized knowledge)	• Functional home for team members	• Team pride, motivation, and commitment are high
	• Policies of the parent organization are followed	
Disadvantages	*Disadvantages*	*Disadvantages*
• Aspects of the project that are not directly related to the functional area get short-changed	• Project team members have multiple bosses	• Duplication of resources
	• Success depends on project manager's negotiating skills	• Organizational goals and policies are ignored
• Needs of the client are secondary and are responded to slowly (no one involved in details is ultimately responsible for the final results)		• Difficult to transfer technology / learning
		• Team members have no functional area "home"
• Motivation of team members is often weak		

management is sometimes referred to as the "accidental profession." Training, disciplined work on areas of weakness, and a wide variety of experiences in different functional areas of the firm are helpful in giving the project manager a broader view, along with the opportunity to build relationships across the organization. Informal relationships with key resource managers are invaluable to project managers. Training programs offered by companies and by societies such as the Project Management Institute can also be helpful (www.pmi.org).

Selecting a project manager for a given project can be tricky. Many times the "perfect" person isn't available or doesn't exist. Good project managers are a rare commodity. Usually the stature of the project manager should match the priority and importance of the project. Major projects should be led by top executives, whereas small projects provide a good training ground for junior managers. Sometimes it is useful to match the personal characteristics of the manager with those of the project. For example, the development of a new technology is best led by someone with an advanced technical background, coupled with a strong understanding of business strategy. It is important to create a profile of all of the technical and social factors that might be important for a given project so that a manager who best fits the profile can be identified.

Organizing Project Teams

What makes a good project team? The following list provides some of the best practices identified in research for creating high-performance project teams.

relationships

• Break the overall project group into teams, each with less than 10 members.
• Make sure that team members are committed; use volunteers if possible.

- To the extent possible, ensure that team members serve on the project from beginning to end.
- Try to get team members assigned full-time to the project, and have them report to only one boss.
- Design teams such that all relevant functional areas and needed skills are represented on the team; this includes interpersonal skills and roles as well as technical skills.
- Help the team members understand the importance of their team, and pick team leaders who foster cooperation and trust.
- Colocate team members within conversational distance of each other.

Though there is a wealth of research on this topic, it is still difficult to guarantee team success, even if all the "known" best practices are followed. Through preproject training, team members learn about the different roles they might play on the team. Training helps team members learn how to handle conflict. Importantly, they can recognize their need to evolve quickly as team members to become productive. By setting early milestones and deliverables, the project manager can encourage the team to coalesce into a productive working unit.

global

Globally Dispersed Project Teams

Throughout this book we have discussed the increasing roles of outsourcing and low-cost country suppliers. Due to these trends, project teams increasingly involve members in different companies and in different locations around the world. For example, a software development project initiated by a U.S. company might involve programmers and design personnel in India and other parts of the world. Managing such globally dispersed project teams involves unique challenges. Cultural, organizational, and technological barriers often must be overcome in order to meet project goals.

In addition to the obvious challenges associated with team members who speak different languages, one of the biggest cultural barriers involves a reluctance of personnel in one company or location to share information or ask for help from personnel in other companies or locations. Often, this reluctance stems either from an unwillingness to trust project partners or from the "not invented here" syndrome, which discounts the value of ideas that are not homegrown. The project manager must try to instill in the project team members a longer-term perspective that shifts the focus away from short-term gains and win-lose thinking, which can impede project progress.

At the same time, it is imperative that the team at the center of the project does not force its culture and perspectives on its project partners. The value of collaboration in projects comes from diversity in culture, perspectives, and skills, not from similarities. Training programs can help members of all companies involved to appreciate their differences, especially when constituents represent different national cultures, languages, and work norms. In addition, a focus and priority placed on project goals and customer satisfaction can help personnel overcome barriers due to cultural differences.

Organizational boundaries sometimes stifle globally dispersed projects. Even if partners trust each other and are culturally compatible, stiff hierarchies and long lines of communication can prevent the collaboration from being as effective as it could be. Companies sometimes have strict guidelines regarding who can talk to whom in order to ensure that secrets are kept and organizational hierarchies are respected. The consequence is that project details may be lost, leading to mistakes, incorrect assumptions, and project delays. Project managers need to ensure that team members establish appropriate working contacts in all functional areas across the respective organizational structures.

Finally, physical and temporal boundaries can pose difficulties in managing globally dispersed projects. The ability to use **24/7 project operations** (where groups in one time zone work while groups in other time zones sleep) is one of the potential benefits that entices firms to pick project partners located in distant locations. However, project managers need to develop the systems for effectively passing work back and forth. Information technologies have come a long way in establishing systems to enable secure and accurate

24/7 project operations Globally dispersed projects where groups in one time zone work while groups in other time zones sleep.

knowledge transfer. In addition, video conferencing and other communication technologies offer some of the benefits of face-to-face communications. Managers of globally dispersed projects need to make sure that different information systems talk to each other and that everyone on the team knows where to go to get questions answered.

Establishing a Project Charter

An excellent way to summarize the project definition and organizational design is by means of a project charter. A project charter can be thought of as a contract that signals the authority to launch a project. Many examples of project charters can be found through an Internet search of the term "project charter." A good charter includes several key elements.

project charter A document that establishes the initial plan for a project, including its purpose and priority, its customers and project team members, and its budget, schedule, and major deliverables.

- First, it concisely defines the purpose of the project and establishes its role and priority among all projects for the organization.
- It describes the customers, project team members, and other key stakeholders in the project, along with their roles.
- Finally, it presents the budget, high-level schedule, and major deliverables for the project.

A charter serves an important role in establishing the initial plan for the project. As the project unfolds and new opportunities or problems arise, proposed changes to the project must be compared with the project scope as specified in the original charter. Without this sort of initial anchoring documentation, it is easy for a project to turn into something that was never originally intended. Also, by reading and signing the charter, team members understand their roles in achieving the project goals.

student activity

Find examples of project charters on the Internet. How many of them have all of the important elements we have identified?

PROJECT PLANNING

Once the major elements of a project are defined and approved, the project management team can begin detailed planning by developing a work breakdown structure (WBS). As shown in Figure 15-3, the WBS is a hierarchical listing of project activities. This particular project is designed to install a new supply chain planning system software program.

work breakdown structure (WBS) A hierarchical listing of project activities.

WBS Level	Project Tasks
0–Project	Planning System Installation
1–Task	System Design
2–Work Package	Select system modules
2–Work Package	Set system protocols
1–Task	Prepare Data
2–Work Package	Gather legacy system data
2–Work Package	Translate data
1–Task	Training
2–Work Package	Design training program
2–Work Package	Hold training sessions
1–Task	Prepare Documentation
1–Task	System Rollout
2–Work Package	Populate system data
2–Work Package	Test system
2–Work Package	Debug system
2–Work Package	Pilot test
2–Work Package	Hold "go live" meeting

FIGURE 15-3
Work Breakdown Structure for a Planning System Installation Project

LO15-4 Develop a comprehensive project plan, evaluating trade-offs, uncertainties, and risks.

The project includes steps needed to (1) tailor the design of the software to the specific company's needs, (2) make adjustments to data that will be used in the system, (3) train the users and prepare user manuals, and (4) solve problems once the system is initiated (system rollout). While this is a fairly small project, a larger WBS hierarchy might include many levels, including tasks and subtasks, that are ultimately broken down to the lowest-level tasks, known as *work packages.*

Small projects may include only two or three levels in a WBS, whereas larger projects typically require many more levels of detail. The Get Real boxes in this chapter give an idea of the scope of work involved in huge projects, such as staging the Olympics and expanding an airport. A work package defined at the lowest level of the WBS should have a measurable outcome that is assignable to a single individual or group. Responsibility for each work package should be unambiguous, and metrics should be clear. Here are some of the best practices for developing a WBS:

- Involve all project leaders in developing the WBS. This will instill ownership and provide creativity.
- Each work package should include a noun and a verb to imply action (e.g., "Meet with customers" rather than "Customers").
- As a rule of thumb, low-level tasks should be designed to be between 8 and 80 work hours in duration.[3]
- Include a risk analysis (discussed later in the chapter) at the WBS stage.
- Include any and all activities that consume resources, including project planning and management activities.
- Think hierarchically (top-down) or in a pure brainstorming mode. A hierarchical approach starts with major tasks and then identifies all subtasks related to each major category. A brainstorming approach allows for a rapid-fire listing of all activities that come to mind.
- Don't worry about the sequencing or time-phasing of activities. Scheduling comes later.
- A flexible and effective way to capture activities is to write them on sticky notes and paste them onto a wall. Then the notes can be reorganized to create the WBS hierarchy.
- For complex projects, it may be helpful to have two separate teams develop WBSs independently. Then bring the teams together and compare results.

student activity

Develop a WBS for a small project such as painting a house. You might start by writing down each task on a sticky note. Then arrange the notes on a wall in a hierarchical (top-down) fashion. How can you ensure that you have not forgotten any tasks?

business case A well-developed justification of the financial and strategic reasons for pursuing a project.

Budgeting for Time and Cost

The WBS can be used to estimate, allocate, and ultimately monitor resources for each of the work packages and major tasks in the project. The business case typically includes a preliminary budget based on rough cost estimates. The detailed WBS provides the framework for developing both time and cost estimates and for monitoring the progress of the project once activities begin. Usually time estimates are needed first, in order to then calculate the costs of needed workers, equipment, and so on. Time estimates can be based on similar projects when many have been completed. For example, in the construction industry an experienced estimator can forecast the time and the cost required to construct a building just by knowing the type of construction and the number of square feet of floor space. For really new projects, estimating is more difficult, and it is usually beneficial to have a team of people to develop estimates together.

[3]E. Verzuh, *The Fast Forward MBA in Project Management* (New York: Wiley, 1999).

GET REAL

Managing an "Olympic"-Sized Project

Imagine the work needed to develop a WBS for the Olympic Games. The host country must construct secure accommodations for 17,000 athletes and judges from 205 countries. In the case of the 2008 Summer Olympics in Beijing, China, 31 individual venues were needed. Of those 31 venues, 12 were permanent structures constructed specifically for the Games, another 10 were renovated existing structures, and 9 were temporary sites. Each of these locations required electrical, water, and waste disposal systems to support them.

The management and planning that goes into the Olympics does not stop when all of the buildings have been completed, nor does it only start again when the athletes take the field. PC-maker Lenovo spent the entire year leading up to the Games providing and testing IT systems to support both the competition and the media associated with the events. Lenovo provided 20,000 pieces of computing equipment to help run 56 Olympic venues. To further complicate the project, several of the venues—especially the National Aquatics Center, also known as the "Water Cube"— had to have IT infrastructure that could handle 90 percent indoor humidity.

If testing all of the equipment was not difficult enough, the 580 engineers sent to run and troubleshoot the system also required training and work scheduling. Projects with this kind of multilayered complexity demand strong project management skills.

The "Water Cube" National Aquatics Center in Beijing.

© Li wei–imaginechina/AP Images

Once the time and cost estimates have been produced, the planning team makes initial adjustments based on overall budget and schedule constraints. Figure 15-4 shows a cost-allocated WBS for the planning system project introduced in Figure 15-3. Typically, the costs for project tasks are initially estimated by work package managers and then added up to compute the costs for the major tasks and for the project as a whole. Then, adjustments and reallocations are made if the costs do not meet budget limitations or expectations. There may be some negotiations between project managers and customers, or between managers of major tasks in the project, in order to arrive at an overall resource allocation that is reasonable and achievable. Managers typically use a combination of cost data from past similar projects and detailed resource analyses to make their cost estimates.

Detailed Scheduling Using the Critical Path Method

Once the overall budget and time estimates for tasks have been established, a detailed schedule can be created. A useful way to plan and communicate schedules is the **critical path method (CPM)**. The nearby Get Real box describes the historical origins of this method. Critical path scheduling techniques display a project in graphic form in a way that identifies the activities that are most important and should receive focused attention. Critical path scheduling is based on several key assumptions:

critical path method (CPM) A project planning technique that identifies in graphic form the activities that are most important and should receive focused attention.

1. The project tasks have well-defined beginnings and endings.
2. The tasks are independent; the duration of one task is not dependent on the duration of another.
3. A required sequence of the tasks can be established.

FIGURE 15-4 WBS for a Planning System Installation Project with Allocated Budget

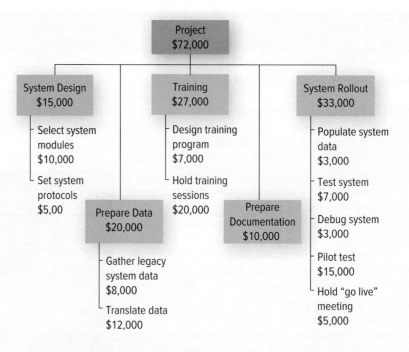

For small projects, a formal schedule may be unnecessary; a simple checklist may be sufficient. For larger projects, however, a special set of scheduling tools can clarify planning and help ensure that tasks are completed in the proper sequence. One such tool is a **network diagram**. A network diagram is constructed using the task definitions, estimated lengths, and precedence relationships (the definition of what has to come first, second, and so on).

network diagram A graphical display of project tasks and their interrelationships.

Table 15-2 shows project information for the planning system installation project. Figure 15-5 shows a network diagram for the planning system installation project. Each circle (or *node*) represents a task, and the arrows connecting the tasks show the precedence relationships among them. A parallel relationship between two tasks means that they can be performed simultaneously. For example, when building a house, one crew can landscape the yard at the same time that another crew installs the light fixtures indoors. On the other hand, sequential activities depend on each other—pouring the concrete for the foundation of a house cannot be done until the site excavation is completed.

GET REAL

The History of CPM and PERT

The critical path method (CPM) and its close relative, the project evaluation and review technique (PERT), were developed in the 1950s and 1960s at DuPont Corporation and at the U.S. Navy. Both techniques use network diagramming to graphically display and analyze projects, with a few differences. Managers at DuPont were scheduling fairly predictable facilities cleaning operations, so they developed the CPM with a focus on making time-cost trade-offs using fixed task time estimates. Naval officers were scheduling highly uncertain activities associated with the development of the Polaris missile system, so they developed PERT with a focus on managing uncertainties in the project by using probabilistic time estimates. The CPM approach typically uses "activity-on-node"

notation, like we are using in this chapter. The PERT approach uses "activity-on-arc" diagramming, where each project task is represented by an arc or arrow. The advantage of activity-on-arc diagramming is that arrows can have different lengths representing the different lengths of task durations; this gives a more visual representation of the lengths of various paths in the project network. The disadvantage is that these networks are more difficult to draw, and some task interrelationships are difficult to represent.

Both DuPont and U.S. Navy operations gained large improvements in project outcomes through the use of these techniques. These early methods have been refined and computerized to provide the tools that thousands of managers use today.

TABLE 15-2   Task Information for the Planning System
Implementation Project

Task	Task Label	Estimated Duration (days)	Immediate Predecessors
Start	Str	0	None
Select system modules	SSM	9	Str
Prepare data	PDat	5	Str
Populate system data	PSD	5	PDat, SSM
Test system	TS	6	PSD
Debug system	DS	4	TS
Pilot test	PT	3	DS, PDoc, HTS
Hold "Go Live" meeting	HGL	1	PT
Set system protocols	SSP	3	SSM
Prepare documentation	PDoc	14	SSM
Design training program	DTP	2	SSM
Hold training sessions	HTS	1	DTP

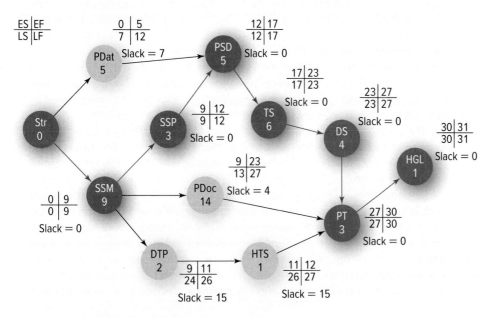

FIGURE 15-5   Network Diagram for the Planning System Installation Project

Red nodes are critical path (zero slack) activities.

EXAMPLE 15-1

Let's use the information given in Figure 15-5 to understand how to use the critical path method. The **critical path** is defined as the longest path (or paths, if two or more paths tie for longest path) from the beginning node to the end node in the project. The longest path is deemed *critical* because, assuming all tasks are executed according to plan, the longest path of activities will determine the final completion date for the project. Thus, if one of the tasks on the critical path is late, then the entire project will be late.

critical path The longest path of activities reaching from the beginning node to the end node in a project.

(continued)

earliest start date The earliest date that an activity can be planned to start given the requirements of its predecessors.

earliest finish date The earliest date that an activity can be planned to finish given the requirements of its predecessors.

latest start date The latest dates that an activity can be planned to start given the requirements of its successors.

latest finish date The latest dates that an activity can be planned to finish given the requirements of its successors.

task slack The amount of time that a task duration can be increased without affecting the length of the project.

(continued)

The nodes and arrows colored in red in Figure 15-5 form the longest path in the network and, therefore, constitute the critical path. The critical path indicates that the current estimated project length is 31 days (add up the durations along the critical path).

The data given next to each of the nodes in the diagram indicate the earliest start date and earliest finish date for each task, and the latest start date and latest finish date for each task. The earliest start date for a task is simply the next period after the completion of the latest of the task's predecessors. For example, the earliest date that the "Populate System Data" task can start is on the day that the "Set System Protocols" task is completed, because that task must finish at the same time or later than the "Prepare Data" task. Earliest starts for tasks can be computed by adding up the durations of tasks along the network paths from left to right. This is known as a *forward pass* analysis. The longest path leading up to a given task determines that path's earliest possible start date. The earliest possible completion date for any task is simply its earliest start date plus the expected duration of the task.

Task slack (also called *float*) is the amount of time (working days) that a task duration can be increased without affecting the length of the project. Notice that the task slack for each of the activities on the critical path is zero. An increase in the duration of any of these activities lengthens the overall project. Therefore, a project manager must pay special attention to these tasks to ensure that they take no longer than their planned durations. There is no freedom in the schedule that allows any of the activities on the critical path to be completed late without delaying the overall project. On the other hand, the tasks not on the critical path all have slack. For example, the "Prepare Data" task has seven days of slack. Why seven days? Notice that the length of the start to finish path containing the "Prepare Data" task is 24 days long. This means that the "Prepare Data" task could be lengthened by seven days (31 days − 24 days) and the project would still finish in 31 days. Looking at it another way, we could postpone the start of the "Prepare Data" task by as much as seven working days. As long as the task itself takes no more than the planned five days, the task that follows, "Populate System Data," can still be started on its planned date.

Both the "Design Training Program" and "Hold Training Sessions" tasks have 15 days of slack. This is because the path that they are on is 15 days shorter than the critical path. However, this does not mean that both tasks have 15 days of slack *independently*. Instead, these two tasks *share* a total of 15 days of slack. If the "Design Training Program" starts late or takes longer than planned, then the slack available at the subsequent task, "Hold Training Sessions," is reduced. Some of the slack can be used at either of the noncritical tasks and not affect the overall project duration.

Such sequential and parallel relationships are indicated in Figure 15-5 as well. For example, the start of "Debug System" must follow the completion of "Test System." However, the start of "Prepare Documentation" is not dependent on the start or completion of "Set System Protocols," so parts of these two tasks could be done simultaneously. It is important for every project to have a single starting point and a single ending point. The "Start" activity at the left end of the project consumes zero days because it is simply a node that indicates the proposed start date of the project.

The latest start date and latest finish date for any task are computed by adding the task slack to the earliest start and earliest completion dates possible for the task. Another way to compute the latest start and completion dates for all the tasks in the project network is to make a *backward pass* analysis. The backward pass is done by starting with the project completion date (defined by the critical path), and then subtracting the task times from right to left along the paths in the network.

We can summarize all of these network relationships in the following equations, which make up the critical path algorithm:

- *Forward pass:* Calculating the earliest start and finish dates.

  Earliest start date for a task = Maximum (latest) earliest finish date for all predecessors of that task (Earliest start date for tasks at the beginning of the network = 0)

  Earliest finish date for a task = Earliest start + Task duration

  Project completion date = Maximum (latest) earliest finish date for all tasks
- *Backward pass:* Calculating the latest start and completion dates.

  Latest finish date for a task = Minimum (earliest) latest start date for all followers of that task

  Latest start date for a task = Latest finish date − Task duration
- *Calculating task slack:*

  Task slack = Latest start date − Earliest start date, or

  $\qquad\quad$ = Latest finish date − Earliest finish date

Practice using these equations to verify the numbers shown in Figure 15-5. Another detailed example of how to use these equations is provided in the solved problem at the end of the chapter.

The information detailing the critical activities, earliest and latest starts and completions, and task slack helps project managers know where to focus their attention and how much flexibility they have in scheduling noncritical tasks. Frequently re-analyzing a project in this way as tasks are completed helps project managers more effectively allocate resources. For example, if a critical task is completed late, then a manager might decide to move resources from a noncritical activity to other activities on the critical path in order to get the project back on schedule.

Figure 15-6 shows how the planning system implementation project network diagram looks when it is created using Microsoft Project, a widely used project management software program. In Figure 15-6, each box (or *node*) represents an activity. Each box contains the task slack, the earliest start and earliest complete dates, and the estimated duration of the task. Note that a tool such as this can automatically calculate calendar dates, accounting for weekends and holidays. Figure 15-6 shows that, assuming no work is done on weekends, the estimated completion date is Monday, December 4. Since many project managers use software programs like this one to manage project information, we will use this format for the rest of the examples in this chapter.

FIGURE 15-6
MS Project CPM Network for the Planning System Installation Project

Analyzing Resources and Trade-Offs

Once an initial project schedule is created, project managers review the resource requirements implied by the schedule to see if they are compatible with project constraints and goals. If a specific resource for a critical path activity is not available during the scheduled time period, the delay affects the entire project. For example, suppose that the "Populate System Data" task in Figure 15-6 is assigned to the marketing department, yet they will not have personnel available to work on this task until Friday, November 10. The project will be completed two days late, assuming nothing else changes. As another example, suppose that the person who is given the task of "Select System Modules" is also given the task of "Prepare Data." Because "Select System Modules" is a critical activity, the person will do that task first, taking nine days. Unfortunately, this means that the "Prepare Data" task will be completed late (because it has only seven days of slack). The start of "Populate System Data" will be postponed by two days, and again the project will be completed two days late, assuming nothing else changes.

Initial estimates of task durations are often made assuming certain resource availabilities, without a clear understanding of the schedule. Parallel activities can create overlapping and conflicting resource requirements at certain points in time. For this reason, managers need to evaluate the scheduled requirements and find solutions for resource conflicts. Important resources could include people (skill types), materials, technology (equipment), and capital (cash). Some useful questions to ask are:

- Are resources available in the windows of time identified by the schedule?
- Is the same resource required on parallel paths?
- Is a resource frequently used only a little at a time (e.g., part-time need for an electrician at multiple stages)?
- Should resources be dedicated full-time or part-time?

Making Time-Cost-Scope Trade-Offs

Remember the "faster-better-cheaper" trade-off discussed earlier in the chapter? If resource conflicts exist in the schedule, or if the current plan exceeds the budget or schedule requirements, changes to the plan may be required. Suppose that the current plan exceeds the available budget for the project. A simple change would be to reduce the scope of activities and eliminate some of the deliverables for the project. If that is not an option, the project managers often make trade-offs between budget (cost) and schedule (time). Suppose that current project activities are running late, or that the client has moved up the due date so that the current plan no longer meets the required deadline. In either case, more money could be spent to hasten project activities to meet the required completion date. In project management terminology, speeding up an activity is known as *crashing* the activity. When many activities are *crashable,* the decision regarding exactly which activities to crash can be complicated. However, by following a simple set of rules the project manager can usually find the lowest cost way to speed up a project in order to meet its deadline. The supplement for this chapter illustrates the procedure for crashing projects in detail.

Planning for Uncertainty

Up to this point we have assumed that estimates of task durations are fixed and accurate. In reality, it can be very difficult to accurately estimate durations, especially when tasks are new or when they are dependent on circumstances outside the control of the project team. In this section we will discuss three tools for managing uncertainty in projects: probabilistic estimates, buffering, and risk analysis.

Probabilistic Task Duration Estimates

One method for analyzing the impacts of uncertainty on projects is to use **probabilistic task duration estimates**, which include a range of possible task durations for each task,

probabilistic task duration estimates A tool for conveying uncertainty that includes a range of possible task durations for each task, rather than relying on a single point estimate.

Project Management Software Helps Get the Job Done

Hartsfield-Jackson Atlanta International Airport (ATL), one of the busiest air terminals in the world, is in the midst of a major development and expansion program that culminates in 2030. One of the key projects of this comprehensive program was the addition of a fifth runway to meet expanding demand at this major hub. Building a nearly two-mile runway in a major metropolitan area like Atlanta required not just constructing the runway itself, but also rerouting through a newly constructed tunnel under the tarmac.

The project encompassed some 15,000 interdependent schedule items and 23 subprojects, including working with important government and local constituencies to prevent delays, raw material delivery, and subcontractor schedules. Getting the project done on time, despite the massive complexity of the task, was particularly important because each week of delay was estimated to cost the airline industry $5 million in revenue, and each day of delay carried a $5 million penalty for the bidding company.

Project managers used a software program to manage this massively complex task. The software allowed users to plan the project in great detail, see how delays in one subproject might impact the entire project, and run scenarios to attempt to work around delays. The software also helped manage payment to contractors by having them check off their progress as they completed

each task. This documentation made it easy to check whether contractors had made all the progress they claimed on schedule.

The result of this close and efficient project supervision aided by project management software was extremely positive. Despite the complexity of the task both from a political and engineering standpoint, the runway was completed 11 days early and $102 million under budget.

© Alberto Riva/Bloomberg via Getty Images

rather than relying on a single point estimate. "Best case," "worst case," and "most likely case" durations are estimated for each task in the project. By making some assumptions about the statistical properties of these estimates, project analysts can create distributions of possible outcomes for each project task and, ultimately, for the project as a whole. Instead of simply expecting the project to be completed on a certain date, the project manager can use this new statistical information to estimate the probability that the project will be completed on or before a given date. If the probability of completion by a given deadline is unacceptably low, then the manager can use project crashing, buffering, or other techniques to improve the project's chances of on-time completion. The calculations for probabilistic task duration estimations are illustrated in the supplement to this chapter.

Buffering the Project

When managers are asked to submit estimates of task durations for project planning, they sometimes build in extra time (a buffer) "just to be safe." For example, if a manager expects that a task may take four days, he might tell his boss five days (have you ever done this?). However, because these buffers are hidden from the project manager, they often are wasted in terms of helping complete projects on time. A more useful approach is to design buffers into the project plan, making them plain for everyone on the project to see and utilize. A **project buffer** is simply a designated time period that provides some slack along paths that are critical or highly variable.

project buffer A time period set aside to provide slack along activity paths that are critical or highly variable.

Risk Analysis

Risk analysis is an important thing to do early on in project definition, at the development of the WBS, and after a detailed schedule is created. Project managers should

EXAMPLE 15-2

Consider the revised planning system installation project plan shown in Figure 15-7. In this example, the project will most likely take 31 days, yet the due date for delivery of the survey is 35 days. This leaves four days for buffering. As the figure suggests, it is usually a good idea to place explicit buffers in the following parts of the network:

- Immediately after high uncertainty tasks.
- Where noncritical tasks merge with the critical path.
- Where scarce resources are needed.
- At the end of the project.

    Project buffers are a means for hedging against unforeseen problems in the project execution. By making buffers visible and by managing them closely, the project team can have a better idea of where uncertainties lie and how the project is doing relative to its schedule.[4]

FIGURE 15-7   Revised Planning System Installation Project Plan Including Buffers (Due date for the project: December 8)

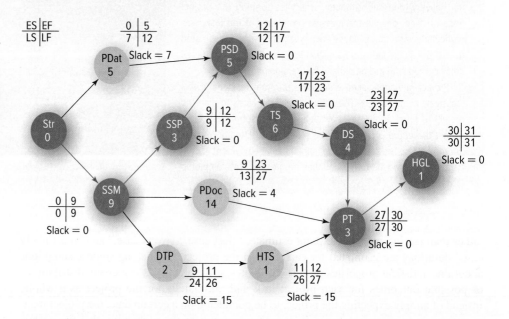

always consider Murphy's Law: What can go wrong, will go wrong! There are numerous tools available for assessing project risk. A simple risk analysis technique[5] involves several steps:

Step 1: Hold a team brainstorming session to identify the possible risks associated with technologies, resources of all kinds, markets and customers, and competitors.

Step 2: Establish the probability that each risk event will occur.

Step 3: Establish the potential impacts of each risk event on the budget, schedule, and deliverables of the project.

Step 4: Determine plans for dealing with the risk events that are of highest probability and impact. Risk mitigation plans could include:

- Preventive measures
- Contingency plans

---

[4]Eli Goldratt discusses the technical and behavioral issues associated with buffering projects in his book, *The Critical Chain* (Great Barrington, MA: North River Press, 1997).

[5]This technique is an application of the failure modes and effects analysis (FMEA) approach discussed in Chapter 4, "Product/Process Innovation."

TABLE 15-3   Risk Analysis for Shooting of Winter Scenes in a Movie

Risk	Outcome/Impact	Likelihood	Strategies/ Responses	Cost*	Triggers
No snow for winter scenes	• Delay filming • Incomplete storyline	• 50% in October (current schedule) • 20% in December	1. Film winter scenes in December 2. Move location 3. Rent snow-making machines	$10,000 to change schedule $100,000 move cost $20,000 rental charge	• Schedule delay of 1 week • Weather forecast showing <20% chance of snow

*Note that costs do not necessarily have to be indicated in monetary terms.

- Emergency funds
- Time buffers

Step 5: Select the risk mitigation plans that give the best prevention or protection against risk for the minimum investment required.

The final steps of this analysis can be communicated as a risk table. An example of a risk table is shown in Table 15-3. In addition to the steps above, the risk planning team should establish a signal or metric that determines the circumstances under which a contingency or risk mitigation plan should be invoked. These "triggers" establish concrete decision points for the project team. For example, in Table 15-3, the team might decide that a schedule delay of one week will be the trigger for renting snowmaking machines. Risk assessment is typically one of the most important, and most neglected, activities in project management.

PROJECT EXECUTION

Project execution is the phase in which the project work is actually done. At this point, the project manager plays the important roles of encouraging, monitoring, and controlling performance. For small projects, performance monitoring can be fairly informal; the project manager can frequently speak with each of the project team members. In larger projects, however, it is important to determine the levels of reporting frequency and formality that project managers will require. This is often a question of balance. Managers don't want project team members to be so busy preparing status reports that they never get any work done. On the other hand, more frequent reports give managers a more up-to-date picture of the project's status.

One way to achieve balance is for project managers to give most of their attention to critical path activities, and less to others, unless they are particularly risky. For example, a large project might require weekly reports from owners of critical path activities and only monthly reports from owners of noncritical activities. It is also especially important to get regular status updates early on in the project. Research shows that early budget and schedule performance are strong predictors of the ultimate completed project performance.

Status reports should contain updates on budget, schedule, and the quality of output. Though many more sophisticated reporting formats exist, a common and simple way to communicate schedule status is through the use of a bar chart (also known as a **Gantt chart**) showing percentage completion for each activity. Figure 15-8 displays an example of an MS Project bar chart. Note that the dark line through the center of any task bar indicates the percentage of the task that is complete. For example, task 2, "Prepare Data," is

Gantt chart A bar chart that shows the timing, relationships, and percentage completion for activities in a project.

FIGURE 15-8   MS Project Bar Chart for the Planning System Installation Project

ID	Task Name	Duration	Oct 22 10/22	Oct 29 10/29	Nov 5 11/5	Nov 12 11/12	Nov 19 11/19	Nov 26 11/26
1.	Start	0d	▮ 10/23					
2.	Prepare Data	5d	▭					
3.	Populate System Data	5d			▭			
4.	Test System	6d				▭		
5.	Debug System	6d					▭	
6.	Prepare Documentation	14d		▭				
7.	Design Training Program	2d			▭			
8.	Hold Training Sessions	1d			▭			
9.	Pilot Test	3d						▭
10.	Hold "Go Live" Meeting	1d						
11.	Select System Modules	9d	▭					
12.	Select System Protocols	3d		▭				

50 percent complete. "Select System Protocols" (task 12) has been completed entirely. "Populate System Data" awaits the completion of "Prepare Data" before it can start.

In addition to monitoring the budget, schedule, and quality/scope conditions of an ongoing project, it is often important to monitor other key indicators of project progress and success. Sometimes project managers routinely estimate the financial returns of a project using metrics like net present value and return on investment. It is also important to frequently answer questions like:

sustainability

- Is our customer happy?
- Are the project sponsors/leaders still committed?
- Are we overcoming technical hurdles and avoiding risks?
- How is the project team's morale?
- Do we have issues that are not being resolved?
- Is the project receiving the resources that it needs?
- Are we being socially responsible (safe and environmentally friendly)?

When to Kill a Project

Sometimes the best way to execute a project is to actually "execute" it, that is, to kill it. This can be a very difficult decision and process. Consequently, unhealthy projects are often allowed to persist for too long. Projects are often aggressive efforts that involve lots of uncertainty, and conditions that initially made the project attractive can quickly change. For this reason, it is important for project sponsors and managers to periodically gauge the progress of a project from a strategic perspective. If a project is no longer expected to meet its objectives, it should be killed quickly to avoid wasted resources. There are many reasons to kill a project, including:

- *Consistent budget or schedule overruns.* This can be an indication that resource needs and costs were severely underestimated at the beginning of the project. Or perhaps conditions have changed so that inexpensive resources are no longer available. At some point rising costs may exceed the value of the project.
- *Failure to create value.* Projects sometimes involve technical hurdles that just cannot be surmounted at a reasonable cost. On the other hand, the project may be meeting its objectives, but those objectives are no longer valuable. For example, suppose that a competitor introduces a new product that makes your new product project obsolete. Customers and clients may also change their minds about a project based on changing needs and market trends.

- *Changing priorities.* Organizations change their priorities over time, and these changes may make a current project less attractive. For example, if a company falls on hard times financially, it may need to scrap projects that do not provide immediate benefits. In another case, a new project idea may come along that is actually more important or gives a better return than the current project. In this case it would be prudent to kill the current project and shift the resources to the new opportunity.
- *Wrong resources.* Perhaps the project idea still has merit, but the organization does not currently have the skills or talent needed to bring the project to a successful conclusion. Sometimes political forces come into play that stifle a project's progress. As some point it may be better to kill the current project and start again when proper resources and a unified commitment become available.

PROJECT COMPLETION

Project completion occurs when all project deliverables have been completed to the satisfaction of the client, sponsor, and other decision makers with acceptance authority. Project managers should make sure that project team members stay motivated at this stage, as it is easy for them to experience burnout or to turn their attention to other projects prematurely. It is usually a good idea to hold reviews of all activities, with checklists and other reports, to make sure that no final deliverables are missed.

Immediately after project completion is also the best time to evaluate the key successes and failures of the project. This activity is commonly known as a **postproject review** (also called a *postmortem*). Ideally, an independent team should review the project and develop a detailed report of lessons learned. The purpose of this team is not to second-guess or place blame, but to identify both effective and ineffective practices that can be compared against other project reviews. This will help ensure that the good practices are repeated and that the weaker practices are corrected in future projects. In addition, the postproject review can be the time to recognize the contributions of project team members and to highlight the success of the project to executives throughout the organization. Points to be addressed in a postproject review include:

> **postproject review** An effort to capture the lessons learned from the project experience and to recognize the contributions of project team members.

- How well were deliverables met in terms of scope, quality, and dealing with changes throughout the project?
- How well was the project budget met? Where were the important variances?
- Was the project on time? What were the constraining resources?
- Have all remaining project tasks been completed? Have results been communicated to all important stakeholders?
- Is the customer happy? How has this project affected our relationships with customers?
- Are the project team members satisfied? What specific morale issues need to be addressed? In what ways were employees' skills and knowledge enhanced?
- What problems were solved on this project? What new market or technical knowledge needs to be documented and used in future projects?
- What was learned regarding new management approaches or use of new project management technologies (organizational approach, software, information systems, and so on).

MANAGING A PORTFOLIO OF PROJECTS

> **LO15-5** Fashion criteria to guide project selection and management of a portfolio of projects.

Large organizations typically have many projects going on at the same time, at many locations across the supply chain. A business development unit, for example, could be developing several new products simultaneously. Supply chain managers typically have many process improvement and relationship management projects going on, potentially involving product suppliers, customers, consultants, and technology vendors. It is important for managers to view such a mix of projects as a portfolio of efforts that are used to execute the organization's overall strategy. Each project's unique contribution to the overall goals of the business unit should be clearly established.

Too often in businesses, projects are not managed strategically. Team members on various projects often do not understand how projects relate to one another and to the business strategy. There are many reasons for this. A primary cause is that often the criteria used to select projects are not consistent with higher-level business goals. For example, projects are often selected using financial criteria alone. Figure 15-9 shows a mix of projects positioned according to their probability of success (risk) and value if successful (contribution). If these were the only important criteria, then we would select only projects that are in the upper right-hand quadrant of the figure.

There are other, more strategic, reasons to select and include projects in the portfolio. Projects can be viewed as opportunities to learn new things, build technical capabilities, develop new partnerships, and identify the strengths and weaknesses of people in the organization. Projects also can be designed to build upon previous successes or failures in order to move the organization toward long-term strategic goals.

In general, managers should evaluate potential new projects by considering three categories of factors:

1. The project's fit with the organization's overall strategy and existing portfolio of projects.
2. Financial returns or other benefits associated with the project.
3. The feasibility of the project, including availability of required resources.

Project selection should be based on a business case. As described earlier in the chapter, a business case is a well-developed justification including both financial and strategic reasons for the project. A comprehensive business case includes:

- Financial and market analyses identifying required resources, costs, and benefits of the project.
- Description of assumptions, risks, and how risks will be managed.
- Importance of the project to the organization's strategic mission.

Small projects may not require such a formal analysis, but some evaluation of benefits, costs, and risks should always precede the start of a project.

FIGURE 15-9

Estimating the Value of a Portfolio of Projects

Portfolio value $= \Sigma\, P_i(\text{Success}) \times NPV_i$

CHAPTER SUMMARY

A project is a one-time or infrequently occurring set of activities that creates outputs within prespecified time and cost schedules. Project management is the combination of planning, directing, and controlling resources (people, equipment, information, and material) in a project to meet technical objectives within budget and schedule constraints. To make projects successful, project managers should keep the following facts in mind:

- Most projects are important processes for managing change. Such projects are often challenging because most organizations are not configured for projects; they are configured for routine operations and processes.

- A large part of the project manager's ability to influence the success of a project comes in the definition and planning stages that occur before project execution. In defining the project objectives and in assigning resources, project managers should remember that both social and technical factors contribute to a project's success.

- Projects can be organized and executed in three different ways: as pure (autonomous) projects, functional projects, and matrix projects. Each of these organizational structures offers advantages and disadvantages that should be matched to the requirements of the project at hand.

- Project managers need to be aware of tools and techniques for budgeting, scheduling, and controlling projects. These include the work breakdown structure, the critical path method, time-cost trade-offs, probabilistic methods, and risk analysis.

- Large organizations typically must manage a portfolio of projects at the same time. Selection and prioritization of projects should be seen as ways to strategically manage change and generate new capabilities for the organization.

KEY TERMS

business case   518, 530

critical path   000

critical path method
   (CPM)   519

earliest finish date   522

earliest start date   522

functional project   513

Gantt chart   527

latest finish date   522

latest start date   522

matrix project   514

network diagram   520

postproject review   529

probabilistic task duration
   estimates   524

project   510

project buffer   529

project charter   517

project objective
   statement   513

pure (autonomous)
   project   513

social factors   511

task slack   522

technological factors   511

24/7 project
   operations   516

work breakdown structure
   (WBS)   517

QUESTIONS

1. What are some of the assumptions underlying the critical path method (CPM)? Can you think of situations in which the CPM assumptions would not be valid?

2. Think of the last project in which you participated that did not go as well as planned (e.g., this could be a team assignment for a class). Were the causes of failure mainly social or technical in nature? Explain.

3. At what point in the life of a project does the project manager have the greatest ability to influence the success of the project? Name three things you would try to get executive sponsors of a project to agree to before you accepted the job as project manager.

4. Suppose that you are the leader of a project designed to quickly develop and explore radical new business opportunities that exploit the company's strengths in supply chain management. What types of personnel would you want on your team? How would you organize the project?

5. What strengths do you possess that would make you an excellent project manager? In what areas would you need to improve?

PROBLEM

Bill and Judy are planning their upcoming wedding. They have laid out the following tasks and estimated durations:

Task	Task Label	Estimated Duration (days)	Immediate Predecessors
Book the wedding site and date	A	2	None
Purchase rings and gifts	B	5	None
Hire a caterer	C	2	A
Select wedding party	D	7	A
Hire a videographer	E	2	A
Select dresses and tuxedos	F	10	D
Alter dresses and tuxedos	G	15	F
Hold rehearsal	H	1	B, E, G
Hold wedding	I	1	C, H

What is the earliest date that Bill and Judy can get married? What activities are critical, and by how many days can the noncritical activities be late or postponed? To answer these questions, you will need to take the following steps:

1. Draw the network diagram.

2. Identify the critical path.

3. Compute the project length, along with earliest and latest start and finish dates for each task.

Using the information provided in the preceding table, draw the network diagram starting from left to right. The following diagram shows the paths and durations in an activity-on-node format.

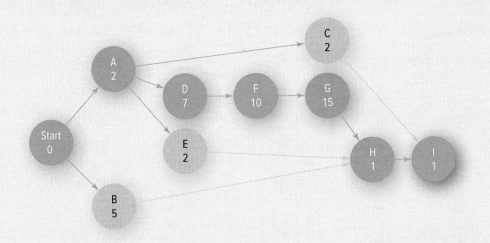

Solution:

By adding up the path lengths, we see that the critical (longest) path is A-D-F-G-H-I, with a length of 36 days. Bill and Judy could get married in as little as 36 days if all tasks go as planned.

Using the critical path algorithm, we can compute the earliest start, earliest completion, latest start, and latest completion dates for all the tasks, as shown in Table 15-4.

The slack values given in Table 15-4 indicate by how many days the noncritical tasks can be late or postponed. For example, task B can be postponed as much as 29 days without making the project late.

TABLE 15-4   Forward and Backward Pass Calculations

Forward pass:

Task	Immediate Predecessors	Earliest Start (ES)	Earliest Completion (EC) = ES + Task Duration
A	None	0	2
B	None	0	5
C	A	2	4
D	A	2	9
E	A	2	4
F	D	9	19
G	F	19	34
H	B, E, G	34	35
I	C, H	35	36

Backward pass:

Task	Immediate Successors	Latest Completion (LC)	Latest Start (LS) = LC − Task Duration	Slack = LS − ES
I	None	36 (proj length)	35	35 − 35 = 0
H	I	35	34	34 − 34 = 0
G	H	34	19	19 − 19 = 0
F	G	19	9	9 − 9 = 0
E	H	34	32	32 − 2 = 30
D	F	9	2	2 − 2 = 0
C	I	35	33	33 − 2 = 31
B	H	34	29	29 − 0 = 29
A	C, D, E	2	0	0 − 0 = 0

PROBLEMS

1. Suppose that you have been given the task of organizing a graduation open house party for your younger brother who is graduating from high school. Write an objective statement and develop a WBS for the project, with at least three levels of detail. Write a few sentences describing how the elements in the WBS support the project objective statement.

2. Somewhere in the United States, committee members in a voting precinct have decided to conduct a vote recount following an election. They have developed a preliminary WBS and have asked you to critique it. What are the weaknesses of this WBS?

Vote Recount Project

Task	Subtask	Work Package
1. Personnel	1.1 Establish criteria for selection 1.2 Bipartisan 1.3 Select Democratic Party Representatives 1.4 Contact Republican Party 1.5 Training	1.1.1 Screen criteria for redundancy 1.3.1 Contact Party 1.3.2 Ask for nominees 1.3.3 Select nominees

Task	Subtask	Work Package
2. Process	2.1 Local and state requirements / hisory	2.1.1 Examine local historical practices 2.1.2 Determine state legal requirements
	2.2 Procedures	2.2.1 Benchmark procedures in other states 2.2.2 Select best procedures 2.2.3 Make modifications to best procedures selected 2.2.4 Document procedures 2.2.5 Test procedures 2.2.6 Modify procedures as needed
	2.3 Maintain objectivity	
3. Facilities	3.1 Nice work environment 3.2 Search for available space	3.2.1 Contact real estate agents 3.2.2 Contact government agencies 3.2.3 Scan real estate websites 3.2.4 Contact failed dot-coms
	3.3 Prepare rental agreement	3.3.1 Install utilities
	3.4 Contract for support services	3.4.1 Janitorial service
4. Budget	4.1 Determine budget needs	4.1.1 Prepare formal budget proposal 4.1.2 Request budget allocation from county
5. Media and Public Relations		

3. For the following simple set of project tasks, answer the questions below. (Task times are shown in hours.)

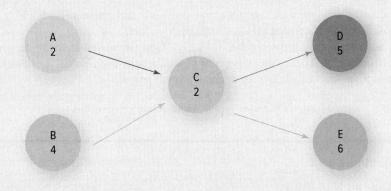

a. What is the expected time that all five tasks will be completed?
b. What is the earliest start date for task C?
c. What is the latest start date for task A?

4. For the following network, answer the questions below. (Times shown are in days.)

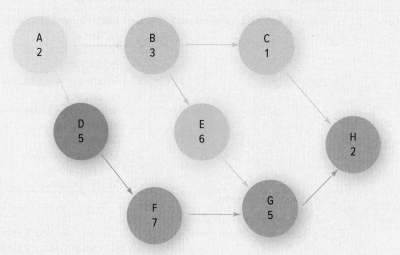

a. What is the length of the critical path?
b. What are the earliest and latest start dates for task E?
c. What is the latest start date for task B?
d. If all other tasks are completed in their expected durations, will the project length be affected if task B actually takes five days instead of the expected three?

5. Suppose that you and two other students are working on a team research project for a course you are taking. To complete the project, you expect that the three of you will need to work together on reviewing related literature for about five days. Then, you will divide the work into three parts: collecting financial data (2 days), writing the text of the paper (5 days), and preparing the figures and tables (2 days). Then the team will work together in assembling and editing the paper (2 days).

a. Assuming that none of the work can be done in parallel (i.e., collecting data must precede writing, which must precede preparing figures and tables), how many days will it take to complete your research project?
b. Ideally, the work would be best accomplished serially (as in question [a] above) so that all information created in one task is available for the processing of the next task. However, assuming for the moment that collecting data, writing text, and preparing figures and tables can be done in parallel (i.e., each task can be done by a different team member independently and simultaneously), how many days will it take to complete your research project?
c. Suppose that the project is due in 14 days. How would you structure the project in order to make sure the paper is of highest quality and also delivered on time?

6. Consider the following information about a small project:

Task	Duration Estimates	Immediate Predecessors
A	2 days	None
B	5 days	A
C	1 day	B
D	2 days	A
E	3 days	B & D
F	12 days	E & C

a. Draw a network diagram.
b. Identify the critical path, the earliest start and finish dates, and the slack for each task.
c. Which of these activities should the project manager track most closely?
d. What would happen if a new estimate for task D increases its expected duration from two days to six days? Would the project take longer? Would anything else change?

7. Consider the following table of precedence relationships for a portion of a house-building project:

Task	Duration Estimates	Immediate Predecessor(s)
Prepare Site	4 days	None
Install Rough Plumbing	3 days	Prepare Site
Pour Concrete Foundation	2 days	Install Rough Plumbing
Concrete Curing Time	3 days	Pour Concrete Foundation
Preassemble Wall Frames	8 days	None
Erect Wall Frames	4 days	Preassemble Wall Frames, Cure Concrete
Install Roof	2 days	Erect Wall Frames
Install Wiring	3 days	Install Roof
Install Exterior Siding	4 days	Install Roof
Install Insulation	2 days	Install Exterior Siding
Hang Drywall	3 days	Install Insulation, Install Wiring
Install Windows	1 day	Hang Dry Wall
Paint Interior	6 days	Install Windows
Paint Exterior	5 days	Install Exterior Siding
Level Yard	2 days	Cure Concrete
Landscape Yard	4 days	Level Yard

a. Draw a network diagram for this project and identify the critical path.
b. What assumptions may have been made in the development of the time estimates?
c. What will happen to the project if the materials needed for the frame preassembly are not available until the second day of the project? What if the materials are delayed until the tenth day?
d. Do you see any potential resource conflicts in this schedule? Will there be any incompatible tasks occurring simultaneously?

8. Based on the precedence table below, draw a network diagram for this project. Identify the critical path, the earliest start and finish dates, and the slack for each task.

Activity	Duration (Days)	Immediate Predecessor
A	2	None
B	3	None
C	4	None
D	5	A
E	3	B
F	7	C
G	2	D, E
H	4	F
I	3	F
J	1	H
K	3	I
L	1	G, J, K

9. Given the following project network:

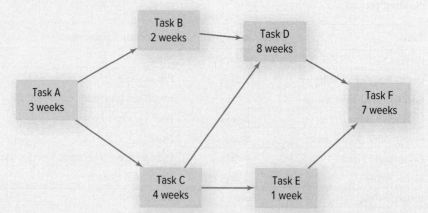

a. Identify the critical path and the earliest start and finish dates for each task.
b. Calculate the slack for every project activity.
c. Draw this network as a Gantt chart.

10. Given the network in problem 9, enter project data into a project management software program such as MS Project. Print a network and a bar chart (Gantt) view. Interpret the results.

11. Professor Bill is planning to launch a new research project that he hopes will culminate in a high quality published article. He and his collaborators have identified the research steps below. Bill will be considered for tenure in 18 months time, and getting another publication is critical to his success. If all goes according to plan, will the article be published in time to be considered a part of Bill's case for tenure?

Activity	Expected Duration	Precedence Requirements
Refine research question	1 month	None
Complete literature review	2 months	None
Formulate theory and hypotheses	2 months	Must complete refining research question and at least half of the literature review
Design experiment	1 month	Must complete literature review and formulation of theory and hypotheses
Recruit students for participation in experiment	0.5 months	Must complete literature review and formulation of theory and hypotheses
Run experiment	1 month	Must complete experiment design and recruit students
Conduct preliminary analysis of results	2 months	Must complete running the experiment
Write the article	3 months	Must first complete the preliminary analysis of results
Final analysis of results	1 month	Must complete the preliminary analysis of results
Submit article to journal and get reviews	4 months	Must complete writing the article and final analysis of the results
Revise article using reviewers' comments	3 months	Must receive the reviews
Resubmit article and get acceptance	1 month	Must revise the article
Article appears in print after acceptance	2 months	Article must be accepted

12. Given the project data below, which activities are critical and what is the length of the critical path? If activity E is reduced by 2 days, what additional activities become critical?

Activity	Duration	Precedents
A	4	None
B	5	None
C	2	B
D	3	A, B
E	6	C, D
F	3	C, D
G	5	F
H	3	E, F
I	4	G, H

CASE

Derek's European Tour

Derek had a busy summer ahead of him. It was February 1, and Derek was planning out a summer full of activities that included a backpacking tour of Europe, doing some work for his father, and completing an online summer course offered by his university. Derek was in the midst of the spring semester of his senior year at State University, and he looked forward to taking a once-in-a-lifetime trip to Europe before starting a job in August that year. He had already secured a position as a drummer for a musical group on Holland America Cruise Lines. The job required him to report for training on August 1.

After completing his spring semester and going through graduation ceremonies on May 15, Derek planned to visit most of the larger countries in Western Europe and also attend a couple of key events while there. His tentative plan was to spend a week in Spain, two weeks in the UK, two weeks in Italy, a week in France, a week in Benelux (Belgium, Netherlands, Luxembourg), and two weeks in the area of Germany, Switzerland, and Austria. In addition to travel, Derek had two passions in his life, jazz and tennis. It was his dream to attend all three days of the largest jazz event on the planet, the North Sea Jazz Festival, to be held in Rotterdam on July 13–15. He also wanted to spend at least a couple of days watching matches at Wimbledon, the most prestigious tennis tournament in the world. This year's tournament was scheduled for June 22 through July 6 in Wimbledon, England.

Derek also had some work to do this summer. He had promised that he would help his father, a professor, by preparing figures and tables for a new textbook that he was writing. His father expected that the work would take Derek about four weeks to complete, given that he did the work on his laptop computer while traveling. Derek preferred to complete the work in one four-week period, rather than starting and stopping the work multiple times over the summer. His father did not care when Derek did the work, as long as it was completed before he started his new job on August 1.

Derek also had one last course to take in order to finish his degree (even though he attended graduation ceremonies in the spring). He had to complete the course this summer in order to be eligible to start his job in the fall. Fortunately, his university offered an online course on ecology that would fulfill the general education requirement he needed. The course was self-paced and only required the completion of four online examinations. Derek expected that this course would take about four weeks, and he very much wanted to complete the course before attending the North Sea Jazz Festival, so that he could give full attention to networking with many of the jazz legends who would be playing there. He could start the course any time after June 1, but he felt that it would be quite difficult to take the course at the same time that he did the work for his father.

As he considered all the things he had planned for the summer, Derek started to wonder if it was all even feasible. He also began to think of all the things he needed to do to prepare for the trip. He had been told that he needed to apply for a passport at least 12 weeks before leaving the country. He wanted to book his airline flights at least eight weeks in advance in order to get low fares. And he estimated that it would take at least three weeks for him to procure and pack all the things he needed for his trip.

Fortunately, his planning was made simpler by the fact that he could fly into and out of Europe from just about any country. While in Europe, he would simply buy a Eurail pass, which would allow him to travel to all of his planned destinations by train.

Questions

1. Draw a network diagram that gives a workable plan for Derek's trip and work.

2. Can Derek achieve all the things he wants to do this summer? What is the first thing he needs to do? In what order should he visit the various countries he wants to see?

3. When should Derek start doing the work for his father? When should he take the class?

4. What things might happen that would put Derek's plans at risk? How can he mitigate or respond to these risks?

CASE

Monolith Productions*

The summit meeting at Monolith Productions started promptly on August 20 at 10:45 a.m. The president of the company, Hugo Monolith III, called the meeting of his vice presidents to order. "Ladies and gentlemen, thank you for meeting here on such short notice. A most important contract has been won by our company. Monolith has been signed to produce a new made-for-TV version of Charles Dickens's *A Christmas Carol*. The movie will be broadcast during prime time on Christmas Eve on the nationwide BAA Network.

"We are in complete control of the project. We will write a screenplay version of the story (with the BAA having final approval), produce the film, and support BAA's promotion of the film. We also have the rights to release a picture book based on the film. Steven Playhill will be the director, Bill Quinn will handle the promotion, and Kim Yoshikawa will be in charge of production and release of the picture book. It is now my privilege to introduce one of the most popular film producers of our time, Steven Playhill. Steven?"

The introduction of Playhill brought further applause. It was acknowledged by a slight, bearded man in rumpled casual clothing who walked to the front of the conference room and started to speak. "Thank you. I would like to explain the production process. We are targeting the completion of the film for December 17. The film is to be shown on the evening of December 24, but BAA wants one week in case last-minute rescheduling during Christmas week is necessary. The first task is to write a screenplay. The screenplay, with revisions, should take about four weeks to complete. The next step is to cast the leading roles according to the screenplay. Casting for the project should take about two weeks. Casting can occur while the screenplay is being written. Interior scenes requiring only the primary characters can be shot at a studio using soundstages. I expect we can comfortably complete the interior scenes in about four to five weeks. Exterior shots, depicting the streets of 19th-century London, will be shot in

Boston. We are already committed to at least seven weeks of soundstage and equipment rental. Because of the long scheduling lead time, we signed a guaranteed rental agreement to assure their availability for our project.

"The shooting in Boston will probably take about three weeks. However, we want good amounts of fog and some snow available, so we cannot begin Boston shooting before November."

Playhill considered the other activities needed for the movie. "Let's see . . . well, some props would have to be constructed. I'd say that should take a week, but it can be done while the screenplay is being written and prior to renting shooting sites. After each stage of filming is completed, we will need at least one week to edit the film that was shot. We'll need an additional week at each stage for shooting any retakes. Has anyone requested a preview?"

Mr. Monolith spoke up. "BAA always requires its films to be previewed. Why?"

Playhill answered, "Because we should allow another week for staging the preview here in Burbank and processing any reedits they request. That should produce us a made-for-TV film. Again, this all has to be completed by December 17. Any questions? Thank you."

Playhill took his seat and Bill Quinn began to discuss the promotion of the film. "BAA has requested two forms of promotion. They would like us to produce a 60-second and a 30-second commercial including actual film footage. The 60-second spot must include scenes from both interior and location shooting. The 30-second spot should contain only close-ups of the primary characters. They want to run these commercials from December 3 through December 24. I have set aside one week to complete this task, although an abbreviated schedule could be used. Using the abbreviated plan, the commercials can be completed in as little as three days, but the production staff

---

*Revised with permission from V. A. Mabert and M. J. Showalter, *Cases in Operations Management* (Plano, TX: BPI, 1984).

size would have to expand, probably increasing the commercial cost."

Playhill asked, "Bill, does that mean the film must be completed by December 3?"

"No, it means we'll take some action shots during the editing stage, produce copies, and expect those shots to appear in the film," Quinn replied.

He continued, "For the second phase of promotion, BAA will air several talk shows, including Jay Tenno and David Postman. They would like two or three of the stars of the movie to make the rounds of these shows after shooting is complete. They will appear, discuss the film, and introduce a film clip. The film clip accompanying a star has to spotlight that star. Arranging these talk shows (i.e., booking the appearance, completing the film clips, filming the shows) will require two weeks and must be completed by December 10. The shows will air during the two weeks leading up to the movie premier."

Next, Kim Yoshikawa discussed the development of the book. "Ladies and gentlemen, this portion of the project is not exactly a 'picture book.' What we plan to do is develop a novella from the screenplay. Basically, we're editing Dickens into an action novel. Then we will combine this prose with color photos taken from the film. Similar products have been quite successful. Because we have total control over this part of the project, we are its sole benefactor and collect all revenues. We anticipate maximum sales if the book is finished and shipping begins during the week of November 26. A delay of one week would cost us about half our revenues due to missed holiday sales."

"Kim, are you saying now that the film has to be done by the third week of November?" asked Monolith.

Kim replied, "No, all that must be completed is the filming. Like the commercial, we can then take stills from the footage. Once we have the photos, it will take one week to put the photos in the book and print copies."

Monolith asked, "What about the prose portion of the book, Kim?"

She replied, "The book has to be written from the original screenplay. Although some changes may occur during shooting, such changes should not affect the book significantly. The 'prose-ifying' of the screenplay should take about one week. We need another three weeks to choose an appropriate layout and composition for the book, which can also be shortened by one week for the same cost. Then it's all done except photos and printing. Are there any questions?"

Mr. Monolith rose to wrap up the meeting. "Ladies and gentlemen, we have one week to schedule and budget this project. We plan to let the people who made presentations here begin their work one week from today."

Questions

1. What analytical tools can be used to schedule the project? Is any tool more advantageous than others?

2. Using the most conservative estimates (longest times) for the timing of projects, can the movie be completed on time? Can the book be released on time to capture all holiday sales?

3. Which activities would you try to shorten? Why?

4. What are the most likely risks that threaten the completion of this project? As project manager, which activities should receive your greatest attention?

SELECTED READINGS & INTERNET SITES

Goldratt, E. *The Critical Chain.* Great Barrington, MA: North River Press, 1997.

Gray, C. F., and E. W. Larson. *Project Management,* 4th ed. New York: McGraw-Hill/Irwin, 2007.

Meredith, J. R., and Mantell, S. J. *Project Management,* 6th ed. Hoboken, NJ: John Wiley & Sons, 2006.

Project Management Journal, Project Management Institute.

Swink, M. "Product Development—Faster, On Time." *Research-Technology Management,* July–August 2002, pp. 50–58.

Swink, M.; S. Talluri; and T. Pandejpong. "Faster, Better, Cheaper: A Study of NPD Project Efficiency and Performance Tradeoffs." *Journal of Operations Management* 24, no. 5 (2006), pp. 542–62.

Verzuh, E. *The Fast Forward MBA in Project Management,* 3rd ed. Hoboken, NJ: John Wiley & Sons, 2008.

Project Management Institute
www.pmi.org

15

Chapter Supplement: Advanced Methods for Project Scheduling

LEARNING OBJECTIVES *After studying this supplement, you should be able to:*

LO15S-1 Make time and cost trade-offs in projects.

LO15S-2 Schedule projects using probabilistic task time estimates.

This supplement illustrates two of the more quantitative techniques for scheduling project tasks and resources. First, the reasoning for making time and cost trade-offs in projects is presented. This approach, called **crashing** a project, is useful when project managers need to speed up projects that are behind schedule or when deadlines have been changed. The second technique, **probabilistic scheduling**, is useful when the durations of project tasks are uncertain. Such uncertainty is common in "really new" projects or in projects involving tasks that are subject to many factors outside the direct control of the project team (e.g., weather, competitor actions, regulators, and so on). Probabilistic scheduling uses statistics to model the uncertainty in the project and to estimate the likelihood of various project outcomes.

crashing Adding resources to efficiently speed up a project.

probabilistic scheduling The use of statistics to model the uncertainty in the project and to estimate the likelihood of various project outcomes.

To illustrate these techniques we will use the example project from Chapter 15. Figure 15S-1 shows the original network diagram for the supply chain planning system installation project.

PROJECT CRASHING: MAKING TIME-COST TRADE-OFFS

LO15S-1 Make time and cost trade-offs in projects.

Revisions to a project schedule are often necessary due to many possible factors. Initial project activities may have taken longer than originally planned, project deadlines may have been changed, or critical resources may have become unavailable. Any of these causes can make the original plan no longer feasible or desirable, so the project manager needs to decide how to shift resources in ways that achieve project objectives in the most efficient way possible.

A common decision managers must make is how best to spend more money (resources) to speed up the project. The following steps provide a process for making such a decision:

1. List the crash costs for each task in the project.
2. Choose the task or the combination of tasks on the critical path that has the lowest crash cost, and reduce that task's duration by one period.
3. Update the lengths of all affected paths in the network. Identify any paths that have become critical.
4. Repeat this process until the plan meets the required deadline, or until the cost of reducing the project's length exceeds the benefit.

FIGURE 15S-1 Network Diagram for Planning System Installation Project

EXAMPLE 15S-1

Let's apply this decision process to the planning system installation project introduced in Chapter 15. Suppose that the client wants this project completed one week early (five working days). The current plan indicates that it will take 31 days to finish the project. What is the least expensive way to reduce the project length by five days?

Step 1. Assume that we have investigated the possibilities and created the crash cost information shown in Table 15S-1. The **crash cost** per day data are estimates of the additional costs (adding workers, overtime pay, etc.) required to speed up each task by one day. Note that several activities cannot be crashed, and all activities have some lower duration limit.

Steps 2 and 3. Start by examining the critical path tasks (marked by asterisks in the Table). Because "Set System Protocols" can be reduced by one day for a cost of $500, it offers the cheapest alternative. Note that reducing "Prepare Data" for a cost of $200 does not affect the project length because this task is not on the critical path. Planning to spend $500 to reduce "Set System Protocols" will change the planned project completion to 30 days. This change also reduces the slack in the noncritical tasks by one day each. This reduction is not enough to cause any of the noncritical tasks to become critical.

Repeating Steps 2 and 3. The best next step would be to reduce the "Set System Protocols" task by an additional day, as it remains the cheapest option on the critical path. Now the "Set System Protocols" task is planned to be done at its fastest (minimum) duration of one day, and the project will complete in 29 days.

Repeating Steps 2 and 3. The next cheapest crash option is "Test System." Crashing this task from six days to five days costs $600. This brings the critical path length down to 28 days. Note that by reducing the project a total of three days so far, we have reduced the slack in noncritical activities by the same amount.

crash cost Estimated cost to reduce a project task by one time unit (e.g., a day or a week).

TABLE 15S-1 Crash Schedule for Planning System Installation Project

Task	Current Planned Duration	Minimum Duration	Crash Cost per Day
*Select System Modules	9	6	$1,200
Prepare Data	5	4	$ 200
*Set System Protocols	3	1	$ 500
*Populate System Data	5	3	$ 700
Prepare Documentation	14	10	$ 400
Design Training Program	2	2	_____
Hold Training Sessions	1	1	_____
*Test System	6	3	$ 600
*Debug System	4	2	$ 800
*Pilot Test	3	2	$ 900
*Hold "Go Live" Meeting	1	1	_____

*Critical path task

Repeating Steps 2 and 3. The next cheapest crash option is still "Test System." Crashing this task from five days to four days costs $600. This brings the critical path to 27 days. Note that the path containing the "Prepare Documentation" is also 27 days long. In reducing the critical path by four days, the "Prepare Documentation" has now become critical. Any further efforts to crash the project must address both critical paths.

Repeating Steps 2 and 3. Consider the options for reducing the project further. We could reduce the "Test System" task by one more day at a cost of $600, but doing this would still leave the path with "Prepare Documentation" at 27 days long. To reduce the project by one day, we would need to reduce *both* activities "Test System" and "Prepare Documentation" by one day each, at a total cost of $1,000 ($600 + $400). However, a better option would be to crash the "Pilot Test" task by one day at a cost of $900. Because "Pilot Test" is on all paths leading to the completion of the project, we can reduce the overall project by reducing this one activity.

Now we have a plan to reduce the project length by a total of five days. The plan is summarized in Table 15S-2 and the crashed project network is shown in Figure 15S-2. If we wanted to crash the project further, we would have to crash both "Test System" and "Prepare Documentation" by one day each, because the "Pilot Test" task has already been reduced to its minimum duration.

You may have noticed that the cost to crash the project length each additional day increases as the planned project length gets shorter and shorter. This increasing incremental crash cost phenomenon is true in almost all projects. Consequently, it is important to continuously compare the costs and benefits of crashing a project to ensure that the most economical plans are made. Suppose, for example, that our client decided that he would only be willing to pay a maximum of $2,000 to complete the project earlier. Our crash schedule in Table 15S-2 shows that a project time reduction of three days would be justified, because it would cost a total of $1,600. However, to crash the project any further would cost more than the client is willing to pay.

TABLE 15S-2   Summary of Crash Plan for the Planning System Installation Project

	Activity to Crash	Crash Cost	Critical Path Length	Notes:
0			31 days	No tasks crashed
1	Set System Protocols	$ 500	30 days	Cheapest task on critical path
2	Set System Protocols	$ 500	29 days	Cannot crash this task any further
3	Test System	$ 600	28 days	Cheapest task on critical path
4	Test System	$ 600	27 days	Prepare Documentation becomes a critical path
5	Pilot Test	$ 900	26 days	Crashing this task reduces both critical paths. Planned deadline met.
	Total Cost:	$3,100		

FIGURE 15S-2 Planning System Installation Project Crashed to 26 Days

SCHEDULING A PROJECT WITH PROBABILISTIC TASK DURATION ESTIMATES

LO15S-2 Schedule projects using probabilistic task time estimates.

best-case duration Estimate of the task time given everything goes as planned.

worst-case duration Estimate of the task time given all possible delays are realized.

most likely case duration Estimate of the most probable task time.

Sometimes it is difficult to accurately estimate the durations of project tasks. In these situations, it can be helpful to analyze the impacts of uncertainty on the project by developing a range of possible task durations for each task, rather than relying on a single point estimate. Using this approach, managers estimate the **best-case duration**, **worst-case duration**, and **most likely case duration** for each task in the project. The best-case duration is the manager's estimate of the time the task will take assuming everything goes exactly as planned. For example, the weather is perfect, no one on the project team gets sick, no technical problems arise, and so on. The worst-case duration is the expected time should all possible delays be realized, that is, if every imaginable thing goes wrong. The most likely duration is the manager's estimate of the most probable task time. By making some assumptions about the statistical properties of these estimates, project analysts can create distributions of possible outcomes for each project task and, ultimately, for the project as a whole.

Table 15S-3 recasts the original planning system installation project data using ranges of task time estimates. Some of the ranges are symmetrically distributed around the most likely duration, whereas others are skewed to the left or right. The distribution of durations for a task is often a result of resource uncertainties and dependencies. For example, suppose that we are dependent on an outside consultant for help with the task "Select System Modules." The duration estimates suggest that if all goes well and the consultant is available when we need her, the task may be finished in as little as seven working days. However, if the consultant is as much as a week late in becoming available, it might take up to 15 days to select the system modules. Using this kind of reasoning, managers can create ranges of task durations and, using some simple formulas and rules of thumb, assign probabilities to various outcomes.

Here's how the probabilistic analysis works.

1. Compute the expected duration and standard deviation for each task using the following formulas:

(15S.1) $t_i = (w + 4 * m + b) / 6$

(15S.8) $\sigma_i = (w - b) / 6$

where:
  w = worst-case duration
  m = most likely duration
  b = best-case duration

TABLE 15S-3   Probabilistic Time Estimates for the Planning System
Installation Project

Task	Best-Case Duration	Most Likely Duration	Worst-Case Duration
*Select System Modules	7	9	15
Prepare Data	4	5	10
*Set System Protocols	2	3	5
*Populate System Data	3	5	7
Prepare Documentation	10	14	16
Design Training Program	2	2	3
Hold Training Sessions	1	1	2
*Test System	4	6	8
*Debug System	2	4	6
*Pilot Test	2	3	4
*Hold "Go Live" Meeting	1	1	1

*Critical path task

2. Compute the expected duration and standard deviation for each path.

(15S.3)
$$t_{path} = \Sigma \, t_i$$

(15S.4)
$$\sigma_{path} = \sqrt{(\Sigma \, \sigma_i^2)}$$

3. Use these estimates and the standard normal curve to evaluate probabilities for given completion dates.

EXAMPLE 15S-2

We know from the prior analysis that the planning system installation project is most likely to be completed in about 31 days. Suppose that the client has determined that the project absolutely must be finished within 33 days. Given the range estimates in Table 15S-3, what is the probability that the project will be finished on time? We can follow the three steps above to answer this question.

Step 1. Table 15S-4 shows the expected durations and standard deviations computed using the formulas above.

For example, the results for "Select System Modules" are:

$$t_i = (15 + 4 * 9 + 7) / 6 = 9.67 \text{ days}$$
$$\sigma_i = (15 - 7) / 6 = 1.33 \text{ days}$$

Note that the expected duration for a given task might be longer or shorter than the most likely time, depending on the range of duration estimates. The expected time gives the "50/50" estimate of task duration. That is, the actual duration of the task has a 50 percent chance of being longer or shorter than the expected time.

Step 2. This step involves adding up the expected times for various paths in the project to identify the *expected* longest path. The expected length and standard deviation for the most likely critical path is:

$$t_{path} = 9.67 + 3.17 + 5 + 6 + 4 + 3 + 1 = 31.84 \text{ days}$$
$$\sigma_{path} = \sqrt{(1.33^2 + 0.5^2 + 0.67^2 + 0.67^2 + 0.67^2 + 0.33^2 + 0^2)}$$
$$= 1.86 \text{ days}$$

(continued)

(continued)

TABLE 15S-4   Expected Duration and Standard Deviations for Planning System Installation Project

Task	Best-Case Duration	Most Likely Duration	Worst-Case Duration	Expected Duration	Standard Deviation
*Select System Modules	7	9	15	9.67	1.33
Prepare Data	4	5	10	5.67	1
*Set System Protocols	2	3	5	3.17	0.5
*Populate System Data	3	5	7	5	0.67
Prepare Documentation	10	14	16	13.67	1
Design Training Program	2	2	3	2.17	0.17
Hold Training Sessions	1	1	2	1.17	0.17
*Test System	4	6	8	6	0.67
*Debug System	2	4	6	4	0.67
*Pilot Test	2	3	4	3	0.33
*Hold "Go Live" Meeting	1	1	1	1	0

*Critical path task

This result indicates that there is a 50 percent chance that the project will last longer than 31.84 days, and a 50 percent chance that the project will be completed before 31.84 days. This assumes, of course, that the project length is determined by this one path. There is a possibility that one of the noncritical paths could in fact become critical, if those tasks are at their worst-case conditions and the critical path tasks are at their best-case conditions. For now we will concentrate only on the expected critical path.

Step 3. To estimate the probability that the project will take 33 days or less to finish, we use the information from a standard normal table (given in Appendix A). We can assume that the length of a path in the network will vary normally around its mean (expected) value. The *z*-score for our expected critical path is:

(15S.5) $Z = (\text{target completion time} - t_{path}) / \sigma_{path}$

$$= (33 - 31.84) / 1.86 = .624$$

From the partial *z*-table shown in Table 15S-5, a value of .624 corresponds to a probability of approximately .73, or 73 percent. Figure 15S-3 illustrates this probability upon a standard normal curve. The result indicates that there is about a 73 percent chance that the project duration will last no more than 33 days, given our estimates of best-case, worst-case, and most likely scenarios. If this probability is unacceptable to us or our client, then we would want to investigate the potential for crashing critical activities to the point that an acceptable probability of completion on time is achieved.

(continued)

(continued)

TABLE 15S-5   Standard Normal Table

z	F(z)	1 − F(z)	z	F(z)	1 − F(z)
0.0	0.5000	0.5000	1.9	0.9713	0.0287
0.1	0.5398	0.4602	2.0	0.9772	0.0228
0.2	0.5793	0.4207	2.1	0.9821	0.0179
0.3	0.6179	0.3821	2.2	0.9861	0.0139
0.4	0.6554	0.3446	2.3	0.9893	0.0107
0.5	0.6915	0.3085	2.4	0.9918	0.0082
0.6	0.7257	0.2743	2.5	0.9938	0.0062
0.7	0.7580	0.2420	2.6	0.9953	0.0047
0.8	0.7881	0.2119	2.7	0.9965	0.0035
0.9	0.8159	0.1841	2.8	0.9974	0.0026
1.0	0.8413	0.1587	2.9	0.9981	0.0019
1.1	0.8643	0.1357	3.0	0.9987	0.0013
1.2	0.8849	0.1151	3.1	0.9990	0.0010
1.3	0.9032	0.0968	3.2	0.9993	0.0007
1.4	0.9192	0.0808	3.3	0.9995	0.0005
1.5	0.9332	0.0668	3.4	0.9997	0.0003
1.6	0.9452	0.0548	3.5	0.9998	0.0002
1.7	0.9554	0.0446	3.6	0.9998	0.0002
1.8	0.9641	0.0359	3.7	0.9999	0.0001

F(z) is the standard normal cumulative probability from the left tail of the distribution to the value of z.

FIGURE 15S-3   Probability that the Planning System Installation Project Will Take 33 or Fewer Days

$p(t < D) = 73\%$

$p(t > D) = 27\%$

Target Completion Date $D = 33$

$t_{path} = 31.84$

$Z\sigma$

In this example we have assumed that the expected critical path will define the project length. If the critical path is much longer than other paths, then this is likely to be the case. As noted previously, however, each path in a project has some probability that it will actually turn out to be the longest path. What project managers really want to know, then, is: What is the probability that *all* paths will be completed by a given target deadline? This is usually difficult to estimate directly because paths in projects are usually not independent (several paths share certain tasks in common). Instead, project managers often use simulation tools to automatically simulate thousands or millions of scenarios that randomly vary different task lengths according to their best, worst, and most likely case parameters. This type of analysis provides an overall distribution of project length. If the distribution is normal, then managers can use the *z*-table in the same way as shown above to estimate project completion probabilities.

SUPPLEMENT SUMMARY

This supplement provides brief explanations and examples of two quantitative means for analyzing projects and rearranging resources in order to achieve desired completion time goals. While much more sophisticated methods exist, these approaches are useful in many situations. Importantly, the logic underlying these methods helps the project manager to understand the nature of trade-offs between resources, time, and risk.

KEY TERMS

best-case duration   546
crash cost   544
crashing   543

most likely case duration   546
probabilistic scheduling   543

worst-case duration   546

DISCUSSION QUESTIONS

1. When does it make economical sense to *crash* project activities? How do you know when to stop?
2. Why does it never make sense to crash activities that are not on the critical path?
3. Suppose that your project has two activity paths of about the same length, but one path is made up of more uncertain activities while the other path is fairly routine. How would you manage the activities on these two paths differently?
4. What project factors would make you more or less comfortable with a lower probability that the project will be completed on time?

Suppose that one of your professors has hired you as part of a team of students for a summer research project, for a total payment of $2,000. The preliminary project plan is presented in the network diagram shown in Figure 15S-4. Based on an hourly pay rate agreed upon by you and your teammates, you have estimated the cost for each activity as shown in Table 15S-6. It is possible to speed up certain activities. However, to do so you will have to add more teammates and work on weekends. Table 15S-6 also shows the costs for making these changes.

Part A. The critical path of the project (shown in red) indicates that the project will take 16 working days to complete. However, your professor must have the report in no more than 13 working days. Come up with the lowest cost way to meet the 13-day goal.

FIGURE 15S-4 Network Diagram for Research Project

TABLE 15S-6 Crash Costs for Research Project

Activity	Planned Duration	Cost	Minimum Possible Duration	Crash Cost per Day
Library Research	5	$300	4	$250
Online Research	3	$100	2	$100
Create Manager Questions	2	$200	1	$400
Interview Managers	5	$300	5	____
Write Report	3	$200	1	$150
Prepare Tables and Figures	2	$100	1	$150
Finalize Report	1	$100	1	____

Solution:

As currently planned, the project will cost $1,300 (netting your team a $700 profit) and will be completed in 16 working days. Your challenge is to complete the project in 13 days without spending all of your profit.

1. The cheapest critical path activity to crash initially is "Write Report," for a cost of $150. If we crash this activity by one day, then the critical path becomes 15 days long.

2. Now the cheapest way to reduce the project is to reduce "Library Research" by one day at a cost of $250. This brings the project length to 14 days. The alternative would be to crash both "Write Report" and "Prepare Tables and Figures" by one day each, but that total cost would be $300. We could also crash "Create Manager Questions" by one day, but that would cost $400.

3. Because "Library Research" is now at its shortest duration (four days), the cheapest way to reduce the project by a final day is to crash both "Write Report" and "Prepare Tables and Figures" by one day each, for a total cost of $300.

Figure 15S-5 shows the crashed project with a 13-day duration. The total crash costs are $150 + $250 + $300 = $600, which leaves $100 in unspent profit.

Part B. Your professor has reviewed your crash plan and is not convinced that you will complete the project on time. He asks you to develop a probabilistic analysis of the project. As a start, you and your team have used the current duration estimates as most likely times, adding the best-case and worst-case time estimates as shown in Table 15S-7. Use this information to provide your professor with your estimated probability that you will finish the project in 13 days or less.

FIGURE 15S-5 Network Diagram for Crashed Research Project

TABLE 15S-7 Probabilistic Time Estimates for Research Project

Activity	Best-Case Duration	Most Likely Duration	Worst-Case Duration
Library Research	3	4	6
Online Research	2	3	4
Create Manager Questions	2	2	3
Interview Managers	4	5	8
Write Report	1	1	2
Prepare Tables and Figures	1	1	2
Finalize Report	1	1	1

Solution:

The first step is to calculate the expected duration and standard deviation for each activity. For example, the calculations for the "Library Research" activity are:

$$t_i = (w + 4 * m + b) / 6$$
$$= (3 + 4 * 4 + 6) / 6 = 4.17$$
$$\sigma_i = (w - b) / 6$$
$$= (6 - 3) / 6 = 0.50$$

Using the same calculations, the expected durations and standard deviations for the other activities are shown below:

	Expected Duration	Standard Deviation
Library Research	4.17	0.50
Online Research	3.00	0.33
Create Manager Questions	2.17	0.17
Interview Managers	5.33	0.67
Write Report	1.17	0.17
Prepare Tables and Figures	1.17	0.17
Finalize Report	1	0

The next step is to compute the expected duration and standard deviation for the longest path in the network. The two critical paths shown in Figure 15S-5 are formed by the two parallel activities, "Write Report" and "Prepare Tables and Figures," that have equal expected lengths and equal standard deviations. Thus, either path will give the same overall result. We compute the results for either path as:

$$t_{path} = \Sigma\ t_i = 4.17 + 2.17 + 5.33 + 1.17 + 1 = 13.84 \text{ days}$$
$$\sigma_{path} = \sqrt{(\Sigma\ \sigma_i^2)} = \sqrt{(0.50^2 + 0.17^2 + 0.67^2 + 0.17^2 + 0^2)}$$
$$= 0.87 \text{ days}$$

Given these characteristics, we calculate the z-score for the path as

$$z = (\text{Target completion time} - t_{path}) / \sigma_{path}$$
$$= (13 - 13.84) / 0.87 = -0.97$$

The negative sign indicates that there is a less than 50 percent chance that the path will be completed in less than or equal to 13 days. From the standard normal table (z-table), the probability associated with a positive value of this z-score is approximately 0.83. Because our z-score is negative, this means that the probability of completing the path in 13 days or less is given by $1 - 0.83 = 0.17$, or 17 percent. Because there are two paths in the project with this low probability of success, the team should probably consider crashing another activity in order to increase the odds of completing the project on time.

PROBLEMS

1. Bill needs to schedule a meeting for tomorrow afternoon, but he also has a tee time for golf at 10:00 a.m. Bill usually finishes a round of golf in 4.25 hours. If the course is empty and he doesn't spend too much time looking for lost balls, he can finish in 3.25 hours. However, if the course is crowded, there are rain delays, and/or he hits many bad shots, a round can take as much as 5.5 hours.
   a. What is the expected time that Bill will complete his round of golf tomorrow?
   b. If Bill schedules a meeting to begin at 3:30 p.m. tomorrow and it takes 30 minutes for him to get from the golf course to his office, what is the probability that he will make it to the meeting on time?

2. In problem 1 we assumed that it would take Bill 30 minutes to get from the golf course to his office. Assume now that this is the most likely time, but traffic and other factors could make the commute time as little as 25 minutes or as much as 45 minutes. What is the probability that Bill will make it to his meeting on time if you take this variability into account?

3. Consider the supply chain planning system installation project depicted in Figure 15S-1. Suppose that the client has offered a $4,000 bonus to us if we can complete the project seven working days early. Based upon the crash cost information provided in Table 15S-1, would you accept the client's proposal? By how many days could you profitably shorten the project?

4. Annie is planning a large surprise party for her sister Gwendolyn. She has developed the plan below, including estimates of the time (in hours) and cost necessary to perform each of the activities required at the currently planned pace and at the crashed pace.

Activity	Predecessor	Current Planned Duration (hours)	Minimum Duration if Crashed (hours)	Current Planned Cost	Total Cost If Crashed to Minimum Duration
A. Create Guest List	—	8	4	$200	$310
B. Send Invitations	A	2	1	$125	$150
C. Buy Decorations	A	8	6	$300	$370
D. Plan Menu	A	3	2	$150	$210
E. Purchase Food	D	4	2	$475	$550
F. Prepare Food	E	5	3	$225	$475

   a. Annie is most interested in reducing the time associated with creating the guest list. What is the crash cost per hour for that activity?
   b. Annie will save $40 for every hour she can reduce from her plan. Annie has decided to crash her project and use the money she saves to purchase a larger gift for Gwendolyn. Which activity should she crash first?
   c. Annie has now crashed activity A by four hours at a cost of $110. What other activity could she crash to further reduce the project?
   d. Annie has now crashed activity A by four hours at a cost of $110 and activity E by two hours at a cost of $75. What other activity could she crash to further reduce the project?
   e. How much money did Annie save by crashing the project?
   f. What is the duration of the fully crashed project?

5. Given the data in Table 15S-3, what is the probability that the project will be completed in 32 days or less? What is the probability that the project will take longer than 32 days?

6. Jude and Pat Strohsal have a crack in their water line and need to replace it. This will require digging up the water line, replacing it, filling the hole, leveling the soil, and reseeding the grass. The Strohsals' plumber suggests that, because they will have the water line dug up, they also should replace the foot valve. Following are the plumber's estimates of the time (in hours) necessary to perform each of the activities required.

Activity	Description	Predecessor	Optimistic (Best Case)	Most Likely	Pessimistic (Worst Case)
A	Digging	–	2	3	4
B	Replace line	A	1	1.5	2
C	Replace foot valve	B	.5	1	1.5
D	Fill hole	C	1.5	2	5.5
E	Level soil	D	.5	1	1.5
F	Reseed lawn	E	.4	.5	.6

a. If the plumber and his crew begin working at 7:00 a.m., what time are they expected to finish?
b. The plumber has scheduled another small job at 6:00 p.m. If it takes 1/2 hour to drive from the Strohsals' to the other job, what is the probability the plumber will be able to make the 6:00 p.m. appointment on time?
c. Jude Strohsal can't bear to see her lawn all dug up, so she has decided to visit her mother on the day the work is to be done. Jude wants to return home at 6:45 p.m. What is the probability the work will be complete when she arrives home?

7. Consider the following software development plan.

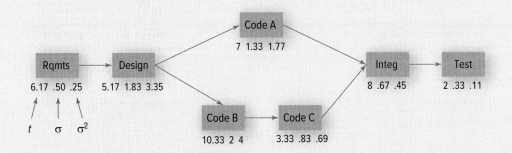

a. The client has asked for an estimated completion date. What would you tell her?
b. The client would like to have the completed software in 37 weeks. What is the likelihood that the *critical path* will be completed in that time frame?
c. The client has just asked if it would be possible to have the completed software in 36 weeks. What is the likelihood the *project* will be completed in that time frame?
d. Now the client wants to know if it would be possible to complete the project in 33 weeks. What is the probability of meeting the client's demand?
e. You are concerned about the accuracy of your calculations because the paths are not independent. What is the likelihood that all of the coding activities will be completed on time?

8. Marty and Marge are renovating their house. They hope for all work to be completed before the Thanksgiving holiday, which is 55 days away. Given the data below, what is the probability that the house will be completed before Thanksgiving? Assume that only one activity can be done at a time. How many days would Marty and Marge need

to crash the project (reducing the expected duration) in order to achieve at least a 90 percent probability of completing the renovation before Thanksgiving? Assume that crashing the project does not affect the uncertainty associated with activities.

Activity	Best-Case Duration	Most Likely Case Duration	Worst-Case Duration
Demolition	1 day	2 days	3 days
Framing	5 days	8 days	15 days
Plumbing	5 days	10 days	15 days
Wiring	13 days	20 days	25 days
Drywalling	4 days	8 days	15 days
Painting and Finish	2 days	4 days	8 days

9. Frank owns and operates a company that installs audio visual equipment for corporate clients. He is currently working on a job that must be completed in 17 days. However, the project is running behind (see the remaining task information below). Equipment installation must be completed first. Then software installation and network connection can happen concurrently. After these are both completed, then system test can take place.

    a. How much will it cost Frank to crash the project enough to meet the 17-day deadline? Which tasks should he crash, and in what order?
    b. If the client offers Frank an incentive of a $500 bonus for completing the project one day early, should he do it?

Remaining Project Activities	Planned Duration	Crash Cost
Equipment installation	10 days	$600 per day, max reduction of 1 day
Software installation	5 days	$300 per day, max reduction of 2 days
Network connection	7 days	$400 per day, max reduction of 3 days
System test	2 days	Cannot be crashed

Gray, C. F., and E. W. Larson. *Project Management,* 4th ed. New York: McGraw-Hill/Irwin, 2007.

Meredith, J. R., and S. J. Mantell. *Project Management,* 6th ed. Hoboken, NJ: John Wiley & Sons, 2006.

Project Management Journal, Project Management Institute.

Project Management Institute
www.pmi.org

16

Sustainable Operations Management—Preparing for the Future

LEARNING OBJECTIVES

After studying this chapter, you should be able to:

LO16-1 Define sustainability using the triple bottom line and explain what this approach means not only for operations management but also the entire supply chain.

LO16-2 Explain the reasons why operations managers are increasingly focusing on the environmental impact of their activities.

LO16-3 Evaluate products using life cycle waste composition assessment.

LO16-4 Discuss the approaches used by operations managers to ensure social responsibility while improving performance in the "people" aspect of sustainability.

LO16-5 Understand the challenges operations managers face as they seek to develop and maintain a sustainable competitive advantage.

LO16-6 Understand the process by which the triple bottom line is transformed into appropriate measures, metrics, and standards.

Most people know Unilever, an Anglo-Dutch multinational consumer goods company whose products include food, beverages, cleaning agents, and personal care products. It is the world's third-largest consumer goods company (just after Procter & Gamble and Nestlé). Over 200 billion times a day someone in the world uses a Unilever product.

Less than 10 years ago, Unilever was relatively unknown. Consumers knew the company's brands, such as Popsicle, VO5, Cup a Soup, Suave, Ben & Jerry's, Noxzema, Pears, and Pond's (to name a few), but few could name the company. That changed in 2009 when Paul Polman became the new CEO. One of the first changes that Polman introduced was to focus on making Unilever and its various brands sustainable. The goal was for Unilever to become the "trusted mark of sustainable living." More importantly, Unilever was to half its environmental footprint while doubling the size of its business by 2020. At the heart of this new strategic initiative were the following objectives:

- *Health and Hygiene:* Help more than a billion people improve their hygiene habits and bring safe drinking water to 500 million people.

- *Nutrition:* Double the proportion of the Unilever product portfolio that meets the highest nutritional standards, thus helping people to achieve a healthier diet.

- *Greenhouse Gases:* Halve the greenhouse gas impact of Unilever products across their life cycles (from sourcing to product use and disposal).

- *Water:* Halve the water usage associated with consumers' use of Unilever products, especially in developing countries, where the company expects much of its future growth to be.

- *Waste:* Halve the waste associated with the disposal of Unilever products.

- *Sustainable Sourcing:* Increase the amount of agricultural raw materials sourced sustainably from 10 percent today to 100 percent.

- *Better Livelihoods:* Link into the supply chain more than 500,000 small farmers and small-scale distributors so that they can benefit by working with Unilever.

> **Unilever Strikes Gold in Green**
> Unilever finds that being sustainable is good for both the planet and the bottom line.

In addition to these objectives, Polman announced that Unilever would produce reports for Wall Street only once yearly, rather than producing the normal quarterly reports. While this was regarded as radical by many on Wall Street, Polman and the employees of Unilever saw this move as being consistent with the longer term view that is needed to promote sustainability.

By 2015, the early results were in. Unilever's share price has increased 60 percent. It is the third most looked up company on LinkedIn, outperformed only by Google and Apple and ahead of

Facebook and Microsoft. In May 2015, the Gartner Group placed Unilever at No. 3 on its Top 25 Supply Chains, highlighting Unilever's *Sustainable Living Plan* as an exemplar of corporate leadership in both the market and in sustainability. By January 2015, five years ahead of schedule, Unilever announced that it had achieved zero waste to the landfill across 242 industrial sites located in 67 countries. Finally, Unilever's portfolio of sustainable brands is showing more growth than its other products.

It is evident that for Unilever, being green is gold!

This chapter discusses future developments in Operations and Supply Chain Management. We begin the discussion by focusing on sustainability, which has now become one of the major drivers in operations and the supply chain. As illustrated by Unilever's experiences, sustainability is not only good for the planet, it is also good for business. It is attractive to customers, and it has helped Unilever to reduce waste. In addition, the Unilever story highlights another critical element discussed in this chapter–the importance of organizational culture and values. Finally, the chapter concludes by examining how changes in customer expectations, supply chain strategies, and technologies are creating new levels of customization and customer service.

THE TRIPLE BOTTOM LINE

LO16-1 Define sustainability using the triple bottom line and explain what this approach means not only for operations management but also the entire supply chain.

triple bottom line An approach to corporate performance measurement that focuses on a company's total impact measured in terms of profit, people (social responsibility), and the planet (environmental responsibility). Also referred to as the **TBL**, the **3BL**, or the **3Ps**.

global

The **triple bottom line** (3BL) approach (first discussed in Chapter 2 of this book) seeks to reduce the potentially negative impacts of a firm's processes and products on the environment (planet) and society (people). Put in a more positive light, the sustainability approach strives to improve the quality of life for people, in terms of health, fairness, and opportunity, especially for people who are disadvantaged or who live in developing countries.

For companies that are based in the developed world where markets are already saturated with products and services (such as Unilever), sustainability provides a new opportunity for differentiation. It also addresses the needs of markets in developing countries that represent most future business opportunities. At the same time, a shift toward sustainability is not without risks. Sometimes sustainability initiatives involve costs that customers may not be willing to pay. Sometimes the immediate and direct benefits to customers are difficult to identify. Financial markets are notoriously focused on short-term results, and this can be at odds with the long-term focus that sustainability requires.

The primary message of this chapter is that operations managers need to develop systems that simultaneously reduce our demands on the limited (and shrinking) resources of this Planet, play positive roles in providing safe and fair opportunities for People, and continuously create Profits by providing critical customers with compelling reasons to buy sustainable products. Too much focus on any one of these Ps (planet, people, profit), to the exclusion of the other two, creates an unsustainable strategy. Consequently, sustainability must be tightly integrated into the thinking and actions of operations managers (especially those who work in a global environment).

Figure 16-1 illustrates the triple bottom line (3BL) approach and the topics addressed in this chapter. Other terms used to describe this approach include: corporate social responsibility (CSR), sustainability, ethical business practices, social/environmental responsibility, and environmental social stewardship. Critical to this approach, as shown in Figure 16-1, are the intersections of the three sometimes competing objectives. In the next sections of this chapter we examine each of the three Ps and the potential trade-offs among them.

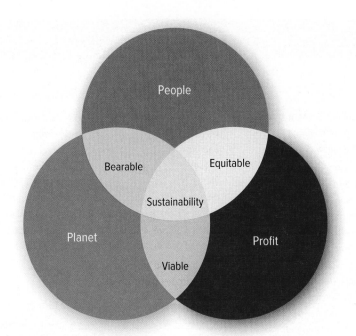

FIGURE 16-1
The Triple Bottom Line

THE FIRST P—PLANET

Environmental sustainability involves more than simply reducing air or water pollution. The United Nations Brundtland Commission defines sustainability as being able to meet "the needs of the present without compromising the ability of future generations to meet their own needs." With world population growth and increasing economic development, there is greater demand for all types of raw materials that are in short supply, including metals, petroleum, and natural gas. The more we use, the less there will be for future generations. Companies like Unilever, Dell, Steelcase, Philips, Walmart, Coca-Cola, Ford, Toyota, Disney (see the nearby Get Real box), and the Inter-Continental Hotels include environmental sustainability as a core aspect of strategic and operational planning.

The awareness of, and emphasis on, environmental sustainability has grown tremendously in recent years, due to several factors:

Customer expectations: Customers (especially in economically developed markets) are now demanding products that are environmentally sustainable. Consider the following statistics:

- 54 percent of shoppers indicate that they consider elements of sustainability (sourcing, manufacturing, packaging, product use, and disposal) when they select products and stores.[1]

- 80 percent of consumers are likely to switch brands to ones that support a cause when the brands are equal in quality and price.[2]

- Approximately 75 percent of consumers say that they have bought products from a socially or environmentally responsible company, up from 47 percent a few years ago.[3]

sustainability The ability or capacity of the system (the firm and its supply chain) to maintain or sustain itself by improving its performance in terms of how it manage pollution (planet), people, and changes in the business model (profit).

LO16-2 Explain the reasons why operations managers are increasingly focusing on the environmental impact of their activities.

---

[1]http://www.greenbiz.com/sites/default/files/document/US_CP_GMADeloitteGreenShopperStudy_2009.pdf (accessed July 11, 2012).
[2]http://www.coneinc.com/files/2010-Cone-Cause-Evolution-Study.pdf (accessed July 11, 2012).
[3]http://www.tillerllc.com/pdf/TillerGreenSurvey2009.pdf (accessed July 12, 2012).

GET REAL

Disney Sustainability

Walt Disney is the world's largest media and entertainment company. Recently, it decided to become a leader in environmental sustainability. To this end, Disney has taken the following steps:

- **Cutting Emissions:** Disney plans to cut carbon emissions by half, reduce electricity consumption by 10 percent, reduce fuel use, halve the garbage at its parks and resorts, and ultimately achieve net zero direct greenhouse gas emissions and landfill waste. Consequently, Walt Disney World has been designated as Florida Green Lodging Certified.

- **Recycling and More:** The Disney Harvest Program distributes nearly 50,000 pounds of food to the Second Harvest Food Bank every month (taken from food that has been prepared but not served at Disney's various restaurants and convention centers). All used cooking oil at Walt Disney Resort is recycled into biofuel and other products that are used by local companies. Food scraps are recycled into compost, which is used locally as fertilizer. The Walt Disney Healthy Cleaning Policy has the goal of minimizing the environmental impact of its cleaning products. The majority of props, vases, and containers used by the Disney floral team for events are made from reusable

glass and plastics. Finally, every day, 10 million gallons of wastewater are reclaimed and used in irrigation systems and other similar applications.

- **Preserving the Wildlife:** When building the Walt Disney World Resort in Orlando, the company set aside more than one-third of the land for a wildlife conservation habitat. This habitat forms the basis for Disney's Animal Kingdom Theme Park, which is used to educate guests on the importance of conservation and preserving the future.

Ultimately, these and other initiatives are part of the following long-term environmental goals at Walt Disney:

1. Create zero waste.
2. Produce zero net direct greenhouse gas emissions from fuels.
3. Reduce indirect greenhouse gas emissions from electricity consumption.
4. Have a net positive impact on ecosystems.
5. Minimize water use.
6. Minimize product footprint.
7. Inform, empower, and activate positive action for the environment.

activity

student

Look up the listing of Global 100 most sustainable corporations in the world at www.global100.org. Review how the rankings were generated. Using Pareto analysis, determine in which geographic regions (Europe, the United Kingdom, Africa, the Middle East, the Far East, Australia, South America, North America) most of the 100 firms are found. Why do you think this is the case?

The economics of environmental sustainability: Instead of viewing environmental protection as a drag on business performance, managers are increasingly noting that environmental sustainability can lead to cost savings and other benefits. For example, Walmart, Ikea, Wawa, Google, and eBay are switching to solar power because it is renewable, and after the initial investment, the actual cost to produce electricity is inexpensive. Investments in commercial solar products are frequently seeing payback periods of between four and five years (which equates to an annual rate of return in excess of 20 percent).

Diminishing natural resources: Consumers, governments, and firms are becoming increasingly aware of our world's limited resources. Most people are aware that petroleum resources are finite. Some estimates indicate that, with no other changes, global petroleum resources will be exhausted by 2056.[4] The United Nations Environmental Program recently reported that, if nothing changes, the world will demand 140 billion tons of minerals, ores, fossil fuels, and biomass every year by 2050—amounts that far exceed what the earth

---

[4]http://www.ncpa.org/pdfs/bg159.pdf (accessed July 11, 2012).

eBay's solar power system.
© Steve Proehl/Proehl Studios/Corbis

can provide.[5] Producing your smartphone or LCD television may not be possible in the future unless something is done to preserve or replace scarce resources. Industrial materials such as platinum, indium, zinc, gallium, tantalum, and antium are important for these uses, and these resources are expected to run out in the next 10 to 20 years. Further, as demand increases for nonrenewable materials, prices can be expected to increase and become more volatile, making budgeting very difficult.

Water, the most basic of all resources, is also becoming scarce. While salt water is plentiful, there is only a limited amount of easily accessible fresh water, most of which is found in the Great Lakes in North America. Safe drinking water is becoming scarce, especially in developing countries.

Increased business demand for scarce resources: Further complicating matters is the increasing demand for resources from developing countries such as China, Vietnam, India, and various countries in Africa. This demand is not only for the resources needed to build products such as LCD televisions; demand also exists for resources needed to build infrastructure projects such as roads, power generation plants, airports, and ports. For example, consider China's demand for steel. Over the past decade, China's average 15 percent annual growth in demand for steel means that China now accounts for over 40 percent of the global demand for steel.[6] Similar situations exist for concrete and the rare minerals.

New initiatives/programs: Programs and initiatives launched by governments, nongovernmental organizations (NGOs) such as the International Organization for Standardization (ISO), and professional societies are raising expectations for environmental sustainability among firms. Table 16-1 identifies some of these programs.

Global climate change: There is growing evidence that the world is experiencing global climate change, potentially caused by increased concentrations of carbon dioxide and other greenhouse gases produced by the burning of fossil fuel for heating, production, and transportation. The problem is worsened by deforestation, which reduces the earth's capacity to remove carbon from the atmosphere. Global climate change contributes to problems such as extreme weather (e.g., hot summers, droughts, violent storms, wildfires) and rising sea levels. Heat waves increase fatalities and illnesses. Rising sea levels may displace millions, and droughts can contribute to famines, especially in developing countries. These and other factors compel operations managers to take actions to become more environmentally responsible.

---

[5]C. Barnatt, "Resource Depletion," *ExplainingtheFuture.com* (February 18, 2012), www.explainingthefuture.com/resource_depletion.html (accessed July 9, 2012).

[6]L. Hook, "China's Steel Appetite Set to Wane," *Financial Times* (www.ft.com), http://www.ft.com/cms/s/0/2712469a-6377-11e1-9686-00144feabdc0.html (accessed July 12, 2012).

TABLE 16-1 Examples of Environmental Initiatives/Programs

Program/Initiative	Source	Summary
Kyoto Protocol	United Nations	Initially adopted on December 11, 1997, 37 countries committed to the reduction of four greenhouse gases. The accord introduced emissions trading, clean development mechanisms, and joint implementation to allow the countries to meet their limitations.
Responsible Care	Chemical industry	Global, voluntary initiative developed by the chemical industry (currently operating in 52 countries) to improve health, safety, and environmental effects.
Renewable Fuel Standard Program	EPA (USA)	Regulations designed to ensure that transportation fuel sold in the United States contains a minimum volume of renewable fuel.
Greenhouse Gas Reporting Program	EPA (USA)	Implemented in 2008, requires the mandatory reporting of greenhouse gases emitted by U.S. firms.
ISO 14000 (http://www.iso.org/iso/iso_14000_essentials)	ISO	A set of environmental management standards intended to help firms minimize their operations' impact on the environment.
Electronic Product Environmental Assessment Tool (EPAT) (www.epeat.net)	Green Electronics Council	A method for evaluating the environmental impact of computers and other electronic equipment. Certifies that electronic products are recyclable and designed to maximize energy efficiency and minimize environmental harm. EPEAT rating is becoming a requirement for purchases by the U.S. government and state and city governments.
Cradle to Cradle Standard (www.mbdc.com/c2c/)	McDonough Braungart Design Chemistry	A set of standards intended to ensure that products are designed to make use of renewable resources and that the resulting products can be easily disassembled and the outputs converted back into inputs for future production (rather than being returned to the ground).
LEED Certification (Leadership in Energy and Environmental Design) (www.usgbc.org/LEED/)	U.S. Green Building Council (USGBC)	LEED is intended to provide building owners and operators a concise framework for identifying and implementing practical and measurable green building design, construction, operations, and maintenance solutions. Certification at three levels.

Demand from governments and states for sustainable companies: Finally, not only is the demand for sustainability coming from consumers, economics, and companies, it is coming from governments and cities. For example, consider Switzerland. The government there has made sustainability an integral, formal, and key element of its national planning process. In addition, some Swiss cities have now established sustainability as one of the criteria that they use when evaluating and marketing to companies considering moving into the area.

activity

student

Examine one of the programs presented in Table 16-1, or find one of your own. What is the goal of the program? How will this program affect operations management and the supply chain? What are the advantages and shortcomings in the program? What did you learn?

Implications for Operations Management: A Broader View of Waste

LO16-3 Evaluate products using life cycle waste composition assessment.

Chapter 8 describes how lean systems reduce wastes within the operating system. Environmental sustainability expands the concept of waste to include waste generated across a product's life cycle. For example, the waste created by the customer in using the product and the disposal waste produced at the end of the product's life are both considered in life cycle assessment (LCA).

Life cycle assessment is a tool that helps managers assess the full impact of waste by quantifying its costs in five product stages: extraction, production, packaging/transportation, usage, and disposal.

- *Extraction* considers all the costs of getting the inputs that are used by the operations management system. Suppliers' harvesting, mining, or production processes may differ. For example, some processes may use more water or produce higher scrap levels. Prices paid do not necessarily reflect these differences because of differences in regulations, costs, and practices in different countries. The cost of inbound shipping of materials is also considered.

- *Production* considers the costs incurred by the firm that produces the finished good or service. These are the costs typically considered by most lean systems.

- *Packaging/transportation* includes wasted material and energy for packaging, which can sometimes be more damaging than the product itself (consider bottled water). Transportation can also contribute mightily to the overall waste picture in terms of energy consumption and CO_2 emissions.

- *Usage* consists of waste-related costs in use, including maintenance, repair, and operation (for example, CO_2 emissions). This element of waste is strongly influenced by the habits of the person using the product. For example, a person who performs regular maintenance on the product may generate a lower level of pollution compared to someone who does not.

- *Disposal and/or recycling* costs are incurred at the end of a product's life. These costs are difficult to estimate, for several reasons. First, disposal costs for a product sold today will occur in the future, sometimes in the distant future. Emerging technologies may radically change the limitations of recyclability today. Second, remanufacturing and recycling may make it difficult to determine when a product will finally have to be disposed of. Third, recycling often means *downcycling*. That is, recycling often results in lower-grade outputs—products that cannot be used in the same way that the original product was used. For example, recycled paper is usually not as bright as original paper; it is thus a lower grade of paper that can be used in fewer applications.

Life cycle assessment captures these various forms of waste using a common unit of measure. This unit can be monetary (dollars or euros), a measure of energy (barrels of oil or kilowatt-hours), or a simple rating of environmental impact. Gathering the data for such an analysis is not a trivial undertaking. However, products such as Herman Miller's Mirra chair (see the nearby Get Real box) are now being designed and built with the goal of minimizing life cycle costs.

When performing life cycle assessment, it is important to recognize that not all waste is equal. Every form of waste creates its own set of problems and issues. Wastes can be classified into five categories: (1) material choice (e.g., lead creates more environmental problems than steel), (2) energy usage, (3) solid residuals, (4) liquid residuals, and (5) gaseous residuals. Good materials choices use materials that are not toxic, are amply available, and can be recycled. This point is illustrated in the Get Real box "Paper or Plastic?". These five types of wastes can be assessed across the five life cycle stages to create a 5 × 5 *Environmentally Responsible Process/Material Matrix,* as shown in Figure 16-2. Ideally, a monetary cost of waste should be entered in each cell, but this is usually difficult to do. Alternatively, analysts can enter a value ranging from 0 (no impact, no effect—the desired state) to 4 (dangerous/extremely high environmental impact) into each cell, resulting in a total waste assessment score ranging from 0 to 100.

Using the process/material matrix approach, operations managers can quickly assess various production and material options and identify issues affecting environmental sustainability. In practice, the values are provided by users who draw on their experiences. In contrast, a full-blown LCA can be very expensive and time-consuming because it requires data that most firms do not regularly collect.

A similar approach is **carbon footprinting**. Rather than creating a monetary value for environmental issues, the carbon footprint is the total set of GHG (greenhouse gas)

life cycle assessment A tool for quantifying the various costs generated by waste in extraction, production, packaging/transportation, usage, and disposal.

carbon footprinting An analysis that evaluates environmental impact by calculating the greenhouse gas emissions caused directly and indirectly by a product.

GET REAL

Herman Miller Designs a "Green" Chair

The Mirra chair is the result of a four-year design process by Herman Miller. From the outset, this chair was designed from the ground up to meet the Design for the Environment (DfE) criteria set down by Herman Miller. The chair is comfortable (it automatically shapes itself to every user), attractive, and easy to recycle (since it is designed using only a few components, each of which can be easily disassembled and recycled). The chair is also a sales hit, proving that you can be green (environmentally responsible) while earning green (money).

The Mirra Chair by Herman Miller
© Herman Miller, Inc.

GET REAL

Paper or Plastic?

Many times we are asked, "paper or plastic?" when checking out at the grocery store. Which choice is more environmentally friendly? It turns out that answering this question for even a "simple" project such as grocery bags is not that simple after all. The following table summarizes some of the key findings of different life cycle assessments for these two options. Several studies indicate that plastic seems to be the overall better choice because over its life cycle it consumes less energy, less fossil fuel, and less fresh water. In addition, it produces less solid waste and lower greenhouse gas emissions. However, the *best* choice is to use neither type of bag but instead to use reusable cloth bags or plastic crates. Unfortunately, many of us (at least in the United States) are not willing to give up the convenience of "disposable" bags.

Life Stage	Paper Bags	Plastic Bags
Extraction	Paper comes from trees, a renewable resource if obtained from sustainably managed forests.	Plastic bags come from polyethylene, a nonrenewable petroleum by-product.
Manufacturing	Paper bag production generates 70% more air and 50% more water pollution and consumes 20 times more fresh water.	It takes only one-fourth the energy to produce a plastic bag that it does to produce a paper bag.
Transportation	It takes seven trucks to transport the same number of bags that are in a single truck full of plastic bags.	A plastic bag weighs about 10% of the weight of a paper bag, therefore requiring less energy to transport.
Usage	A paper bag can hold almost twice as many items as a plastic bag can, so fewer bags are needed.	Plastic bags usually cost one-third to one-fourth the cost of paper bags.
Disposal/ Recycling	Paper bags are biodegradable, but few landfills allow the air and water to reach the product (due to potential air and groundwater pollution). About 10% of paper bags currently get recycled.	Plastic bags take less space in landfills, but stray bags are found almost everywhere. They especially pose threats to marine life. About 1% of plastic bags currently get recycled, even though recycling consumes less energy and produces about half the pollutants of paper bags.

Life Stage	Material Choice	Energy Choice	Solid Residues	Liquid Residues	Gaseous Residues
Resource Extraction					
Product Manufacture					
Product Packaging/ Transportation					
Product Use					
Reburbishment Recycling & Disposal					

FIGURE 16-2

The Environmentally Responsible Process/ Material Matrix

emissions caused directly and indirectly by a product. This footprint can be evaluated across any of the five phases of the life cycle.

Identifying and Eliminating Environmental Wastes

A guiding principle of environmental sustainability is that it is better to prevent the creation of waste than to minimize its effects. Waste is a symptom of deficiencies in product designs, operational processes, and packaging. Root causes must be identified and appropriate corrective actions aimed at preventing waste must be introduced. Chapter 3 describes a process for identifying and improving wasteful processes.

In many cases, organizations are unaware of how well or poorly they are doing in terms of environmental sustainability. The reason—their supporting cost accounting/ information systems often do not record the needed data, such as energy consumption and waste disposal. These data are often hidden as they are incorporated into overhead costs. Along with direct costs, environmental sustainability typically affects indirect costs of storage, sorting, recording, information system management, and procedures for documenting, controlling, and dealing with environmental problems. Consequently, justifying sustainability improvement projects involves identifying, quantifying, and reporting these indirect costs. It is commonly believed that every dollar saved in direct sustainability costs creates many more dollars' worth of indirect savings.

ISO 14000—The Standard for Environmental Management Systems

As is the case for quality, there is an international standard for environment management: **ISO 14000**. Most firms are interested in ISO 14001:2015 and ISO 14004:2016, standards that deal with the **environmental management system (EMS)**. The EMS is responsible for:

- Identifying and controlling the environmental impact of a firm's activities, products, or services.

ISO 14000 A family of standards related to environmental management.

environmental management system (EMS) The formal system responsible for the planning, documentation, and management of an organization's environmental program. It covers areas such as systems, software, and information databases.

- Improving corporate environmental performance on a continuous basis.
- Implementing a systematic approach for setting environmental objectives and targets and for demonstrating that these targets have been achieved.

global

ISO 14001:2015 provides the requirements for an EMS, while ISO 14004:2016 gives general EMS guidelines. Being certified according to ISO 14001:2015 standards, while consistent with the goal of environmental sustainability, does not necessarily ensure sustainability performance. These standards simply ensure that the firm has a formal EMS—a necessary step toward improved environmental performance.

ISO 14000 standards are global in nature and significantly affect international trade. They lower trade barriers due to differences in environmental requirements. For more information on the overall ISO 14000 standards, see www.iso.org, the website for the International Organization for Standardization, the organization responsible for this certification standard.

Challenges of Being Environmentally Sustainable

In spite of its importance, it is not easy to be environmentally responsible. The trade-offs among choices are not always clear. For example, an "obvious" improvement in environmental sustainability might be to replace cardboard packing cases with returnable packaging. However, one must also consider the environmental impact of shipping empty containers back to the supplier. No matter how "green" you try to make a product, there will still be some form of environmental impact. Consider the following:

- PepsiCo undertook an initiative to ensure that Aquafina's bottles (even the caps and labels) are 100 percent recyclable, only to find that 80 percent of water bottles are not recycled.
- GE's new CFLs (compact fluorescent lights) use 75 percent less energy than a traditional incandescent light. However, CFL bulbs contain a hazardous substance, mercury, which poses a potential health concern if bulbs are broken or disposed of in traditional landfills. Is this health risk worth the energy savings?
- Patagonia, the outdoor-apparel company, decided to minimize the environmental impact of its fibers. It found that the most harmful fiber was cotton (not petroleum-based synthetics), because of the pesticides used. So it switched to organic cotton, only to find that to grow this type of cotton requires a great deal of water. A single pair of jeans, for example, requires 1,200 gallons of water.

As these examples illustrate, environmental sustainability requires managers to consider the complex interactions of product design and operations across the entire supply chain and throughout a product's life cycle.

THE SECOND P—PEOPLE

LO16-4 Discuss the approaches used by operations managers to ensure social responsibility while improving performance in the "people" aspect of sustainability.

The second element of the triple bottom line focuses attention on people, specifically human rights, health and safety, and quality of life in communities. Think of all the people groups that a typical business directly affects: (1) customers, (2) workers, (3) suppliers, and (4) investors. In addition, businesses can indirectly affect the larger community and society as a whole. Each of these stakeholder groups has its own needs and priorities (see Table 16-2).

As the examples in Table 16-2 illustrate, operations managers need to consider the needs and demands of many stakeholders when they make choices about sources, process designs, labor policies, and so on. Media stories often point out potential inequities, or even oppressive conditions, that operations managers and their suppliers have possibly created, either knowingly or unknowingly. For example, in recent years the media have brought attention to the exploitation of workers and small businesses in developing countries. As a result, more and more operations managers are participating in established Fair Trade practices. The Fair Trade movement focuses on helping producers in developing countries by improving trading conditions and promoting sustainability. The nearby Get Real box examines how Fair Trade practices have affected the way in which Starbucks buys coffee.

Fair Trade An organized social movement that seeks to help producers in developing countries, thus making for better trading conditions and promoting sustainability.

TABLE 16-2   People: Four Key Stakeholders and Their Expectations

Customers	Workers	Suppliers	Investors
Good "value" for their money	Fair labor practices and a "living wage" that affords a reasonable standard of living	Working with firms that share similar values	Competitive returns on investments
Products that are safe		Opportunities for supplier development and improvement	A sustainable business model so that investors can expect consistent returns over time
Privacy and protection of personal information	Safe working and living environment (both for themselves and the community)		
Honesty in marketing and sales communications	Equal opportunities for advancement	Opportunities to grow—shared success	Integrity in reporting operating and financial conditions
Integrity in fulfilling contracts and obligations	Support for social and economic developments (e.g., schools, arts, parks, charities)	Consistent application of rewards and punishments	Reduction of unreasonable risks and uncertainties (due to poor practices on the part of the firm and its operations management system)
Quick response to questions		Receiving a "fair" payment for goods and services provided	
System transparency			

GET REAL

Starbucks and "Fair Trade"[7]

Fair Trade is an organized social movement that seeks to help producers in developing countries, thus making for better trading conditions and promoting sustainability. Through Fair Trade efforts, farmers are paid a price for their products that allows them to invest in better equipment, buy better food for their families, and send their children to school (rather than keeping them working on the farm to support the family). Many of the farmers affected grow commodity products such as coffee.

Starbucks Corporation is an international coffee company and coffeehouse chain. It is currently the world's largest coffeehouse company. In 2000, the company introduced a line of Fair Trade products. Since then, this practice has evolved into a corporatewide system aimed at ethical sourcing. To this end, it has worked with Conservation International to develop *Coffee and Farmer Equity (C.A.F.E.) Practices.* This comprehensive set of coffee-buying guidelines focuses attention on four areas:

- Product quality
- Economic accountability
- Social responsibility (measures evaluated by third-party verifiers to ensure safe, fair, and humane

working conditions and adequate living conditions; covers minimum wage, child labor, and forced labor requirements)
- Environmental leadership

In 2011, Starbucks bought over 428 million pounds of coffee, 367 million pounds of which were from C.A.F.E. Practices–approved suppliers. The company paid an average price of $2.38 per pound in 2011, up from $1.56 per pound in 2010. According to Conservation International, this premium has enabled farmers to keep their children in school and to preserve remaining forests on their land, while achieving higher performance. This program spans some 20 countries and affects over one million workers each year. It is affecting practices on 102,000 hectares each year (a hectare is about 2.47 acres). Starbucks has paid an additional $16 million in Fair Trade premiums to those producer organizations for social and economic investments at the community and organizational levels.

_____

[7]http://www.starbucks.com/responsibility/sourcing/coffee (accessed July 20, 2012).

The seven objectives of Unilever's new strategic initiative, as described at the start of this chapter, are interlinked with people. Unilever strives to improve the lives of its consumers through better nutrition, reduced waste, reduced greenhouse gases, access to fresh water, and better health and hygiene. Further, Unilever has developed a supplier code to require that its suppliers comply with all labor laws, do not use forced or child labor, and provide safe and healthy working conditions. Unilever's suppliers are required to apply this code with their own suppliers as well.

Unfortunately, the supply chains in some industries, including electronics, textiles, cocoa, and coffee, involve developing countries that are plagued by human rights and health and safety violations. Human rights issues include excessive overtime, low wages, unsafe working conditions, and even forced child labor. For example, in 2012, an audit supported by Nestlé found violations of its labor code of conduct, including the use of child labor by suppliers in the Ivory Coast, which is the world's largest producer of cocoa. Stating that eliminating child labor in its supply chain is its number one priority, Nestlé is collaborating with the Fair Labor Association to train and certify suppliers, increase monitoring, and work with the Ivory Coast's government.

activity

student

Many companies are currently implementing versions of the triple bottom line (e.g., IKEA, Hewlett-Packard, GE, Citigroup, FedEx Kinko's, PepsiCo, Anheuser-Busch, Dow Chemical, and Weyerhaeuser Company). Select two companies (do a search on the Internet) and review their triple bottom line reports. What did you learn? What new practices were introduced? How did the pursuit of the triple bottom line affect financial performance?

Human rights and health and safety problems in the supply chain are complex challenges that are typically driven by underlying economic, social, and political issues. Companies try to combat these problems in a number of different ways. Most large companies have detailed codes of conduct for themselves and their direct suppliers. Many have extensive training programs for their own employees and their suppliers and use external agencies to regularly audit suppliers. Companies also work closely with nongovernmental organizations (NGOs) and industry associations to help address some of the broader economic, social, and political issues. Some companies such as Nike evaluate how their own business practices, such as short deadlines, poor forecasting, and last-minute changes, contribute to problems such as excessive overtime.

An important part of the people aspect of the triple bottom line is supporting the communities in which companies operate. By supporting the local community, companies contribute to the health and wellness of their employees as well as their quality of life. For example, Marathon Petroleum is a major supporter of United Way as a way to improve health and human services. Walmart provides volunteers and financial support to over 100,000 community-based organizations and charities. Delta Airlines is a strong supporter of the arts and helps to fund museums, orchestras, and music festivals.

For the second P to be successfully addressed, people-focused initiatives must first be ingrained in the organization's corporate culture; they must be part of the widely accepted way of doing things within the company. Second, initiatives must recognize and adapt to differences in the ways that people in different countries deal with issues. Country cultures, norms, and values can vary drastically, leading to different expectations and requirements for social responsibility.

Organizational Culture

Organizations affect how their members see issues, deal with problems, and identify what is important. People are influenced by organizational goals, structure, training, coworkers' attitudes, successes and failures, and a host of other aspects of organizational life. Operational programs such as those we have discussed in this book can have large impacts on organizational culture, and a given set of goals may be more or less appropriate for different cultures. For example, the organizational culture that evolves over time in a lean system emphasizes waste and variance reduction, along with process standardization and discipline. Such an approach may seem stifling to employees who wish to be rewarded for radical innovations. Operational initiatives can greatly affect the culture and work life of employees. Operations managers must often address conflicts between changing organizational goals and existing cultural norms. In fact, preexisting cultural norms often form serious impediments to organizational change. This is why in environments of rapid change, operations managers have to be so attuned to the strengths and weaknesses of their organization's culture. These strengths and weaknesses are often difficult to identify. As one manager put it, "organizational culture is what the employees do when the boss is not around."

While culture can be difficult to change, it can also be a key source of competitive advantage. For example, consider the success of Apple. Many people believe that the reason that Apple has been successful is because it has developed a culture of innovation. Similarly, as discussed in the nearby Get Real box, much of Zappos's success is attributed to its spirited culture.

Organizational culture is an increasingly important issue as operations managers seek to integrate partners in the supply chain. Culture affects supply chain–related issues like trust and compliance. In general, people in an organization work most comfortably with those who they regard as being like them. They tend to have less trust when dealing with people who are perceived as having different goals or motivations. For this reason, operations managers have to carefully consider differences in the organizational cultures of potential partners before they enter into long-term collaborative agreements.

relationships

Organizational culture plays a critical role in achieving sustainability goals. People within the organization must embrace and support the organization's view of sustainability in order for goals to be met. This is not always easy. There is disagreement and controversy surrounding some sustainability issues (global warming, for example). Leadership plays an important role in defining the culture and related sustainability goals. For example, the Michigan furniture company Herman Miller (see the earlier Get Real box) has had extensive success with sustainability. One of the founders of Herman Miller was a minister who believed strongly in corporate stewardship and responsibility. In large part, the company's commitment to sustainability stems from the values and corporate culture created by this founding leader. Similarly, one of the reasons that Unilever, the subject of the opening vignette in this chapter, has been so successful in its sustainability initiatives is that this commitment to sustainability is consistent with the cultural values of Unilever—values that can be traced back to the values of its founders, William Hesketh Lever (UK) and Antoon Jurgens and Simon van den Bergh (the Netherlands).

National Culture

Throughout this book we have maintained that globalization is a primary change driver in operations management. Most supply chains are now global and involve interactions among multiple national cultures. Supply chains often source from suppliers and provide

global

GET REAL

Zappos Culture Sows Spirit[8]

Zappos.com is considered one of the leading online company success stories. It has developed a loyal following of customers by selling them something that many consider hard to sell online: shoes. Its website describes each shoe in great detail. Another important feature is its liberal return policy (customers have one year in which to return the shoes, and Zappos pays shipping both ways).

Critical to Zappos's success is its highly regarded customer service group. An extremely high level of customer service is a direct result of the Zappos culture. All new corporate employees receive four weeks of customer loyalty training—answering phones in the call center—before starting their jobs. After training, they are offered $2,000 to leave the company—no questions asked. This "quit now" bonus is designed to ensure that employees stay at Zappos for the right reasons. About 97 percent decline the offer.

Zappos.com annually publishes a "Culture Book" in which employees describe what the company culture means to them. Among the company's 10 core values are: "Create fun and a little weirdness," "Be adventurous, creative and open-minded," and "Build a positive team and family spirit." CEO Tony Hsieh views company culture as the number one priority. A great culture translates into great service, and great service is what Zappos is all about. Culture matters because it means attracting great people, motivating them to continue giving their best as well as retaining them, and giving customers an experience that brings them back to Zappos. So far, it is working.

[8]C. Gergen and G. Vanourek, "Zappos Culture Sows Spirit," *The Washington Times*, July 16, 2008, http://www.washingtontimes.com/news/2008/jul/16/zappos-culture-sows-spirit/print/, (accessed February 26, 2009).

products and services to customers located all around the world. Therefore, it is important to recognize that people from different nations or regions often differ from each other in a number of important ways:

- Different ways of looking at things.
- Different ways of dressing.
- Different ways of expressing personality and what constitutes goodness or success.
- Different ways of interacting with each other.
- Different skills.

These differences in national culture can have major effects on operations management. Processes that work in one country may not necessarily work in another. For example, when designing supply chains for North America, managers typically assume that all the people involved can read and write. This assumption is not always valid in some parts of the world (for example, read about dabbawallahs in the nearby Get Real box). Thus, labor practices that are sustainable in one region might not be sustainable in another.

Culture also affects how people deal with problems. In an American/British/Canadian setting, problems are usually identified explicitly. In a Japanese setting, people are likely to deal with problems less directly. Dave Barry, a famous American humorist, describes a situation that he encountered on a trip to Japan. When he requested that he be booked on a flight between two cities, the clerk asked if he would rather take the train. Barry rejected this option; he wanted to fly. The clerk then pointed out that there were numerous options available for going between the two cities. Dave insisted that he wanted to fly. To this, the clerk replied that it would be difficult to accommodate this request. After a great deal of discussion (that greatly frustrated both parties), the clerk finally stated that there were no direct flights between the two specific cities (a source of embarrassment for the clerk). The problem was that each person was operating in a manner appropriate to their culture, but their notions of what was appropriate did not mesh. To the Japanese clerk, it was impolite to tell Dave Barry that there was no direct flight. To Dave Barry, it was important to know whether or not he could fly between the two cities.

GET REAL

Dabbawallahs—Managing the Lunchtime Food Supply Chain in Bombay, India

Five thousand people, 150,000 lunch boxes per day, almost zero errors—that is the bottom line for Bombay's dabbawallas. In the large cities of India, business managers want hot, homemade lunches, not cafeteria-bought meals. Given the crowded conditions of Bombay, this would seem to be a difficult, if not impossible, task—were it not for dabbawallahs. Dabbawallahs (translated, the term means "box people") are a group of individuals responsible for picking up the meals from the homes and bringing them to the offices and then picking up the dishes and returning them home. They must do this every day; they must do it fast; and they must do it without error (for a mistake means that someone goes hungry). What makes this supply chain and service unique is that nearly all dabbawallas are illiterate. To provide this service, they have developed a system that relies on simple color-coding and a few other codes readily understood by the people involved. The results are amazing; only one delivery in a million goes wrong. That is good performance anywhere.

© Rob Elliott/AFP/Getty Images

http://trak.in/tags/business/2009/02/08/
mumbai-dabbawallahs-inspire-their-us-counterparts/.

The challenge for operations managers is to understand and anticipate differences in national cultures that have the potential to make operational processes less effective and to lower the quality of work life for employees. Conversely, it is also important for managers to build upon the strengths of different cultures as they relate to the demands of different operational processes. The meshing of cultures continues to be a very important issue as supply chains become more and more interconnected and global.

To successfully bring about changes related to sustainability, operations managers must be prepared to invest not only in new systems, processes, tools, and technology, but also in efforts to change culture when possible and adapt to it when necessary.

THE THIRD P—PROFIT AND LONG-TERM COMPETITIVE ADVANTAGE

The third P, profit, is the one that operations managers and their businesses have typically prioritized in the past, at least in "for-profit" organizations. Profit (or funding, for nonprofit organizations) is critically important for the long-term sustainability of an enterprise. No matter how noble a firm's ambitions may be, it will not survive if it is consistently unprofitable, and maintaining profits can be difficult in rapidly changing conditions. Ultimately, an organization's business model must change if it is to maintain a *sustainable competitive advantage.* The use of the word "sustainable" in this context is no less important than in its connotations of environmental and social good.

Developing and maintaining a sustainable competitive advantage is not easy, and it requires continual renewal. Every year since 1955, *Fortune* magazine (http://money.cnn.com/magazines/fortune/) has published a list of the 500 largest publicly traded companies. Consider the following statistics:

- It took 20 years to replace one-third of the Fortune 500 companies listed in 1960. Starting in 1998, it took only four years to replace one-third of the Fortune 500.[9]
- According to Peter Senge, MIT professor, the average life of a Fortune 500 firm is only 30 years.[10]
- Jim Collins, the author of *Built to Last,* noted that only 71 companies of the original 1955 Fortune 500 still exist.[11]

In preparing for the future, operations managers have to anticipate and manage changes in the elements of their business models. Recall from Chapter 2 that these elements include key customers, value propositions, and the organization's operational capabilities.

Changes in Key Customers

Over time, an organization might begin to serve new key customers (due to the introduction of new products and services or the firm's movement into new geographic markets, for example). Alternatively, the expectations of an organization's existing key customers might change, for a number of reasons:

- *Changes in economic conditions:* During the recession that began in 2008, many firms found that cost had become an order winner (where previously it was an order qualifier).
- *Changes in competitors' actions:* Suppose that a competitor offers a new feature to your customer. Now that customer expects you to do the same.

LO16-5 Understand the challenges operations managers face as they seek to develop and maintain a sustainable competitive advantage.

- *Changes in income levels:* As income levels increase, customers can afford more and, as a result, they expect more (this is common in rapidly developing countries).
- *Changes in educational levels:* As customers' educations increase, they are exposed to, and may develop tastes for, new and different things and experiences.
- *Changes in fashion and lifestyles:* As societies evolve and interact, customers' demands for particular products and services grow and decline.

Changes in Value Propositions

Firms frequently change or update their value propositions, either leading or responding to customer changes. Consider the current development of value propositions for consumers that emphasize highly customized experiences. For example, companies such as Blue Apron, Plated, and HelloFresh offer home-delivered meals that involve the customer in menu planning and preparation. The customer works with the chefs to select a meal plan for the week. The company then ships the ingredients, which are locally sourced, along with instructions for preparation. The design and preparation become the experiences that these companies offer their customers, along with the eating!

Increasingly companies are revising their value propositions to accommodate individual customer demands and expectations. Starbucks offers an example of this kind of change in its new Starbucks Reserve brand. This new type of coffee shop enables each customer to select a specific type of coffee and be involved in how it is made (see the nearby Get Real box).

Changes in Operational Capabilities

Changes in customers and in value propositions usually call for supporting changes in operational capabilities. Conversely, sometimes changes in operational capabilities offer opportunities for new value propositions and new customers. As noted in Chapter 2, a firm's capabilities stem from its resources, assets, and processes and its investments in new management practices, new supply chain relationships, and new technological advances.

GET REAL

Starbucks Reserve

Having Coffee Your Way!

In December 2014, Starbucks introduced a new type of Starbucks store—Starbucks Reserve. The first one was opened in Seattle, Washington—just nine blocks from the original store. What makes this Starbucks so unique? It is more than simply a place where you can get a cup of coffee. Rather, it is designed to be an experience for the consumer—one in which the supply chain is highly visible. When you enter the Starbucks Reserve, you are given a menu of the different coffees, which are unique to Starbucks Reserve, currently being roasted on-site. You can even watch the coffee beans being roasted, grounded, and packaged. You are told the origins of the coffee beans and their taste characteristics. You are also informed that the coffee beans have been sourced from Fair Trade certified suppliers. When you decide on which coffee to try, you are given a choice of one of five different methods for preparing it. Then, the coffee is prepared just for you: You watch and are involved in the entire process. The Starbucks Reserve barista explains every step in the

Starbucks Reserve—the main coffee preparation area.
© Steve Melnyk

process. The result is a truly unique customer experience, which is a direct reflection of Starbucks's new value proposition and approach.

Technology is especially important, because it enables the firm to develop and implement new business models that would not have been possible otherwise.

Of the many major technological advances that have occurred in the last few years, one of the most important is the **Internet of Things (IoT)**—the network of physical objects or "things" that are embedded with software, sensors, and network connectivity that enable the IoT to collect, exchange, and analyze data. The "things" that make up the IoT include smartphones, sensors in cars, equipment and appliances, fitness monitors (such as Fitbit and Vivofit), smart watches (e.g., Apple's iWatch), and product tags. A recent Gartner report estimates that there will be over 201 billion such devices by 2020.[12]

Consider how the IoT is changing business models in the following examples:

Internet of Things (IoT) The network of physical objects or "things" that are embedded with software, sensors, and network connectivity resulting in the generation and analysis of large datasets about the system (and its status) and the customer.

- HydroPoint Data Systems, a water management company, has developed an IoT application that eliminates water waste by installing sensors to monitor leaks and runoff. The system, called WeatherTRAK, has more than 25,000 subscribers who, in 2013, saved more than 20 billion gallons of water, 77 million kilowatt hours of electricity, and about $143 million in expenses.

- Pirelli, one of the world's largest tire manufacturers, is learning about the durability and performance of its products from sensors embedded in the tires. Targeted to fleet managers, this system is also used for vehicle protection and control; information about traffic, road conditions, and parking; remote vehicle behavior and diagnostics; management of logistics and industrial vehicle fleets; and automated emergency calls.

- Florida Hospital Celebration Health, a hospital in Kissimmee Florida, is using IoT to track the location of critical medical equipment as well as to collect information on hand hygiene compliance and how nurses spend their time during a shift. It is also helping to uncover patterns that can lead to increased efficiency and improved customer satisfaction.

- Ford Motor Co. launched Connected Car Dashboards to collect information from vehicles to gain insights into driving patterns and vehicle performance. Meanwhile, companies such as Verizon (Hum), Zubie, and Automatic are producing modules that plug into cars to enable consumers to monitor conditions within the car and to enable insurance companies to adjust rates based on consumers' driving behaviors.

The IoT is helping firms learn more about consumers' desires and behaviors, thereby affecting product design, promotion, and customization. IoT also enables hardware firms to offer more information-based services. These kinds of business model opportunities, spawned from technological developments such as the IoT, are truly changing the future of operations management along with the nature of sustainable advantage.

Balancing the 3 Ps

Today, environmental and social concerns are increasingly important drivers of changes in customers, value propositions, and operational capabilities. These investments can affect a firm's profit in two fundamental ways. First, a firm's efforts to be more environmentally and socially sustainable can improve its value proposition and associated sales revenues, because customers place importance on these aspects and are willing to pay more for them. Think of paying a higher price for "organic" foods, for example. Second, more sustainable practices can either lower or raise the costs of providing a good or service. For example, minimizing the transportation of products might simultaneously lower both cost and carbon emissions—a "win-win." In other cases, however, a firm might have to choose between a high-cost, highly sustainable option and a lower cost, less sustainable one. The value proposition, and its effect on profit, should not get lost in a firm's efforts to become

---

[12] Gartner Group, 2015. "Gartner Says 6.4 Billion Connected 'Things' will be in use in 2016, Up 30 Percent from 2015." Gartner Press Release. November 10, 2015. http://www.gartner.com/newsroom/id/3165317.

GET REAL

Patagonia Outdoor Sportswear

Please Don't Buy This Jacket!

Patagonia is an American outdoor apparel company and a leader of the sustainability charge in the clothing industry. Its commitment to sustainability is evidenced in its actions:

- Patagonia donates 1 percent of its sales to environmental charities.
- It helped found the Sustainable Apparel Coalition to measure environmental impact in member firms' supply chains.
- It created a fund, $20 Million and Change, to assist sustainable start-up companies.
- Patagonia was one of the first Californian firms to register as a B Corporation, freeing it from the legal requirement to maximize shareholder returns.
- It encourages customers to return gently worn clothing so that it can be repaired and resold—emphasizing reuse over new production.
- It has eliminated its internal sustainability department, instead making sustainability the responsibility of all workers throughout the firm.

© Patagonia

In a somewhat counter-intuitive move, Patagonia recently launched a marketing campaign with the slogan, "Don't Buy Our Jackets." The point of the campaign was to emphasize the need to reduce overconsumption, suggesting that consumers should not buy more products than they actually need. Rather than reducing demand, Patagonia argued that the campaign actually strengthened its relationships with existing customers and attracted new ones who were impressed by the company's commitment to environmental issues.

As part of the campaign, Patagonia also launched its Common Threads Initiative, which asks customers to partner with the company in the following agreement: Patagonia promises to "make great stuff, fix it when it breaks, and recycle it when you're done with it," while customers promise to "buy only what you need, repair it when it breaks, and recycle it when you're through."

Patagonia is a company truly committed to sustainability and, at the same time, it engages its customers in this mission in such a compelling way as to secure strong loyalty, thereby creating sustainable advantage and excellent profitability. Patagonia has tripled its profits in the last five years!

---

more environmentally and socially sustainable. Consider the ways in which Patagonia considers people, the planet, and profit in its messaging to its customers (see the nearby Get Real box).

LO16-6 Understand the process by which the triple bottom line is transformed into appropriate measures, metrics, and standards.

MEASURING AND REPORTING SUSTAINABILITY THROUGH THE TRIPLE BOTTOM LINE

For an organization to pursue its mission sustainably, it needs to measure its progress in each of the three Ps. Comprehensive measures of sustainability are being developed. For example, Walmart is developing a sustainability index that consumers can use to assess products and the firms that produce them. As a first step, it has surveyed its first-tier suppliers on energy and climate, material efficiency, nature and resources, and people and community. Walmart is now working with a consortium to develop a database of information on product life cycles. The ultimate goal is to develop a simple, easy-to-understand tool for customers.

More broadly, many organizations have launched initiatives seeking to make the sustainability performance of businesses and products more visible, either to better inform potential investors or to put pressure on firms to raise their levels of sustainability. For example, the Dow Jones Sustainability Index evaluates and rates applying firms by

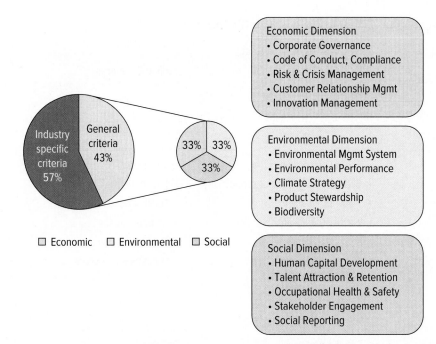

FIGURE 16-3
Criteria for the Dow
Jones Sustainability Index
Source: http://www.sustainability-
indexes.com/sustainability-assessment/
corporate-sustainability-assessment.jsp.

administering a survey questionnaire and by scanning media reports. Figure 16-3 shows
the breakdown of criteria assessed by the Dow Jones index. Economic criteria include
issues such as the degree to which the firm protects the privacy and security of its customers (e.g., against fraud or identity theft). Social issues include how well the firm provides access to its products for underprivileged customers (e.g., in developing countries).
A unique aspect of the Dow Jones Sustainability Index is that many of the criteria are
tailored to specific industry contexts.

To provide a sense of the breadth of issues addressed under sustainability, Table 16-3
shows the criteria used by three other rating organizations to evaluate sustainability
performance.

- The Global Reporting Initiative (GRI) is a nonprofit organization founded in the
  United States in 1997 by the Coalition of Environmentally Responsible Economies
  (CERES) and the United Nations Environment Program (UNEP). The GRI produces
  a sustainability reporting framework to enable greater organizational transparency,
  with the goal of developing a standard practice for reporting which allows stakeholders to compare sustainability-related data.

- The Global 100 Most Sustainable Companies is an annual project initiated by
  Corporate Knights Inc., a company that promotes clean capitalism. Inclusion in
  the Global 100 is limited to a select group of the top 100 large-cap companies
  in the world.

- The Ethical Consumer is but one example of many watchdog groups that seek
  to make global businesses more sustainable through consumer pressure. Such
  organizations research and report on what they deem to be good and bad company
  behaviors.

Operations managers need to be aware of these kinds of independent assessments.
They can have a large impact on a business's financial success as a growing number of
investors and consumers pay attention to them. In many cases, groups create "scorecards," "buyers' guides," or "stamps of approval" in order to signal sustainability practices to consumers, and they can organize boycotts and other grassroots movements.
Such programs are increasing the visibility and quantification of issues associated
with sustainability. In doing so, they are forcing organizations not only to measure and
report different aspects of sustainability, but also to take actions aimed at improving
their performance.

TABLE 16-3   Examples of Sustainability Criteria Used by Rating Organizations

Global Reporting Initiative (GRI)	Global 100 Most Sustainable Companies	Ethical Consumer
Economic • Market presence • Indirect economic impacts	• % Taxes paid	
Environmental • Materials • Energy • Water • Biodiversity • Emissions, effluents, and waste • Products and services • Compliance • Transport	• Energy productivity • Greenhouse gas (GHG) productivity • Water productivity • Waste productivity • Innovation capacity	Environment • Environmental reporting • Nuclear power • Climate change • Pollution & toxics • Habitats & resources
Labor Practices and Decent Work • Employment • Labor/management relations • Occupational health and safety • Training and education • Diversity and equal opportunity • Equal remuneration for women and men Human Rights • Investment and procurement practices • Nondiscrimination • Freedom of association and collective bargaining • Child labor • Forced and compulsory labor • Security practices • Indigenous rights • Assessment • Remediation	• Safety productivity • Employee turnover • Leadership diversity • Clean capitalism paylink • CEO to average employee pay	People • Human rights • Workers' rights • Supply chain management • Irresponsible marketing • Arms & military supply Animals • Animal testing • Factory farming • Animal rights & cruelty
Society • Local communities • Public policy • Compliance Product Responsibility • Customer health and safety • Product and service labeling • Marketing communications • Customer privacy • Compliance		Politics • Antisocial Finance • Boycott calls • Genetic engineering • Political activity Sustainability • Company ethos • Product sustainability (organic, fair trade, energy efficient, vegan & vegetarian products)
https://www.globalreporting.org/	http://www.global100.org/	http://www.ethicalconsumer.org/

CHAPTER SUMMARY

Operations management must be dynamic in dealing with a changing world. Further, to be sustainable, operations management must address issues that go beyond standard accounting and financial objectives. These are the primary messages of this chapter:

1. Both today and in the increasingly competitive environment of the future, operations managers must be concerned with sustainability. We defined sustainability in terms of the triple bottom line: planet, people, and profit.

2. Environmental sustainability, the first P, is becoming increasingly critical as resources are becoming more scarce, population and demand for these resources are increasing, and products and processes are creating environmental problems (such as global warming). Tools like life cycle assessment and standards such as ISO 14001 can help guide operations managers' decisions.

3. The people aspect of sustainability, the second P, focuses on issues such as human rights, health and safety, and quality of life in the community. Each organization should consider at least four key stakeholders: customers, workers, suppliers, and investors.

4. In addressing the people aspect of sustainability, operations managers need to stay mindful of the need to manage and adapt to differences in both corporate and national cultures.

5. In order to sustain profits, the third P, operations managers need to continually improve or change the firm's business model, ensuring that it continues to offer critical customers a value proposition that is both attractive and supportable by the organization's capabilities. Maintaining the fit between customers, value propositions, and capabilities is difficult over time, because these elements are always changing.

6. Technological advances offer new ways to improve the 3 Ps. Developments such as the Internet of Things (IoT) are helping to create greater operational visibility and greater knowledge of what customers want (and do not want).

7. Organizations and agencies are growing in their influence and power in making the sustainability practices of a given firm visible to the public. Operations managers need to be cognizant of the criteria that these organizations are using and the ways in which their businesses are being perceived.

KEY TERMS

carbon footprinting 565
environmental management system (EMS) 567
Fair Trade 568
Internet of Things (IoT) 575
ISO 14000 567
life cycle assessment 565
sustainability 561
triple bottom line 560

DISCUSSION QUESTIONS

1. Review the new strategic direction for Unilever, as presented at the beginning of this chapter. What are the economic rationales for the company's seven key strategic imperatives? What are the risks? To what extent are these initiatives driven by concerns of environmental as compared to business sustainability?

2. Why does the concept of "cradle to grave" no longer make business and environmental sense?

3. What would a firm's business model look like if we were to compete primarily on environmental sustainability?

4. In a recent study by MIT, it was found that the Toyota Prius, a hybrid, was less environmentally responsible than a Hummer SUV. How could this be? You might want to consider using the AT&T Environmental Assessment Matrix in addressing this question.

5. What are some operations/supply chain management strategies that can be used to deal with the challenges of diminishing natural resources?

6. Why is it that some managers are not willing to more aggressively pursue environmental sustainability even when presented with compelling reasons for its need? (*Hint:* Think about issues such as level of resources available, risk of failure, and how the managers are measured and rewarded.)

7. The triple bottom line can be viewed as a three-legged stool in that each element must be present or, if one or more elements are removed, then the entire structure collapses. To what extent do you agree with this approach? Why is it important that each element be present?

8. Do you think companies should invest in community-based programs such as support for the arts? Why or why not?

9. One common approach that companies use to protect human rights is a supplier code of conduct. How can you increase the effectiveness of a code of conduct?

10. In the United States, the South and the Midwest experience natural disasters on a regular basis (hurricanes, such Hurricane Katrina, in the South and tornadoes in the Midwest). Whenever such a disaster takes place, organizations such as the American Red Cross must respond. Part of this response is to set up a supply chain structure. Identify and discuss several of the factors that can influence the design and deployment of such a supply chain. How can technology be used to improve and enhance the operation of this supply chain?

11. Recently, companies such as Verizon, Automatic, and Zubie have introduced a module that plugs into the diagnostic port of most cars. This module keeps track of the status of the car and informs the user of any problems (explaining the problems in plain English). In some cases, companies such as Verizon have introduced a version that is connected to a cellular network. How could such a product potentially affect the customer and the management of automotive maintenance? Think about issues such as how this development could affect activities such as the ordering of spare parts and the monitoring of vehicles to identify systematic problems in product design or component reliability.

12. How could the Internet of Things affect activities such as your visit to a store to buy a product?

CASE

EuroConstellation Electronics

"Welcome everyone. Robert, please turn on the television." Vice President of Global Procurement, Stefan Schrettle, started the meeting with these words. The components sourcing and procurement team had been hurriedly assembled at Schrettle's request. Robert Schmidt walked to the control center of the rather cramped conference room and clicked the icons needed to project the BBC World News onto the screen at the front of the room. The face of a well-known anchorperson for the BBC filled the screen. While he talked, pictures of factory workers appeared.

The BBC had been repeatedly airing a special report focused on the working conditions at a large electronics supplier located in Mongolia, MongTronics. MongTronics had rapidly become one of the leading suppliers of electronic toys, subassemblies, and components to consumer goods manufacturers around the world, including EuroConstellation Electronics, the company that Robert worked for. The BBC was reporting that a worker at the MongTronics facility had committed suicide a day earlier by throwing himself off the roof of the seven-story dormitory where workers were housed. Alarmingly, this was the ninth suicide at the factory in the past 12 months. A BBC correspondent was raising questions about the working conditions at MongTronics. Though the facilities were toured regularly by MongTronics's major customers, little was actually known about the policies and work practices employed at the company. The correspondent was interviewing the general manager at the MongTronics plant. He had a concerned look on his face as he explained that worker safety and quality of life were important priorities for the company. The camera quickly cut to video of workers installing large nets around the dormitory walls to catch workers who might contemplate similar forms of suicide in the future.

After a few more minutes, Schrettle walked over to the control panel, turned off the projector, and raised the lights. He stated, "This is a serious situation, and we need to decide what, if anything, we can and should do about it. I'm putting Robert in charge of a task force to develop immediate responses to this situation, as well as a longer-term sourcing strategy for the parts we buy at MongTronics." As Mr. Schrettle spoke, the hairs on the back of Robert's neck stood up. He knew that this was an important assignment and his first real opportunity to demonstrate his leadership skills. Since joining the company almost a year earlier, Robert had mostly been learning the ropes as he participated in some sourcing trips to China and other locations in Eastern Asia.

Later that afternoon, Robert considered the facts that he had about the business that EuroConstellation did with MongTronics. EuroConstellation designed and assembled many different kinds of remote-controlled toys and equipment, including small robots, toy vehicles, and also monitoring and control systems for industrial equipment. Numbers from its ERP system showed that it had spent 25 million euros on purchases from MongTronics in the last year. MongTronics was its largest supplier, and this amount accounted for almost 30 percent of EuroConstellation's total materials purchasing spend. The items that EuroConstellation purchased included completely finished and packaged electronic toys (such as radio-controlled airplanes and cars), as well as a large number of subassemblies and components that were assembled into finished products by EuroConstellation's own factories. Low labor costs were the most attractive part of doing business with MongTronics. On average, Robert figured that his company was able to purchase items at about half the unit cost that it would pay to suppliers in Europe and the United States. Even after taking transportation and inventory costs into account, he figured that the Mongolian source still offered about a 30 percent cost advantage. On the other hand, labor costs were rising in the country; some analysts estimated that labor costs there would match those of low-cost Eastern European locations within five years.

As he dug into Internet and newspaper articles about MongTronics and the surrounding areas of Mongolia, Robert noted that most of the articles were quite positive regarding the economic benefits that the company had brought to a previously depressed region of the country. Before the growth of MongTronics, the population in the area had very low standards of living, at least from a Western perspective. Most people lived by subsistence farming or by raising horses. Many still lived as nomads in temporary shelters. Few individuals were educated beyond very basic levels. MongTronics had provided relatively high paying and stable employment for the people. In addition, it had built living quarters, a hospital, and schools for employees and their children.

Representatives from EuroConstellation had toured the MongTronics facility as recently as six months earlier. As Robert read the trip report written by the visiting team he noted that facilities were clean, processes seemed to be disciplined, and the workers seemed to be fairly satisfied with their conditions. In fact, the team had noted that the factory was a fine example of a lean operation.

Several questions floated around in Robert's head. How bad could this BBC report be for EuroConstellation? Was there a need for the company to respond? How would continuing to do business with MongTronics affect Euro-Constellation financially? Were there ethical issues to be considered too?

Questions

1. What are the possible ramifications of the BBC story for EuroConstellation's business prospects?

2. What is the socially responsible thing to do regarding future business with MongTronics?

3. Outline an action plan that Robert can give to his task force. What further information will the task force need? What actions, if any, should be taken immediately?

CASE

The Problem with Plastics

"Lucy, I thought that you told me and the planning committee that this move to recycle storage plastics was going to save us money. But, look here. I just got the bill for last month's disposal of our plastic. We wound up paying $3,000, rather than being paid for the value of the recycled material. This is the third month in a row that this has happened. I want to know what is going on and I want to know by Friday. If you can't solve the problem, we are going to simply throw out the plastic with the garbage, the way we used to do. It was less hassle for us and we would recover the space now being used for the recycling bins. Again, I want recommendations by Friday."

With those words, Fred Morgenstern, plant manager for the Novi plant of Voiture Automotive Supplies, turned around and walked out the door. Lucy Po, the environmental, health, and safety (EHS) manager for this facility, sat in her office considering what had just happened. What a way to start the week. It was Monday and she knew that she had five days to get to the heart of the problem. It was her initial analysis that had led to the decision to sell the various plastics to a recycler. It should have been a winner, but she must have missed something. In her mind, she reviewed the chain of events leading up to the meeting with Fred this morning.

The Novi plant, located in a suburb of Detroit, used over 40,000 square meters of 40 different plastics for storage. These various plastics were used to cover the parts during storage and in transportation. Once used, they were collected and thrown out. With landfills in Michigan becoming scarcer (especially in the Detroit area), landfill costs were increasing. Lucy could have recommended that the Novi plant truck the plastics out to Mount Pleasant, where landfill space was still available. But that seemed to attack the symptom of the problem, rather than the root cause.

As she looked around for options, she was approached by R-CYCL, a new start-up recently founded by a husband and wife team. The purpose of the start-up was to provide employment for chronically unemployed people in Detroit. Their proposal was simple but attractive. R-CYCL would pick up the plastic and pay the Novi plant a recovery price, provided that the plastics were properly sorted. If the plastics were not properly sorted, then the personnel at R-CYCL would sort the plastic and charge the plant for the labor required. This charge would be deducted from any recovery prices.

There was the problem. The Novi plant used 40 different types of plastic. It seemed that every time a new part was designed, the engineers would specify a new storage plastic. Whenever a new plastic covering was introduced, a number of things happened: a new item master had to be developed and entered into the system; inventory storage locations had to be identified (the Novi facility generally used a fixed inventory location system); and operators had to be trained on the material. Because of the high usage of plastic, the purchasing department had been aggressive in looking for the lowest-priced suppliers. They were currently buying much of the required materials from low-cost Chinese suppliers. Lucy was told that purchasing was generally happy with these suppliers, though on-time delivery was an issue (causing an increase in safety stock).

When it came time to recycle the plastic, the processes in place clearly described what was supposed to happen. The operator was to take the plastic to the recycling storage area, where 40 large bins were located next to the operation and parts storage areas. The operator was to review the code and then put the plastic into the appropriate bin. Once a week, R-CYCL would empty the bins and recycle the material. Lucy remembered how plant management had almost rejected the recycling plan because of the space requirements to locate 40 storage bins. Facility management had argued that this space would be better used for production.

That was the theory. The practice was different. Though each plastic item was stamped with a code, the material differences between the plastics were slight. Sometimes the codes got covered by grease or paint. Because the operators often could not read the codes (or they did not care), they often stuffed the plastic into the first bin available. Operators could be "written up" if they persistently failed to put plastics in the correct bin, but it was difficult to know when, or how often, this happened. When bins were nearly full, items often fell out onto the floor. This created problems for housekeeping, and plastic on the floor had contributed to several workplace injuries (thus increasing workers' compensation charges). In two cases the injuries resulted in fines being assessed against the plant. Lucy could see why Fred wanted to return to the old system. She had to recommend a better, more sustainable, approach. She also knew that the Novi plant was R-CYCL's biggest customer; if the plant stopped recycling plastic it would effectively put this start-up out of business.

After reviewing the facts, Lucy spoke to the engineers to get an idea of what types of plastic film they could consider at least minimally acceptable. With this information, she worked with purchasing to ask several suppliers for proposed solutions within 48 hours. Only one supplier responded—FilmTech.

FilmTech was located in Lapeer, Michigan (about 50 miles from the Novi plant). The company proposed to replace all 40 plastics with one plastic that could meet all of the technical requirements. Lucy wondered whether the engineers at the plant would accept the one substitute plastic material. An even larger problem with the proposal was that the new film, while recyclable, was higher quality and cost almost twice as much as the average material provided by the Chinese suppliers. Lucy figured that such a cost differential might make the FilmTech proposal a loser right away.

Questions

1. Review FilmTech's proposal from a triple bottom line perspective. What opportunities and costs are exposed that Lucy may have overlooked? How would these hidden costs affect the economic analysis being developed by Lucy?

2. What else can Lucy do to reduce the cost of buying and using FilmTech's plastic?

3. What else can Lucy do to make these operations truly sustainable?

CASE

The HyperCar

Photo courtesy of Rocky Mountain Institute (www.rmi.org)

How do you convince the auto industry to accept and support the need to develop and build a super efficient sport utility vehicle (SUV)? At first glance, this would be a no-brainer. Everyone wants an SUV that is fuel efficient. All that is needed is a quarter of a billion dollars to get this thing out of the lab and into the hands of the users. That

is the challenge facing Amory Lovins, the developer and champion of the Hypercar and the CEO of Hypercar, Inc., a car company with a plan to build this new car—a car that he is convinced will revolutionize the auto industry. It is also a challenge that is currently frustrating Lovins.

At first glance, you would not think that Lovins would have a problem raising such funding. After all, he has the "right" credentials. He has a degree from Oxford University, a MacArthur foundation "genius" grant, and a worldwide reputation as one of the premier environmental consultants. He has written or co-written 27 books and co-founded an environmental think tank that has successfully spun off several for-profit businesses. He has the right stuff to bring this revolutionary product to market—and revolutionary it is!

To begin with, the Hypercar is an earth friendly SUV that gets the equivalent of 99 miles per gallon of gas and emits nothing but drinkable water. It is powered by a fuel cell that converts hydrogen into electricity. The body is made from lightweight carbon fiber—the kind used in fighter planes, tennis rackets, and skis (to help industry, Lovins's group has even developed a method for converting carbon fibers into sheets of material ready to be used in making the Hypercar). Even the process of driving the Hypercar is revolutionary. The steering wheel has been replaced by two joy sticks; a sophisticated brain links and coordinates all activities—controlling everything from maintenance to entertainment. The car windows are insulated, thus reducing the need for air conditioning and heating. Even the tires have been redesigned. Gone are the big, bulky tires. These have been replaced by high tech, high pressure tires designed to increase rolling resistance and increase fuel efficiency—they can even run flat safely for short distances. Lovins's company has rethought every aspect of the car and it shows.

The challenge is that the very features that make the car revolutionary are also ones that have never been done before. To make this car a commercial success, all that is needed is money—and that is something that has not been coming from industry. Some corporate funding has been obtained. For example, BP Amoco PLC has invested about $500,00 in the Hypercar in the hopes that this project will encourage the auto industry to build cleaner products. Terra Trust, an environmentally focused Swiss investment fund, has pledged to invest $1.5 million of the $5 million that Hypercar has currently raised (unfortunately, Terra has only come up with $100,000 to date). While many executives, especially those with deep corporate pockets, are impressed with what Lovins has done, they are still hesitant to support the Hypercar.

Why does Hypercar need a quarter of a billion dollars? There are several reasons. First, the funds are needed to build about 20 Hypercars so it can be determined that the car really works. In addition, full scale production will cost around $140 million. Then there is the money needed to encourage suppliers to participate in this endeavor. After all, nearly everything that the Hypercar needs would have to be provided by suppliers—from the carbon fiber doors to the new engine plant to the dual joystick steering system to the computer control system. Then there are the costs of establishing the fueling system. After all, a system for refueling the Hypercar with hydrogen will have to be set up. Hypercar, Inc., has focused on the challenges of bringing such a product to the market. However, it has not even considered post-production issues such as insuring, servicing, and repairing (i.e., dealing with body repairs).

These considerations are part of the reason that Hypercar, Inc., has decided to target truck fleet users as potential key customers for this new product. They could help set up the necessary fueling infrastructure, while being drawn to the Hypercar by its very high level of energy efficiency.

Recently, the Hypercar team convened for a three-day summit in Basalt. Because of the problems with raising money, some of the young staffers suggested scaling back the company's do-or-die production goal. It was agreed that the company will start trying to license its technology to other automakers in two years, regardless of whether it is ever able to build a fleet of Hypercars. In part, this decision was based on the realization that, if the company is to successfully raise the funds needed, it must offer a short-term way for investors to reap a profit.

Question

It is now three years later and you have been approached by Amory Lovins for advice (address your report to him). As you prepare your recommendations, assume that the Hypercar is technically feasible (that is, it can and will work within the next two years). You should also assume that the purchase price for this car would be within $2,000 of a comparable, conventional car.

Source: Adapted from "One Quest to Build a Truly 'Clean' Car Has Gathered Steam," by Jeffrey Ball, Staff Reporter of The Wall Street Journal.

SELECTED
READINGS & INTERNET SITES

Elkington, J. "Towards the Sustainable Corporation: Win-Win-Win Business Strategies for Sustainable Development." *California Management Review* 36, no. 2 (1994), pp. 90–100.

Hayes, R.; G. Pisano; D. Upton; and S. Wheelwright. *Operations, Strategy, and Technology: Pursuing the Competitive Advantage.* Danvers, MA: John Wiley and Sons, 2005.

Keegan, P.; J. Dawsey; and B. Feldman. "The Trouble with Green Product Ratings." *Fortune* 164, no. 2 (2011), pp. 130–34.

Lee, H. L. "The Triple-A Supply Chain." *Harvard Business Review* 82, no. 10 (2004), pp. 102–12.

McDonough, W., and M. Braungart. *Cradle to Cradle: Remaking the Way We Make Things.* New York: North Point Press, 2002.

Murrary, S. "Textiles Industry: How to Be the Solution, Not the Problem." *The Financial Times,* June 19, 2012, **http://www.ft.com/intl/cms/s/0/d609cf9e-a434-11e1-84b1-00144feabdc0.html#axzz20dJYCDo3.**

"Nestlé Sets Out Actions to Address Child Labour in Response to Fair Labour Association Report on the Company's Cocoa Supply Chain." June 29, 2012, **http://www.nestle.com/Media/NewsAndFeatures/Pages/fla-report-cocoa.aspx.**

Schein, E. *Organizational Culture and Leadership.* Fort Worth, TX: Harcourt College Publishers, 1993.

http://www.delta.com/about_delta/global_good/arts_culture/index.jsp

http://www.marathonpetroleum.com/Corporate_Citizenship/Philanthropy/

http://www.walmartstores.com/communitygiving/

http://www.walmartstores.com/Sustainability/9292.aspx

Appendix

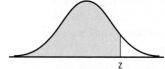

Table of Cumulative Probability of the Normal Distribution (one-tail)

Z	0.00	0.01	0.02	0.03	0.04	0.05	0.06	0.07	0.08	0.09
0.0	0.5000	0.5040	0.5080	0.5120	0.5160	0.5199	0.5239	0.5279	0.5319	0.5359
0.1	0.5398	0.5438	0.5478	0.5517	0.5557	0.5596	0.5636	0.5675	0.5714	0.5753
0.2	0.5793	0.5832	0.5871	0.5910	0.5948	0.5987	0.6026	0.6064	0.6103	0.6141
0.3	0.6179	0.6217	0.6255	0.6293	0.6331	0.6368	0.6406	0.6443	0.6480	0.6517
0.4	0.6554	0.6591	0.6628	0.6664	0.6700	0.6736	0.6772	0.6808	0.6844	0.6879
0.5	0.6915	0.6950	0.6985	0.7019	0.7054	0.7088	0.7123	0.7157	0.7190	0.7224
0.6	0.7257	0.7291	0.7324	0.7357	0.7389	0.7422	0.7454	0.7486	0.7517	0.7549
0.7	0.7580	0.7611	0.7642	0.7673	0.7704	0.7734	0.776	0.7794	0.7823	0.7852
0.8	0.7881	0.7910	0.7939	0.7967	0.7995	0.8023	0.8051	0.8078	0.8106	0.8133
0.9	0.8159	0.8186	0.8212	0.8238	0.8264	0.8289	0.8315	0.8340	0.8365	0.8389
1.0	0.8413	0.8438	0.8461	0.8485	0.8508	0.8531	0.8554	0.8577	0.8599	0.8621
1.1	0.8643	0.8665	0.8686	0.8708	0.8729	0.8749	0.8770	0.8790	0.8810	0.8830
1.2	0.8849	0.8869	0.8888	0.8907	0.8925	0.8944	0.8962	0.8980	0.8997	0.9015
1.3	0.9032	0.9049	0.9066	0.9082	0.9099	0.9115	0.9131	0.9147	0.9162	0.9177
1.4	0.9192	0.9207	0.9222	0.9236	0.9251	0.9265	0.9279	0.9292	0.9306	0.9319
1.5	0.9332	0.9345	0.9357	0.9370	0.9382	0.9394	0.9406	0.9418	0.9429	0.9441
1.6	0.9452	0.9463	0.9474	0.9484	0.9495	0.9505	0.9515	0.9525	0.9535	0.9545
1.7	0.9554	0.9564	0.9573	0.9582	0.9591	0.9599	0.9608	0.9616	0.9625	0.9633
1.8	0.9641	0.9649	0.9656	0.9664	0.9671	0.9678	0.9686	0.9693	0.9699	0.9706
1.9	0.9713	0.9719	0.9726	0.9732	0.9738	0.9744	0.9750	0.9756	0.9761	0.9767
2.0	0.9772	0.9778	0.9783	0.9788	0.9793	0.9798	0.9803	0.9808	0.9812	0.9817
2.1	0.9821	0.9826	0.9830	0.9834	0.9838	0.9842	0.9846	0.9850	0.9854	0.9857
2.2	0.9861	0.9864	0.9868	0.9871	0.9875	0.9878	0.9881	0.9884	0.9887	0.9890
2.3	0.9893	0.9896	0.9898	0.9901	0.9904	0.9906	0.9909	0.9911	0.9913	0.9916
2.4	0.9918	0.9920	0.9922	0.9925	0.9927	0.9929	0.9931	0.9932	0.9934	0.9936
2.5	0.9938	0.9940	0.9941	0.9943	0.9945	0.9946	0.9948	0.9949	0.9951	0.9952
2.6	0.9953	0.9955	0.9956	0.9957	0.9959	0.9960	0.9961	0.9962	0.9963	0.9964
2.7	0.9965	0.9966	0.9967	0.9968	0.9969	0.9970	0.9971	0.9972	0.9973	0.9974
2.8	0.9974	0.9975	0.9976	0.9977	0.9977	0.9978	0.9979	0.9979	0.9980	0.9981
2.9	0.9981	0.9982	0.9982	0.9983	0.9984	0.9984	0.9985	0.9985	0.9986	0.9986
3.0	0.9987	0.9987	0.9987	0.9988	0.9988	0.9989	0.9989	0.9989	0.9990	0.9990

Appendix

ANSWERS TO SELECTED PROBLEMS

Chapter 2

1. a. 16.67%.
   b. 2.09 times.
   c. 34.78%.
   d. $23,000,000.

Chapter 3

7. a. 70 minutes.
   b. The desired waiting time is 30 minutes; yet, the actual expected waiting time is 70 minutes, which is greater than the desired 30 minutes. To bring the actual and promised waiting times into agreement, we can do the following:

   - Reduce the processing time for jobs from 6 to less than 2.6 minutes.
   - Reduce either of the coefficients of variation.
   - Reduce the utilization from 70 to 50 percent by increasing the staffing levels in the health center.

9. a. 2.86, rounded to 3.
   b. 42.
   c. 70.
   d. If we were to set the resources to the levels indicated in the preceding calculations, then we should not have any bottlenecks. However, in reviewing the numbers, where the potential bottleneck emerges can be identified based on how sensitive the calculations are to violations in the assumptions. With that perspective, we can see if we were to have 3 cash registers, we are assuming that each order will have 4 people on the order. If this assumption is violated (e.g., we have a number of checks where there are less than 4 people per check), then this becomes the bottleneck.

11. a. 32 jobs per day.
    b. 10 days.
    c. 6.25 days.
    d. Process A (less labor).
    e. Process B (15 minutes per job compared to 24 minutes per job under Process A).

13. a. If we have an inventory of $200 and daily sales of $400, then the flow rate of 1 day could not be supported.
    b. To keep the flow times constant, we have to increase the inventory.

Chapter 3S

3. a.

Process Flow Chart

Page _____ of _____

Overall Description of Process Charted:

Date Charted: _____   Charted by: _____

Check appropriate box: Current Process: (x)   Proposed Process: ( )

Dist FT Meters	Time (avg.)	Symbol	Pers Invol.	Value Code V/W/N/?[1]	Description of Activity (indicate outcome)
		O ➡ □ D ▽		?	Transport in the raw materials
		O ⇒ □ D ▼		N	Store the raw materials
		O ⇒ ■ D ▽		?	Inspect the material
		O ⇒ □ D ▼		N	Put the raw materials in storage
		O ➡ □ D ▽		W	Move the materials to the area where mixed
	60 min	● ⇒ □ D ▽		V	Mix the items, place in pans
50 yds.		O ➡ □ D ▽			Move to shipping area
		O ⇒ □ D ▽			Put into inventory
		● ⇒ □ D ▽		V	Order, rearrange the number of bagels, match to an order
		O ➡ □ D ▽			Move to trucks
		O ⇒ □ ◗ ▽			Wait to be loaded into trucks
	20 min	● ⇒ □ D ▽			Place into trucks
	40 min	O ➡ □ D ▽			Transport (while allowing bagels to rise)
		O ⇒ □ ◗ ▽			Wait to be unloaded
		● ⇒ □ D ▽			Unload trucks
		O ➡ □ D ▽			Move to work areas
	40 min	● ⇒ □ D ▽		V	Mix, cook
		O ➡ □ D ▽			Move to cooling area
		● ⇒ □ D ▽		N	Allow bagels to cool
		O ➡ □ D ▽			Move to retail area displays
		O ⇒ □ D ▼		V	Sit in displays and wait to be sold
		6 8 1 2 4			

b. Value-adding activities are indicated in the preceding chart.

---

[1]The value code indicates the extent to which the activity is value-adding (V), waste-creating (W), not value-adding but necessary (N), or unknown (?).

Chapter 5

1. a. 50 seconds.
   b. 82.8%.
   c. 72 units per hour.
   d. 45 seconds per unit.
   e. The time at workstation 4 needs to be reduced by 5 seconds so that it does not exceed the TAKT time of 45 seconds.

3. a.

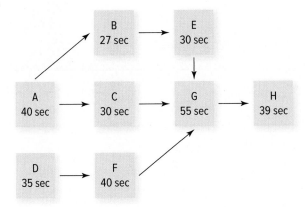

   b. 96 seconds per unit.
   c. 3.08, round up to 4 workstations.
   d.

Workstation	Tasks in Order	Workstation Time (Seconds)	Idle Time (Seconds)
1	A, D	75	21
2	F, C	70	26
3	B, E	57	39
4	G, H	94	2

   e. 77.1%.

9. V = 2,667 claims.
   Use the newer, more automated process because the total cost will be lower because the volume of 3,500 claims per year exceeds the indifference point.

Chapter 6S

1.

2. Histogram

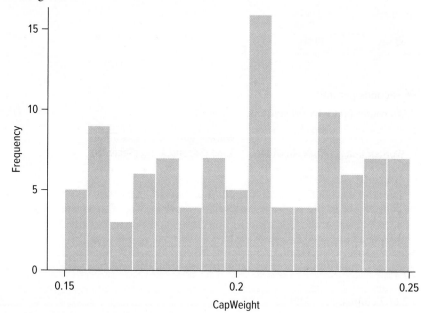

3. $C_p = S/P = 1/.6 = 1.67$
   $C_{pk} = 1.64$

13.

Data Points	*x*-bar Chart	*R*-bar Chart
Central line	12.94	1.35
Lower control limit (LCL)	12.14 − .58*1.35 = 11.36	0
Upper control limit (UCL)	12.14 + .58*1.35 = 12.92	2.12*1.35 = 2.86

14. For this table, we would construct a Pareto chart with the following information:

Reject Cause	Number
Contamination	15
Oxide defect	9
Misc	3
Corrosion	2
Metallization	2
Doping	1
Silicon defect	1

Focus on contamination and oxide defect. Tools to use here include:

- Cause-and-effect analysis.
- Checksheets.

15. Number of defects decreased from 33 to 19.
    Significant decrease in oxide defects (from 9 → 1).
    Significant decrease in contamination (from 15 → 8).
    Increases in silicon defects.

Chapter 7

1. Inventory turnover rate: 7 times.
   Inventory carrying cost: $150,000.

3. Item 1 = $607,500.
   Item 2 = $540,000.
   Item 3 = $81,900.
   Item 4 = $333,000.
   Item 5 = $9,900.
   Total annual inventory carrying cost = $1,572,300.

6. a. EOQ = 1,789 cases.
      Average inventory = 894.5 cases.
      Inventory turnover = 223.6 times.
   b. EOQ at $18 = 1,886 cases.
      However, Foods Galore must order 10,000 cases to receive this price. Therefore, the calculated EOQ for the $18 price is not relevant.
      TAC of ordering at the $20 price = $4,008,944.27.
      TAC of ordering at the $18 price = $3,623,300.00.
      Foods Galore should order 10,000 cases at a time because they would save $385,644.27.
   c. Standard deviation of demand during lead time = 1,211.94 or 1,212 cases.
      5% risk of stockout equals 1.65 deviations of safety stock = 2,000 cases.
      Inventory carrying cost = $9,000.
          1% risk of stockout = 2,824 cases.
      Inventory carrying cost = $12,708.

8. Production order quantity 73.03 = 74 units.
   Producing 74 units in a production run at a rate of 16 per day requires 74/16 = 4.625 days.

10. Standard deviation of demand during lead time = 204.27 = 205 units.

    SS = 339 units.

    EOQ = 707.11 = 708 units.

    TAC of ordering 708 units = $628,535.54.

    Average cycle stock = 354 units.

    Average inventory = 693 units.

Chapter 9

1. Unit fill rate = 95%.

    Line fill rate = 90%.

    Order fill rate = 80%.

3. 62.2%.

5. Unit fill rate = 96%.

    Line fill rate = 97.6%.

    Order fill rate = 96.6%.

Chapter 10

1. Supplier A's score is 2.7, Supplier B's is 3.15, Supplier C's 3.2. Judgment should be used to decide between Supplier B and Supplier C.

3. WebTex score is 3.25, CoolWeb is 2.6, Dazzling Designs is 4.05, and Major Marketing is 3.7. Dazzling Designs has the highest score and may be the best supplier to select.

Chapter 11

1. a. $99.66

    b. The 2-day shipment total cost = $109.86. The 2-day shipment is more expensive than the 5-day shipment. If the manager chose this option, the company would lose $10.20.

5. Air = $910.96

    Ground = $1,432.88

    Other considerations involved besides cost are the availability of these modes of transportation, customer desire for rapid delivery, and their dependability. If the customer wants the diamonds delivered as soon as possible and to ensure their safety, air is probably the best option. Although there are chances of delays, air transportation will probably deliver the diamonds more quickly with less handling and chances of damaging these expensive items.

8. Single shipments cost = $1,440.

    Consolidated shipment cost = $1,420.

    The consolidated shipment offer is the better choice. The company would save $20 by combining all 10 shipments into one.

10. $X^* = 47.647$

    $Y^* = 32.647$

Chapter 12

1. The weight put on one time period older than the most recent period is .24. Two periods older 0.096.

3. Forecast error = 3.

    $F_{t+1} = 28.5$, or 29 rounded up.

5. a.

Week	Demand	2-Week	Error	Absolute	4-week	Error	Absolute	6-week	Error	Absolute
1	232									
2	263									
3	271	247.5	23.5	23.5						
4	248	267	−19	19						
5	235	259.5	−24.5	24.5	253.5	−18.5	18.5			
6	261	241.5	19.5	19.5	254.3	6.8	6.8			
7	207	248	−41	41	253.8	−46.8	46.8	251.7	−44.7	44.7
8	243	234	9	9	237.8	5.3	5.3	247.5	−4.5	4.5
9	237	225	12	12	236.5	0.5	0.5	244.2	−7.2	7.2
10	293	240	53	53	237.0	56.0	56.0	238.5	54.5	54.5
11	243	265	−22	22	245.0	−2.0	2.0	246.0	−3.0	3.0
12	260	268	−8	8	254.0	6.0	6.0	247.3	12.7	12.7
13	253	251.5	1.5	1.5	258.3	−5.3	5.3	247.2	5.8	5.8
14	270	256.5	13.5	13.5	262.3	7.8	7.8	254.8	15.2	15.2
15	230	261.5	−31.5	31.5	256.5	−26.5	26.5	259.3	−29.3	29.3
16	253	250	3	3	253.3	−0.3	0.3	258.2	−5.2	5.2
17	238	241.5	−3.5	3.5	251.5	−13.5	13.5	251.5	−13.5	13.5
18	272	245.5	26.5	26.5	247.8	24.3	24.3	250.7	21.3	21.3
19	222	255	−33	33	248.3	−26.3	26.3	252.7	−30.7	30.7
20	243	247	−4	4	246.3	−3.3	3.3	247.5	−4.5	4.5
21	289	232.5	56.5	56.5	243.8	45.3	45.3	243.0	46.0	46.0
22	238	266	−28	28	256.5	−18.5	18.5	252.8	−14.8	14.8
23	262	263.5	−1.5	1.5	248.0	14.0	14.0	250.3	11.7	11.7
24	234	250	−16	16	258.0	−24.0	24.0	254.3	−20.3	20.3
			−14.0	20.5		−19.0	17.5		−10.5	19.2
			MFE	MAD		MFE	MAD		MFE	MAD

The four-week moving average has the lowest MAD. It also has the highest level of bias, in that the forecast tends to overestimate the demand. In this situation, it would be better to overforecast than to underforecast.

b. The alpha of 0.25 results in the lowest MFE value of 76.5. Although the MAD of 18 is not the lowest, it is very close to the lowest value. Thus, 0.25 is the best choice for the alpha value.

13. $FIT_7 = 69.3$.

15. $b = 7.8$, $a = 14.3$.

17. a. Sales (1000s) = 1.182 (PMI) + 71.99, $R^2 = 0.65$.
    b. Sales (1000s) = 1.73 (PMI) + 49.65, $R^2 = 0.91$.
    c. 133.

Chapter 13

1. Total level plan cost = $271,400.
    Total chase plan cost (adjust workforce) = $257,400.
    Total overtime plan cost = $288,480.
    Total subcontract cost = $260,640.
    Total hybrid cost = $269,640.

3. Total cost = $24,400,000.

5. a. 350 units per month.
    b. The maximum end-of-period inventory experienced would be 300 units.
        Total cost = $539,000.
    c. Total cost = $534,000.

7. Total level plan cost = $29,610,000.
    Total case with overtime cost = $30,500,000.
    Total Chase (Hiring/firing) Cost = $28,960,000

Chapter 14

1. Es are components in Bs and Ds. Start with the Bs. 20 As × 2 Bs for each A = 40 Bs. 40 Bs × 4 Es for each B = 160 Es. Then determine the Es needed for the Ds. 20 As × 2 Ds for each A = 40 Ds. 40 Ds × 2 Es for each D = 80 Es. The total number of Es = 160 + 80 = 240.

    Cs are used directly to make As and also are used to make Ds. 20 As × 1 C for each A = 20 Cs. 20 As × 2 Ds for each A = 40 Ds. 40 Ds × 1 C for each D = 40 Cs. The total number of Cs = 20 + 40 = 60.

4. Fs are used in component Ds and component Cs. 15 As × 1 B for each A = 15 Bs. 15 Bs × 2 Ds for each B = 30 Ds. 30 Ds × 4 Fs for each D = 120 Fs. 15 As × 4 Cs for each A = 60 Cs. 60 Cs × 1 F for each C = 60 Fs. 60Cs × 3 Ds for each C = 180 Ds. 180 Ds × 4 Fs for each D = 720 Fs. Total Fs = 120 + 60 + 720 = 900 Fs.

    If part D is purchased, the number of levels in the BOM will be reduced from four levels to three levels. The components that are used to make Ds (E and F) will not be shown in the BOM.

    If D is purchased, C is the only parent of F in the BOM. 15 As × 4 Cs for each A = 60 Cs. 60 Cs × 1 F for each C = 60 Fs. Only 60 Fs will be needed. The other Fs will be purchased and used by the supplier who provides component D.

10.

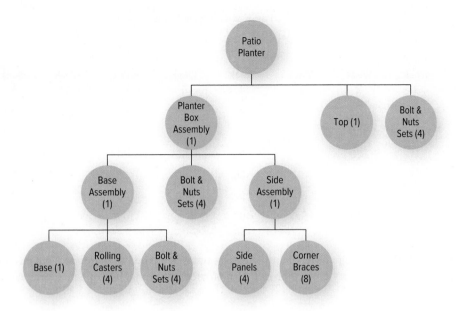

The total number of bolt and nuts sets = 32 + 32 + 32 = 96 sets.

11.

MRP Record				Part Name: Bicycle frame				
Lead time = 2 weeks On hand = 0 Safety stock = 0 Order quantity: L4L	Week 1	Week 2	Week 3	Week 4	Week 5	Week 6	Week 7	Week 8
Gross requirements	70	50	80	80	70	60	80	80
Scheduled receipts	70	50						
Available inventory								
Net requirements			80	80	70	60	80	80
Planned order receipts			80	80	70	60	80	80
Planned order releases	80	80	70	60	80	80		

MRP Record	Part Name: Bicycle frame						
Lead time = 2weeks On hand = 0 Safety stock = 0 Order quantity: FOQ = 100	Week 1	Week 2	Week 3	Week 4	Week 5	Week 6	Week 7	Week 8
Gross requirements	70	50	80	80	70	60	80	80
Scheduled receipts	100	100						
Available inventory	30	80		20	50	90	10	30
Net requirements				80	50	10		70
Planned order receipts				100	100	100		100
Planned order releases		100	100	100		100		

Compared to the FOQ strategy, the L4L strategy orders more often (six times compared to four times) but has no inventory costs. The FOQ strategy has inventory costs. The L4L also provides a truer picture of actual demand to the supplier.

17.

	Part Name: Computer keyboard						
Processing time = 9 minutes	Week 1	Week 2	Week 3	Week 4	Week 5	Week 6	Week 7	Week 8
Planned order releases	1,000	1,200	900	1,300	1,400	1,000	800	1,100
Processing load (hours)	150.0	180.0	135.0	195.0	210.0	150.0	120.0	165.0
Available capacity (hours)	200	200	200	200	200	200	200	200

The load exceeds capacity in week 5, and there are significant levels of excess capacity in weeks 1, 3, 6, and 7. Perhaps product can be made in week 3 and held in inventory for week 5.

Chapter 15

6. a.

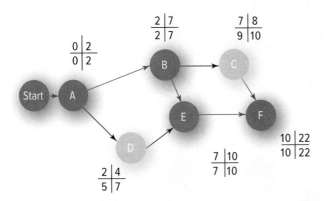

  b. The critical path is A, B, E, F

Task	Immediate Predecessors	Earliest Start (ES)	Earliest Completion (EC) = ES + task duration
A	None	0	2
B	A	2	7
C	B	7	8
D	A	2	4
E	B, D	7	10
F	C, E	10	22

Task	Immediate Successors	Latest completion	Latest Start (LS) = LC − task duration	Slack = LS − ES
F	None	22	10	10−10 = 0
E	F	10	7	7−7 = 0
D	E	7	5	5−2 = 3
C	None	10	9	9−8 = 1
B	E	7	2	2−2 = 0
A	B, D	2	0	0−0 = 0

  c. The activities that the project manager should track most closely are A, B, E, and F. They are on the critical path.

  d. Increasing the time required for D from 2 days to 6 days is an increase of 4 days. Activity D currently has 3 days of slack [LC − EC (7 − 4 days) or LS − ES (5 − 2 days)]. Thus, D will now be on the critical path and the overall project time will increase by 1 day and activity B is no longer on the critical path. The ES and LS time for activity E becomes 8 rather than 7 days.

8. The critical path tasks are C, F, H, I, K.

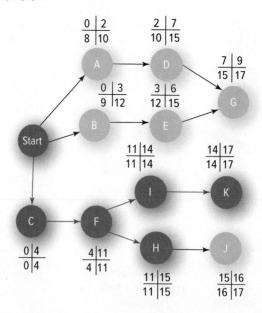

Task	Immediate Predecessors	Earliest Start (ES)	Earliest Completion (EC) = ES + task duration
A	None	0	2
B	None	0	3
C	None	0	4
D	A	2	7
E	B	3	6
F	C	4	11
G	D, E	7	9
H	F	11	15
I	F	11	14
J	H	15	16
K	I	14	17

Task	Immediate Successors	Latest Completion (LC)	Latest Start (LS) = LC − task duration	Slack = LS − ES
K	None	17	14	14 − 14 = 0
J	None	17	16	16 − 15 = 1
I	K	14	11	11 − 11 = 0
H	J	15	11	11 − 11 = 0
G	None	17	15	15 − 7 = 8
F	H, I	11	4	4 − 4 = 0
E	G	15	12	12 − 3 = 9
D	G	15	10	10 − 2 = 8
C	F	4	0	0 − 0 = 0
B	E	12	9	9 − 0 = 9
A	D	10	8	8 − 0 = 8

Chapter 15S

3. The project must be crashed by an additional two days. To do this, you must crash Prepare Documentation by 2 days at a cost of $400/day and Populate System Data by 1 day at a cost of $700. Thus, the total cost of crashing the project by 7 days is $4,600, which is more than the $4,000 bonus. The project could be shortened to 6 days by crashing Prepare Documentation by 1 day at a cost of $3,500.

5. The probability that the project will take less than 32 days is 53%, so the probability that the project will take more than 32 days is 47%.

7. a. 35 weeks.
    b. The likelihood that the critical path will be completed in 37 weeks is 75%.
    c. The likelihood that the project will be completed in 36 weeks is 63%.
    d. The likelihood that the project will be completed in 33 weeks is 37%.
    e. Because the two paths share several activities, it is difficult to estimate the likelihood that both paths will complete the project on time. However, because the duration of the "Code A" task is much shorter than the combined duration of tasks "Code B" and "Code C," we can be fairly sure that "Code A" will always be completed before both "Code B and "Code C" are completed. Using the expected durations, "Code A" has 6.66 days of slack. Therefore, we can be confident that the expected critical path will always dictate the actual length of the project, and we can be assured of the correctness of our estimates of project completion in parts a-d above that are based on the critical path alone.

Name Index